# A West African Model to Address Human Trafficking

Paul VI Sidlawinde Karenga

# A West African Model to Address Human Trafficking

Springer

Paul VI Sidlawinde Karenga
Saint Thomas University
Miami Gardens, FL, USA

ISBN 978-3-030-88119-1 ISBN 978-3-030-88120-7 (eBook)
https://doi.org/10.1007/978-3-030-88120-7



This Springer imprint is published by the registered company Springer Nature Switzerland AG.
The registered company address is: Gewerbestrasse 11, 6330 Cham, Switzerland

# Foreword by Thomas Wenski, Archbishop Metropolitan of Miami

Trafficking in persons is a form of modern-day slavery, threatening the lives of our children. This book titled *A West African Model for the World to Address Trafficking in Persons* is a timely and groundbreaking work that draws abundantly from literature, field trip work, and pastoral experiences to illustrate and inform the reader on trafficking trends in West Africa and around the world. In these pages, we discover unexpected trafficking offenders such as family members, friends, children, and even people living with physical handicaps. The detailed study also highlights the structural causes of inequality and exploitation as well as the legislative challenges that prevent meaningful change. This book fills a substantial gap as the author brings to light many other forms of trafficking underexplored in the existing literature such as forced marriage, begging, child soldiering, trafficking for blood money, trafficking for body parts, and trafficking for ritual bondage. This makes the writing one of the most thorough narratives of trafficking in persons.

The book's originality consists of arguing that trafficking in persons cannot be dealt with by over-relying on criminal justice frameworks and recommends the use of law in tandem with religious values to craft effective responses that ultimately prevent harm. In effect, cultural norms and religious values are highly influential over individual behavior in the context of human trafficking and its prevention, as norms create an environment that can address crime and its deleterious effects.

Ultimately, the greatest value of *A West African Model for the World to Address Trafficking in Persons* lies in its insightful human dignity-centered approach to trafficking in persons calling for concerted, collaborative efforts of all stakeholders. Indeed, human dignity is a universally shared value with the potential of fostering a culture of dialogue across secular and religious traditions. With discussion-provoking questions, this narrative is an eye-opening writing that moves readers from awareness to advocacy and action. The book awakens in readers a sense of moral responsibility in purchasing. I urge you, therefore, to use our consumer power by downloading an anti-trafficking app on our phones to scan the barcode of the items we buy. Our feedback on social media sites such as Yelp and Facebook can force unethical companies to take steps to ensure their supply chains are slavery-free.

This would be our way to join in the fight. I hope this book is helpful in introducing this disturbing social issue.

Miami Shores, FL, USA Thomas Wenski

# Foreword by John Makdisi, Professor Law Emeritus

The trafficking of human beings is a major problem in the world today, particularly in certain areas of the world such as West Africa. The 15 countries of West Africa suffer from food insecurity and malnutrition, political tensions and instability, chronic poverty, inter-ethnic violence, and transnational organized crime, all of which exacerbate the problem of human trafficking. Fr. Karenga relates the horrors of this trafficking through selected stories, punctuated by a disturbing set of statistics. Through careful analysis of the well-organized cycle and flows of human trafficking coupled with the extreme vulnerability and hiddenness of its victims, he shows several intricate patterns of trafficking that are well-integrated into society. Unfortunately, the legal system can only do so much to address the problem. Fr. Karenga examines in detail what the legal system is doing through the policing regulations, strategies, protections, preventions, and other actions made possible by the legal and institutional framework that the West African States have on an international, transnational, regional, and national levels. It is not enough, and Fr. Karenga shows why in a powerful yet fair critique of the system. In fact, human trafficking is increasing in West Africa and begs for extra-legal solutions to complement existing law in order to achieve a more holistic approach to the problem. Towards this end, Fr. Karenga examines how insights from the Catholic tradition can and are contributing to such solutions. Just a few of the many solutions elaborated by Fr. Karenga are the use of the Church's global influence to help organize anti-trafficking networks, extensive education in human dignity and responsibility, and the conversion of hearts from entrenched customary beliefs that promote human trafficking by reaching people through their deeply held religious convictions. With deep insight himself into the differences between the cultural tradition of West Africa and the Catholic tradition of the Church, Fr. Karenga sees not a negative but a positive transforming dialogue that will lead to stronger social structures hopefully capable of resisting the problem of human trafficking.

Fr. Karenga has researched a massive amount of data (including personal interviews with key people in West Africa) and organized and analyzed it in a clear, understandable, and interesting manner to produce a convincing argument for the value of the Catholic Church's contribution to the solution of trafficking as a complement to the existing legal system in West Africa. Having been trained in the Intercultural Human Rights Program at St. Thomas University School of Law, Fr. Karenga follows the methodology of the New Haven School of Jurisprudence in using a disciplined sequence of tasks to analyze and evaluate the problem in a holistic manner. As a result of his careful work on the case in West Africa, his book significantly advances our understanding of how we can tackle one of the most serious problems in society today by thinking outside the box of mere legal solutions. It is a must-read for all who seek truly to stem the tide of the human disease of trafficking.

St. Thomas University School of Law
Miami Gardens, FL, USA
April 2, 2021

John Makdisi

# Acknowledgment

This book was made possible by the Grace of God and the assistance and support of many persons.

The Synod of Koupéla conducted in 2000 by the Most Reverend Séraphin Rouamba, Archbishop Emeritus of Koupéla inspired me to produce this academic paper. I owe him a depth of gratitude for his continued support and follow up with my academic career. Grateful thanks for his many years of dedicated service to the Church as Parish Priest and Archbishop. I am extremely grateful to the Most Reverend Thomas Wenski, Archbishop of Miami who generously offered me an assignment in the Archdiocese of Miami and a scholarship to complete my studies at Saint Thomas University. His ongoing interest and commitment to the cause of this book have been a blessing for me. Thanks should also go to the Most Reverend Gabriel Sayaogo, Archdiocese of Koupéla for his paternal benevolence and his significant support to my studies.

This book is a revised version of my JSD dissertation submitted to the School of Law, Saint Thomas University, in Miami, Florida. Subsequently, I am particularly grateful to my supervisor Professor, Dr. John Makdisi for his expert guidance throughout this endeavor. It would have been extremely difficult to complete this research project without his intellectual input and cheerful disposition. Sincere thanks to Professor Dr. Juris, Siegfried Wiessner who welcomed me to law school and whose scholarship provided the resources which helped me succeed in my studies. I must also thank Professor Dr. Roza Pati whose guidance from the onset contributed to the writing of this academic paper. Her wealth of knowledge and experience in Human Trafficking has shaped my thoughts and enriched this work. I wish to thank Ms. Haydee Gonzalez, Program Manager at the Graduate Program in Intercultural Human Rights, Saint Thomas University who provides unwavering support to students. Thanks to the Committee and all the Reviewers for their critical reviews, useful suggestions, and insightful remarks that contributed to the improvement of the manuscript draft.

I also had great pleasure collaborating and working with Non-Government Organizations, Government Institutions, priests and religious nuns from Burkina

Faso, Ghana and the Archdiocese of Miami in the U.S.A. In this regard, l would like particularly to commend Mr Paulin Bambara, Permanent Secretary to the Superior Council of the Judiciary in Burkina Faso, for his unwavering support and rich contribution to this research paper. I am deeply indebted to Father Ernest Biriruka for his mediation regarding my coming to the USA and I am grateful he encouraged me to further my studies. May God bless his ministry and St John XXIII Parish Community. My heartfelt gratitude goes to Irma and Joseph Verga's Family for their unwavering support. I also wish to thank Father Andrew and Saint St Bartholomew Parish for hosting me as a student priest. Particularly helpful to me during this time was Saint Mark's Parish Community, who provided me in a singular way with a conducive atmosphere for both my priestly ministry and academic studies. Their generous support helped to bring this work to completion. In this regard, I am sincerely grateful to Father Jaime Assevedo, Pastor of Saint Mark Parish, and to the late Monsignor Edmond Whyte, former Pastor.

Finally, I would like to extend my gratitude to my family, especially my Father and Grandfather whom I wish were still alive, friends and colleagues for their helpful contributions which made this achievement possible.

# Contents

# Chapter 1
# Introduction

On April 2, 2015, the Guardian[1] reported that African women from Sierra Leone, Cameroon, Kenya, and Ethiopia paid recruitment agents approximately US $1500 to secure lucrative jobs in nursing or the hotel industry in foreign countries. Upon their arrival, the women instead learned they were to be offered to families as housemaids and forced to work for long hours without a day off. They were not allowed to leave the house and were prohibited from using mobile phones. One of the victims recounted that her employer did not pay anything for her work and, in addition, deliberately spilled hot oil on her because she cooked too slowly.[2]

The same report also described how, in the basement of an old tower block near Kuwait City, recruitment agents presented files containing the profiles of healthy, work-ready domestic workers from West Africa. When advertising their merchandise, the agents made the following promise, "Choose the one you want. . .I will give you a hundred days' guarantee. If you don't like her you can send her back [and get your money back]". In addition to keeping employers happy, this complex has created a growing "second-hand" market in which returned workers domestic can be resold multiple times to other families for up to two years. According to the report, other offices in the building served as showrooms in which the women were displayed to clients; once selected by a Kuwaiti family,[3] they were taken to their house and treated 'like slaves'.

---

[1] Pattison (2015).

[2] *Walls at Every Turn: Abuse of Migrant Domestic Workers through Kuwait's Sponsorship System*, Human Rights Watch (Oct. 6, 2010). Human Rights Watch reports that the embassies of labor-sending countries in Kuwait received more than 10,000 complaints from domestic workers in 2009. Their grievances included "nonpayment of wages; withholding of passports; working excessively long hours without rest; and physical, sexual, and psychological abuse."

[3] *Id.* Kuwait allegedly has the highest ratio of domestic workers to citizens in the Middle East, with one domestic worker for every two Kuwaiti citizens. Once enslavement begins, it is extremely difficult for women to escape because the Kuwait's *kafala* sponsorship system prevents them from being able to leave or change jobs without the permission of their employer.

 
P. VI. S. Karenga, *A West African Model to Address Human Trafficking*,
https://doi.org/10.1007/978-3-030-88120-7_1

In all West African Countries, women and girls are trafficked primarily for domestic servitude, restaurant labor, forced street vending, and commercial sexual exploitation. Conversely, boys migrate to the Ivory Coast to be enrolled in forced agricultural and mining labor. In 2018, the US Department of State reported that the authorities in Guinea had identified an increasing number of trafficking networks fraudulently recruiting Guinean, Liberian, and Sierra Leonean women for work in West Africa, Europe, the Middle East, and the United States where they would be exploited for domestic servitude and prostitution.[4] In the same year, an international organization in Guinea stated that it had "repatriated more than 3756 Guineans from Libya and northern Mali, and the organization estimated more than 560 were victims of trafficking."[5]

Trafficking in Persons (TIP) Report (2018) states that all West African nations are source, transit and destination countries for victims of forced labor and sex trafficking with some tribes perpetuating traditional and ritual slavery. For example, experts allege that in the Volta delta of Ghana as many as 3000 virgin girls and young women still live in bondage as part of the *Trokosi* tradition which subjects them to forced labor and sexual exploitation to atone for sins committed by their relatives. Similarly, the longstanding practice of debt bondage in the salt mines of *Taoudenni* in northern Mali enslaves people of *Songhai* ethnicity, servitude that is reportedly extended to their children.

This brief look at just a handful of reports provides considerable evidence that the incidence of slavery and its new manifestations persist all around the world and especially in West Africa. In this latter region, figures on trafficking in persons are particularly challenging to policy makers because they reflect the "survival of traditional forms of servitude, but also relate to extreme poverty, a high incidence of child labour, and a context of severe political violence."[6] Moreover, populations in countries where armed conflicts are fared up, inevitably experiences the forced recruitment of child soldiers, abductions, and enslavement. In response to urgent concerns raised with regard to trafficking in persons, the United Nations created a legal definition to formalize the crime and established legal frameworks to outlaw this practice. However, one troubling issue within the evolving trafficking discourse is that the significant uncertainty regarding the crime results in a lack of action or an improper response.[7] Consequently law enforcement, prevention, and protection measures worldwide have failed to realize their objectives, especially in West Africa. The current research on trafficking in persons has therefore been conducted to provide an impetus for action on behalf of its victims.

Numerous scholars have noted that the criminal law model required by the Palermo Protocol focuses heavily on perpetrators at the expense of other issues that sustain the practice of trafficking in persons, such as gender based violence,

---

[4] US Department of State, 2018 *Trafficking in Persons Report - Guinea*, (June 28, 2018).

[5] *Id.*

[6] *Forced Labour in Africa: Between Poverty and Tradition*, ILO, (May 15, 2005).

[7] Bassiouni (2010), p. 425.

various forms of socio-economic exclusion and discrimination, education, and political forces.[8] Additionally, prevention or assistance programs for victims incur financial costs and social burdens that developing countries struggle to meet. Consequently, "a legal regime of human rights can never be said to fully capture the entire picture of human trafficking."[9] The contribution to knowledge of this research thus lies in analyzing how the Church participates significantly in solving the problem of trafficking in persons in preventing, reducing the demand and protecting. It also aims to show how the Church contributes to increasing the effective prosecution of traffickers and the identification of victims. Although slavery (trafficking in persons) is abolished in law it still occurs de facto around the world and continues to be a salient issue for all individuals in one form or another. Notably, Martin Luther King Junior stated that the law cannot make a person love others but it can prevent the heartless from harming others. He stated that "if the problem is to be solved then in the final sense, hearts must be changed. Religion and education must play a great role in changing the heart."[10] The Church is committed to abolishing slavery for the benefit of all people and to addressing the conditions that foster the trafficking and exploitation of others.

The scope of the present research is limited to West Africa; more specifically, to the Economic Community of West African States (ECOWAS). It is based on insights gathered through field research conducted in Togo, Benin, Nigeria, Burkina Faso, Ghana, and the Ivory Coast in 2017. The methodology consists primarily of a review of academic research related to the topic and an analysis of legislation, national and international reports, and other relevant documents. It also incorporates findings from an analysis of semi-structured interviews conducted with stakeholders including victims and members of (Non-Governmental Organizations) NGOs who deal with the issues that arise in relation to trafficking in persons.

Part I describes the forms and manifestations of the trafficking of persons in West Africa, identifying the actors taking part in this criminal activity and their fundamental motivations for doing so. It also discusses the methods used by traffickers to recruit and control their victims. By exploring different dimensions of victims' vulnerability, this dissertation argues that gender discrimination, poverty, lack of equal opportunities, political unrest, underemployment, poor educational achievement, and culturally engrained slavery-like practices make West African people particularly vulnerable to trafficking.

Part II examines the evolving interpretation of the legal definition of trafficking in persons in Courts' jurisprudence and discusses related issues such as whether coercion should be an element or whether crossing international borders is required. It also considers the challenges involved in establishing the *mens rea* requirement to convict perpetrators of trafficking. The analysis outlines the law enforcement and human rights frameworks that have been tailored to combat trafficking in persons

---

[8] *See* Todres (2006), p. 885.

[9] Lutenco (2012).

[10] Martin Luther King, (December 18, 1963).

along with the state obligations arising from these. Finally, this section assesses the strengths and weaknesses of each framework and argues that a faith-based approach has the potential to enhance international efforts to curb this crime.

Part III then develops the major claim of this dissertation. Whereas the Palermo Protocol emphasizes the prosecution of offenders and provides limited protections for the human rights of victims, the Catholic Church in Africa has initiated actions to bolster the prevention of trafficking and facilitated the protection and rehabilitation of victims. To some extent, religion is a powerful means of social control as it impels members of a society to accept and conform to dominant moral values and social norms. The discussion in Part III will describe the best practices taken by the Catholic Church to implement social reform and discourage the demand for goods and services derived from exploitation. Because the prevention of trafficking in persons and assistance of victims poses psychological and ethical challenges, this dissertation will also show how the Church and its members play a significant role in the corresponding networks and support work needed at both international and national levels.

## References

Bassiouni CM (2010) Addressing international human trafficking in women and children for commercial sexual exploitation in the 21st century. Int Rev Pen Law 81:417, 425

ECOWAS — Basic Information, History, Economic Community of West African States (ECOWAS), http://www.ecowas.int. Accessed 1 July 2021

*Forced Labour in Africa: Between Poverty and Tradition*, Int'l Labour Org. (ILO) (May 15, 2005), Shttp://www.ilo.org/global/about-the-ilo/newsroom/news/WCMS_075494/lang%2D%2Den/index.htm

Lutenco A (2012) The extend of state obligations in preventing and combating trafficking in human beings: challenges and perspectives for a European human rights-based approach, pp 29–33 (unpublished LL.M., Central European University) (on file in Central European University at: https://eige.europa.eu/docs/54_HU.pdf)

Martin Luther King, Jr.'s address at Western Michigan University, December 18, 1963

Pattison P (2015) Women from Sierra Leone 'sold like slaves' into domestic work in Kuwait, The Guardian (Apr. 2, 2015), http://www.theguardian.com/global-development/2015/apr/02/women-sierra-leone-sold-like-slaves-domestic-work-kuwait

Todres J (2006) The importance of realizing other rights to prevent sex trafficking. Cardozo J Law Gender 12

US Department of State, 2018 Trafficking in Persons Report - Guinea, (June 28, 2018) https://www.refworld.org/docid/5b3e0b304.html. Accessed 4 June 2021

*Walls at Every Turn: Abuse of Migrant Domestic Workers through Kuwait's Sponsorship System*, Human Rights Watch (Oct. 6, 2010), https://www.hrw.org/report/2010/10/06/walls-every-turn/abuse-migrant-domestic-workers-through-kuwaits-sponsorship-system

# Part I
# The Problem of Trafficking in Persons and Respective Stakeholders

In Part I, the following questions are addressed in relation to the problem of trafficking in persons. What is the prevalence of such trafficking in West Africa? Who are the traffickers and how do they organize their operations? What makes victims vulnerable to trafficking and how do traffickers coerce and exploit them? What drives people into the trafficking business? Each of these question is now addressed in turn.

# Chapter 2
# Delimiting the Problem of Trafficking in Persons

West Africa is also known as the "Bulge of Africa" and comprises the countries of Benin, Burkina Faso, Cameroon, Côte d'Ivoire, The Gambia, Ghana, Guinea, Guinea-Bissau, Liberia, Mali, Niger, Nigeria, Senegal, Sierra Leone, and Togo. There are many different tribes in Western Africa spanning a diversity of cultures. More than a thousand local languages are spoken including cross-border native tongues such as *Ewe, Fulfulde, Hausa, Mandingo, Wolof, Yoruba, Ibo,* and *Ga*. Comprising approximately 5% of the world's population (over 300 million people) in a vast territory covering over 40% of sub-Saharan Africa (about 5.1 million square kilometers), West Africa is the most densely populated on the continent. This gives rise to diverse socio-cultural and ecological dimensions of development that seriously challenge the establishment of peace and security in the region.[1]

On May 28, 1975, the desire for economic integration leading to political and cultural cooperation inspired the creation of The Economic Community of West African States (ECOWAS) in Lagos, Nigeria. This geographical entity, which constitutes the focus of this study, is composed of an aggregation of states that have emerged from different colonial experiences and administrations. The current membership includes fifteen countries: Benin, Burkina Faso, Cape Verde, The Gambia, Ghana, Guinea, Guinea Bissau, Ivory Coast, Liberia, Mali, Niger, Nigeria, Senegal, Sierra Leone, and Togo. (The countries that make up the Economic Community of West African States (ECOWAS) region are illustrated in Fig. 2.1). Existing member states use three different imported official languages (English, French, and Portuguese).

The vision of the Economic Community of West African States (ECOWAS) is to create a borderless region governed in accordance with the principles of democracy, rule of law, and good governance; a region where the population enjoys free movement, has access to efficient education and health systems, and engages in

[1] *See* About ECOWAS—Basic Information, History, Economic Community of West African States (ECOWAS), http://www.ecowas.int (accessed July 1, 2021).



P. VI. S. Karenga, *A West African Model to Address Human Trafficking*,
https://doi.org/10.1007/978-3-030-88120-7_2

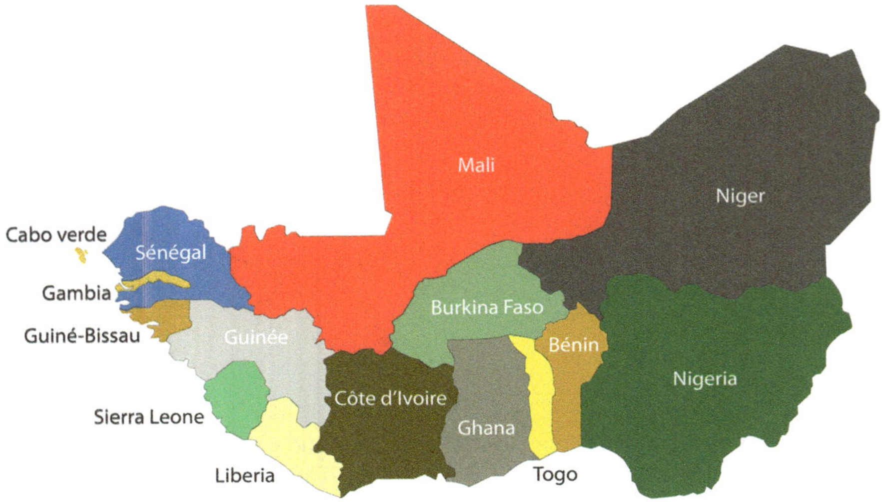


**Fig. 2.1** The Economic Community of West African States (ECOWAS) (Source: ECOWAS Map at http://www.euractiv.com/sections/development-policy/west-african-states-close-trade-deal-eu-301206)

economic and commercial activities while living in dignity in an atmosphere of peace and security.[2] To that end, the Declaration of Political Principles of the Revised Treaty undertakes to protect and promote human rights and provides a powerful tool for the enforcement of human rights through the establishment of ECOWAS' Community Court of Justice (ECCJ) in accordance with Article 25.[3]

The organization is now globally acknowledged as a successful regional body. In 2013, West Africa registered an economic growth of 6.3%, the highest rate in the entire continent and this was largely due to the collective prosperity drive of the Economic Community of West African States (ECOWAS).[4] However, despite its strong economic performance, West Africa remains trapped in a spiral of high levels of poverty, unequal distribution of wealth, escalating rates of youth unemployment,

---

[2] *Basic Information*, ECOWAS, http://www.ecowas.int/about-ecowas/basic-information/; *see also* ECOWAS—Revised Treaty art. 2, 2015, http://www.ecowas.int/wp-content/uploads/2015/01/Revised-treaty.pdf.

[3] Declaration of Political Principles art. 25, ECOWAS A/DCL 1/7/91 [hereinafter *Declaration of Political Principles*]. The ECOWAS Community of Court of Justice (ECCJ) held that individuals can bring complaints against ECOWAS member states for violations of human rights protected in the African Charter on Human and Peoples' Rights (African Charter). Among other cases, Ghana also brought a complaint against the Gambia for human rights abuses of its citizens. *See* Alter et al. (2013), p. 737.

*See also* Nwauche (2009), pp. 319–347; Nwauche (2011), p. 30; Ebobrah (2010), p. 1.

[4] *Id.* at 11; *see also* U.N. Security-General, *Activities of the United Nations Office for West Africa*, ¶ 13, U.N. Doc. S/2013/384 (Jun. 28, 2013) [hereinafter *Activities of the U.N. Office for West Africa*].

and recurrent natural disasters. At the same time, the living conditions of large segments of the population continue to be affected by ongoing constraints on access to food and high fuel prices that threaten the fundamental prerequisite for development and peace. With the exception of Cape Verde and Ghana, all countries in this region are on the United Nations list of the "least developed countries", including five countries with the lowest levels of human development.[5]

The humanitarian situation in West Africa is dominated by food insecurity and the malnutrition crisis in the Sahel, displacement resulting from the operation of extremist groups in the vast desert Nord, and insecurity in north-eastern Nigeria. An estimated 11.4 million people across the Sahel lack secure sources of food and require assistance. "In some regions of Burkina Faso, Guinea, Guinea-Bissau, Liberia, and Sierra Leone, children under five years of age suffer from global acute malnutrition that is above the emergency threshold."[6] The International Organization for Migration reports that between February 2011 and April 2012, nearly 790,000 migrant workers and their families crossed the Libyan border into other countries to escape ongoing conflict.[7]

Efforts toward achieving economic integration and protecting human rights in West Africa have been hampered by political tensions, election-related instability, inter-ethnic violence, and the increasing threat of terrorist activities and transnational organized crime in the Sahel, especially following the fall of Muammar al-Qadhafi's regime.[8] In some countries in West Africa, concern has been raised over a number of alleged incidents of extrajudicial killings and forced disappearances, intimidation, threats, restrictions on freedom of expression and assembly, impunity, and serious violations of political and cultural human rights.[9] Coups and attempted coups along with unconstitutional changes in government are also a prevalent phenomenon in the region; indeed, since independence, the Economic Community of West African States (ECOWAS) has experienced at least 52 coups and attempted coups.[10]

---

[5] *Human Development Report 2014: Sustaining Human Progress: Reducing Vulnerabilities and Building Resilience*, United Nations Development Programme (UNDP) 164–167 (2014), http://hdr.undp.org/sites/default/files/hdr14-report-en-1.pdf; *see Activities of the U.N. Office for West Africa*, *supra* note 4, at ¶ 14; *see also* Human Development Index for the Year 2013, to *List of African countries by Human Development Index*, Wikipedia, https://en.wikipedia.org/wiki/List_of_African_countries_by_Human_Development_Index (2014).

[6] *Activities of the U.N. Office for West Africa*, *supra* note 4 at ¶ 15.

[7] *Migrants Caught in Crisis: The IOM Experience in Libya*, International Organization of Migration (IOM) 5 (2012), http://publications.iom.int/system/files/pdf/migrationcaughtincrisis_forweb.pdf.

[8] U.N. Security-General, *Transnational organized crime and illicit drug trafficking in West Africa and the Sahel Region*, ¶¶ 16-19; U.N. Doc. S/2013/359 (Jun. 17, 2013), http://www.securitycouncilreport.org/atf/cf/%7B65BFCF9B-6D27-4E9C-8CD3-CF6E4FF96FF9%7D/s_2013_359.pdf) [hereinafter *West Africa and the Sahel Region Report*].

[9] U.N. Secretary-General, *Activities of the United Nations Office for West Africa*, *supra* note 4 at ¶ 16.

[10] *Transnational Trafficking and the Rule of Law in West Africa: A Threat Assessment*, United Nations Office of Drugs and Crime (UNDOC) 9 (Jul. 2009), https://www.unodc.org/documents/

In 2012, a report by the Security Council portrayed a grim picture of a West Africa region where peace and security are constantly threatened by "instability as a result of States' corruption, bad governance, hunger, poverty, ill-defined borders, combined with terrorist attacks, piracy, organized crime, the uncontrollable circulation of small arms and light weapons, border friction and severe human rights violations..."[11] Moreover, reports indicate that "[s]ome 5,000 West African women have been trafficked into sexual exploitation in Europe annually in recent years, generating around $200 million [dollars in profit business]. Organized criminal syndicates from Nigeria continue to dominate those networks."[12] Chronic poverty and armed conflicts that increase the number of refugees and internally displaced persons in the region continue to exacerbate the trade in human beings and render women, children, and migrants more vulnerable to these types of crimes.

In conjunction with these issues, the flourishing tourism industry and growth in the international market for gold, cocoa, cotton, diamond, and oil has created avenues in the sub-region for the trafficking of men for forced labor and of women and children for prostitution. For instance, the 2014 Global Slavery Index estimated that 1,239,400 of the global population of 231,122,782 in the Economic Community of West African States (ECOWAS) are currently enslaved, most in agricultural or mineral production and domestic service.[13] Western African countries, including Ghana, Nigeria, and the Ivory Coast, provide more than 70% of the world's cocoa. Consequently, the Ivory Coast's large economy attracts vulnerable workers, mostly children, who ultimately end up enslaved in agriculture, cocoa plantations, mining, fishing, construction, and domestic work.[14]

The manifestations of modern slavery in West Africa take various forms and exhibit particular characteristics; in fact, the endemic and challenging pattern is less the exploitation of foreigners than the enslavement of citizens through culturally institutionalized or tolerated forms of slavery or slavery-like practices. These include the persistent cultural and economic practices of both caste and debt bondage in Mali and Niger; the exploitation of children through *vidomegon* in Benin and all African countries, and trafficking for the purposes of religious rituals. In global terms, this region has the highest measured level of forced and child marriages in the world; practices that are both prevalent and culturally tolerated in almost every country in the Economic Community of West African States (ECOWAS).

---

data-and-analysis/Studies/West_Africa_Report_2009.pdf; *see also List of Coups d'état and Coup Attempts by Country*, Wikipedia, https://en.wikipedia.org/wiki/List_of_coups_d%27%C3%A9tat_and_coup_attempts_by_country.

[11] *See West Africa and the Sahel Region Report, supra* note 8.

[12] *Id.* at ¶ 12. *See also Joint Action to Tackle West African Human Trafficking Network*, Europol (Jun. 12, 2014), https://www.europol.europa.eu/content/joint-action-tackle-west-african-human-trafficking-networks-0.

[13] *The Global Slavery Index 2013*, Walk Free Foundation, https://s3-ap-southeast-2.amazonaws.com/walkfreefoundation.org-assets/content/uploads/2016/03/14153121/Global-Slavery-Index-2013.pdf, [hereinafter *Slavery Index 2013*].

[14] *Id.* at 62.

At an international level, the United Nations (UN) has adopted a range of measures, including the specific Supplementary Protocol of the United Nations Convention against Transnational Organized Crime to Prevent, Suppress, and Punish Trafficking in Persons (Palermo Protocol),[15] especially in relation to women and children. Their aim is to provide solutions that contribute to strengthening the fight against trafficking in persons. At a regional level, West African countries have taken initiatives to address transnational organized crime and trafficking in persons within the framework of the Economic Community of West African States (ECOWAS), which established a special Trafficking in Persons Unit, drafted a declaration, and formulated an action plan against trafficking in persons. The declaration emphasizes "criminal prosecution, increased control of trafficking in the region and the importance of children as a vulnerable group."[16] Its "implementation has influenced the development and adoption of national legislation against trafficking in persons in the member countries."[17]

However, since the convention against Transnational Organized Crime and the Palermo Protocol first came into force, followed by the adoption of the first Action Plan of the Economic Community of West African States (ECOWAS) (2002–2003) and national legislation against trafficking in persons; these legal instruments and mechanisms have not been able to achieve the expected results. Thus, despite such initiatives, trafficking in persons remains a critical problem in West Africa: the persistence of harmful cultural practices, the growth and influence of organized crime networks, obsolete democracies, weak and corrupted governments that lack resources, and increasing poverty have hindered the efforts of West African countries to implement effective mechanisms to fight trafficking in persons.

Such trafficking is without doubt a lucrative business and extremely difficult to combat because the "dragnet of the traffickers is so wide."[18] No single organization or government can overcome the phenomenon on its own. It is a problem that exists at all levels of society and thus needs a coordinated and unified commitment from everyone if it is to be resolved. In addition to the legal approaches adopted by the United Nations (UN) and the Economic Community of West African States (ECOWAS), this dissertation proposes a Catholic faith-based response to effectively fight trafficking in persons in West Africa. The choice of a Catholic faith-based response is grounded in recognition of the role played by the Catholic Church and Catholic institutions in education, shaping people's opinions and behavior, raising

---

[15] Adopted in 2000, the United Nations Convention against Transnational Organized Crime came into effect on September 29, 2003.

[16] *Review of the Norwegian Ministry of Foreign Affairs Portfolio on Human Trafficking*, NORAD (Sept. 2009), http://www.norad.no/globalassets/import-2162015-80434-am/www.norad.no-ny/filarkiv/vedlegg-til-publikasjoner/review-of-the-norwegian-ministry-of-foreign-affairs-portfolio-on-human-trafficking.pdf.

[17] *Trafficking in Persons in West Africa: Analyzing the Legal and Policy Framework for the Protection of Victims*, UNOWA 9 (Dec. 31, 2013), http://www.womencount4peace.org/en/bibliographies/publications/unowa/trafficking_persons_west_africa_analyzing_legal_and_policy.

[18] *See* Agbu (2003), p. 1, 2 (quoted by Titi Atiku Abubakar, Wife of Nigeria's Vice-President).

public awareness, protecting and assisting the victims, and influencing the development of public policy in West Africa.

## 2.1 Scope and Magnitude of Trafficking in Persons

The Global Slavery Index highlights the fact that 16.36% of the estimated 29.8 million people trapped in modern slavery live in Sub-Saharan Africa. Moreover, Benin, The Ivory Coast, and The Gambia are among the ten worst countries in the world based on their policies and risk of enslavement. ECOWAS therefore has the largest modern slavery figures of all the regions measured and is also the most diverse in terms of the risk and forms of enslavement.[19] People are trafficked for a variety of reasons including forced labor and sexual exploitation. Some patterns of slavery are especially challenging because they are rooted in socio-cultural practices. In several countries, child and forced marriages continue to be tolerated in the context of informal or 'traditional' legal systems.

Despite the fact that outright slavery in the modern world has decreased significantly, the wholesale abduction of individuals and communities continues to take place in a handful of countries such as Liberia and Sierra Leone. The states of Mali and Niger, for example, are both known to have high levels of caste-based slavery and hereditary forms of debt bondage in rural areas; as well as trafficking in persons to other African states.[20] A Verité Study investigating forced labor in Ivory Coast reported the significant involvement of children in cocoa-related labor along with the widespread practice of debt bondage and slavery-like conditions.[21]

Although in West Africa the trend in trafficking is for children to be voluntarily handed over to intermediaries or to make the contact themselves; there are a growing number of instances of children being kidnapped for trafficking or recruited for armed conflict. For example, in 2014 the US Department of Labor reported that children are "abducted and forcibly recruited for use in armed conflict in northern Mali by armed rebels and extremist Islamic militia groups."[22] The risk of enslavement in the majority of ECOWAS countries is increasing as a result of ongoing conflicts, extreme poverty, corrupt government officials, porous borders, a lack of

[19] *The Global Slavery Index 2014*, Walk Free Foundation 25, http://reporterbrasil.org.br/wp-content/uploads/2014/11/GlobalSlavery_2014_LR-FINAL.pdf, [hereinafter *Slavery Index 2014*].

[20] UN General Assembly, *Report of the Special Rapporteur on contemporary forms of slavery, including its causes and consequences, Addendum: Mission to the Niger*, para.36–37 (30 July, 2015), A/HRC/30/35/Add.1, https://www.refworld.org/docid/55f7d4044.html [accessed August 16, 2021].

[21] See *Assessment of Forced Labor Risk in the Cocoa Sector of Côte d'Ivoire*, Verité, February 2019. https://www.verite.org/wp-content/uploads/2019/02/Verite-Report-Forced-Labor-in-Cocoa-in-CDI.pdf.

[22] *Findings on the Worst Forms of Child Labor 2014*, U.S. Dept. of Labor, http://www.dol.gov/ilab/reports/child-labor/findings/2014TDA/2014TDA.pdf.

adequate legislation and political will to enforce existing mandates, harmful cultural practices, the involvement of international organized crime networks, and the impact of resource exploitation to feed global markets.[23]

### 2.1.1 A Global Overview of the Problem of Trafficking in Persons

Sex trafficking is the most common form of trafficking reported in the mass media; however, this is just the tip of the iceberg as the problem is massive, complex and encompasses a wide range of exploitation. Humans are trafficked for a multitude of other purposes including labor exploitation, marriage, begging, services as child soldiers, ritual services, and the removal of organs.[24] Trafficking in persons is a worldwide problem and no country is exempt, with cases even occurring in isolated countries such as Iceland, which has a population of just 320,000 inhabitants. The scale of trafficking has also increased significantly; with ILO 2012[25] data estimating that 20.9 million trafficking victims across the world have been coerced into performing work they cannot leave. This means that around 3 out of every 1000 inhabitants in the world are engaged in forced labor at any given point in time. Women and girls are particularly affected by forced sexual exploitation; nearly 11.4 million (55%) are involved in this practice compared to 9.5 million (45%) men and boys. Adults are more likely to be trafficked than children; about 74% (15.4 million) of the victims are aged 18 years and above, while children below 17 years represent 26% (5.5 million) of the total number of victims.

The global distribution of trafficking indicates that 18.7 million (90%) out of 20.9 million forced laborers are exploited in the private economy by individuals or enterprises. Of these, 4.5 million (22%) are trafficked for the purpose of sexual exploitation and 14.2 million (68%) are victims of labor exploitation in economic sectors such as agriculture, construction, domestic work, or manufacturing. The remaining 2.2 million (10%) are involved in state-imposed forms of forced labor in prisons, enrolled in the state military, or are performing compulsory work for rebel armed forces.

Regarding regional repartition, the Asia-Pacific region (AP) has a larger number of forced laborers than other regions and accounts for the largest number of forced laborers – 11.7 million or 56% of the total global figure. The second most affected

---

[23] *Measures to Combat Trafficking in Human Beings in Benin, Nigeria, and Togo*, UNODC 65 (2006), https://www.unodc.org/documents/human-trafficking/ht_research_report_nigeria.pdf.

[24] *See* Everts (2003), pp. 149–158; Aronowitz (2009), pp. 110–121; Jackson S H (2007), p. 895.

[25] *Global Estimate of Forced Labour—Executive Summary*, ILO (2012), http://www.ilo.org/wcmsp5/groups/public/%2D%2D-ed_norm/%2D%2D-declaration/documents/publication/wcms_181953.pdf. The Global Slavery Index 2013 estimated there are 29.8 million people trapped in modern slavery. *See* Slavery Index 2013, *supra* note 13.

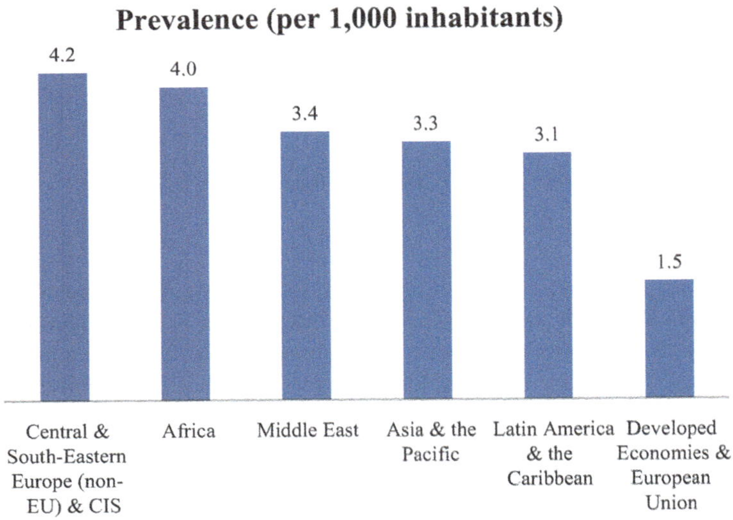


**Fig. 2.2** Prevalence of Trafficking in Persons across the World (ILO, *supra* note 25)

region is Africa (AFR) at 3.7 million (18%), followed by Latin America and the Caribbean (LA) with 1.8 million victims (9%). In the Developed Economies and European Union (DE&EU), 1.5 million (7%) people are subjected to forced labor while countries in the Central, Southeast, and Eastern Europe region (CSEE) and the Commonwealth of Independent States (non-EU) account for 1.6 million (7%). There are also an estimated 600,000 (3%) victims of labor exploitation in the Middle East (ME).

The prevalence[26] of trafficking in persons has been estimated to be 4.2 per 1000 inhabitants in the Central and South Eastern Europe region (CSEE) and 4.0 per 1000 in Africa; these appear to be the regions with the highest records (Cf. Fig. 2.2). The lowest rate is in the Developed Economies and European Union at 1.5 per 1000 inhabitants. This comparative analysis shows that Central and South Eastern Europe (CSEE) and the Commonwealth Independent States (non-EU) have a relatively high prevalence of forced labor. This variation can be explained by the low population; whereas in Asia, for example, reports of trafficking for labor and sexual exploitation and of state-imposed forced labor appear to be far greater.

Globalization has also spurred the development of tourism along with an expanded transportation infrastructure; improvements and innovations in information and transportation technologies have further promoted cross-border travel, making it faster, easier, and more affordable. This, however, has enabled pedophiles to travel and engage in sex tourism. The opening of borders has also increased business activities and the level of migration of people across borders. This has

[26]Number of victims per thousand inhabitants.

meant that the illicit trade in human beings is now expanding whilst also being hidden within the overall mass movement of people. In addition, wealth and demographic disparities among regions and countries caused by a globalized economy, the feminization of poverty, discrimination, and a lack of job opportunities for the mass population of rural communities are among several factors that continue to boost migration and the trafficking of persons into forced labor.

Since the end of the Cold War, regional conflicts have greatly increased, creating an ever growing number of economic and political refugees, an outcome that is conducive to trafficking in persons. Indeed, many rebel groups have turned to the business of trafficking in human beings to fund their military actions and to recruit soldiers. Furthermore, because consumers continually seek cheap goods and services, including easily available and accessible sexual services, producers turn to the lowest-cost labor to stay competitive, which also creates a market for trafficking in persons.[27]

The global sexual exploitation of women and girls and the desire for cheap labor has created a flourishing supply and demand for traffickers; who prefer trading in humans due to the low start-up costs, minimal risks, huge profit margin, and large demand. For organized crime groups in particular, human beings have an additional advantage over drugs in that they can be sold repeatedly. In drug trafficking, profits flow to the top of organizations whereas the small-scale entrepreneurship that characterizes trafficking in persons means that more profits go to individual criminals (making this trade more attractive for all involved).[28]

Trafficking affects every region of the world and, according to a report published the International Labor Organization (ILO) on 20 May 2014, forced labor in private economy generates US $150 billion per annum in illegal profits for criminals; approximately three times higher than previously estimated.[29] Trafficking in persons is one of the most flourishing and profitable global businesses, with a widely-quoted UN Office of Drugs and Crime report estimating it to be the third most profitable business for organized crime after drugs and the arms trade (US $32 billion per year).[30]

However, those who traffic in persons are not always motivated exclusively by pecuniary profit. Some deliberately engage in this activity for ideological purposes in order to fund terrorist groups, a guerrilla movement, or a mere insurgency. Others trade in people to serve as soldiers, militias, and suicide bombers in war-torn

---

[27] Shelley (2010); *see* Galli et al. (2010), pp. 114, 115–136 (available at: https://www.amherst.edu/media/view/247221/original/Economics+of+Human+Trafficking.pdf).

[28] *Id.*

[29] *ILO says that Forced Labor Generates Annual Profits of US$ 150 Billion*, ILO (May 20, 2014), http://www.ilo.org/global/about-the-ilo/newsroom/news/WCMS_243201/lang%2D%2Den/index.htm.

[30] Child/sex trafficking and trafficking in persons is allegedly a billion-dollar industry that makes more money than McDonalds, Wal-Mart, and Google combined. *See Id.*

countries from Colombia, Africa, the Middle East, and South Asia.[31] The consequences of trafficking are devastating for victims and have a wide-reaching social impact. It is a criminal offense that robs individuals of their rights, their human dignity, and their dreams. World leaders increasingly perceive transnational crime as an ongoing major threat to global peace and security; a crime that undermines the economic and cultural development of the international community and weakens the principles of a democratic society and the rule of law.[32]

### 2.1.2 *Regional Overview of Trafficking in Persons in West Africa*

Except for Nigeria and The Ivory Coast, West African countries share several characteristics with small scale populations and economies. For instance, private sector activity and entrepreneurship have been stifled by the dominance of an inefficient public sector, which provides limited sustainable employment opportunities for the continually growing labor force. The majority of the population live in rural areas, are illiterate, and depend on subsistence agriculture that employs about 70% of the labor force.[33] Situated within sub-Saharan Africa, West Africa is a region with a long tradition of human mobility; short- and long-term migration are driven by trading, labor migration, cyclical drought and desertification, poverty, poor economic performances, and endemic conflicts.[34] Faced with a multitude of political, social and economic challenges, the issue of trafficking has recently become a priority on the agendas of African governments.

Since the enactment of the Trafficking Victims Protection Act of 2000, the U.S. State Department has created an annual TIP report, ranking nearly every country on its efforts to achieve minimum standards for the elimination of trafficking in persons (prosecution, protection, and prevention). Following the inception of the TIP Report and coordinating efforts to combat trafficking with funding from the US government, West African countries have enacted anti-trafficking laws and taken

[31] Carter Sara A, *Taliban Buying Children for Suicide Bombers*, Washington Times, (Jul. 2, 2009), http://www.washingtontimes.com/news/2009/jul/02/taliban-buying-children-to-serve-as-suicide-bomber/?page=all; *see also* Adepelumi B P (2015), https://www.unodc.org/documents/congress//workshops/workshop2/Presentation_P_Adepelumi_African_Center_.pdf; O'Neill (2007), http://www.cnn.com/2007/WORLD/africa/02/12/child.soldiers.

[32] Shelly (2010), p. 3.

[33] Adepoju (2005a), p. 1, http://www.iom.int/jahia/webdav/site/myjahiasite/shared/shared/mainsite/policy_and_research/gcim/rs/RS8.pdf.

[34] *Id.* (2005) [available at: https://www.zef.de/uploads/tx_zefportal/Publications/a127_New%20patterns%20in%20the%20Human%20migration%20in%20West%20Africa.pdf]; Fong (2004), p. 1.

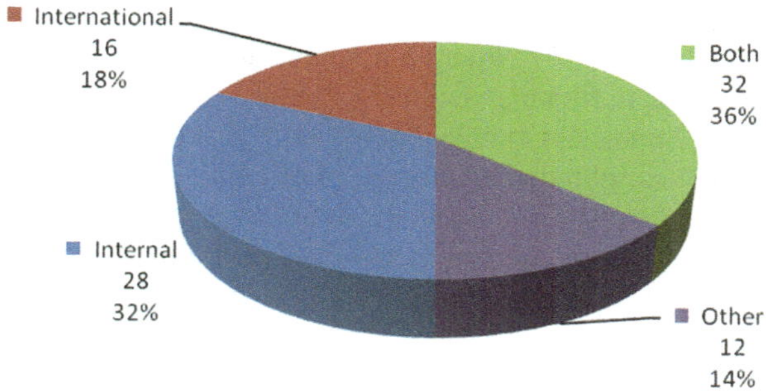


**Fig. 2.3** Migrants who are trafficked and ultimately receive IOM Assistance, 2011 (Source: IOM, Counter Trafficking and Assistance to Vulnerable Migrants Annual Report of Activities 2011, IOM 2012, p. 60 at https://www.iom.int/files/live/sites/iom/files/What-We-Do/docs/Annual_Report_2011_Counter_Trafficking.pdf)

other steps required to improve their rankings.[35] Trafficking in persons constitutes an enormous issue in West Africa insofar as all 15 states are countries of origin, transit, and destination in the trafficking supply chain.[36] Although a substantial number of people in the sub-region are trafficked across continents to Western Europe, the United States of America, Middle Eastern countries, and South America;[37] most exploitative practices take place within the national borders, close to home (Cf. Fig. 2.3). Available data show that intra-regional and domestic trafficking are the major forms of trafficking in West Africa, driving the population to neighboring countries and from rural areas to the capital cities.[38] The routes used for trafficking are continually changing according to the availability of transportation, communication, monitoring, and border control.

Precise figures for trafficking in persons at a regional level remain elusive due to its illegal and clandestine nature and variations in how trafficking is defined. However, in 2006 the National Agency for the Prohibition of Trafficking in Persons (NAPTIP) report estimated that about 200,000 to 800,000 people were trafficked

---

[35] *Report on Human Trafficking Issues to the 2015 Winter Meeting of the OSCE Parliamentary Assembly*, OSCE 8 (Feb. 18, 2015), https://www.oscepa.org/documents/all-documents/winter-meetings/2015-vienna/reports-3/2740-2015-sr-on-human-trafficking-issues-report-eng/file.

[36] Danso (2013), http://www.kaiptc.org/kaiptc-publication/the-human-being-as-a-commodity-responding-to-the-trafficking-and-trading-of-persons-in-west-africa; *see also* Office to Monitor and Combat Trafficking in Persons, *Tier Placements—Trafficking in Persons Report 2014*.

U.S. Dept. of State, http://www.state.gov/j/tip/rls/tiprpt/2014/226649.htm (Tier 2: Benin, Burkina Faso, Cabo Verde, Cote d'Ivoire, Ghana, Liberia, Niger, Nigeria, Senegal, Sierra Leone, Togo. Tier 2 Watch list: Mali, Guinea. Tier 3: Guinea-Bissau, the Gambia).

[37] *Id.* at 2; *see also Human Trafficking in Nigeria: Root Causes and Recommendations*, United Nations Educational, Scientific, and Cultural Organization (UNESCO) 11 (2006), http://unesdoc.unesco.org/images/0014/001478/147844e.pdf.

[38] Danso (2013), p. 2.

each year in the sub-region.[39] In 2017, the International Organization for Migration (IOM) assisted a total of 8, 277 Nigerian migrants arriving in Italy by sea; of which 6599 were identified as trafficking victims.[40] The business of trafficking in persons is driven loosely by "Organized Criminal Networks"[41] that are also involved in dealing weapons and narcotics, plundering property, colluding with government officials, arming local militia groups,and conducting summary executions in dozens of countries.[42] Poverty and tradition' are commonly cited as the major causes of trafficking in Africa, along with unscrupulous employers and weak state capacity or regulatory failure.[43] These are the driving forces "behind this trade, propelling vulnerable people into the hands of traffickers, who belong to both small-scale local enterprises with extensive criminal networks and to large scale multi-commodity businesses."[44]

Only a limited amount of reliable data exists on the nature and extent of trafficking in persons at regional and domestic levels; moreover, the nature of such trafficking varies from country to country. In contrast to the international trade, where 80% of victims are trafficked into prostitution, trafficking in West Africa is far more complex; men, women and children are exploited for a wide range of purposes, including forced labor in construction, forestry, fishing, mining, and agriculture, domestic servitude, street begging, child soldiers and forced recruitment into militias and armed forces, child prostitution, forced marriage, false adoption, sex tourism and entertainment, pornography, the harvesting of body organs, and other criminal activities.[45] However, anti-trafficking policies in West Africa mostly focus on children, in particular on child migration and child trafficking for the purpose of sexual exploitation. The definition of trafficking and the interventions undertaken to combat this phenomenon are rarely extended to other forms of exploitation.[46]

In the West African region, approximately 50% of victims are trafficked either internally or internationally, with 36% of victims experiencing both.

---

[39] Sessay and Olayode (2012), p. 74. "In 2006, a total of 570 West African victims were detected in 11 European countries. If one in 30 were detected, this suggests a pool of some 17,000 victims per year. Multiplying this by the average debt they are expected to repay results in a market just under US$300 million."

[40] *Human Trafficking through the Central Mediterranean Route: Data, Stories and Information Collected by the International Organization for Migration*, U.N. Migr. Agency 8–9 (2017) https://italy.iom.int/sites/default/files/news-documents/IOMReport_Trafficking.pdf.

[41] G.A. Res. 55/25 at art. 2 (a) (November 15, 2002). The U.N. Convention Against Transnational Organized Crime states: "Organized Criminal Group" shall mean a structure group of three or more persons, existing for a period of time and acting in concert with the aim of committing one or more serious crimes or offences established in accordance with the convention, in order to obtain, directly or indirectly, a financial or other material benefit.

[42] NORAD, *supra* note 16*; see also* Agbu (2003), p. 2.

[43] *Combating Forced Labour and Trafficking in Africa*, ILO 12 (Nov. 19, 2013), http://www.ilo.org/wcmsp5/groups/public/%2D%2D-africa/documents/meetingdocument/wcms_229620.pdf.

[44] UNESCO, *supra* note 37, at 12.

[45] Id.

[46] Fong (2004), p. 2.

## 2.2 Definition of Trafficking in Persons

Trafficking in persons can be defined as a process of people being recruited in their community and country of origin and moved within national borders or across international borders to an unfamiliar environment where they are controlled and exploited for purposes of forced labor, prostitution, domestic servitude and other forms of exploitation. Until the mid-1990s, trafficking was often described as a form of human smuggling and a type of illegal migration[47] An international definition of trafficking as a distinct phenomenon emerged in December 2000, with the establishment of the United Nations Protocol to Prevent, Suppress, and Punish Trafficking in Persons, supplementing the Convention against Transnational Organized Crime (UNCOC).[48] This Protocol provides a definition of trafficking in persons for the international community and frames the profile of trafficking victims.

---

[47] Laczko (2002), http://www.migrationpolicy.org/article/human-trafficking-need-better-data.

[48] G.A. Res. 55/25 at art. 3 (November 15, 2000) [hereinafter *Palermo Protocol*]. Prior to the drafting of the Palermo Protocol in 2000, other international treaties have provisions that address human rights violations taking place in the context of trafficking. These include inter alia:

the Convention on the Suppression of White Slave Trade of May 18, 1904;

the Convention on the Abolition of Slavery, the Slave Trade, and Institutions similar to Slavery, 1956; International Convention for the Suppression of the Traffic in Women and Children, 1921; the International Convention for the Suppression of the Traffic in Women of Full Age, 1933;

the Slavery Convention, 1926; and the Convention for the Suppression of the Traffic in Persons and the Exploitation of the Prostitution of Others 1949.

These early agreements were later consolidated into:

the Convention for the Suppression of the Traffic in Persons and of the Exploitation of the Prostitution of Others; ILO Convention 105 (Abolition of Forced Labour Convention), 1957;

the International Covenant on Civil and Political Rights, 1966; the International Covenant on Economic, Social and Cultural Rights, 1966; the Convention on the Elimination of all form of Discrimination Against Women, 1979; the Convention Against Torture and other Cruel, Inhuman or Degrading Treatment, 1984; the Convention on the Rights of the Child, 1989; the Convention on the Protection of the Rights of All Migrant Workers and their Families, 1990; ILO Convention 182 on Elimination of Worst Forms of Child Labor, 1999; and the Protocol Against the Smuggling of Migrants by Land, Sea and Air, supplementing the United Nations Convention Against Transnational Organized Crime, 2000.

### 2.2.1 The International Definition of Trafficking in Persons

The legally binding definition provides a framework for a comprehensive range of international, regional, and national norms and standards[49] on which to implement successful anti-trafficking policies. It is set forth in Article 3:

(a) Trafficking in persons shall mean the recruitment, transportation, transfer, harboring or receipt of persons, by means of the threat or use of force or other forms of coercion, of abduction, of fraud, of deception, of the abuse of power or of a position of vulnerability or of the giving or receiving of payments or benefits to achieve the consent of a person having control over another person, for the purpose of exploitation. Exploitation shall include, at a minimum, the exploitation of the prostitution of others or other forms of sexual exploitation, forced labor or services, slavery or practices similar to slavery, servitude or the removal of organs;
(b) The consent of a victim of trafficking in persons to the intended exploitation set forth in subparagraph (a) of this article shall be irrelevant where any of the means set forth in subparagraph (a) have been used;
(c) The recruitment, transportation, transfer, harboring or receipt of a child for the purpose of exploitation shall be considered "trafficking in persons" even if this does not involve any of the means set forth in subparagraph (a) of this article;
(d) "Child" shall mean any person under 18 years of age.[50]

As set out in the convention, the crime of trafficking in persons comprises three pronged elements, the first of which is an *action:* "recruitment, transportation, transfer, harboring or receipt of persons." The second element is the *means* used to achieve that action: "threat or use of force or other forms of coercion, of abduction, of fraud, of deception, of the abuse of power or of a position of vulnerability or of the giving or receiving payments or benefits to achieve the consent of a person having control over another person." The third element relates to the *purpose* of the intended action/means, namely exploitation.[51] All three of the listed components must be present to be considered trafficking in persons in international law and for the Trafficking Protocol and Organized Crime Convention to become operational.[52]

---

[49] *Id.*

[50] *Palermo Protocol, supra* note 48, at arts 1–5; *see also* Gallagher Anne (2010), p. 24. Gallagher, drawing heavily on the Special Rapporteur on Violence against Women, noted that the separation of the victims from their nuclear family must be included as the defining factor of trafficking: "placing or holding such person whether for pay or not, in forced labour or slavery-like practices, in a community other than the one in which such person lived at time of the original act" of transferring. This is particularly relevant in the context of West Africa where children belong to a large community, and trafficking for domestic servitude occurs close to home.

[51] Trafficking in human beings is distinct from human smuggling, and abuses of contracts and hazardous conditions of employment for laborers do not necessarily constitute trafficking in persons.

[52] Gallagher Anne (2010), p. 29; *see also* Perrin et al. (2012), p. 25.

In discussing the role of a victim's consent in the crime of trafficking in persons, the United Nations Office on Drugs and Crime (UNODC) explains that "[c]onsent of the victim can be a defence in domestic law, but as soon as any of the improper means of trafficking are established, consent becomes irrelevant and consent-based defences cannot be raised."[53] This disposition "reflects a long-standing principle of international human rights law: The intrinsic inalienability of personal freedom renders consent irrelevant to a situation in which that person's freedom is taken away;"[54] it is not possible under international law to consent to enslavement, torture, abuse, and exploitation.[55]

In effect, the free consent of trafficking victims can always be called into question owing to their social and economic vulnerabilities. During the field research in West Africa a large number of those interviewed who used the services of domestic servants and mine laborers claimed that the labor transaction is not exploitative because laborers chose their work on their own volition. Accordingly, if a transaction between two parties is strictly voluntary on both sides, it is considered to be mutually beneficial However, closer scrutiny of trafficking in persons in West Africa reveals that these children come from desperate households and therefore are being paid half the minimum wage, which is better than not being paid at all; or enjoy left overs rather than having nothing to eat at all. It is beneficial to the workers to accept this deal; the same applies for any adverse working conditions.[56]

It is telling that, when these abusers are confronted with moral quandaries, such as being asked whether they would like their own children to be in this situation or whether they would like to be involved in this kind of exploitative labor transaction, they always say no. It is clear, for example, that if a gun is pressed to someone's chest with the choice between his/her money or his/her life, it is to his/her benefit to

[53] *Toolkit to Combat Trafficking in Persons*, UNODC, https://www.unodc.org/documents/human-trafficking/Toolkit-files/08-58296_tool_1-3.pdf (accessed on August 2, 2021).

[54] Gallagher Anne (2010), p. 28. This issue came before the drafters of both the Supplementary Slavery Convention (Supplementary Convention on the Abolition of Slavery, the Slave Trade, and Institutions and Practices Similar to Slavery (1956) and the ICCPR (International Covenant on Civil and Political Rights) (1966), in the context of proposals to add the qualification "involuntary" to the term "servitude". The proposal was rejected in both instances on the grounds that "[i]t should not be possible for any person to contract himself into bondage." Ovey C and White Robin CA (2006); *See also* debate around "Consent, Coercion and the Position of Vulnerability", in ILO *supra* note 43, at 6–10; Elliot (2014), pp. 123–128.

[55] Gallagher Anne (2010), p. 34. *See also Human Trafficking for Labour Exploitation/Forced and Bonded Labour Identification—Prevention—Prosecution of Offenders, Justice for Victims,* Office of the Special Representative and Coordinator for Combating Trafficking in Human Beings (OSCE) (Nov. 7, 2005), http://www.osce.org/cthb/31923?download=true. In the case of a child, the permission of the parents should be irrelevant in situations where parents consent because they think it is in the interest of the child but are not aware they have entered into an agreement that constitutes a form of child trafficking.

[56] *Human Trafficking: Issues Beyond Criminalization*, Vatican 478–479 (2016), https://dyhyjqmcimsyl.cloudfront.net/assets/files/6179/vatican-humantrafficking.pdf.

choose the latter. However, it cannot then be claimed that he or she consented to a transaction in which he or she hands his or her money over to the robber.[57]

From the above definition of trafficking in persons, "another legal question which arises is whether under domestic law the subject had the capacity to consent to the recruitment or subsequent treatment."[58] According to Article 3(c) of the Trafficking in Persons Protocol, a child under 18 is a victim as they cannot legally give their consent to trafficking, owing to their particularly vulnerable status, even if no means of coercion or deception are involved. Furthermore, parents cannot give their consent to the use of their child for labor, which is of fundamental relevance in West Africa where child trafficking often occurs with the consent of the parents and, sometimes, with the voluntary agreement of the children themselves.[59]

The 2000 Anti-trafficking instrument provides several valuable insights when compared to the former, as the Protocol has shifted from prostitution *per se* to exploitation as fundamental to the trafficking experience. Moreover, the definition includes a wide range of non-prostitution-related trafficking offenses that can affect any human being irrespective of age and gender such as trafficking for forced labor or services, slavery, servitude, removal of organs, begging, unlawful adoption, child recruitment into military service, or forced marriage.[60] Furthermore, the Legislative Guide for the Implementation of the Palermo Protocol makes it clear that trafficking in persons occurs both across borders and within a country and takes place with or without the involvement of organized crime groups.[61]

This definition of human trafficking makes it is easier to understand the challenge involved in producing comprehensive and accurate data worldwide regarding the extent of the problem and the number of victims. Trafficking in persons, within but especially across international borders, always involves illegal and clandestine activities, even if per se it does not constitute a criminal offense in the country (for example, for agricultural work or mining). Traffickers often resort to fraudulent and deceptive means to recruit people, including illegal entry into a country and involvement in prohibited jobs such as prostitution. In addition to these conditions, trafficking by nature involves coercion or deception, which is sometimes hard to prove as victims are reluctant to report it or to seek assistance from local authorities.

---

[57] *Id.*

[58] UNODC, *supra* note 53.

[59] *Child Trafficking in West Africa: Policy Responses*, United Nations Children's Fund (UNICEF) 3 (Apr. 2002), http://www.unicef-irc.org/publications/pdf/insight7.pdf.

[60] Edwards (2008), p. 1, 14.

[61] *Legislative Guides for the Implementation of the United Nations Convention against Transnational Organized Crime and the Protocol Thereto*, Part IV, Chapter II, ¶ 25; U.S. DEP'T OF STATE, TRAFFICKING IN PERSONS REPORT 2019, https://www.state.gov/reports/2019-trafficking-in-persons-report/.

### 2.2.2 *The Relevance of the Definition of Trafficking in Persons in West Africa*

By providing an internationally agreed definition, the Palermo Protocol established common standards in approaches to fight trafficking in persons; this is a prerequisite for efficient international cooperation when investigating and prosecuting trafficking cases and also assists in the development of indicators and providing a uniform basis for statistical and research purposes. As expected, this Protocol provides the baseline for a legal conceptual framework from which most regional and national anti-trafficking legislations have either been replicated or modified to suit idiosyncratic local realities. For instance, Article 28(j) of the Protocol on Amendments to the Protocol on the Statute of the African Court of Justice and Human Rights incorporates explicitly the definition of trafficking in persons anchored in the Palermo Protocol.[62] Definitions of trafficking therefore vary in practice among different sectors and countries may apply them differently according to their social, cultural, political and legal traditions. This has practical implications as "these variations can lead to fragmented approaches in combating human trafficking in Africa and make regional law enforcement cooperation more difficult."[63]

From 2000, the Economic Community of West African States (ECOWAS) operated using the so-called Palermo Protocols, which prohibit trafficking in persons and set guiding standards that enable domestic law to address this criminal offense. However, in the ECOWAS region, "[t]he concept of trafficking of adult men and women for labor exploitation, whether internally, within the region or outside the region, is clearly not well understood or recognized as a significant form of trafficking".[64] Given the African practice of migration and the fostering of children with family members, a "sub-regional workshop on trafficking in child domestics in West and Central Africa" held in July 1998 in Cotonou, Benin described the parameters used to determine victims of trafficking in persons and, consequently, the rights and protections to which they are entitled.

---

[62] African Union, Protocol on Amendments to the Protocol on the Statute of the African Court of Justice and Human Rights, 27 June 2014, Article 28 J.

[63] Obokata (2019), p. 538.

[64] *Counter-Trafficking Baseline Assessment*, FMM West Africa 6 (Aug. 2017), http://rodakar.iom.int/oimsenegal/sites/default/files/reports/fmm%20west%20africa%20-%20counter%20traffcking.pdf; Shu-Acquaye (2012–2013), pp. 1, 4; *see West Africa and the Sahel Region Report, supra* note 8; *see also, Trafficking in Persons Report 2009*, U.S. Dep't of St. 113–115 (Jun. 2009) http://www.state.gov/documents/organization/123357.pdf. The U.S. Department of State's Trafficking in Persons Report, June 2009, lists Cote d'Ivoire as a Tier 2 Watch List for a third consecutive year because the country does not fully comply with minimum standards for the elimination of trafficking. For example, it has never reported a single prosecution or conviction for trafficking in persons. There is a lack of understanding among police and officials who have in the past characterized children found in a brothel raid as "voluntary prostitutes," rather than presumptive victims of trafficking, and for a third consecutive year there has been a failure to investigate NGO reports that police harass undocumented foreign women forced into prostitution by demanding sex in exchange for not being arrested.

In line with the Palermo Protocol, the regional legal definition considers the "action of moving" to be an important element when referring to trafficking in persons; this reflects the social and cultural patterns of migratory movements within and beyond the borders of West African countries. Additionally, for this transfer to take place, specifically with regard to the trafficking of children, there should be:[65]

Firstly, the conclusion of a transaction referring to "any institution or practice through which young people, below 18 years, are handed over by either or both parents, or by a guardian to a third person, whether for a fee or not, with the intention of exploiting the person or the work of the young person."[66] The sub-regional consultation identified six different types of criminal offenses that fall under the definition of child trafficking in West and Central Africa, depending on the means by which traffickers to lure their victims:

**Abduction of Children** Although in most cases children are voluntarily handed over, and some children decide to contact the third parties themselves, a growing number of children are reported to have been abducted from their homes. For instance, the kidnapping of children has taken place in Sokoto State, Nigeria, where they are sold to businessmen for amounts ranging from ₦50,000 to 100,000 (US $500–1000) to be used as laborers or as ritual or sex objects.[67] Furthermore, in Liberia, children have been kidnapped to become soldiers and sex slaves in armed conflicts.

**Placement as Sale** This involves the payment of money to impoverished parents who bond their children to a third party for a set price. Parents are promised that the child will be treated well and will receive education or vocational training skills. From one country to another, the amounts paid to parents vary between 10,000 and 100,000 FCFA (US $14–140);

**Bonded Placement or Transfers of Pawns** The practice of offering the labor of children as reimbursement for debt is a custom embedded in South Asia. However, cases of bonding of children for debt have also been reported in Benin and Ghana;

**Temporary Placement for a Token Sum or for Gift Items** "The child is handed over to a third party for a set period of time, for a token sum paid in cash or kind. The amount depends on the duration agreed upon and the age of the child. The intermediary collects the wages paid by the employer, which he keeps for himself."[68]

**Placement as a Service for a Fee** At the request of parents, the agent places the child in domestic work for a fee. The parents also have to bear "handling costs". In

---

[65] *Combating Trafficking in Children for Labour Exploitation in West and Central Africa: Synthesis Report*, ILO 3–4 (Dec. 1, 2001), http://www.ilo.org/ipec/Informationresources/WCMS_IPEC_PUB_776/lang%2D%2Den/index.htm. [hereinafter *Children for Labour*].

[66] Economic and Social Council Res. 608 (XXI), at art. 1(d) (April 30, 1957).

[67] *Ibid.*

[68] ILO, *supra* note 65, at 3.

Cameroon, it has been reported that parents will pay up to 100,000 FCFA (US $140) for a child that is placed by a so-called "matrimonial agency";[69]

**Placement as Embezzlement** A professional employment agent or an intermediary deceive the parents by declaring that the child will be sent to school, receive vocational training, and be taken care of by the host household. Instead, the child is enrolled in paid work, which often provides no scope for skill development. The intermediary collects the wages directly from the employer and does not pay the parents anything. Ghanaian women are operating in this way in the Makola, Nima, Maamobi, and Agbogloshie markets in the suburbs of Accra.

Secondly, the intervention of an intermediary (a third person or group other than the child's parents); this distinctive characteristic described by the regional anti-trafficking workshop is anchored in the ILO Convention No. 189. Any work undertaken by a child is not necessarily trafficking. Children in their own homes who undertake an excessive workload as a direct consequence of coercion by those close to them are in a situation of child labor.[70]

Thirdly, the motive to exploit and make profit from trafficking. The purpose of trafficking places great emphasis on exploitation. In effect, exploitation occurs in "a situation where someone makes someone else work in unfavorable conditions in order to earn as much money as possible."[71] Thus, trafficking in human beings "relates to excessively degrading circumstances in employment or service relationships involving fundamental breaches of human rights."[72]

Some commentators have argued that the international definition, tailored on the model of transnational trafficking with the involvement of large networks of organized crime, does not entirely fit the contextual situation in Africa. Trafficking in Africa is usually (but not always) managed by small, family-related networks and does not always take place across national borders.[73] To dispel any ambiguity, "[t]he provisions of both the Convention and the Protocol operate require that the offense of trafficking be established in the domestic law of every State Party, independently

---

[69] *Id.*

[70] *Hard to See, Harder to Count—Survey Guidelines to Estimate Forced Labour of Adults and Children*, ILO 17 (Jun. 1, 2012), http://ilo.org/global/topics/forced-labour/publications/WCMS_182096/lang%2D%2Den/index.htm; Int'l Programme on the Elimination of Child Labour (IPEC), *Child Labour and Domestic Work*, ILO, http://ilo.org/ipec/areas/Childdomesticlabour/lang%2D%2Den/index.htm (accessed on August 5, 2021).

[71] Boot-Matthijssen et al. (2008), p. 149, http://hrlibrary.umn.edu/research/Netherlands/Netherlands-Trafficking_Fifth%20Report%20Rapporteur.pdf.

[72] *Id.* at 150; *see also* Keo (2013), p. 65.

[73] *Legislative Guides for the Implementation of the United Nations Convention against Transnational Organized Crime and the Protocol Thereto*, UNODC 2, ¶ 23 (2004), https://www.unodc.org/pdf/crime/legislative_guides/Legislative%20guides_Full%20version.pdf [hereinafter *UNODC-Protocol*]; *see also* Angeles Maria B & Truong T-D, *Searching for Best Practices to Counter Human Trafficking in Africa: A Focus on Women and Children*, UNESCO 18 (Mar. 2005), http://humantraffickingsearch.org/wp-content/uploads/2017/06/138447e.pdf.

of its transnational nature or the involvement of the organized criminal group."[74] Despite these conceptual challenges, the adoption of the UN Protocol has facilitated discussion on trafficking in persons. Notably, the conceptual insight that can be extracted from the UN definition is that "the purpose of exploitation as well as the presence of movement"[75] are two associated elements used to determine when trafficking occurs.

Controversies regarding the definition of trafficking revolve around the question of whether movement within or across the borders is a requirement for the conduct to constitute trafficking; or whether any physical movement from one location to another is even involved. Interpreting the Protocol conjointly with the UN Convention, Jean Allain concluded that the provisions of the Protocol include situations where a person is trafficked across an international border or within national jurisdictions. Thus, the victim may be moved solely within one state and the crime would be 'transnational in nature' when, for instance, it involves an organized criminal group that operates in more than one State.[76] Therefore, trafficking in persons requires some degree of movement or social isolation as the strategy of traffickers consists of moving those trafficked away from familiar surroundings to restrict their ability to seek help or escape, and to facilitate the control and exploitation of trapped victims (Chap. 4 of this dissertation will discuss this issue further).[77] For this reason, social isolation or movement of the trafficked person to an unfamiliar location forms part of the definition of the crime.

Furthermore, "movement" for the purpose of facilitating "control and exploitation" of the trafficked person distinguishes trafficking in persons from other crimes such as forced labor. For example, what is the difference between a victim of forced labor, who is recruited by means of deception, force, or coercion and subsequently exploited for profit; and a victim of trafficking for forced labor? Exploitation by means of coercion and deception are intrinsic to both activities; however physical movement of the victims to unfamiliar places, away from home while being controlled by the trafficker, appears to distinguish labor trafficking from forced labor. "Workers who are subject to forced labor are abused, but nonetheless free to leave or

---

[74] Gallagher Anne (2010), p. 79; *UNODC—Protocol, supra* note 73, at pt 2, ¶ 25.

[75] Some sources argue that the international definition enshrined in the Trafficking Protocol or the United States' definition 103(8) of the Trafficking Victims Protection Act of 2000 do not require physical movement. Localized trading within a specific area may meet all the requirements. With reference to the definitions of "severe forms of trafficking" in the Trafficking Victims Protection Act, the 2007 and 2008 TIP Reports explicitly state that "a victim need not be physically transported from one location to another in order for the crime to fall within these definitions." (*See Trafficking in Persons Report*, U.S. State Dept. (2008), 6, https://www.state.gov/documents/organization/105501.pdf, and *Trafficking in Persons Report*, U.S. State Dept. (2007), 7, https://www.state.gov/documents/organization/82902.pdf).

[76] Allain (2014), p. 111, 114.

[77] *Breaking the Cycle of Vulnerability: Responding to the Health Needs of Trafficked Women in Eastern and Southern Africa*, Int'l Org. Migr. 20 (2006), http://publications.iom.int/system/files/pdf/iom_breakingthecycleofvulnerability.pdf; *see also* Allais et al. (2010).

resign, while trafficked persons cannot leave, because they are kept under control of the trafficker."[78]

Moreover, the migration and placement of children in the home of a better-off relative or acquaintance is a traditional practice in Africa; the foster child or adolescent performs light housework in exchange for education and training opportunities. Only the concept of "exploitation" distinguishes children at work placed within this custom and those that are trafficked for the purposes of exploitation. Unfortunately, many of these children become victims of trafficking for forced labor when they are placed in exploitative situations.[79] It is therefore evident that trafficking remains intricate in nature and often entails a complex process involving multiple actors. Palermo's definition of trafficking not only requires force, fraud, or coercion to satisfy its "means element"; it also includes a broader list of potential means, such as the "abuse of power or of a position of vulnerability." In developing countries, traffickers often exploit the vulnerabilities of a trafficked person; for example, through poverty, starvation, or survival affecting themselves or their families, including situations where the victim "has no real and acceptable alternative but to submit to the abuse."[80]

In terms of legal support, the African Charter on Human and Peoples' Rights is a regional instrument that can be invoked to combat trafficking in persons. This Charter is supported by two relevant instruments: The African Charter on the Rights and Welfare of the African Child and the Protocol of the Rights of women, both of which secure legal provisions for the protection of women and children against trafficking. The African Union Commission Initiative against Trafficking (AU. COMMIT) calls upon states to ratify the Palermo Protocol through the Ouagadougou Action Plan to Combat Trafficking in Persons (November 2006). At a sub-regional level, the Economic Community of West African States (ECOWAS) operates using the so-called Palermo Protocols, which prohibit trafficking in persons and aim to set guiding standards that enable domestic law to address this criminal offense. However, in the Economic Community of West African States (ECOWAS) region, "[t]he concept of trafficking of adult men and women for labor exploitation,

---

[78] *Id.*

[79] *Combating Trafficking in Children for Labour Exploitation in West and Central Africa: Synthesis Report*, ILO 2 (Dec. 1, 2001), http://www.ilo.org/ipec/Informationresources/WCMS_IPEC_PUB_776/lang%2D%2Den/index.htm. [hereinafter *Children for Labour*].

[80] Jane K, Prosecuting Human Trafficking as a Crime Against Humanity (2011), 9, (unpublished J.D. thesis, Columbia Law School) (on file with Columbia Law School library system) (available at: http://blogs.law.columbia.edu/gslonline/files/2011/02/Jane-Kim_GSL_Prosecuting-Human-Trafficking-as-a-Crime-Against-Humanity-Under-the-Rome-Statute-2011.pdf); the Palermo Protocol addresses the evidentiary burden imposed by the traditional means standard of force, fraud, and coercion that is often difficult to prove in the context of trafficking in persons, and also offers no loophole enabling traffickers to use the alleged consent of the victim in their own defense.

whether internally, within the region or outside the region, is clearly not well understood or recognized as a significant form of trafficking".[81]

## 2.3 The Cycle and Flows of Trafficking in Persons

Trafficking in persons thus refers to the process of people being abducted or recruited in their country of origin, transferred through transit regions, and then exploited in the destination country for forced and/or sexual labor. An additional phase may consist of laundering the criminal proceeds, depending on the size and sophistication of the trafficking operation.[82] This section discusses the major stages of the process, describes related actions, and identifies the countries and regions most widely reported in association with each stage of the process.

### *2.3.1 Trafficking of Persons Across International Borders*

Transnational trafficking of persons requires substantial levels of organization, especially if this entails trafficking a group of victims across borders with exploitation taking place over an extended period of time. It involves a series of actions carried out by different actors. Trafficking across borders is carried out by organized crime networks that "have operational capacity in source, transit, and destination countries and the capability to perform all aspects of trafficking from the recruitment and exploitation of victims to document forgery, [safe houses], money laundering and high-level corruption."[83]

A typical case is the Nigerian organized crime ring, which is directly involved in managing the trafficking of young women from rural areas of Benin City to Italy via Lome' (Togo). The traffickers have connections with the family members of victims

---

[81] *Counter-Trafficking Baseline Assessment*, FMM West Africa 6 (Aug. 2017), http://rodakar.iom.int/oimsenegal/sites/default/files/reports/fmm%20west%20africa%20-%20counter%20traffcking.pdf; Shu-Acquaye (2012–2013); *see West* U.N. Security-General, *Transnational organized crime and illicit drug trafficking in West Africa and the Sahel Region*, U.N. Doc. S/2013/359 (Jun. 17, 2013) (available at: http://www.securitycouncilreport.org/atf/cf/%7B65BFCF9B-6D27-4E9C-8CD3-CF6E4FF96FF9%7D/s_2013_359.pdf) [hereinafter *West Africa and the Sahel Region Report*]; *see also*, U.S. Dep't of State, 2009 Trafficking in Persons Report 113–115 (Jun. 2009) http://www.state.gov/documents/organization/123357.pdf.

[82] *Trafficking in Persons: Global Patterns*, UNODC 57 (Apr. 2006), http://www.unodc.org/pdf/traffickinginpersons_report_2006ver2.pdf.

[83] U.N. Global Initiative to Fight Human Trafficking (U.N. GIFT) *The Vienna Forum to Fight Human Trafficking*, UNODC 11 (Feb. 2008), https://www.unodc.org/documents/human-trafficking/2008/BP027TransnationalOrganizedCrimeandHumanTrafficking.pdf; U.N. Gift, *Analyzing the Business Model of Trafficking in Human Beings to Better Prevent the Crime,* OSCE (2010), https://www.osce.org/cthb/69028?download=true.

in the origin country, along with the smuggling route, and control their exploitation in brothels throughout different areas of Europe. A ritual oath is used to ensure the victims remain compliant.[84] The large number of victims involved and the high prevalence of women compelled into prostitution and men into forced labor are also characteristics of the crime.

#### 2.3.1.1 Recruitment in Countries of Origin

The first criminal action involved in trafficking in persons begins in the origin countries with the recruitment of victims or potential victims, whether by deception or by physical or psychological coercion. These criminal offenses are associated with the provision of fraudulent or deceptive information to induce the victim to cooperate, abduction or kidnapping, and document forgery.[85] This lament by a Togolese mother reported by ILO reflects the typical pattern of child trafficking in West and Central Africa:

> . . .when she (the intermediary) came, she gave me 25,000 FCFA (US $35) to take care of my children. She promised to find my son a job and said that I would receive some money every month. I thanked God, because I thought that I had at last found a way of taking care of my seven children. I had no idea what she really had in mind for my child![86]

There have been numerous reports of women and children being lured by criminals into leaving their countries of origin with false promises of education, employment as dancers or waitresses, and false marriages.[87] Migrant workers in rural areas are highly likely to rely on recruitment agencies due to extremely complex visa procedures, or a general lack of familiarity and connection with the destination country. In addition, recruiters and recruitment agencies are alleged to have taken advantage of migrant workers' lack of education, language skills, and information by enticing them with offers of well-paid jobs abroad.[88]

The United Nations Office on Drugs and Crime (UNODC) (2006) reports that Western Africa is the predominant region for the origin of trafficking in persons, both inter-regionally and intra-regionally. Among the reported origin countries in Africa, Nigeria is the only country ranked "very high", according to the United Nations Office on Drugs and Crime (UNODC) citation index, followed by Benin and

---

[84] *Global Report on Trafficking in Persons 2014*, UNODC 56, http://www.unodc.org/res/cld/bibliography/global-report-on-trafficking-in-persons_html/GLOTIP_2014_full_report.pdf.

[85] *Trafficking in Persons: Global Patterns*, UNODC 57 (Apr. 2006), http://www.unodc.org/pdf/traffickinginpersons_report_2006ver2.pdf.

[86] *Combating Child Trafficking in West and Central Africa*, 39 ILO World of Work 1, 6 (Jun. 2001).

[87] Fitzgibbon (2003), p. 81, 84.

[88] *The Role of Recruitment Fees and Abusive and Fraudulent Recruitment Practices of Recruitment Agencies in Trafficking in Persons*, UNODC 6 (Jun. 20, 2015), https://www.unodc.org/documents/human-trafficking/2015/Recruitment_Fees_Report-Final-22_June_2015_AG_Final.pdf; Qerimi (2012); Adebayo Adeyemi (2015).

Ghana, each reported as having a "high" incidence of trafficking.[89] These countries are characterized most prominently by economic poverty and unemployment; rank higher on corruption indices; have experienced recent political transitions, civil wars, and civil disruptions; and are generally more rural.[90] Individuals from these countries and geographic areas are particularly vulnerable to being lured by traffickers.

Whereas intra-regional trafficking occurs within the African continent and among countries such as South Africa, Libya, Gabon, and Equatorial Guinea, inter-regional trafficking involves the movement of victims across the African continent. This encompasses the trafficking of victims to Italy, Spain, United Kingdom, France, the Middle East, Gulf states, and other countries in the European Union.[91] Of the 39 sources collected in the Trafficking Database reporting the trafficking in persons in Africa, 33 report the sub-region as an origin of trafficking, and 12 as a destination.[92] For instance, the Moroccan police reported that out of the 27,000 migrants apprehended in 2004, over half were of West African origin, with most migrants coming from the Gambia, Ghana, Mali, and Senegal regions, respectively.[93]

In general, cross border trafficking occurs within a well organized criminal network where different actors are involved in navigating trafficked people across the border; indeed, there is a well-established organized criminal ring that runs the business of trafficking around the West African hub. One of the most recent and widely publicized child trafficking scandals in West Africa occurred on October 30, 2007, when Zoé's Ark (*L'Arche de Zoé*), a French charity organization providing aid for children affected by the conflict in Darfur, attempted to take 103 children to Paris under the pretense that they were orphans; the government of Chad arrested six of its members for the abduction of children.[94]

Women are often visible actors within a trafficking ring, as traffickers are usually expected to be men.[95] The modus operandi of the Nigerian organized crime network provides an illustrative example of this. Within this network, recruitment is

---

[89] *Trafficking in Persons: Global Patterns*, UNODC 87 (Apr. 2006), http://www.unodc.org/pdf/traffickinginpersons_report_2006ver2.pdf; *see also* Davies (2012), p. 14, https://www.gov.uk/government/uploads/system/uploads/attachment_data/file/115923/occ103.pdf.

[90] UN-Habitat (2007), p. 63 https://www.un.org/ruleoflaw/files/urbansafetyandsecurity.pdf.

[91] de Haas (2008), p. 32, http://publications.iom.int/system/files/pdf/mrs-32_en.pdf; *see also* Territoriality and Migration in the E.U. Neighbourhood: Spilling Over the Wall 104 (eds., Margaret Walton-Roberts & Jenna Hennebry, Springer Science & Business Media 2013).

[92] UNODC, *supra* note 85, at 85.

[93] Territoriality and Migration in the E.U. Neighbourhood: Spilling Over the Wall 104 (eds., Margaret Walton-Roberts & Jenna Hennebry, Springer Science & Business Media 2013), at 105.

[94] *Profile: Zoe's Ark*, BBC News (Oct. 29 2007), http://news.bbc.co.uk/2/hi/europe/7067374.stm.

[95] *Money Laundering Risks Arising from Trafficking in Human Beings and Smuggling of Migrants*, Financial Action Taskforce (FATF) 12 (Jul. 2011), http://www.fatf-gafi.org/media/fatf/documents/reports/Trafficking%20in%20Human%20Beings%20and%20Smuggling%20of%20Migrants.pdf.

organized by so-called "madams"[96] who organize girls and women trafficked for sexual exploitation, control their activities, and collect the proceeds.[97] The trafficker recruits victims related to her own community or citizenship, and moves them to a destination country where she resides and maintains her business dealings. She always uses commercial carriers and ostensibly legitimate methods to circumvent immigration controls and secure a visa for the potential travelers through visa shopping: the persons then overstay their visa once they reach the destination country.[98] This is a common trend in transnational and transregional trafficking in all West African countries with cases of Beninese, Togolese, Nigerian, Burkinabe, Senegalese, and Nigerian recruiters settling in Gabon, Angola, Guinea Equatorial, The Ivory Coast, and Europe; where they engage in commercial activities and regularly return to their country of origin to go around villages to recruit girls and children.

The recruitment of trafficking victims usually peaks during the dry season, which is the agricultural off season when children are available and parents have little income. These women return to their native villages during traditional festivals, bringing with them new victims. Women of a high social status generally offer presents to the families and parents who, in return, entrust them with their children.[99] When necessary, they resort to the recommendation and notoriety of the community or village leaders to support their recruitment campaign.[100] More forceful recruitment methods such as kidnapping the children from their home village or on streets in the cities to which they have migrated, or the enrollment of child soldiers, are also ways in which people are trafficked into forced labor or commercial sexual exploitation in West Africa.[101]

Along with recruitment through personal contact, another means used to recruit persons in cities for exploitation is the Internet. New technologies offer a broader range of approaches to recruitment from offers aimed at a wide audience, such as employment opportunities overseas, to more targeted spaces, chatrooms, spam mail,

---

[96] Prina (2003), p. 30, http://www.unicri.it/topics/trafficking_exploitation/archive/women/nigeria_1/research/rr_prina_eng.pdf. A "Madam" is a wealthy woman usually running a business abroad and who may represent an ideal for young girls. Sometimes this *madam* - who always remains in Nigeria—also assumes the role of *sponsor*, financially guaranteeing the journey towards Europe: in this latter case we are faced with a subject who has acquired a certain amount of importance and considerable prestige in the eyes of the community and has vital economic resources.

[97] *Money Laundering Risks Arising from Trafficking in Human Beings and Smuggling of Migrants*, Financial Action Taskforce (FATF) (Jul. 2011), 12 http://www.fatf-gafi.org/media/fatf/documents/reports/Trafficking%20in%20Human%20Beings%20and%20Smuggling%20of%20Migrants.pdf.

[98] Visa shopping is the act of filing visa petitions with more than one of a state's Embassies or Consulates in a region. The theory behind visa shopping is twofold. One is that some consular officials may not adjudicate visa applications as strictly as others. Second, that by only applying for one or two visas at a time, the trafficker is less likely to draw attention to him or herself.

[99] Loungou (2011), p. 256 (available at: http://com.revues.org/6389).

[1C0] *Id.*

[1C1] U.S. Dept. of Labor, *supra* note 22.

and Internet dating.[102] As social means, they are user-friendly, effective, unrestricted, cheap, extremely fast, and anonymous;, they deliver victims "on a plate" to traffickers, who no longer have to leave their homes to find them.[103] Online employment agencies, promising work abroad or seeking fashion or artists' models, and marriage agencies can also be used to lure victims.[104]

'Friending' on web-based social networks and appearing benevolent are often astute ways to persuade West African young people and teenagers to travel abroad of their own free will. "The main attractions of sham marriages are the promises made to women by recruiters that create the illusion of considerable gain made with little effort."[105] West African women and girls also travel to Europe with men they are in a romantic relationship with, who then force them into the sex industry.[106] In conclusion, resources and expertise to combat human trafficking in countries of origin are aimed at legal, infrastructural, and political capacity-building. This enables them to address the conditions that render individuals vulnerable to trafficking and empowers them to resist potentially dangerous situations by offering viable alternatives.[107]

#### 2.3.1.2 Transferring Persons Through Countries of Transit

The second stage of the trafficking process is the movement of the potential victim within or across borders; this is important to the trafficker as it enables them to isolate the victims and keep them in a state of total dependency. This can be achieved by transporting potential victims within their own country to a region or town with which they are unfamiliar and where they are culturally, linguistically, or physically isolated.[108]

---

[102] *Trafficking in Human Beings: Internet Recruitment*, Council of Europe 21 (2007), http://www.coe.int/t/dghl/monitoring/trafficking/Source/THB_Internetstudy_en.pdf.

[103] *Id.*

[104] *Id.*

[105] *A Report Concerning The Macro And Micro Analyses Of Human Trafficking*, Trafficking as a Criminal Enterprise (TRACE) 48 (Nov. 25, 2014), http://trace-project.eu/wp-content/uploads/2014/11/TRACE_D1.3_Final.pdf.

[106] The Nature and Scale of Human Trafficking in 2013, National Crime Agency (NCA) 12 (Sept. 30, 2014), http://www.nationalcrimeagency.gov.uk/publications/399-nca-strategic-assessment-the-nature-and-scale-of-human-trafficking-in-2013/file.

[107] *Ensuring Human Rights Protection in Countries of Destination: Breaking the Cycle of Trading*, OSCE 13 (Sept. 23, 2004), https://www.osce.org/odihr/16201?download=true; *An Introduction to Human Trafficking: Vulnerability, Impact and Action*, United Nations Office on Drugs and Crime (UNODC) (2008), 78, at https://www.unodc.org/documents/human-trafficking/An_Introduction_to_Human_Trafficking_-_Background_Paper.pdf.

[108] Human Trafficking is a Modern Day Form of Slavery, IOM 8, https://ec.europa.eu/anti-trafficking/sites/antitrafficking/files/train_the_trainers_manual_1.pdf (accessed on August 30, 2021).

Once the recruitment phase is successfully completed, the victim is smuggled through transit countries characterized by corruption and porous borders affiliated with organized crime groups involved in trafficking. In general, organized criminals smuggle victims over any border that facilitates their passage.[109] Victims primarily travel to Europe by plane from West African international airports; they may also be transported by land and sea across the Mediterranean.[110] Several transit countries may be involved and alternative routes may vary significantly to avoid detection. In reports by the United Nations on transnational Human Trafficking, 'transit countries' "refers to the countries that make up the transnational route by which a victim is transported from their country of origin to a destination country determined by the traffickers."[111] During the transportation process, victims may be transferred from one group of traffickers to another or harbored in a transit country for an undetermined period of time. The transit country may eventually become the destination where they are placed into forced labor. Some trafficking cases may involve several transit and destination phases.

Irregular migration by air always involves abuse and fraud in relation to official traveling documents; this can include the lending of stolen passports with photos that resemble the migrants (the use of "look-alikes"),[112] acquisition of genuine travel documents through bribery or other forms of corruption, the alteration of genuine documents, or outright forgery.[113] Another method employed to bring trafficked persons into a destination country is to apply for visa status on the basis of fraudulent

---

[109]Nikolic-Ristanovic V et al., *Trafficking in People in Serbia, Belgrade*, OSCE 63 (2004), http://www.osce.org/documents/fry/2004/07/3290_en.pdf.

[110]*Trafficking in Persons to Europe for Sexual Exploitation*, UNODC, p.4, https://ec.europa.eu/anti-trafficking/sites/antitrafficking/files/trafficking_in_persons_to_europe_for_sexual_exploitation_1.pdf.

[111]UNODC, *supra* note 89, at 60.

[112]*Trafficking in Human Beings, Especially Women and Children,* United Nations Asia and Far East Institute (UNAFEI) 158, http://www.unafei.or.jp/english/pdf/RS_No62/No62_19RC_Group1.pdf (accessed on August 14, 2021); Aronowitz (2009), p. 56. Picture substitution in passports or passport rental from young women to smuggle lookalikes into a country have also been reported by law enforcement officials. Although an increasing number of passports contain bio-information printed on chips, this is clearly not the case in many developing nations where funds are scarce, and the verification of a person's identity is difficult—birth records in rural villages are often nonexistent.

[113]*The Role of Organized Crime in the Smuggling of Migrants from West Africa to the European Union*, UNODC 11 (2011), http://www.unodc.org/documents/human-trafficking/Migrant-Smuggling/Report_SOM_West_Africa_EU.pdf; *Leveraging Anti-Money Laundering Regimes to Combat Trafficking in Human Beings*, Organization for Security and Co-operation in Europe (OSCE) (2014), https://www.osce.org/secretariat/121125?download=true; "Travelling on falsified documents renders the migrant/trafficked person extremely vulnerable to abuse. They will likely be told by traffickers that because of their false documents they cannot approach the police for fear of arrest or deportation. This serves to keep trafficked persons in their trafficking situation." *Child Trafficking in Sierra Leone 2005*, UNICEF 89, http://lastradainternational.org/lsidocs/244%20Child%20Trafficking%20in%20Sierra%20Leone%20(UNICEF).pdf.

supporting documents.[114] Traffickers may, under false pretenses, attempt to acquire legal visas into a desired country from the embassy, or use this country as a point of entry into Western Europe.[115] Thus, regular three-month tourist visas,[116] entertainment visas, or student visas may be used for travel and to move across national borders. The holders of visas can overstay and work unlawfully or change their visa status as required to remain in the country.[117]

Finally, entering furtively into a country is a way to cross the border without an immigration check, and without being noticed by the immigration officer. Studies conducted by Customs and Immigration officials indicate that "some pass through the immigration booth at the airport by sinking down out of sight, and in the case of sneaking at sea, stowaways pass the immigration check at the seaport by hiding in the container of the ship."[118]

For a variety of reasons, including lower costs for this type of transportation, traffickers can also move their victims across vast distances[119] using cars, buses,

---

[114] *Id.* at 9–10.

[115] Aronowitz (2009), pp. 55–56.

[116] *Id*, at 55–56. In 2000 the embassy personnel of EU member states, when assessing the problem of trafficking in women in Nigeria, reported that Nigerian traffickers resort to "visa shopping" for the embassy to obtain travel visas for women's study groups or tours. When embassies began coordinating their efforts to place restrictions on obtaining visas from EU countries, Nigerian traffickers began moving their victims to neighboring states such as Benin and overland to Northern Africa to secure visas from the embassies of EU member states in these countries. The following is an example of an attempt at a visa shopping prototype: The application of a Nigerian who sought visas for members of his young women's badminton team was being processed at the embassy. The consular officer invited the young women to take part in individual interviews to test their knowledge of the sport. It then transpired that the women had no idea what a badminton shuttlecock looked like. *See also Smuggling of Migrants from West Africa to Europe*, UNODC, http://www.unodc.org/documents/toc/Reports/TOCTAWestAfrica/West_Africa_TOC_MIGRANTS.pdf (accessed on Apr. 15, 2021).

[117] *The Role of Organized Crime in the Smuggling of Migrants from West Africa to the European Union*, UNODC 10 (2011), http://www.unodc.org/documents/human-trafficking/Migrant-Smuggling/Report_SOM_West_Africa_EU.pdf.

[118] *Id.* at 158.

[119] *Id.* at 26. UNODC describes at least 5 geographical routes along which smugglers have historically moved migrants from West Africa to enter Europe without a visa:

- By sea to the Canary Islands (Spain)
- By land to Spanish North African enclaves (Spain)
- By land and sea across the Straits of Gibraltar (Spain)
- By land and sea across the Mediterranean to Lampedusa (Italy) or Malta
- By land and sea across the Mediterranean to Greece

The prominence of these routes has changed substantially over the past decade.

- In 2000, the chief points of entry were the Spanish enclaves (Ceuta and Melilla), small areas of Spanish soil along the coast of Morocco. Over 47,000 irregular migrants were detected entering the enclaves in 2000. Access to these entry points is facilitated by the free movement in ECOWAS, as citizens of ECOWAS countries can visit any other ECOWAS country for 90 days before requiring a residence permit.

trucks, rented cars, minibus, or even by making them walk. "They often require numerous safe houses along the way where they can lodge their human cargo until it is safe to move them further."[120] Describing the typical trafficking of West African people to Europe, Fitzgibbon asserts that traffickers establish a safe-house network across the region and move people through the desert to Morocco or by vehicle to other parts of North Africa. They may cross the Mediterranean to Spain by fast-boats; hundreds of illegal immigrants and trafficked persons travel from West African countries en route to Spain, become stranded in Morocco for up to 4 or more years, and many die in the desert or when crossing the ocean.[121] For example, the US Department of State reports that networks "traffic women from Nigeria, India, and Greece through Guinea to the Maghreb and onward to Europe, notably Italy, Ukraine, Switzerland, and France for forced prostitution and involuntary domestic servitude."[122] Routes are often indirect and change over time, "as traffickers carefully avoid policed roads, border checkpoints, and jurisdictions where there is efficient and honest law enforcement."[123]

Related criminal offenses and human rights violations on their journey "include abuses of immigration and border-control laws, corruption of officials, document forgery, acts of coercion against the victim, unlawful confinement and the withholding of identity papers,[ money] and other documents[in order to prevent their escape]."[124] Traffickers undertake to provide the travel documents needed to cross the borders, to find persons to accompany the victims during their journey, to control the victims, and ensure accommodation at their place of stay to prevent them from seeking help.[125]

"During the trip, people might be squeezed into exceptionally small spaces in trucks or onto unseaworthy boats"[126] in order for traffickers to maximize their

---

[120] Shelley (2014), p. 7, https://www.migrationpolicy.org/sites/default/files/publications/BadActors-ShelleyFINALWEB.pdf.

[121] Fitzgibbon (2003), p. 85. *See also* Adepoju (2005b), p. 76, 78 (available at: http://women.humantrafficking.org/uploads/publications/IOM_Data_Research_Human_Trafficking.pdf#page=76).

[122] Trafficking in Persons Report, U.S. State Dept. (2010), http://www.state.gov/documents/organization/142981.pdf.

[123] Shelley (2014), p. 7.

[124] *Id.* at 60–61.

[125] Constantinou A et al., *Deliverable D2.1: Report on the Relevant Aspects of the Trafficking Act (Geographical Routes and Modus Operandi) and on its Possible Evolutions in Response to Law Enforcement*, Trafficking as A Criminal Enterprise (TRACE) 41 (Feb. 27, 2015), http://trace-project.eu/wp-content/uploads/2015/03/TRACE-D2.1_FINAL.pdf.

[126] Cohen (2003), p. 8, 19, (available at: http://www.hrw.org/sites/default/files/reports/togo0403.pdf). Togolese trafficked children described the boats that transported them to Gabon as wooden barks, overloaded, and lacking any navigational equipment or sanitation facilities. "There were no toilets," one said. "There were girls defecating on each other and vomiting in the boat. It was impossible to vomit into the sea without falling in." There was no medicine on board and no clean water to drink. Some girls even traveled in *pirogues*, which are long, narrow canoes made from a single tree trunk.

"cargo".[127] A UN Special Rapporteur on a mission to Gabon reported that "[a] ccording to accounts of victims of trafficking, the journey to Gabon takes several days in cramped boats, where victims sit without moving and are not provided with any sanitation facilities. The boats do not have adequate navigational equipment and capsizing or drowning of victims is not uncommon."[128]

Trafficked persons might be raped or beaten during the trip, sold from one trafficker to another without their knowledge, transported without a precise destination, or left to die in the desert. It has been reported that children from Burkina Faso who were trafficked to Ivory Coast were transported across national borders without travel documents and then forced to walk long distances in the wilderness to avoid immigration patrol guards; these children were also subjected to physical and psychological violence. Children transported by boat reported that their companions had succumbed to thirst or had drowned.[129] "Likewise, Nigerian women reported being raped while in transit overland to Northern Africa to 'groom and prepare' them for what awaits them in their destination country in Western Europe or to force them to pay for their upkeep during the transport phase."[130]

Remarkably, the lack of visa requirements for entry into a transit country has reportedly facilitated the illegal movement of trafficking victims to destination countries.[131] Specific challenges in the countries of transit therefore consist of

---

[127] Human Rights Watch described the terrible journey undertaken by a child trafficked from Togo to Nigeria.

> On the other side, another truck was waiting for us. It had no seats, so we had to stand up in the truck. We were 250 people in one truck, all standing. It was hot and we were falling on each other. The truck became so full that some boys had to sit on the edge. The boys on the edge would sometimes get hit by a tree and fall down—one boy fell from the truck and broke his leg. There was no hospital because we were in the bush, so we just picked him up and put him back on the truck. We drove in that truck for seven days, taking detours to avoid the soldiers. Sometimes we took the same route used to herd cattle from Nigeria to Benin. At night we got off the truck and slept in the bush.

*Id.* at 31. *See also Smuggling of Migrants: The Harsh Search of a Better Life*, UNODC, http://www.unodc.org/toc/en/crimes/migrant-smuggling.html (accessed on August 16, 2021).

[128] *See also* Report of the Special Rapporteur Trafficking in Persons, especially Women and Children), *Mission to Gabon*, ¶ 10, U.N. Doc. A/HRC/23/48/Add.2 (Mar. 18, 2013) (by Joy Ngozi Ezelio).

[129] Cohen (2003), p. 8, 20 (available at: http://www.hrw.org/sites/default/files/reports/togo0403.pdf). The Togolese government reported that in two separate incidents, 700 trafficked children from Nigeria drowned in the sea during their journey to Gabon in March 2001; half of whom were Togolese and came from the country's central region. *See also Country Reports on Human Rights Practices in Togo for 2001*, U.S. Dept. of State, http://www.state.gov/j/drl/rls/hrrpt/2001/af/8408.htm. "These mishaps are caused by the fact that the boats that freight the children are tiny old rickety wooden boats with two old outboard and forty horsepower engines . . . [T]he boats are overloaded with goods and people without any life jacket or navigational facility."

[130] Aronowitz (2009), p. 57.

[131] Perrin B, *Trafficking in Persons & Transit Countries: A Canada-U.S. Case Study in Global Perspective* No. 10- 05, 18 (April 2010) http://mbc.metropolis.net/assets/uploads/files/wp/2010/WP10-05.pdf.

strengthening cooperation among border control agencies, exchanging information on trafficking routes, and undertaking measures to prevent transport operated by commercial carriers from being used in the commission of trafficking offenses.[132]

#### 2.3.1.3 Exploitation in Destination Countries

The third stage occurs in the destination countries in which the exploitation primarily takes place and where most of the profits are generated. Two major forms of exploitation have been identified: sexual exploitation and forced labor.[133] There are also reports of members of gangs and organized criminal networks forcing vulnerable people to perform illicit acts, particularly in the sale and transportation of illegal narcotics. For example, people are trafficked from Cape Verde to Brazil, Portugal, and other European countries as drug couriers.[134] Similarly, Nigerian women are recruited and moved to Malaysia, where they are coerced into prostitution and forced to work as drug mules for their traffickers.[135] Other forms of trafficking include child soldiers and trafficking for the purposes of rituals.

Trafficking in persons is predominantly aimed at extorting the labor and services of victims for economic benefit. The 'loverboy' who traffics his girlfriend in a scenario of sexual exploitation is also leveraging his power over her for profit. Similarly, families exploiting the domestic help of foster children "*vidomegon*" in West Africa or housing "*restavek*" children in the Caribbean are benefiting from their labor and services. Finally, "the debt bondage schemes behind some West African or East Asian trafficking networks are leveraging the migration dream of the victims to exploit them in forced labour or in the commercial sex market."[136]

Whether domestically or abroad, trafficking in persons is always organized by traffickers striving to maximize the benefits and minimize costs of exploiting their victims. However, doing so in relatively richer countries is economically more advantageous due to the higher monetary value of the services traffickers demand from the victims. In the case of a "local national exploiting his girlfriend on his own in Canada, the authorities estimated that this trafficker profited about US $180,000 during the 8 months of the victim's exploitation in the commercial sex market"[137]

---

[132] UNODC, *supra* note 89, at 12.

[133] According to the ILO definition, forced labor comprises two basic elements: "(a) the work or service of the trafficked person is exacted under the menace of penalty; and, (b) it is undertaken involuntarily". *See also What is Forced Labour, Modern Slavery, and Human Trafficking*, ILO, http://www.ilo.org/global/topics/forced-labour/definition/lang%2D%2Den/index.htm (accessed on Apr. 20, 2018).

[134] *Trafficking in Persons Report*, U.S. Dept. of State (June 2013), https://www.state.gov/documents/organization/210737.pdf.

[135] *Trafficking in Persons Report*, U.S. Dept. of State (June 2015), https://www.state.gov/documents/organization/245365.pdf.

[136] UNODC *supra* note 83 at 46–47.

[137] *Id.* at 47.

(an average of US $750 per day). Similarly, 11 South-East Asian citizens who were trafficked to Australian brothels for approximately 2 years generated a net profit of between US $55,000–65,000. It would not be possible to earn such amounts of money from prostitution in poorer countries. In the Philippines and Chile for example, the national authorities reported that victims of sexual exploitation were forced to serve their clients at a price of US $10–20 per encounter.[138]

Debt bondage is commonly reported as a major enforcement tactic used on victims in the commercial sex industries. In addition to the fees prospective victims incur when being transported to their destination, the debt accumulates through arbitrary charges for food, accommodation, bills for the prostitution workspace or other places where prostitution takes place, protection taxes or taxes paid to other criminal groups for offering prostitutes within "their territories", and their transport to work. Investigations have revealed that victims trafficked into Europe (Italy, the Netherlands, Belgium, Spain. . .) by the Nigerian organized crime network are forced to pay inflated smuggling charges.[139] For example, in Italy "some Nigerian women are trapped in a cycle of debt bondage in the sex industry, with little hope of clearing €50–60,000 (US $65–75,000) debts owed to their exploiters."[140] To free themselves from the debt contracted with their exploiters, the girls have to pay an average of €50–60,000.[141]

Furthermore, a Human Rights Watch study on Nigerian girls and women trafficked to brothels in Ivory Coast reported that "the traffickers demanded that the women and girls engage in prostitution to pay off an exorbitant 'debt' of generally 1.5 to 2 million CFA francs (US $3000 to $4000), even though the cost of overland transportation to Ivory Coast is only roughly 100,000 CFA (US $200)."[142] Several victims stated they had not yet been able to pay off their "debt" despite engaging in prostitution in Ivory Coast for between 2 and 6 years, and despite attending as many as 30 clients a night.[143] This is tantamount to debt bondage, a practice similar to slavery under the 1956 United Nations Supplementary Convention on the Abolition of Slavery.

Traffickers are also known to use voodoo practices or "juju" to coerce and subjugate their victims.[144] This practice is specific to a number of West African

---

[138] *Id.* at 47.

[139] *Trafficking in Persons—TOCTA*, UNODC, http://www.unodc.org/documents/data-and-analysis/tocta/2.Trafficking_in_persons.pdf (accessed on August 20, 2021); *see also* Aronowitz (2009), pp. 57–58.

[140] Slavery Index 2014, *supra* note 19, at 50; *see also Trafficking in Persons and Exploitation of Migrants*, UNICRI, http://www.unicri.it/topics/trafficking_exploitation/ (accessed on August 20, 2021).

[141] *Id.* at 50.

[142] *Côte d'Ivoire/Nigeria: Combat Trafficking for Prostitution*, Human Rts Watch (Aug. 26, 2010), http://www.hrw.org/news/2010/08/26/c-te-d-ivoirenigeria-combat-trafficking-prostitution.

[143] *Id.*

[144] Aronowitz (2009), p. 60. *See Human Trafficking in 2013—Nigeria-France*, U.S. Dept. of State, http://www.state.gov/j/tip/rls/tiprpt/2013/210546.htm. *See also* Beyer C, *An Introduction to the*

countries, in particular, Niger, Ghana, and Benin where the traditional belief in witchcraft remains extremely strong. Nigerian organized crime rings that engage in trafficking in persons operate as business models and control the victims they have recruited through ritual bondage. Prior to their departure to Europe, the traffickers who are sponsoring the trip force the victims to participate in a magic religious ceremony and make them swear oaths to a particular deity in a shrine before a juju priest is called upon to enforce the contract terms; they are then compelled to sign to pay back the debt.[145] This ritual creates a sense of fear in victims, in addition "to secrecy and confidentiality that binds them to their traffickers, ensures compliance, and guarantees they will work to repay the huge sums of money claimed to be owed for transporting them to Europe and for their upkeep."[146] Many victims, fearful of any misfortune falling upon themselves or their families, are compelled to endure their suffering in silence without recourse to help or support. Their fear of breaking ritual oaths makes it extremely difficult for human rights advocates to support victims and for the authorities to investigate and bring suspected traffickers to justice for prosecution and punishment.[147] The practice of ritual bondage is the most common psychological tool used to control Nigerian trafficked persons in the UK.

The common trends among international destinations for trafficking appear to be that they are well-developed, prosperous, and industrialized areas in great demand for labor, where the financial return for traffickers per victim is also the highest. In its 2014 report the UNODC observed that, the 'global north' attracts mainly victims from the 'global south'.[148] Traffickers have an economic interest in moving victims to wealthier countries such as Western Europe, North America, or the Middle East; as trading them in poorer countries is less competitive. Other conditions that have an impact on the directions in which trafficking flows "include issues related to job

*Basic Beliefs of the Vodou (Voodoo) Religion*, ThoughtCo. (May 2, 2018), https://www.thoughtco.com/vodou-an-introduction-for-beginners-95712; *Human Trafficking & Modern-Day Slavery (Nigeria)*, GVNET, http://gvnet.com/humantrafficking/Nigeria.htm (accessed on Apr. 18, 2021); *Global Report on Trafficking in Humans*, UNDOC 56 (2014), https://www.unodc.org/documents/data-and-analysis/glotip/GLOTIP_2014_full_report.pdf.

[145] Prina (2003), p. 35. The victim declared: "*Before leaving they take you to a witch doctor who tells you "you are obliged to pay" and you haven't yet left. Then he says «when you arrive in Italy all the money which you earn (you must give them), if you take one euro you will die (. . .) Swear!» And you swear, they all swear.*" (Interview Victim No. 5). *See also "Breaking the Cycle of Fear", Witchcraft, Juju and Safeguarding Victims of Human Trafficking*, Africans Unite Against Child Abuse (AFRUCA) 6–7 (Mar. 9, 2011), http://www.afruca.org/wp-content/uploads/2013/07/Breaking-the-cycle-of-fear.pdf.

[146] AFRUCA, *supra* note 145, at 6–7.

[147] Peachey (2012), www.independent.co.uk/news/uk/crime/jailed-the-slave-trader-in-britain-whosold-women-around-europe-for-sex-under-the-spell-of-his-juju-witchcraft-8228574.html. *See also Examining the UK's Criminal Justice—Response to Trafficking*, Anti-Slavery (June 2013), http://www.antislavery.org/includes/documents/cm_docs/2013/i/inthedock_final_small_file.pdf. Harrop (2012), http://lastradainternational.org/lsidocs/Witchcraft%20and%20Trafficking%20in%20Africa.pdf.

[148] UNODC, *supra* note 144, at 7.

markets, migration policy, regulation, prostitution policy, legal context, law enforcement and border control efficiency."[149]

Two significant outbound flows of trafficking from West Africa have been identified: one is to Western and Central Europe, and the other to North Africa and the Middle East. However, it is important to note that West African victims have been found in almost all Western European countries and are largely comprised of women and girls trafficked for sexual exploitation.[150] The primary European end points are Belgium, Italy, the United Kingdom, and the Netherlands although some women are also trafficked to Lebanon, Libya, and the United States.[151] While Nigerian women travel to Italy as agricultural laborers,[152] a significant number of Malian women are moved to Kuwait and Saudi Arabia to serve as domestic workers.[153]

In terms of the trans-regional trafficking of human beings, Benin, Burkina Faso, Guinea-Bissau, Guinea, Ghana, Mali, Nigeria, and Togo are listed as major source countries of child victims recruited from rural areas and transported to Equatorial Guinea, Côte d'Ivoire, Gabon, Nigeria, Senegal and South Africa for domestic services in the cities and forced labor in commercial farms.[154] These sub-regional patterns can be understood in terms of geographical proximity, ease of movement and transport, and cultural and linguistic patterns that may lead some people to an English or French speaking country.

The challenges facing destination countries consist of recognizing trafficking for exploitation in all its forms and "the development of adequate countermeasures for victim identification, protection, and assistance, as well as the prosecution of offenders."[155] In fact, destination countries are often less concerned with the problem of trafficking as their own nationals are not at risk. They assume they have no jurisdiction and are reluctant to investigate these crimes. Public opinion and policy makers in these countries tend to perceive "the problem of trafficking as clandestine migration organized by foreigners, a reality which should not divert political

---

[149] *Id,* at 48.

[150] *Id*, at 83.

[151] *Nations Hospitable to Organized Crime and Terrorism*, Int'l Org. Migr. 29, http://www.loc.gov/rr/frd/pdf-files/Nats_Hospitable.pdf (accessed on August 20, 2021); *see also* UNODC, *supra* note 89, at 87.

[152] *Id*, at 29.

[153] *Id*, at 29.

[154] Sawadogo (2012), p. 1. *See also* Adepoju (2005b), p. 77.

[155] *OSCE, supra* note 55, at 9. *See also* Pearson E, *The Mekong Challenge Human Trafficking: Redefining Demand*, Int'l Labour Org. (ILO) (2005), http://un-act.org/publication/view/the-mekong-challenge-human-trafficking-redefining-demand/. The report, regarding the demand-side of trafficking in persons, stated that offenders encompass three categories of people: employer (employers, owners, managers, or subcontractors); consumer (clients (sex industry), corporate buyers (manufacturing), household members (domestic work)); third parties involved in the process (recruiters, agents, transporters and those who participate knowingly in trafficking persons at any stage of the process).

attention from the needs of their own citizens."[156] Once the exploitation phase generates ongoing substantial proceeds, traffickers may embark on a fourth stage which consists of laundering the revenues to conceal their criminal origins and then using these as legitimate funds or capital to invest in trafficking in persons or other related criminal activities.

#### 2.3.1.4 Laundering the Proceeds of Crime

The laundering of proceeds from criminal activities is often carried out as a clandestine operation that takes place across borders and is thus extremely difficult to quantify. Reliable estimates for Africa are especially hard to obtain.[157] However, experts agree that trafficking in human beings is the third largest source of illicit profits after narcotics and arms trafficking, although estimating its total revenues remains difficult. A report issued by the International Labor Organization (ILO) in May 2014 estimated that trafficking in human beings generates US $150 billion in gross proceeds each year for those individuals or groups carrying out this crime[158] This data shows a threefold increase on the ILO's previous estimate of US $32 billion in 2005–2006.[159]

The trade in human beings thrives in West Africa because of its low risks and high profits; depending on the source country, destination, age, gender, and "use" of those trafficked. An African child delivered to the United States, for example, might net a trafficker US $10,000–$20,000.[160] According to the United Nations Office on Drugs and Crime (UNODC), the trafficking in persons from Africa to Europe alone generates an annual turnover in excess of $300 million.[161] However, by using assets derived from this serious violation of human rights, human traffickers risk drawing authorities' attention to their criminal activity and exposing themselves to criminal prosecution. To remain hidden from law-enforcement agencies and benefit freely from the proceeds of their crime, they must therefore conceal the illicit origin of these funds by laundering the proceeds of their crimes.[162] "Money laundering" is the

---

[156] *Trafficking in Human Beings, Especially Women and Children, in Africa*, UNICEF 16 (2005), https://www.unicef-irc.org/publications/pdf/trafficking-gb2ed-2005.pdf.

[157] Moshi Humphrey (2007), p. 2, https://issafrica.s3.amazonaws.com/site/uploads/Paper152.pdf.

[158] *Profits and Poverty: The Economics of Forced Labour*, ILO (May 2014), http://www.ilo.org/global/topics/forced-labour/publications/WCMS_243391/lang%2D%2Den/index.htm.

[159] Belser (2005), https://digitalcommons.ilr.cornell.edu/cgi/viewcontent.cgi?article=1016&context=forcedlabor.

[160] O'Neill-Richard (2000), p. 22, https://www.cia.gov/library/center-for-the-study-of-intelligence/csi-publications/books-and-monographs/trafficking.pdf.

[161] *Smuggling of Migrants*, UNODC 25 (Jan. 2011), https://www.unodc.org/documents/human-trafficking/Migrant-Smuggling/Smuggling_of_Migrants_A_Global_Review.pdf.

[162] *Anti-Money Laundering/Combating the Financing of Terrorism – Topics*, International Monetary Fund (IMF), https://www.imf.org/external/np/leg/amlcft/eng/aml1.htm#moneylaundering (accessed on August 20, 2021).

act of disguising the source or true nature of money obtained through prohibited means.[163] According to the Vienna Convention and the provisions of the Palermo Protocol, money laundering usually involves three distinct, alternative stages:

> 1) the introduction of the proceeds of crime into the financial system (placement); 2) transactions to convert or transfer the funds to other locations or financial institutions (layering); and 3) reintegrating the funds into the legitimate economy as 'clean' money and investing it in various assets or business ventures.[164]

Only the integration stage is applicable in West Africa as the banking financial sector in the region is relatively sophisticated and cash-based transactions predominate in its economies.

There are a wide range of money laundering techniques including "the use of internet services, online banking, and new electronic payment technologies; international companies and shell companies; and trade in and false invoicing for the supply of goods or services, real estate, art, diamonds, gold, and other precious metals."[165]

The *2015 National Money Laundering Risk Assessment* (NMLRA) identifies the following common methods of laundering money:[166]

- Use of cash, making it difficult for authorities to differentiate between the licit and illicit use and movement of bank notes;
- Structured transactions below applicable thresholds to avoid reporting and recordkeeping obligations;
- Individuals and entities that disguise the nature, purpose, ownership, and control of accounts;
- Occasional Anti-Money Laundering (AML) compliance deficiencies, which are an inevitable consequence of a financial system with financial services in hundreds of thousands of locations;
- Complicit violators within financial institutions;

---

[163] *Introduction to Money-Laundering*, UNODC (2015), https://www.unodc.org/unodc/en/money-laundering/introduction.html (accessed on August 20, 2021); *see also Risks and Methods of Money Laundering and Terrorist Financing*, UNODC, http://learningmatrixatcampus.co.in/COURSES_DATA/IMSContent/Anti%20Money%20Laundering%20Srilanka-Lesson3240/AMLSL/Files/PDF/Chapter_2.htm (accessed on August 20, 2021). Those involved in the fight against money laundering or the financing of terrorism rely on the most current information on "typologies", which refer to the various techniques used to launder money or finance terrorism. Criminals are extremely creative and the methods they use to launder money and finance terrorism vary from place to place and over time.

[164] *Id.* at 3–5; *see also* Moshi Humphrey (2007), p. 2.

[165] *Id.*; *see also Terrorist Financing in West Africa*, FATF (Oct. 2013), http://www.fatf-gafi.org/Media/Fatf/Documents/reports/tf-in-west-africa.pdf.

[166] *National Money Laundering Risk Assessment 2015*, U.S. Dep't. of Treasury 4, http://www.treasury.gov/resource-center/terrorist-illicit-finance/Documents/National%20Money%20Laundering%20Risk%20Assessment%20%E2%80%93%2006-12-2015.pdf; *see also Risks and Methods of Money Laundering and Terrorist Financing*, *supra* note 163.

– Complicit merchants, particularly wholesalers who facilitate Trade-Based Money Laundering (TBML), and financial services providers.

The United Nations Office on Drugs and Crime (UNODC) analysis of crime and development in Africa (2005a) highlights the extent as well as the range of illicit activities undertaken by organized criminal networks in five countries in the region—Côte d'Ivoire, Ghana, Nigeria, Senegal, and Sierra Leone.[167] Two recent international reports from the International Labor Organization (ILO) and the Organization for Security and Cooperation in Europe (OSCE) have claimed that substantial sums of money are earned from trafficking in persons; however, the offenders misuse complex financial and commercial structures in order to hamper financial investigations into money laundering and trafficking in persons. Among the many examples mentioned are the use of shell companies, cash mules, hidden beneficial ownership, and offshore companies and accounts.[168]

Money laundering can also take place through banks[169] and financial institutions. For example, to move funds into an account at a bank or broker-dealer, criminals "may use an individual, serving as a nominee, to open the account and shield the identities of the criminals who own and control the funds. Alternatively, the account may be opened in the name of a business that was created to hide the beneficial owner who controls the funds."[170] African criminal enterprises (Nigeria, Ghana, and Liberia) that have been identified by the Federal Bureau of Investigation (FBI) in major metropolitan areas across the United States are typically involved in these kinds of illicit financial transactions. For example, one of techniques used by the Nigerian-group for financial frauds and money laundering consists of "check cashing/funds transfer fraud". This involves a person outside the United States asking for help transferring funds. The victim, who is contacted as a result of posting a résumé online, receives money orders, checks, or fund transfers and is then asked to take a percentage and transfer the funds offshore; the funds received are typically laundered.[171]

In 2014, more than a dozen members of a Nigerian criminal organization were charged in Mississippi with fraud, account takeovers, and money laundering.[172] Primarily located in South Africa with alleged co-conspirators in the United States and Canada, the criminal network was connected via the Internet. The group bought

[167] *Transnational Organized Crime in the West African Region*, UNODC (2005), https://www.unodc.org/pdf/transnational_crime_west-africa-05.pdf.

[168] *Leveraging Anti-Money Laundering Regimes to Combat Trafficking in Human Beings*, Organization for Security and Co-operation in Europe (OSCE), 19 (2014), https://www.osce.org/secretariat/121125?download=true.

[169] *Id.* In its study, the OSCE observed that "[i]n one experiment, it took only two hours to transfer money around the world, but it took two years to re-trace the process using mutual legal assistance between countries".

[170] U.S. Dep't. of Treasury, *supra* note 166, at 3–4.

[171] U.S. Dep't. of Treasury, *supra* note 166, 18–19.

[172] *U.S. v. Oladimeji Seun Ayelotan, etal.* 917 F.3d 394 (5th Cir. 2019).

**Fig. 2.4** Example of Trade Based Money Laundering (TBML) used extensively by Colombian drug cartels

stolen credit card numbers, bank and brokerage account data, and personal identity information online. This stolen information was used to open new accounts; thus transferring value from the hacked accounts to accounts opened with altered or forged foreign passports. The stolen funds they received were used to buy consumer electronics, or were transferred to prepaid cards.[173]

Another method of laundering money practiced by African organized crime is that of trade-based money laundering (TBML). This process consists of disguising the origin of criminal proceeds through the import or export of merchandise and trade-related financial transactions.[174] Trade-based money laundering (TBML) is one of the more complex methods of money laundering to investigate, primarily because it involves complicit merchants falsifying the value of merchandise, misrepresenting trade-related financial transactions, and ultimately placing the funds into the financial system. Figure 2.4 provides is an illustration of this process. The African criminal group in Mississippi alleged that they asked their victims to receive a shipment of fraudulently acquired merchandise and then reship the same goods to Africa. In a similar manner, other victims received counterfeit checks and were asked to deposit them into their bank accounts and then transfer the proceeds to recipients in Africa.

Finally, the Economic Community of West African States (ECOWAS) region is a fertile environment for transnational and domestic crime syndicates because its

---

[173] U.S. Dep't. of Treasury, *supra* note 166, 18–19.

[174] *Id.*

economies are cash-based. Cash (bank notes) is omnipresent in financial transactions; it is also an inherently fungible monetary instrument that carries no record of its source, owner, or legitimacy. Cash generated from trafficking in persons can be held and spent as cash, therefore cash-based economies are attractive to money launderers "as the dominance of cash transactions, coupled with the narrowness of the financial sector (low levels of penetration), makes it easier [and quicker] for the proceeds of crime to be integrated into the rest of economy, without the involvement of the financial system in the initial stages."[175]

Mortgage financing is underdeveloped in the Economic Community of West African States (ECOWAS) and most residential and nonresidential buildings are built on a cash basis.[176] In the context of booming real estate deals, criminals have chosen to launder money in real estate property for several reasons. Not only is the lack of an audit appealing, real estate property also provides an excellent investment for those who have funds at their disposal, irrespective of whether these funds are derived from criminal or legitimate activities, due to the rising prices of both land and houses.[177]

In conclusion, money laundering activities have a significant impact on developing countries with relatively small or fragile financial systems or weak economies that are particularly susceptible to instability. These illicit activities are detrimental to development because they increase the profitability of these crimes, promote corruption, and negatively affect governance. They impair the development of "critical financial sector institutions,[178] and may [even] scare away foreign investors and reduce a country's access to both foreign investment and foreign markets."[179]

This example depicts the exchange of U.S. drug dollars for Colombian pesos to pay Colombian Drug Trafficking Organizations (DTOs) and is referred to as the Black-Market Peso Exchange (BMPE)[180]

---

[175]Moshi Humphrey (2012), p. 3, https://issafrica.s3.amazonaws.com/site/uploads/SitRep2012Oct.pdf.

[176]*The West African Economic and Monetary Union WAEMU (UEMOA)*, Housing Finance Africa 1 (2013), https://housingfinanceafrica.org/app/uploads/UEMOA-REGION-2013-Profile.pdf.

[177]Moshi Humphrey (2007), p. 4.

[178]*See* UNODC, *supra* note 163, at 5–10. Banking institutions, insurance companies, securities firms, and financial investment management firms are particularly vulnerable to the adverse consequences of money laundering.

[179]Moshi Humphrey (2007), p. 2.

[180]*Combating Trade Based Money Laundering: Rethinking the Approach*, Bankers Association for Finance and Trade (BAFT) 8 (Aug. 2017), http://baft.org/docs/default-source/marketing-documents/baft17_tmbl_paper.pdf?sfvrsn=2.

### 2.3.2 Trafficking of Persons within National Borders

While richer countries in the North attract victims from a variety of origins, global trends reveal that poorer countries are affected by domestic or sub-regional trafficking flows.[181] For instance, US Department of State reports indicate that the Economic Community of West African States (ECOWAS) are significant countries for internal trafficking.[182] In many cases, internal trafficking generally flows from rural to capital cities or tourist centers or labor sites within a country. All three stages of the process of trafficking persons; namely abduction or recruitment of people, transfer, and then exploitation, occur within the borders of a single country. Furthermore, for one out of every three trafficking cases; the exploitation takes place in the victim's country of citizenship. Transnational trafficking activities involve a significant risk of being arrested, especially if the border crossings require the control of travel documents. Such elaborate organization is not required if victims are exploited within the national border or in a neighboring Economic Community of West African States (ECOWAS) country, resulting in a lower risk of detection.

Therefore, trafficking within the borders of Economic Community of West African States (ECOWAS) countries is more prevalent than transnational trafficking and the majority of victims are children. Within each country, while girls are trafficked from rural provinces to towns and mining areas for domestic servitude and sexual exploitation, boys are frequently trafficked for forced labor in diamond mines, petty trading, petty crime, and for forced begging (US State Department 2009). Women and children may also be trafficked to serve as forced labor in agriculture, commercial farms, and the fishing industry.

Human Rights Activists and United Nations (UN) Agencies report that children are recruited by people who visit their villages and negotiate the children's placement and terms with parents who have little means, to whom they offer advance payments for the child as domestic worker. This method of recruitment especially affects children.[183] Girls may be recruited by women through kinship relationships or trading activities to work in their own household. Female recruiters could also act as intermediaries for a relative or friend who is seeking a child domestic worker. Such recruitment may sometimes amount to trafficking in children according to the sub-regional workshop organized by UNICEF, especially if the recruiters earn money by placing girls in domestic service as is the case in Ghana and The Ivory

---

[181] *Report of the Special Rapporteur on trafficking in persons, especially women and children*, ¶ 9, U.N. Doc. A/HRC/29/38 (March 2015) (by Maria Grazia Giammarinaro).

[182] It has been estimated that 15 million young people are involved in child labor in Nigeria, 40% of whom, around 6 million children, are estimated to be at risk of internal or external trafficking (*See Child Labour UNICEF Nigeria*, UNICEF (2006), https://www.unicef.org/wcaro/WCARO_Nigeria_Factsheets_ChildLabour.pdf).

[183] Kippenberg (2007), p. 33 (available at: https://www.hrw.org/report/2007/06/15/bottom-ladder/exploitation-and-abuse-girl-domestic-workers-guinea); ILO, *supra* note 75, at 25.

Coast.[184] Parents have often alleged to resort to non-kin agencies to secure the placement of their children in domestic work.[185]

The most prevalent form of internal trafficking in West Africa is related to the traditional schemes and widespread practice of child fostering in extended families; this is in exchange for the promise of an education, a wage, or lodgings for the house boy or girl.[186] The vast majority of children working in domestic service are girls. There are also boys and girls who come to the cities to learn a trade or receive a religious or secular education, or help out the urban extended family *through fostering arrangements*. In exchange for better living conditions and expectations of a better future, fostered children help out in the receiving household with chores that itself leads to their subsequent socialization and training. Most of the children working in urban cities, such as apprentices for boys and domestic workers for girls, are natural extensions of the indigenous system of education.[187]

Instructive data from a Benin village show that West African children are increasingly leaving rural areas through arrangements made outside the traditional kinship pattern of securing children's well-being. For example, the proportion of children fostered by a relative decreased from 62% in 1996 to 46% in 1999. Countering this trend, the proportion of children fostered by a stranger increased significantly from 18% to 27% over the same period while those children who left with a friend of the family also increased from 19% to 25%.[188] The urban domestic

---

[184] Thorsen (2012a), p. 6, http://sro.sussex.ac.uk/43303/1/Briefing_paper_No_1_-_child_domestic_workers.pdf. See also HRW, *supra* note 183, at 33; ILO, *supra* note 79, at 33–34.

> In placement as embezzlement, the child is handed over by his/her parents to a third party who may be a professional employment agent or an intermediary on the understanding that the child will be sent to school, receive vocational training, and be taken care of by the host household. Instead, the child is put into paid work, which often provide no scope for skills development. The intermediary collects the wages directly from the employer and does not pay the parents anything. According to the Ghana study, women are operating in this way in the Makola, Nima, Maamobi and Agbogloshie markets in the suburbs of Accra.

ILO, *supra* note 79, at 3.

> A human rights watch investigation on child trafficking in Togo found that girls trafficked to Gabon are employed either by Beninese or Togolese nationals who trade in various merchandise, or by Gabonese families who require a cheap, domestic workforce for housework. In the case of the latter, any salary paid by the girl's host family, on average 50,000 CFA (US $76) per month, is reportedly paid to the child's trafficker.

HRW, *supra* note 129, at 21. *See also* Jacquemin M Y (2004), pp. 383, 383–397. The author describes three types of child domestics in Abidjan, Côte d'Ivoire: the *little niece*, who works for kin; the *hired help*, who works for strangers and whose payment goes directly to her guardian; and the *little paid maid* who also works for strangers but is paid directly in cash.

[185] Bass Loretta (2004), pp. 89–90.

[186] Cherti M et al. (2013), p. 24, http://www.ippr.org/files/images/media/files/publication/2013/01/nigeria-trafficking_Jan2013_10189.pdf?noredirect=1.

[187] Bass Loretta (2004), p. 22. Alain Morice found that apprentices comprise 85% of the labor force in the leather industry in Nigeria.

[188] Bass Loretta (2004), p. 90.

work of girls (known as *mbindaan* in Senegal, *Kalifa* in Mali, and *vidomegon* in Benin), where children placed with and entrusted to someone who is meant to protect them so that they can have access to an education and a more or less decent life; often ends up transforming the girls into slaves for their urban host families.[189] In all these cities today,"[t]his informal approach to fostering has created conditions of "hard trafficking", involving households completely unknown to the domestic servants, and "soft trafficking", where the child lives with an extended family or in households originally known to them (WHO 2011)."[190]

An analysis conducted by the Committee on the Rights of the Child observed that the cultural tradition of placing a child in another household for a better future is often "synonymous with the exploitation of children as domestics and exposure to several forms of abuse and violence."[191] A specialized (non-governmental organization) NGO has also expressed concern that, "taking charge of the education of an underage child becomes a false pretense leading to his or her exploitation in a foreign country."[192] In a different context but involving circumstances and experiences of child domestic work similar to those in West Africa, the Committee of Experts on the Application of Conventions and Recommendations (CEACR) in 2011 considered Paraguay's criadazgo system—"which legitimizes the quasi-adoption practice of children working in domestic work in exchange for food, board and education – to be a violation of the ILO Convention No. 182 on the worst forms of child labour."[193]

In general, the pattern of internal trafficking can be as simple as a single individual recruiting and exploiting a single victim in the same city or country of origin.[194] However, in terms of magnitude, existing reports suggest that domestic trafficking victimizes a very large proportion of people and accounts for more than three quarters of the total number of victims identified in Sub-Saharan Africa.[195] Internal trafficking is characterized by recruitment carried out by the acquaintances

---

[189] *La Souffrance des "Restaveks"*, Courrier Int'l (May 26, 2009), https://www.courrierinternational.com/breve/2009/05/26/la-souffrance-des-restaveks; *Haiti—J'aime Nettoye: L'enfer des Enfants Domestiques Habitués à Obéir*, UNICEF (2009), http://www.unicef.fr/en/node/734>; *see also Unprotected Work, Invisible Exploitation: Trafficking for the Purposes of Domestic Servitude*, OSCE 23–24 (Jun. 17, 2010) http://www.osce.org/secretariat/75804?download=true [hereinafter *OSCE Rep.*].

[190] Derby Nana (2012), p. 23.

[191] *Conclusion Observations of the Committee on the Rights of the Child: Burkina Faso*, U.N. Comm. Rts. of the Child (UNCRC) 48 (Jan. 2010), https://www.crin.org/en/library/publications/burkina-faso-persistent-violations-childrens-rights; *Spotlight on Claudine Akakpo: "Confiage" is a Modern Form of Child Slavery*, Int'l Trade Union Confederation (ITUC) (Jan 4, 2010), https://www.ituc-csi.org/spotlight-on-claudine-akakpo-cstt.

[192] *Le Travail Domestique des Mineurs en France*, Comité Contre l'Esclavage Moderne (CCEM) 17 (2009), http://www.esclavagemoderne.org/media/Etude-Travail-domestique-des-mineurs-2.pdf.

[193] *Ending Child Labour in Domestic Work and Protecting Young Workers from Abusive Working Conditions*, Int'l Labour Org. 28 (Jun. 12, 2013), http://www.ilo.org/ipec/Informationresources/WCMS_207656/lang%2D%2Den/index.htm.

[194] Aronowitz (2009), p. 65.

[195] UNODC, *supra* note 84, at 83.

of victims. In the Gambia, "[f]or generations, parents sent their sons to live with Koranic teachers or marabouts, who often forced children to beg instead of ensuring their progress in religious studies."[196]

Human Rights Watch studies in West Africa (Guinea and Togo) also report incidences of children being sold by their parents, family members, or acquaintances to traffickers to ensure the subsistence of the rest of the family or to pay off debts. A US Department of State report corroborates this, stating that in Benin "many traffickers are relatives or acquaintances of their victims, exploiting the traditional system of *vidomegon*, in which parents allow their children to live with and work for richer relatives, usually in urban areas."[197] This report also observes that Ghanaian traffickers of internal labor "are commonly freelance operators, and may be known to members of the source community. Uninformed parents may not understand that by cooperating with trafficking offenders, they may expose their children to bonded placement, coercion, or outright sale."[198]

In a number of situations, the trafficking endures and is intrinsically linked to descent-based slavery. This is the case in Mali, where the US Department of State 2010 reports that adult men and boys, primarily of Songhai ethnicity, are sent to provide forced labor in the salt mines of Taoudenni in northern Mali, which is related to the longstanding practice of debt bondage. "Some members of Mali's black *Tamachek* community are [also] subjected to traditional slavery-related practices rooted in hereditary master-slave relationships".[199] Even today some people are born into hereditary slavery, a caste-based slavery practice rooted in ancestral master-slave relationships. According to the US Department of State report, this practice primarily persists in the northern part of Niger.[200]

Another challenging practice occurring in all Western African countries that renders children, especially women and girls, vulnerable to trafficking, is the custom of early marriage. This traditional practice can also contribute to trafficking in persons.[201] "When poverty is severe, girls are often perceived to be an economic burden of the family. It can be a survival strategy for a family to sell their daughters for the purpose of marriage; it is estimated that in Western Africa 49% of girls were married under 19 years."[202] According to the Special Rapporteur, a number of reports have been published on trafficking for forced marriages in West Africa;. For example, the highest proportion of child marriages in the world is found in the

[196]Trafficking in Persons Report—Gambia, U.S. Dept. of State (2010), https://www.state.gov/j/tip/rls/tiprpt/2010/142760.htm.

[197]Trafficking in Persons Report—Benin, U.S. Dept. of State (83–85) (Jun. 2010), http://www.state.gov/documents/organization/142981.pdf.

[198]U.S. Dept. of State, *supra* note 197, at Ghana.

[199]U.S. Dept. of State, *supra* note 197, at Mali.

[200]Special Rapporteur on Contemporary Forms of Slavery, including its Causes and Consequences, *Addendum—Mission to Niger*, U.N. Doc. A/HRC/30/35/Add.1 (Jul. 30 2015) (by Mothusi Bruce Rabasha Palai).

[201]UNICEF, *supra* note 157P.

[202]Fong (2004), p. 3.

ECOWAS region, namely Niger, where approximately 75% of girls under 18 are married. Child marriage occurs mostly in southern regions and among girls who are the least educated, poorest, and living in rural areas.[203]

In conclusion, trafficking in persons threatens the security of states and the protection and promotion of human rights.[204] Moreover, the process of trafficking in persons affects territorial integrity as it involves "the facilitation of crossing of borders and remaining in a State in violation of national criminal and immigration laws."[205] Additionally, it constitutes a violation of rights inherent to all human beings, the dignity and worth of the human person as recognized in the Universal Declaration of Human Rights. Traffickers treat victims like a commodity, depriving them of their freedom, security and wages; and subjecting them to the withholding of documents, threats and violence; including forced prostitution, sexual assaults, rape, and even death. Moreover, victims are frequently compelled to work in indecent and inhuman conditions; and are often denied access to medical care, basic social services, and education.[206]

## 2.4 Physiognomy of Victims in West Africa and the Root Causes of Their Vulnerability

There are several factors that make potential victims vulnerable to trafficking in West Africa, including age, gender, mental and physical disability, and poverty. Children in Africa are totally dependent on the demands and expectations of those in authority, such as their parents and extended family; and therefore constitute a group vulnerable to trafficking.[207] Women are also at risk "because they are often excluded from employment, higher education, and legal as well as political parity."[208] Many gender-based violations and harmful cultural and religious practices contribute to the vulnerability of women being trafficked.[209] Migrant workers are also the targeted victims of trafficking and forced labor; in all West African countries, the largest

---

[203] Palai, *supra* note 200. The percentage of women aged 20 to 24 married by the age of 18 is highest in the regions of Diffa (89%), Zinder (88%), Maradi (87%) and Tahoua (83%), followed by Dosso (74%), Tillabéry (69%), Agadez (48%), and Niamey (28%). *See Marrying Too Young: End Child Marriage*, United Nations Population Fund (UNPF) (2012), https://www.unfpa.org/sites/default/files/pub-pdf/MarryingTooYoung.pdf. *See also Trafficking in Persons Report 2015—Niger*, U.S. Dept of State 263–267, http://www.state.gov/documents/organization/243561.pdf.

[204] UNODC, *supra* note 84, at 14.

[205] Touzenis K (2010), p. 52 [available at: http://unesdoc.unesco.org/images/0018/001883/188397e.pdf].

[206] OSCE, *supra* note 168, at 12.

[207] *Human Trafficking: An Overview*, UN.GIFT 18 (2008), http://www.ungift.org/doc/knowledgehub/resource-centre/GIFT_Human_Trafficking_An_Overview_2008.pdf.

[208] *Id.*

[209] *Id.*

group of men and women migrating for economic purposes end up becoming exploited workers. The following discussion describes the physiognomy of victims and delineates the permanent factors driving the trafficking of persons in West Africa.

### *2.4.1 Profile of the Victims*

There is no single profile for a trafficking victim; trafficking involves men and women, adults and children, foreign nationals and citizens. As identified in studies conducted by the International Organization for Migration (IOM), victims of trafficking in West Africa can be divided into two populations: children under the age of 18 and adults trafficked primarily for farm labor (men) and domestic work (women) within and across countries. Apart from the cases in Nigeria, the trafficking of adults in the West African region has remained largely unexplored.[210] These victims are trafficked mainly outside the region for the sex industry.[211]

Information on the profiles of victims reported in the Economic Community of West African States (ECOWAS) may be relatively limited and affected by uneven legislation on trafficking in persons. Some countries such as Togo and the Ivory Coast have legislation that criminalizes only child trafficking, whereas Burkina Faso has recently included adult trafficking in their criminal codes.[212] Consequently, children are predominantly reported as victims. Moreover, when considering countries in West Africa with long-standing and comprehensive legislation on trafficking in persons, the incidence of child trafficking was still found to be higher than the global average. In Ghana and Sierra Leone for example, the vast majority of trafficking victims were identified as children. During the same period, Nigeria reported that children accounted for about half of the victims identified.[213]

Additional information from other intergovernmental organizations have confirmed that child trafficking is the major form of trafficking in West Africa. In 2009, the United Nation Operation in Cote d'Ivoire reported 15 cases of trafficking in persons; all involved children aged 8 to 16 from countries neighboring Cote d'Ivoire who had been trafficked for child labor and forced prostitution.[214] Similarly, in 2012 an operation coordinated by the International Criminal Police Organization's (INTERPOL) Trafficking in Persons Unit rescued nearly 400 child trafficking

---

[210]Council of Europe Convention on Action against Trafficking in Human Beings, *Counter Trafficking and Assistance to Vulnerable Migrants'* Annual Report of Activities 2011, Int'l Org. Migr. (ILO) 59, (2012), at https://www.iom.int/files/live/sites/iom/files/What-We-Do/docs/Annual_Report_2011_Counter_Trafficking.pdf.

[211]Adepoju (2005b), p. 76.

[212]UNODC, *Global Report on Trafficking in Persons 2012*, 74 UNODC, Sales No.E.13.IV.1.

[213]*Id.*

[214]*Id.*

victims in Burkina Faso, some as young as 6 years old, who were forced to work in illegally-operated gold mines and cotton fields under extremely dangerous conditions.[215] Field research worldwide indicates that the groups most vulnerable to trafficking in persons are prostitutes, domestic servants, *talibés*, street children, Internally Displaced Persons (IDPs) and refugees, migrants, elderly people, disabled persons, and groups experiencing structural discrimination within their community.[216]

## 2.4.2 Factors Increasing Vulnerability

Although trafficking appears to be applied indiscriminately to minors and adults, males and females, there are certain circumstances or vulnerabilities that exist that make some people more susceptible to victimization. The judicial summit dealing with access to justice for trafficking victims, which was held in Brazil in 2008, defines vulnerable people "as those who, due to reasons of age, gender, physical, or mental state, or due to social, economic, ethnic, and/or cultural circumstances, find it especially difficult to fully exercise their rights before the justice system as recognized to them by law."[217] The following conditions may increase people's vulnerability to trafficking: age, disability, belonging to indigenous communities or minorities, victimization, migration and internal displacement, poverty, gender, and the deprivation of liberty.

### 2.4.2.1 Chronic Unemployment

West Africa achieved a relatively high economic growth rate in 2014 with the sub-regional average peaking at 6% despite the challenge posed by the Ebola virus. For instance, the growth rate in Nigeria's of 6.3% came mainly from non-oil sectors, indicating that the sources of its economy are diversifying.[218] Despite this

---

[215] *Nearly 400 Victims of Child Trafficking Rescued across Burkina Faso in INTERPOL-led Operation*, Interpol (Nov. 22, 2012), http://www.interpol.int/News-and-media/News/2012/PR096.

[216] UNICEF, La Strada Int'l, *supra* note 113, at 62–67; Moens (2004), p. 9, https://www.mensenhandelweb.nl/system/files/documents/09%20dec%202014/moens_2004_study_practice_trafficking_senegal_4.pdf. *See also* Kanth Amod (2004), http://www.cyc-net.org/cyc-online/cycol-0904-Homelessness.html; *International Migration Law: Glossary on Migration*, IOM 42 (2004), http://www.iomvienna.at/sites/default/files/IML_1_EN.pdf.

[217] *Abuse of a Position of Vulnerability and Other "Means" within the Definition of Trafficking in Persons*, UNODC 14 (2013), https://www.unodc.org/documents/human-trafficking/2012/UNODC_2012_Issue_Paper_-_Abuse_of_a_Position_of_Vulnerability.pdf; *see also* UNODC, *supra* note 107, at 71–75.

[218] *African Economic Outlook 2015*, African Economic Outlook (AEO), http://www.africaneconomicoutlook.org/sites/default/files/content-pdf/AEO2015_EN.pdf.

significant improvement, national policies on the redistribution of wealth, poverty reduction, and expansion of the labor market have remained static. The productive sectors of the economy in many countries "have been unable to create the jobs needed to reduce the levels of youth unemployment. Moreover, neither the public nor the private structures in place can provide strong enough support for youth job creation efforts."[219] The government, which in the past was the primary employer in the formal labor market, is unable to provide new jobs to absorb the growing number of young graduates into the civil service; and the poorly developed private sector with its precarious industries has reached its limits in addressing the employment issue. These structural constraints are exacerbated by numerous crises facing the countries of the sub-region, including the deficiencies of educational systems that fail to provide youths with the skills they need to secure decent employment; such youths are also affected by the food, economic, financial, and energy crises.[220]

According to ILO standards, unemployment has increased in West Africa and affects almost 12% of the total workforce (people between 16 and 65 years of age) compared to 8% and 10%, respectively (ILO, 2007).[221] Although this is slightly lower than the global youth unemployment rate of 12.4%, it does not reflect the realities of unemployment in the region. Many people are employed in the informal sector and work under precarious conditions earning a low income, less than US $2 a day, with inadequate social protection, insufficient hygiene and occupational safety, non-compliance with the provisions of labor codes, and a high incidence of child labor.[222]

Macro-economic policies solely focused on the growth and economic stability of the sub-region have failed to promote the creation of decent[223] jobs in sufficient numbers to absorb the unemployed workforce as well as new arrivals entering the labor market. For instance, records in Senegal show that 100,000 newly qualified youths enter the labor market every year. In the Republic of Benin, the Ministry for

---

[219] *Strategies to Promote Youth Self-employment in West Africa*, UN Economic Commission for Africa (UNECA) 11 (2010), http://repository.uneca.org/bitstream/handle/123456789/16552/bib.%2020457.pdf?sequence=1.

[220] *Id*, at 16.

[221] *Implementation of Decent Work Agenda in West Africa,* ILO 23 (May 2013), http://www.ilo.org/wcmsp5/groups/public/%2D%2D-africa/%2D%2D-ro-addis_ababa/documents/publication/wcms_235308.pdf.

[222] *Implementation of Decent Work Agenda in West Africa,* ILO 23 (May 2013), http://www.ilo.org/wcmsp5/groups/public/%2D%2D-africa/%2D%2D-ro-addis_ababa/documents/publication/wcms_235308.pdf; *Strategies to Promote Youth Self-Employment in West Africa*, Int'l Org. Migr. (ILO) 15, 21 (2018), https://rodakar.iom.int/sites/default/files/LHD%20Strategy.pdf.

[223] The ILO defines decent work as the sum of

> the aspirations of the people in their professional lives. Decent work involves opportunities for work that is productive and delivers a fair income; provides security in the workplace and social protection for workers and their families; offers better prospects for personal development and encourages social integration; gives people the freedom to express their concerns, to organise and to participate in decisions that affect their lives; and guarantees equal opportunities and equal treatment for all, both men and women. ILO, *supra* note 280.

Youth estimates this figure to be 30,000 while the ILO suggests that 100,000 young graduates enter the labor market each year in Mali.[224]

Consequently, the informal sector has become the sole source of opportunity for young graduates, including those with neither degrees nor other forms of qualification. Difficulties in finding work puts increased pressure on vulnerable people to take exploitative work at all costs; and some try to smuggle their way into Europe or neighboring countries under tragic conditions that involves risking their lives. The unemployed and people seeking opportunities to migrate are targeted by human traffickers who promise employment with good pay, high income, and better living standards for potential victims and their dependents.[225]

#### 2.4.2.2 Lack of Birth Registration

Birth registration refers to the official recording of the birth of a child by the government, establishing formal proof of a child's name, existence, and age. The Convention of the Rights of the Child, the African Charter on the Rights and Welfare of the Child, and other international treaties recognize the right to a name and nationality[226] as a fundamental human right and an essential means of protecting children's right that also enables family relations.[227] Without legal registration and recognition, other rights are difficult to claim.[228] It provides access to citizenship, travel documents, and basic social services such as school enrolment and health care. Birth registration may be required for children to access citizenship, health care, school enrolment, prove their right to inherit property, and other social services and forms of social assistance. Official identification documents also provide a life-long passport throughout the life of an individual, enabling them to enter into marriage or the labor market, to obtain a passport, to vote, and to open a bank account.[229] Birth

---

[224] UNECA, *supra note* 219, at 15.

[225] Ndiaye (2010).

[226] Convention on the Rights of the Child art. 7(1), Nov. 20, 1989, 1577 U.N.T.S. 3 [hereinafter *CRC*]. "The child shall be registered immediately after birth and shall have the right from birth to a name, the right to acquire a nationality and, as far as possible, the right to know and be cared for by his or her parents". *See also* International Covenant on Civil and Political Rights art 24(2), Dec.16, 999 U.N.T.S. 17 (1967) [hereinafter *ICCPR*]; Universal Declaration of Human Rights, G.A. Res. 217A (III), U.N. Doc. A/810 at art. 6 (1948) [hereinafter *UDHR*]; *see also* Office of the U.N. High Comm. for Human Rts, Report on Birth registration and the right of everyone to recognition everywhere as a person before the law, ¶ 4, U.N. Doc. A/HRC/27/22, (June 2014).

[227] It is anchored in Article 7 of the CRC that all children should be registered immediately upon birth, including being provided with a name and nationality. Birth registration is to be free for all children.

[228] *Child Protection*, UNICEF, http://www.unicef.org/wcaro/english/overview_6592.html (accessed August 20, 2021). *See also Birth Registration and Armed Conflict*, UNICEF (2007), https://www.unicef.org/protection/birth_registration_and_armed_conflict(1).pdf.

[229] *Every Child's Birth Right: Inequities and Trends in Birth Registration*, UNICEF 6 (Dec. 11, 2013), https://www.unicef.org/publications/files/Birth_Registration_11_Dec_13.pdf.

registration also contributes significantly to gender equality, reinforcing the equal treatment of girls and boys.

Birth registration is also a crucial first step in building a culture of protection against violence, abuse, neglect, exploitation and discrimination. Proof of age can prevent adolescents from being prosecuted and sentenced as adults and can also assist in tracing support for unaccompanied and separated children. In a similar vein, identity proof "can help protect the child against child marriage, under-age recruitment into the armed forces, and against child labour."[230] Having a national identity aids the fight against child trafficking and gives trafficking victims access to social services and rehabilitation.

Additionally, it provides the state with a tool to record and update statistics on children within its territory to facilitate effective planning of social services and policymaking. In effect, "[a]n effective civil registration system provides demographic data that allow a country to keep track of the condition of its population, including vital information about the situation of children."[231] This can ensure more accurate planning and implementation of development policies and programs such as school building to support communities and families in their child-rearing responsibilities. Despite efforts to promote universal birth registration in West and Central Africa, only 40% of children across the region are registered at birth. According to recent estimates by UNICEF, two out of three children below the age of five are not registered; leaving more than 48 million children each year without a legal identity thus no legal proof of their existence. Across the region, birth registration rates range from 57% in urban areas and better-off families to 33% in poor households situated in rural areas.[232]

The main obstacles preventing the registration of infants in West Africa include: state succession and border disputes;[233] discrimination against ethnic or religious minorities or refugee populations; the exclusive use of official languages in birth registration forms and procedures; fear of discrimination and persecution; conflicting laws; and migration with a prolonged residence abroad that can lead to loss of civil status.[234] In some cases, traditional or religious practices also create obstacles to civil registration and the establishment of a legal identity. For example, in Niger the birth registration rate is low among the Muslim population, where children are only named several weeks after birth. The historical systems of slavery and caste discrimination in that country and across the Sahel region, known as *wahaya*, also deny identity documents to "additional wives" of servile origin. Their children are not

---

[230] *Ibid.*

[231] *Id.*

[232] *Id.*

[233] "Birth registration rates in Côte d'Ivoire fell from 72 per cent in 2000 to 58 per cent in 2006, with a slight increase (to 65 per cent) in 2011–2012. This general decline is attributed to the political and military crisis between 2002 and 2011, which effectively divided the country in half and temporarily halted civil registration services in the north." *See* UNICEF, *supra* note 229 at 32.

[234] *Regional Conference on Statelessness in ECOWAS Member States*, UNHCR 2 (Feb. 23, 2015), http://www.unhcr.org/ecowas2015/Background-Agenda-Detailed-ENG.pdf.

considered legitimate children of the "master", which means they remain domestic servants to the family (and if they are girls they may themselves be sold as *wahayu*) and are excluded from registration.[235]

Finally, "the failure to acknowledge significant colonial-era population transfers and to grant nationality systematically to the populations residing in West African countries at the time of transition to independence still has consequences today."[236] Similarly, "more recent transfers of territory following adjustments to borders have failed to take sufficient account of the people living in those zones."[237] Since independence in West Africa, The International Court of Justice has dealt with several such cases. One of the well-known cases of nationality transfer that has affected numerous people relates to the Bakassi area bordering Nigeria and Cameroun.[238]

A child with no legal identity or proof of age and family relations lacks protection from the State, which in turn facilitates trafficking in several important ways. In Sierra Leone, the trafficking of unregistered children abroad is organized using falsified documents in which their ages are falsified to those of adults to facilitate their movement.[239] Without proper documentation, it is difficult for these children to approach authorities while abroad; they are also reluctant to identify themselves to the police as victims of trafficking out of fear of being arrested and deported, a situation exploited by traffickers.

The Economic Community of West African States (ECOWAS) region has significant advantages when it comes to addressing the issue of statelessness. For instance, all member states are parties to treaties that provide the right to a nationality;[240] they have achieved inter-state cooperation in the regulation of migration and promotion of free movement, residence and work. The common law and civil law models of nationality applied in ECOWAS combine two basic principles, *jus soli* (law or right of the soil), whereby an individual obtains nationality because he or she was born within the territory of the State; and *jus sanguinis* (law or right of blood), where nationality is conferred according to the official nationality of the child's parents.[241]

In addition to the framework of its treaty on free movement, the Economic Community of West African States (ECOWAS) adopted a protocol in 1982

---

[235] Manby B (2015), pp. 79–80, http://www.unhcr.org/ecowas2015/Nationality-Migration-and-Statelessness-in-West-Africa-REPORT-EN.pdf.

[236] *Id.* at 1.

[237] *Id.*

[238] *Id.* at 67.

[239] UNICEF, *supra* note 114, at 48.

[240] Convention on the Reduction of Statelessness arts 1-6, 989 U.N.T.S. 175, *entered into force* Dec. 13, 1975.

[241] Manby B (2015), p. 5.

addressing the concept of citizenship;[242] however, the implementation of these measures remains a challenge for member states. Current efforts to reform the civil registration system by adopting a common biometric Economic Community of West African States (ECOWAS) national identity card and abolishing the requirement to obtain a residence permit, represent a significant step toward addressing these problems.[243]

#### 2.4.2.3 Lack of Educational Opportunities and Prevalence of Ignorance

Differences in the education system from rural to urban areas is notable because of geographical disparities, both in terms of the enrollment rate and in infrastructure coverage. There are also inequalities related to gender—in Burkina Faso 65.2% of boys attend school compared to 61.1% of girls;[244] this region experiences high dropout rates with only 66% of students surviving primary school.[245] Although primary education in public schools is officially free and compulsory until 16 years of age, in many cases fees are paid to parent-teacher committees.[246] Parents also incur other direct costs in relation to activities, uniforms, paper and pens, text books, transport, lunches, and other expenses which often result in the exclusion of poor children from school.[247] In fact, there is an ongoing major problem with over-subscription in secondary schools. Although students take a test, 70% of those who pass are still not able to attend due to a lack of places.

Basic education is therefore not within everyone's means in the country and is not always available for all children; especially in remote rural areas. Private schools are also expensive. In Mali, the percentage of children out-of-school in the 7–14 years age group stands at 56%; it is around one-half that in Niger and Burkina Faso, and at least one-third of this figure in Senegal, Guinea Bissau, and Guinea. Overall, 16 million children were out of school in the Economic Community of West African States (ECOWAS) region in 2009, the largest number of out-of-school children in the continent: "[a]t least one-fifth of children are out of school in all countries except

[242] Economic Comm. of W. Afr. St. [ECOWAS], Protocol relating to the Definition of Community Citizen art. 1, ECOWAS Doc. A/P.3/5/82 (May 29, 1982). Article 1 states four possibilities for becoming a community citizen: (1) descent, (2) place of birth (providing one parent is a national), (3) adoption, or (4) naturalization.

[243] Manby B (2015), p. 2.

[244] *Burkina Faso, Statistics*, UNICEF, http://www.unicef.org/infobycountry/burkinafaso_statistics.html#117 (accessed on August 20, 2021).

[245] *Second Decade of Education for Africa*, UNESCO (2015), http://www.unesco.org/new/fileadmin/MULTIMEDIA/FIELD/Dakar/pdf/AU%20SECOND%20DECADE%20ON%20EDUCTAION%202006-2015.pdf.

[246] Stuart E (2010), https://oxfamilibrary.openrepository.com/oxfam/bitstream/10546/111984/1/a-crisis-multiplied-poverty-burkina-faso-240610-en.pdf.

[247] Melnick (2010), http://www.triplepundit.com/2010/12/gasp-benefits-child-labor-developing-world.

Ghana and Togo, underscoring the distance the region must still travel to reach universal primary enrolment."[248]

Many of these ostensibly inactive children are likely to be performing unskilled work such as household chores, agricultural work, and animal herding in their own families; thus, increasing their vulnerability to labor exploitation. There may also be worse forms of child labor that fall beyond the scope of standard household surveys; for instance, a lack of access to quality education is a major factor increasing the trafficking of children into the worst forms of child labor in plantations and mines in the West African region.[249] Therefore, children may be sent to neighboring countries or into cities for a lack of alternative options, including the opportunity to pursue primary and secondary schooling. Additionally, there are often no mechanisms in place to enforce the requirements for compulsory primary education. Where schools are available, the quality of education is good but the content not relevant; in situations where education is not affordable, or parents see no immediate value in education, children are sent to the Ivory Coast, Nigeria, Equatorial Guinea, and Gabon rather than to school.[250]

Furthermore, studies in numerous countries have established a close correlation between trafficking in persons and low levels of education, inadequate training and educational opportunities. For example, in Nigeria most of the trafficked victims in prostitution are primary or secondary school drop outs.[251] In addition to their limited educational qualifications, they do not have access to vocational training as their limited skills exclude them from the work market. An overwhelming majority also have no access to capital and become vulnerable prey to traffickers who entice them with the possibility of a better life.[252]

Finally, research has shown that the majority of trafficked people largely come from poorly educated families with illiterate parents living in rural areas. The general public in West Africa lacks overall knowledge of the trafficking phenomenon and holds different perceptions as to what it actually entails. Some people are clearly ignorant regarding what constitutes trafficking in persons, believing that it is a western perception of the migration of Africans for work purposes.

By the same token, "[t]he majority of trafficked persons are unaware of the forms of labor to which they will be subjected; most people trafficked to Europe for

---

[248] *The Twin Challenges of Child Labour and Educational Marginalisation in the ECOWAS Region*, ILO 36 (Jan. 1, 2016), http://documents.worldbank.org/curated/en/424061467993168177/pdf/103602-WP-PUBLIC-ECOWAS-child-labour-educational-marginalisation20140709-130339.pdf.

[249] *Id.*

[250] *Stop Trafficking in Child Labor*, Human Rts. Watch (Apr. 1, 2003), https://www.hrw.org/news/2003/04/01/west-africa-stop-trafficking-child-labor.

[251] Women Trafficking and Child Labour Eradication Foundation (WOTCLEF), The Rape of the Innocents: Evolving an African Initiative against Human Trafficking: Proceedings of the First Pan-African Conference on Human trafficking, 168 (WOTCLEF, 2001).

[252] *Unbearable to the Human Heart: Child trafficking and Action to Eliminate it*, ILO (2002), http://www.unicef.org/violencestudy/pdf/2002_traff_unbearable_en.pdf.

prostitution did not foresee entry into the sex industry."[253] A study on the impact of the reintegration program that forms part of the ALNIMA project of the Transnational AIDS/STD Prevention Among Migrant Prostitutes in Europe Project (TAMPEP) in Nigeria has shown that most of the women and girls trafficked to Italy were in fact shocked by the nature of the job they had to perform.[254]

#### 2.4.2.4 Physical and Mental Disabilities

Article 1 of the Convention on the Rights of Persons with Disabilities and Optional Protocol states that "Persons with disabilities include those who have long-term physical, mental, intellectual, or sensory impairments which in interaction with various barriers may hinder their full and effective participation in society on an equal basis with others."[255] The World Bank and World Health Organization (WHO) estimate that 15% of the world's population lives with a disability, of which a staggering 106 million children are estimated to have moderate and severe disabilities. Most are living in developing countries with little to no access to services.[256] In the Economic Community of West African States (ECOWAS) region, there is a notable number of disabled persons, which includes victims of devastating war injuries or who have been maimed by rebel forces; and those suffering from debilitating diseases, such as polio or birth defects.[257]

Multiple levels of prejudice exist throughout communities, towards children with disabilities, leading to profound levels of discrimination and exclusion. Attitudes and the language used to describe people with disabilities are overwhelmingly negative and based on false assumptions and beliefs; this includes shocking reports of infanticide and the trading in body parts of children with disabilities.[258] A social worker in Togo reported that in his community, children who have cerebral palsy and cannot stand are referred to as snakes because they lie on the ground. To eliminate such children, ceremonies are organized at the river where the child is left to drown, following which it is said that the snake is gone.[259]

West African cultural tradition considers any disability to be a punishment of the individual or family members for the sins they have committed. Examples of beliefs

---

[253] UNESCO, *supra* note 37, at 37.

[254] *Id.*

[255] Convention on the Rights of Persons with Disabilities and Optional Protocol art. 1, 2515 U.N.T.S. 3 (Dec. 13, 2006).

[256] *World Report on Disability*, World Health Organization (WHO) 29 (2011), http://apps.who.int/iris/bitstream/handle/10665/70670/WHO_NMH_VIP_11.01_eng.pdf?sequence=1.

[257] UNICEF, *supra* note 113, at 64; *see also* Convention on the Rights of the Child art. 7(1), Nov. 20, 1989, 1577 U.N.T.S. 3 [hereinafter *CRC*], at General Comment No. 9, ¶ 1.

[258] *Outside the Circle*, Plan Int'l 8 (Sept. 2, 2013), https://plan-international.org/publications/outside-circle#download-options.

[259] *Id.* at 23–24; Davinder (2013), http://www.aljazeera.com/indepth/features/2013/09/2013922121017135639.html.

about children's impairments include beliefs that they derive from the "sins" committed by parents, that they are an act of the devil, that the child is a sorcerer, that witchcraft has been performed on the child or family, or that the mother had looked at a disabled child during pregnancy.[260] Consequently, the families of children with disabilities become both victims and perpetrators of discrimination and stigmatization.

Across the region, people with disabilities are widely excluded from social life; deprived of emotional and physiological support; and denied access to basic human rights such as education.[261] These actions constitute a violation of the right to life, the right to be included in the community, and the right to equality and non-discrimination anchored in Art 10, Art 19, and Art 5 of the Convention on the Rights of Persons with Disabilities (CPRD). All children have the same right to develop their potential and access to education as outlined in both the United Nations Convention on the Rights of Persons with Disabilities (CRPD) (Article 7, 24) and the United Nations Convention on the Rights of the Child (CRC) (Article 2, 23). Art 25 (CRPD) protects the right of people with disabilities to access health services. Research shows that people with disabilities are subject to extreme levels of poverty, disproportionately represented among the unemployed, and therefore particularly vulnerable to being recruited for work such as begging. In most cases, parents or guardians drop disabled persons off on street corners and at major intersections to beg for money; girl beggars have been located in Senegal having been recruited in Mali by blind persons to whom they serve as guides and for whom they beg under abusive conditions.[262]

In addition to the high risk of disabled persons being trafficked, there is also potential vulnerability amongst the children of disabled parents; who often represent the sole source of support for parents who are unable to work and are vulnerable to promises of work and good salaries either in their own country or abroad. Furthermore, s no consistent definition of "disability" has been formulated by the official authorities in West Africa, and the stigma and shame associated with this plight often prevent parents from disclosing the existence of such children in any public documents. Children with disabilities are therefore not adequately accounted for in any government records or databases. Consequently, children with disabilities remain invisible to authorities and are more vulnerable to abuse and violation of their rights.

---

260 *Id.* In ECOWAS, Human Rights Watch reports the widespread belief that people are afflicted have a mental health condition as a result of evil spirits or curses. Children and adults are put in shackles at home or in unregulated prayer camps, deprived of food and water, and denied medication. When visiting Ghana in November 2013, the UN Expert on Torture described the shackling, denial of food and medicine, inadequate shelter and involuntary treatment as forms of torture and called on governments to act promptly to end these abuses. *See* Barriga Shantha (2015), https://www.hrw.org/news/2015/06/29/torture-comes-many-forms.

261 Ankinrimisi B. et al. (2012), http://www.odi.org/sites/odi.org.uk/files/odi-assets/publications-opinion-files/7579.pdf.

262 Moens (2004), p. 9.

Moreover, the services for such children are substantially under-resourced.[263] The stigmatization of people with disabilities is widespread across society in West Africa and is not given adequate attention by parents, guardians, siblings, peers, teachers, pastors, imams, and governments.[264]

#### 2.4.2.5 Family Disruptions and Domestic Violence

The family is often characterized as a safe place where individuals seek love, security, and shelter. However, evidence shows that it is also a place where an ever-present threat of violence exists against women and children, denying them their human rights and robbing them of their lives.[265] Poverty and an extremely low household income might induce parents to "sell" daughters for the purpose of marriage or to send their children into worse conditions of labor on the street. In general, girls are placed as domestic servants or street traders while boys work in plantations, construction, or mines. Many girls and boys in West Africa run away from their parents to avoid an unwanted marriage or to escape domestic violence, as a result of which they may end up on the street and be trafficked in brothels.

According to NGOs and research studies, a street child is primarily defined as "any girl or boy who has not reached adulthood, for whom the street... has become his or her habitual abode and/or source of livelihood, and who is inadequately protected, directed, and supervised by responsible adults."[266] In West Africa, there are three categories of "Street children":[267]

*Market children*: Children working in the streets and markets of cities selling or begging during the day may return to relatives in the evening for sleep and/or food. They spend most days and some nights on the street due to poverty and low household income, family size, sexual or physical abuse at home, and the need to work.[268]

[263] Davinder (2013).

[264] *Id.* at 7–8.

[265] UNICEF, *Domestic Violence against Women and Girls*, 6 Innocenti Digest 1 (2000) (available at: https://www.unicef.org/malaysia/ID_2000_Domestic_Violence_Women_Girls__6e.pdf).

[266] *Street Children and Homelessness*, CYC-Net, http://www.cyc-net.org/cyc-online/cycol-0904-Homelessness.html (accessed on August 20, 2021); *see also Rapid Situation Assessment Report—Street Children of Cairo & Alexandria, including the Children's Drug Abuse and Health/Nutritional Status* UNODC 7 (Jun. 2001), https://www.unodc.org/pdf/youthnet/egypt_street_children_report.pdf.

[267] In West Africa, "street children" refers both to *market children*, who work in the streets and markets of cities selling or begging during the day and return to relatives in the evening for sleep and/or food, and *homeless street children* who permanently work, live, and sleep on the streets, often lacking any contact with their families. *See* Worldwide Stats, *Exploitation of Children*, Casa Alianza (Sept. 2000), http://www.childtrafficking.com/Docs/casa_allianca_statistics_7.pdf.

[268] UNICEF, *supra* note 169, at 62.

*Homeless street children*: These children have no home other than the streets and move from place to place. They permanent work, live, and sleep on the streets, and often lack family support and ties; which makes them extremely vulnerable.[269]

*Children who are part of a Street Family*: These children live on sidewalks or in the halls of public buildings with the rest of their families because they cannot afford to rent a shelter. They may be displaced due to poverty, wars, or natural disasters. These families are nomad, carrying their possessions with them; children in these families often beg on the streets with other family members.[270]

The major factors forcing children onto the streets include dysfunctional families, intense poverty, child abuse and neglect, the death of one or both parents, the need to work to support the household income, lack of (or limited) opportunities in education, and banishment for an unplanned pregnancy. Additional factors include rivalry between spouses in polygamous families, a large family size of more than five children, forced marriage, drug use by children,and peer influence.[271] Uneducated or school drop outs with few job prospects live in extremely precarious conditions. These children are vulnerable to physical and sexual abuse and to becoming victims of trafficking;[272] many resort to begging in order to survive. In Senegal for example, some street children pretend to be *talibés* by finding their own tin tomato cans, the signature begging bowl used to ask for a pittance on the street.[273]

Many children are taken from their parents with the promise of school enrollment in the city; however, instead of being sent to school they must work and "are often punished if they don't bring enough money and are also often abused at home which can then lead them to leave the home and end up as a street child."[274] Equally salient is the fact that children living and working on the street are desperately looking for someone to care for them (support or affection or money) and are easy prey for traffickers who promise them work, study, or overseas adventures; but then subject them to exploitative labor conditions, which may include prostitution, sex tourism, forced begging, and criminal activities.

The incidence of street children across West Africa has been poorly documented due to the constant mobility of street children between major cities. In addition, various social and legal terms have been used to refer to street children resulting in an inconsistency in definitions and estimates regarding their numbers. Although there are no official statistics on the magnitude of the problem of street children in the Economic Community of West African States (ECOWAS), several efforts have

---

[269] *Id.*

[270] Moens (2004), p. 9. *See also* CYC-Net, *supra* note 323.

[271] *A Civil Society Forum for Anglophone West Africa on Promoting and Protecting the Rights of Street Children*, Consortium for Street Children 10 (Oct. 2003), http://www.streetchildrenresources.org/wp-content/uploads/2013/01/civil-society-forum-for-anglophone-west-africa.pdf; UNICEF, *supra* note 169, at 62; UNODC, *supra* note 323.

[272] Moens (2004), p. 8.

[273] *Id.*

[274] Surtees R, Child Trafficking in Sierra Leone, UNICEF 62 (fn. 123) (Jul. 28, 2005), https://nexushumantrafficking.files.wordpress.com/2015/03/child-trafficking-in-sierra-leone.pdf.

been made to estimate their demographics. For instance, the Consortium for Street Children (CSC) report on the population of street children in Greater Accra paints a grim picture for the entire sub-region. A "count of street children in Ghana's capital [in 2003] alone revealed that there are 21,140 street children, 6,000 street babies, and 7,170 street mothers under age 20."[275] Members of street families or entire families may be trafficked for labor purposes, begging, and petty crime.

#### 2.4.2.6 Poor or Non-Existent Social Services

The growing populations of young people in ECOWAS face high unemployment and an absence of social protection[276] that prevents them from supporting themselves and their families. Such limited economic and social opportunities has increased the pressures on adolescents and youths to migrate to the sub-region and out of the continent.[277] The current trends in demographic transitions, the aging of work forces, and international migration; as well as evolving economic and employment crises, underscores the need to ameliorate the risks and mitigate the vulnerabilities these nationals encounter by implementing legislative and practical measures that extend social protection coverage to all members of society.

UNICEF defines social protection as a set of public and private policies and programs aimed at reducing and eliminating economic and social vulnerabilities to poverty and deprivation. This translates into the provision of support for social protection components, which are social transfers; programs to ensure economic and social access to services; social support and care services; legislation and policies to ensure equity and non-discrimination in children, and access by families to services and employment/livelihoods.[278] Social protections play an essential role in realizing the human right to social security for all, thus reducing poverty and

[275] Alenoma G (2012), p. 74 (available at: http://www.iiste.org/Journals/index.php/RHSS/article/view/2805/2829).

[276] The terms social protection and social security are interchangeable, encompassing both contributory and noncontributory benefits. *See Social Security Programs throughout the World: Africa,* Social Security Administration (U.S.) (SSA) (2017), https://www.ssa.gov/policy/docs/progdesc/ssptw/2016-2017/africa/ssptw17africa.pdf; *Annual Review 2011-2012*, International Social Security Association (ISSA) 11, http://www.social-protection.org/gimi/RessourcePDF.action;jsessionid=RPF1rO9-rdieg9X0heZG0WxKwUS-VJVX3wGnwBxvhyw9ypJDXeH6!2055178518?id=31009.

[277] *Youth and International Migration: Role and Relevance of Social Protection*, United Nations Children's Fund (UNICEF) 6 (2014) http://www.globalmigrationgroup.org/sites/default/files/6._Chapter_3.pdf.

[278] *Integrated Social Protection Systems – Enhancing Equity for Children*, UNICEF 4 (Feb. 20, 2012), https://www.unicef.org/socialpolicy/files/Presentation_Jennifer_Yablonski_UNICEF__20_Feb_2012.pdf.

inequality, contributing to decent living conditions, and supporting inclusive economic growth and sustainable development.[279]

Social security is recognized as a human right in the Universal Declaration of Human Rights (1948) (Art. 22 and 25) and the International Covenant on Economic, Social and Cultural Rights (1966) (Art. 9, 11 and 12), as well as in UN conventions promoting the rights of specific groups such as the Convention on the Rights of the Child (CRC, 1989) and the International Convention on the Protection of the Rights of All Migrant Workers and Members of their Families (ICRMW, 1990). Regional initiatives include the African Union's Social Policy Framework for Africa, which has made recommendations on ways to strengthen coordination between national and regional policy initiatives,[280] and the adoption of the ECOWAS General Convention on Social Security, which aims to provide better coordination of social security schemes in the region.

Given the critical importance of human health both to individuals and to social and economic development, health coverage has been at the core of the ILO mandate since its foundation in 1919. The first formulation of guidance to achieve universal coverage dates back to 1944, when ILO constituents adopted Medical Care Recommendation (No. 69), which states: "The medical care service should cover all members of the community, whether or not they are gainfully occupied."[281] ILO data on health coverage and access deficits "reveal that nearly four-tenths (38.9%) of the world's population are without any form of legal health coverage". The largest gaps in coverage can be in sub-Saharan African countries such as Burkina Faso, where approximately 80% of the population is excluded from legal coverage as they are not enrolled in any health system or scheme.[282] Further analyses reveal that countries with the highest levels of poverty among their populations are more likely to experience gaps in the coverage of social health protection; whereas the highest

---

[279] *Migration and Youth: Challenges and Opportunities*, 2014 Global Migration Group (GMG), chapt. 3 (Youth and International Migration: Role and Relevance of Social Protection); The definition in the Constitution of the International Social Security Association (ISSA) ISSA reads,

> any scheme or programme established by legislation, or any other mandatory arrangement, which provides protection, whether in cash or in kind, in the event of employment accidents, occupational diseases, unemployment, maternity, sickness, invalidity, old age, retirement, survivorship, or death, and encompasses, among others, benefits for children and other family members, health care benefits, prevention, rehabilitation, and long-term care.

The full text of the ISSA Constitution is available at: http://www.issa.int/details?uuid=da0af86b-b150-4313-938d-185ce2316fbb.

[280] *Social Policy Framework for Africa*, African Union (Oct. 27, 2008), http://www.un.org/esa/socdev/egms/docs/2009/Ghana/au2.pdf.

[281] ILO, *Medical Care Recommendation No. 69*, ¶ 8 (1944).

[282] *World Social Protection Report 2014/15—Building Economic Recovery, Inclusive Development and Social Justice*, Int'l Labour Org. (ILO) 102 (2014), http://www.ilo.org/wcmsp5/groups/public/%2D%2D-dgreports/%2D%2D-dcomm/documents/publication/wcms_245201.pdf.

rates of coverage are achieved in countries with low poverty levels, such as those of Western Europe (Cf. Fig. 2.5).[283]

It is often the case that even simple basic care involves out-of-pocket payments, including facility-based maternity care. For example, in Burkina Faso, where most of the population earns less than US $1 a day, women were officially supposed to pay 900 F CFA (€1.4), the amount of the residual fee in health centers, for normal deliveries in 2010; although the indigent were supposed to be exempted. More than 50% of women reported that they had paid more than 900 F CFA due to expenses for medical products bought directly from the care provider or from the CSPS's community pharmacy.[284] Evaluating the health care situation in West Africa, even people who are legally covered experience limited health benefits; and medical assistance is frequently unavailable due to a lack of infrastructures and human resources to deliver services, or is unaffordable (as it requires high out of pocket payments). Ensuring access to essential services can lead to poverty. Lack of social support is therefore another source of trafficking in children, who may become trapped in the worst form of labor to support the elderly.

However, in recent years, increased social protection coverage in numerous developing countries with a strong tradition in contributory social insurance and a labor market characterized by persistent levels of high informality has been achieved through the expansion of a combination of programs.[285] Notably, recent significant reductions in income inequality in Latin America, which has the world's highest and persistent levels of socioeconomic inequality, have been attributed in part to the expansion of public cash transfers targeted at the poor, improved macroeconomic conditions that have fostered employment, the expansion of coverage in basic education, and stronger labor institutions.[286] In the African region, Ghana has embraced a dynamic social security approach to improve coverage and support sustainability in order to achieve critical social security objectives.[287] Ghana's experience provides an important model for the progressive realization of social

[283] Significant gaps in the funding of health care are also apparent in this group of wealthy and poor countries. The threshold required to provide access to quality health care is estimated by the ILO to be US $239 per person per year. Notably, the current financial deficit in low-income countries exceeds 90% of the expenditure necessary to cover the costs of minimum health care. The global average annual cost per capita on health is US $948; Eritrea, the country with the lowest total expenses per year on health, invests just US$12. *World Health Statistics,* WHO (2016), http://apps.who.int/iris/bitstream/10665/206498/1/9789241565264_eng.pdf.

[284] Ridde et al. (2012), p. 3. The mean medical expenditure for a delivery is equivalent to seven days of consumption for the 46% of the population living under the poverty threshold. Annuaire Statistique 2009, INSD, http://www.insd.bf/n/contenu/pub_periodiques/annuaires_stat/Annuaires_stat_nationaux_BF/Annuaire_stat_2009.pdf.

[285] Gasparini and Lustig (2011), http://www.ecineq.org/milano/WP/ECINEQ2011-213.pdf.

[286] *Id.* at 22.

[287] *Good Practice Review: Extending Social Security Coverage in Africa,* International Social Security Association, Geneva, 2009; Insurance Scheme brings Relief to Ghana's Informal Sector, *Ghana Business News*, 2008.

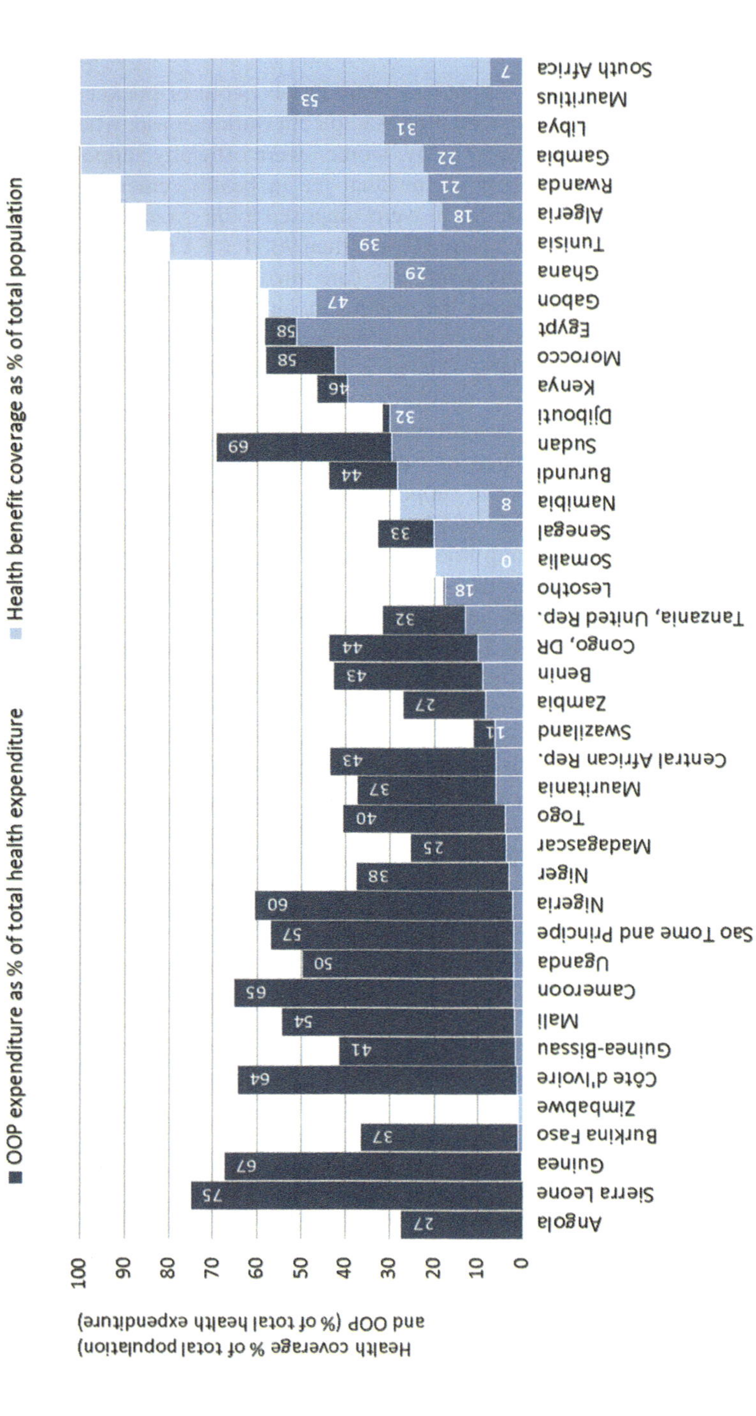


**Fig. 2.5** Out of pocket expenditure and health benefit coverage (Sources: Health coverage: OECD and national sources; OOP: WHO. http://www.social-protection.org/gimi/gess/RessourceDownload.action?ressource.ressourceId=43300)

protection from which other middle- and low-income countries may draw useful lessons.

#### 2.4.2.7 Varying Gender Roles in Society

An in-depth understanding of trafficking in West Africa is associated with an understanding of gender roles and the relative values ascribed to females and males in the community; gender shapes the way in which power and violence are used and perceived in African society, as well as in the context of trafficking in persons. "Most research concludes that girls and women are at high risk of being trafficked in Africa and removed from school to provide income for the family, while boys are favored for educational opportunity."[288] This inequality "causes a lifelong economic and social disadvantage to women."[289]

Thus, women in West African societies experience extensive discrimination at social, economic, and political levels which reinforces their disadvantaged position, especially with respect to access to resources; participation in decision making in the family, community, and national spheres; and non-recognition of their labor in national accounting processes.[290] Schools have been challenged by significant, regional negative gender gaps for girls; and the problem of retention prevents girls from attaining professional and academic qualifications. The vulnerability of women is also reflected in a lack of employment opportunities; compared to men, lower proportions of women can be found in higher educational institutions, high-status occupations, and top managerial and administrative positions in the West African region. Although women comprise more than half of the population, gender disparities are prevalent in formal representation in governance institutions; for instance, data regarding the parity of men and women in the legislature and local government indicate the presence of indirect discrimination in Cape Verde. In the 2006 Legislative Elections, women represented 15.2% of those elected, while in the 2008 Local Elections, 22% of those elected were women. This represents approximately one fifth of those elected in the country.[291]

Moreover, in the Federal Civil Service in Nigeria, 76% of workers on the payroll are men and just 24% are women, while less than 14% of women run the management level offices. Additionally, in the medical profession (despite a recent inflow of women) gender statistics report that women represent less than 20% of workers, especially in highly skilled positions. Women also face discrimination in obtaining

---

[288] Msuya (2017), p. 25 (available at: https://digitalcommons.uri.edu/cgi/viewcontent.cgi?article=1007&context=dignity).

[289] *Id.*

[290] Fayomi (2009), p. 65, 67 (available at: http://eprints.covenantuniversity.edu.ng/3970/1/Dr.%20Fayomi%20O.%20O.%204.pdf).

[291] *Plan of Action on Gender and Trade 2010-2020*, ECOWAS 7, http://www.ccdg.ecowas.int/wp-content/uploads/Plan-of-Action_Gender-and-Trade.pdf (accessed on August 20, 2021).

employment, credits[292] and equal pay, and in owning or managing businesses in West Africa. Urban women dominate the informal trading sector while those living in rural areas carry out domestic work, which is traditionally a female job. Such gender discrimination and disparities continue to increase women's proclivity to migrate in order to seek a better life.[293]

The UN Special Rapporteur on violence against women, Radhika Coomaraswamy, has observed that all cultures foster certain harmful practices that deny women their rights and dignity. The most prevalent forms of violence in Burkina Faso and the West African region are domestic violence, rape, early and forced marriages, polygamy, the custom of levirate marriage, the use of the dowry, and clandestine Female Genital Mutilation (FGM).[294] Caste-based slavery practices, rooted in ancestral master-slave relationships, continue to exist in parts of Niger. An estimated 8800 to 43,000 Nigerians live in conditions of traditional servitude that range in practice from societal discrimination to outright slavery.[295] Other demeaning practices classified as psychological violence towards women include: demeaning post-menopausal spouses by favoring younger spouses, desertion of infertile women, the repudiation of women who have given birth to girls, wrongful widowhood rites, and accusations of sorcery.[296]

Additionally, in these heavily patriarchal societies, most customary laws do not allow women the right to own or inherit land or property. Regarding women's role in relation to land ownership and farming in Nigeria, statistics on land registration show that 90% of all land in the country is registered to men[297] Islamic laws allow for a woman to inherit her husband's property, except in divorce cases. Such cultural practices restrict women's economic autonomy and increase their vulnerability to poverty. The dire need to meet economic demands and escape poverty, persecution, and discrimination at home may drive women and girls to seek solace in trafficking. In effect, trafficking becomes a survival strategy, an alternative to poverty

---

292 Niger government automatically provides "social benefits to male heads of household, but women are required to initiate Court proceedings to prove that they qualify as heads. Women's property rights predominantly derive from their status as wives, mothers, and wards rather than individuals." *Id.*

293 Fayomi (2009).

294 FGM practices remove part of or the whole clitoris. *See* Radhika Coomaraswamy (Special Rapporteur on Violence Against Women), *Integration of the Human Rights of Women and the Gender Perspective of Violence Against Women*, U.N. Doc. E/CN.4/2002/83 (Jan. 31, 2002).

295 *Trafficking in Persons Report—Niger*, U.S. Dept. of State (2009), https://www.state.gov/j/tip/rls/tiprpt/2009/123137.htm.

296 *Country report for the Task force on Violence against Women*, Inter-Agency Network on Women and Gender Equality (IANWGE) (Nov. 3, 2010), http://www.un.org/womenwatch/ianwge/taskforces/tf_vaw.htm; *see also* Convention on the Elimination of Discrimination against Women (CEDAW), *Country Reports*, U.N. Women (Dec. 28, 2007), http://www.un.org/womenwatch/daw/cedaw/reports.htm.

297 Fayomi (2009), pp. 67–69.

alleviation, and also offers the hope of obtaining personal freedom and a better standard of living.[298]

Finally, findings have revealed that men and boys can also become victims of trafficking, particularly for forced labor. "However, lack of awareness about the involvement of men as trafficked persons has resulted in identification failures, as well as significant discrimination against male victims, particularly in terms of access to protection and assistance."[299]

#### 2.4.2.8 War and Trafficking for Body Parts

Since the 1960s, West Africa has experienced serious food insecurity, acceleration of drought, desertification in the Sahel, socio-political crises, pandemic diseases, and natural calamities leading to substantial refugee movements. The various wars and conflicts that have persisted for more than two decades have resulted in a vulnerability to trafficking as citizens seek to escape the country.[300] Thus intra-regional armed conflicts such as the *Biafran* War in Nigeria (1967–1970), the liberation struggle in Guinea-Bissau (1963–1973), the Casamance independence movement in Senegal (1980s to present), the Mauritanian conflict in 1989, and the terrible conflicts that tore apart the River Mano countries (Sierra Leone and Liberia) from 1989 to 2000, resulted in the trafficking of adults and children into rebel factions as soldiers, porters, messengers and 'wives'.[301] For example, in Sierra Leone, World Vision 2002 reported that 31% of child laborers in the mines were refugees and 52% were Internally Displaced Peoples (IDPs), many of whom may be seen as victims of trafficking.[302]

Following his visit to the Ivory Coast, the UN Representative reported in 2005 that the armed conflict affecting the country since 2002 had caused between 500,000 and 1,000,000 IDPs, the overwhelming majority of whom (98%) were living with host families.[303] In 2014 the United Nations High Commissioner for Refugees (UNHCR) assisted more than 12,900 refugees to return to Mali after the humanitarian crisis caused by political and social unrest. An additional 42,000 refugees in 2015, along with an estimated 74,000 Internally Displaced People (IDPs) and migrants, have also returned to their countries of origin.[304]

---

[298] *Id.* at 70; Innocenti Insight, *Trafficking in Human Beings, especially Women and Children, in Africa*, UNICEF 7 (Sept. 2003), http://www.unicef-irc.org/publications/pdf/insight9e.pdf.

[299] Giammarinaro, *supra* note 181, ¶ 23.

[300] ECOWAS and the Dynamics of Conflict and Peace-Building (eds., Stella Amadi, Dauda Garuba, and Thomas Jaye, CODESRIA 2011).

[301] Charrière F, Frésia M (2008), pp. 9–10, http://www.unhcr.org/49e479c311.pdf.

[302] *Id.* at 64–65.

[303] UNGA, *Protection of and Assistance to Internally Displaced Persons—Note by the Secretary-General*, ¶ 14-15, U.N. Doc. A/61/276 (Aug. 21, 2006).

[304] *Global Appeal—West Africa*, UNHCR (2015), http://www.unhcr.org/5461e602b.html.

A related yet hidden dimension of trafficking consists of the plundering of the bodies of the enemy. In times of war and instability, severe rights abuses occur as a result of the theft and plunder of organs and tissues from captive prisoners of war and unwanted dead bodies.[305] Documented sources have shown that trafficking chains involving human body parts operate across West African national boundaries to diaspora communities in Europe and the United States as part of an income generation scheme. Traditional healers use body parts in black-magic rites and witchcraft rituals to cure ailments, protect their clients from misfortunes, or gain more wealth and power. War and conflicts in the region primarily meet the demand for this illicit trade in body parts of the dead and the living.

In 2015, the United Nations High Commission for Refugees (UNHCR) reported violent clashes between government forces and armed groups in the north of Nigeria which triggered large waves of displacement. More than half-a-million civilians were internally displaced, while others sought safety in neighboring Cameroon, Chad, and Niger.[306] Forced displacement increases trafficking vulnerability by weakening family support structures, community bonds, and self-protection mechanisms that might otherwise serve as a buffer to trafficking and related activities undertaken by criminal organizations. Given the dire economic circumstances of asylum countries, refugees may be particularly vulnerable to traffickers who appear to offer life-saving access to employment opportunities or may fall prey to traffickers who claim to offer a route to safety.[307]

In addition to these violent conflicts, a number of states have taken stringent measures to regulate immigration at a time of economic recession, bringing fundamental changes to the stability of the sub-region. These include the massive expulsion of foreigners from Ghana in 1969 and Nigeria in 1983, the birth of the notion of "Ivority" as early as 1986, the expulsion of Moorish traders in Senegal in 1989, and the expulsion of West Africans by the Libyan authorities in the 1980s.[308]

Alongside these conflicts, the rapidly evolving outbreak of Ebola in Guinea, Liberia, Nigeria, Senegal, and Sierra Leone in 2014 killed 3000 people. This pandemic crisis had dramatic consequences for social and economic activities in West Africa, as several borders were closed and many farmers were unable to tend their fields in affected areas. On a large scale, "war results in an amplification of factors that contribute to and cause trafficking, including poverty, social vulnerability, decimated government infrastructure and services, impunity, corruption, and social dislocation (refugees and IDPs)."[309]

---

[305] Scheper-Hughes (2016), http://www.ia-forum.org/Files/HDSQLC.pdf; *see also* Scheper-Hughes (2015), http://www.endslavery.va/content/endslavery/en/publications/acta_20/scheper_hughes_panel.pdf; Cockayne J, Walker S (2016), https://collections.unu.edu/eserv/UNU:5780/UNUReport_Pages.pdf.

[306] UNHCR, *supra* note 304.

[307] UNICEF, *supra* note 274, at 64–65.

[308] Charrière F, Frésia M (2008).

[309] UNICEF, *supra* note 129, at 48.

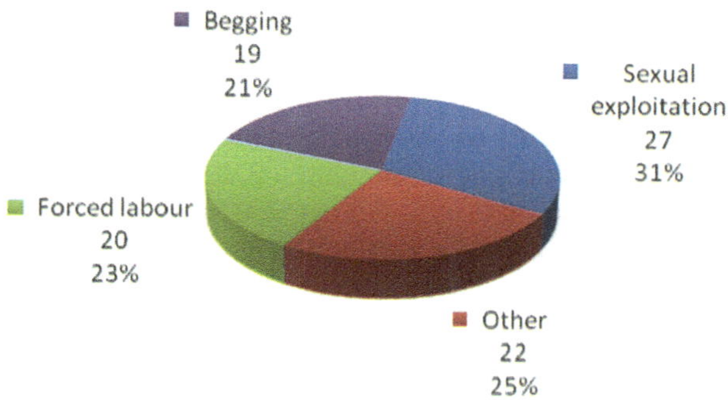


**Fig. 2.6** IOM Assistance to Persons Trafficked from West and Central Africa in 2011 (Source: IOM, Counter Trafficking and Assistance to Vulnerable Migrants Annual Report of Activities 2011, IOM 60 (2012), https://www.iom.int/files/live/sites/iom/files/What-We-Do/docs/Annual_Report_2011_Counter_Trafficking.pdf)

## 2.5 Forms of Trafficking in West Africa

The international community recognizes that people are being trafficked across international borders in abusive and illegal circumstances for a variety of purposes. Human Rights Watch observed that child trafficking in West Africa "typically begins with a private arrangement between a trafficker and a family member, one driven by the family's economic struggle and the trafficker's desire for profit and cheap labor."[310] Trafficking occurs for a myriad of exploitative purposes for which trafficked victims have not consented, including forced and/or bonded labor, including within the sex trade, forced marriage, and other slavery-like practices (cf. Fig. 2.6).[311]

### *2.5.1 Trafficking for Commercial Sexual Exploitation*

Commercial sexual exploitation has become a massive transnational industry, especially in the last 20 years. The potential and high profits that arise from sex trafficking stem in part from the low cost and the resalable nature of the commodity. Another advantage is the remarkable stability of the sex market in both good and bad economic times. "The demand does not seem to decline, and customers appear to be willing to pay the going price, again regardless of the state of the economy."[312] Furthermore, the sex industry is proliferating, expanding beyond club and brothel prostitution around the world to include mail-order brides, women for rent, and sex tour businesses and their common interrelated forms, all of which may involve trafficking for prostitution, pornography, and sex tourism.

---

[310] Cohen (2003), p. 9.

[311] *Id.*; *see also Type of Modern Day Slavery Crime*, National Crime Agency (UK), http://www.nationalcrimeagency.gov.uk/crime-threats/human-trafficking/types-of-human-trafficking (accessed on August 20, 2021).

[312] Farr (2005).

#### 2.5.1.1 Prostitution and Sex Trafficking

A review of trafficking flows by the US State Department report shows that domestic trafficking for the commercial sexual exploitation of women and children is prevalent in all Economic Community of West African States (ECOWAS) countries[313] and many West African children and women, mostly girls from Nigeria, are trafficked to Europe for sexual purposes. According to Nigeria's National Agency for Prohibition of Traffic in Persons (NAPTIP) and the United Nations Inter-regional Crime and Justice Research Institute (UNICRI) over 10,000 Nigerians are engaged in prostitution in Italy and Belgium. This number accounts for more than 60% of street prostitutes in these countries. The business of trafficking in persons "has become so profitable in Italy that a Nigerian mafia has formed, which coordinates the trafficking of girls through "madams," who lure the girls from Nigeria with promises of a better future."[314]

Reliable data from the National Referral Mechanism (NRM)[315] along with recent prosecutions also demonstrate the very real incidence of transnational trafficking in West Africa. For instance, UK Human Trafficking Referral Mechanism statistics for the years 2012–2013 show that a number of West African countries are ranked among the highest in terms of country of origin for trafficking (cf. Table 2.1). In 2013, the UK National Referral Mechanism recorded 250 people as possibly having been trafficked from Nigeria, Ghana, Sierra Leone, the Gambia, or the Ivory Coast.[316] Ghanaian girls between 16 and 25 years of age have also been reported as having been trafficked to neighboring countries in West Africa for the purpose of commercial sexual exploitation, for example to brothels in the capital cities. Others are moved to Gambia for prostitution in tourist locations. Alarming flows in the trafficking of children for sexual exploitation has been taking place from Ghana to Togo, Ivory Coast and Nigeria, and vice versa.[317] A rapid assessment carried out in Mali in 2005 highlighted the increasing expansion of the commercial sexual exploitation of girls between 12 and 18 year-old. Most were Malian citizens, although

---

[313] U.S. Dept. of State 2015, Report on ECOWAS.

[314] *Nigeria*, Global Monitoring 13 (2011), http://www.ecpat.net/sites/default/files/A4A2011_AF_NIGERIA_FINAL.pdf; *see also Women of Nigerian Origin in Finland who have been subjected to Trafficking for Sexual Exploitation: Practice in Applying the Aliens Act*, Syrjintä (2017), https://www.syrjinta.fi/documents/14490/0/Nigeriaselvitys_englanti/6ea936c8-462d-47a8-a73a-535af377ffd0.

[315] The UK Decision-Making Office, which has been operational since 2009, is where people identified as possible victims of trafficking can be referred to a competent authority to judge their case.

[316] Cherti M et al. (2013), p. 24, http://www.ippr.org/files/images/media/files/publication/2013/01/nigeria-trafficking_Jan2013_10189.pdf?noredirect=1.

[317] Dr. M'Jid (2008), p. 6, https://www.unicef.org/wcaro/english/ESEWCAROFinalReport_EN_corrige.pdf; *Global Monitoring Status of Action against Commercial Sexual Exploitation of Children, Ghana,* ECPAT, 13 (2014) https://www.ecpat.org/wp-content/uploads/legacy/A4A2011_AF_GHANA_FINAL2.pdf.

**Table 2.1** United Kingdom Human Trafficking Referral Mechanism Statistics 2018: All Referrals- 132 Countries of Origin[a]

| Rank of 132 | Claimed Nationality | Domestic servitude | Labor Exploitation | Organ harvesting | Sexual exploitation | Unknown exploitation | **Total 2018** | Total 2017 |
|---|---|---|---|---|---|---|---|---|
| 8 | Nigeria | 47 | 38 | 0 | 103 | 20 | **208** | 264 |
| 21 | Ghana | 12 | 14 | 0 | 14 | 7 | **47** | 45 |
| 38 | Sierra Leone | 5 | 4 | 0 | 5 | 2 | **16** | 7 |
| 39 | Gambia | 3 | 4 | 0 | 3 | 5 | **15** | 10 |
| 51 | Guinea | 2 | 3 | 0 | 2 | 1 | **8** | 9 |
| 65 | Benin | 2 | 0 | 0 | 2 | 0 | **4** | 1 |
| 71 | Ivory Coast | 0 | 1 | 0 | 0 | 2 | **3** | 13 |
| 87 | Senegal | 0 | 0 | 0 | 2 | 0 | **2** | 6 |
| 95 | Burkina Faso | 1 | 0 | 0 | 0 | 0 | **1** | 2 |
| 98 | Cape Verde | 1 | 0 | 0 | 0 | 0 | **1** | 0 |
| 111 | Liberia | 0 | 1 | 0 | 0 | 0 | **1** | 2 |
| | **Total** | **73** | **65** | **0** | **131** | **37** | **306** | 359 |

[a]*National Referral Mechanism Statistics- End of Year Summary 2018*, National Crime Agency (NCA) UK, (20 Mars 2019), file:///C:/Users/irie/Downloads/NCA%20-%20Stats%20End%20of%20Year%20Summary%202018%20(1).pdf

some also came from neighboring countries such as Burkina Faso, Cameroon, Ivory Coast, Guinea, Nigeria, and Sierra Leone.

Prostitution in West Africa is street-based but also occurs in brothels and rooms alongside bars and clubs harboring prostitutes to attract clients.[318] Some sources have asserted that street trading is sometimes used as a front for prostitution; with girls and women supplementing their trade revenues through the sale of sexual services at night. Another commonly reported location for prostitution is that of maritime ports, where some women provide sexual services on port roads while the ship or truck is in port; this involves the movement of people from rural to prosperous urban areas or from one town to another. In many cases, prostitutes, particularly girls under 18 years of age, are moved for sexual exploitation from rural to prosperous urban areas, tourist locations, or to places where there is a concentration of migrant male workers such as mining camps, plantations, and oil-extraction zones.

Trafficking victims are kept in bondage through a combination of fear, intimidation, abuse and psychological control; the traffickers lure innocent and ignorant girls into their clandestine networks through fraud, deception, false passports, visas, and false promises of attractive working conditions at irresistible salaries by working as nannies, maids, dancers, models, or other service worker occupations. The victims unknowingly end up being forced by threats and violence into sex acts or slavery. Women trafficked to Europe are frequently under debt bondage to their traffickers; the experience of Nigeria shows that victims generally pay a deposit and then agree (sign a contract) to pay back the outstanding balance by working in prostitution.

To illustrate the incidence of trafficking in persons in West Africa, this figure presents a selective summary of the number of potential victims referred to in the UK National Referral Mechanism (NRM) in 2018. It is broken down into exploitation types and the claimed nationality of the first respondent at the time of referral.

#### 2.5.1.2 Sex Trafficking: Act, Means, and Purpose

Under international law, three essential elements constitute the criminal act defined as trafficking in persons: **act**, **means,** and **purpose**. Whenever a person is charged with the offense of trafficking in persons, the prosecutor must prove "under 'activity' what the accused did (the action). Under 'means', the burden is to prove how the accused did what they did and, under 'purpose', the reason for doing so."[319] Even though trafficking in persons often includes all three phases, prosecutors do not need to prove all the constituents listed under each of the three elements. The proof of one activity, one means, and one purpose is enough to support the prosecution.

---

[318] Dr. M'Jid (2008), p. 16.

[319] Justice of the High Court, *The Republic v. Rauf Ibrahim et al.*, Suit No. D2/447/15 [Ghana].

#### 2.5.1.2.1 Deceptive Recruitment and Social Isolation

Sex trafficking comprises an inherently coercive environment. As noted previously, victims of trafficking are lured by deception with false promises of attractive working conditions at irresistible salaries as nannies, maids, dancers, or models. "Only when they were far away from their homes were they told the truth – that they would have to work as prostitutes,"[320] Those recruited to work abroad—whether in a legal or illegal manner are not aware they will be forced into sex work until they reach the destination country where the exploitation occurs. The victims then realize that the initially promised job and working conditions differ considerably from reality; and find themselves trapped in abusive situations and debt bondage without the ability to escape.[321] The *Attorney General of the Federation and Toyin Ogbebor* case recorded that on October 22, 2005, the offender deceitfully induced four victims, promising them higher earnings abroad by working in a saloon and selling herbs. In her statement to NAPTIP (National Agency for Prohibition of Traffic in Persons), she admitted having been duly cautioned and was fully aware that the girls were going to be used for prostitution in Libya.[322]

In cases of smuggling or the facilitated migration of victims between African countries and European countries for work or to engage in prostitution, experience shows that in certain cases victims may have consented at some point to traveling abroad. For example, in the *AG v. Samuel Emwiovbankhoe* case, Samuel made an agreement with Nigerian girls to take them to Italy for the purpose of prostitution;[323] The use of such a method by traffickers to procure their victims raises two legal issues of crucial importance: the question of legal capacity and giving consent to contractual transactions. In the first case, it is a fundamental principle of law that a

[320] Lupton (2016), http://www.reuters.com/article/us-britain-trafficking-witchcraft/woman-jailed-for-22-years-for-trafficking-nigerian-girls-for-sex-trade-idUSKCN10F21A.

[321] Constantinou et al., *Report on the Relevant Aspects of the Trafficking Act (Geographical Routes and Modus Operandi) and on its Possible Evolutions in Response to Law Enforcement*, Trafficking as A Criminal Enterprise (TRACE) 49 (Feb. 27, 2015), http://trace-project.eu/wp-content/uploads/2015/03/TRACE-D2.1_FINAL.pdf. *See also* Report of the Special Rapporteur on Trafficking in Persons, especially Women and Children), *Mission to Italy*, ¶ 9 U.N. Doc. A/HRC/26/37/Add.4 (Apr. 1, 2011) (by Joy Ngozi Ezelio).

[322] *High Court of Justice, Between A.G. Federation and Toyin Ogbebor*, Suit No. NCT/140/06 (Nigeria) (available at: https://www.unodc.org/res/cld/case-law/nga/2008/attorney_general_of_the_federation_and_toyin_ogbebor_suit_no__nct14006.html/Attorney_General_of_the_Federation_and_Toyin_Ogbebor_Suit_No._NCT.140.06.pdf); *see also PO (Nigeria) v. Secretary of State for the Home Department* [2011] 132 EWCA 22 (U.K.).

[323] *High Court of Justice, Between Attorney-General of the Federation and Samuel E.*, Suit No. B/20C/2005 (Nigeria) (available at: https://www.unodc.org/res/cld/case-law/nga/2008/attorney_general_of_the_federation_and_samuel_emwirovbankhoe_suit_no__b20c2005_.html/Attorney_General_of_the_Federation_and_Samuel_Emwirovbankhoe_Suit_No._B.20C.2005.pdf).

minor cannot enter into a valid legal contract.[324] The purpose of this provision is to "protect the minor against his [or her] inexperience, which may enable an adult to take unfair advantage of him [or her], or to induce him [or her] to enter into a contract which, though in itself fair, is simply improvident."[325]

Secondly, expressive agreement raises the question of consent to "contractual documents" in regard to the adult women and men who are victims of this practice. To give valid consent to an original work offer, a person must have full knowledge of the nature and scope of the transaction. Thus, if a victim's consent is obtained by fraud, deception, or similar conduct, this alleged agreement is impaired and lacks legal effect.[326] In this respect, Court jurisprudence accepts economic pressure exerted on a party to agree to a contract as one of the conditions for invalidating the contract. Interpreting Art 3 of the Trafficking Protocol, which states that the consent of the person being trafficked is irrelevant when deception, coercion, and exploitation are present, Lord Goff of the English House of Lords declared in the *Evia Luck Case (No 2)*, "it is now accepted that economic pressure may be sufficient to amount to duress ... provided at least that the economic pressure may be characterised as illegitimate and has constituted a significant cause inducing the [claimant] to enter into the relevant contract."[327]

The matter of consent or voluntariness on the part of the victims is also emphasized by the International Organization for Migration (IOM), which offers this important analysis: "[i]n many instances, trafficked migrants are lured by false promises, misled by misinformation concerning migration regulations, or driven by economic despair or large-scale violence. In such cases, the migrant's freedom of choice is so seriously impaired that the 'voluntariness' of the transaction must be questioned."[328] It therefore follows from this discussion that the dimension of

---

[324] Peel (2007), p. 567. This fundamental principle of law is embedded in Art 3(c) of the UN Trafficking Protocol which renders a child's apparent consent to exploitation irrelevant. However, there are limited exceptions to the general rule under which contracts with minors are not void but voidable.

[325] Okogbule (2013), p. 57.

[326] Peel (2007), p. 456.

[327] *Dimskal Shipping Co SA v. International Transport Workers Federation* [1992], 2 AC 152, 165 (U.K.). Moreover, undue influence exerted on a party to agree to a contract can lead to the setting aside of the contract in equity. *See* Royal Bank of Scotland v. Etridge [2002], 2 AC 773 (U.K.). The UNODC 2013 paper explains the concept of vulnerability as follows:

> ... the vulnerability may be of any kind, whether physical, psychological, emotional, family-related, social, or economic. The situation might, for example, involve insecurity or illegality of the victim's immigration status, economic dependence, or fragile health. In short, the situation can be any state of hardship in which a human being is impelled to accept being exploited. Persons abusing such a situation flagrantly infringe human rights and violate human dignity and integrity, which no-one can validly renounce.

UNDOC, *supra* note 217.

[328] *Trafficking in Women to Italy for Sexual Exploitation*, IOM 2 (Jun. 1996), https://childhub.org/en/system/tdf/library/attachments/iom_1996_trafficking_in_wo2.pdf?file=1&type=node&id=16371; *see also The Cost of Coercion: Global Report on the ILO Declaration on Fundamental*

trafficking found in West Africa, with purported "contractual documents" usually signed between the traffickers and the victims and induced by the undue influence of intermediaries and accomplices, are voidable in law.[329]

Victims of trafficking are moved from their familiar surroundings and sent on a journey that has been arranged by someone else to a foreign country where they experience feelings of social isolation. The intent of the traffickers is to maintain women's dependence on them by taking away their sense of agency or any feeling that they have some control over their lives.[330] Steps toward social isolation include the confiscation of identification papers, which renders them illegal migrants and places them in a difficult position regarding their relationship with the police, as approaching authorities for assistance may result in them being deported back to their home countries.[331]

Furthermore, restrictions on freedom of movement and contact with the outside world, including from friends and family and people with the same background, may be discouraged or strictly controlled. To achieve this, trafficked persons are frequently moved around to avoid detection and also to disorientate them so that they are less inclined to attempt to escape.[332] Unfortunately, "the very cause of their being trafficked – the desire to make more money to support their families – is also often the chain with which they lock themselves into the position of trafficked [persons]."[333] This usually happens to West African women and girls smuggled into Western countries as potential tourists, students, and artists.

Additionally, with the advent of new technologies, victims' accommodation or workplaces may be closely monitored by GPS, cameras, or guards. Travel to and from work may also be controlled to reinforce their feelings of isolation and helplessness; the traffickers may also further debilitate the victim by giving them addictive drugs or alcohol to control them.[334]

#### 2.5.1.2.2 Control Through Ritual and Debt Bondage

Furthermore, traffickers exploit the debt bondage aspect to force victims to work in prostitution for extremely low wages; and withhold their wages to prevent them from leaving their job. Indeed victims have reported paying their traffickers amounts of

---

*Principles and Rights at Work*, ILO 6-8 (May 12, 2009), http://www.ilo.org/global/topics/forced-labour/publications/WCMS_106268/lang%2D%2Den/index.htm.

[329] Okogbule (2013). *See also* Elliot (2014).

[330] Kathryn (2005), p. 37.

[331] UNAFEI, *supra* note 112, at 159.

[332] Anti-Slavery *supra* note 147, at 24; *see also A Serious Crime Against Humanity and a Global Issue*, Counter Trafficking in Persons (CTIP) 7 (Jun. 2012), http://www.aptireland.org/wp-content/uploads/2012/06/ctip_syllabus_for_high_schools.pdf.

[333] *Id.*

[334] Anti-Slavery *supra* note 147, at 24; CTIP, *supra* note 332, at 7.

money ranging from €30,000–60,000 to reach Europe; for which their families had provided collateral guarantees in the expectation that the victims would not only pay off the debt but also provide financial assistance to the family at a later stage.[335] To make this easier, traffickers often sponsor the traveling expenses of potential victims. Upon their arrival in the destination country, the traffickers overcharge them the fees for providing transportation and false documentation to get them out of the country of origin to their destination; creating a scenario of lifelong debt-bondage. In the *AG v Samuel Emwiovbankhoe* case, Samuel made an agreement with Nigerian girls to take them to Italy for the purpose of prostitution. The defendant was placed on trial accused of the offense of placing persons in servitude as a security for debt owed. He never denied the fact that he charged each of the girls €35,000. He declared that he made them take an oath stating they would not escape from the place they were going to and that they would pay the amount of money he had agreed with them.[336]

Experience in Nigeria shows that prior to procuring traveling passports and visas, the victims undergo ritual oaths at shrines and swear to pay back the money owed to the traffickers, and to obey their "madam sponsors" or "trolley" under all circumstances.[337] Sex trafficking networks in West Africa use psychological and ritual witchcraft (voodoo)[338] to intimidate victims into believing that misfortune will befall them or their families if they reveal their experiences and disclose the identity of their traffickers to the police. Court jurisprudence considers the taking of "juju" oaths to be a means of coercion, resulting in victims feeling that they have no real or acceptable alternative other than to submit to the exploitation, although this is not necessarily categorized as "deceit", "threat" or other particular type of coercion.[339] Trafficking expert Siddharth Kara from Harvard University stated that: "[Juju] exerts

---

[335] Ezeilo, *supra* note 321.

[336] Nigeria, *supra* note 323.

[337] Olaide A. Gbadamosi Esq., *International Perspectives and Nigerian Laws on Human Trafficking*, Network for Justice and Democracy (2006), http://www.justiceanddemocracy.org/Trffic%20Bk.pdf.

[338] The girls are made to undergo special black magic juju rites in which parts of their bodies (pubic hair, nails, menstrual blood, hair, and pieces of intimate clothing) are taken and placed before traditional shrines. The girls are made to swear an oath not to disclose the origin of their trip abroad, to pay their 'debt' (usually not stated at the moment of stipulating the 'blood contract'), and never to reveal the identity of their traffickers and madams to the police. Their failure to respect this oath means that some grave ill or misfortune will befall themselves and/or their families. *See* Aghatise (2005), http://www.koed.hu/mozaik15/esohe.pdf. *See also* U.S. Dept. of State, *Trafficking in Persons Report,* Nigeria 2014; Ezeilo, *supra* note 321; Nagle Luz and Owasanoye (2016), p. 561 (available at: http://www.swlaw.edu/sites/default/files/2017-04/5%20Fearing%20the%20Dar.pdf).

[339] *See A.G. v. Felicia Okafor*, Nigeria Court of High Justice, Suit No. A.12C.06, Judgment (2006); *Federal Republic of Nigeria v. Favour Anware Okwuede*, Nigeria Court of High Justice, Charge No. FHC.ASB.24C.09, Judgment (2009); *AG v Samuel Emwirovbankhoe*, Nigeria Court of High Justice, Suit No. B.20C.2005, Judgment (2005); and *Attorney General of the Federation v. Omoruyi,* High Court Edo State of Nigeria, Suit No. B/31c/2004 (2006); UNODC, *supra* note 227, at 39.

a kind of control that's so much more potent than chains or locking someone up; it's control of the spirit which is far more powerful and insidious."[340]

For example, the Italian Police observed that victims from Nigeria, Ghana and Benin "undergo much less physical control/check-up from their exploiters, compared to other foreign girls trafficked into prostitution. They have no need of physical control because the rites they are made to undergo psychologically impose the control on them."[341] They are enslaved and controlled through the psychological and economic powers of 'ownership' exercised over them. The successful investigation and prosecution of a trafficking case depends heavily on the victim's testimony. Unfortunately, many victims who are fearful of a misfortune falling upon themselves or their families endure their suffering in silence.[342] Investigations supported little evidence result in short sentences for the traffickers. Furthermore, psychological coercion of the victims is so subtle that the judge may have no evidence on which to convict the offenders.

#### 2.5.1.2.3 Exploitation of Labor

Importantly, the transnational criminal law applicable to trafficking in persons prohibits exploitation where consent has been obtained by significant deception, coercion, and so on.[343] Although consent can clearly be deemed valid, an agreement to work in a situation or provide a service that may be considered exploitative will still constitute trafficking. Consent in that situation does not necessarily render the activity harmless or justified because the exploitative conditions remain.[344] This position reflects a long-standing principle of international human rights law, which declares that "it is not possible to meaningfully consent to certain violations of human dignity."[345] "Frequently, those involved are the victims of trafficking and are forced to work in slave-like conditions, virtually owned by their employers and without any choice over their "customers", the numbers served, acts performed, or

[340] *Juju magic 'more controlling than chains', says Harvard expert*, BBC News (Oct. 14, 2014), http://www.bbc.com/news/uk-wales-29599158.

[341] Aghatise (2005).

[342] Peachey (2012); Willmott (2012), http://lastradainternational.org/lsidocs/Witchcraft%20and%20Trafficking%20in%20Africa.pdf.; *see also* AFRUCA, *supra* note 145.

[343] Elliot (2014); *See* for instance the Case of *AG v Hussaina Ibrahim* and Idris Aminus Suit No. K.1TPP.2003, Case of *AG v Samson Ovensari*, Suit No. B.15c.06 and Case *AG v Samuel Emwiovbankhoe*, Suit No. B.20C.2005. The latter case is an outstanding example of conflicting evidence as to whether or not the victims and their families knew they would work in prostitution abroad.

[344] *Id.*

[345] *The Role of Consent in Trafficking in Persons Protocol*, UNODC 35 (2014), https://www.unodc.org/documents/human-trafficking/2014/UNODC_2014_Issue_Paper_Consent.pdf.

hours worked."[346] As such the victims of trafficking are subjected to verbal, physical and sexual violence by their pimps and by their clients. They work in conditions involving intimidation, unsafe sexual practices, and long hours, often in dangerous and precarious environments for very low wages or sometimes no wages at all.

A human rights activist and lawyer in Nigeria has described the threat to human dignity caused by a trafficking syndicate based in Delta State, which reportedly abducted over 40 underage girls as sex slaves for gold miners at a mining field in Burkina Faso. The girls reported that the madam informed them that the cost of sleeping with a man is 2000F CFA, which is equivalent to US $3.55, and forced them to sleep with about 16 men a day, remitting not less than US $56.67 in total. If they failed to meet the daily target, the girls were beaten mercilessly and starved. These 40 girls had to undergo this awful experience on a daily basis as sex slaves to the miners in Burkina Faso.[347] Victims of trafficking in prostitution in a foreign country are also unable to show any identity documents. In the *Hon. Attorney General of the Federation v. Franca Edith Asiboja* case, involving the deceitful procurement of girls from Edo State, Nigeria, for the purpose of prostitution in Ouagadougou, Burkina Faso; one of the victims stated that on arrival in Burkina Faso, they were not allowed to go outside the house, especially at night, because of the police, as they had no travel papers.[348] Without identification documents and with nothing else for them to do, they had no choice but to work as prostitutes.

Trafficking in prostitution occurs generally under the form of bonded labor; this type of enslavement takes place when migrant workers reach the destination country. In the *Hon. Attorney General of the Federation v. Franca Edith Asiboja* case, the offender "provided the money for the transportation of the girls to Burkina Faso and the victims were to pay 500,000F CFA (approximately US $955) to her in order to earn their freedom."[349] To ensure they remained loyal, she made them take an oath with a native doctor. Upon their arrival in Burkina Faso, the offender received and controlled the earnings of the girls and kept a record of their payments; however, she was unable to present a labor contract between the victims and their employer or the records of wages paid to workers.

Additionally, workers had to pay food or accommodation, the costs of which were deducted from their wages. In the *Hon. Attorney General of the Federation v. Franca Edith Asiboja* case, when the victim explained that she wanted to go back

---

[346] *Human Trafficking and Forced Labour Exploitation: Guidance for Legislation and Law Enforcement*, ILO 25 (Apr. 1, 2005), http://digitalcommons.ilr.cornell.edu/cgi/viewcontent.cgi?article=1021&context=forcedlabor.

[347] Chijioke J (2017), http://dailypost.ng/2017/07/18/lawyer-reveals-40-warri-girls-trafficked-burkina-faso-sex-slaves/.

[348] High Court of Justice (2007), Between Hon. Attorney General of the Federation and Franca Edith Asiboja, 11, Charge No. B/31C/2005 (Nigeria) (available at: https://www.unodc.org/res/cld/case-law/nga/2007/_hon__attorney_general_of_the_federation_and_franca_edith_asiboja_charge_no._b31c2005.html/Hon._Attorney_General_of_the_Federation_and_Franca_Edith_Asiboja_Charge_No._B.31C.2005.pdf).

[349] *Id.* at 6.

to Nigeria, the offender promised to help her on the condition that she hand over all the money she had earned to make up the sum of money that would be required to take her back. Under this arrangement, the girl worked as a prostitute and gave whatever she made; however, the offender deducted payments for house rent, electricity, and water charges while continuing to tell her that the money saved was insufficient to return her to Nigeria.[350]

### 2.5.2 Sex Tourism

Reports show that sex tourism is growing exponentially in West Africa, especially in the coastal areas. According to the African network of End Child Prostitution And Trafficking (ECPAT) studies, the West African countries most affected by sexual tourism are Benin, Ivory Coast, the Gambia, Ghana, Nigeria, Senegal, and Cabo Verde. The West African Atlantic coasts of the Gambia and Ghana that contain holiday resorts and tourist hotspots are considered to be the most popular destinations for child sex tourism; while Nigeria appear to be a country of origin for sexual tourists visiting neighboring countries.[351] In Gambia, for example, the Child Protection Alliance, ECPAT, and Terre des Hommes have confirmed that the sexual industry in the country involves domestic travelers or foreigners (middle-aged men and women from Europe and America) traveling on organized trips looking for a "holiday romance" with young Gambian men and little boys in exchange for money, expensive gifts, or visas.[352] The national coordinator of the Sex Workers Intervention Project in Gambia reports that it is common to see extremely young boys approaching tourists and offering an under-age "sister", promising she is a virgin. Tourists who are homosexual go for the boys.

Campaigners report that "sponsoring a child" has become a means for abusers to initiate a sexual relationship; tourists typically offer to pay for a year's schooling, which for them is only the cost of an expensive meal; as well as offering electronic devices, promises of jobs, or educational opportunities overseas in exchange for sexual favors. The US Department of State reported that a judge in Gambia "sentenced one convicted trafficker to life imprisonment for rape under the 2005 Children's Act. The trafficker, a Scandinavian child sex tourist, sexually exploited two Gambian girls in exchange for paying their schooling fees."[353] Unfortunately, many parents regard the exhibition of their offspring to holiday makers as an "opportunity" rather than a threat. Despite the risk of trauma, risk of contracting AIDS, and ruined

---

[350]Nigeria, *supra* note 348, at 13.

[351]Dr. M'Jid (2008), p. 15.

[352]*Id.*

[353]*The Gambia*, U.S. Dept. of State (2017), https://www.state.gov/j/tip/rls/tiprpt/countries/2017/271191.htm.

marriage prospects, prostitution has for many young Gambian women become an aspirational lifestyle choice.

Similarly, research conducted by the Ghana NGO Coalition on the Rights of the Child (GNCRC) and the End Child Prostitution And Trafficking (ECPAT) group has drawn attention to the fact that Ghana is becoming famous on pedophile websites as an attractive and 'safe' destination for child sex because of the low prevalence rate of HIV/AIDS. A high rate of sexual exploitation and abuse of boys between 10 and 17 years old in the tourism sector has been observes, particularly in the central region of Ghana.[354] The situation seems to have worsened dramatically inasmuch as local boys deliberately hang around hotels, guesthouses, and tourist areas soliciting foreign tourists. Members of the Coalition witnessed little boys in Cape Coast handing out 'business cards' to tourists proposing sexual services. Approximately 70% of their clients were males and 30% were females. This includes African tourists from the sub-region, including Ghanaians, Nigerians and Liberians; those outside the sub-region come mainly from China, the Americas, and Europe.[355]

Although tourism is not the cause of child sexual exploitation, child-sex exploiters make use of the facilities offered by tour companies, hotels, resorts, restaurants, clubs/bars, airlines and other tourism-related services that facilitate contact with children and enable the exploiter to remain anonymous in the surrounding population and environment.[356] Some businesses may even foster sex tourism; for example, a hotel that does not include a policy opposing the sexual exploitation of children on its premises or travel agents that knowingly arrange sex tours abroad. Child sex tourism and trafficking in children for sexual purposes are inextricably linked and the end purpose of domestic and cross-border trafficking of minors in West Africa is primarily to service sex tourists who are wealthier than locals.

### 2.5.3 Forced Marriage

Forced marriage refers to induction into a marriage that may be exploitative and demeaning without the free or valid consent of one or both of the partners and

[354] *Global Monitoring Status of Action against Commercial Sexual Exploitation of Children, Ghana*, ECPAT, 13 (2014) https://www.ecpat.org/wp-content/uploads/legacy/A4A2011_AF_GHANA_FINAL2.pdf; *Global Study on Sexual Exploitation of Children in Travel and Tourism Country, Ghana 2015*, Ghana NGOs Coalition on the Rights of the Child (GNCRC) 2015. https://ssa.riselearningnetwork.org/wp-content/uploads/sites/5/2017/01/SECTT-GHANA.pdf.

[355] *Global Monitoring Status of Action against Commercial Sexual Exploitation of Children, Ghana*, ECPAT, 12 (2014) https://www.ecpat.org/wp-content/uploads/legacy/A4A2011_AF_GHANA_FINAL2.pdf.

[356] Sakulpitakphon (2007), p. 6, http://www.ecpat.net/sites/default/files/confronting_csec_eng_0.pdf.

involves either physical or emotional duress.[357] According to the Special Rapporteur on Slavery, early marriage is related to forced marriage because, under international human rights law, minors are deemed incapable of giving informed consent to a marriage. "The marriage is therefore considered forced and falls under the slavery-like practices defined in the Convention [against Slavery]."[358] Forced and early marriages are serious human rights violations that deny the free and informed consent of both parties to a marriage.[359] The parents or guardians arrange the union for financial gain or for other forms of social advantage.[360]

Servile marriage involves adults as well as children being sold, transferred, inherited into marriage, or forced into marriage by either the person they are marrying or another person such as a parent. In Africa, it encompasses early marriage; young girls forcibly married to a local god represented by a priest (Ghana and India) in *trokosi*;[361] levirate (marriage of a widow to her deceased husband's brother); sororate (*marriage* of a widow to his deceased wife's sister),[362] forced marriages; and, to a certain extent, polygamy. Gender prejudices mean that the overwhelming majority of those in servile marriage are girls and women; although boys and men can also be victims. Reliable statistics on forced marriage are difficult to compile due to the unofficial and undocumented nature of most of these cases. The absence of a birth certificate is another obstacle to reliable data

[357] The Art 1(1) of the 1964 Convention on Consent to Marriage provides that "[n]o marriage shall be legally entered into without the full and free consent of both parties, such consent to be expressed by them in person after due publicity and in the presence of the authority competent to solemnize the marriage and of witnesses, as prescribed by law." G.A. Res. 1763 A (XVII), Nov. 7, 1962. *See also*, the 1995 Beijing Platform for Action para. 274 (e); ICCPR, *supra* note 226, at article 23; UDHR, *supra* note 226, at art 16(2). The Art. 21 (2) of the Org. of Afr. Unity (OAU), African Charter on the Rights and Welfare of the Child, Doc. No. CAB/LEG/24.9/49 (Jul. 11, 1990) [African Charter on the Rights and Welfare].

[358] Gulnara Shahinian (Report of the Special Rapporteur on Contemporary Forms of Slavery, including its Causes and Consequences), *Thematic Report on Servile Marriage*, ¶ 14, U.N. Doc. A/HRC/21/41 (Jul. 10 2012).

[359] A forced marriage differs from an arranged marriage in which families arrange meetings between two partners in the hope of fostering a voluntary relationship that will lead to marriage. In these situations, although the initial meetings are arranged by the families and a marriage is encouraged, the ultimate decision to marry lies with the individuals getting married. By contrast, in a forced marriage, one or both parties are threatened or coerced into marrying against their will and may suffer honor-related violence if they resist or refuse the marriage. *See* Report of the Special Rapporteur on the Human Rights Aspects of the Victims of Trafficking in Persons, especially Women and Children), *Implementation of General Assembly Resolution 60/251 of March 15 2006 entitled "Human Rights Council*, ¶ 26, U.N. Doc. A/HRC/4/23, (Jan. 24, 2007) (by Huda Sigma).

[360] Because a child under the age of 18 is not capable of giving their valid consent to enter into marriage, child marriages are considered to be forced marriages. *See* Convention on Consent to Marriage, Minimum Age for Marriage, and Registration of Marriages, 32 U.N.T.S. 231 (Nov. 7, 1962).

[361] *Devadasi* is the equivalent of this practice in India.

[362] Husband engages in marriage with the sister of his wife, usually after the death of his wife or if his wife has proven infertile.

inasmuch as the victim has no way of proving that they are a child victim or were forced into an early marriage.

Early marriage has been primarily documented in Economic Community of West African States (ECOWAS) countries; six million child brides in the world live in West Africa, where early marriage affects 49% of girls under 19.[363] In parts of this region, children are also likely to be married off at the extremely early age of seven or 8 years. According to the State of the World's Children 2007 report by UNICEF, the average rate of women aged 20 to 24 years-old across the region who were married before the age of 18 was 28% in urban zones and 56% in rural zones (44% globally). The highest rates of child marital unions are in Niger (77%), Guinea (65%), and Burkina Faso (52%); with a declining proportion in Togo (31%), Côte d'Ivoire (33%), Gabon (34%), Senegal (36%), and Benin (37%).[364] In Nigeria, a national survey found that in cases where the wife married before 15 years of age, the mean age difference between husband and wife is 12 years;. This large age gap increases the unequal power dynamics within a relationship where the younger the spouse, the less likely it is she will have a full understanding of her choice to enter into marriage, which increases her vulnerability to becoming subjected to control and lifelong servitude within marriage.[365]

In addition to the moral reasons, forced marriage in West Africa has financial incentives and is used as an economic survival strategy for poor families. In most parts of West Africa, the dowry consists of clothes, animals, kola-nuts, drinks, or daily labor, voluntarily given to the bride's family as a sign of appreciation for the girls' upbringing. Cash is never given. Most importantly, "dowry is the legal exchange which validates a marriage and confirms the consent of both the parents of the bride and bridegroom. Without the payment of dowry, no marriage is recognized as valid."[366] In Burkina Faso, families marry off their daughters to kings in exchange for favors or in gratitude for friendship. In Niger and Nigeria, economically disadvantaged families will often give their young girls in marriage in exchange for financial compensation, which is a form of Commercial Sexual Exploitation of Children.[367]

---

[363] *Mapping Early Marriage in West Africa: A scan of trends, interventions, what works, best practices and the way forward*, Girls Not Brides 7 (Sept. 2013), http://www.girlsnotbrides.org/wp-content/uploads/2013/10/Ford-Foundation-CM-West-Africa-2013_09.pdf.

[364] Dr. M'Jid (2008), p. 23.

[365] Turner (2013), p. 11, http://www.antislavery.org/includes/documents/cm_docs/2013/c/child_marriage_final.pdf; Msuya (2017); In High Court of South Africa (2014), Nvumeleni Jezile v. the State, High Court Case No: A 127/2014 (S. Afr.) (available at: https://www.unodc.org/res/cld/case-law-doc/traffickingpersonscrimetype/zaf/2015/jezile_v__s_and_others_a_1272014_2015_zawchc_html/2015.03.23_Jezile_v_S.pdf.

[366] Theological Advisory Group, *Payment of Dowry and the Christian Church*, 15 Afr. J. Evangelical Theology 128 (Feb. 15, 1996) (available at: https://biblicalstudies.org.uk/pdf/ajet/15-2_128.pdf).

[367] Global Monitoring, *supra* note 314, at 16.

Polygamy is another traditional practice that affects a large percentage of the population in West African countries; this describes a form of marriage where the husband has more than one wife. The high-polygamy zone is concentrated in West Africa along the coast, as well as inland in the Sahel, where nearly one in every two married woman lives in a polygamous union, even in the cities. Polygamy is a common practice in Togo, Benin, Burkina Faso, Senegal and Mali.[368] Multiple wives have become a status symbol denoting wealth, power, achievement, and prestige for privileged social classes in Africa.[369] A polygamous family is a household characterized by wariness due to dependence and submissiveness of co-wives, and jealousy, inequalities and rivalry among children.[370] Moreover, it denies women some of their fundamental rights including sexual and reproductive rights, the right to equality and non-discrimination, protection against domestic violence and unjustified domestic work burdens; and in some cases, the right to health and even the right to life (as polygamy exposes women to the risk of sexually transmitted infections such as HIV/AIDS). Polygamy goes hand in hand with other cultural practices that violate the sexual and reproductive rights of women including sororate marriage[371] and levirate marriages.[372] These also include harmful practices relating to childbirth and dietary taboos during pregnancy and lactation.

Closely related to the custom of early marriage is the equally abhorrent practice of *trokosi*.[373] This outlawed custom, practiced in Benin, Ghana, Togo, and southwestern Nigeria requires a family to offer a virgin daughter as a *trokosi*[374] to a traditional fetish shrine in payment for services or as religious atonement for alleged crimes or moral wrongdoings committed by a family member. The misdeeds (stealing, adultery, failure or omission to keep a pledge made to a deity, having sex with a *trokosi*) for which atonement is sought may often date back generations before the birth of

[368]Caselli G et al. (2005), p. 361.

[369]*Id.* at 359–360. *See also* Hayase and Liaw (1997), p. 293, 298.

[370]A controversial debate currently exists with proponents arguing that those who enter into polygamous marriages do so freely and consensually. Indeed, marriage activists claim that consenting to adult polygamous relationships is a matter of private choice and the state should not interfere with such a personal decision. They consider anti-bigamy laws to restrict the freedom to make decisions about intimate adult relationships. Opponents of polygamy argue that a polygamous family structure is inherently abusive and demeaning to women and children. Coercion or a lack of consent is necessarily present in polygamy because polygamous families are so harmful to women that no woman would freely consent to such a relationship. *See* Hahn Hans and Kastner (2012), pp. 80–81. *See also* Ba (1979).

[371]Where a man is married to two or more sisters, usually simultaneously or successively after the first wife has been found to be barren or has died.

[372]Upon the husband's death, a wife in a servile marriage may be inherited by his brother.

[373]Msuya (2017).

[374]The *Ewe* word *trokosi* can be translated alternatively as "slave to the gods" or "wife to the gods". The practice is alleged to date back to the seventeenth century as a means to attract the favor of the gods, especially in times of crisis and war. *See also* Kwame (2004).

the child.[375] Girls designated to become *trokosi* are usually committed at a very young age (6 to 10 years-old). An initiation ritual betrothing them to the gods is performed in the shrine to establish a relationship of spiritual bondage between the girls and the shrine. From the moment of their betrothal, vestal virgins must wear special insignia indicating their status, following which outsiders are prohibited from having any sexual contact with them.[376]

Reports estimate that more than 5000 girls and women are bound to various shrines within Ghana alone, and as many as 29,000 to 35,000 in the four countries in which the practice continues.[377] In addition to performing ritual duties, the girls are forced, under threat of death, to live as domestic and sexual slaves to the priests in the shrine: daughters born from such sexual relations also have certain obligations to the shrine. *Trokosi* are also expected to work long hours on farmland belonging to the priest. They are 'usually in poor health' due to the absence of medical facilities and do not receive anything in return for their labor; their families are required to provide them with food and all other necessities.[378]

## 2.5.4 *Trafficking for Domestic Servitude*

In an African cultural setting driven by a subsistence economy, child labor is regarded as a critical economic asset and children are enlisted into the family labor pool.[379] One proverb states that: "When the orphan becomes big enough to work, those who want him become numerous."[380] Within the Economic Community of West African States (ECOWAS) region, the magnitude of trafficking for domestic servitude is unknown and extremely difficult to assess. Domestic work carried out by children has only recently become a national concern; and distinctions among trafficking, child fostering, placement with relatives, and employees makes it extremely difficult to obtain reliable statistical information on the number of about children working as domestics. This is compounded by the fact that domestic work is a form of employment that takes place out of sight and often form part of the informal economy. This labor sector is not recognized as real work in West African countries and is therefore unregulated. As such, domestic workers, who most often

---

375 Special Rapporteur on Violence against Women, its Causes and Consequences), Addendum—Mission to Ghana, ¶ 42, U.N. Doc. A/HRC/7/6/Add.3 (Feb. 21, 2008) (by Yakin Ertürk).

376 *Id. See* Dogbadzi J, *Speak Truth To Power: Sex Slavery*, Washington Post, http://www.washingtonpost.com/wp-srv/photo/onassignment/truth/st/09.htm (accessed on August 20, 2021).

377 Aird Sarah (1999) http://www.wcl.american.edu/hrbrief/v7i1/ghana.htm; *see also* Asomah (2015), p. 129.

378 ECPAT Int'l, *supra* note 356, at 23; *Findings on the Worst Forms of Child Labor, Report on Ghana 2014*, U.S. Dept. of Labor, http://www.dol.gov/ilab/reports/child-labor/ghana.htm.

379 Adepoju (2005b).

380 Dambia and Nare (1999), p. 318.

live with their employers who provide them with accommodation and subsistence, are vulnerable to abuse and exploitation.[381]

#### 2.5.4.1 Challenges to the Definition of Domestic Work

Article 1 of the ILO Convention No. 189 draws on the definition of domestic workers as "engaged in domestic work within an employment relationship" by third private households for pay or in-kind remuneration, and provide services chores, caring for children and running errands, among other tasks.[382] Although this definition seems obvious, the line between domestic workers and trafficked persons in domestic servitude can be a difficult one to draw. In West Africa, both boys and girls undertake household chores in their own homes as well as farming and the rearing of livestock. This forms an integral part of family life and of growing up. It is common for young girls to work not only in the household but also in trade activities and to do so from morning to nightfall, alongside their mothers or under the direction of female kin. However, this is not considered domestic service because there is no agreement regarding pay.[383]

However, under the same circumstances, girls who are fostered into the same family (in a third party household) may spend their days performing similar tasks. The question that arises is: are they servants? What about girls as young as seven in Benin, who want to escape the poverty of their rural towns and voluntarily move through the system of *vidomegon* with an aunt in the city and work as domestic servants in exchange for housing? Are they classified as servants because they have been harbored by a third person?[384] The point here is that these girls and boys are not necessarily called servants by the people for whom they are performing services; yet they may be performing exactly the same tasks as those who are called servants.[385]

Moreover, what about girls and boys who, when staying with relatives, only carry out domestic work for part of each day and attend school for the remainder to pursue an education? Do they count as domestic workers? Given that this custom is a widespread practice in many families and communities, it may be difficult for people to recognize this as exploitation and trafficking.

---

[381] Adepoju, *supra* note 121.

[382] International Labour Organization (ILO), Domestic Workers Convention, art. 1 Doc. C189, No. 11 (2011); Langer and Levison (2009), p. 2, https://pop.umn.edu/sites/pop.umn.edu/files/wp-2009-1.pdf; *see also Definition—Child Labour and Domestic Work*, ILO, http://www.ilo.org/ipec/areas/Childdomesticlabour/lang%2D%2Den/index.htm (accessed on August 20, 2021); UNICEF, *Child Domestic Work*, Innocenti Digest No. 5, 2 (May 17, 1999), https://www.unicef-irc.org/publications/pdf/digest5e.pdf.

[383] Langer and Levison (2009).

[384] Bureau of Int'l Labor Affairs, *Child Labor and Forced Labor Reports—Benin*, U.S. Dept. of Labor, http://www.dol.gov/ilab/reports/child-labor/benin.htm#ENREF_4 (accessed on August 20, 2021).

[385] Langer and Levison (2009).

#### 2.5.4.2 Manifestations of Domestic Trafficking

The vast majority of children working in domestic service are girls as well as boys; these are girls who come into the cities to learn a trade or receive a religious or secular education, or to help out the urban extended family *through fostering arrangements*. In exchange for better living conditions and expectations of a better future, fostered children help the receiving family with household chores that then constitute their socialization and training. Most of the children working in urban cities, as apprentices for boys and domestic workers for girls, are natural extensions of the indigenous system of education.[386] This practice still prevails across much of sub-Saharan Africa, including networks of extended families resident in immigrant African communities abroad. Instructive data from a Benin village show that West African children are increasingly leaving rural areas through arrangements made outside the traditional kinship pattern of securing children's well-being.

In all cities today,"[t]his informal approach to fostering has created conditions of "hard trafficking", involving households completely unknown to the domestic servants, and "soft trafficking", where the child lives with an extended family or in households originally known to them (WHO, 2011)."[387] The urban domestic work of girls (known as *mbindaan* in Senegal, *Kalifa* in Mali, and *vidomegon* in Benin), where they are placed with and entrusted to someone who is meant to protect them so that they can have access to an education and a more or less decent life, often results in them becoming the slaves of their urban host families.[388] With minimal parental supervision, these child workers run the risk of enduring exploitative situations in unsafe living conditions that interfere with their education or their ability to participate in social activities, thus denying them their inalienable rights.[389] Smucker's and Murray's findings from a study in Haiti portrays a characteristic picture of child domestic labor in West Africa and around the world:

> . . .[servant] children living outside the home tended to have a heightened risk of treatment as second class citizens and also a heightened risk of physical and sexual abuse–though neither is inevitable. According to field interviews, the living conditions of servant children tend to be distinctly different from other children in the same household. They sleep in the least desirable places, e.g., on a section of carpet in the outside kitchen or on the floor at the foot of

---

[386] Bass Loretta (2004). Alain Morice found that apprentices comprise 85% of the labor force in the leather industry in Nigeria.

[387] Derby Nana (2012). *See also* Innocenti Digest No. 5, *supra* note 382, at 4. For example, the proportion of children fostered by a relative decreased from 62% in 1996 to 46%in 1999. Countering this trend, the proportion of children fostered by a stranger increased significantly from 18% to 27% over the same period while the proportion of children who left with a friend of the family also increased from 19% to 25%. Bass Loretta (2004), p. 90.

[388] *Haiti, Le calvaire des "Restaveks"*, Courrier Int'l (Feb. 24, 2011), https://www.courrierinternational.com/article/2011/02/24/le-calvaire-silencieux-des-restaveks; *J'aime Nettoyer: L'enfer des Enfants Domestiques Habitués à Obéi*r, UNICEF France (Dec. 28, 2015), https://www.unicef.fr/article/j-aime-nettoyer-l-enfer-des-enfants-domestiques-habitues-obeir. *See* OSCE, *supra* note 189, at 24.

[389] Derby Nana (2012), p. 22. *See also* Bass, *supra* note 185, at 22–23.

> a bed. They eat different food. They do significantly more work than other children in the household. They may well carry the workload of adult domestic servants and more. According to direct observation by informants, such children are subject to public humiliation and corporal punishment including beatings with cooking pots, shoes, whips, or fists. They may well not go to school, or if they do, it is an inferior school and in any case a different school from those attended by other children in the household. They are subject to sexual abuse by other children in the household and sometimes by adults, yet they would not be likely to be allowed to marry the sons or daughters of the household served.[390]

Mindful of the importance of distinguishing common forms of exploitation from trafficking in domestic servitude, the Organization for Security and Cooperation in Europe (OSCE) has identified three main criteria to determine the threshold beyond which a specific exploitative situation in a household falls within the legal requirements for trafficking, slavery, or forced labor.[391]

##### 2.5.4.2.1 Poor Living and Working Conditions

Victims of domestic servitude are subjected to working and living conditions that are incompatible with human dignity, such as extremely long working hours that usually extend beyond 12 hours and can be as much as 18 hours per day. The definition of domestic slavery is not related to the nature of the tasks but the excessive burden of work and the long hours required to perform it. In Guinea, Burkina Faso, Mali and several other countries in West Africa, Human Rights Watch has documented young girls working for more than 12 hours a day, without holidays, no weekly day off, and little rest during the day.[392] Domestic workers of all ages are made to work around the clock and are on-call day and night as they are expected to be at the employer's disposal at all times. Susanne K., who is 16 years-old, describes her working hours:

> As a domestic worker, I had to clean the house, cook the food, wash the dishes, and go to the market. I had no breaks. I was the first one to get up and the last one to go to bed. I got up around 4:30 in the morning, with the first prayer call. In the evening I worked sometimes until midnight, while the other children were watching TV.[393]

---

[390] Murray and Smucker (2004), pp. 35–36, https://pdf.usaid.gov/pdf_docs/Pnadf061.pdf.

[391] *How to Prevent Human Trafficking for Domestic Servitude in Diplomatic Households and Protect Private Domestic Workers*, Office of the Special Representative and Coordinator for Combating Trafficking in Human Beings (OSCE) (2014), http://www.osce.org/handbook/domesticservitude?download=true; *see also Human Trafficking Indicators*, U.N. Office on Drugs & Crim., https://www.unodc.org/pdf/HT_indicators_E_LOWRES.pdf (accessed on August 20, 2021).

[392] Kippenberg (2007); Derby Nana (2012), p. 23.

[393] Kippenberg (2007), p. 53. *See also O.O.O. et al. v Commissioner of Police for the Metropolis* [2011], EWHC 1246 (QB) (dealing with transnational trafficking for domestic servitude) (available at: https://ec.europa.eu/anti-trafficking/sites/antitrafficking/files/o.o.o_and_others_v_commissioner_of_police_for_the_metropolis_1.pdf; *Siliadin v. France*, European Court of Human Rights, Application No. 73316/01, Judgment (2005); *U.S. v. Bello*, 503 F. App'x 910, 911-13 (11th Cir. 2013).

Domestic workers in all West African countries carry out a wide range of tasks within as well as outside the household; they sweep the Courtyard and the house; wash the laundry; pound rice, maize, and cereals to prepare food; do the dishes: and go to the market to buy groceries. The task of fetching water from deep wells or other sources is very demanding work for children because of the distances covered, the physical labor involved in lifting and carrying the buckets, and the potential threats during the journey.[394]

Furthermore, girl domestic workers often look after small children during the day and at night so that their parents can go to work. "Children working in low-income households often engage in income-generating activities in addition to the household chores assigned to them, especially if the woman of the house is a trader or runs a restaurant."[395] They are employed all day by the *tutrice* to sell goods in the market or in the street, and are expected to hand over the money earned.[396] The stark reality of total dependence and ownership is expressed in this West African proverb: "The slave is not the master of his eye, even less of what he found."[397] This means that slaves in African society have no rights, own nothing, and have no control over their labor, or their children. Their bondage is lifelong and it is hereditary.

In France, 38% of children enslaved in domestic servitude are also obliged to perform additional work in other households. In most cases, employers lend their services to their circle of family members and friends during holidays or school days. The employer may also force children to work as waitresses, hairdressers in cafes/lounges, or for the benefit of a third party; the profits of this work are earned exclusively by the employer. Finally, in two cases analyzed by CCEM (Comité Contre l'Esclavage Moderne),[398] the victims were subject to sexual exploitation and forced into prostitution alongside their domestic tasks.[399] Although labor rights assist child domestic workers in times of sickness, children trafficked in domestic servitude always receive inadequate medical treatment.[400] In West Africa, they lack access to basic health and are never taken to the doctor when they are ill. In the Human Rights Watch report, many girls testified that they did not receive adequate care in time of sickness; their employer simply accused them of faking the illness and demanded that they continue working.[401]

---

[394] Cohen (2003).

[395] Thorsen (2012a), p. 3.

[396] Kippenberg (2007), p. 51.

[397] Dambia and Nare (1999), p. 268.

[398] CCEM is an anti-slavery comity combating domestic slavery in Europe.

[399] *Le Travail Domestique des Mineurs en France*, Comité Contre l'Esclavage Moderne (CCEM) 28 (2009), http://www.esclavagemoderne.org/media/Etude-Travail-domestique-des-mineurs-2.pdf.

[400] Ending child labor in domestic work and protecting young workers from abusive working conditions. *Id.* at 29.

[401] Kippenberg (2007), p. 60.

> Nine-year-old Rosalie Y. stated that she was beaten with a whip when she was tired or sick. Dora T., 14 years old, remembers what happened to her when she fell ill. 'Once I fell ill, I

#### 2.5.4.2.2 Low or No Wages

The existence of domestic servitude is not necessarily dependent on the complete absence of remuneration. A *Mossi* proverb that elucidates this states: "The slave says that he is paid but his salary is meager."[402] Indeed, their master gives them only shelter and food. Even if the worker receives a certain amount of money, insufficient wages can still be considered an important component of domestic servitude when the amount given, in addition to not being commensurate with working hours, does not extend beyond the mere subsistence of the worker or does not make it possible for the worker to achieve—even partially—the objectives related to the migration project, namely to send home what is sufficient for the survival of the family.[403]

In the case of *Siliadin v. France*,[404] a French national of Togolese origin who procured a Togolese national for domestic work, the applicant stated that she was never paid; except by Mrs B.'s mother, who gave her one or two 500 French franc (FRF) notes. The household couple were prosecuted on charges of having obtained, from July 1995 to July 1998, the services of a minor either without payment or in exchange for remuneration that was clearly disproportionate to the work carried out; as well as taking advantage of that person's vulnerability or state of dependence.[405]

It is common for girl domestic workers in West African countries to have no written contract with their employers. Of the forty-one girl domestic workers interviewed by Human Rights Watch staff in Togo, few recalled receiving any remuneration for their labor; one declared earning 12,000F CFA (US $18) for 3 months' work in a boutique in Benin, while another received a salary of 48,000 CFA (US $70) for 6 months' work in a market in Nigeria.[406] In Conakry, children over 15 who had been promised remuneration or payment in kind did not receive a salary; their employers frequently found ways to avoid payment and made the victims believe they were saving their wages or sending stipends to their parents back home.[407] "False promises are very often used in domestic servitude, to strengthen control over the worker and to ensure that the forced labor continues."[408] To justify the non-payment of wages, the traffickers used to argue that they would

---

had malaria. I was taken to hospital and I needed treatment. My aunt refused and said she had no money. Because my cousin intervened in my favor, my aunt finally paid for the treatment.

[402] Dambia and Nare (1999), p. 401.

[403] *Unprotected Work, Invisible Exploitation: Trafficking for the Purposes of Domestic Servitude*, OSCE 23 (Jun. 17, 2010), http://www.osce.org/secretariat/75804?download=true.

[404] *Siliadin*, *supra* note 393.

[405] *Id.*

[406] Cohen (2003).

[407] Kippenberg (2007), p. 46.

[408] OSCE, *supra* note 403.

send the money to the children after they returned home at the end of the contract, or they were included in a tontine.[409]

It was often the case that the girls themselves did not ask for a salary and even seemed surprised when asked about this. Parents and the employers often defined the situation more in terms of child fostering than child domestic work. Those who had jobs were expected to give all of their earnings to the employer who hosted them and to be grateful for having a place to stay. Research has found that harsh debt-bondage[410] arrangements are common practice, especially in Nigeria, Togo, and the Ivory Coast.[411]

Traffickers are particularly ingenious in creating circumstances that make the worker totally dependent on them. For instance, all children enslaved in domestic servitude in West Africa are required to address members of their employer's family as "uncle" or "auntie" and they are indoctrinated to consider themselves part of this family.[412] Thus, a parent-child relationship develop between the children and their offenders, and victims may not perceive themselves as trafficked. Even though the servants are sometimes very much older than their masters, they come to believe that their employers are surrogate parents and that they are part of the family.

#### 2.5.4.2.3 Violation of Human Dignity and Autonomy

The threat to human dignity is described in *Bidemi Bello, Movant, v. United States Of America*; a case involving the trafficking of two Nigerian women, where the evidence showed that Bello secured Laome's loyalty and labor compliance through violence or threats of violence. Whenever the household chores dissatisfied Bello, the domestic servant was hit and beaten by the employer "with the back of her hand, a shoe, a wooden spoon, an extension cord, a belt, a hanger, a broom, or any item close at hand. On occasion, Bello stood on Laome's stomach while beating her."[413] The autonomy and self-determination of the domestic servant are also denied or restricted and their travel documents are confiscated. In the case cited above, Laome never left the house for social occasions; she could not come and go freely from the house, she had no cell phone, no keys to Bello's home, and no personal money. Consequently, Laome made no friends of her own in the United States. Bello warned

[409] A tontine is a special arrangement in which moneys are collected and distributed directly to an individual on a rotational basis among the group.

[410] The UN's 1956 Supplementary Convention on the Abolition of Slavery defines debt bondage, the Slave Trade, and Institutions and Practices Similar to Slavery as: "the status or condition arising from a pledge by a debtor of his personal services or of those of a person under his control as security for a debt, if the value of those services as reasonably assessed is not applied towards the liquidation of the debt or the length and nature of those services are not respectively limited and defined." *See* UNESC Res. 608(XXI), art. 1(a)) (Sept. 7, 1956).

[411] Cohen (2003).

[412] Anti-Slavery, supra note 147, p. 24.

[413] Bello, *supra* note 403. *See also U.S. v. Adaboi Stella Udeozor*, 515 F.3d 260 (4th Cir., 2008).

Laome "that if she answered the door or talked to the neighbors, the police would take Laome to jail. . .One day Laome reported that her father called the house, Bello beat and kicked her for hours and forced her to stand naked for a day with one hand and one foot on the ground, and the other foot in the air."[414] Victims of domestic servitude are also subjected to constant verbal abuse and to humiliation., Laome, for instance was subjected to insults, abuse, and threats, such as when Bello called her "dumb, stupid, poor, dirty, ugly, demonic, a slave, a witch, and a bitch. . ."[415]

The denial of schooling is another efficient means by which to cut off ties with the outside world and obtain total control of a minor. Of the 92% of child domestic workers who do not have access to schooling in France, 26% have never been educated in their country of origin and only 22% have attended school until seventh grade.[416] Most do not have language skills and such illiteracy creates difficulties in communication as they have only a basic knowledge of French. Like minors from non-French speaking countries, they often speak only the dialect of their country of origin; these language deficiencies contribute to cultural isolation and strengthen their dependence vis-à-vis their employer. The latter effectively becomes the only intermediary between the child and society; consequently, it is extremely difficult for a minor to escape this condition of servitude.

In addition, the worker also experiences daily living conditions in the home of the employer that are discriminatory, involving exclusion, disrespect, ingratitude, and sexual and physical violence.[417] Even if their relationship with members of the household is good, it cannot be conducted on equal terms; a typical manifestation of this discrimination is that the employer's children go to school whilst the domestic

---

[414] *Id.*

[415] *Id.*

[416] *Le Travail Domestique des Mineurs en France*, Comité Contre l'Esclavage Moderne (CCEM) 31 (2009), http://www.esclavagemoderne.org/media/Etude-Travail-domestique-des-mineurs-2.pdf.

[417] *Id.* at 27. OSCE noted that the exploiter resorts to verbal, physical, and sometimes sexual violence and mistreatment of the domestic worker as a means of strengthening the relationship of domination and submission with the victim. In fact, consultations with children in domestic labor have revealed that they have suffered maltreatment consisting of extreme physical punishment, and psychological (emotional) and sexual harassments from male household members. In West and Central Africa, psychological violence towards child domestics takes the form of name-calling, insults, threats, swearing, humiliation, bullying, screaming, shouting insults, obscene language, fines for damages, or being forced to remain outdoors. Many girls reported that they were accused of lying, stealing, being witches, sleeping with men, and being lazy. Physical violence may include beating (with wooden whips, electric cords, belts, sticks, brooms), cigarette burns, crushing the feet with high heels, whipping, pulling hair, scalding with water or an iron, pinching, extreme overwork, and denial of food. The girls are often subjected to sexual harassment and abuse by the men (even the spouse of their employer) or the boys of the household, including fondling and sometimes rape. In cases of pregnancy, the girls are always forced to have an abortion or are thrown out of the household. Unwelcome at home because their situation has brought dishonor on the family, they are forced to fend for themselves on the streets or engage in sexual commercial exploitation.

child stays home to do chores, or the family's children watch TV while the servant is busy washing dishes.[418]

Furthermore, the segregated child always eats alone in the kitchen, separate from the employing family; she serves meals to employers and waits until they have finished, only then can she consume the leftovers or food of low-quality. Trafficked children are not allowed to use the same plates and bowls as other members of the household or even the same seats.[419] An outside visitor cannot fail to see them: they can be seen lying on the floor or seated in the corner of the house and, in most cases, they are dressed in used clothing given them by the employer, which can often be highly unsuitable for the season.

Commonly, child domestics are referred to by a derogatory label and some employers prefer to change the given name of child domestic workers in their homes. In numerous countries in West Africa, the term "boy" or "bonne" is often used as synonymous with slave; these experiences adversely affect children, instilling in them deep feelings of inferiority and chronically low self-esteem, impeding them from challenging the situation.[420] A former Malian domestic servant describes her experience thus:

> They weren't willing to give me food. When they served the food, they would put my portion in the lid of the bowl to give me. When they'd give me mine in the lid of the bowl, I'd eat it and sit and cry. I would just eat mine like that. When I was done eating, I'd go and lay down. They would show me where to sleep, and I'd go and lay down there. The house they showed me was bad. Nobody could sleep there. But I'd sleep there by myself.[421]

Due to their young ages and because they are unaware of their rights, children become particularly vulnerable and totally dependent when they migrate a lengthy distance from their families or relocate to another country. Often coming from a rural family with few economic resources and ethnic origins typically perceived as being of lower social status than those of the employing family, they find themselves in unfamiliar surroundings. One survey shows that 26% of the victims of domestic servitude have not attended school in their home country prior to their entry into French territory and could neither read nor write.[422] These inequalities of power are usually compounded by the employers' beliefs that they are generous to the children and are doing them a favor.

Although some child domestic servants have positive and harmonious relationships within the households they serve, children working as domestics remain particularly vulnerable to trafficking, forced labor, the worst forms of child labor; which makes domestic work one of the most widespread and potentially exploitative

---

[418] *Ending Child Labour in Domestic Work and Protecting Young Workers from Abusive Working Conditions*, Int'l Labour Org. 29 (Jun. 12, 2013), http://www.ilo.org/ipec/Informationresources/WCMS_207656/lang%2D%2Den/index.htm.

[419] Derby Nana (2012), p. 23.

[420] ILO, *supra* note 418, at 35–36.

[421] Derby Nana (2012), pp. 23–24.

[422] CCEM, *supra* note 416, at 23.

forms of child labor across the world today.[423] In Africa, domestic work is not even seen as an occupation; it is even considered light work reserved for children and women. Moreover, some parents still believe that the contribution of their offspring's chores forms part of their education. However, the working conditions invoked under domestic servitude far exceed the concept of domestic help.

### 2.5.5 Trafficking for Forced Labor

According to observations by the International Program on the Elimination of Child Labor (IPEC), most forced labor in the Economic Community of West African States (ECOWAS) is now implemented by private individuals and entities rather than the State. It occurs through the informal economy, including trafficking in persons for forced labor in agriculture, domestic work, mining and quarrying, fishing, construction, street-related activities such as head loading, begging, and the involvement of children in armed conflicts and commercial sexual exploitation.[424] The International Labor Organization (ILO) Forced Labor Convention, 1930 (No. 29), defines forced labor as "all work or service that is exacted from any person under the menace of penalty and for which the said person has not offered her or himself voluntarily."[425] The circumstances of the enslaved person are crucial in identifying which practices are tantamount to slavery. ILO provides six[426] useful criteria that can be better understood when divided into three dimensions: coercive

---

[423] *Id.*

[424] Casentini G (2015), https://www.human-dignity-foundation.org/wp-content/uploads/2016/04/InterPol-AKOMA-Final-assessment-report-Casentini.pdf; *ECOWAS Regional Action Plan for the Elimination of Child Labour Especially the Worst Forms*, ILO, http://www.ilo.org/wcmsp5/groups/public/%2D%2D-africa/documents/publication/wcms_227737.pdf (accessed on August 20, 2021); *see* Astrid de Bruycker, *Slave-free Chocolate in the Making? The Worst Forms of Child Labour present in the cocoa sector of Ivory Coast and Ghana*, MLB (2008), http://www.tsr.ch/xobix_media/files/tsr/abe/2009/worst_forms_of_child_labour_-_master_thesis.pdf; *see also* Okyere (2017), pp. 92–105.

[425] ILO, Forced Labor Convention art. 2, 39 UNTS 55 (May 1, 1932).

[426] The ILO suggests six indicators of forced labor:

> (i) Threats or actual physical harm to the worker; (ii) Restriction of movement and confinement to the workplace or to a limited area; (iii) Debt bondage: where the worker works to pay off a debt or loan and is not paid for his or her services. The employer may provide food and accommodation at such inflated prices that the worker cannot escape the debt; (iv) Withholding of wages or excessive wage reductions that violate previously made agreements; (v) Retention of passports and identity documents so that the worker cannot leave or prove his/her identity and status; (vi) Threat of denunciation to the authorities as the worker is of irregular immigration status.

*See ILO Indicators of Forced Labour*, ILO, http://www.ilo.org/wcmsp5/groups/public/@ed_norm/@declaration/documents/publication/wcms_203832.pdf (accessed on August 20, 2021).

recruitment, work and life under duress, and the impossibility of leaving an employer through penalty or the threat of penalty.

#### 2.5.5.1 Forced Labor in Mining and Quarries

Mining and quarrying are traditional activities for West African people in Senegal, Sierra Leone, Mali, Burkina Faso, Ghana, Liberia, and Guinea, all of which have been mining for centuries.[427] Over the last few years, gold mining in this region has undergone a remarkable expansion following a the strong rise in gold prices to their current high levels: this has stimulated exploration and attracted increasing numbers of migrants looking for work on small-scale mines along the West African gold belt.[428] Thus, the West Africa region has experienced a significant growth in gold production over the last two decades to 6.7 million ounces in 2010; accounting for nearly 8% of the global supply. Continued growth is forecast to approximately 11 million ounces by 2015. Artisanal mining is a poverty-alleviating activity that directly and indirectly employs thousands of people in every West African country. In Mali, Human Rights Watch staff estimate that between 20,000 and 40,000 children are involved in mining production.[429] In Burkina Faso, the potential of artisanal gold mining production is extremely substantial; it provides jobs to over 100,000–200,000 active miners as a minimum of 200 sites across the country.[430] However, these mines are also the sites of modern-day slavery where many people are forced, often through debt bondage, to work in hazardous conditions.

##### 2.5.5.1.1 Coercive Recruitment

In the context of trafficking, the invalidation of "freely" given consent is dependent upon false promises from the traffickers and their accomplices. However, the interference with consent may be obscured by coercive circumstances, particularly economic disadvantages, resulting in the appearance of freely given consent. This is the case with respect to trafficking in mines and other forced labor in West Africa where the consenting agent is motivated by dire poverty.[431]

---

[427] Since 300 AD, the old empires of Ghana, Mali, and Songhai in West Africa have built their prosperity on their artisanal small scale mining tradition. ASM in Africa falls into two broad categories. The first is the mining of high value minerals such as gold, diamond, and precious stones, generally for export. The second comprises mining and quarrying for industrial minerals and construction materials, mostly for local markets.

[428] Daffé L (2012), https://www.iom.int/jahia/webdav/shared/shared/mainsite/projects/showcase_pdf/Global-Eye-Issue11-Mar2012.pdf.

[429] *A Poisonous Mix: Child Labor, Mercury, and Artisan Gold Mining in Mali*, HRW (Dec. 2011), https://www.hrw.org/sites/default/files/reports/mali1211_insert_LOWRES_WITH_COVER.pdf.

[430] Gueye Dj (2001), p. 25, http://pubs.iied.org/pdfs/G00717.pdf.

[431] Elliot (2014).

West African boys and girls are involved in mining production through deceptive and forced recruitment; while some laborers migrate to the mining areas seeking work, others are recruited, taken, or sold there by family members or former commanders.[432] As reported by Human Rights Watch staff, the vast majority of mines in West Africa operate illegally without a license and are part of the informal sector. Recruitment occurs through people who are informally engaged in the business or through victims' friends or family. No contract is signed between an employer and an employee, putting the laborers at high risk of abuse. An extremely common practice on these sites consists of migration to mining camps, which is a characteristic of trafficking. "One such example is the relocation of boys aged 6–18 years-old from Benin to Nigeria, where they work in quarries outside Abeokuta."[433] An external analysis considers the people with whom the children travel to be 'traffickers/employers' because they recruit[434] harbor, and employ the victims; and make a profit. The boys call such persons their boss.[435]

#### 2.5.5.1.2 Abusive Working and Living Conditions

Forced labor victims, according to ILO guidance, "are likely to endure living and working conditions that workers would never freely accept."[436] Work may be performed under degrading, substandard, and hazardous living conditions that are in severe breach of labor law. IOM and Human Rights Watch staff have observed that all laborers (men, women, and children) engaged in mining activities in West

---

432 UNICEF, *supra* note 274, at 35.

433 Thorsen (2012b), http://www.unicef.org/wcaro/english/Briefing_paper_No_4_-_children_working_in_mines_and_quarries.pdf.

434 The mere fact of being unable to contact his or her parents puts the child in a position of vulnerability and may constitute isolation.

435 Thorsen (2012b), p. 5.

436 ILO, *supra* note 426.

Africa experience adverse living and working conditions. For instance, miners working in these traditional artisanal mines use rudimentary tools and perform labor-intensive and hazardous work. Typically, men and children who are 15 years-old dig shafts that run over 80 meters underground, using makeshift pulleys to haul up buckets of ore, carry heavy loads of ore, and then crush it.[437] In the tunnels and mineshafts, life is difficult as there is poor ventilation and lighting; minors risk death when setting explosives to blast rock; and also from rock falls, floods, and tunnel collapse. They breathe air filled with dust and, on occasion, toxic gases.[438] On the gold sites, the business policy is that work begins at 6 a.m. and ends at 6 p.m.[439] According to Terre des Hommes, children as young as 5 years-old work overtime 6–14 hours each day, beyond the limits prescribed by national law.[440] In Burkina Faso, for example, children and adults directly involved in mining work full-time every day, occasionally getting to rest on Friday only because of a superstition that associates this day with misfortune.

Due to their location in remote areas, laborers in mining sites live in deplorable conditions in camps with plastic sheeting and have little or no access to health care, including basic public services such as water and sanitation, even though mining has significant health consequences. Consequently, they suffer from headaches; back, shoulder, and muscle pain, and all the diseases related to a lack of hygiene. Women and children, who perform most of the gold washing, are at risk of being poisoned by toxic mercury and cyanide. Women and girls working at the sites also jeopardize their reproductive health as mercury can harm fetuses in utero and infants through breastfeeding.[441] Accidents such as shaft collapses or those caused by the unsafe use of tools happen regularly, often leading to injuries.[442] The United Nations International Children's Emergency Fund (UNICEF) report in Burkina Faso, the Human Rights Watch report from Ghana and Mali, and the International Organization for Migration (IOM) study in Senegal have noted that "[t]he poor working conditions in the mines, combined with the absence of government services and regulation in the area, pose serious risks of exploitation and abuse."[443]

---

[437] Daffé L (2012), p. 1.

[438] Child Labour in Gold Mining, Int'l Labour Org. (ILO), http://www.ilo.org/ipec/areas/Miningandquarrying/MoreaboutCLinmining/lang%2D%2Den/index.htm (accessed on Apr. 28, 2021).

[439] *Permanent Secretariat Plan for National Action for Children—Burkina Faso*, UNICEF 48 (Dec. 2006), https://www.unicef.org/french/worldfitforchildren/files/Burkina_Faso_WFFC5_Report.pdf.

[440] Bureau of International Labor Affairs, *Project to Reduce Child Labor in Burkina Faso*, U.S. Dept. of Labor, https://www.dol.gov/ilab/reports/child-labor/findings/2013TDA/burkinafaso.pdf (accessed on August 20, 2021).

[441] In Burkina Faso, women have continually assisted men in all activities, especially in business ventures such as artisanal mining. About 45% of those working onsite are women (45,000–85,000 individuals) who carry out various tasks, including domestic chores, mineral treatment (crushing, washing and extracting), and trading. *Id.*

[442] Daffé L (2012), p. 1, 5.

[443] *Id.* at 4.

Mining activities are also associated with an increase in prostitution, often involving women and girls as young as 12 years-old. This has inevitably led to an increased number of teenage pregnancies, single parenting, and sexually transmitted diseases, particularly HIV/AIDS.[444] Artisanal mining activities have also been cited as a factor influencing school attendance in West Africa; where many children attend school irregularly, skipping classes or entire school days. Some pupils leave school and engage in these lucrative activities to earn quick money. The miners may also force their young offspring to drop out of school entirely in order to provide a helping hand.[445]

##### 2.5.5.1.3 Control Through Sanctions or Threats of Violence

A survey in the *Kono* district, a primary area for diamond mining in Sierra Leone, revealed that trafficking is one means by which children become mine workers. The commanders who recruited the children reported that they hold sway over them and would not let the child miners stop working for them if someone came to put an end to child mining.[446] The manipulation of debt constitutes a strong indicator of forced labor; indeed, debt bondage or forced labor imposed as repayment for a loan is common in several countries throughout West Africa through a system of abusive pay practices that are intended to increase indebtedness and condemn the worker to slavery for life. This is an extreme exploitation and control mechanism that prevents victims of trafficking from leaving. Claims have emerged from Nigeria, Ghana, Liberia, and Sierra Leone of mining laborers working in an attempt to pay off an incurred or sometimes even inherited debt. New workers are required to borrow money to purchase food, supplies, and the tools and equipment needed to remain employed. In other situations, debt bondage occurs as a result of inheriting the debt of deceased family members.[447] Thus, for those mining laborers that are paid, the cost of food, tools, and medication is deducted from their earnings such that they are left with virtually nothing; the borrower is unable to save, unable to pay off the debt, and falls further into debt over time. Thus, they are held in a situation of precariousness and total dependence. As happens in most of these cases, workers' documents are supposedly retained as a guarantee for the payment of their debts; in practice, they are actually withheld to prevent them from leaving the site.

Irregular or delayed wages imply a forced labor situation.[448] Mining workers are obligated to remain with their abusive employers while waiting for the wages that are

---

[444] *Precious Metal, Cheap Labor: Child Labor and Corporate Responsibility in Ghana's Artisanal Gold Mines*, HRW (Jun. 10, 2015), https://www.hrw.org/report/2015/06/10/precious-metal-cheap-labor/child-labor-and-corporate-responsibility-ghanas.

[445] HRW, *supra* note 453.

[446] UNICEF, *supra* note 113, at 35.

[447] ILO, *supra* note 43, 23.

[448] ILO, *supra* note 426.

owed to them. In the context of forced labor, wages are systematically and deliberately withheld as a means to compel the worker to remain; rendering victims too impoverished to leave and denying them the opportunity to change employers. In some cases, the victims are not physically isolated and many travel back and forth between their home and the mining sites. The production of gold may involve no restrictions on worker movement; nevertheless, the former victim who is re-trafficked is in a vulnerable position as they lack alternative livelihood options.

#### 2.5.5.2 Trafficking for Begging

In West Africa, informal networks and Islamic religious teachers take advantage of the vulnerable condition of orphans, under aged children, and old people; as well as people with intellectual and physical disabilities to earn higher amounts of money from begging. Forced begging can be classified into two different types. First, children and people who are physically challenged are trafficked into begging either informally or in an organized manner. This type of trafficking, observed in Nigeria, has spread beyond the country's borders to the Middle East, in particular to Saudi Arabia.[449] Contractual beggars include adult men and women. "Physically challenged or handicapped persons are hired on a daily basis for begging assignments with a token fee of often no more than ₦500 (some US $3.8)."[450] Children are sent out to beg by parents who realize that they can acquire a substantial share of profits from this activity. The perpetrators carry the physically challenged on their back or in a wheelbarrow or wheelchair and carry them around town from sunrise to sunset, often in harsh weather and dangerous traffic conditions.[451]

Second, disabled persons or experienced beggars can traffic children in their custody; reports indicate that little girls and boys in Nigeria and Senegal have been recruited in Mali by blind persons who compel them to guide the handicapped in a form of organized begging.[452] They are forced into this business without any financial reward other than the daily meals that may be handed out to them on the streets.

Children sent to live in Koranic boarding schools are forced to beg by their teachers. This is forms part of a traditional practice in which families send their children to religious teachers (marabouts) for the purpose of Koranic education. The arrangement between parent and religious teacher is similar to that of fosterage; the pupil becomes a member of the teacher's household.[453] Research by Human Rights Watch staff has found that many marabouts conscientiously fulfill their role of providing young boys with a religious and moral education. However, in Konaric

[449] UNESCO, *supra* note 37, at 30.

[450] *Id.*

[451] *Id.*

[452] *Id.* at 31; Moens (2004), p. 9.

[453] Saul M (2009), p. 199.

school (*daaras*) in the cities, numerous other marabouts are using education as a cover for economic exploitation of the children entrusted to their custody.[454]

The Department of Labor Report estimates there are tens of thousands of Koranic school pupils (*talibés*), mostly under age 12, in situations of forced begging in Senegal.[455] Evidence of boys living in Koranic schools and begging has also been found in several other West African countries including the Gambia, Guinea-Bissau, Mali, Niger, Nigeria, Burkina Faso, Sierra Leone, and Benin. Although more specific information needs to be documented, there are confirmed elements of trafficking within the practice of forced begging organized by a third person or religious teachers.

#### 2.5.5.2.1 Coercion and Abuse of Power

Begging is closely linked to the abuse of power and consists of assigning young children low-status work, often against their will. Indeed, in Senegal, when the (*talibés*) Konaric school pupils grow older, they are either sent back to their villages having completed their Koranic schooling or take on a different role in the Koranic school (*daara*) by supervising the younger children. They are no longer assigned to beg because younger children are likely to evoke more pity and because the shame associated with begging at an older age makes it embarrassing for the boys.[456] In addition, most of the pupils in the Konaric school live far away from their families and see their parents only a few times a year. This separation places the children in a situation of total dependence on their guardians. Consequently, they will be reluctant to walk away from their abusive situation due to a sense of loyalty or fear of reprisals.

The traffickers, either the religious teacher or the relatives, have total control over the pupils, their belongings, and income. *Talibés* are moved to major cities from rural areas within and from neighboring countries. Senegalese children, for example, are trafficked to Gambia and to Mauritania where religious teachers force them to beg. The Special Rapporteur on contemporary forms of slavery also identified cases of marabouts "renting" *talibés* to work in gold mines in Niger.[457] Moreover, studies on forced begging report that people who abuse and exploit the situation supervise their victims permanently and visit them to collect the earned cash. All of the money collected by the pupils is handed over to the religious teacher. The children will not

[454] *Senegal: Boys in Many Quranic Schools Suffer Severe Abuse*, HRW (Apr. 15, 2010), https://www.hrw.org/news/2010/04/15/senegal-boys-many-quranic-schools-suffer-severe-abuse.

[455] Bureau of International Labor Affairs, *Senegal*, U.S. Dept of Labor, http://www.dol.gov/ilab/reports/child-labor/findings/2011TDA/senegal.pdf (Accessed on August 20, 2021).

[456] Delap (2009), p. 9, https://ec.europa.eu/anti-trafficking/sites/antitrafficking/files/anti-slavery_international_2009_-_begging_for_change_en_1.pdf.

[457] Bhoola Urmila (Special Rapporteur on Contemporary Forms of Slavery, including its Causes and Consequences), *Mission to the Niger*, ¶ 61, U.N. Doc. A/HRC/30/35/Add.1 (Nov. 11-21, 2014).

steal any of the money because they fear the teacher and that, if they do, misfortune will befall them and they will be cursed.[458]

#### 2.5.5.2.2 Dismal Living Conditions

The pupils also endure abusive and precarious living conditions; those boys called to work up to 14 hours per day are obliged to hand over the money they have earned to their teachers.[459] On the streets, they are vulnerable to car accidents, disease, and severe weather, including scorching heat. Reports describes pupils who are living "in overcrowded, unsanitary conditions; receive inadequate food and medical care; and are vulnerable to sexual exploitation."[460]

Rural Koranic schools are among the largest farming enterprises thanks to a stable labor force of pupils. The pupils work on the teacher's farm or contribute to their upkeep in several ways. In addition to being obligated to work in construction or agricultural fields or to sell goods on the market, some children are forced by their teachers to beg on the streets and therefore do not receive the education promised to their parents.[461]

Finally, long hours spent in farms or on the street have sometimes evolved into a practice of forced begging where children are required to beg for long hours and receive very little or no education. Across the major cities of West Africa, these trafficked children are denied access to formal education and a proper social upbringing. Often studies are "done in the blaze of a bonfire, the symbol of these schools, which is said to bring blessings on the community and defend the pupils on Judgment Day."[462] Marabouts who send the children out to beg are unceasing in their demand for daily quotas to be met; the methods used to persuade the children to raise more money vary from psychological abuse to cruel physical punishment.

#### 2.5.5.2.3 Abuse and Exploitation

Not all forced labor is trafficking; in its 2007 General Survey, the ILO Committee of Experts on the Application of Conventions and Recommendations (CEACR) underlines the fact[463] that the common denominator between forced labor and trafficking

---

[458] UNICEF, *supra* note 113, at 43.

[459] Department of Labor, 2012 Benin, at http://www.dol.gov/ilab/reports/child-labor/findings/2012TDA/benin.pdf.

[460] HRW, *supra* note 454; U.S. Dept. of Labor, *supra* note 455.

[461] UNICEF, *supra* note 113, at 43.

[462] UNESCO, *supra* note 37, at 30–31; Saul M (2009), p. 199.

[463] *ILO: Eradication of forced labour, General Survey concerning the Forced Labour Convention, 1930 (No. 29), and the Abolition of Forced Labour Convention, 1957* (No. 105), ILO (2007), http://www.ilo.org/wcmsp5/groups/public/%2D%2D-ed_norm/%2D%2D-relconf/documents/meetingdocument/wcms_089199.pdf.

is exploitation.[464] In Senegal, Koranic students as young as 5 or 6 years-old spend most of the day begging and receive religious education in the mornings or evenings. They earn 250-300F CFA (US $0.60–0.70)[465] per day and hand over the revenues to their marabout. Research suggests that some marabouts make vast profits from children begging; marabouts with a large number of students in their schools can earn more than is needed to maintain the Konaric school (*daara*). For instance, "with a *daara* of 50 *talibés*, a marabout might earn 350,000F CFA (US $770) per month."[466] Taking into account rent and other costs "a marabout could still expect to earn well in excess of the 125,000F CFA (US $275), which matches the average monthly salary of primary school teachers in Senegal."[467]

### 2.5.6 Other Forms of Trafficking

As suggested in the Palermo Protocol definition, trafficking includes various forms that force, coercion, fraud, or exploitation may take. Subsequently, the following list of other forms of trafficking in West Africa is illustrative rather than exhaustive.[468]

#### 2.5.6.1 Child Soldiers

In times of armed conflict or social unrest, trafficking in children may also occur in the form of forced recruitment of child soldiers into armies or rebel groups. In West Africa, children who are forcibly recruited have fought for militias, clan-based or

---

[464] *Harder to See, Harder to Count: Survey Guidelines to Estimate Forced Labour of Adults and Children*, ILO 19 (2012), http://www.ilo.org/wcmsp5/groups/public/%2D%2D-ed_norm/%2D%2D-declaration/documents/publication/wcms_182096.pdf.

[465] The equivalent amounts of US Dollars given here were calculated based in currency exchange rates in December 2008.

[466] Delap (2009), p. 11.

[467] *Id.*

[468] There have been incidental UNESCO reports of the trafficking of young children from Nigeria to Saudi Arabia for blood money known as "diya". The trafficker, often female, takes a child trafficked to Saudi Arabia to have him/her run over and possibly killed by the car of a wealthy person. On behalf of the victim's family, the trafficker claims monetary compensation prescribed by Shari'a for the crime. The trafficker obtains an equivalent of about ₦3,500,000 (local currency, equivalent to US $27,000) in compensation for injury or death. Back in Nigeria the trafficker informs the parents that the child died of natural causes and pays about ₦100,000 (the equivalent of US $775) as the child's wages while in Saudi Arabia. Many parents simply accept the supposed wages and consider the death of the child to be the will of Allah. Although less prevalent than sex and labor trafficking, people are also trafficked in West Africa for the purpose of removing their organs and body parts for use in witchcraft or traditional medicine. Media reports have linked the trafficking of West African children such as albinos to Europe for organs and body parts including skulls, hearts, eyes, and genitals which are sold and used by deviant practitioners to increase wealth, influence, power, health, or fertility.

factional groups, and government and armed political opposition forces in Côte d'Ivoire, Guinea, Liberia, Mali, and Nigeria. After the war in Sierra Leone ended in 2002, the Child Soldiers Global Report 2004 reported that approximately 21,000 child soldiers were enlisted during the decade of conflict.[469] In the same period, an estimated 30,000 child soldiers were drawn into new conflicts in Ivory Coast and Liberia; some were recruited among child refugees and veteran child soldiers from the Sierra Leonean conflict.[470]

Child soldiers recruited for armed conflicts assume various roles; many are recruited by armed groups not to fight but to be engaged in forced labor. Their tasks range from serving as porters, guards hunting and looting for food, deployment as lookouts, as messengers and spies, and as raiders of infantry troops. Reports indicate that armed forces have also compelled children to work in the diamond mines of Sierra Leone.[471] In Liberia, several girls were reportedly recruited as both soldiers and helpers; and faced routine rapes and sexual assaults. The armed groups in Sierra Leone who abducted girls in large numbers to become fighters also forced them into marriages as "wives" to commanders, for whom they worked long hours as domestic servants.[472] Similarly, the rebel and Islamic extremist groups who invaded and occupied northern Mali in 2012, used girls for sexual exploitation and forced them to marry members of armed groups. Militias and pro-government groups also recruited and used children to carry assault rifles, staff checkpoints, guard prisoners, and conduct patrols.[473] Trafficking for the purpose child soldiering affects every aspect of a child's development as they may be injured or killed, beheaded, maimed, and mutilated. They are uprooted from their communities, separated from their parents and families, subjected to sexual abuse and exploitation, and are victims of trauma as a result of being exposed to violence and deprived of both an education and medical assistance.[474]

#### 2.5.6.2 Baby Farming and Surrogacy

y Nigeria has recently become notorious for a new trend in trafficking, consisting of the exploitation of "baby factories" and "baby harvesting."[475] The first cases of "baby harvesting" in the three states of Abia, Ebonyi, and Lagos were officially

[469] *Child Soldiers Global Report 2004*, Child Soldiers 22, https://www.child-soldiers.org/Handlers/Download.ashx?IDMF=c5f157d3-4b56-457c-a2d8-31601ffc1b9e.

[470] *Id.* at 15; UNICEF, *supra* note 113, at 38–39.

[471] Child Soldiers, *supra* note 469.

[472] UNICEF, *supra* note 113, at 40.

[473] Trafficking in Persons Report, Mali, U.S. Dept. of State (2015), http://www.state.gov/j/tip/rls/tiprpt/countries/2015/243487.htm.

[474] SOS Children's Villages, Children in Conflict: Child Soldiers, http://www.child-soldier.org/.

[475] UNESCO, *supra* note 37, at 31; Shitu S (2016), p. 224 (available at: http://www.journalijar.com/uploads/373_IJAR-9473.pdf).

reported in 2006 by UNESCO of doctors, nurses, and orphanages who help teenagers with unwanted pregnancies by promising safe abortions or jobs. Other young women were later impregnated by men specifically hired for such purposes; the traffickers confine and care for these women during pregnancy and provide money and shelter. Upon delivery, their babies are sold for international or domestic adoptions, rituals, slave labor, or sexual exploitation. The young mothers are paid off after having signed papers repudiating their claims to the babies or swearing oaths of secrecy.[476]

These "baby factories" are operated by well-organized criminal syndicates who run their "business" with the help of employees. The traffickers, some of whom are medical doctors, are also usually the owners of these facilities. "Baby factories" are often disguised as maternity homes, orphanages, social welfare homes, clinics, and even water bottling factories. A notorious case that caught the government's attention was that of two sisters who approached a doctor in Lagos with an offer to sell the unborn child of one of them. They demanded ₦500,000 (about US $3875) if the baby was born a boy and ₦300,000 (about US $2325) if the baby was a girl; they later raised the stakes for a baby girl to ₦400,000 (about US $3100) due to "the rising cost of living." Similar allegations were reported in a case involving the Good Shepherd Orphanage which engaged in the illegal adoption of babies.[477]

Media reports of police raids confirm that "baby factories" as an industry are flourishing in Nigeria and affect multiple victims. For example, in May 2008, police freed 25 teenage girls who were confined to a hospital in Enugu. Police conducted another raid in June 2011, rescuing 32 teenage girls from a "baby factory" located in the city of Aba, Abia state. In May 2013, law enforcement officers saved 6 teenage girls held in captivity in a "baby factory" in Enugu, 17 pregnant teenage girls and 11 babies in Southern Imo province, and 26 teenage girls in Umuaka village, Imo State. In July 2013, police arrested the owner of "Moonlight Maternity Home", an illegal home with a nurse working for the owner to help sell babies from unwanted pregnancies.[478]

---

476 Svetlana (2013), p. 11, http://www.internationalcrimesdatabase.org/upload/documents/20131030T045906-ICD%20Brief%203%20-%20Huntley.pdf. *See* Uduma Kalu, *How Child Trafficking Network Operates in South East*, Vanguard (Jul. 30, 2011), http://www.vanguardngr.com/2011/07/how-child-trafficking-network-operates-in-south-east; Madike I, *The ABC of Baby Factories (National Mirror Investigation)*, CKN Nigeria (May 26, 2013), http://www.cknnigeria.com/2013/05/the-abc-of-baby-factories-national.html; *Nigeria "Baby Factory" raided in Imo State*, BBC (May 10, 2013), http://www.bbc.co.uk/news/world-africa-22484318; Tucker Reals, *32 Teens Freed in Nigeria "Baby Factory" Raid*, CBS News (Jun. 2, 2011), http://www.cbsnews.com/8301-503543_162-20068184-503543.html; Nigeria Frees 16 in "Baby Factory" Raid, news24 (Jun. 20, 2013), http://www.news24.com/Africa/News/Nigeria-frees-16-in-baby-factory-raid-20130620; Caulfield P, *Police in Nigeria Free 32 Pregnant Teens from "Baby Factory": Newborns Sold into Labour, Sex Markets*, Daily News (Jun. 2, 2011), http://www.nydailynews.com/news/world/police-nigeria-free-32-pregnant-teens-baby-factorynewborns-sold-labour-sex-markets-article-1.127079#ixzz2VH1sr4f1.

477 UNESCO, *supra* note 37, at 31.

478 Svetlana (2013).

The question that arises is whether "baby factories" constitute a trafficking in persons offense or merely violate adoption rules. This phenomenon is a real issue as there is no legal definition of "baby factories" or "baby harvesting" under Nigerian domestic law or in international law. These terms were created by journalists to describe criminal activities in Nigeria involving the restriction of a person's freedom of movement, forced impregnations, sale of babies, and illegal adoptions.[479] Public media has provided insightful descriptions evidencing the core elements of trafficking in this criminal practice. According to these reports, traffickers usually approach their victims with false promises of jobs or safe abortions and lure women and girls into "factories" through deception and by exploiting the vulnerability of underage children and out of wedlock pregnancies.

Furthermore, girls and women are locked up at facilities used as "baby factories," allowing their traffickers to establish full control over them and detain until they give birth to babies that are subsequently sold to a third party. Those victims who are not pregnant upon their arrival at the "baby factory" are forcibly and repeatedly impregnated while being held at the facility for extended periods. These babies are primarily sold for the purposes of adoption or used for sacrifices in black magic rituals, the sex trade, and manual labor. They may also become victims of trafficking along with their biological mothers.[480] Victims have also claimed that the traffickers took away their cell phones and deleted stored contacts to prevent them from asking their friends and relatives for help; they also complained about malnutrition and poor care. The underlying factors that motivate traffickers and those who participate or aid in this crime and human rights violations need to be exposed. Additionally, customers and clients who purchase the services or goods, who abuse their power, and who dehumanize trafficking victims must be unmasked and brought to justice.[481]

## References

(AU), African Charter on the Rights and Welfare of the Child, Doc. No. CAB/LEG/24.9/49 (Jul. 11, 1990), Art. 21 (2)

*A Civil Society Forum for Anglophone West Africa on Promoting and Protecting the Rights of Street Children*, Consortium for Street Children 10 (Oct. 2003), http://www.streetchildrenresources.org/wp-content/uploads/2013/01/civil-society-forum-for-anglophone-west-africa.pdf

*A Poisonous Mix: Child Labor, Mercury, and Artisan Gold Mining in Mali*, HRW (Dec. 2011), https://www.hrw.org/sites/default/files/reports/mali1211_insert_LOWRES_WITH_COVER.pdf

[479] *Id.* at 10.

[480] Svetlana (2013), pp. 10–11.

[481] U.N. Gift, *Analyzing the Business Model of Trafficking in Human Beings to Better Prevent the Crime,* OSCE 15 (2010), https://www.osce.org/cthb/69028?download=true.

*A Report Concerning the Macro and Micro Analyses of Human Trafficking*, Trafficking as a Criminal Enterprise (TRACE) 48 (Nov. 25, 2014), http://trace-project.eu/wp-content/uploads/2014/11/TRACE_D1.3_Final.pdf

*A Serious Crime Against Humanity and a Global Issue*, Counter Trafficking in Persons (CTIP) (Jun. 2012), http://www.aptireland.org/wp-content/uploads/2012/06/ctip_syllabus_for_high_schools.pdf.

*A.G. v. Felicia Okafor*, Nigeria Court of High Justice, Suit No. A.12C.06, Judgment (2006)

*Abuse of a Position of Vulnerability and Other "Means" within the Definition of Trafficking in Persons*, UNODC 14 (2013), https://www.unodc.org/documents/human-trafficking/2012/UNODC_2012_Issue_Paper_-_Abuse_of_a_Position_of_Vulnerability.pdf

Adebayo Adeyemi E, Ph.D., Terrorism and Transnational Security Threats in West Africa: A Global Perspective (Xlibris US 2015)

Adepelumi BP (2015) The Root Causes of Human Trafficking in Nigeria. African Center For Advocacy & Human Development (ACAHD) (Apr. 13, 2015), https://www.unodc.org/documents/congress//workshops/workshop2/Presentation_P_Adepelumi_African_Center_.pdf

Adepoju A (2005a) Migration in West Africa. Global Commission on Int'l Migration 1 (Sept. 2005), http://www.iom.int/jahia/webdav/site/myjahiasite/shared/shared/mainsite/policy_and_research/gcim/rs/RS8.pdf

Adepoju A (2005b) Review of research and data on human trafficking in sub-Saharan Africa. Int Migr 43:76, (available at: http://women.humantrafficking.org/uploads/publications/IOM_Data_Research_Human_Trafficking.pdf#page=76)

African Economic Outlook 2015, African Economic Outlook (AEO), http://www.africaneconomicoutlook.org/sites/default/files/content-pdf/AEO2015_EN.pdf

African Union, *Protocol on Amendments to the Protocol on the Statute of the African Court of Justice and Human Rights*, 27 June 2014, art. 28 J

*AG v Hussaina Ibrahim* and Idris Aminus Suit No. K.1TPP.2003

AG v Samson Ovensari, Suit No. B.15c.06

AG v Samuel Emwiovbankhoe, Suit No. B.20C.2005

*AG v Samuel Emwirovbankhoe*, Nigeria Court of High Justice, Suit No. B.20C.2005, Judgment (2005)

Agbu O (2003) Corruption and human trafficking: the Nigerian Case. West Afr Rev 4(1):2

Aghatise E (2005) Women trafficking from West Africa to Europe: cultural dimensions and strategies. Moziak, http://www.koed.hu/mozaik15/esohe.pdf

Aird Sarah C (1999) Ghana's slaves to the gods. Human Rights Brief http://www.wcl.american.edu/hrbrief/v7i1/ghana.htm

Akinrimisi B, Cooke N, Jones N, Presler-Marshall E (2012) Promoting synergies between child protection and social protection in Nigeria. Overseas Development Institute (ODI) (Feb. 2012), http://www.odi.org/sites/odi.org.uk/files/odi-assets/publications-opinion-files/7579.pdf

Alenoma G (2012) Parental perspectives on children streetism in Tamale in Ghana. Res Human Soc Sci 2:74 (available at: http://www.iiste.org/Journals/index.php/RHSS/article/view/2805/2829)

Allain AJ (2014) No effective trafficking definition exists: domestic implementation of the Palermo Protocol. Albany Gov Law Rev 7:111, 114

Allais C et al (2010) Tsireledzani: Understanding the Dimensions of Human Trafficking in Southern Africa 4 (the Democracy and Governance Program of the Human Sciences Research Council of South Africa 2010)

Alter KJ, Helfer LR, McAllister JR (2013) A new international human rights court for West Africa: the ECOWAS community court of justice. Am J Int Law 107:737

*An Introduction to Human Trafficking: Vulnerability, Impact and Action*, United Nations Office on Drugs and Crime (UNODC) (2008), 78 at https://www.unodc.org/documents/human-trafficking/An_Introduction_to_Human_Trafficking_-_Background_Paper.pdf

Annuaire Statistique 2009, INSD, http://www.insd.bf/n/contenu/pub_periodiques/annuaires_stat/Annuaires_stat_nationaux_BF/Annuaire_stat_2009.pdf

Annual Review 2011-2012, International Social Security Association (ISSA) 11, http://www.social-protection.org/gimi/RessourcePDF.action;jsessionid=RPF1rO9-rdieg9X0heZG0WxKwUS-VJVX3wGnwBxvhyw9ypJDXeH6!2055178518?id=31009

*Anti-Money Laundering/Combating the Financing of Terrorism – Topics*, International Monetary Fund (IMF), https://www.imf.org/external/np/leg/amlcft/eng/aml1.htm#moneylaundering (accessed on August 24, 2021)

Aronowitz A (2009) Human trafficking, human misery: the global trade in human beings. Prager, pp 110–121

Asomah JY (2015) Cultural rights versus human rights: a critical analysis of the Trokosi practice in ghana and the role of civil society. Afr Human Rights Law J 15:129. (*see also*)

*Assessment of Forced Labor Risk in the Cocoa Sector of Côte d'Ivoire*, Verité, February 2019. https://www.verite.org/wp-content/uploads/2019/02/Verite-Report-Forced-Labor-in-Cocoa-in-CDI.pdf

*Attorney General of the Federation v. Omoruyi,* High Court Edo State of Nigeria, Suit No. B/31c/2004 (2006)

Ba M (1979) So long a letter. Waveland Press, Inc. (*See also*)

Barriga Shantha R (2015) Torture Comes in Many Forms. HRW (Jun. 29, 2015), https://www.hrw.org/news/2015/06/29/torture-comes-many-forms

*Basic Information*, ECOWAS, http://www.ecowas.int/about-ecowas/basic-information/.

Bass Loretta E (2004) Child Labor in sub-Saharan Africa. Lynne Rienner, pp 89–90

Belen AM, Thanh-Dam T (2005) Searching for Best Practices to Counter Human Trafficking in Africa: A Focus on Women and Children, UNESCO 18 (Mar. 2005), http://humantraffickingsearch.org/wp-content/uploads/2017/06/138447e.pdf

Belser P (2005) Forced labour and human trafficking: estimating the profits. International Labour Organization, https://digitalcommons.ilr.cornell.edu/cgi/viewcontent.cgi?article=1016&context=forcedlabor

Benjamin P (2010) *Trafficking in Persons & Transit Countries: A Canada-U.S. Case Study in Global Perspective* No. 10- 05, 18 (April 2010). http://mbc.metropolis.net/assets/uploads/files/wp/2010/WP10-05.pdf

Beyer C (2018) An introduction to the basic beliefs of the Vodou (Voodoo) religion. ThoughtCo. (May 2, 2018), https://www.thoughtco.com/vodou-an-introduction-for-beginners-95712

Birth Registration and Armed Conflict, UNICEF (2007), https://www.unicef.org/protection/birth_registration_and_armed_conflict(1).pdf

Boot-Matthijssen M et al (2008) Trafficking in human beings—fifth report of the dutch national rapporteur. Dutch National Rapporteur 149 (Feb. 12, 2008), http://hrlibrary.umn.edu/research/Netherlands/Netherlands-Trafficking_Fifth%20Report%20Rapporteur.pdf

"*Breaking the Cycle of Fear", Witchcraft, Juju and Safeguarding Victims of Human Trafficking*, Africans Unite Against Child Abuse (AFRUCA) 6-7 (Mar. 9, 2011), http://www.afruca.org/wp-content/uploads/2013/07/Breaking-the-cycle-of-fear.pdf

*Breaking the Cycle of Vulnerability: Responding to the Health Needs of Trafficked Women in Eastern and Southern Africa*, Int Org. Migr. (2006), http://publications.iom.int/system/files/pdf/iom_breakingthecycleofvulnerability.pdf

Bureau of Int'l Labor Affairs, *Child Labor and Forced Labor Reports—Benin*, U.S. Dept. of Labor, http://www.dol.gov/ilab/reports/child-labor/benin.htm#ENREF_4 (accessed on August 20, 2021)

Bureau of International Labor Affairs, *Project to Reduce Child Labor in Burkina Faso*, U.S. Dept. of Labor, https://www.dol.gov/ilab/reports/child-labor/findings/2013TDA/burkinafaso.pdf (accessed on August 20, 2021a)

Bureau of International Labor Affairs, *Senegal*, U.S. Dept of Labor, http://www.dol.gov/ilab/reports/child-labor/findings/2011TDA/senegal.pdf (Accessed on August 20, 2021b)

*Burkina Faso, Statistics*, UNICEF, http://www.unicef.org/infobycountry/burkinafaso_statistics.html#117 (accessed on August, 2021)

Carter Sara A (2009) Taliban buying children for suicide bombers. Washington Times, (Jul. 2, 2009), http://www.washingtontimes.com/news/2009/jul/02/taliban-buying-children-to-serve-as-suicide-bomber/?page=all

Caselli G, Vallin J, Wunsch G (2005) Demography analysis and synthesis: a treatise in population. Academic Press, p 361

Casentini G (2015) Combating child trafficking in the Cocoa Industry and other vulnerable sectors in Ghana and Côte d'Ivoire. Human Dignity Foundation (Jul. 2015), https://www.human-dignity-foundation.org/wp-content/uploads/2016/04/InterPol-AKOMA-Final-assessment-report-Casentini.pdf

Caulfield P (2011) Police in Nigeria Free 32 pregnant teens from "Baby Factory": newborns sold into labour, sex markets. Daily News (Jun. 2, 2011), http://www.nydailynews.com/news/world/police-nigeria-free-32-pregnant-teens-baby-factorynewborns-sold-labour-sex-markets-article-1.127079#ixzz2VH1sr4f1

Charrière F, Frésia M (2008) *West Africa as a Migration and Protection Area*, UNHCR 9-10 (Nov. 2008), http://www.unhcr.org/49e479c311.pdf

Cherti M, Pennington J, Grant P (2013) Beyond borders: human trafficking from Nigeria to the UK. Inst Public Policy Res (IPPR) 24 (Jan. 2013), http://www.ippr.org/files/images/media/files/publication/2013/01/nigeria-trafficking_Jan2013_10189.pdf?noredirect=1

Chijioke J (2017) Lawyer reveals how 40 Warri Girls were trafficked to Burkina Faso as Sex Slaves. Daily Post (Jul. 18, 2017). http://dailypost.ng/2017/07/18/lawyer-reveals-40-warri-girls-trafficked-burkina-faso-sex-slaves/

*Child Labour in Gold Mining*, Int'l Labour Org. (ILO), http://www.ilo.org/ipec/areas/Miningandquarrying/MoreaboutCLinmining/lang%2D%2Den/index.htm (accessed on August 20, 2021)

*Child Labour UNICEF Nigeria,* UNICEF (2006), https://www.unicef.org/wcaro/WCARO_Nigeria_Factsheets_ChildLabour.pdf)

*Child Protection*, UNICEF, http://www.unicef.org/wcaro/english/overview_6592.html (accessed August 20, 2018)

Child Soldiers Global Report 2004, Child Soldiers 22, https://www.child-soldiers.org/Handlers/Download.ashx?IDMF=c5f157d3-4b56-457c-a2d8-31601ffc1b9e

Child Trafficking in Sierra Leone 2005, UNICEF 89, http://lastradainternational.org/lsidocs/244%20Child%20Trafficking%20in%20Sierra%20Leone%20(UNICEF).pdf

*Child Trafficking in West Africa: Policy Responses*, United Nations Children's Fund (UNICEF) 3 (Apr. 2002), http://www.unicef-irc.org/publications/pdf/insight7.pdf

Cockayne J, Walker S (2016) Fighting human trafficking in conflict. United Nations University, https://collections.unu.edu/eserv/UNU:5780/UNUReport_Pages.pdf

Cohen J (2003) Borderline Slavery—child trafficking in Togo. Human Rights Watch 15:8, 19, (Available at: http://www.hrw.org/sites/default/files/reports/togo0403.pdf)

Cohen J (2003) Borderline Slavery—child trafficking in Togo. Human Rights Watch 15:8, 20, (available at: http://www.hrw.org/sites/default/files/reports/togo0403.pdf)

*Combating Child Trafficking in West and Central Africa.* ILO World of Work 39:1, 6 (Jun. 2001)

*Combating Forced Labour and Trafficking in Africa*, ILO 12 (Nov. 19, 2013), http://www.ilo.org/wcmsp5/groups/public/%2D%2D-africa/documents/meetingdocument/wcms_229620.pdf

*Combating Trade Based Money Laundering: Rethinking the Approach*, Bankers Association for Finance and Trade (BAFT) 8 (Aug. 2017), http://baft.org/docs/default-source/marketing-documents/baft17_tmbl_paper.pdf?sfvrsn=2

*Combating Trafficking in Children for Labour Exploitation in West and Central Africa: Synthesis Report*, ILO 3-4 (Dec. 1, 2001), http://www.ilo.org/ipec/Informationresources/WCMS_IPEC_PUB_776/lang%2D%2Den/index.htm

*Conclusion Observations of the Committee on the Rights of the Child: Burkina Faso*, U.N. Comm. Rts. of the Child (UNCRC) 48 (Jan. 2010), https://www.crin.org/en/library/publications/burkina-faso-persistent-violations-childrens-rights.

Constantinou A et al (2015a) Deliverable D2.1: Report on the Relevant Aspects of the Trafficking Act (Geographical Routes and Modus Operandi) and on its Possible Evolutions in Response to Law Enforcement. Trafficking as A Criminal Enterprise (TRACE) 41 (Feb. 27, 2015), http://trace-project.eu/wp-content/uploads/2015/03/TRACE-D2.1_FINAL.pdf

Constantinou A et al (2015b) Report on the Relevant Aspects of the Trafficking Act (Geographical Routes and Modus Operandi) and on its Possible Evolutions in Response to Law Enforcement. Trafficking as A Criminal Enterprise (TRACE) 49 (Feb. 27, 2015), http://trace-project.eu/wp-content/uploads/2015/03/TRACE-D2.1_FINAL.pdf

Convention on Consent to Marriage, Minimum Age for Marriage, and Registration of Marriages, 32 U.N.T.S. 231 (Nov. 7, 1962)

Convention on the Elimination of Discrimination against Women (CEDAW), *Country Reports*, U.N. Women (Dec. 28, 2007), http://www.un.org/womenwatch/daw/cedaw/reports.htm

Convention on the Reduction of Statelessness arts 1-6, 989 U.N.T.S. 175, *entered into force* Dec. 13, 1975

Convention on the Rights of Persons with Disabilities and Optional Protocol art. 1, 2515 U.N.T.S. 3 (Dec. 13, 2006)

Convention on the Rights of the Child art. 7(1), Nov. 20, 1989, 1577 U.N.T.S. 3

Convention on the Rights of the Child art. 7(1), Nov. 20, 1989, 1577 U.N.T.S. 3, at General Comment No. 9, ¶ 1

Coomaraswamy R (Special Rapporteur on Violence Against Women), *Integration of the Human Rights of Women and the Gender Perspective of Violence Against Women*, U.N. Doc. E/CN.4/2002/83 (Jan. 31, 2002)

*Côte d'Ivoire/Nigeria: Combat Trafficking for Prostitution*, Human Rts Watch (Aug. 26, 2010), http://www.hrw.org/news/2010/08/26/c-te-d-ivoirenigeria-combat-trafficking-prostitution

Council of Europe Convention on Action against Trafficking in Human Beings (2012) Counter Trafficking and Assistance to Vulnerable Migrants' Annual Report of Activities 2011. Int Org Migr (ILO) p 59, at https://www.iom.int/files/live/sites/iom/files/What-We-Do/docs/Annual_Report_2011_Counter_Trafficking.pdf

*Counter-Trafficking Baseline Assessment*, FMM West Africa 6 (Aug. 2017), http://rodakar.iom.int/oimsenegal/sites/default/files/reports/fmm%20west%20africa%20-%20counter%20traffcking.pdf

*Country report for the Task force on Violence against Women*, Inter-Agency Network on Women and Gender Equality (IANWGE) (Nov. 3, 2010), http://www.un.org/womenwatch/ianwge/taskforces/tf_vaw.htm

Country Reports on Human Rights Practices in Togo for 2001, U.S. Dept. of State, http://www.state.gov/j/drl/rls/hrrpt/2001/af/8408.htm

Daffé L (2012) Gold Rush in Kédougou, Senegal: protecting migrants and local communities. Int Org Migr. (Mar. 11 2012), https://www.iom.int/jahia/webdav/shared/shared/mainsite/projects/showcase_pdf/Global-Eye-Issue11-Mar2012.pdf

Dambia FX, Nare L (1999) Proverbes Mossi, Une Sélection 318. Abidjan

Danso SO (2013) The human being as a commodity: responding to the trafficking and trading of persons in West Africa. Kofi Annan Peacekeeping Training Centre. http://www.kaiptc.org/kaiptc-publication/the-human-being-as-a-commodity-responding-to-the-trafficking-and-trading-of-persons-in-west-africa

Davies P (Mar. 2012) An evidence assessment of the routes of human trafficking into the UK. Home Office (UK) (Mar. 2012), https://www.gov.uk/government/uploads/system/uploads/attachment_data/file/115923/occ103.pdf

Davinder K (2013) Africa's disabled cursed by apathy and abuse. AlJazeera, http://www.aljazeera.com/indepth/features/2013/09/2013922121017135639.html

de Haas H (2008) Irregular migration from West Africa to the Maghreb and the European Union: an overview of recent trends. IOM, p 32. http://publications.iom.int/system/files/pdf/mrs-32_en.pdf

Declaration of Political Principles art. 25, ECOWAS A/DCL 1/7/91

Delap E (2009) Begging for change: research findings and recommendations on forced child begging in Albania/Greece, India and Senegal. Anti-Slavery Int'l 9, https://ec.europa.eu/anti-trafficking/sites/antitrafficking/files/anti-slavery_international_2009_-_begging_for_change_en_1.pdf

Department of Labor, 2012 Benin, at http://www.dol.gov/ilab/reports/child-labor/findings/2012TDA/benin.pdf

Derby Nana C (2012) Are the barrels empty? Are the children any safer?' Child domestic labor and servitude in Ghana. In: Ensor MO (ed) African childhood: education, development, peacebuilding, and the youngest continent. Palgrave McMillan, p 23

Dogbadzi J. Speak truth to power: sex slavery. Washington Post, http://www.washingtonpost.com/wp-srv/photo/onassignment/truth/st/09.htm (accessed on August 20, 2021)

*Dimskal Shipping Co SA v. International Transport Workers Federation* [1992], 2 AC 152, 165 (U.K.)

Ebobrah S (2010) Critical issues in the human rights mandate of the ECOWAS Court of Justice. J Afr Law 54:1

Economic and Social Council Res. 608 (XXI), at art. 1(d) (April 30, 1957)

Economic Comm. of W. Afr. St. [ECOWAS], Protocol relating to the Definition of Community Citizen art. 1, ECOWAS Doc. A/P.3/5/82 (May 29, 1982)

ECOWAS and the Dynamics of Conflict and Peace-Building (eds., Stella Amadi, Dauda Garuba, and Thomas Jaye, CODESRIA 2011)

*ECOWAS Regional Action Plan for the Elimination of Child Labour Especially the Worst Forms*, ILO, http://www.ilo.org/wcmsp5/groups/public/%2D%2D-africa/documents/publication/wcms_227737.pdf (accessed on August 20, 2021)

ECOWAS — Basic Information, History, Economic Community of West African States (ECOWAS)., http://www.ecowas.int (accessed August 1, 2021)

ECOWAS—Revised Treaty art. 2, 2015., http://www.ecowas.int/wp-content/uploads/2015/01/Revised-treaty.pdf

Edwards A (2008) Traffic in human beings: at the intersection of criminal justice, human rights, asylum/migration and labor. Denv J Int Law Policy 36:1, 14

Elliot J (2014) The role of consent in human trafficking. Routledge, pp 123–128

*Ending Child Labour in Domestic Work and Protecting Young Workers from Abusive Working Conditions*, Int'l Labour Org. 28 (Jun. 12, 2013), http://www.ilo.org/ipec/Informationresources/WCMS_207656/lang%2D%2Den/index.htm

*Ensuring Human Rights Protection in Countries of Destination: Breaking the Cycle of Trading*, OSCE 13 (Sept. 23, 2004), https://www.osce.org/odihr/16201?download=true

Everts D (2003) Human trafficking: the ruthless trade in human misery. Brown J World Aff 10:149–158

*Every Child's Birth Right: Inequities and Trends in Birth Registration*, UNICEF 6 (Dec. 11, 2013), https://www.unicef.org/publications/files/Birth_Registration_11_Dec_13.pdf

*Examining the UK's Criminal Justice—Response to Trafficking*, Anti-Slavery (June 2013), http://www.antislavery.org/includes/documents/cm_docs/2013/i/inthedock_final_small_file.pdf

Farr K (2005) Sex trafficking: the global market in women and children. Worth Publishers

Fayomi OO (2009) Women, poverty and trafficking: a contextual exposition of the Nigerian situation. J Manage Soc Sci 5:65, 67. http://eprints.covenantuniversity.edu.ng/3970/1/Dr.%20Fayomi%20O.%20O.%204.pdf

*Federal Republic of Nigeria v. Favour Anware Okwuede*, Nigeria Court of High Justice, Charge No. FHC.ASB.24C.09, Judgment (2009)

Findings on the Worst Forms of Child Labor 2014, U.S. Dept. of Labor, http://www.dol.gov/ilab/reports/child-labor/findings/2014TDA/2014TDA.pdf

Fitzgibbon K (2003) Modern-day slavery? The scope of trafficking in persons in Africa. Afr Sec Rev 12:81, 84

Fong J (2004) Literature review on trafficking in West and East Africa. Bangkok, p 1

G.A. Res. 1763 A (XVII), Nov. 7, 1962

G.A. Res. 55/25 at art. 2 (a) (November 15, 2002)

G.A. Res. 55/25 at art. 3 (November 15, 2000)

Gallagher Anne T (2010) The international law of human trafficking. Cambridge University Press, p 24

Galli TV, Schauer EJ, Wheaton EM (2010) Economics of human trafficking. Int Migrat 48(114):115–136. available at: https://www.amherst.edu/media/view/247221/original/Economics+of+Human+Trafficking.pdf

Gasparini L, Lustig N (2011) The rise and fall of income inequality in Latin America. Society for the Study of Economic Inequality (Aug. 2011), http://www.ecineq.org/milano/WP/ECINEQ2011-213.pdf

Gbadamosi Olaide A (2006) Esq., International perspectives and Nigerian laws on human trafficking. Network for Justice and Democracy, http://www.justiceanddemocracy.org/Trffic%20Bk.pdf

*Global Appeal—West Africa*, UNHCR (2015), http://www.unhcr.org/5461e602b.html

*Global Estimate of Forced Labour—Executive Summary*, ILO (2012), http://www.ilo.org/wcmsp5/groups/public/%2D%2D-ed_norm/%2D%2D-declaration/documents/publication/wcms_181953.pdf

*Global Monitoring Status of Action against Commercial Sexual Exploitation of Children*, Ghana, ECPAT, 12 (2014a). https://www.ecpat.org/wp-content/uploads/legacy/A4A2011_AF_GHANA_FINAL2.pdf

Global Monitoring Status of Action against Commercial Sexual Exploitation of Children, Ghana, ECPAT, 13 (2014b). https://www.ecpat.org/wp-content/uploads/legacy/A4A2011_AF_GHANA_FINAL2.pdf

Global Report on Trafficking in Persons 2014, UNODC 56, http://www.unodc.org/res/cld/bibliography/global-report-on-trafficking-in-persons_html/GLOTIP_2014_full_report.pdf

*Global Study on Sexual Exploitation of Children in Travel and Tourism Country*, Ghana 2015, Ghana NGOs Coalition on the Rights of the Child (GNCRC) 2015., https://ssa.riselearningnetwork.org/wp-content/uploads/sites/5/2017/01/SECTT-GHANA.pdf

*Good Practice Review: Extending Social Security Coverage in Africa,* International Social Security Association, Geneva, 2009; Insurance Scheme brings Relief to Ghana's Informal Sector. *Ghana Business News*, 2008

Gueye D (2001) Small-Scale mining in Burkina Faso, mining. Miner Sustain Dev (MMSD) 73:25. http://pubs.iied.org/pdfs/G00717.pdf

Gulnara Shahinian (Report of the Special Rapporteur on Contemporary Forms of Slavery, including its Causes and Consequences), *Thematic Report on Servile Marriage*, ¶ 14, U.N. Doc. A/HRC/21/41 (Jul. 10 2012)

Hahn Hans P, Kastner K (2012) Polygamous family life in senegal. In: Urban life-worlds in motion: African perspectives. Global Studies, pp 80–81

*Haiti, Le calvaire des "Restaveks"*, Courrier Int'l (Feb. 24, 2011), https://www.courrierinternational.com/article/2011/02/24/le-calvaire-silencieux-des-restaveks

*Haiti—J'aime Nettoye*: *L'enfer des Enfants Domestiques Habitués à Obéir*, UNICEF (2009). http://www.unicef.fr/en/node/734>

*Hard to See, Harder to Count—Survey Guidelines to Estimate Forced Labour of Adults and Children*, ILO 17 (Jun. 1, 2012), http://ilo.org/global/topics/forced-labour/publications/WCMS_182096/lang%2D%2Den/index.htm

*Harder to See, Harder to Count: Survey Guidelines to Estimate Forced Labour of Adults and Children*, ILO 19 (2012), http://www.ilo.org/wcmsp5/groups/public/%2D%2D-ed_norm/%2D%2D-declaration/documents/publication/wcms_182096.pdf

Harrop EW (2012) Ties that bind: African Witchcraft and contemporary slavery. Liberty Humanity (Sept. 17, 2012), http://lastradainternational.org/lsidocs/Witchcraft%20and%20Trafficking%20in%20Africa.pdf

Hayase Y, Liaw K-L (1997) Factors on polygamy in sub-Saharan Africa: findings based on the demographic and health surveys. Dev Econ 3:293, 298

High Court of Justice (2007) *Between Hon. Attorney General of the Federation and Franca Edith Asiboja*, 11, Charge No. B/31C/2005 (Nigeria) (available at: https://www.unodc.org/res/cld/case-law/nga/2007/_hon__attorney_general_of_the_federation_and_franca_edith_asiboja_charge_no._b31c2005.html/Hon._Attorney_General_of_the_Federation_and_Franca_Edith_Asiboja_Charge_No._B.31C.2005.pdf)

High Court of Justice, *Between A.G. Federation and Toyin Ogbebor*, Suit No. NCT/140/06 (Nigeria) (available at: https://www.unodc.org/res/cld/case-law/nga/2008/attorney_general_of_the_federation_and_toyin_ogbebor_suit_no__nct14006.html/Attorney_General_of_the_Federation_and_Toyin_Ogbebor_Suit_No._NCT.140.06.pdf)

High Court of Justice, *Between Attorney-General of the Federation and Samuel E.*, Suit No. B/20C/2005 (Nigeria) (available at: https://www.unodc.org/res/cld/case-law/nga/2008/attorney_general_of_the_federation_and_samuel_emwirovbankhoe_suit_no__b20c2005_.html/Attorney_General_of_the_Federation_and_Samuel_Emwirovbankhoe_Suit_No._B.20C.2005.pdf)

High Court of South Africa (2014) *Nvumeleni Jezile v. the State*, High Court Case No: A 127/2014 (S. Afr.) (available at: https://www.unodc.org/res/cld/case-law-doc/traffickingpersonscrimetype/zaf/2015/jezile_v__s_and_others_a_1272014_2015_zawchc_html/2015.03.23_Jezile_v_S.pdf

*How to Prevent Human Trafficking for Domestic Servitude in Diplomatic Households and Protect Private Domestic Workers*, Office of the Special Representative and Coordinator for Combating Trafficking in Human Beings (OSCE) (2014), http://www.osce.org/handbook/domesticservitude?download=true

Human Development Index for the Year 2013, to *List of African countries by Human Development Index*, Wikipedia, https://en.wikipedia.org/wiki/List_of_African_countries_by_Human_Development_Index (2014)

*Human Development Report 2014: Sustaining Human Progress: Reducing Vulnerabilities and Building Resilience*, United Nations Development Programme (UNDP) 164–167 (2014), http://hdr.undp.org/sites/default/files/hdr14-report-en-1.pdf

*Human Trafficking & Modern-Day Slavery (Nigeria)*, GVNET, http://gvnet.com/humantrafficking/Nigeria.htm (accessed on August 18, 2021)

*Human Trafficking and Forced Labour Exploitation: Guidance for Legislation and Law Enforcement*, ILO 25 (Apr. 1, 2005), http://digitalcommons.ilr.cornell.edu/cgi/viewcontent.cgi?article=1021&context=forcedlabor

*Human Trafficking for Labour Exploitation/Forced and Bonded Labour Identification—Prevention—Prosecution of Offenders, Justice for Victims,* Office of the Special Representative and Coordinator for Combating Trafficking in Human Beings (OSCE) (Nov. 7, 2005), http://www.osce.org/cthb/31923?download=true

Human Trafficking in 2013—Nigeria-France, U.S. Dept. of State, http://www.state.gov/j/tip/rls/tiprpt/2013/210546.htm

*Human Trafficking in Nigeria: Root Causes and Recommendations*, United Nations Educational, Scientific, and Cultural Organization (UNESCO) 11 (2006), http://unesdoc.unesco.org/images/0014/001478/147844e.pdf

*Human Trafficking Indicators*, U.N. Office on Drugs & Crim., https://www.unodc.org/pdf/HT_indicators_E_LOWRES.pdf (accessed on August 20, 2021)

Human Trafficking is a Modern Day Form of Slavery, IOM 8, https://ec.europa.eu/anti-trafficking/sites/antitrafficking/files/train_the_trainers_manual_1.pdf (accessed on August 13, 2021)

*Human Trafficking through the Central Mediterranean Route: Data, Stories and Information Collected by the International Organization for Migration*, U.N. Migr. Agency 8–9 (2017). https://italy.iom.int/sites/default/files/news-documents/IOMReport_Trafficking.pdf

*Human Trafficking: An Overview*, UN.GIFT 18 (2008), http://www.ungift.org/doc/knowledgehub/resource-centre/GIFT_Human_Trafficking_An_Overview_2008.pdf

*Human Trafficking: Issues Beyond Criminalization*, Vatican 478–479 (2016), https://dyhyjqmcimsyl.cloudfront.net/assets/files/6179/vatican-humantrafficking.pdf

ILO, Forced Labor Convention art. 2, 39 UNTS 55 (May 1, 1932)

*ILO Indicators of Forced Labour*, ILO, http://www.ilo.org/wcmsp5/groups/public/@ed_norm/@declaration/documents/publication/wcms_203832.pdf (accessed on Agust 17, 2021)

*ILO says that Forced Labor Generates Annual Profits of US$ 150 Billion*, ILO (May 20, 2014), http://www.ilo.org/global/about-the-ilo/newsroom/news/WCMS_243201/lang%2D%2Den/index.htm

*ILO: Eradication of forced labour, General Survey concerning the Forced Labour Convention, 1930 (No. 29), and the Abolition of Forced Labour Convention, 1957* (No. 105), ILO (2007), http://www.ilo.org/wcmsp5/groups/public/%2D%2D-ed_norm/%2D%2D-relconf/documents/meetingdocument/wcms_089199.pdf

*Implementation of Decent Work Agenda in West Africa*, ILO 23 (May 2013), http://www.ilo.org/wcmsp5/groups/public/%2D%2D-africa/%2D%2D-ro-addis_ababa/documents/publication/wcms_235308.pdf

Innocenti Insight, *Trafficking in Human Beings, especially Women and Children, in Africa*. UNICEF 7 (Sept. 2003), http://www.unicef-irc.org/publications/pdf/insight9e.pdf

Int'l Programme on the Elimination of Child Labour (IPEC), *Child Labour and Domestic Work*, ILO, http://ilo.org/ipec/areas/Childdomesticlabour/lang%2D%2Den/index.htm (accessed on August 5, 2021)

*Integrated Social Protection Systems – Enhancing Equity for Children*, UNICEF 4 (Feb. 20, 2012), https://www.unicef.org/socialpolicy/files/Presentation_Jennifer_Yablonski_UNICEF__20_Feb_2012.pdf

International Covenant on Civil and Political Rights art 24(2), Dec.16, 999 U.N.T.S. 17 (1967)

International Labour Organization (ILO), Domestic Workers Convention, art. 1 Doc. C189, No. 11 (2011)

*International Migration Law: Glossary on Migration*, IOM 42 (2004), http://www.iomvienna.at/sites/default/files/IML_1_EN.pdf

*Introduction to Money-Laundering*, UNODC (2015), https://www.unodc.org/unodc/en/money-laundering/introduction.html (accessed on August 24, 2021)

Jackson SH (2007) Marriages of convenience: international marriage brokers, "Mail-Order Brides", and domestic servitude. Univ Toledo Law Rev 38:895

Jacquemin MY (2004) Children's domestic work in Abidjan, Côte d'Ivoire: the 'Petit Bonnes' have the floor. Inst Res Dev 11:383–397

*J'aime Nettoyer: L'enfer des Enfants Domestiques Habitués à Obéir*, UNICEF France (Dec. 28, 2015), https://www.unicef.fr/article/j-aime-nettoyer-l-enfer-des-enfants-domestiques-habitues-obeir

*Joint Action to Tackle West African Human Trafficking Network*, Europol (Jun. 12, 2014), https://www.europol.europa.eu/content/joint-action-tackle-west-african-human-trafficking-networks-0

*Juju magic 'more controlling than chains', says Harvard expert*, BBC News (Oct. 14, 2014), http://www.bbc.com/news/uk-wales-29599158

Justice of the High Court, *The Republic v. Rauf Ibrahim et al.*, Suit No. D2/447/15 [Ghana]

Kanth Amod K (2004) Street Children and Homelessness. E-Journal of the International Child and Youth Care Network (CYC-Net) (Sept. 2004), http://www.cyc-net.org/cyc-online/cycol-0904-Homelessness.html

Keo C (2013) Human trafficking in Cambodia (Routledge Contemporary Southeast Asia Series). Routledge, p 65

Kim J (2011) Prosecuting Human Trafficking as a Crime Against Humanity (unpublished J.D. thesis, Columbia Law School) p 9 (on file with Columbia Law School library system) (available at: http://blogs.law.columbia.edu/gslonline/files/2011/02/Jane-Kim_GSL_Prosecuting-Human-Trafficking-as-a-Crime-Against-Humanity-Under-the-Rome-Statute-2011.pdf)

Kippenberg J (2007) Bottom of the ladder: exploitation and abuse of girl domestic workers in Guinea. Human Rights Watch 33 (available at: https://www.hrw.org/report/2007/06/15/bottom-ladder/exploitation-and-abuse-girl-domestic-workers-guinea)

Konseiga A (2005) New Patterns in the human migration in West Africa, Center for development research. In: Lang P (ed) Regional integration beyond the traditional trade benefits: labor mobility contribution. Frankfurt am Main, 2005 [available at: https://www.zef.de/uploads/tx_zefportal/Publications/a127_New%20patterns%20in%20the%20Human%20migration%20in%20West%20Africa.pdf]

Kwame AR (2004) Human rights, gender and traditional practices: the Trokosi system in West Africa. In: Kalunta-Crumpton A, Agoni B (eds) Pan-African issues in crime and justice. Routledge

*La Souffrance des "Restaveks"*, Courrier Int'l (May 26, 2009), https://www.courrierinternational.com/breve/2009/05/26/la-souffrance-des-restaveks

Laczko F (2002) Human trafficking: the need for better data, migration policy. Institute (MPI) (Nov. 1, 2002), http://www.migrationpolicy.org/article/human-trafficking-need-better-data

Langer A, Levison D (2009) Child domestic servants – numbers and trends. Minnesota Population Center, p 2. https://pop.umn.edu/sites/pop.umn.edu/files/wp-2009-1.pdf; *see also Definition—Child Labour and Domestic Work*, ILO, http://www.ilo.org/ipec/areas/Childdomesticlabour/lang%2D%2Den/index.htm (accessed on August 20, 2021)

*Le Travail Domestique des Mineurs en France*, Comité Contre l'Esclavage Moderne (CCEM) 17 (2009), http://www.esclavagemoderne.org/media/Etude-Travail-domestique-des-mineurs-2.pdf

Legislative Guides for the Implementation of the United Nations Convention against Transnational Organized Crime and the Protocol Thereto, Part IV, Chapter II, ¶25

Legislative Guides for the Implementation of the United Nations Convention against Transnational Organized Crime and the Protocol Thereto, UNODC 2, ¶ 23 (2004), https://www.unodc.org/pdf/crime/legislative_guides/Legislative%20guides_Full%20version.pdf.

*Leveraging Anti-Money Laundering Regimes to Combat Trafficking in Human Beings*, Organization for Security and Co-operation in Europe (OSCE) (2014), https://www.osce.org/secretariat/121125?download=true

List of Coups d'état and Coup Attempts by Country, Wikipedia, https://en.wikipedia.org/wiki/List_of_coups_d%27%C3%A9tat_and_coup_attempts_by_country

Loungou S (2011) Children's Traffic, an Aspect of West African Migration in Gabon. Cahier d'Outre-Mer, p 256 (available at: http://com.revues.org/6389)

Lupton A (2016) Woman jailed for 22 years for trafficking Nigerian girls for sex trade. Reuters (Aug. 4, 2016), http://www.reuters.com/article/us-britain-trafficking-witchcraft/woman-jailed-for-22-years-for-trafficking-nigerian-girls-for-sex-trade-idUSKCN10F21A

M'Jid NM (2008) Sexual abuse and exploitation of children in West and Central Africa. UNICEF 6, https://www.unicef.org/wcaro/english/ESEWCAROFinalReport_EN_corrige.pdf

Madike I (2013) The ABC of Baby Factories (National Mirror Investigation). CKN Nigeria (May 26, 2013), http://www.cknnigeria.com/2013/05/the-abc-of-baby-factories-national.html; *Nigeria "Baby Factory" raided in Imo State*, BBC (May 10, 2013), http://www.bbc.co.uk/news/world-africa-22484318

*Mapping Early Marriage in West Africa: A scan of trends, interventions, what works, best practices and the way forward*, Girls Not Brides 7 (Sept. 2013), http://www.girlsnotbrides.org/wp-content/uploads/2013/10/Ford-Foundation-CM-West-Africa-2013_09.pdf

Manby B (2015) Nationality, migration and statelessness in West Africa. U.N. Refugee Agency (UNHCR) pp 79–80, http://www.unhcr.org/ecowas2015/Nationality-Migration-and-Statelessness-in-West-Africa-REPORT-EN.pdf

*Marrying Too Young: End Child Marriage*, United Nations Population Fund (UNPF) (2012), https://www.unfpa.org/sites/default/files/pub-pdf/MarryingTooYoung.pdf

*Measures to Combat Trafficking in Human Beings in Benin, Nigeria, and Togo*, UNODC 65 (2006), https://www.unodc.org/documents/human-trafficking/ht_research_report_nigeria.pdf

Melnick L (2010) Gasp! The benefits of child labor in the developing world. Triple Pundit (Dec. 5, 2010), http://www.triplepundit.com/2010/12/gasp-benefits-child-labor-developing-world

*Migrants Caught In Crisis: The IOM Experience in Libya*, International Organization of Migration (IOM) 5 (2012), http://publications.iom.int/system/files/pdf/migrationcaughtincrisis_forweb.pdf
Moens B (2004) Study on the practice of trafficking in persons in senegal. U.S. Agency for Int'l Development (USAID) 9 (Sept. 2004), https://www.mensenhandelweb.nl/system/files/documents/09%20dec%202014/moens_2004_study_practice_trafficking_senegal_4.pdf
*Money Laundering Risks Arising from Trafficking in Human Beings and Smuggling of Migrants*, Financial Action Taskforce (FATF) (Jul. 2011), 12 http://www.fatf-gafi.org/media/fatf/documents/reports/Trafficking%20in%20Human%20Beings%20and%20Smuggling%20of%20Migrants.pdf
Moshi Humphrey PB (2007) Fighting money laundering: the challenges in Africa. Inst Sec Stud 2 (Oct. 2007), https://issafrica.s3.amazonaws.com/site/uploads/Paper152.pdf
Moshi Humphrey PB (2012) Implications of cash-dominated transactions for money laundering. Inst Sec Stud 3 (Oct. 19, 2012), https://issafrica.s3.amazonaws.com/site/uploads/SitRep2012Oct.pdf
Msuya HN (2017) Tradition and culture in Africa: practices that facilitate trafficking of women and children. Dignity J Sex Exploit Viol 2:25 (available at: https://digitalcommons.uri.edu/cgi/viewcontent.cgi?article=1007&context=dignity)
Murray GF, Smucker GR (2004) The uses of children: a study of trafficking in haitian children. USAID 35–36, https://pdf.usaid.gov/pdf_docs/Pnadf061.pdf
Nagle Luz E, Owasanoye B (2016) Fearing the dark: the use of witchcraft to control human trafficking victims and sustain vulnerability. South West Law Rev 45 (available at: http://www.swlaw.edu/sites/default/files/2017-04/5%20Fearing%20the%20Dar.pdf)
Nancy S-H (2015) Neo-cannibalism, organ theft, and military-biomedical necropolitics. EndSlavery, http://www.endslavery.va/content/endslavery/en/publications/acta_20/scheper_hughes_panel.pdf
Nancy S-H (2016) Organ trafficking during times of war and political conflict. International Affairs Forum, http://www.ia-forum.org/Files/HDSQLC.pdf
National Money Laundering Risk Assessment 2015, U.S. Dep't. of Treasury 4, http://www.treasury.gov/resource-center/terrorist-illicit-finance/Documents/National%20Money%20Laundering%20Risk%20Assessment%20%E2%80%93%2006-12-2015.pdf
*National Referral Mechanism Statistics- End of Year Summary 2018*, National Crime Agency (NCA) UK, (20 Mars 2019), file:///C:/Users/irie/Downloads/NCA%20-%20Stats%20End%20of%20Year%20Summary%202018%20(1).pdf
*Nations Hospitable to Organized Crime and Terrorism*, Int'l Org. Migr. 29, http://www.loc.gov/rr/frd/pdf-files/Nats_Hospitable.pdf (accessed on August 20, 2021)
Ndiaye N (2010) Labor migration, human trafficking and multinational corporations within the ECOWAS region: challenges and opportunities. In: Quayson A, Arhin A (eds) Labour migration, human trafficking and multinational corporations: the commodification of illicit flows. Routledge
*Nearly 400 Victims of Child Trafficking Rescued across Burkina Faso in INTERPOL-led Operation*, Interpol (Nov. 22, 2012), http://www.interpol.int/News-and-media/News/2012/PR096
*Nigeria*, Global Monitoring 13 (2011), http://www.ecpat.net/sites/default/files/A4A2011_AF_NIGERIA_FINAL.pdf
Nigeria Frees 16 in "Baby Factory" Raid, news24 (Jun. 20, 2013), http://www.news24.com/Africa/News/Nigeria-frees-16-in-baby-factory-raid-20130620
Nwauche ES (2009) Regional economic communities and human rights in West Africa and the African Arabic countries. In: Windhoek N (ed) Human Rights in Africa: legal perspectives in their protection and promotion. Macmillan Education, pp 319–347
Nwauche ES (2011) The ECOWAS community court of justice and the horizontal application of human rights. Afr Human Rights Law J 13:30
*O.O.O. et al. v Commissioner of Police for the Metropolis* [2011], EWHC 1246 (QB) (dealing with transnational trafficking for domestic servitude) (available at: https://ec.europa.eu/anti-

trafficking/sites/antitrafficking/files/o.o.o._and_others_v_commissioner_of_police_for_the_metropolis_1.pdf
O'Neill Ann (2007) Stolen Kids Turn into Terrifying Mascots, CNN (Feb. 12, 2007), http://www.cnn.com/2007/WORLD/africa/02/12/child.soldiers
O'Neill-Richard A (2000) International Trafficking in Women to the United States: A Contemporary Manifestation of Slavery and Organised Crime. Center for the Study of Intelligence (CSI) 22 (Apr. 2000), https://www.cia.gov/library/center-for-the-study-of-intelligence/csi-publications/books-and-monographs/trafficking.pdf
Obokata OT (2019) Human Trafficking in Africa. In: Jalloh CC et al (eds) The African Court of Justice and Human and Peoples' rights in context. Cambridge University Press, p 538
Office of the U.N. High Comm. for Human Rts, Report on Birth registration and the right of everyone to recognition everywhere as a person before the law, ¶ 4, U.N. Doc. A/HRC/27/22, (June 2014)
Office to Monitor and Combat Trafficking in Persons, *Tier Placements—Trafficking in Persons Report 2014*, U.S. Dept. of State, http://www.state.gov/j/tip/rls/tiprpt/2014/226649.htm
Okogbule NS (2013) Combating the "New Slavery" in Nigeria: an appraisal of legal and policy responses to human trafficking. J Afr Law 57
Okyere S (2017) A critique of the ghana-centric child trafficking discourse. Anti-Traff Rev:92–105
*Outside the Circle*, Plan Int'l 8 (Sept. 2, 2013), https://plan-international.org/publications/outside-circle#download-options
Ovey C, White Robin CA (2006) Jacobs &white: the European convention on human rights. OUP, Oxford
Peachey P (2012) Jailed: the Slave Trader in Britain who Sold Women around Europe for Sex under the spell of his 'Juju' Witchcraft. The Independent (Oct. 26, 2012), www.independent.co.uk/news/uk/crime/jailed-the-slave-trader-in-britain-whosold-women-around-europe-for-sex-under-the-spell-of-his-juju-witchcraft-8228574.html
Pearson E (2005) The mekong challenge human trafficking: redefining demand. International Labour Organization (ILO), http://un-act.org/publication/view/the-mekong-challenge-human-trafficking-redefining-demand/
Peel E (2007) The law of contract. Sweet & Maxwell, p 567
*Permanent Secretariat Plan for National Action for Children—Burkina Faso*, UNICEF 48 (Dec. 2006), https://www.unicef.org/french/worldfitforchildren/files/Burkina_Faso_WFFC5_Report.pdf
Perrin B, John W, Philip R (2012) Human trafficking: exploring the international nature, concerns, and complexities. CRC Press, p 25
*Plan of Action on Gender and Trade 2010-2020*, ECOWAS 7, http://www.ccdg.ecowas.int/wp-content/uploads/Plan-of-Action_Gender-and-Trade.pdf (accessed on August 20, 2021)
*PO (Nigeria) v. Secretary of State for the Home Department* [2011] 132 EWCA 22 (U.K.)
*Precious Metal, Cheap Labor: Child Labor and Corporate Responsibility in Ghana's Artisanal Gold Mines*, HRW (Jun. 10, 2015), https://www.hrw.org/report/2015/06/10/precious-metal-cheap-labor/child-labor-and-corporate-responsibility-ghanas
Prina F (2003) Trafficking of Nigerian girls to Italy. Trade and exploitation of minors and young Nigerian women for prostitution in Italy. United Nations Interregional Crime and Justice Research Institute (UNICRI), p 30. http://www.unicri.it/topics/trafficking_exploitation/archive/women/nigeria_1/research/rr_prina_eng.pdf
*Profile: Zoe's Ark*, BBC News (Oct. 29 2007), http://news.bbc.co.uk/2/hi/europe/7067374.stm
*Profits and Poverty: The Economics of Forced Labour*, ILO (May 2014), http://www.ilo.org/global/topics/forced-labour/publications/WCMS_243391/lang%2D%2Den/index.htm
Qerimi B (2012) Countering strategies against transnational organized crime: the danger we face multifaceted challenges and unprecedented. LAP LAMBERT Academic Publishing
*Rapid Situation Assessment Report—Street Children of Cairo & Alexandria, including the Children's Drug Abuse and Health/Nutritional Status* UNODC 7 (Jun. 2001), https://www.unodc.org/pdf/youthnet/egypt_street_children_report.pdf

Reals T (2011) 32 Teens Freed in Nigeria "Baby Factory" Raid. CBS News (Jun. 2, 2011), http://www.cbsnews.com/8301-503543_162-20068184-503543.html

*Regional Conference on Statelessness in ECOWAS Member States*, UNHCR 2 (Feb. 23, 2015), http://www.unhcr.org/ecowas2015/Background-Agenda-Detailed-ENG.pdf

Report of the Special Rapporteur on the Human Rights Aspects of the Victims of Trafficking in Persons, especially Women and Children), *Implementation of General Assembly Resolution 60/251 of March 15 2006 entitled "Human Rights Council*, ¶ 26, U.N. Doc. A/HRC/4/23, (Jan. 24, 2007) (by Huda Sigma).

Report of the Special Rapporteur on Trafficking in Persons, especially Women and Children), *Mission to Italy*, ¶ 9 U.N. Doc. A/HRC/26/37/Add.4 (Apr. 1, 2011) (by Joy Ngozi Ezelio)

*Report of the Special Rapporteur on trafficking in persons, especially women and children*, ¶ 9, U.N. Doc. A/HRC/29/38 (March 2015) (by Maria Grazia Giammarinaro)

Report of the Special Rapporteur Trafficking in Persons, especially Women and Children, *Mission to Gabon*, ¶ 10, U.N. Doc. A/HRC/23/48/Add.2 (Mar. 18, 2013) (by Joy Ngozi Ezelio)

*Report on Human Trafficking Issues to the 2015 Winter Meeting of the OSCE Parliamentary Assembly*, OSCE 8 (Feb. 18, 2015), https://www.oscepa.org/documents/all-documents/winter-meetings/2015-vienna/reports-3/2740-2015-sr-on-human-trafficking-issues-report-eng/file

*Review of the Norwegian Ministry of Foreign Affairs Portfolio on Human Trafficking*, NORAD (Sept. 2009), http://www.norad.no/globalassets/import-2162015-80434-am/www.norad.no-ny/filarkiv/vedlegg-til-publikasjoner/review-of-the-norwegian-ministry-of-foreign-affairs-portfolio-on-human-trafficking.pdf

Ridde V et al (2012) Reducing the medical cost of deliveries in Burkina Faso is good for everyone, including the poor. PLoS One 7:3

*Risks and Methods of Money Laundering and Terrorist Financing*, UNODC, http://learningmatrixatcampus.co.in/COURSES_DATA/IMSContent/Anti%20Money%20Laundering%20Srilanka-Lesson3240/AMLSL/Files/PDF/Chapter_2.htm (accessed on August 24, 2021)

*Royal Bank of Scotland v. Etridge* [2002], 2 AC 773 (U.K.)

Sakulpitakphon P (2007) Confronting the commercial sexual exploitation of children in Africa. ECPAT Int 6 (Sept. 2007), http://www.ecpat.net/sites/default/files/confronting_csec_eng_0.pdf

Saul M (2009) Koranic schools and child labour in West Africa. In: Hindman HD (ed) The World of child labor: an historical and regional survey. ME Sharp, p 199

Sawadogo WR (2012) The challenges of transnational human trafficking in West Africa. Afr Stud Q 13:1

*Second Decade of Education for Africa*, UNESCO (2015), http://www.unesco.org/new/fileadmin/MULTIMEDIA/FIELD/Dakar/pdf/AU%20SECOND%20DECADE%20ON%20EDUCTAION%202006-2015.pdf

*Senegal: Boys in Many Quranic Schools Suffer Severe Abuse*, HRW (Apr. 15, 2010), https://www.hrw.org/news/2010/04/15/senegal-boys-many-quranic-schools-suffer-severe-abuse

Sessay A, Olayode K (2012) Regionalization and efforts to combat human trafficking in West Africa: the Nigerian experience. In: Challenging issues and accountability in Nigeria's public administration. AuthorHouse, p 74

Shelley L ( 2010) Human trafficking: a global perspective. Cambridge University Press, p 3

Shelley L (2014) Human smuggling and trafficking into Europe: a comparative perspective. Migr Policy Inst. (MPI), p 7, https://www.migrationpolicy.org/sites/default/files/publications/BadActors-ShelleyFINALWEB.pdf

Shitu S (2016) Entrepreneurship as a tool for mitigating baby factory: human trafficking in Nigeria. Int J Adv Res 4:224 (available at: http://www.journalijar.com/uploads/373_IJAR-9473.pdf)

Shu-Acquaye F (2012–2013) Human trafficking: trends in Africa. Gonzaga J Int Law 16:1, 4

*Siliadin v. France*, European Court of Human Rights, Application No. 73316/01, Judgment (2005)

*Slave-free Chocolate in the Making? The Worst Forms of Child Labour present in the cocoa sector of Ivory Coast and Ghana*, MLB (2008), http://www.tsr.ch/xobix_media/files/tsr/abe/2009/worst_forms_of_child_labour_-_master_thesis.pdf

*Smuggling of Migrants*, UNODC 25 (Jan. 2011), https://www.unodc.org/documents/human-trafficking/Migrant-Smuggling/Smuggling_of_Migrants_A_Global_Review.pdf
*Smuggling of Migrants from West Africa to Europe*, UNODC, http://www.unodc.org/documents/toc/Reports/TOCTAWestAfrica/West_Africa_TOC_MIGRANTS.pdf (accessed on Ausgust 15, 2021)
*Smuggling of Migrants: The Harsh Search of a Better Life*, UNODC, http://www.unodc.org/toc/en/crimes/migrant-smuggling.html (accessed on August, 2021)
*Social Policy Framework for Africa*, African Union (Oct. 27, 2008), http://www.un.org/esa/socdev/egms/docs/2009/Ghana/au2.pdf
*Social Security Programs throughout the World: Africa*, Social Security Administration (U.S.) (SSA) (2017), https://www.ssa.gov/policy/docs/progdesc/ssptw/2016-2017/africa/ssptw17africa.pdf
SOS Children's Villages, Children in Conflict: Child Soldiers, http://www.child-soldier.org/
*Special Rapporteur on Contemporary Forms of Slavery, including its Causes and Consequences, Addendum—Mission to Niger*, U.N. Doc. A/HRC/30/35/Add.1 (Jul. 30 2015) (by Mothusi Bruce Rabasha Palai)
*Special Rapporteur on Violence against Women, its Causes and Consequences*, Addendum—Mission to Ghana, ¶ 42, U.N. Doc. A/HRC/7/6/Add.3 (Feb. 21, 2008) (by Yakin Ertürk)
*Spotlight on Claudine Akakpo*: *"Confiage" is a Modern Form of Child Slavery*, Int'l Trade Union Confederation (ITUC) (Jan 4, 2010), https://www.ituc-csi.org/spotlight-on-claudine-akakpo-cstt
*Stop Trafficking in Child Labor*, Human Rts. Watch (Apr. 1, 2003), https://www.hrw.org/news/2003/04/01/west-africa-stop-trafficking-child-labor
*Strategies to Promote Youth Self-employment in West Africa*, UN Economic Commission for Africa (UNECA) 11 (2010), http://repository.uneca.org/bitstream/handle/123456789/16552/bib.%2020457.pdf?sequence=1
*Strategies to Promote Youth Self-Employment in West Africa*, Int'l Org. Migr. (ILO) 15, 21 (2018), https://rodakar.iom.int/sites/default/files/LHD%20Strategy.pdf
*Street Children and Homelessness*, CYC-Net, http://www.cyc-net.org/cyc-online/cycol-0904-Homelessness.html (accessed on August 20, 2021)
Stuart E (2010) A crisis multiplied how the global economic crisis, coming on top of other shocks, is worsening poverty in Burkina Faso. Oxfam International, https://oxfamilibrary.openrepository.com/oxfam/bitstream/10546/111984/1/a-crisis-multiplied-poverty-burkina-faso-240610-en.pdf
Surtees R (2005), *Child Trafficking in Sierra Leone*, UNICEF 62 (fn. 124) (Jul. 28, 2005), https://nexushumantrafficking.files.wordpress.com/2015/03/child-trafficking-in-sierra-leone.pdf
Svetlana HS (2013) The Phenomenon of "Baby Factories" in Nigeria as a New Trend in Human Trafficking. Int Crim Datab (ICD) 11 (Oct. 2013), http://www.internationalcrimesdatabase.org/upload/documents/20131030T045906-ICD%20Brief%203%20-%20Huntley.pdf. *See* Uduma Kalu, *How Child Trafficking Network Operates in South East*, Vanguard (Jul. 30, 2011), http://www.vanguardngr.com/2011/07/how-child-trafficking-network-operates-in-south-east
Territoriality and Migration in the E.U. Neighbourhood: Spilling Over the Wall (2013) Walton-Roberts M, Hennebry J (eds) Springer Science & Business Media, p 104
*Terrorist Financing in West Africa*, FATF (Oct. 2013), http://www.fatf-gafi.org/Media/Fatf/Documents/reports/tf-in-west-africa.pdf
*The Cost of Coercion: Global Report on the ILO Declaration on Fundamental Principles and Rights at Work*, ILO (May 12, 2009), http://www.ilo.org/global/topics/forced-labour/publications/WCMS_106268/lang%2D%2Den/index.htm
*The Gambia*, U.S. Dept. of State (2017), https://www.state.gov/j/tip/rls/tiprpt/countries/2017/271191.htm
The Global Slavery Index 2013, Walk Free Foundation, https://s3-ap-southeast-2.amazonaws.com/walkfreefoundation.org-assets/content/uploads/2016/03/14153121/Global-Slavery-Index-2013.pdf

The Global Slavery Index 2014, Walk Free Foundation 25, http://reporterbrasil.org.br/wp-content/uploads/2014/11/GlobalSlavery_2014_LR-FINAL.pdf

The Nature and Scale of Human Trafficking in 2013, National Crime Agency (NCA) 12 (Sept. 30, 2014), http://www.nationalcrimeagency.gov.uk/publications/399-nca-strategic-assessment-the-nature-and-scale-of-human-trafficking-in-2013/file

*The Role of Consent in Trafficking in Persons Protocol*, UNODC 35 (2014), https://www.unodc.org/documents/human-trafficking/2014/UNODC_2014_Issue_Paper_Consent.pdf

*The Role of Organized Crime in the Smuggling of Migrants from West Africa to the European Union*, UNODC 10 (2011a), http://www.unodc.org/documents/human-trafficking/Migrant-Smuggling/Report_SOM_West_Africa_EU.pdf

*The Role of Organized Crime in the Smuggling of Migrants from West Africa to the European Union*, UNODC 11 (2011b), http://www.unodc.org/documents/human-trafficking/Migrant-Smuggling/Report_SOM_West_Africa_EU.pdf

*The Role of Recruitment Fees and Abusive and Fraudulent Recruitment Practices of Recruitment Agencies in Trafficking in Persons*, UNODC 6 (Jun. 20, 2015), https://www.unodc.org/documents/human-trafficking/2015/Recruitment_Fees_Report-Final-22_June_2015_AG_Final.pdf

*The Twin Challenges of Child Labour and Educational Marginalisation in the ECOWAS Region*, ILO 36 (Jan. 1, 2016), http://documents.worldbank.org/curated/en/424061467993168177/pdf/103602-WP-PUBLIC-ECOWAS-child-labour-educational-marginalisation20140709-130339.pdf

The West African Economic and Monetary Union WAEMU (UEMOA), Housing Finance Africa 1 (2013), https://housingfinanceafrica.org/app/uploads/UEMOA-REGION-2013-Profile.pdf

Theological Advisory Group (1996) Payment of Dowry and the Christian Church. Afr J Evangelical Theol 15:128 (Feb. 15, 1996) (available at: https://biblicalstudies.org.uk/pdf/ajet/15-2_128.pdf)

Thorsen D (2012a) Child domestic workers—evidence from West and Central Africa. UNICEF 6 (Apr. 2012), http://sro.sussex.ac.uk/43303/1/Briefing_paper_No_1_-_child_domestic_workers.pdf

Thorsen D (2012b) Children working in mines and quarries: evidence from West and Central Africa. UNICEF (Apr. 2012), http://www.unicef.org/wcaro/english/Briefing_paper_No_4_-_children_working_in_mines_and_quarries.pdf

*Toolkit to Combat Trafficking in Persons*, UNODC, https://www.unodc.org/documents/human-trafficking/Toolkit-files/08-58296_tool_1-3.pdf (accessed on August, 2021)

Touzenis K (2010) Trafficking in human beings: human rights and trans-national criminal law, developments in law and practices. UNESCO, p 52 [available at: http://unesdoc.unesco.org/images/0018/001883/188397e.pdf]

*Trafficking in Human Beings, Especially Women and Children,* United Nations Asia and Far East Institute (UNAFEI) 158, http://www.unafei.or.jp/english/pdf/RS_No62/No62_19RC_Group1.pdf (accessed on August 14, 2021)

*Trafficking in Human Beings, Especially Women and Children, in Africa*, UNICEF 16 (2005), https://www.unicef-irc.org/publications/pdf/trafficking-gb2ed-2005.pdf

*Trafficking in Human Beings: Internet Recruitment*, Council of Europe 21 (2007), http://www.coe.int/t/dghl/monitoring/trafficking/Source/THB_Internetstudy_en.pdf

*Trafficking in Persons and Exploitation of Migrants*, UNICRI, http://www.unicri.it/topics/trafficking_exploitation/ (accessed on August 20, 2021)

*Trafficking in Persons in West Africa: Analyzing the Legal and Policy Framework for the Protection of Victims*, UNOWA 9 (Dec. 31, 2013), http://www.womencount4peace.org/en/bibliographies/publications/unowa/trafficking_persons_west_africa_analyzing_legal_and_policy

Trafficking in Persons Report, U.S. State Dept. (2010), http://www.state.gov/documents/organization/142981.pdf

*Trafficking in Persons Report*, U.S. Dept. of State (June 2013), https://www.state.gov/documents/organization/210737.pdf

*Trafficking in Persons Report*, U.S. Dept. of State (June 2015a), https://www.state.gov/documents/organization/245365.pdf

Trafficking in Persons Report, Mali, U.S. Dept. of State (2015b), http://www.state.gov/j/tip/rls/tiprpt/countries/2015/243487.htm

*Trafficking in Persons Report 2009*, U.S. Dep't of St. 113–115 (Jun. 2009). http://www.state.gov/documents/organization/123357.pdf

Trafficking in Persons Report 2015—Niger, U.S. Dept of State 263-267, http://www.state.gov/documents/organization/243561.pdf

Trafficking in Persons Report—Benin, U.S. Dept. of State (Jun. 2010), http://www.state.gov/documents/organization/142981.pdf

Trafficking in Persons Report—Gambia, U.S. Dept. of State (2010), https://www.state.gov/j/tip/rls/tiprpt/2010/142760.htm

*Trafficking in Persons Report—Niger*, U.S. Dept. of State (2009), https://www.state.gov/j/tip/rls/tiprpt/2009/123137.htm

Trafficking in Persons to Europe for Sexual Exploitation, UNODC, 4, https://ec.europa.eu/anti-trafficking/sites/antitrafficking/files/trafficking_in_persons_to_europe_for_sexual_exploitation_1.pdf

*Trafficking in Persons: Global Patterns*, UNODC 57 (Apr. 2006), http://www.unodc.org/pdf/traffickinginpersons_report_2006ver2.pdf

*Trafficking in Persons: Global Patterns*, UNODC 87 (Apr. 2006), http://www.unodc.org/pdf/traffickinginpersons_report_2006ver2.pdf

*Trafficking in Persons—TOCTA*, UNODC, http://www.unodc.org/documents/data-and-analysis/tocta/2.Trafficking_in_persons.pdf (accessed on August 20, 2021)

*Trafficking in Women to Italy for Sexual Exploitation*, IOM (Jun. 1996), https://childhub.org/en/system/tdf/library/attachments/iom_1996_trafficking_in_wo2.pdf?file=1&type=node&id=16371

*Transnational Organized Crime in the West African Region* (2005) UNODC, https://www.unodc.org/pdf/transnational_crime_west-africa-05.pdf

*Transnational Trafficking and the Rule of Law in West Africa: A Threat Assessment*, United Nations Office of Drugs and Crime (UNDOC) 9 (Jul. 2009), https://www.unodc.org/documents/data-and-analysis/Studies/West_Africa_Report_2009.pdf

Turner C (2013) Out of the shadows: child marriage and slavery. Anti-Slavery Int 11 (Apr. 2013), http://www.antislavery.org/includes/documents/cm_docs/2013/c/child_marriage_final.pdf

*Type of Modern Day Slavery Crime*, National Crime Agency (UK), http://www.nationalcrimeagency.gov.uk/crime-threats/human-trafficking/types-of-human-trafficking (accessed on August 20, 2021)

U.N. Gift (2010) Analyzing the business model of trafficking in human beings to better prevent the crime. OSCE, https://www.osce.org/cthb/69028?download=true

U.N. Global Initiative to Fight Human Trafficking (U.N. GIFT) *The Vienna Forum to Fight Human Trafficking*, UNODC 11 (Feb. 2008), https://www.unodc.org/documents/human-trafficking/2008/BP027TransnationalOrganizedCrimeandHumanTrafficking.pdf.

U.N. Security-General, *Activities of the United Nations Office for West Africa*, ¶ 13, U.N. Doc. S/2013/384 (Jun. 28, 2013)

U.N. Secretary-General, *Activities of the United Nations Office for West Africa*, ¶ 16, U.N. Doc. S/2013/732 (Dec. 11, 2013)

U.N. Security-General, *Transnational organized crime and illicit drug trafficking in West Africa and the Sahel Region*, ¶¶ 16-19, U.N. Doc. S/2013/359 (Jun. 17, 2013), http://www.securitycouncilreport.org/atf/cf/%7B65BFCF9B-6D27-4E9C-8CD3-CF6E4FF96FF9%7D/s_2013_359.pdf)

U.S. Dep't of State, TRAFFICKING IN PERSONS REPORT 2019., https://www.state.gov/reports/2019-trafficking-in-persons-report/
U.S. Dept of State, 2009 Trafficking in Persons Report 113-115 (Jun. 2009). http://www.state.gov/documents/organization/123357.pdf
U.S. State Dept, *Trafficking in Persons Report*, (2007), 7, https://www.state.gov/documents/organization/82902.pdf)
U.S. State Dept, *Trafficking in Persons Report* (2008), 6, https://www.state.gov/documents/organization/105501.pdf
*U.S. v. Adaboi Stella Udeozor*, 515 F.3d 260 (4th Cir., 2008)
*U.S. v. Bello*, 503 F. App'x 910, 911-13 (11th Cir. 2013)
*U.S. v. Oladimeji Seun Ayelotan, etal.* 917 F.3d 394 (5th Cir. 2019)
UN General Assembly, *Report of the Special Rapporteur on contemporary forms of slavery, including its causes and consequences, Addendum: Mission to the Niger*, para.36–37 (30 July, 2015), A/HRC/30/35/Add.1, https://www.refworld.org/docid/55f7d4044.html [accessed Agust 20, 2021]
*Unbearable to the Human Heart: Child trafficking and Action to Eliminate it*, ILO (2002), http://www.unicef.org/violencestudy/pdf/2002_traff_unbearable_en.pdf
UNESC Res. 608(XXI), art. 1(a)) (Sept. 7, 1956)
UNGA, *Protection of and Assistance to Internally Displaced Persons—Note by the Secretary-General*, ¶ 14-15, U.N. Doc. A/61/276 (Aug. 21, 2006)
UN-Habitat (2007) Enhancing Urban Safety and Security: Global Report on Human Settlements 2007. United Nations Human Settlements Programme (UNHSP), p 63. https://www.un.org/ruleoflaw/files/urbansafetyandsecurity.pdf
UNICEF (1999) Child Domestic Work, Innocenti Digest No. 5, 2 (May 17, 1999), https://www.unicef-irc.org/publications/pdf/digest5e.pdf
UNICEF (2000) Domestic Violence against Women and Girls. Innocenti Digest 6:1 (available at: https://www.unicef.org/malaysia/ID_2000_Domestic_Violence_Women_Girls__6e.pdf)
Universal Declaration of Human Rights, G.A. Res. 217A (III), U.N. Doc. A/810 at art. 6 (1948)
*Unprotected Work, Invisible Exploitation: Trafficking for the Purposes of Domestic Servitude*, OSCE 23-24 (Jun. 17, 2010). http://www.osce.org/secretariat/75804?download=true
Urmila B (2014) (Special Rapporteur on Contemporary Forms of Slavery, including its Causes and Consequences), *Mission to the Niger*, ¶ 61, U.N. Doc. A/HRC/30/35/Add.1 (Nov. 11-21, 2014)
Vesna N-R et al (2004) Trafficking in people in Serbia, Belgrade. OSCE, p 63 http://www.osce.org/documents/fry/2004/07/3290_en.pdf
West U.N. Security-General (2013) Transnational organized crime and illicit drug trafficking in West Africa and the Sahel Region. U.N. Doc. S/2013/359 (Jun. 17, 2013) (available at: http://www.securitycouncilreport.org/atf/cf/%7B65BFCF9B-6D27-4E9C-8CD3-CF6E4FF96FF9%7D/s_2013_359.pdf)
*What is Forced Labour, Modern Slavery, and Human Trafficking*, ILO, http://www.ilo.org/global/topics/forced-labour/definition/lang%2D%2Den/index.htm (accessed on August 20, 2021)
*Women of Nigerian Origin in Finland who have been subjected to Trafficking for Sexual Exploitation: Practice in Applying the Aliens Act*, Syrjintä (2017), https://www.syrjinta.fi/documents/14490/0/Nigeriaselvitys_englanti/6ea936c8-462d-47a8-a73a-535af377ffd0
Women Trafficking and Child Labour Eradication Foundation (WOTCLEF), The Rape of the Innocents: Evolving an African Initiative against Human Trafficking: Proceedings of the First Pan-African Conference on Human trafficking, 168 (WOTCLEF, 2001)
World Health Statistics, WHO (2016), http://apps.who.int/iris/bitstream/10665/206498/1/9789241565264_eng.pdf

*World Report on Disability*, World Health Organization (WHO) 29 (2011), http://apps.who.int/iris/bitstream/handle/10665/70670/WHO_NMH_VIP_11.01_eng.pdf?sequence=1
*World Social Protection Report 2014/15—Building Economic Recovery, Inclusive Development and Social Justice*, Int'l Labour Org. (ILO) 102 (2014), http://www.ilo.org/wcmsp5/groups/public/%2D%2D-dgreports/%2D%2D-dcomm/documents/publication/wcms_245201.pdf
Worldwide Stats, *Exploitation of Children*, Casa Alianza (Sept. 2000), http://www.childtrafficking.com/Docs/casa_allianca_statistics_7.pdf
*Youth and International Migration: Role and Relevance of Social Protection*, United Nations Children's Fund (UNICEF) 6 (2014). http://www.globalmigrationgroup.org/sites/default/files/6._Chapter_3.pdf

# Chapter 3
# Relevant Actors and Their Interests

The previous chapter focused on the definition of trafficking in person and described the different forms in which it was manifested in West Africa. It also strived to ascertain why trafficking occurs by identifying the underlying economic, social, political, environmental, and cultural factors that render people vulnerable to exploitation. To carry out their criminal activities, traffickers often interact with legitimate individuals and institutions who inadvertently or deliberately benefit from or support this illicit enterprise. This begins with the recruitment process where recruiters including housewives pose as labor brokers. Travel agents facilitate the movement of victims through hotels, night clubs, brothels, and restaurants whose owners and pimps harbor or engage them. Legitimate businesses may also purchase the products made or harvested by trafficked victims; customers are the end users of the trafficked victims' services. Health care practitioners may also be involved in the trafficking business by providing specialized services to the victims. Other actors include corrupt border guards, police or embassy personnel, the investors who finance the operations, and financial institutions such as banks that launder the illegal proceeds.[1] The ensuing discussion will provide an analysis of factors that contribute to trafficking in persons through the prism of the perpetrators. It will focus on the traffickers and their cohorts and examine the motivations for becoming involved in the trade, as well as the environments conducive to organized criminal activity.

---

[1] Aransiola and Zarowsky (2014), pp. 509, 517; Mensah-Ankrah and Sarpong (2017), p. 5; Madevi Sun-Suon, Human Trafficking and the Role of Local Governments, U.N. Insti. Training & Res. (UNITAR) 12, https://unitar.org/sites/default/files/media/publication/doc/SDP-publication3.pdf.



P. Vl. S. Karenga, *A West African Model to Address Human Trafficking*,
https://doi.org/10.1007/978-3-030-88120-7_3

## 3.1 Individual Traffickers: Relatives or Employers

As reported by Human Rights Watch staff, increased levels of education and employment among middle class urban women in West Africa have created a higher demand for domestic workers.

> Nowadays, many African women in the city have a job and want cheap help at home to look after their children and the household. Rather than employing adults who are more likely to demand a salary, they use girl domestic workers. . . . Employers are mostly women from the urban middle classes. They tend to demand a girl from their poorer relatives in the countryside, or send intermediaries to find a girl in the home village or in Conakry.[2]

In a case presented to the Court of Cassation in France, a Senegalese couple based in France traveled to Senegal and recruited their cousin to travel to France to take care of the house and their three children. The couple instructed and assisted their cousin in obtaining a false passport to enter France. The couple then seized the victim's true identity documents and subjected her to forced labor and services without remuneration.[3] *Siliadin v. France*[4] cases involving Togolese national abduction into domestic servitude follow similar patterns.

Numerous cases illustrate that trafficking in persons can be easily conducted by one, two or three people acting simultaneously as recruiters, transporters, and exploiters with only a limited organization in place.[5] For example, the traffickers of domestic workers are often a wife and husband who coerce girls from the same village by promising their parents that they will receive an education or enjoy a better life in the city.[6] However, once the child arrives at the couples' residence, she is denied access to school, is compelled to perform domestic work, is not fed properly, and on occasion is also abused. Some perpetrators may use the victims for domestic services and sexual gratification. For example, the phenomenon of forced marriage is usually not for the purpose of making money as the victim is trafficked for personal reasons such as domestic servitude and sexual exploitation.

Furthermore, peers who have already made the journey may also be involved in the recruitment process.[7] In Burkina Faso, Nigeria, Benin, Ivory Coast, Guinea, Mali, Ghana and Liberia, for example, young migrant workers often return to their villages to recruit new children for work in the cacao and cotton plantations, fisheries, artisanal quarries, and mines. These migrant workers exhibit outward signs of wealth (clothes and jewels, motorcycles or used cars, and having lived in

---

[2] Kippenberg (2007), p. 33.

[3] LegiFrance, at https://www.legifrance.gouv.fr/affichJuriJudi.do?idTexte=JURITEXT000033143954.

[4] *Siliadin v. France*, European Court of Human Rights, Application No. 73316/01, Judgment (2005).

[5] Strategies against human trafficking: The role of the security sector, Cornelius Friesendorf, Vienna and Geneva, 130 (September, 2009).

[6] Touzenis (2010), p. 57.

[7] de Lange (2009), p. 195.

pretty decent houses) and lure and recruit young people for migration abroad. This efficient method of recruitment is sometimes used in trafficking for sexual exploitation. Traffickers send former victims to their hometown or village to recruit other victims.

Finally, it "is also possible for a victim to be trafficked through the collaboration of family members working with professional gangs or organized crime affiliates who may have been posing as concerned friends of the family."[8] In the *Federal Republic of Nigeria v. Favour Anware Okwuede*[9] a case involving the prostitution of others, the victim (H.O.) testified that, sometime in 2006, the brother of the accused came to her brother and told him that the accused was looking for girls to take back to Italy to work in a fashion-designing store and also a hairdresser salon. The brother then introduced the victim (H.O.) to his sister who said that she wanted to take H.O to Italy at the cost of ₦60,000 (approximately US $370) for transportation. When H.O. expressed her inability to afford the trip, the accused promised to help her. The victim met J.O.P., another prospective prostitute, and together they were taken to a traditional religious house where they underwent certain religious rituals and took an oath of allegiance to ensure they would remain loyal. The accused was able to collect ₦16,000 (approximately US $98) from J.O.P. but received nothing from H.O. as she said she had no money. The next day, H.O., J.O.P., and the accused left for Lagos to travel to Cotonou and Togo. The accused then took them to Niger Republic, where she forced them into prostitution in a hotel room she had rented. She then collected all the money the women earned.[10]

Surprising as it may be, analyses have shown that the family, who are usually considered to be people who care the most, but are those responsible for trafficking the vast majority of people exploited in domestic servitude and forced labor; either out of perversity or a state of necessity.[11] This indicates that economic vulnerability is a driving cause of trafficking in persons; a situation portrayed in "Les Miserables" by Victor Hugo. In the 19th century, Fantine, who no longer has any money, sells herself into prostitution, also selling her hair and her teeth to feed and protect her family. This continues to occur in is in contemporary society. Greed and the "get rich quick virus" can also lead parents to traffic their own children. For instance, the *Attorney General of the Federation v. Felicia Okafor* case dealt with the situation of a woman who trafficked three women, including her own daughter, from Nigeria to Senegal for the purpose of prostitution.[12] The Court commented that "[t]he facts of

---

[8] Cherti et al. (2013), p. 38.

[9] *Federal Republic of Nigeria v. Favour Anware Okwuede*, Nigeria Court of High Justice, Charge No. FHC.ASB.24C.09, Judgment (2009).

[10] *Id.*

[11] Cherti et al. (2013), p. 38. *See also Global Report on Trafficking in Humans*, UNDOC 43–44 (2014), https://www.unodc.org/documents/data-and-analysis/glotip/GLOTIP_2014_full_report.pdf; Alexander et al. (2016).

[12] *See*, Attorney General of the Federation v. M.A., Nigeria High Court, Suit No. B/13c/2004, Judgment (2005) (available at: https://www.unodc.org/cld/case-law-doc/traffickingpersonscrimetype/nga/2005/hon._attorney_general_of_the_federation_v._m.a.html).

this case offer another example of the moral decay in our society and how deep the 'get rich quick virus' has eaten into our social fabric. That a mother will recruit her own daughter to travel to Senegal for the purpose of prostitution shows the level of moral decadence in our society."[13] This example reflects the fact that the family unit is not necessarily a safe haven that protects its members against trafficking.

## 3.2 West African Transnational Organized Crime Networks

The transnational organized crime model captures the complexity of trafficking in persons. The best known is that of Nigerian organized crime, which draws women from several neighboring countries for prostitution in Europe and the Middle East;[14] these networks consist mainly of Nigerians, and have extended their reach through established trade networks in the region and ties to large West African populations in the United States and in parts of Europe.[15]

"During the 2007–2012 period, Nigerian victims constantly accounted for more than 10 percent of the total number of detected victims in Western and Central Europe, making this the most prominent transregional flow in this subregion."[16] Since the late 1990s, these trafficking rings have been operating in several different European countries. Many cases reported by UNODC indicate that "the victimization of more persons at the same time, and the endurance in conducting the criminal activity are all indicators of a high level of organization of the trafficking network behind the flow."[17]

Unlike hierarchical organizational models, which are common among Chinese or Italian groups, Nigerian organized criminals utilize a network model. Furthermore, hierarchical groups may tumble like a house of cards; whereas the loose organizational form of the Nigerian networks enables them to rapidly restructure into new constellations, thus making them extremely efficient.[18] It is therefore important to consider how Nigerian organized crime is initially set up?

---

This case involved a woman who took three girls including her own sister to the Niger Republic for the purpose of prostitution.

[13] *See A.G. v. Felicia Okafor*, Nigeria Court of High Justice, Suit No. A.12C.06, Judgment (2006); *Federal Republic of Nigeria v. Favour Anware Okwuede*, Nigeria Court of High Justice, Charge No. FHC.ASB.24C.09, Judgment (2009) at 17.

[14] Farr (2005), pp. 115–117; *see also* Shelly (2010), pp. 128–129. *See also* Abadinsky (2010).

[15] *Migration, Human Smuggling and Trafficking from Nigeria to Europe*, Int'l Org. Migr. (IOM) 42 (2006), https://www.iom.int/files/live/sites/iom/files/What-We-Do/idm/docs/MRS23.pdf.

[16] *Global Report on Trafficking in Persons 2014*, UNODC 56, http://www.unodc.org/res/cld/bibliography/global-report-on-trafficking-in-persons_html/GLOTIP_2014_full_report.pdf.

[17] *Id.* at 45.

[18] IOM, *supra* note 15, at 42.

Typically, the trafficker is a woman called "*Madam*"[19] although it may also be a man. Sometimes there is a *sponsor* who intervenes and is responsible for paying all the costs of the journey and settling abroad; this creates a debt that the woman is required to pay back.[20] In general, the *Madam* also assumes the role of sponsor and carries out the criminal activities closely associated with a legitimate business. This was the case for Mrs. Lasiru Rossato Dolly, an Italian-based Nigerian lady, who was arrested by the National Agency for the Prohibition of Trafficking in Persons (NAPTIP) for her alleged involvement in trafficking in persons. The suspect, said to be one of the most notorious traffickers in Nigeria, is a mother of one child and married to an Italian man. She operates a phony company, African Choice and Import Market, through which she recruits most of her victims and procures forged travel documents to enable them to travel to Italy. The *Madam,* who claims to own three businesses in Italy, is also said to own properties in both Italy and Nigeria.

In August 2014, she recruited a 25 year-old girl and made the victim's parents give an affidavit of parental consent to changing her name. The parents also signed several agreements with the suspect's lawyer in Benin City, stating that the victim was going to work in the suspect's shop in Italy and not for prostitution; and that she would pay back the sum of €62,000 to Mrs. Dolly Rossato in two-and-a-half years before regaining her freedom. Prior to traveling to Italy, the victim was taken successively to two shrines where she deposited her finger nails, pubic hair, and hair; and then further asked to take an oath of secrecy binding her to the *Madam*; it was later discovered that the suspect was only interested in female victims whom she used as sex slaves.[21] he *Madam* in Nigeria generally has close connections with a *Madam* in the country of exploitation, who is responsible for the trafficked woman once she has arrived. These two partners are often a large group of *Madams* who belong to the same extended family. The other active members in Nigeria are a religious leader (*ohen*) who seals the pact acts, human smugglers who are responsible for the journey (*trolleys*), and a male assistant to the *Madam* in Italy (*Madam's black boy*).[22] Investigations by Italian authorities into a criminal organization of Nigerians dedicated to trafficking young Nigerian women forced into prostitution revealed that an Italian lawyer was involved in the trafficking. His role was to

---

[19] Kienast et al. (2014).

[20] IOM, supra note 15, pp. 26–28. "Required documents normally cost between US $500 and US $3000. In addition, smugglers often charge as much as US $10,000 for the trip. The debts the women incur, however, are considerably larger, usually in the range US $40,000 to US $100,000. It normally takes between one and three years as a prostitute in Europe to pay back this amount. Many women do not understand the extent of their commitment as they are not familiar with European currencies."

[21] Ebegbulem (2017).

[22] IOM, *supra* note 15.

represent the Nigerian girls (most of whom were known to be prostitutes) and request political asylum for them.[23]

Women who are trafficked to Europe are forced into the most dangerous type of prostitution as streetwalkers. The trade is very effective as it allies traditional tribal customs to sophisticated forms of modern technology; and it generates significant financial profits through debt bondage. The documents required for the trip normally cost between US $500 and US $3000. The smuggler then increases the debt to between €40,000 and 70,000 to cover travel, protection, and alleged additional expenses; this amount can be paid off after one two three years' work as a prostitute in Europe.[24]

For example, in the *PO (Nigeria) v. Secretary of State for the Home Department* case, Osagie brought a national Nigerian to the United Kingdom on January 10, 2005. He had persuaded the victim that she would be employed in his factory; at the time, the appellant was living in dire poverty in Benin City. Her father had died before she was born and her mother had died when giving birth. She was brought up by an aunt with whom she was very close. Convinced by Osagie's promises of financial security. which would enable her and her aunt to escape from poverty, she arrived in the UK and discovered the true purpose of her journey. Osagie and two of his associates intended to use her for sexual gratification and to deploy and exploit her for purposes of prostitution. She was required to earn and hand over large sums of money, initially fixed at £20,000 but later raised to £50,000.[25] Similarly, a Human Rights Watch study on Nigerian girls and women trafficked to brothels on the Ivory Coast confirmed that "the traffickers demanded that the women and girls engage in prostitution to pay off an exorbitant 'debt of generally 1.5 to 2 million CFA francs (US $3000 to $4000), though the cost of overland transportation to Côte d'Ivoire is only roughly 100,000F CFA ($200)."[26] Small amounts of earnings "are occasionally returned to family members of the girls and women, while some profits are passed on to the local operations of the crime groups" and "other illicit activities and are laundered."[27]

Nigerian trafficking is primarily characterized by female leadership and a self-reproducing organizational structure. The strength of this network lies in an ambivalent relationship of reciprocity between traffickers (*Madam*) and victims (prostitutes). For instance, although, the *Madam* holds the victims under slave-like conditions, she may actually support the prostitutes so that they can earn money and establish themselves as a *Madam* once the debt is paid. A *Madam* can also help a

[23] *Explanatory Note—Crime Type: Trafficking in Persons*, U.N. Office of Drugs & Crime (UNODC) (2012), https://www.unodc.org/res/cld/case-law-doc/criminalgroupcrimetype/ita/2012/r_g__ass__nr_1110_-_trafficking_case_html/Trafficking_in_persons_-_explanatory_note.pdf.

[24] IOM, *supra* note 15, at 28; UNODC, *supra* note 16, at 56.

[25] *PO (Nigeria) v. Secretary of State for the Home Department* [2011] 132 EWCA 22 (U.K.).

[26] *Côte d'Ivoire/Nigeria: Combat Trafficking for Prostitution*, Human Rts Watch (Aug. 26, 2010), http://www.hrw.org/news/2010/08/26/c-te-d-ivoirenigeria-combat-trafficking-prostitution.

[27] Aronowitz (2009), pp. 74–76.

woman get married and obtain her residence permit and/or facilitate a relationship with a customer who offers to pay all or parts of the remaining debt. The possibility of "promotion" from being a prostitute to becoming a supervisor, and later a *Madam*, constitutes an important motivation to "stick it out."[28] Both prospects help maintain the relationship between the *Madam* and the prostitutes. As a young Nigerian who had worked in Italy described it, "when a woman asks you to work the street, you accept because she is like you; she has done so herself."[29] In addition to the prospects for a better life when the indentured prostitution ends, the religious and legal sanctioning of the pact between the two parties gives the majority of victims a strong motivation to comply. Consequently, Nigerian trafficking networks are less reliant on the use of violence than their Eastern European counterparts.[30]

Reports from various European criminal justice authorities confirm that Nigerian crime syndicates are extremely well organized and difficult to detect. Like other groups, Nigerian transnational networks involve a chain of actors and have been found to engage in ancillary services such as document fraud, money laundering, cyber-crime, corruption, and other criminal activities, including drug trafficking, diamond smuggling, counterfeiting, arms smuggling, and transnational financial scams.[31] Remarkably, the transnational nature of organized crime cases makes them extremely difficult to prosecute. For instance, in the *NIGERIA Attorney General v. Kingsley Edegbe* case, following the successful prosecution of three members of the trafficking syndicate in the Netherlands who worked with Kingsley Edegbe as their partner in Nigeria, the Government of the Netherlands made a request to the Attorney General of the Federation and Minister of Justice for the extradition of Mr. Kingsley Edegbe to face trial in the Netherlands for his involvement in trafficking in persons. The judge stated that the application by the Netherlands was not based an extradition treaty between the two countries; he also insisted that the mere signing and ratification of UNTOC by the two countries did not qualify as a treaty for the purposes of extradition. The judge ruled that under Nigerian Law, i.e. section 12(1) of the constitution of the Federal Republic of Nigeria, for a treaty to become part of Nigerian Municipal laws, it had to be domesticated through ratification and made enforceable by an Act of the National Assembly. Therefore, in the absence of domestication, the UNTOC convention and its protocols are not part of Nigerian law. The Judge concluded that the application was therefore not made

[28] In Italy, *Madams* running sex industries are aged between 25 and 35 years-old. In the Netherlands, where many Nigerians prostitutes arrive as minors, some become *Madams* at just 19 years of age. *See also* Carling (2005).

[29] IOM, *supra* note 15, at 49.

[30] Carling (2005).

[31] *Combating International Crime in Africa*, Committee on International Relations, http://commdocs.house.gov/committees/intlrel/hfa50884.000/hfa50884_0.HTM (accessed on August 20, 2021).

according to the provisions of the Extradition Act of Nigeria and thereby declared the extradition application incompetent.[32]

Trafficking in persons is condemned and is widely considered a social evil. In response, traffickers often "argue that they serve important needs by alleviating the shortage of laborers or prostitutes in specific markets."[33] Traffickers in West Africa emphasize the benefits of their actions such as enabling their clients to realize their goals and helping to provide labor for vital occupations in developed countries. They consider themselves to be facilitators for families looking for an extra income.[34] Traffickers involved in forced marriage also argue that they are doing a good deed for widows by finding a partner for them to marry. Although some express remorse for their crimes, others consider themselves to be the victims of circumstances such as poverty. Overall, the socio-demographic profiles of traffickers in West Africa show that they are essentially poor, uneducated, unemployed persons who were earning very little no income at all. The low profile of their primary jobs provided just enough to modestly support their large families of five to eight children.

Many convicted traffickers claimed they were unaware their behavior constituted trafficking in persons and were completely ignorant of the existence of the anti-trafficking legislation. Others knew that their activity was reprehensible, but had assumed they would be given a light punishment. Had they known the severity of the punishment they would not have engaged in these criminal activities, while others recounted that this was the first time they had engaged in the trafficking business and were apprehended for their actions.[35] Recruiters and transporters involved in trafficking invoke denial of injury to "minimize the criminal act by implying no one has been harmed by the act" and argue that they "are only helping them to realize their dreams."[36] Housewives who traffic young girls from impoverished villages to towns and cities for domestic labor argue that they have improved the living conditions for these girls by taking them out of a slum area to a beautiful home.

"Denial of victim" is also an argument individuals uphold to justify their involvement in crime. In the case of forced labor, "injury is not wrong in light of the circumstances" if it is claimed a victim is receiving more money for the same services he or she would have performed at home.[37] Offenders falsely believe that women who have engaged in prostitution in their home countries and seek work abroad to improve their lives are not trafficking victims. They have been told that

[32] High Court (2014), Between Nigeria Attorney General and Kingsley Edegbe, 11–24, Charge No. FHC/ABJ/CS/907/2012 (available at: https://www.unodc.org/res/cld/case-law-doc/criminalgroupcrimetype/nga/2014/attorney_general_of_the_federation_and_kingsley_edegbe_html/NIGERIA_Attorney_General_vs_Kingsley_Edegbe_2014.pdf).

[33] Chenda (2013), p. 27.

[34] *Id.*; David (2012), p. 9; Mollema (2013), p. 56.

[35] Chenda (2013), p. 148.

[36] U.N. Gift (2010), p. 31.

[37] *Id.*

they will be working in the sex industry in another country and even consented to sign an employment contract.[38]

Finally, trafficking in persons bears financial costs to traffickers, including establishing routes, bribing police and other officials to turn a blind eye on their activities, outfitting individuals for travel and providing falsified documents, and housing, feeding, and clothing forced laborers. In addition, all traffickers live under constant threat of exposure to the police with the consequential loss of social status, financial investment, and future income, and penalties including prison time and fines.[39]

## 3.3 The Role of Corrupt Law Enforcement Agents

From a law enforcement perspective, trafficking in persons is an offense that involves "document forgery, violation of immigration and labor laws, corruption of government officials, smuggling of migrants, money laundering and tax evasion."[40] For instance, in the case of international trafficking, victims are transported illegally across state borders in violation of immigration laws. Facilitating this criminal activity also requires the falsification of documents or the corruption of government officials. Thus, government actors and traffickers may act jointly in the trafficking process; police, border guards, prosecutors, judges, labor and immigration officials charged with law enforcement activities can all benefit from the continued exploitation of human beings. In practice foreigners attempting to obtain visas face enormous obstacles in most consulates in West Africa. To overcome these, traffickers often bribe officials in order to execute their operations.[41]

Before the trafficking takes place embassy officials may have knowingly supplied falsified travel documents for persons taken to destination countries. During the trafficking process, border guards may facilitate the transit of individuals from one country to the next; or, once the exploitation has occurred, police may actively aid the trafficking operation by deliberately failing to shut it down, rescue victims or investigate and arrest perpetrators.[42] In a United Nations Office on Drugs and Crime (UNODC) report on the smuggling and trafficking of Persons in West Africa, the consular staff of two different EU member states in Senegal allegedly sold visas, resulting in the admission of perhaps thousands of people to the EU over the years. In one consulate, the sale of visas was carried out specifically to facilitate the illegal

[38] *Id.*; An example of a letter with a victim's promise can be read in U.N. Gift (2010), p. 49.

[39] Galli et al. (2010), pp. 124, 129.

[40] *Id.* at 18.

[41] Shelly (2010), p. 129.

[42] Aronowitz (2009), pp. 26–27; *Corruption and the Smuggling of Migrants*, U.N. Office on Drugs and Crime (UNODC) 3 (2013) https://www.unodc.org/documents/human-trafficking/2013/The_Role_Of_Corruption_in_the_Smuggling_of_Migrants_Issue_Paper_UNODC_2013.pdf.

movement of West African women as sex workers.[43] Studies in Senegal revealed that, in the mid-2000s, tourist visas for Italy could be illicitly obtained for 2.5,000,000F CFA (€3811) and a Portuguese visa for €5000, while a Turkish visas cost 600,000F CFA francs (€915). Two million CFA francs (€3049) were quoted for French visas. Similar reports in Mali in 2009 found that a United States visa could be acquired for 3 million CFA francs (€4573), compared to 1,250,000F CFA (€1905) for a South African visa and 1,000,000 CFA (€1524) for a Libyan visa.[44]

Additionally, the diplomats and employees of multinational organizations and government contractors may also participate in the trafficking of young women for domestic labor. In 2013, "allegations arose that an Ivorian diplomat stationed in Copenhagen subjected his domestic employee to forced labor and sexual abuse."[45] A June 2010 article in the United Kingdom's Daily Mail reported that a Sierra Leone envoy in the UK was accused of trafficking in persons.[46] Low ranking military personnel, members of the security apparatus, and law enforcement personnel who once supplemented their low salaries can all facilitate trafficking in human beings. Although moving significant numbers of individuals across guarded borders is especially challenging, border posts can be crossed in exchange for small payments. NGOs and media reports indicate that corruption among police and *gendarmes* may have facilitated the illicit movement of people in 2014 to the Ivory Coast.[47] Additionally, peacekeeping troops may also carry out trafficking activities. Deployed peacekeeping units in Liberia were reportedly involved in fueling a demand for sex workers and the use of commercial sexual services while on missions in the country.[48]

Government officials, especially those from developing countries, may consider trafficking to have an enormous socio-economic potential for the individual child; families; communities, and the nation as a whole. Ghana, for example, recognizes that child labor "creates and sustains a vulnerable population that has no employable skills, and who therefore cannot be gainfully employed, many of whom, out of frustration in an attempt to survive may become a social menace by engaging in armed robberies, drug use and prostitution."[49] Subsequently, many violations of the human rights of women and children may occur largely due to the complicity or

---

[43] *Trafficking in Persons Report 2015, Benin US Dept. of State*, http://www.state.gov/j/tip/rls/tiprpt/countries/2015/243397.htm.

[44] *The Role of Organized Crime in the Smuggling of Migrants from West Africa to the European Union*, UNODC 11 (2011), http://www.unodc.org/documents/human-trafficking/Migrant-Smuggling/Report_SOM_West_Africa_EU.pdf; *see also Smuggling of Migrants: The Harsh Search of a Better Life*, UNODC, http://www.unodc.org/toc/en/crimes/migrant-smuggling.html (accessed on August 20, 2021).

[45] *Trafficking in Persons Report 2015—Ivory Coast*, U.S. Dept. of State, http://www.state.gov/j/tip/rls/tiprpt/countries/2015/243421.htm.

[46] Walker (2010).

[47] U.S. Dept. of State, *supra* note 45.

[48] d'Estree and Kirby (2008), pp. 221, 233.

[49] GNA (2004).

indifference of the State. For example, laws and policies in the destination countries can inadvertently create a demand for exploited labor and prostitution that allows trafficking markets to flourish. Importantly, a state law that does not prohibit trafficking in persons allows this crime to thrive.[50]

## 3.4 The Victims of Trafficking and Their Families

Insightful research in West Africa "suggests that household members who migrate can facilitate investments in new activities by providing rural households with liquidity, in the form of remittances, as well as income security,"[51] to overcome an adverse income shock. In essence it is the need to improve the living conditions for their children that impel parents to accept the prospects of a transfer. An implicit contractual arrangement may exist wherein the household will finance migration in order to receive remittances at a later stage. Research studies have shown that women in particular can be active migrant workers in the trafficking process as they are prepared to take risks by moving abroad to improve their living standards.[52]

Trafficking has led many families out of extreme poverty into the appearance of having achieved success and wealth in the local community. For instance, the emigration of young tribal people (Bissa) from Niaogho and Béguédo to Italy, initially to engage in horticulture around Naples, has been highly lucrative in terms of the remittances sent back to the household. The success of many immigrants who travelled to Europe is visible in the form of cars and grand houses built with remittances from Italy or by queues of people in the Post Office sending parcels to their family members back home or long lines of people picking up cash from the Western Union Agency and other banks.[53]

---

[50] *Read* U.N. Gift (2010).

[51] Taylor and Wouterse (2006), p. 3; IOM, *supra* note 556, at 30; *A Survey on Migration Policies in West Africa*, Econ. Comm. W. Afr. St. (ECOWAS) 34 (2015), http://publications.iom.int/system/files/pdf/survey_west_africa_en.pdf.

[52] *Trafficking in Women to Italy for Sexual Exploitation*, IOM 6 (Jun. 1996), https://childhub.org/en/system/tdf/library/attachments/iom_1996_trafficking_in_wo2.pdf?file=1&type=node&id=16371.

[53] IOM, *supra* note 52, at 3. The decision for a woman to leave to work in Europe is often made by the family, and parents encourage their daughters to do this as it is seen as an investment for them all. Many families pride themselves on having a daughter, sister, or other relation in Europe earning money, pointing to things they have acquired with the money sent by these women. Sending daughters abroad has become a type of status symbol for some families. Women who return from Europe wealthy do not necessarily hide the fact that the money stems from prostitution and this has become socially acceptable in Edo State. The success of many women who have been to Europe is visible—for instance, in the form of grand houses—and this tempts others to leave for Europe. These successful women easily become role models for young girls. According to Cherti et al., as the pressure to succeed financially increases, trafficking in persons has become an accepted, even respected, way to earn money, and families involved in such trafficking are ready to sacrifice one or

The Government of Senegal has estimated that remittances received in the country through unofficial channels amount to "approximately 242 billion FCFA (7 per cent of the gross domestic product), representing an important source of income for the country and providing people with a strong incentive to migrate."[54] Remittances transferred through official channels represent between 40 and 50% of overall Senegalese remittances. In 2006 it was reported that there were more than 500 wire-transfer points (banks, post offices and others) operating in money transfer in Senegal.[55]

In the case of trafficking in children, it is important to understand the role parents may play in their life; family members who are unable to support their children induce them into trafficking as the only strategy to improve the household income. For instance, in Togo, parents are actively involved in trafficking and accepting money from traffickers, and distant relatives pay intermediaries with promises of paid work abroad, professional training, or education.[56] They seek financial benefits for themselves and to support the other children as well as improve the general well-being of the household.

A potential victim in a precarious position who is seeking "help" to escape from a situation of oppression, desperation or persecution may be led to contact a trafficker. Research shows that the majority of young women who migrate within the trafficking network or who seek a job outside their community do not do this solely for economic reasons. Rather, they base their decisions on a profound need to obtain personal freedom and better living opportunities. Desperate economic situations can also put people at risk of exploitation. In effect, parents living in dire poverty "will exchange almost anything that they can for the basic necessities of survival, and sometimes, the only thing that they can trade is sexual access to their children's bodies."[57]

In addition to economic reasons, the pressures associated with social prestige, consumerism, and personal well-being can also be a force that drives trafficking crimes. In Burkina Faso and most West African countries, parents give their daughters to kings and wealthy people in exchange for social positions. There have also been instances "of parents exchanging their children for a television set or a refrigerator. This is not an action born of desperate poverty but one stemming from the pressure of consumerism."[58] In Togo, Human Rights Watch reported that in exchange for "[p]romised highly coveted goods such as bicycles, radios and

---

more family members as long as it is lucrative to do so. *See also* Immigration Acts [2016], no. 25, CG UKUT 00454 (IAC) (Nigeria) (available at: http://www.refworld.org/pdfid/580724ed4.pdf); Ezeh (2017). [hereinafter Prostitution Among Women and Girls].

[54] Special Rapporteur on the Human Rights of Migrants, *Addendum - Mission to Senegal*, ¶ 17, U.N. Doc. A/HRC/17/33/Add.2 (Feb. 23, 2011) (by Jorge Bustamante); Fall (2003).

[55] *Id.*

[56] Innocenti Insight, *Trafficking in Human Beings, especially Women and Children, in Africa*, UNICEF 9 (Sept. 2003), http://www.unicef-irc.org/publications/pdf/insight9e.pdf.

[57] Prostitution Among Women and Girls, *supra* note 53 at 23.

[58] *Id.*

sheet-metal roofing, [parents] readily succumbed to the offers of child traffickers and in some cases encouraged their friends to accompany them abroad."[59] Victims can also be accomplices in the crime as some are attracted by the prospects of a substantial business in trafficking in persons and become traffickers themselves. Thus, some victims who find themselves in exploitative situations may accept such a status and not report the traffickers to the authorities because they believe that, one day, this system will work in their favor and they will run their own trafficking ring.[60]

There are also people in Mali, Niger who are born into a state of servitude as a result of caste-based slavery. Slave masters see this as the natural order of things and, surprisingly, victims also "believe it is their place in the world to work as slaves, without pay, and without rights to their children."[61] In effect, many cannot imagine a life without the assistance of their master. They ignore what freedom is and are afraid to take the risk. The situation for victims born into slavery is far more sinister than for those held by physical restraints because the shackles of slavery are mental and are transmitted across generations. Religion can also be used to justify enslavement. For example, in Northern Ghana and parts of Togo, girls are 'donated' to traditional priests and compelled to live as 'wives of gods' in return for the protection of the family.[62]

## 3.5 Economic Benefits from Trafficking-Related Transactions

Naylor noted that

> ... profit-driven crime is not an isolated act, but a complex series of interrelated actions in which various participants perform a host of different roles that have different degrees of importance and show different degrees of awareness and involvement.[63]

Drawing on the premises of classical criminology it can be argued that those who traffic in persons "choose to commit a crime after weighing the costs, benefits, and risk of committing these crimes."[64] The activities of offenders are supported by a range of intermediaries and facilitators operating in legal and legitimate business settings as well as in underground markets. In effect, illicit or legitimate travel, employment, or marriage agencies may promote or otherwise facilitate the recruitment and movement of victims. Businesses markets such as hotels, night clubs, taxi

[59] Human Rights Watch (2003).

[60] UNODC (2014), p. 56.

[61] Sutter (2013).

[62] Innocenti Research Centre (2000), p. 6.

[63] Naylor (2003), pp. 81, 83.

[64] U.N. Gift (2010), p. 36.

services, and restaurants, along with owners and landlords who rent apartments to traffickers or trafficked victims, may (knowingly or unknowingly) support the activity and/or benefit from trafficking and procuring.[65]

Researchers have provided evidence to show that the sending and hosting of immigrant communities helps support the processes of irregular migration that can ultimately involve migrant smuggling and trafficking in persons. Nigerian diaspora members "facilitate the trade, especially in Italy, which has the largest Nigerian immigrant community and the greatest number of enslaved women in Europe of Nigerian nationality."[66] Many of the trafficking cases investigated in France were reportedly inter-familial, in that families exploited family members brought from Africa to work in their households.[67] In Saint-Louis in Senegal in 2008, women were reported to have set up a tontine association (a savings club) to assist with the often phenomenal cost of migration by their own children; similar arrangements also exist in other cities throughout West Africa.[68]

Trafficking in persons is a business and traffickers ultimately need to market victims to clients who seek the services of prostitutes. Advertisements can be placed in newspapers the internet, or any informal channel in a covert manner to avoid identification, arrest, and prosecution. The legitimate economy, which engages in subcontracts with these smaller operations, also benefits financially from the use of irregular labor workers. At this stage of exploitation, revenues are generated, stored, transferred, or spent through financial structures. Therefore, a symbiotic relationship exists between the legal and illicit economies with, for example, banks operating predominantly in the legitimate world and laundering illegal proceeds.[69]

Finally, the culture that condones or promotes pornography, sexual exploitation, and the exploitation of child domestic workers is an environment conducive to trafficking in persons. In a material sense, within the community the men and women who migrate to Europe are often considered models of achievement. The *madam* who lives in Europe owns grand houses in her origin country in West Africa. By the same token, a consumer culture is spreading, leading many to crave quick wealth, and this has produced favorable conditions for trafficking.

---

[65] David (2012); Aronowitz (2009), pp. 26–27.

[66] Shelly (2010), p. 129.

[67] *Trafficking in Persons Report 2011, France*, European Commission, https://ec.europa.eu/anti-trafficking/sites/antitrafficking/files/us_trafficking_in_persons_report_2011_france_en_1.pdf.

[68] *The Role of Organized Crime in the Smuggling of Migrants from West Africa to the European Union*, UNODC 11 (2011), http://www.unodc.org/documents/human-trafficking/Migrant-Smuggling/Report_SOM_West_Africa_EU.pdf.

[69] Aronowitz (2009), p. 33.

## 3.6 Conclusion

This discussion has described the scope and prevalence of trafficking in persons across West Africa as well as the complexity of its various forms. People are moved from their communities through coercion, threat, and abuse for the purposes of forced prostitution, forced or bonded labor in mines and plantations, domestic servitude, forced marriage, the exploitation of children and disabled persons in begging, the trafficking of children for warfare, and the use of body parts for rituals and, in some cases, for human sacrifice. This criminal activity is often conducted by individuals close to the victims or organized criminal groups.

There are many factors that lead potential victims into a situation o trafficking. Poverty, social exclusion, environment-related circumstances, lack of education, domestic violence, and various forms of persecution can all drive individuals to take the risk of migrating illegally in search for a better life for themselves and their families. Traffickers play upon the desires and aspirations of the victims to compel them into forced labor or sexual exploitation. Another common pattern observed in trafficking in persons is that people flow from impoverished regions to wealthier countries. Many young girls and women are trafficked from rural to urban areas to meet the demand for cheap domestic labor and sex work.

Political instability and internal armed conflict that generate a demand for child soldiers and the use of organs or body parts for rituals also contribute to trafficking in persons. In West Africa, social and cultural practices such as child fostering, the custom of early marriage for girls, the servitude of girls for ritual religious purposes, and gender discrimination that excludes women from inheriting land makes both women and girls disproportionately vulnerable to trafficking. Broadly speaking, trafficking in persons is created by structural causes that lead potential victims to seek the services of traffickers. The latter appear to be opportunistically responding to the tension that exists between the pressure placed on potential victims to migrate in search of viable economic options, and governments' politically motivated restrictions on migration.[70]

Due to the criminal nature and structural causes of trafficking in persons, the primary responsibility for combating trafficking rests with states that have the capacity to create effective policing solutions. Thus, an anti-trafficking effort requires states that undertake actions and play a leading national and international role in simultaneously address the underlying inequalities and discrimination that facilitate trafficking while targeting organized crime and related criminal activities. To this end, governments have developed law enforcement strategies reflected in approaches to criminal justice, the support and assistance provided to victims, human rights protection, the implementation of development strategies, migration policy, and labor market regulation. Part II of the discussion explores the provisions of the international legal and institutional framework that guide national governments in the creation of anti-trafficking policies.

[70] Chuang (2006), p. 140.

## References


*A.G. v. Felicia Okafor*, Nigeria Court of High Justice, Suit No. A.12C.06, Judgment (2006); *Federal Republic of Nigeria v. Favour Anware Okwuede*, Nigeria Court of High Justice, Charge No. FHC.ASB.24C.09, Judgment (2009) at 17

Abadinsky H (2010) Organized crime. Wadsworth Cengage Learning

Alexander A, Malinowski RL, Mogambi AM, Otube SN (2016) Displacement, violence and vulnerability: trafficking among internally displaced persons in Kenya. Awareness Against Hum. Trafficking (HAART) (May 2016), https://ssa.riselearningnetwork.org/wp-content/uploads/sites/5/2016/04/HT-IDP-Research-2016.pdf

Aransiola J, Zarowsky C (2014) Human trafficking and human rights violations in South Africa: stakeholders' perceptions and the critical role of legislation. Afr Hum Rights Law J 14:509, 517

Aronowitz A (2009) Human trafficking, human misery: the global trade in human beings. Prager

*Attorney General of the Federation v. M.A.*, Nigeria High Court, Suit No. B/13c/2004, Judgment (2005) (available at: https://www.unodc.org/cld/case-law-doc/traffickingpersonscrimetype/nga/2005/hon._attorney_general_of_the_federation_v._m.a.html)

Carling J (2005) Trafficking in women from Nigeria to Europe. Migration Policy Institute (Jul. 1, 2005), http://www.migrationpolicy.org/article/trafficking-women-nigeria-europe

Chenda K (2013) Human trafficking in Cambodia (Routledge Contemporary Southeast Asia Series). Routledge, p 27

Cherti M, Pennington J, Grant P (2013) Beyond borders: human trafficking from Nigeria to the UK. Insti. Pub. Pol'y Res. (IPPR), p 38., http://www.ippr.org/files/images/media/files/publication/2013/01/nigeria-trafficking_Jan2013_10189.pdf?noredirect=1

Chuang J (2006) Beyond a snapshot: preventing human trafficking in the global economy. Indiana J Global Leg Stud 13:140, http://www.repository.law.indiana.edu/ijgls/vol13/iss1/5

*Combating International Crime in Africa*, Committee on International Relations., http://commdocs.house.gov/committees/intlrel/hfa50884.000/hfa50884_0.HTM (accessed on August 20, 2021)

*Corruption and the Smuggling of Migrants*, U.N. Office on Drugs and Crime (UNODC) 3 (2013). https://www.unodc.org/documents/human-trafficking/2013/The_Role_Of_Corruption_in_the_Smuggling_of_Migrants_Issue_Paper_UNODC_2013.pdf

*Côte d'Ivoire/Nigeria: Combat Trafficking for Prostitution*, Human Rts Watch (Aug. 26, 2010), http://www.hrw.org/news/2010/08/26/c-te-d-ivoirenigeria-combat-trafficking-prostitution

d'Estree C, Kirby KM (2008) Peacekeepers, the military and human trafficking: protecting whom? Univ St. Thomas Law J 6:221, 233

David F (2012) Organised crime and trafficking in persons. Australian Instit. of Crim. (AIC) (Mar. 2012), https://aic.gov.au/file/6266/download?token=HDZcIrNF

de Lange A (2009) Trafficking for labor exploitation in West and Central Africa. In: Hindman HD (ed) The world of child labor: an historical and regional survey. ME Sharpe, p 195

Ebegbulem S (2017) NAPTIP arrests Italian-based Nigerian lady over human trafficking. Vanguard (Jul. 26, 2017), https://www.vanguardngr.com/2017/07/naptip-arrests-italian-based-nigerian-lady-human-trafficking/

*Explanatory Note—Crime Type: Trafficking in Persons*, U.N. Office of Drugs & Crime (UNODC) (2012), https://www.unodc.org/res/cld/case-law-doc/criminalgroupcrimetype/ita/2012/r_g__ass__nr_1110_-_trafficking_case_html/Trafficking_in_persons_-_explanatory_note.pdf

Ezeh MD (2017) Human trafficking and prostitution among women and girls of Edo State, Nigeria possibility of rehabilitation through education and prevention. Xlibris UK

Fall AS (2003) Enjeux et dÈfis de la Migration Internationale de Travail Ouest-Africaine. Cahiers de Migrations Internationales, http://lartes-ifan.org/pdf/Abdou_Salam_Fall_Enjeux_et_defis_de_la_migration_internationale_de_travail_ouest_africaine.pdf

Farr K (2005) Sex trafficking: the global market in women and children. Worth Publishers, pp 115–117

*Federal Republic of Nigeria v. Favour Anware Okwuede*, Nigeria Court of High Justice, Charge No. FHC.ASB.24C.09, Judgment (2009)

Galli TV, Schauer EJ, Wheaton EM (2010) Economics of human trafficking. Int Migr 124, 129, https://www.amherst.edu/media/view/247221/original/Economics%2Bof%2BHuman%2BTrafficking.pdf

Global Report on Trafficking in Humans, UNDOC 43–44 (2014), https://www.unodc.org/documents/data-and-analysis/glotip/GLOTIP_2014_full_report.pdf

Global Report on Trafficking in Persons 2014, UNODC 56, http://www.unodc.org/res/cld/bibliography/global-report-on-trafficking-in-persons_html/GLOTIP_2014_full_report.pdf

GNA (2004) Combating child labour in Ghana. Modern Ghana (May 28, 2004), https://www.modernghana.com/news/114338/combating-child-labour-in-ghana.html

High Court (2014), Between Nigeria Attorney General and Kingsley Edegbe, 11–24, Charge No. FHC/ABJ/CS/907/2012 (available at: https://www.unodc.org/res/cld/case-law-doc/criminalgroupcrimetype/nga/2014/attorney_general_of_the_federation_and_kingsley_edegbe_html/NIGERIA_Attorney_General_vs_Kingsley_Edegbe_2014.pdf)

Human Rights Watch (2003) Borderline slavery child trafficking in Togo, Vol. 15, No. 8 (A), 29 (April 2003). https://www.hrw.org/sites/default/files/reports/togo0403.pdf

Immigration Acts [2016], no. 25, CG UKUT 00454 (IAC) (Nigeria) (available at: http://www.refworld.org/pdfid/580724ed4.pdf)

Innocenti Insight (2003) Trafficking in human beings, especially women and children, in Africa. UNICEF 9 (Sept. 2003), http://www.unicef-irc.org/publications/pdf/insight9e.pdf

Innocenti Research Centre (2000) Domestic violence against women and girls, Innocenti Digest 6. UNICEF, Florence, p 6

Kippenberg J (2007) Bottom of the ladder: exploitation and abuse of girl domestic workers in Guinea. Hum. Rts. Watch, p 33 (available at https://www.hrw.org/report/2007/06/15/bottom-ladder/exploitation-and-abuse-girl-domestic-workers-guinea)

Kienast J, Lakner M, Neulet A (2014) The role of female offenders in sex trafficking organizations. Regional Academy of the U.N. (RAUN) (Dec. 20, 2014), http://www.ra-un.org/uploads/4/7/5/4/47544571/the_role_of_female_offenders_in_sex_trafficking_organizations.pdf

LegiFrance, at https://www.legifrance.gouv.fr/affichJuriJudi.do?idTexte=JURITEXT000033143954

Mensah-Ankrah C, Sarpong RO (2017) The modern trend of human trafficking in Africa and the role of the African Union (AU). Eban Center for Human Trafficking Stud:5 https://www.researchgate.net/publication/322050335_The_Modern_Trend_of_Human_Trafficking_in_Africa_and_the_Role_of_the_African_Union

*Migration, Human Smuggling and Trafficking from Nigeria to Europe*, Int'l Org. Migr. (IOM) 42 (2006), https://www.iom.int/files/live/sites/iom/files/What-We-Do/idm/docs/MRS23.pdf

Mollema N (2013) Combating human trafficking in South Africa: a comparative legal study (Jun. 2013), p 56 (unpublished LL.D thesis, University of South Africa) (on file with University of South Africa at: https://nfnresources.yolasite.com/resources/2013%20-%20Thesis%20-%20Nina%20Mollema%20-%20A%20comparative%20legal%20study%20of%20Human%20Trafficking%20in%20South%20Africa.pdf)

Naylor RT (2003) Towards a general theory of profit-driven crimes. Br J Criminol 43:81, 83

PO (Nigeria) v. Secretary of State for the Home Department [2011] 132 EWCA 22 (U.K.)

Shelley L (2010) Human trafficking. A global perspective. Cambridge University Press

*Siliadin v. France*, European Court of Human Rights, Application No. 73316/01, Judgment (2005)

*Smuggling of Migrants: The Harsh Search of a Better Life*, UNODC., http://www.unodc.org/toc/en/crimes/migrant-smuggling.html (accessed on July, 2021)

Special Rapporteur on the Human Rights of Migrants, *Addendum - Mission to Senegal*, ¶ 17, U.N. Doc. A/HRC/17/33/Add.2 (Feb. 23, 2011) (by Jorge Bustamante)

Strategies against human trafficking: The role of the security sector, Cornelius Friesendorf, Vienna and Geneva, 130 (September, 2009)

Sun-Suon M, Human trafficking and the role of local governments. U.N. Insti. Training & Res. (UNITAR), p 12, https://unitar.org/sites/default/files/media/publication/doc/SDP-publication3.pdf

Sutter JD (2013) Slavery's last stronghold. CNN, http://www.cnn.com/interactive/2012/03/world/mauritania.slaverys.last.stronghold/index.html
Taylor JE, Wouterse F (2006) Migration and income diversification evidence from Burkina Faso. Dept. of Agricultural & Resource Economics Uni. of CA. (Dec. 2006), p 3, http://ageconsearch.umn.edu/bitstream/190914/2/WP06-003.pdf;
*The Role of Organized Crime in the Smuggling of Migrants from West Africa to the European Union*, UNODC 11 (2011), http://www.unodc.org/documents/human-trafficking/Migrant-Smuggling/Report_SOM_West_Africa_EU.pdf
Touzenis K (2010) Trafficking in human beings: human rights and trans-national criminal law, developments in law and practices. UNESCO, p 57. (available at http://unesdoc.unesco.org/images/0018/001883/188397e.pdf)
Trafficking in Persons Report 2011, France, European Commission, https://ec.europa.eu/anti-trafficking/sites/antitrafficking/files/us_trafficking_in_persons_report_2011_france_en_1.pdf
Trafficking in Persons Report 2015, Benin US Dept. of State, http://www.state.gov/j/tip/rls/tiprpt/countries/2015/243397.htm
Trafficking in Persons Report 2015—Ivory Coast, U.S. Dept. of State, http://www.state.gov/j/tip/rls/tiprpt/countries/2015/243421.htm
*Trafficking in Women to Italy for Sexual Exploitation*, IOM 6 (Jun. 1996), https://childhub.org/en/system/tdf/library/attachments/iom_1996_trafficking_in_wo2.pdf?file=1&type=node&id=16371
U.N. Gift (2010) Analyzing the business model of trafficking in human beings to better prevent the crime. OSCE, https://www.osce.org/cthb/69028?download=true
UNODC (2014) Global Rep. on Trafficking in Persons 2014, at 56 (Nov. 2014), https://www.unodc.org/documents/data-and-analysis/glotip/GLOTIP_2014_full_report.pdf
Walker K (2010) Crimes of untouchable diplomats accused of sex assaults, human trafficking and £36 million in unpaid fines. Daily Mail (29 June 2010) Google Scholar, online: Daily Mail, http://www.dailymail.co.uk/news/article-1290341/Diplomats-accused-sex-assaults-human-trafficking-36m-unpaid-fines.html (accessed August 20, 2021)

# Part II
# Legal and Institutional Response to Trafficking in Persons

The UN Trafficking Convention has subsumed slavery within the manifestations of trafficking in persons, which gives an added significance to its traditional notion. It is important, therefore, to read the 1926 Slavery Convention in such a way as to encompass genuine conditions of slavery and new manifestations of human exploitation. However, given the wide sociological manifestations of modern slavery and the varying jurisdictions, the adoption of international and regional legal instruments, along with specific definitions and distinctions between slavery, trafficking in persons, and forced labor, can be challenging.

For instance, an overly inclusive interpretation of the concept of slavery would subsume forced domestic service and other practices similar to slavery within current legal provisions on slavery without any further analysis, whereas the *Travaux Préparatoires* of the slavery Convention show that it was not an instrument used to combat all forms of exploitation.[1] Hypothetically, the fact that many regional codes are open to different interpretations means that any lack of clarity would undermine the implementation and enforcement of the law designed to change the behavior of offenders and provide protection or satisfaction for the victims. Most importantly, ambiguity in the understanding "of slavery, servitude and forced labor in the modern context is likely to limit, rather encourage applications by individuals for breach of their right not to be enslaved; the potential applicant being unable to identify whether their treatment would engage the relevant legal provisions."[2] Finally, because international discourse is reflected at a domestic level, a common understanding will presumably result in consistency of implementation from state to state and equality of protection.

---

[1] Andrea Nicholson, *Reflections on Siliadin v. France: Slavery and Legal Definition*, 14 Int'l J. Hum. Rts. 705, 714 (2010).

[2] *Id.*

# Chapter 4
# Understanding Trafficking in Persons in International Law

As already referred to in the introduction, the Palermo Protocol is the cornerstone framing the legal definition of trafficking in persons for the international community. Article 3 of the Convention sets forth:

> (a) Trafficking in persons shall mean the recruitment, transportation, transfer, harboring or receipt of persons, by means of the threat or use of force or other forms of coercion, of abduction, of fraud, of deception, of the abuse of power or of a position of vulnerability or of the giving or receiving of payments or benefits to achieve the consent of a person having control over another person, for the purpose of exploitation. Exploitation shall include, at a minimum, the exploitation of the prostitution of others or other forms of sexual exploitation, forced labor or services, slavery or practices similar to slavery, servitude or the removal of organs;
> (b) The consent of a victim of trafficking in persons to the intended exploitation set forth in subparagraph (a) of this article shall be irrelevant where any of the means set forth in subparagraph (a) have been used;
> (c) The recruitment, transportation, transfer, harboring or receipt of a child for the purpose of exploitation shall be considered "trafficking in persons" even if this does not involve any of the means set forth in subparagraph (a) of this article;
> (d) "Child" shall mean any person under eighteen years of age.[1]

Analyzing the definition of the UN Palermo Protocol Allain explains that criminal liability for trafficking in human beings requires three distinctive and correlated elements. First, the individual must engage in any of the activities of 'recruitment, transportation, transfer, harbouring, or receipt of persons.' Secondly, this criminal act must be carried out by means 'of the threat or use of force or other forms of coercion, of abduction, of fraud, of deception, of the abuse of power or of a position of vulnerability or of the giving or receiving of payments or benefits to achieve the consent of a person having control over another person.' Thirdly, the ultimate purpose of the process must be the exploitation of the person in prostitution or other forms of sexual exploitation, forced labor or services, slavery or practices

[1] G.A. Res. 55/25 at art. 3 (November 15, 2000).

 
P. VI. S. Karenga, *A West African Model to Address Human Trafficking*,
https://doi.org/10.1007/978-3-030-88120-7_4

similar to slavery, servitude, or the removal of organs.[2] Although this definition is widely accepted by the international community, several issues can be raised about its practical application and the development of a national understanding of the nature and extent of trafficking in human beings.

With regard to the increasing number of transnational criminal activities that span multiple nations and numerous jurisdictions, states have come to realize that criminal sanctions are nonoperational "without modifications to the substantive criminal law, including the creation of extraterritorial offences, and elaborate cooperation between national investigatory and prosecution authorities of States."[3] Unlike domestics crime such as burglary, theft, and assault committed within a single country, a transnational crime is planned or committed in more than one state, controlled by a group operating in multiple countries, or has substantial effects on several countries,[4] and for this reason several states might claim criminal jurisdiction over the case.[5] Transnational criminal law is the corresponding branch of law dealing with this criminal matter and operates through domestic criminal Courts in imposing individual liability on the traffickers and obligations on the state to prevent this crime, prosecute the individuals involved, and protect the human rights of the victims.[6] The UN Protocol to Prevent, Suppress and Punish Trafficking in Persons, especially Women and Children (2000)[7] is the principal example of this branch of law. This is the first international legally binding instrument to develop a definition of trafficking in persons that covers all trafficking of forced labor, slavery, and servitude, whether it occurs within or across national borders, and to recognize the rights of trafficking victims and meet their needs.

The Trafficking Protocol places the protection of all human rights of trafficked persons at the center of any measures taken to prevent and combat trafficking. Accordingly "[a]nti-trafficking measures should not adversely affect the human rights and dignity of persons and, in particular, the rights of those who have been trafficked, migrants, internally displaced persons, refugees and asylum seekers."[8]

---

[2] Allain (2010), p. 546.

[3] Elliot (2014), p. 56.

[4] UN Convention against Transnational Organized Crime, art.3(2), entered into force Sep. 29, 2003, U.N.T.S.3957.

[5] Elliot (2014), p. 57.

[6] *Id.*

[7] Other sources of transnational criminal laws include: United Nations Convention against Transnational Organised Crime (2000); Protocol against the Smuggling of Migrants by Land, Sea and Air, supplementing the United Nations Convention against Transnational Organised Crime (2000); Protocol against Illicit Manufacturing and Trafficking in Firearms, their Parts and Components and Ammunition, supplementing the United Nations Convention against Transnational Organised Crime (2001); Council of Europe Convention on Cybercrime (2001); Council of Europe Convention on Action against Trafficking in Human Beings (2005); African Union Convention on Cyber-Security and Personal Data Protection (2014).

[8] OHCHR, *Recommended Principles and Guidelines on Human Rights and Human Trafficking*, p. 3, http://www.ohchr.org/Documents/Publications/Traffickingen.pdf.

This victim-centered approach "has the potential to promote a holistic approach which seeks not only legal, but also political, economic and social solutions"[9] to the problem of trafficking in persons.

In addition to fostering national legislative reform and domestic actions, another purpose of the Protocol is to facilitate and strengthen international cooperation in investigating and prosecuting trafficking in persons. Because such trafficking may have potential trans-boundary implications, the national criminal response may be remote due to jurisdictional restrictions: it must therefore be supplemented with criminal cooperation between affected states if offenders are to be deprived of a safe haven.[10] To enhance prosecutorial efforts, Art 16 of the United Nations Convention on Transnational Crimes (UNCTC) prescribes the formation of bilateral and multilateral treaties calling for extraterritorial jurisdiction over traffickers.[11] Where criminal activities occur within domestic jurisdictions, it is possible to prosecute the offenders under the dispositions of the ordinary criminal law.

One of the distinguishing features of transnational criminal law is the relevance of human rights that impose certain specific duties on states for the protection of victims and provide the framework for criminal investigation and fair trials for suspected offenders."[12] The status of international human rights law is such that non-state actors such as organized criminal groups do not bear legal obligations and cannot be held directly responsible for their criminal activities. However, human rights norms and principles can be enforced indirectly in national courts and tribunals through civil and criminal proceedings against traffickers.[13]

## 4.1 Trafficking in Persons as a Process

The definition of trafficking in persons set out in the Palermo Protocol is arguably open to substantial interpretation. For instance, the *travaux préparatoires* leading to the adoption of the Convention adduce very little guidance, which suggests that the intentions of drafters needs to be inferred from the overall structure of the protocol.[14] Like to "drug trafficking", the term "human trafficking" implies the illicit movement of people for commercial or material gain. Although the term refers to movement, controversies may arise as to what degree of movement is required for the offense of

[9] Touzenis (2010a), p. 72.

[10] Elliot (2014), p. 57.

[11] UNODC, *United Nations Convention Against Transnational Organized Crime And The Protocols Thereto,* UNITED NATIONS New York, Art 16 2004, https://www.unodc.org/documents/middleeastandnorthafrica/organised-crime/UNITED_NATIONS_CONVENTION_AGAINST_TRANSNATIONAL_ORGANIZED_CRIME_AND_THE_PROTOCOLS_THERETO.pdf.

[12] Elliot (2014), pp. 56–57.

[13] Obokata (2006), pp. 377, 381.

[14] Bassiouni et al. (2010), pp. 417, 425.

trafficking to have taken place.[15] Central to the debate is whether some form of travel, transportation, or movement across state or national borders or within the community is a required element for the crime of trafficking in persons. Understanding the role that physical movement of the victims can play in the trafficking process lie s in the formulation of anti-trafficking law and policy.

The first approach to the definition of the Palermo Protocol involves extending the concept of trafficking to all situations of exploitation in which individuals are coercively or forcibly exploited, whether movement is involved or not. Ann Gallagher advocates this interpretation of the Convention, which emphasizes the provision of harboring and receipt. She argues that "maintaining an individual in a situation of exploitation through any of the stipulated means would, according to the plain meaning of the text, also amount to trafficking."[16] Therefore, as "both the act and means elements would typically be satisfied by the inherently coercive nature of the end result—for example, exploitation in the form of forced labor or slavery-like practices—demonstrating this exploitation would be sufficient to satisfy all three elements of the definition of trafficking."[17] Following the same line of reasoning, a large number of practitioners believe that the trafficking offense is complete if the end purpose (exploitation) has taken place.

Remarkably, this approach anti-trafficking has the compelling result of being able to capture more forms of exploitation, including situations in which people are maintained or born into bonded labor. It also makes labor "policy and the concept of labor itself explicitly relevant to a field that had long been narrowly focused on sexual exploitation"[18] and calls for labor rights and migration policy reforms as means of reducing vulnerability to trafficking. This advocacy with respect to the broader issues of labor exploitation is reflected in regional and domestic anti-trafficking laws and policymaking. For instance, the Council of Europe Convention and the European Directive criminalize "all forms of trafficking in human beings, whether national or transnational, whether or not connected with organized crime."[19] Furthermore, the Explanatory Report states that the smuggling of migrants involves unlawful cross-border transport in order to obtain a financial or other material benefit whereas "the purpose of trafficking in human beings is exploitation. Furthermore, trafficking in human beings does not necessarily involve a transnational element; it can exist at national level."[20] Various states around the world, including the United States of America, have also criminalized trafficking in persons, indicating that although movement across international boundaries may be involved in the crime,

[15] *Id.* at 425.

[16] Gallagher (2010), p. 31.

[17] Chuang (2014), pp. 609, 632.

[18] *Id.* at 613.

[19] Council of Europe, Convention on Action Against Trafficking in Human Beings and Its Explanatory Report art. 2, May 15, 2005, C.E.T.S. 197 [hereinafter *Council of Europe Trafficking Convention*].

[20] *Explanatory Report* to *the Council of Europe Trafficking Convention*, ¶ 7.

it is not a required component for a person to be considered a victim of trafficking. Thus, the TIP Report office declared that "in analyzing trafficking in persons issues and designing effective responses, the focus should be on the exploitation and control of a person through force, fraud or coercion—not on the movement of that person"[21] The ultimate goal of such advocacy is to increase the capacity to address "all forms of forced labor and trafficking through a single-policy framework and coordination body, thereby promoting great coherence in national responses."[22]

In contrast to this interpretation of the Palermo Protocol, another approach entails maintaining the legal limitations whereby trafficking entails some element of movement, therefore conflating trafficking, slavery, and forced labor, which may actually undermine "trafficking" as a freestanding legal concept.[23] The Palermo Protocol in Article 4 lays out clearly the scope of application of the convention as follows:

> This Protocol shall apply, except as otherwise stated herein, to the prevention, investigation and prosecution of the offences established in accordance with article 5 of this Protocol, where those offences are transnational in nature and involve an organized criminal group, as well as to the protection of victims of such offences.[24]

With regard to the legal issue, the UN Protocol describes the crime of trafficking as involving a series of actions, notably "recruitment, transportation, transfer, harboring or receipt of persons."[25] Although these actions do not describe the nature or extent of the movement required for trafficking to take place, they connote the movement and process carried out by multiple actors in concert. Accordingly, trafficking in persons "is the international supply chain into exploitation, it is not a type of exploitation" and "once that chain is broken, it is no longer trafficking in persons."[26] Allain describes the typical example of a prostitute who has been trafficked into another country and then sold to another brothel owner. In this case, the owner can be held liable for "harboring or receiving" a victim of sex trafficking if evidence shows that that they were involved in the original movement across an international border.[27]

Vladislava Stoyanova noted that "the five actions in the definition can all qualify as human trafficking in isolation from each other. In other words, it is enough for a person to commit only one of these actions to qualify as a perpetrator of human

[21] *Trafficking in Persons Report*, U.S. Dep't. St. (2008).

[22] *ILO, Strengthening Action to End Forced Labor*, ILabC.103/IV/1(2014), art. 21.

[23] Chuang (2014), p. 629.

[24] Convention Against Transnational Organized Crime, Protocol to Prevent, Suppress and Punish trafficking in Persons, Especially Women and Children, done Nov. 15, 2000, T.I.A.S.13127, art. 4.

[25] G.A. Res. 55/25, annex II, U.N. GAOR Supp. No. 49, U.N. Doc. A/45/49 (Vol. I) (Nov. 15, 2000) art. 3(a) [hereinafter *Trafficking Protocol*].

[26] Allain (2012), p. 355.

[27] *Id.*

trafficking as long as the other elements of the definition are also present."[28] It is also important to clarify that "[t]he recruitment, transportation, transfer, harbouring or reception does not necessarily have to be exercised by the same person, but each of the acts constitute criminal conduct [and] it is irrelevant whether the act has been committed jointly within an organised criminal group or not."[29]

By the same token, the earliest anti-trafficking treaties evoke cross-border transportation as part of the crime. For example, the 1949 Convention on the Suppression of Traffic in Persons and the Exploitation of the Prostitution of Others requires the punishment of any person who "procures, entices or leads away" and "exploits the prostitution of another person."[30] The expression 'leads away' describes a movement that provides further evidence to show that the crime could involve the transfer of victims across international borders.

Indisputably the definition of trafficking in persons requires a "sense of movement" because the removal of the victim from his safe and familiar environment is a determining factor in the entire trafficking process, as it aims to isolate the victim from the outside world and make them fully dependent on the trafficker. This objective is usually achieved through displacement across national borders or within a territory. In this respect the Special Rapporteur submitted

> that the definition of trafficking should require that the movement or transport involved is such as to place the victim in an unfamiliar milieu where she is culturally, linguistically or physically isolated and denied legal identity or access to justice. Such dislocation increases trafficked women's marginalization and therefore increases the risk of abuse, violence, exploitation, domination or discrimination both by traffickers and by State officials such as the police, the Courts, immigration officials, etc. Although the crossing of geographic or political borders is sometimes an aspect of trafficking, it is not a necessary prerequisite for these elements to be present. Trafficking occurs within, as well as across, national borders.[31]

An illustrative case (*Kawogo v. UK*) involves a Tanzanian woman named Elizabeth Kawogo who was brought to the UK on a domestic worker visa by her employer Mrs Alibhai, a British citizen resident in Tanzania. The applicant was left in the UK with her employer's elderly parents, Mr and Mrs Dhanji who required her to carry out extensive domestic work without payment. Her passport was taken away and she was not allowed to leave the house other than to go to church. With the help of a friend she met in church, she escaped and reported the abuses to the police but was informed there was insufficient evidence to demonstrate the criminal

---

[28] Stoyanova (2017), p. 34; UNODC, *Legislative Guides for the Implementation of the United Nations Convention against Transnational Organized Crime and the Protocol Thereto*, (2004) ¶¶ 31, 33.

[29] Krieg (2009), pp. 775, 779.

[30] Convention on the Suppression of Traffic in Persons and the Exploitation of the Prostitution of Others art. 1, Dec. 2, 1949, 96 U.N.T.S. 271, [hereinafter: *Convention on Suppression*].

[31] Special Rapporteur on Violence against Women, its Causes, and Consequences on Trafficking in Women, Women's Migration, and Violence against women, Fifty-Sixth Sess. on the Commission on Human Trafficking, U.N. Doc. E/CN.4/2000/68, ¶ 15 (Feb. 29, 2000) (by Radhika Coomerswamy).

liability of Mr and Mrs Dhanji as "essentially they did not commit the cross-border element" required for offenses under the Asylum and Immigration (Treatment of Claimants) 2004.[32]

Furthermore, the Inter-American Court of Human Rights (IACHR) jurisprudence on *Hacienda Brasil Verde Workers v. Brazil*[33] case "brings much clarity that the action element (which entails) movement is one that differentiates" trafficking in persons from forced labor, servitude, or slavery, "and this element needs to be corroborated in order to establish that trafficking has indeed taken place."[34] In its analysis to determine whether the facts constituted trafficking, the Court found that the circumstances of the case meet the legal definition of trafficking in persons described in the Palermo Protocol as the victims were recruited from the poorest regions of the country through fraud, deceit, and false promises.[35] Importantly, this assessment explains how the element of recruitment and movement has been fulfilled, and points to the "action" element of trafficking as the distinctive characteristic rather than its forms of exploitation taken per se.[36] In general, trafficked and non-trafficked victims of forced labor often work in the same sectors in countries of destination. Their distinguishing feature is "that trafficking includes the additional element of movement by the action of a third party into the forced labor situation. Merely maintaining a person in forced labor (for example, intergenerational bonded laborers born into debt bondage), by contrast, would be considered 'non-trafficked forced labor'."[37]

Recalling Ann Gallagher and the TIP Office's perception that trafficking is exploitation-based, it is worth noting that this interpretation led non-governmental organizations (NGOs) and institutions to rebrand forced labor and trafficking as modern day slavery, which has been effective in motivating states to pass legislation and calling on public society to take action. However, questions arise as to whether analyzing and designing policies that conflate forced labor, trafficking in persons, and practices similar to slavery has actually increased the capacity to address the sprawling phenomenon of these practices What are the implications of collapsing distinctions between freestanding legal categories?[38]

With regard to recasting all forced labor as trafficking in persons, it is important to highlight that "[i]nternational human rights law has traditionally drawn distinctions between various types and degrees of exploitation, while also implying a hierarchy

---

[32] *Elisabeth Kawogo v. The United Kingdom*, European Court of Human Rights [ECOHR], Application No. 56921, Statement of Facts, ¶ 8 (23 June 2010).

[33] *Hacienda Brasil Verde Workers v. Brazil*, Inter-American Court of Human Rights [IACtHR], Preliminary Objections, Merits, Reparations and Costs, Series C No. 318 (20 October 2016).

[34] Milano (2018), p. 1.

[35] *Hacienda Brazil*, *supra* note 35, ¶¶ 297–303.

[36] Milano (2018), p. 18.

[37] Chuang (2014), pp. 619–620.

[38] *Id.* at 629.

of severity: slavery, servitude, forced labor."[39] Subsequently, international legal developments have preserved the freestanding legal concepts of slavery, forced labor, practices similar to slavery, and trafficking in persons. Thus, the Forced Labor Convention was adopted in 1930 to deal specifically with forced labor or compulsory labor. Similarly, the 1956 Supplementary Convention to Slavery created a separate concept of "a person of servile status" to protect victims of institutions and practices similar to slavery such as debt bondage, child labor, and serfdom.[40] These practices are considered to be less severe than slavery in Article 8 of the International Covenant on Civil and Political Rights.

Consequently, an interpretation that places an emphasis on "harbouring" collapses the three-part definition and renders the 'action' element meaningless from Vladislava Stoyanova's point of view. Accordingly, if Gallagher's arguments are endorsed, it can be argued that the first person is harbored or received by the second through an abuse of their position of vulnerability for the purpose of sexual exploitation. It follows that trafficking in persons would be deprived of its standing as a concept capturing a distinct phenomenon, and it would thus be possible to label individual instances of rape or sexual abuse.[41] The need to draw conceptual limits on trafficking in persons gives weight to the meaning of the 'action' element. It appears that trafficking in persons encompasses various factual circumstances that are unrelated to its original meaning at an international level (coercively moving a victim from one village to the city, from one street corner to the next, or from one house to another for the purpose of exploitation) but might also converge with conduct traditionally criminalized at a national level, such as fraud, deception, abduction, pimping, and procurement.[42] Subsequently, a clear distinction between these offenses in national criminal law is crucial as it can have a significant impact on the identification and protection of victims, the prosecution of offenders, and the eradication of structural factors that lead to exploitation.

Although the United Nations, non-governmental organizations (NGOs), and most governmental bodies states that the crime of trafficking in persons does not require any movement, the most persuasive argument that protects the legal integrity of the definition should include 'some form of movement' "to create a 'constructive' or 'substantive' border crossing of a geographical or political boundary."[43] Indeed "if human trafficking within national borders is to make some sense [. . .] elements denoting distinctiveness have to be included, such as that the perpetrator has moved

---

[39] *Id.*, note 140.

[40] *See* Report of the Advisory Committee of Experts on Slavery, *Fourth Session of the Committee*, Apr. 10, 1935, 159 L.N.T.S. 113 (Doc. C.), at 9–10. ("[O]ne should realize quite clearly that [debt slavery]. . .is not 'slavery' within the definition set forth in. . .the 1926 Convention, unless any or all the powers attaching to the right of ownership are exercised by the master.").

[41] Stoyanova (2017), pp. 38–39.

[42] *Id.* at 41.

[43] Bassiouni et al. (2010), p. 426.

the victim to an unfamiliar milieu where the latter does not have social contacts."[44] The very purpose for traffickers of moving their victims is to ensure additional control by placing them in an unfamiliar environment where they are culturally, linguistically, or physically isolated and ignored by authorities. Such dislocation renders the victims vulnerable to violence and exploitation and increases their domination by traffickers. Furthermore, the historical context of the Palermo Protocol suggests that the international community focused on the issue of trafficking on the "understanding that the problem of abuses was linked with the movement of victims to an unfamiliar milieu which made it difficult for them to access assistance, and had to be faced with the adoption of an international instrument."[45]

There is an inseparable connection between the steps traffickers take to isolate their victims from their social environment and the physical movement of the victim to another place, "as isolation can effectively create a situation in which the victim has nowhere to go and no one to turn to and thus no opportunity to escape."[46] Thus, elements indicating "social isolation" are bound to the process and are relevant to situations of trafficking without physical movement of the victims. Depending on the circumstances, the trafficker can isolate the victims from the outside world by prohibiting them from communicating with family and friends, and not allowing them to read the newspaper or attend church. In the *R. v. Urizar* case, the defendant at one stage moved the victim into his friend's apartment, took her cellular phone each time he left the apartment, insisted that she abandon her studies, and refused to allow her to give her new address to her mother.[47] In West Africa, traffickers may make use of existing barriers that naturally isolate victims such as a lack of education and unfamiliarity with the culture of the place of exploitation or the remote location of the premises.[48] Additionally, cultural stigma or factors relating to vulnerability such as age, gender, illness, and psychological issues may refrain victims of forced marriage, involuntary servitude, and child labor from leaving their abusive situations. Another method of control extensively discussed in Part I is the abuse of victims' vulnerability through witchcraft rituals that form part of the forced labor or trafficking process.

Another argument in support of the inclusion of the 'action element' is that states who are parties to the Trafficking in Persons Convention have a transnational duty to address trafficking in persons as the Protocol states they have a shared responsibility to prevent international trafficking and this responsibility transcends national borders. Stoyanova observed that this "shared responsibility" to prevent international

---

[44] Stoyanova (2017), p. 42.

[45] Stoyanova (2013), pp. 64, 77.

[46] *Evidential Issues in Trafficking in Persons Cases*, U.N. Office of Drugs & Crime (UNODC) 87 (2017), https://www.unodc.org/documents/human-trafficking/2017/Case_Digest_Evidential_Issues_in_Trafficking.pdf.

[47] *Regina v. Urizar*, Québec, District of Longueuil, Criminal Division (J.C.Q.), Judgment, File No. 505-1-084654-090 (13 August 2010), and *Urizar v. Regina*, Quebec Court of Appeal, Judgment, No. 500-10-004763-106 (16 January 2013).

[48] UNODC, Evidential Issues in Trafficking in Persons Cases CASE DIGEST, 87 UNODC (2017).

trafficking in persons has the potential advantage of addressing abuses against migrants that derive from the process of movement and migration across borders.[49] In effect, from a legal perspective, states undertake a legally binding obligation to facilitate international cooperation in combating trafficking, implementing strong border control measures, and ensuring better security and control of travel documents. As such, the definition of trafficking in persons "cannot be interpreted without consideration of the obligations that states adopt in relation to human trafficking, obligations that pertain to movement across borders."[50]

The concept of transnational obligations incumbent to all member states under the Protocol unfolded in the *Rantsev v. Russia* case. Remarkably, the striking feature in this case was that the complaint was simultaneously lodged against parties from two states. Given that trafficking offenses may occur in the state of origin, transit, and the destination, the Court outlined the positive obligation of states arising under Article 4 of the European Court of Human Rights (ECHR) to engage in effective cooperation with any investigation: "member States are also subject to a duty in cross-border trafficking cases to cooperate effectively with the relevant authorities of other States concerned in the investigation of events which occurred outside their territories."[51] Although the endorsement of trafficking as a process that can unfold exclusively within the border of a single state might be challenging in domestic Courts, its invocation has the potential to strengthen the positive obligation of states in cross-border cases.

In short, trafficking refers to the process and can occur without servitude or slave labor exploitation. Among numerous examples of this are attempts and conspiracies relating to trafficking in persons, organ trafficking, trafficking in persons for ritual sacrifice, and the illegal adoption of children. In relation to this, the facts in the *Rantseva* case did not show that exploitation occurred, supporting the Russian Government's objection that "the complaint under Article 4 of the Convention was inadmissible *ratione materiae* as there was no slavery, servitude or forced or compulsory labour in the present case."[52] The Special Rapporteur on Violence against Women explains that the "action" element of the definition is intended to capture all persons and institutions involved in the trafficking chain. It "has the effect of bringing, within potential reach of the definition, not just recruiters, brokers, and transporters but also owners, and managers, supervisors, and controllers of any place of exploitation such as a brothel, farm, boat, factory, medical facility, or household."[53] Criminalizing the activities of all parties engaged in the trafficking process

---

[49]The concept of "shared responsibility" is borrowed from Anne Gallagher in Gallagher (2010), p. 414.

[50]Stoyanova (2017), p. 39.

[51]*Rantsev v. Cyprus and Russia*, European Court of Human Rights, Judgment, Application No. 25965/04, ¶ 289, (7 January 2010) (available at: https://ec.europa.eu/anti-trafficking/sites/antitrafficking/files/rantsev_vs_russia_cyprus_en_4.pdf).

[52]*Id.*

[53]Gallagher (2010), p. 30; Cf. Trafficking in Women, Women's Migration and Violence against Women, UN Doc.E/CN.4/2000/68, 29 February 2000, para. 14 https://www.

facilitates efforts to both prevent the crime and prosecute recruiters as well as other trafficking auxiliaries, including transporters, owners, and supervisors of any place of exploitation.[54] Although some of the actors involved in trafficking "do not exploit or could be physically distanced from the potential or actual exploitation, they can be held criminally liable as perpetrators of human trafficking since they assist by recruiting, transporting, receiving, etc. the victims."[55]

## 4.2 The *Mens Rea* Element: For the Purpose of Exploitation

The criminal intent element required by the Palermo Protocol is the purpose of exploitation. In this section, the main issue that will be discussed is the level of intent required to satisfy the offense. In the criminal justice system, the criminal liability of the offender is usually tested in relation to two criminal law concepts: the *mens rea*—the mental element—and the *actus reus*—the material or physical element (s).[56] In addition to meeting all the *material* elements of a crime, an offender must be shown to have a "guilty mind or culpable mind" when they engaged in the prohibited conduct.[57] The *mens rea* reflects the state of mind of the person charged with a criminal offense. This requires determining the defendant's intent when they committed the crime.

With regard to the criminalization of trafficking in persons, Article 5 of the UN Trafficking Protocol requires states to adopt legislative provisions prohibiting trafficking in persons, but neither the Protocol nor its *travaux préparatoires* elaborate on the mental element of the crime. The UN Special Rapporteur on Violence against Women explained that the mental element required for criminal liability in a case of trafficking is that the person committed the material acts (recruitment, transportation, harboring. . .through coercion) with the intention or purpose that the victim be 'exploited'.[58] Notably, the Unite Nations Office on Drugs and Crime (UNODC)

---

globaldetentionproject.org/wp-content/uploads/2016/06/Special-Rapporteur-on-Violence-against-Women-its-Causes-and-Consequences-Radhika-Coomaraswamy-2000.pdf.

[54] Trafficking in Women, Women's Migration and Violence against Women, UN Doc.E/CN.4/2000/68, 29 February 2000, para. 14 https://www.globaldetentionproject.org/wp-content/uploads/2016/06/Special-Rapporteur-on-Violence-against-Women-its-Causes-and-Consequences-Radhika-Coomaraswamy-2000.pdf.

[55] Stoyanova (2017), p. 43.

[56] UN.GIFT (2009), p. 8. In the crime of trafficking in persons, the *actus reus* requirement includes for the first part recruiting, transporting, transferring, and harboring while the second part must contain at least one of the following means: use of force, threat of force, coercion, abduction, fraud, deception, abuse of power or of a position of vulnerability, and the giving or receiving of benefits.

[57] An act does not make its doer guilty, unless the mind be guilty (*Actus non facit reum, nisi mens sit rea*).

[58] Trafficking in Women, Women's Migration and Violence against Women, UN Doc.E/CN.4/2000/68, 29 February 2000, para. 16.

considers trafficking in persons to be a crime of *dolus specialis* (specific intent) requiring from the perpetrator the specific purpose of exploiting the victim when committing the material acts of the offence.[59] Accordingly, the Legislative Guide to the Protocol that assists domestic legislations in implementing the provisions of the convention requires only the criminalization of intentional conduct and not conduct carrying lower standards such as negligence. It is important to understand that this element of intention refers only to the criminal conduct or action and should not be considered a requirement that excuses offenders who may have been ignorant or unaware of the law.[60] The offense of trafficking in persons "requires a high level of *mens rea*, targeting people who intend to exploit others or who know that others intend to exploit."[61] In general, trafficking in persons offenses were crafted to capture the various actors situated along the trafficking continuum, including those actively involved in organizing, directing and participating as accomplices, as well as those committing the trafficking in persons offense.[62]

Although the UN Protocol sets a high threshold at which to prove the offense of trafficking in persons, it upholds that "countries are not precluded from allowing the mental element of the crime of trafficking to be established on a lesser standard, i.e. via recklessness, willful blindness or even criminal negligence, subject to the requirements of the domestic legal system."[63] For the most part, criminal Courts apply three methods to prove the culpable mental state of a person regarding an offense: (1) that the defendant has committed one of the acts "for the purpose of" or the specific intent of exploiting another person; (2) that the defendant knew the victim would be exploited; or (3) that the defendant recklessly disregarded the fact that the victim would be exploited. Only a suspected perpetrator with a sufficiently "guilty mind" can be convicted in Court of trafficking in persons.

The highest level of *mens rea* required to hold a potential offender liable for the offense of trafficking is intent to exploit. An offender acts intentionally if he or she desires or wants the consequences to follow their actions.[64] This is the highest degree of culpability and is proven by the decided resolve, degree of planning or aforethought involved in the criminal act. With regard to trafficking in persons, the establishment of individual criminal liability requires proof that the alleged offender meant to carry out the act of recruitment, transportation, and so on for the purpose of exploitation where the consequence is very likely to occur. To establish the crime, the Trafficking in Persons Protocol does not require the perpetrator to actually exploit the victim. As soon as a defendant carries out the "acts" and the "means"

[59] UN.GIFT (2009), p. 5, n1.

[60] UNODC The Legislative Guide for the Implementation of the United Nations Convention against Transnational Organized Crime and the Protocol Thereto, 2004, para. 174 (d), p. 471.

[61] https://www.justice.gc.ca/eng/rp-pr/cj-jp/tp/hcjpotp-gtpupjp/p2.html.

[62] *The Legislative Guide for the Implementation of the United Nations Convention against Transnational Organized Crime and the Protocol Thereto*, (2004), para. 36, pp. 269–270.

[63] UN.GIFT (2009), p. 5.

[64] Stoyanova (2013), pp. 44–45.

with the intent of exploitation, the offense of trafficking has been committed. Siller explains that

> [i]t is the actual purpose of the perpetrator, as opposed to the 'practical results' which satisfies the *mens rea* element. For a situation to be considered as trafficking in persons, the exploitation does not necessarily have to take place. The action taken and the means used must be carried out with the specific intention to exploit.[65]

Nevertheless, in cases of intended exploitation it has never ensued that the Court may face particular evidentiary challenges in proving the intention of exploitation and to convict either for the attempted or the completed crime. The *Attorney General of the Federation v. Constance Omoruyi*[66] case mentioned previously is an illustrative example that demonstrates the importance of intention as the Court convicted the defendant for an intended exploitation that had not yet occurred. In this case, the defendant made an agreement with the victims to travel abroad to work as prostitutes. While they were still in Nigeria, the victims were apprehended by law enforcement; they had not yet engaged in any commercial sexual activities. The defendant was convicted for an attempt to organize the trafficking of women abroad for the purpose of prostitution and an attempt to place them in servitude as pledge for a debt payment. The analysis of the case by the Court was supported by the testimony of a native "juju" doctor who proved the defendant's intention to exploit. They girls were bound by an oath not to flee but to pay their debts.[67] Because it is often challenging to prove that a defendant intended the consequences of his or her actions, the concept of recklessness is drawn on to overcome this difficulty.

The lower *mens rea* compared to intent is knowledge. The recruiter or the individual who is transporting acts knowingly if they know that the victim will be exploited. These actors "do not intend to the victim's exploitation; but they are aware that once recruited or transported, exploitation will follow."[68] The borderline between these two "culpability levels is the presence or absence of a *positive desire* to cause the result."[69] Thus, when an offender is aware that exploitation will be a predictable result of their actions, then they are guilty of having criminal knowledge. This is relevant when dealing with aiding and abetting, which is associated with intermediary actors who are aware of a high probability of the consequences but who choose not to confirm what they strongly suspect. In relation to the situation in West Africa, boys in Niger who are trafficked for forced cattle herding sometimes escape their employers and return to their parents. The boys arrive home displaying visible signs of physical and psychological abuse. However, many parents return their sons

---

[65] Siller (2016), p. 418.

[66] *Attorney General of the Federation v. Omoruyi*, High Court Edo State of Nigeria, Suit No. B/31c/2004 (2006).

[67] UNODC, *supra* note 50, at 131.

[68] Stoyanova (2013), p. 45.

[69] Robinson and Grall (1983), pp. 681, 694.

against their will to their employers, angry that the child has abandoned an opportunity to learn a trade.[70]

In other situations, however, establishing this mental state in Court is challenging. Accordingly, Stoyanova raises the following issue. The person recruiting might know that the migrant will work, for example as a prostitute in the destination country; however, at the time of recruitment, did the recruiter know under what conditions the work will be performed and whether these conditions amount to 'sexual exploitation'?[71] While it may be easier in Court to find sufficient evidence proving that the "end exploiter" acted with criminal intent, it appears to be more challenging to demonstrate that actors involved in the process preceding the exploitation, such as the recruiter, transporter, or hotel owner knew that the victim would be exploited.[72] In fact, "it may be difficult, for example, to establish the necessary *mens rea* with respect to a recruiter or transporter, who may, quite reasonably, deny any knowledge of the final end purpose."[73] Furthermore, Courts may be faced with the dilemma of whether to convict alleged traffickers as perpetrators inasmuch as they are themselves vulnerable people. These include relatives of victims, children, and former victims who may be involved in the trafficking chain, as described in Part I.

The third mental state is negligence, recklessness, or disregard. A defendant will be deemed reckless if they have foreseen the occurrence of the undesired consequences of their action yet unreasonably continue to take that risk.[74] The required element "is that the person who recruits or transports manifests negligence or disregard as to what might happen to the person once that person is recruited, transported or transferred or transported in the country of destination."[75] Ordinarily, an alleged trafficking offender will attempt to assert that they were unaware of the risk incurred. For example, in *The State v. Phanat Laojindamanee and others* case, which involved the deceptive recruitment and transportation of young women from Thailand to Fiji for the purpose of prostitution, both defendants convicted for facilitating the trafficking claimed they were "unsophisticated players with no previous criminal history and they were unwittingly caught in this net of international trafficking."[76] In this context, the Court applied the doctrine of "willful blindness" which involves inferring knowledge on the part of a defendant where the evidence indicates that the defendant sought to avoid guilty knowledge.[77] The

[70] U.S. Dept. of St, *Trafficking in Persons Report June 2009*, at 7.

[71] Stoyanova (2017), p. 45.

[72] UNODC, *supra* note 50, at 126.

[73] Gallagher (2010), p. 34.

[74] Stoyanova (2017), p. 45, n. 44.

[75] *Id.* at 45.

[76] *The State v. Phanat Laojindamanee and others*, High Court of Fiji at Suva, Criminal Case No. HAC323, Judgment, ¶ 27.

[77] Justice for Victims of Trafficking Act: A Legal Analysis of the Criminal Provisions of P.L. 114-22, June 9, 2015, https://www.everycrsreport.com/reports/R44064.html#fn22.

issue is not whether the jury believes the defendant, but whether the members of the jury believe in a practical sense that they would have been aware of the risk in the defendant's circumstances. Worded in various ways, the jury are asked to simply decide whether the defendant ought to have been as aware of the risk as any other reasonable person.[78] National legislations may set a low threshold of proof for child trafficking to capture those using the services of trafficking victims. In this regard, it has been articulated in the law in Nigeria that:

> any person who by use of force, deception, threat, coercion, debt bondage (immediate or in the near future) or any means whatsoever[...] keeps detains or harbours any other person with intent, knowing or having reason to know that such person is likely to be forced or induced into prostitution or other forms of exploitation with or by any person or an animal, commits an offence and is liable on conviction to imprisonment for not less than 5 years and a fine.[79]

Remarkably, this low threshold at which to prove culpability has produced some surprising results in terms of effective prosecutions, ranking Nigeria Tier 1 in the TIP Report (June 27, 2011).

The *mens rea* for trafficking in persons requires the offender to know or recklessly disregard the fact that the victim is a minor or has been subject to force, fraud, or coercion to engage in the commercial sex act. For example, in Nigeria the Anti-trafficking Act provides that a body corporate that commits trafficking in persons on the instigation or with the connivance or by any neglect shall be liable to a fine of ₦ 2 million.[80] However, when it comes to prosecuting potential traffickers, Courts face a significant challenge in establishing that all the actors involved in the recruitment and movement, harboring, and receipt of victims possess the requisite mental element for this offense. In criminal Courts, the level of criminal intent is weighed to determine the degree of culpability that results in a fair sentence.[81]

For example, Case No. 8959—2012 (Egypt)[82] from the Criminal Court of Egypt involved a complex chain of actors who colluded to operate a trafficking for prostitution ring, with each defendant fulfilling a specific role. The criminal organization arranged false marriages between young girls in dire economic need and men from the Gulf states. The perpetrators approached the girls and their families under the premise of marrying them to wealthy men. Among those involved in this process was a fake lawyer who issued false *orfy* marriage certificates. Another defendant was

---

[78] All Answers ltd, 'Mens Rea Lecture' (Lawteacher.net, May, 2019) https://www.lawteacher.net/modules/criminal-law/committing-an-offence/mens-rea/lecture.php?vref=1 (accessed August11, 2021).

[79] Nigeria, Act to repeal the Trafficking in persons, Article 14 (b).

[80] TRAFFICKING IN PERSONS (PROHIBITION) LAW ENFORCEMENT AND ADMINISTRATION ACT, Article 28 https://www.refworld.org/cgi-bin/texis/vtx/rwmain/opendocpdf.pdf?reldoc=y&docid=54f98a284.

[81] Robinson and Grall (1983), pp. 681, 682.

[82] Case No. 8959-2012, Criminal Court of Haram and Appeal No. 6772, Judicial Year 82, Egypt. This case is based on a summary and analysis of the decisions of the Criminal Court of Giza Province and the Court of Cassation submitted by an Egyptian expert.

in charge of building an artificial hymen in each of the victims so that they would appear to be virgins, allowing them to charge higher fees and enable the girls to be re-married. Two of these defendants participated in the trafficking by preparing two private apartments where the prostitution occurred. The case also included four clients from the Gulf states who wanted to engage in sexual relations with the young women. Another three defendants implicated in the criminal act were the parents of victims who facilitated the sexual exploitation of their daughters in exchange for financial support by taking them to meet other clients in premises used as brothels.

This case is of particular interest because it involves various actors, including not only professional criminals but also the parents of the victims and clients who intended to engage in sexual relations with the girls under the guise of marriage contracts. The case raises the crucial issue of victim consent and how to prove guilty knowledge of the chain of actors engaged in the trafficking. The Court ruling also raises the question as to whether victims' families should be considered innocent facilitators or complicit in trafficking. Furthermore, in situations of domestic servitude in Africa, children may not consider themselves victims of crime due to their relationship with those who have trafficked them.[83]

Throughout the case, the Court established the *mens rea* or criminal knowledge of all actors in the chain of trafficking regarding the criminal purposes of the operation, as this was the condition on which they were to be convicted. The relationship dynamic between the different perpetrators in carrying out the intended purpose is more likely to fall within the definition of an "organized group" as described in Article 2(a) of the UN Convention on Transnational Organized Crime. Accordingly, an organized group is a:

> structured group of three or more persons, existing for a period of time and acting in concert with the aim of committing one or more serious crimes or offences established in accordance with this Convention, in order to obtain, directly or indirectly, a financial or other material benefit.

In this particular case, the key for the prosecution was to prove a degree of connection between those initially recruiting the victims and those harboring and receiving them, and that all upheld the chain of responsibility as they were, at least seemingly, acting for the same purpose in procuring women for sexual exploitation.[84] Because the third defendant had in his possession 95 unofficial marriage contracts, this evidenced his guilty knowledge. The fourth defendant was responsible for constructing an artificial hymen for each of the victims for the purpose of sexual exploitation and those defendants who admitted knowledge of his actions thus demonstrated their criminal intent. However, the Court acquitted those clients relying on a document issued by a Gulf Embassy officially allowing at least one

---

[83] An analysis of the case can be found in UNODC, Evidential Issues in Trafficking in Persons Cases CASE DIGEST, 162–164 (2017).

[84] Demetriou (2018), p. 8.

client to marry in Egypt, which served to prove his innocent intentions along with those of his brother and friends.

Regarding the consent of victims, the Court noted that they could seemingly be viewed as consenting to their prostitution with the men from the Gulf states even if they were initially deceived and thought they would be married. Thus, to convict the defendant for trafficking, the Court invoked the abuse of a position of vulnerability, which precludes the victim's consent. In its ruling the Court recalled Egyptian law which states that "[t]he consent of the victim to exploitation in any of the forms of human trafficking shall be irrelevant as long as any of the means stipulated in Article 2 of this law have been used and, in regard to minors, consent is irrelevant even if no means have been used."[85] Because some of the victims involved were minors, therefore the matter of consent becomes irrelevant. In convicting the defendants, the trial Court relied on the means of "deception" or "exploitation of a position of vulnerability or need"[86] to prove the commission of the offense.

Another issue dealt with in this case was whether family members who participated in the trafficking process should be convicted as perpetrators or seen as quasi victims whose vulnerabilities are being exploited. When can parents be considered complicit in trafficking? In fact, in this case the parents facilitated the prostitution of their daughters by taking them to one of the brothel houses to offer them to the other defendants. They then selected whomever they wished the girls to engage in sexual activities with in exchange for sums of money. However, the trial Court apparently accepted the parents' claim that they were persuaded the girls would be married. This lack of awareness and the financial vulnerability of the parents negated the special intent required in trafficking crimes. Furthermore, the trial Court acquitted the parents on the assumption that no parent would allow his or her daughter to be exploited in prostitution. The Court of cassation inversely expressed doubt about the parents' innocence in view of the fact that the victims were exploited several times. This complex case illustrates the difficulties in proving the criminal intent of a multiplicity of defendants to secure their convictions. It also reflects the challenge involved in demonstrating the guilty knowledge of family members of victims who participated in the trafficking process.

## 4.3 Means Used: The Issue of Victim's Consent

Before addressing the issue of victim's consent, it is pertinent to explain the conceptual evolution of free labor and coercion. Allain states that, in essence, "free labour is the product of law. It is only through the establishment of domestic and international regulation that a person can assert their right to free choice of

[85] See Law No. 64 of 2010 regarding Combating Human Trafficking, Article 3 https://www.ilo.org/dyn/natlex/docs/ELECTRONIC/89881/103359/F-383089588/eg%2064%20of%202010.pdf.

[86] *Ibid.* Article 2.

labour."[87] In the Middle-Ages, indenture servitude was considered a 'normal' form of consensual, contractual labour "as employees freely consented to a contract which committed them to working for a set number of years."[88] The state through criminal law ensured compliance with the labor contract. Prematurely departing servants could be legally compelled to complete the term of their service or work additional days to make up those lost to illness, and employers were allowed to inflict corporal punishment on non-complying servants.[89] Historians have correspondingly upheld that free labor consisted of moving away from medieval labor systems manifest in indentured forms of servitude such as serfdom to wage labor. However, such assumptions were challenged in the 1990s "as the work of historians showed that labour systems were best understood on a continuum from free to coerced work as opposed to being in binary opposition."[90] Thus, "what would have been termed free labour as late as the Nineteenth Century would be deemed today" unfree in the modern sense of the term and "by its very nature, exploitive."[91] What would have been characterized as legal 'free labour' during this period would be considered 'involuntary servitude' by today's standards, "as nonpecuniary pressures were used to create a form of 'coerced contractual labour'."[92]

From a philosophical perspective it is impossible to attain the ideal of what qualifies as free labor. Jean Allain observed that any labor relationship is coercive, whether the person is physically forced to work or is required to choose between the lesser of two evils.[93] Nevertheless, according to contemporary standards, "having chosen the lesser of two evils is not – in law – deemed coerced labour."[94] Whether a labor is free is "a judgment about what kinds of coercive pressures are legitimate and illegitimate in labour relations."[95] This determination is continuously evolving according to "the subjective standard set by each State, guided by international labour standards."[96] In this respect Jean Allain argues that violations of international labor standards which may be considered exploitive are merely dealt with in domestic Courts as infractions of labor rights that often do not reach the threshold of a criminal law. Instead, these violations are addressed "through administrative sanction, requiring, for instance, the reimbursement of back-wages and the payment of a fine."[97] The debate as to what constitutes free labor and exploitation therefore remains open.

---

[87] Allain (2012), p. 204.

[88] *Ibid.*

[89] Steinfeld (1991), p. 7.

[90] Allain (2012), p. 204.

[91] *Ibid.*

[92] *Ibid.*, at 205.

[93] *Ibid.*, at 204; Steinfeld (1991).

[94] Allain (2012), p. 204.

[95] Steinfeld (2001), p. 16.

[96] Allain (2012), p. 205.

[97] Allain (2012), p. 206.

Returning to the issue of consent, it is important to note that under the law consent is deemed valid when it is informed and freely given, that the person giving consent has the legal or decision-making capacity to do so, and that such consent exists at the time of the act to which consent is given.[98] In the Palermo Protocol, the consent of the victim to the intended exploitation is legally invalid if it is obtained through threats, use of force and other forms of coercion. Thus, evidence of victim consent cannot be raised by the traffickers as a criminal defence in domestic Court.[99] In cases involving children, trafficking in persons is assumed regardless of the use of prohibited means set forth in the Convention. The rationale in both instances rests on the argument that no one can consent to being exploited 'through the use of improper means'[100] and, in the case of children, "their vulnerable position makes it impossible for them to provide consent in the first place."[101] According to the *Travaux Préparatoires*, the Protocol's statement on consent reflected dangers foreseen by member states "that consent would become the first line of defence for those accused of trafficking offences, most particularly in cases where victims may have consented at some point to migrate for work and or to engage in prostitution."[102]

The notion of 'consent' reflected in the Protocol was the subject of controversial debate in negotiations. The discussions revolved around women's agency in terms of "whether or not women can actually choose to work in the sex industry – and, in relation to this, the question whether trafficking should be defined by the nature of the work involved or by the use of deceit and coercion."[103] In fact, the Trafficking Protocol was the target of two competing interest groups concerned about the effect of a new anti-trafficking instrument on the lives of sex workers. The Coalition Against Trafficking in Women (CATW) claimed that prostitution is 'inherently exploitative' and in violation of 'human rights in all circumstances.'[104] This activist group pointed out the necessity of including in the definition language such as 'irrespective of the consent of the person' or 'with or without her consent' to prevent traffickers from using the consent of the victim as a defense to evade accountability.[105] This argument was used to defend the position "that consent should not be permitted to trump fundamental human and social values such as dignity, freedom and protection of the most vulnerable within society."[106]

The other group represented by The (HRC) supported the view that prostitution is a legitimate form of labor. Subsequently, instead of defining trafficking in terms of

---

98 McClean (2007), pp. 20, 322; Elliot (2014).

99 UNODC, Legislative Guides for the Implementation of the United Nations Convention against Transnational Organized Crime and the Protocols thereto, UN Sales No.E.05.V.2 (2004), p. 270.

100 Gallagher (2010), p. 47.

101 UNODC, *supra* note 50, at 8.

102 UNODC, *supra* note 50, at 6.

103 Ditmore and Wijers (2003), pp. 79, 82.

104 *See also*, Elliot (2014), p. 109.

105 Ditmore and Wijers (2003).

106 UNODC, *supra* note 50, at 9.

'the nature of work' involved, the Human Rights Caucus (HRC) argued that legislative policies should focus on the use of coercive or deceptive means when determining whether the alleged victim has voluntarily consented to the recruitment and work conditions.[107] This position upholds the idea that people can consent to migrate or to work in prostitution, even though they cannot consent to forced labor exploitation, slavery, or servitude.

Article 3(b) of the Palermo Protocol, elaborated on by the Ad Hoc Committee at the end of the session, attempted "to draw the line between coercive and voluntary prostitution, and also expands the scope of criminalized activities by broadening the list of coercive means that weaken the weight of the given consent."[108] As a result it encompasses a range of practices including forced labor that are identified as instances of trafficking whereby people have been trafficked or trafficking crimes have been perpetrated.[109]

Although Article 3(b) of the Palermo Protocol[110] considers the victim's consent to engage in prostitution to be irrelevant, in practice such consent is relevant in certain domestic anti-criminal laws when determining whether the person has been trafficked. For example, Gambia, Ghana, Sierra Leone in West Africa, and many other countries have chosen to remain silent on the issue of the victim's consent in trafficking situations. In the absence of statutory norms specifically governing the issue of consent, Courts might consider a victim's consent as relevant in determining the culpability of the defendant for the offense of trafficking in persons.[111] In terms of application, it has been clearly defined that trafficking in persons is carried out with some form of coercion, abuse, or threat to achieve their consent;, however it is difficult to define the conditions indicative of this coercion and the degree of inequity of power between a trafficker and a victim that is required to meet this element of the definition. Definitions of 'lack of consent' and 'coercion' are inherently elusive and are difficult to apply, particularly when coupled with the taxing issue of the effect of pressing economic circumstances.[112]

In practice, most often migrant workers in West Africa might start their journey by consenting in a fully informed and voluntary manner to be smuggled into a foreign country to work in what they believe are legitimate jobs. The facilitators may have given false promises to the prospective workers who, in the destination country, find themselves deceived regarding the nature of the work and end up being forced to

---

[107] Ditmore and Wijers (2003), p. 83.

[108] See also Roth (2012), p. 69.

[109] UNODC, *'The Role of "Consent" in the Trafficking in Persons Protocol' (2014)* Issue Paper, 15-16) accessed August 15, 2021_ (Consent Issue Paper).

[110] Convention Against Transnational Organized Crime, Protocol to Prevent, Suppress and Punish trafficking in Persons, Especially Women and Children, done Nov. 15, 2000, T.I.A.S.13127 [hereinafter Palermo Protocol "Consent of a victim of trafficking in persons to the intended exploitation set forth in subparagraph (a) of this article shall be irrelevant where any of the means set forth in subparagraph (a) have been used."

[111] Bosworth et al. (2012), pp. 137, 149.

[112] Elliot (2014), p. 11.

work for low wages in payment for the travelling fees. Indeed, the defendant will often raise evidence of victim consent to travel and work as a defense. Arguably, "the consent of the victim at one stage of the process cannot be taken as the consent at all stages of the process, and without consent at every stage a trafficking offence has taken place."[113]

A further issue concerns the case of Nigerian girls who consent and even sign contracts to travel abroad to engage in prostitution. In this case the defendant may argue in a domestic Court that migrants who are "well informed" when making their decision to engage in prostitution abroad cannot later claim they were presented with utterly false prospects and were thus victims of a criminal act. A retort in this particular example could be that "the fact that the victim knew in advance that she was going to engage in prostitution" does not absolve the trafficker of criminality "because the victim was aware of the nature of the work but not of the working conditions."[114] In relation to this issue of deception that precludes consent it is instructive to recall the experience of migrant workers in the Middle East. Most of these migrants were recruited by agencies and claimed that they were deceived about the working conditions in their employer's home in the Middle East.[115] This raises the question as whether the recruiters and agents should be held accountable for the harm. Is it the recruitments agency's responsibility to provide all the information and to predict the subsequent exploitative working conditions in the house of the employer or "is the onus on the individual migrant who may be self-delusional or in denial of warnings of the risks involved?"[116] Who should be prosecuted for deception and breach of the contractual arrangements, the employers or also the recruiters?

An extremely challenging situation related to consent is when the victim him/herself asserts their free consent to act which then led them to the alleged trafficking situation. Even though it is well established that is not possible under international law to consent to abuse, slavery, servitude, and exploitation, the evidence might show that victims clearly consented to the subsequent exploitation. For example, apparent consent to work in the prostitution industry, along with evidence that the individual involved received remuneration, may protect a trafficker from prosecution.[117] As noted in the foregoing descriptive analysis, many victims in West Africa do not identify themselves as such. Men involved in forced labor and young girls engaged in domestic wok are unwilling to acknowledge that they have been coerced into a situation of exploitation and are victims of a serious crime. Their

---

[113] *Id.* at 6.

[114] *Toolkit to Combat Trafficking in Persons*, UNODC xvi (2006), https://www.unodc.org/pdf/Trafficking_toolkit_Oct06.pdf.

[115] Demetriou (2018), p. 13.

[116] Touzenis (2010b).

[117] See for example *Regina v Besmir Ramaj and Hasan Atesogullari* [2006] EWCA Crim 448 (U.K.), and *Regina v Makai (Atilla)* [2008] 1 Cr.App.R.(S.) 73 (U.K.).

insistence on their free consent to a particular work arrangement will inevitably impeded the prosecution of exploiters "because it can make the 'means' element very difficult to establish" and "it may also impact on sentencing."[118]

In addition to the means, the type of exploitation carried out is also relevant in consent considerations. The perceived harmfulness and severity of the exploitation is the significant factor at play in this regard.[119] In West Africa and in many other countries it is a social practice that older children aged 16 and 17 years old migrate for work despite international legal dispositions protecting any child under 18.[120] As regards adults, the issue of coercion becomes more complex in labor trafficking cases, particularly where there is an indication that the persons involved have "voluntarily" entered into such situations. For example, migrants who travelled from Africa to work in Europe do not consider themselves exploited and indeed their situation may well have improved. They are at some point responsible for the decisions that resulted in their alleged trafficking. This raises the question as to what constitutes the degree of victimization and exploitation required to satisfy the offense of trafficking in persons. What constitutes exploitation when victims chose to stay in exploitative conditions or, after leaving, choose to return to their former situation. In response to this critical question, it is important to consider that the apparently consensual return of workers to a situation deemed exploitative "does not constitute evidence that the conditions to which the workers were subjected were acceptable" and, moreover,, in some circumstances "is evidence of further exploitation by the offenders of personal circumstances of which they knew they could take advantage."[121]

Thus, Bassiouni et al.'s discussion around adults' consent to forced labor or servitude opens the debate on the wide divergences regarding the question of coercion in relation to exploitation and how to determine whether or not the employment relationship is fundamentally coercive. For example, individuals who pay off their smuggling debts with labor may be perceived as working under coercive conditions and in violation of their fundamental human rights, even though workers might accept working off a debt as a reasonable opportunity to acquire and achieve a better future.[122] This issue is particularly complex in situations where the individuals involved "come from highly vulnerable circumstances and have willingly traded some degree of freedom for what they believe is an improved opportunity for themselves and their families."[123] In addition to the political challenges West African countries encounter "to enacting legislation incorporating a labor

---

[118]UNODC, *supra* note 50, at 51.

[119]*Id.* at 62.

[120]United Nations Convention on the Rights of the Child art. 1, Nov. 20, 1989, 1577 U.N.T.S. 3.

[121]*Regina v Khan, Khan and Khan* [2010] EWCA Crim 2880 ¶ 18 (U.K.)

[122]Chuang (2014), p. 647.

[123]Bassiouni et al. (2010), p. 428.

approach to trafficking, difficult conceptual questions remain concerning the distinction between acceptable labor practices and unacceptable exploitation."[124]

Apart from direct coercion exercised by a trafficker over the individual, there may be 'coercion by circumstances', resulting most notably from economic disadvantage. In West Africa, economic vulnerability is the main factor that leads to trafficking. The question is whether circumstantial coercion resulting from economic conditions may amount to pressure constituting the kind of criminal activity that is defined by reference to a lack of consent.[125] While extreme economic hardship might result in taking the decision to be involved in trafficking situations, it would be inappropriate to claim that the woman 'has freely chosen' her plight. In the final analysis, 'it's better to go and earn money to spend than to stay home and starve.'[126] The role of adverse social and economic conditions in the trafficking process is recognized in The Proposal for the EU 2011 Directive which stipulates that:

> Social vulnerability is arguably the principal root cause of trafficking in human beings. *Vulnerability derives from economic and social factors such as poverty*, gender discrimination, armed conflicts, domestic violence, dysfunctional families, and personal circumstances such as age or health conditions or disabilities. Such vulnerability is used by international organised crime networks to facilitate migration and subsequently severely exploit people by use of force, threat, coercion, or various forms of abuse such as debt bondage. In fact the high level of profits generated is a major underlying driver. The demand for sexual services and cheap labour is a concurrent driver.[127] (Emphasis added)

Arguably, traditional criminal law upholds that 'economic coercion of circumstances' (although influencing decision making) does not invalidate consent as it emanates from the consenting individual and does not derive directly or indirectly from another person.[128] As one scholar explained, "a person's compulsion to choose between working or starving does not render the apparent consent to work involuntary."[129] Provided the person to whom consent is given is not the cause of the starvation or a lack of any reasonable alternative, the consent should be considered valid.[130] Conversely, "for consent to be considered irrelevant, the person to whom consent is given must *have abused* the existing situation of poverty or created such vulnerability in order to secure the exploitation of the victim."[131] In effect '...it is difficult to imagine what a society would be like in which a person would invalidate

[124] Chuang (2014), p. 647.

[125] Elliot (2014), pp. 11–12.

[126] Boonpakdee et al. (1997), p. 91.

[127] Proposal for a Directive of the European Parliament and the Council on preventing and combating trafficking in human beings and protecting victims, repealing Framework Decision 2002/629/JHA, (COM (2010) 95 Final) at 1.2.

[128] Beyleveld and Brownsword (2007), p. 127.

[129] Nozick (1974) as cited in Samuel Vincent Jones, *Human Trafficking Victim Identification: Should Consent Matter?*, 45 Ind. L. R. 483, 508–509 (2012).

[130] *Id.*

[131] UNODC, *supra* note 50, at 22.

a consent simply by showing that she was placed in a position having to choose between unattractive alternatives."[132]

Given that economic vulnerability is a factor increasing susceptibility to trafficking in persons, an alternative suggested by UNODC Model Law to capture the offense of trafficking in persons is relevant in the context of West Africa. This Model Law recommends that:

> In order to better protect the victims, Governments may consider adopting a definition focusing on the offender and his intention to take advantage of the situation of the victim. These may also be easier to prove, as it will not require an inquiry into the state of mind of the victim but only that the offender was aware of the vulnerability of the victim and had the intention to take advantage of it.[133]

This approach may offer an additional advantage in its assessment that "persons should be convicted for crimes they commit or intend to commit, and not be prosecuted because another person is in a vulnerable position."[134]

Furthermore, if it is to be accepted that a more expansive interpretation of the concept of 'coercion' can include 'economic coercion of circumstances, this matter may have implications for countries' immigration policies and for the consent debate. Simply asking that trafficking and smuggling be considered in their proper economic and social context would mean for states to accept the commission of 'legalised immigration offences.'[135] For example, the management of migration by the UK reflects the traditional practices of states in controlling migration flows to ensure national security and the development of the country. While this is not explicitly established in the legislation of the United Kingdom (except with respect to young and vulnerable people) consent is clearly relevant in the identification process of the National Referral Mechanism (NRM). A presumed victim who agrees to come to the United Kingdom for work is considered an irregular migrant despite evidence of deception, coercion, and abuse.[136]

Although a definition of "coercion" that includes economic vulnerability would benefit potentially vulnerable people, "realistically this would not be accepted by States, which have a legitimate interest in protecting their borders against those individuals whom the States will simply view as economic migrants."[137] In fact, "distress of economic circumstances is precisely what border security is designed to

---

[132] Philips (1984), pp. 133, 140.

[133] UNODC, Model Law against Trafficking in Persons, pp. 9–10.

[134] UNODC, *Abuse of a Position of Vulnerability and other "Means" within the Definition of Trafficking in Persons,* 88 (2013) at https://www.unodc.org/documents/human-trafficking/2012/UNODC_2012_Issue_Paper_-_Abuse_of_a_Position_of_Vulnerability.pdf.

[135] Elliot (2014), p. 152.

[136] *Report Concerning the implementation of the Council of Europe Convention on Action against Trafficking in Human Beings by the United Kingdom, First Evaluation Round*, GRETA 52 (2012), https://ec.europa.eu/anti-trafficking/sites/antitrafficking/files/greta_report_united_kingdom_2012_en_0.pdf.

[137] Elliot (2014), p. 153.

protect against – the movement of economic refugees."[138] In general, states label such people as illegal or smuggled migrants, susceptible to peremptory deportation.

Having discussed interpretative questions arising from the Palermo Protocol with regard to the issue of consent, it is useful in this section to draw some valuable insights from case laws. There are two main situations of exploitation worth discussing regarding this element of consent: commercial sexual exploitation and forced labor exploitation.

### 4.3.1 Analysis of Consent in Sex Trafficking Cases

In considering the issue of consent, the judgement of the Australian High Court in the *Queen v. Wei Tang* case[139] highlights how Courts might address the question of victim consent in situations of commercial sexual exploitation. In this case, Ms Tang was convicted of having purchased five women of Thai nationality to work in debt-bondage conditions in a legal brothel in Fitzroy. The women signed a recruitment agreement which stated that each woman would have to work as a prostitute in Australia to pay off a debt of AUD $45,000. Apparently no deception as to the nature of the work was used to secure their consent, and all the women had previously worked in the sex industry in Thailand. Furthermore, they understood that once their debt was paid, they would have the opportunity to work on their own as prostitutes. Two of the women worked off their debts and indeed the restrictions upon them were lifted; their passports were returned and they remained at the brothel to provide their services as free sex workers.

Prior to their departure from Thailand, the women were not aware of the precise terms of the debt or their expected living conditions beforehand. Once in Australia, the workers' passports and returned tickets were taken away. Each woman had to work in the brothel six days per week and the debt would be reduced by $50 for each customer serviced. Although under the contract they could not earn anything in cash other than working one free day per week to keep the $50 per customer for themselves, the defendant provided the five women with reasonable accommodation and adequate food and did not hold them under lock and key.[140]

The salient feature of this case is that the women testified against Ms Tang by explaining that they had voluntarily entered into agreements with a broker in Thailand to whom they owed between AUD $40,000 and 45,000. The case was tried before the amendment to the Australian legislation that explicitly made consent irrelevant. The defense pointed out that no 'severe' means were used to compel the women to work and their contracts were not coercive. Additionally, they had been sex workers in Thailand and were informed that they would be engaged in

---

[138] *Id.* at 153–154.

[139] *The Queen v Tang*, 2008 HCA 39, 22 (28 August 2008).

[140] *Id.*

prostitution in Australia. In relative terms, their lives improved as a resulting of coming to live and work in Australia which was effectively "contradicting a relationship that could be characterised as 'slavery' in any meaningful sense of the word."[141] Therefore, it was argued that evidence of consent should exonerate the defendant.[142]

In line with this argument, the Court pointed out that consent is not inconsistent with slavery given that, in societies where slavery was lawful, a person could bind himself into slavery or debt peonage in exchange for survival. However, in a given case where consent is factually relevant it is necessary to analyze the circumstances and extent of the consent relied upon to establish the element of the offense.[143] The Court on appeal found that voluntarily signing the employment contracts and consenting to work in prostitution in Australia does not equate to consent to enslavement or conditions of servitude. Consent in this particular case is understood in relation to the objective circumstances and conditions attaching to their employment. The Victorian Court of Appeal reinstated the convictions for slavery because the victims lost their freedom of choice in this work relationship. The women "were not free to choose whether or when they worked in the brothel. The evidence of one complainant was that she was not permitted to refuse customers. Two others gave evidence that, although they had never sought to refuse a customer, they did not believe they could do so."[144]

Pertaining to the circumstances, the trial judge noted that the women were financially deprived and vulnerable upon arriving in Australia. Although they "were well-provisioned, fed, and provided for" and "were not kept under lock and key", the trial judge pointed out that they were "effectively restricted to the premises."[145] The circumstances that effectively restricted their freedom included a lack of familiarity with the language, isolation, long hours of work, debt bondage, and the fear of being apprehended by immigration authorities and law enforcement. As a matter of fact, the defendant brought the workers into Australia as illegal immigrants, withholding their passports and return tickets to prevent them from running away and warning them not to leave the premises without supervision.[146]

To conclude this section, it is important to note that the use of "contracts" that force women to provide sexual services is recognized in this jurisprudence as part of the operations of sexual exploitation rather than an acceptable element of

---

[141] Hocking and Muthu (2012), pp. 69, 78.

[142] Australasian Reflections on Modern Slavery, Journal of Politics and Law Vol. 5, No. 4; 2012, read The Dissenting Approach of Justice Michael Kirby in Tang - Exploitation and Consent file:///C:/Users/irie/Downloads/22545-74829-1-PB.pdf.

[143] Tang, *supra* note 141, ¶ 35.

[144] *Id.* at 43.

[145] *Id.* at 7, 8.

[146] *Id.* at 16.

prostitution.[147] The outcome of the Appeal has significant implications for the protection of people from sexual slavery as well as the effective prosecution of trafficking offenders. What also follows from this landmark decision is that attenuate forms of control and possession, besides physical threats and force, can provide evidence of conditions of slavery. In the situation discussed, "[p]hysical and mental control was exercised over these women in a far more subtle but effective way [than imprisonment]. A relationship of dependence existed from the start and was fostered. Fear of the authorities was cultivated."[148]

### 4.3.2 *Analysis of Consent in Labor Trafficking Cases*

Practitioners have speculated that the illegality of the exploitation of prostitution in some countries can facilitate an approach that considers consent irrelevant yet it would be difficult to establish trafficking in relation to activities that are legal and capable of being consented to, such as labor exploitation.[149] For example, in cases involving the exploitation of migrant workers in agriculture, mining, industry, and shops, allegations of consent can be raised to prevent the conviction of the perpetrators. The critical question is whether the person who becomes "voluntarily" involved in a situation of forced labor with a relatively high level of exploitation or through more aggressive means is a victim of trafficking or a mere breach of civil employment regulations? Should the worst forms of child labor in West Africa be interpreted as rural migration patterns or analyzed under a paradigm of trafficking in persons? Some may argue that ending child labor in developing countries does not provide any guarantee that the well-being of the unskilled child will be improved. Moreover, it can be argued that socio-economic improvement of the victims was made possible by the exploitation. Thus, the definition and analysis of trafficking into labor might depend very much on the perspective taken, with one commentator questioning whether "internationally accepted terminology around human trafficking adequately capture the reality that fits the African context" inasmuch as what "the international community often labels as human trafficking are in fact locally acceptable labour practices that offer the only meaningful employment available."[150]

> For many Africans, migration to the Gulf, Europe or North America – no matter how this is achieved – is an exceedingly positive economic and development proposition for themselves, their families, and through remittances paid later, their communities and their nations. African economies benefit from more than $35 billion annually in remittances. The risks and

---

[147] *The Queen v. Wei Tang Information Kit, Media Release: Sex Slave Victims Vindicated by High Court*, Victoria Law Foundation (Aug. 28, 2008), https://acrath.org.au/wp-content/uploads/2011/02/The_Queen_v_Wei_Tang-Information_Kit_Jan2009.pdf.

[148] Tang, *supra* note 141, ¶ 29.

[149] UNODC, *supra* note 50, at 38.

[150] Tuesday Reitano, ENACT project by, Deputy Director, Global Initiative against Transnational Organized Crime, https://reliefweb.int/report/world/does-human-trafficking-need-new-definition.

abuses of the journey are seen as the price to be paid for generational return. When viewed from the perspective of African states and their people, more often than not what the West deems as human trafficking is simply a quest for new opportunities and a better life. And vocal international campaigns are perceived as an effort to restrict those opportunities. So it is no wonder that some African governments do little more than pay lip service to a discourse that is largely shaped outside of Africa.[151]

This explains why some African governments do so little to discourage "job opportunities abroad" that they cannot provide for their populations. The example of the *Chowdury v. Greece* case in the Assize Court illustrates the attitude governments adopt went it comes to addressing forced labor trafficking. The Court acquitted the defendants on the charge of trafficking in persons and also commuted their prison sentences to an insignificant financial penalty of €5 per day of detention."[152]

In terms of specific details, this case involved 42 Bangladeshi men recruited without work permits to pick strawberries in Manolada farm (Southern Greece). Housed in degrading living conditions, they worked excessive hours for seven days a week under the supervision of armed guards. For several months, the workers did not receive the agreed wages. They only received a small amount of money for food which was then deducted from their wages. After six months, the employers hired a new group of workers and told the first group to leave, threatening that the workers would only recover their salaries if they continued working. On April 17, 2013, a group of workers went on strike for the third time to request their salaries from the employer and one of the armed guards opened fire, seriously injuring 30 workers. The two employers together with the guard were tried in the Assize Court for attempted murder and trafficking in human beings.

There are many evidentiary challenges that arise from this case. The first issue pertains to the fact that the alleged victims purportedly consented to work and had initially accepted the terms of the employment contract and the ability to negotiate their salaries.[153] According to the Assize Court it was proven that "the relations between the workers and their employers had been governed by a binding employment relationship" and that "the workers had been in a position to negotiate their conditions of employment at the time of their recruitment."[154] In analyzing the case, the Assize Court added that:

the workers had been informed of their conditions of employment and that they had accepted them after finding them satisfactory. As to the amount of the wages, it found that this was the usual amount paid by the other producers in the region and the workers had not been obliged to accept it. In the Court's view, the information provided to the workers by their team-leaders and their compatriots working for other employers about the reliable payment of

[151] Tuesday Reitano, ENACT project by Deputy Director, Global Initiative against Transnational Organized Crime, https://reliefweb.int/report/world/does-human-trafficking-need-new-definition.

[152] *Chowdury and Others v. Greece*, European Court of Human Rights, Application No. 21884/15, Judgment ¶ 124 (30 Mar. 2017), https://www.unipa.it/scuole/scienzegiur.ecosociali/specializzazioni/professionilegali/.content/documenti/Scaduto-Chowdury-c-Grecia.pdf.

[153] *Id.* at 2.

[154] *Id.* at 26.

> wages constituted a major factor in the choice of T.A. as employer. The Assize Court further noted that, until the end of February 2013, the workers had not made any complaint about their employer, whether concerning his conduct or the payment of wages, and they had only started to complain at the end of February or the beginning of March 2013 about a delay in payment.[155]

Subsequently, consent in criminal law absolves those charged from criminal liability: to those who consent, no wrong is done (*volenti non fit injuria*). Additionally, given the factual circumstances in relation to the "validity of the consent", the question that arises is how can the working conditions and the abusive behavior of the employers be deemed exploitative when the victims stated that they would have continued working for their employers had their wages been paid?[156]

Finally, in analyzing the criterion of coercion to define trafficking in persons, the Assize Court found that elements of physical or mental coercion were lacking as the employers did not use the applicants' unlawful presence in Greece as a means of coercion to force them to continue working and that they had been free to look for an alternative job.[157] Indeed, the workers testified that "during their free time, they were able to move freely around the region, do their shopping in shops which operated by agreement with the defendants, play cricket and take part in an association set up by their compatriots."[158] Additionally, no evidence was shown that the defendant "had, under false pretences and by means of promises, coerced the workers into agreeing to work for him by taking advantage of their situation of vulnerability, especially as it found that they were not in such a situation."[159] Consequently, the Patras Criminal Court found that the employment of the workers was carried out in violation of labor legislation but dismissed the trafficking charge on the grounds that the applicants had signed up willingly without losing the freedom to leave their employer.[160] The United Nations Office on Drugs and Crime (UNODC) commented on the Assize Court decision as follows:

> The Greek domestic Court's acquittal of the accused persons regarding human trafficking charges rested, in a large part, on its assumption that the workers had consented to their situation. The Court stressed that the workers had initially consented to the employment contract and been informed of its terms which they found satisfactory. It noted that the workers had been in a position to negotiate the terms of the contract at the time of their

[155] *Chowdury And Others v. Greece*, (Application no. 21884/15), The European Court of Human Rights (First Section), 30 March 2017, para. 24 https://johan-callewaert.eu/wp-content/uploads/2018/12/CASE-OF-CHOWDURY-AND-OTHERS-v.-GREECE.pdf.

[156] *Id.*

[157] *Chowdury And Others v. Greece*, (Application no. 21884/15), The European Court of Human Rights (First Section), 30 March 2017, para. 24 https://johan-callewaert.eu/wp-content/uploads/2018/12/CASE-OF-CHOWDURY-AND-OTHERS-v.-GREECE.pdf.

[158] *Ibid*., para. 25.

[159] *Ibid*.

[160] *Chowdury and Others v. Greece*, Application to the European Court of Human Rights by the Greek Council for Refugees and the Open Society Justice Initiative on April 27, 2015, para. 19. https://www.justiceinitiative.org/uploads/0a420b3f-35d2-446c-a1e7-302ea0b4fcf2/litigation-echr-chowdury-greece.20170327.pdf.

recruitment and that the amount of the wages was the usual amount paid by other producers in the region, so that the workers were not obliged to accept this particular contract. Moreover, this consent extended to later stages of their employment, as most of the workers stated that they would have continued to work for these employers had their wages been paid. In addition, they were free to come and go and find alternative employment, if they had wished to do so.[161]

As the foregoing case has illustrated, trafficking in forced labor is outlawed in domestic legislations, including in West Africa, but it is tolerated and rarely punished. Accordingly, the Group of Experts on Action against Trafficking in Human Beings (GRETA) noted "that many domestic Courts fail to fully understand the gravity of labour exploitation or the nexus with human trafficking"[162] and highlights the urgent "need for comprehensive legislation on trafficking for the purpose of labour exploitation, including recognition of the irrelevance of the victim's consent to the intended exploitation, and the need for heightened attention to the abuse of a position of vulnerability."[163] The European Court of Human Rights (ECHR) analyzed the issue of "consent" in light of the workers' situation of vulnerability and noted that the migrants were held in situations of trafficking in persons and forced labor.

## 4.4 The Users of Trafficked Persons' Services

Customers and clients are at the end of a long trafficking chain; they are the purchasers and users of services or goods produced by the trafficked victims. The UN Global Initiative to Fight Human Trafficking (UN.GIFT) has identified several types of consumers, including the clients of sex workers or employers; owners and managers of economic activities including agriculture, construction, small scale mining, and fishing; or merely household members requiring access to cheap domestic labor. This list includes those who exploit children, women, and men in the production of pornography. The users can be also third parties involved in the process (i.e., traffickers and their associates, including various brokers or corrupt officials).[164]

---

[161] UNODC, *Further in – depth analysis of selected cases*, p. 4 https://sherloc.unodc.org/res/cld/case-law-doc/traffickingpersonscrimetype/_irb/2017/chowdury_and_others_v__greece_html/In-depth_analysis_of_the_case_ECHR_-_Chowdury.pdf.

[162] Council of Europe, 7th General Report on GRETA's Activities, 6 (2018), https://rm.coe.int/greta-2018-1-7gr-en/16807af20e.

[163] *Ibid.*, at 7.

[164] *Ending Exploitation. Ensuring that Businesses do not Contribute to Trafficking in Human Beings: Duties of States and the Private Sector*, Office of the Special Rep. and Coordinator for Combating Trafficking in Human Beings (OSCE) 17 (2014), http://www.osce.org/secretariat/126305?download=true.

Users may act as individuals or are networked through access to other illegal activities such as prostitution, sexual abuse of children, cheap labor of illegal immigrants, and child labor.[165] To a large extent, "[m]embers of the public are all consumers who can potentially contribute indirectly to the profits of traffickers by paying money for products or services made or provided by people who have been trafficked."[166] Individuals create a demand for specific products and services that breaches the human rights of the person delivering those services including commercial sex, forced labor, domestic work and personal care, the worst forms of child labor, forced marriages, begging, or exploitation of children within the army.

Nevertheless, "few consumers are aware of either the contractual or working conditions involving those generating the products and supplying services."[167] In many cases, they are unaware of or unconcerned about the trafficking process. Often, consumers "do not perceive themselves as part of the trafficking network, although they are, in fact, an engine in the machinery of exploitation."[168] This raises the following questions in relation to the end "users" of the services of trafficking. Should an individual purchasing or obtaining goods produced though trafficking in forced labor be held criminally responsible? Should the "client" of an individual trafficked into sexual activities be included in the category of exploiters? Should the owner of a business that enrolls trafficked workers or buys the low-cost goods produced by trafficked and enslaved workers be liable for criminal prosecution?[169] The challenge lies in establishing that such 'clients' or 'end users' had knowledge of the trafficked status of the victim.

## 4.5 The Role of Parents in Trafficking of Children

As demonstrated in the precedent section, it is assumed that some personal decision-making ability is limited when a person is trafficked. This loss of personal agency by the victim is set out in the UN Protocol statement, "having control over another person". However, the issue of consent becomes much more complex in circumstances in which parents and others make the decision to send out their children to

---

[165] Innocenti Research Center (IRC), *Trafficking in Human Beings, Especially Women and Children, in Africa*, UNICEF 8–9 (2005), http://www.unicef-irc.org/publications/pdf/trafficking-gb2ed-2005.pdf.

[166] OSRCCTHB, *supra* note 166, at 20–21. "It important to understand that the purchasing decisions made by men and boys who pay for sex are qualitatively different to a shopper's decision about which tomatoes or clothes to buy or a care agency's decision about which care workers to hire. Those who assert that paying for commercial sex is intrinsically harmful (and prejudicial to the status of women) regard such consumer decisions as inherently different to ones made about other services or products" *Id.* at 21.

[167] *Id.*

[168] IRC, *supra* note 161, at 8.

[169] Gallagher (2010), pp. 377–378.

work hoping to improve their economic condition. The current discussion will explain how consent is irrelevant in connection with trafficking of children as parents' decisions might undermine the fundamental human and social values of children's individual autonomy, freedom of choice and the protection of the most vulnerable within society.[170]

Child fostering is a customary practice in West Africa whereby children are sent to the households of relatives or others who are expected to provide for their well-being. It is generally the case that children are not transferred in exchange for any reward, but their biological parents or their guardians are aware of the fact their child will be paying with domestic work or any other form of labor to receive schooling, food, shelter, and vocational training. This phenomenon can then pave the way to the exploitation of children or their labor. To address the issue of children enslaved in conditions of domestic work worldwide under the pretext of adoption or a cultural foster care system, Article 1 paragraph (d) of the Supplementary Convention on the Abolition of Slavery, prohibits "any institution or practice whereby a child or young person under the age of 18 years is delivered by either or both of his natural parents or by his guardian to another person, whether for reward or not, with a view to the exploitation of the child or young person or of his labour."[171]

*Prima facie*, the condition of domestic servants and child laborers in general is exploitative; however, this does not automatically mean that it meets the definition of child trafficking prohibited in the 1956 Supplementary Convention to slavery. In considering the application of the definition, the parent or guardian can be held liable for a trafficking offense when they deliver the child to another person "*with a view* to the exploitation of the child or young person or of his labour". In this situation it is important to note that the crime being addressed, "is not the exploitation of a child, but the transferring of that child with the *intent* of their exploitation."[172]

Examination of most child fostering scenarios in West Africa shows that the arrangement is made in good faith for the best interests of the child; the parents or the guardians give the child away to the host family who promise that the well-being of

[170] Cf. UNODC, The Role of 'Consent' in the Trafficking in Persons Protocol, pp. 75–76 https://www.unodc.org/documents/human-trafficking/2014/UNODC_2014_Issue_Paper_Consent.pdf.

[171] The Supplementary Convention on the Abolition of Slavery, Article 1 paragraph (d).

Related to this, Article 3 of the ILO 1999 Worst Forms of Child Labour Convention includes child trafficking in the list of 'the worst forms of child labour':

(a) all forms of slavery or practices similar to slavery, such as the sale and trafficking of children, debt bondage and serfdom, and forced or compulsory labour, including forced or compulsory recruitment of children for use in armed conflict;
(b) the use, procuring, or offering of a child for prostitution, for the production of pornography, or for pornographic performances;
(c) the use, procuring, or offering of a child for illicit activities, in particular for the production and trafficking of drugs as defined in the relevant international treaties;
(d) work which by its nature or the circumstances in which it is carried out, is likely to harm the health, safety, or morals of children.

[172] Allain (2012), p. 197.

that child will be paramount. The parent or the guardian are acting in good faith and do not know that the promises will be broken. Where intent or knowledge requirement is specifically stated in law, if it is considered that actors acted without intention or knowledge at the time of the conduct the requisite *mens rea* was lacking; there is no guilty mind and therefore their conduct is not criminal. However, in a situation where a recruiter acting as guardian during a transfer knows that the child or their labor will be exploited, the *mens rea* of child trafficking is satisfied and the defender is guilty. Maintaining the major distinction between an exploitative practice and the trafficking of a person for such a purpose, Allain argues that the exploitation of children in the household falls most likely in the category of the worst forms of child labor manifested in forced labor or slavery.[173] Depending on the factual circumstances "of exploitation taking place with a [domestic servant], it may meet the definitional threshold of the forced labour as set out in the 1930 Forced Labour Convention or reach to the level of slavery as set out in the 1926 Slavery Convention."[174]

As described in more detail in Part I, forced marriage is another customary practice in West Africa that holds women in conditions of slavery. For instance, the case of *Jezile v. S and Others* describes the situation of a defendant who abducted a 14 year old girl for the purposes of customary marriage (known as *ukuthwala* in South Africa) with the permission of her family. The prospective bride managed to escape twice but was subsequently apprehended by her uncle and returned to the defendant who abused her and locked her up in the house. In analyzing the case, the trial Court convicted the exploiter and found that the involvement of the complainant's male family members including her uncle and "grandmother was nothing more than a neutral factor insofar as the appellant's own blameworthiness was concerned."[175] This example and many other cases that have been dismissed illustrate the role of parents in child trafficking. Regarding this issue, the United States Department of State Office to Monitor and Combat Trafficking in Persons (OMCTP) observed that:

> Parents are often the victims in child trafficking cases. Traffickers convince them to part with their children with false promises of schooling or prosperity. But in some cases parents may also play an active role in the trafficking of children. To combat these types of child trafficking, law enforcement must send a strong message that these practices will not be tolerated.[176]

---

[173] *Ibid*. at 197–198.

[174] *Ibid*. at 198.

[175] *Nvumeleni Jezile v. The State*, High Court Case No: A 127/2014, para. 104 https://sherloc.unodc.org/res/cld/case-law-doc/traffickingpersonscrimetype/zaf/2015/jezile_v__s_and_others_a_1272014_2015_zawchc_html/2015.03.23_Jezile_v_S.pdf.

[176] *TIP Report*, U.S. Dep't. St. 7 (2009), http://www.tipheroes.org/media/1278/single-file.pdf; *Read also* Nigeria: COI Compilation on Human Trafficking December 2017, https://www.refworld.org/pdfid/5a79c7114.pdf.

As described extensively in Part I, family members might give their children to third parties to engage in the worst forms of child labor, including cattle herding, agricultural work, sexual exploitation, domestic servitude, and forced labor in mining. In most cases, economic vulnerability is invoked as a factor leading parents to allow traffickers to take their children for labor or sexual exploitation. Given the circumstances, it is often difficult to draw the line between poverty and neglect, which raises a salient question as to whether is it poverty or neglect when a child has been sent to work in the worst forms of forced labor because their parents lack the financial resources to sponsor their academic education. For example, when victims of forced marriage or domestic servitude are returned to their family, it is to protect family honor and well-being. In Nigeria, the parents of some victims encourage them to obey their traffickers and endure exploitation to earn money (US Department of State, Nigeria, June 2018). In such a situation, should a family member face trafficking charges for failing to protect their children?

In raising concerns about the major role parents can play in the trafficking of children, the Office to Monitor and Combat Trafficking in Persons (OMCTP) highlights the necessity to move beyond the controversies toward the expansion of legislative responses that adequately address the abolition of this crime as well as the punishment of relatives involved in the global trafficking of children and adults. Accordingly, the Office to Monitor and Combat Trafficking in Persons (OMCTP) declared that "Courts should not withdraw cases on the basis of parental consent."[177] With reference to anti-trafficking legislation in West Africa, it is worth noting that countries have adopted various approaches to the issue of coercion and parental responsibility.

The first legislative group adopted the general trafficking standard without further development as regards the parental role. Gambia, Mali, and Niger belong in this category. An analysis of this approach reveals that the sentence is high and the crime has to be committed intentionally, which is a high threshold at which to prove culpability. Consequently, there are no convictions. Another group has taken a step forward to address the involvement of parents in the trafficking process. With respect to parental responsibility for the trafficking of children, the Burkina Faso judicial system prescribes 1 to 5 years imprisonment with a fine for offenders with authority over the victim or custody if they are responsible for the victim's education, intellectual and professional training, and their paid travelling worker.[178] Similarly, Ghana prohibits trafficking by parents in its 2005 Anti-trafficking Act. Clause one, section 4 sets out clearly that:

> Where children are trafficked, the consent of the child, parents or guardian of the child cannot be used as a defence in prosecution under this Act, regardless of whether or not there

[177] U.S. Dep't. St., *supra* note at 7.

[178] Burkina Faso Loi. N.038/2003/AN portant définition et répression du traffic d'enfants, Chapt II, Article 4.

is evidence of abuse of power, fraud or deception on the part of the trafficker or whether the vulnerability of the child was taken advantage of.[179]

Domestic legislation in Ghana gives the state the capacity to prosecute parents and all the intermediaries known or unknown to the family of the trafficked person who "send, take to, consent to the taking to or to receive at any place any person" and "to enter into an agreement whether written or oral" that results in trafficking.[180] Although the legislation is extended to family members, the definition of trafficking in persons does not read the culpability requirement with respect to the offense. Failure to define culpability in relation to trafficking in persons leaves the Court with a crucial difficulty in determining which of the four defined culpable states of mind is appropriate to apply to the case. According to criminal law rules, "in the absence of a general section to supply unstated culpability requirement, it is left to the Court to select the applicable culpability requirement. This delegation to the Courts undercuts predictability and permits inconsistency between similar cases."[181] Another consequence is the risk involved in allowing "the Court to set the culpability requirement higher than the legislature may have intended."[182]

In a continent where some parents encourage their children to obey their traffickers and endure exploitation to earn financial resources for the family, South Africa enacted a ground-breaking law that enriched the debate around the prosecution of parents engaged in this form of criminal conduct. Under the Children's Act, parents who engage in a behavior that facilitates trafficking in persons cannot be exonerated from this criminal offense. Chapter 8, Clause 36, entitled, "Trafficking of child by parent, guardian or other person who has parental responsibilities and rights in respect of child," clearly sets out the parental role.

(1) If a children's Court has reason to believe that the parent or guardian of a child or any other person who has parental responsibilities and rights in respect of a child, has trafficked the child, the Court may— (a) suspend all the parental responsibilities and rights of that parent, guardian or other person; and (b) place that child in temporary safe care in terms of section 152 of the Children's Act, pending an inquiry by a children's Court. (2) Any action taken by a children's Court in terms of subsection (1) does not exclude a person's liability for committing any offence under Chapter 2 of this Act.[183]

The most important avenue of the Children's Act is the clear explanation of liability in the trafficking of children involving parents. A parent is guilty of child trafficking in a situation where he or she "believes that there is a reasonable possibility of the existence" of exploitation and "has failed to obtain information

---

[179] Republic of Ghana, Human Trafficking Act of 2005 (Act 694), Article 1, Subsection 1 (a) and (b).

[180] Republic of Ghana, Human Trafficking Act of 2005 (Act 694), Art.2, Sub.4.

[181] Robinson and Grall (1983), pp. 681, 713.

[182] *Ibid.*

[183] The Children's Act 38 of 2005, section 287. https://www.unodc.org/res/cld/document/prevention-and-combating-of-trafficking-in-persons-act%2D%2D2013_html/Prevention_and_Combating_of_Trafficking_in_Persons_Act_2013.pdf.

to confirm the existence of that fact."[184] As a corollary of this, the Australian Criminal Code Act 1995, Section 271 (2) represents a model of domestic legislation that provides a lower *mens rea* standard of *dolus eventualis* (recklessness) as the criminal culpability required for trafficking offenses. While the law maintains the threshold of "specific intent" in establishing the "aggravated offence of trafficking in persons",[185] in the particular case of trafficking of children the offense is established where the implicated individual "is reckless as to whether the other person will be used to provide sexual services or will be otherwise exploited, either by the first person or another."[186] A person is considered acting recklessly with respect to an outcome "when he is aware of a risk that it will occur; and it is, in the circumstances known to him, unreasonable to take the risk."[187] In most circumstances, the culpability in recklessness is satisfied by the fault of the parents; they predict the need for further inquiry but decline to make this inquiry to avoid knowing the truth.[188] It is worth recalling the aforementioned case of boys trafficked for forced cattle herding in Niger who sometimes managed to escape their exploitative condition and returned to their parents with signs of psychological and physical abuse, yet were frequently returned to their employers by parents angry that had abandoned an opportunity to learn a trade (US Department of State, 2009).[189] In such a situation, a diligent and vigilant parent ought reasonably to have known or suspected the fact by merely inquiring or checking.

In addition to improving the outcomes of prosecutions, the concept of the criminal liability of parents exposes the limits of the legal rights and responsibilities parents have towards their children, and elucidates the meaning of coercion in parent-child relationships. In effect, parents have legal rights to exert some control over the life of their children and even to take decisions regarding their well-being. However, this independent legal right becomes coercion if the right is abused or used to impel children to do something the law considers illegitimate.[190] Although the Children's Act represents a comprehensive legislative tool used to address trafficking in persons, it can be argued that permitting any lower level of intent such as *dolus eventualis* could risk criminalizing innocent people; evidence of criminal conduct is more difficult to prove and the Court's assumption in cases of inadvertent wrong doing rest on delicate foundations. Indeed "to characterize certain conduct as

[184] Prevention and Combating of Trafficking in Persons Act, 2013, (Chapter I section 2. Interpretation of certain expressions) http://www.saflii.org/cgi-bin/disp.pl?file=za/legis/legislation_old/pacotipa2013472/pacotipa2013472.html&query=%20trafficking.

[185] Criminal Code Act 1995 No. 12, 1995, Section 271.3 (1) (a); Sections 271.2 (1B) and (1C)) https://www.legislation.gov.au/Details/C2017C00235/Html/Volume_2.

[186] Criminal Code Act 1995 No. 12, 1995, Section 271.4 (1) (c) (ii).

[187] *Regina v. G and Another*, [2003] UKHL 50, [2004] AC 1034, (2003) 167 JP 621, [2004] 1 Cr App R 21, [2003] 3 WLR 1060, [2004] 1 AC 1034, [2004] 1 Cr App Rep 21, (2003) 167 JPN 955, [2003] 4 All ER 765, para. 41 http://www.bailii.org/uk/cases/UKHL/2003/50.html.

[188] *Sansegret v. The Queen*, [1985] 1 SCR 570, ¶ 22.

[189] U.S. Dep't. St., *supra* note 178.

[190] *See* Wertheimer (1990), p. 172.

'trafficking' has significant and wide-ranging consequences for the alleged perpetrators of that conduct, and for the alleged victims."[191]

Another challenge arising from the implementation of the Children's Act concerns practical difficulty of separating the parents from the children and all the financial and human resources that are entailed in placing that child in temporary safe care. In relation to these issues, the jurisprudence of the children's Court in South Africa noted that "The Courts must be slow in substituting themselves as the parents of the children, especially where the parents are still alive and are staying with their children and there is nothing before the Court placed that shows that the parents are not exercising their parental rights over the children in the best interest of the said minor children."[192] In Togo, Judge Emanuel Edorh expressed his concern regarding the provisions on parental complicity included in the Children's code in these terms:

> it does not further the rights of the child to violate human rights [of parents] in this way. . . . If a father takes a risk with his child, we know he's committed an infraction and has to be punished. But where I part with my fellow committee members is whether such a parent should be imprisoned for six years. The punishment should be six months to a year, not six years.[193]

Togo's Minister of Women's Affairs, Suzanne Aho explained that the punishment of parents might affect children because "children are also stigmatized when they have a parent in prison."[194] Accordingly, the domestic legislation imposes on parents lesser punishments of six months to a year imprisonment or three years of probation if it is proven that they knowingly facilitated the trafficking of their offspring or children under their guardianship.[195] However, these foregoing arguments should not prevail over the necessity to enact comprehensive anti-trafficking laws that impose upon parents a severe punishment to deter them from cooperating with traffickers. In this regard, the Special Rapporteur on trafficking in persons upholds that "there should not be a conflict between the rights of victims and the responses of the criminal justice system, provided that the latter explicitly set out both to challenge the culture of impunity enjoyed by traffickers and to secure justice for the victims."[196]

---

[191] UNODC, *supra* note 50, at 5.

[192] *Kleingeld v Heunis* [2007] 5 SA 559 (T), ¶ 11.

[193] Cohen (2003), p. 40; Article 9(1) of the Convention on the Rights of the Child enshrines that "a child shall not be separated from his or her parents against their will, except when competent authorities subject to judicial review determine, in accordance with applicable law and procedures, that such separation is necessary for the best interests of the child." Article 3(1) of the Convention on the Rights of the Child mandates states to make the best interests of the child the "paramount consideration" in "all actions concerning children."

[194] Cohen (2003), p. 40.

[195] Loi No.2005-009 du 3 août 2005, Chapître III – Article 12.

[196] OHCHR, First decade of the mandate of the Special Rapporteur on trafficking in persons, especially women and children, 17 (2004–2014) https://www.ohchr.org/Documents/Issues/Trafficking/FirsDecadeSRon_%20trafficking.pdf.

## References


All Answers ltd, 'Mens Rea Lecture' (Lawteacher.net, May, 2019) https://www.lawteacher.net/modules/criminal-law/committing-an-offence/mens-rea/lecture.php?vref=1. Accessed 11 Aug 2021

Allain J (2010) Rantsev v Cyprus and Russia: the European Court of Human Rights and trafficking as slavery. Hum Rights Law Rev 10:546

Allain J (2012) Slavery in international law: of human exploitation and trafficking. Brill

*Attorney General of the Federation v. Omoruyi*, High Court Edo State of Nigeria, Suit No. B/31c/2004 (2006)

Australasian Reflections on Modern Slavery, Journal of Politics and Law Vol. 5, No. 4; 2012, read The Dissenting Approach of Justice Michael Kirby in Tang - Exploitation and Consent file:///C:/Users/irie/Downloads/22545-74829-1-PB.pdf

Bassiouni CM et al (2010) Addressing international human trafficking in women and children for commercial sexual exploitation in the 21st century. Int Rev Pen Law 81:417, 425

Beyleveld D, Brownsword R (2007) Consent in the law, p 127

Boonpakdee N, Jantateero C, Skrobanek S (1997) The traffic in women: human realities of the international sex trade. University of Chicago Press, p 91

Bosworth M, Madden MD, Hoyle C (2012) Defining sex trafficking in international and domestic law: mind the gaps. Emory Int Law Rev 26:137, 149

Burkina Faso Loi. N.038/2003/AN portant définition et répression du traffic d'enfants, Chapt II, Article 4

Canada Departement of Justice, A handbook for criminal justice practitioners on trafficking in persons, https://www.justice.gc.ca/eng/rp-pr/cj-jp/tp/hcjpotp-gtpupjp/p2.html

Case No. 8959-2012, Criminal Court of Haram and Appeal No. 6772, Judicial Year 82, Egypt

*Chowdury And Others v. Greece*, (Application no. 21884/15), The European Court of Human Rights (First Section), 30 March 2017, para. 24 https://johan-callewaert.eu/wp-content/uploads/2018/12/CASE-OF-CHOWDURY-AND-OTHERS-v.-GREECE.pdf

*Chowdury and Others v. Greece*, Application to the European Court of Human Rights by the Greek Council for Refugees and the Open Society Justice Initiative on 27 April 2015, para. 19. https://www.justiceinitiative.org/uploads/0a420b3f-35d2-446c-a1e7-302ea0b4fcf2/litigation-echr-chowdury-greece.20170327.pdf

*Chowdury and Others v. Greece*, European Court of Human Rights, Application No. 21884/15, Judgment ¶ 124 (30 Mar. 2017), https://www.unipa.it/scuole/scienzegiur.ecosociali/specializzazioni/professionilegali/.content/documenti/Scaduto-Chowdury-c-Grecia.pdf

Chuang JA (2014) Exploitation creep and the unmaking of human trafficking law. Am J Int Law 108:609, 632

Cohen J (2003) Borderline slavery—child trafficking in Togo. Human Rights Watch 15(8):40 (available at: http://www.hrw.org/sites/default/files/reports/togo0403.pdf)

Convention Against Transnational Organized Crime, Protocol to Prevent, Suppress and Punish trafficking in Persons, Especially Women and Children, done Nov. 15, 2000, T.I.A.S.13127

Convention on the Suppression of Traffic in Persons and the Exploitation of the Prostitution of Others art. 1, Dec. 2, 1949, 96 U.N.T.S. 271

Council of Europe, Convention on Action Against Trafficking in Human Beings and Its Explanatory Report art. 2, May 15, 2005, C.E.T.S. 197 [hereinafter *Council of Europe Trafficking Convention*]

Council of Europe, 7th General Report on GRETA's Activities, 6 (2018), https://rm.coe.int/greta-2018-1-7gr-en/16807af20e

Criminal Code Act 1995 No. 12, 1995, Section 271.3 (1) (a); Sections 271.2 (1B) and (1C)), https://www.legislation.gov.au/Details/C2017C00235/Html/Volume_2

Criminal Code Act 1995 No. 12, 1995, Section 271.4 (1) (c) (ii)

Demetriou D (2018) The Mens Rea of human trafficking: the case of migrant domestic workers. Int Crim Just Rev 29:8

Ditmore M, Wijers M (2003) The negotiations on the UN protocol on trafficking in persons. NEMESIS 4:79, 82 (available at: https://childhub.org/en/system/tdf/library/attachments/ditmor_1_5.pdf?file=1&type=node&id=17261)

*Elisabeth Kawogo v. The United Kingdom*, European Court of Human Rights [ECOHR], Application No. 56921, Statement of Facts, ¶ 8 (23 June 2010)

Elliot J (2014) The role of consent in human trafficking. Routledge, p 56

*Ending Exploitation. Ensuring that Businesses do not Contribute to Trafficking in Human Beings: Duties of States and the Private Sector*, Office of the Special Rep. and Coordinator for Combating Trafficking in Human Beings (OSCE) 17 (2014), http://www.osce.org/secretariat/126305?download=true

*Evidential Issues in Trafficking in Persons Cases*, U.N. Office of Drugs & Crime (UNODC) 87 (2017), https://www.unodc.org/documents/human-trafficking/2017/Case_Digest_Evidential_Issues_in_Trafficking.pdf

Explanatory Report to the Council of Europe Trafficking Convention, ¶ 7

G.A. Res. 55/25 at art. 3 (November 15, 2000)

G.A. Res. 55/25, annex II, U.N. GAOR Supp. No. 49, U.N. Doc. A/45/49 (Vol. I) (Nov. 15, 2000) art. 3(a) [hereinafter *Trafficking Protocol*]

Gallagher AT (2010) The international law of human trafficking. Cambridge University Press

*Hacienda Brasil Verde Workers v. Brazil*, Inter-American Court of Human Rights [IACtHR], Preliminary Objections, Merits, Reparations and Costs, Series C No. 318 (20 October 2016)

Hocking BA, Muthu Y (2012) Australasian reflections on modern slavery. J Pol Law 5:69, 78 (available at: file:///Users/Lamalaw/Downloads/22545-74829-1-PB.pdf)

*ILO, Strengthening Action to End Forced Labor*, ILabC.103/IV/1(2014), art. 21

Innocenti Research Center (IRC), Trafficking in Human Beings, Especially Women and Children, in Africa, UNICEF 8-9 (2005), http://www.unicef-irc.org/publications/pdf/trafficking-gb2ed-2005.pdf

Justice for Victims of Trafficking Act: A Legal Analysis of the Criminal Provisions of P.L. 114-22, June 9, 2015., https://www.everycrsreport.com/reports/R44064.html#fn22

*Kleingeld v Heunis* [2007] 5 SA 559 (T), ¶ 11

Krieg SH (2009) Trafficking in human beings: the EU approach between border control, law enforcement and human rights. Eur Law J 15:775, 779

Law No. 64 of 2010 regarding Combating Human Trafficking, Article 3 https://www.ilo.org/dyn/natlex/docs/ELECTRONIC/89881/103359/F-383089588/eg%2064%20of%202010.pdf

Loi No.2005-009 du 3 août 2005, Chapître III – Article 12

McClean D (2007) Transnational organized crime: a commentary on the UN Conventions on its Protocols. OUP, pp 20, 322

Milano V (2018) Human trafficking by regional human rights courts: an analysis in light of Hacienda Brasil Verde, the first Inter-American Court's ruling in this area. Electron J Int Stud 36:1, https://www.researchgate.net/publication/329658749_Human_trafficking_by_regional_human_rights_Courts_An_analysis_in_light_of_Hacienda_Brasil_Verde_the_first_Inter-American_Court's_ruling_in_this_area. Accessed 20 Aug 2021

Nigeria, Act to repeal the Trafficking in persons, Article 14 (b)

Nozick R (1974) Anarchy, State and Utopia (Basic Books) as cited in Samuel Vincent Jones, Human Trafficking Victim Identification: Should Consent Matter?, 45 Ind. L. R. 483, 508–509 (2012)

*Nvumeleni Jezile v. The State*, High Court Case No: A 127/2014, para. 104, https://sherloc.unodc.org/res/cld/case-law-doc/traffickingpersonscrimetype/zaf/2015/jezile_v__s_and_others_a_1272014_2015_zawchc_html/2015.03.23_Jezile_v_S.pdf

Obokata T (2006) A human rights framework to address trafficking of human beings. Neth Q Hum Rights 24(3):377, 381

Office of the High Commissioner for Human Rights, Recommended Principles and Guidelines on Human Rights and Human Trafficking, p 3, http://www.ohchr.org/Documents/Publications/Traffickingen.pdf

OHCHR, First decade of the mandate of the Special Rapporteur on trafficking in persons, especially women and children, 17 (2004–2014), https://www.ohchr.org/Documents/Issues/Trafficking/FirsDecadeSRon_%20trafficking.pdf

Philips M (1984) Are coerced agreements involuntary? Law Phil 3:133, 140

Prevention and Combating of Trafficking in Persons Act, 2013, (Chapter I section 2. Interpretation of certain expressions) http://www.saflii.org/cgi-bin/disp.pl?file=za/legis/legislation_old/pacotipa2013472/pacotipa2013472.html&query=%20trafficking

*Rantsev v. Cyprus and Russia*, European Court of Human Rights, Judgment, Application No. 25965/04, ¶ 289, (7 January 2010) (available at: https://ec.europa.eu/anti-trafficking/sites/antitrafficking/files/rantsev_vs_russia_cyprus_en_4.pdf)

*Regina v Besmir Ramaj and Hasan Atesogullari* [2006] EWCA Crim 448 (U.K.), and *Regina v Makai (Atilla)* [2008] 1 Cr.App.R.(S.) 73 (U.K.)

*Regina v Khan, Khan and Khan* [2010] EWCA Crim 2880 ¶ 18 (U.K.)

*Regina v. G and Another*, [2003] UKHL 50, [2004] AC 1034, (2003) 167 JP 621, [2004] 1 Cr App R 21, [2003] 3 WLR 1060, [2004] 1 AC 1034, [2004] 1 Cr App Rep 21, (2003) 167 JPN 955, [2003] 4 All ER 765, para. 41, http://www.bailii.org/uk/cases/UKHL/2003/50.html

*Regina v. Urizar*, Québec, District of Longueuil, Criminal Division (J.C.Q.), Judgment, File No. 505-1-084654-090 (13 August 2010), and *Urizar v. Regina*, Quebec Court of Appeal, Judgment, No. 500-10-004763-106 (16 January 2013)

Report Concerning the implementation of the Council of Europe Convention on Action against Trafficking in Human Beings by the United Kingdom, First Evaluation Round, GRETA 52 (2012), https://ec.europa.eu/anti-trafficking/sites/antitrafficking/files/greta_report_united_kingdom_2012_en_0.pdf

Republic of Ghana, Human Trafficking Act of 2005 (Act 694), Art.2, Sub.4

Republic of Ghana, Human Trafficking Act of 2005 (Act 694), Article 1, Subsection 1 (a) and (b)

Robinson PH, Grall JA (1983) Element analysis in defining criminal liability: the model penal code and beyond. Stanford Law Rev, https://scholarship.law.upenn.edu/cgi/viewcontent.cgi?article=1629&context=faculty_scholarship

Roth V (ed) (2012) Defining human trafficking and identifying its victims: a study on the impact and future challenges of international, European and Finnish legal responses to prostitution-related trafficking in human beings. Martinus Nijhoff Publishers, p 69

*Sansegret v. The Queen*, [1985] 1 SCR 570, ¶ 22

*See* Report of the Advisory Committee of Experts on Slavery, *Fourth Session of the Committee*, Apr. 10, 1935, 159 L.N.T.S. 113 (Doc. C.), at 9–10

Siller N (2016) Modern slavery: does international law distinguish between slavery, enslavement and trafficking? J Int Crim Just 14:418

Special Rapporteur on Violence against Women, its Causes, and Consequences on Trafficking in Women, Women's Migration, and Violence against women, Fifty-Sixth Sess. on the Commission on Human Trafficking, U.N. Doc. E/CN.4/2000/68, ¶ 15 (Feb. 29, 2000) (by Radhika Coomerswamy)

Steinfeld R (1991) The invention of free labour: the employment relations in English & American law and culture, 1350–1870. University of North Carolina Press, p 7

Steinfeld R (2001) Coercion, contract and free labour in the nineteenth century. Cambridge University Press, p 16

Stoyanova V (2013) The crisis of a definition: human trafficking in Bulgarian law. Amsterdam Law Forum 5:64, 77

Stoyanova V (2017) Human trafficking and slavery reconsidered: conceptual limits and states' positive obligations in European law, p 34

The Children's Act 38 of 2005, section 287. https://www.unodc.org/res/cld/document/prevention-and-combating-of-trafficking-in-persons-act%2D%2D2013_html/Prevention_and_Combating_of_Trafficking_in_Persons_Act_2013.pdf

*The Legislative Guide for the Implementation of the United Nations Convention against Transnational Organized Crime and the Protocol Thereto*, (2004), para. 36, pp 269–270

*The Queen v Tang*, 2008 HCA 39, 22 (28 August 2008)

*The Queen v. Wei Tang Information Kit, Media Release: Sex Slave Victims Vindicated by High Court*, Victoria Law Foundation (Aug. 28, 2008), https://acrath.org.au/wp-content/uploads/2011/02/The_Queen_v_Wei_Tang-Information_Kit_Jan2009.pdf

*The State v. Phanat Laojindamanee and others*, High Court of Fiji at Suva, Criminal Case No. HAC323, Judgment, ¶ 27

The Supplementary Convention on the Abolition of Slavery, Article 1 paragraph (d)

*TIP Report*, U.S. Dep't. St. 7 (2009), http://www.tipheroes.org/media/1278/single-file.pdf; *Read also* Nigeria: COI Compilation on Human Trafficking December 2017, https://www.refworld.org/pdfid/5a79c7114.pdf

*Toolkit to Combat Trafficking in Persons*, UNODC xvi (2006), https://www.unodc.org/pdf/Trafficking_toolkit_Oct06.pdf

Touzenis K (2010a) Trafficking in human beings: human rights and trans-national criminal law, developments in law and practices. UNESCO, p 72 [available at: http://unesdoc.unesco.org/images/0018/001883/188397e.pdf]

Touzenis K (2010b) Trafficking in human beings – the international legal framework [PowerPoint slides]. Retrived from: https://www.ohchr.org/Documents/Issues/MHR/Consultation2010/Touzenis-OHCHR-MAY2010.ppt

TRAFFICKING IN PERSONS (PROHIBITION) LAW ENFORCEMENT AND ADMINISTRATION ACT, Article 28, https://www.refworld.org/cgi-bin/texis/vtx/rwmain/opendocpdf.pdf?reldoc=y&docid=54f98a284

*Trafficking in Persons Report*, U.S. Dep't. St. (2008)

Trafficking in Women, Women's Migration and Violence against Women, UN Doc.E/CN.4/2000/68, 29 February 2000, ¶ 14 https://www.globaldetentionproject.org/wp-content/uploads/2016/06/Special-Rapporteur-on-Violence-against-Women-its-Causes-and-Consequences-Radhika-Coomaraswamy-2000.pdf

Trafficking in Women, Women's Migration and Violence against Women, UN Doc.E/CN.4/2000/68, 29 February 2000, para. 16

Tuesday Reitano, ENACT project by, Deputy Director, Global Initiative against Transnational Organized Crime, https://reliefweb.int/report/world/does-human-trafficking-need-new-definition

U.S. Dept. of St, *Trafficking in Persons Report June 2009*, at 7

UN Convention against Transnational Organized Crime, art.3(2), entered into force Sep. 29, 2003, U.N.T.S.3957

UN.GIFT (2009) Anti-human trafficking manual for criminal justice practitioners. United Nations Office on Drugs and Crime (UNODC), p 8, https://www.unodc.org/documents/human-trafficking/TIP_module1_Ebook.pdf

United Nations Convention on the Rights of the Child art. 1, Nov. 20, 1989, 1577 U.N.T.S. 3

UNODC, *Abuse of a Position of Vulnerability and other "Means" within the Definition of Trafficking in Persons,* 88 (2013). at https://www.unodc.org/documents/human-trafficking/2012/UNODC_2012_Issue_Paper_-_Abuse_of_a_Position_of_Vulnerability.pdf

UNODC, Evidential issues in trafficking in persons cases CASE DIGEST, 87 UNODC (2017)

UNODC, *'The Role of "Consent" in the Trafficking in Persons Protocol' (2014)* Issue Paper, 15-16) accessed Agust 15, 2021_ (Consent Issue Paper)

UNODC, *Further in – depth analysis of selected cases*, p 4, https://sherloc.unodc.org/res/cld/case-law-doc/traffickingpersonscrimetype/_irb/2017/chowdury_and_others_v__greece_html/In-depth_analysis_of_the_case_ECHR_-_Chowdury.pdf

UNODC, The Role of 'Consent' in the Trafficking in Persons Protocol, pp 75–76, https://www.unodc.org/documents/human-trafficking/2014/UNODC_2014_Issue_Paper_Consent.pdf

UNODC, Evidential Issues in Trafficking in Persons Cases CASE DIGEST, 162–164 (2017)

UNODC, *Legislative Guides for the Implementation of the United Nations Convention against Transnational Organized Crime and the Protocol Thereto*, (2004) ¶¶ 31, 33

UNODC, Legislative Guides for the Implementation of the United Nations Convention against Transnational Organized Crime and the Protocols thereto, UN Sales No.E.05.V.2 (2004), p 270
UNODC, Model law against trafficking in persons, pp 9–10
UNODC, The Legislative Guide for the Implementation of the United Nations Convention against Transnational Organized Crime and the Protocol Thereto, 2004, para. 174 (d), p. 471
UNODC, United Nations Convention Against Transnational Organized Crime And The Protocols Thereto, UNITED NATIONS New York, Art 16 2004., https://www.unodc.org/documents/middleeastandnorthafrica/organised-crime/UNITED_NATIONS_CONVENTION_AGAINST_TRANSNATIONAL_ORGANIZED_CRIME_AND_THE_PROTOCOLS_THERETO.pdf
Wertheimer A (1990) Coercion. Princeton University Press, p 172

# Chapter 5
# Comparative Analysis Between Slavery and Trafficking in Persons

The most expressive analogy to trafficking in persons is certainly the slave trade, as both provide examples of the involuntary movement of people under human control for the purpose of exploitation. Trafficking in persons relates to the slave trade in its substantive allusion to ownership obtained through extreme physical and psychological coercion. Many commentators and indeed popular understanding refer to trafficking in persons as contemporary form of slavery, or the new slave trade.[1] From a legal perspective, the characteristics of trafficking include a spectrum of exploitative activities of which slavery is the most serious. For the purposes of the following discussion, slavery will be defined as the status of a person legally owned as the property of another and may also refer to de facto situations where individuals are held in conditions of analogous slavery. Thus, drawing comparisons between trafficking and the slave trade is a useful approach when analyzing cases to determine whether they constitute conditions of slavery. The critical question addressed in the ensuing discussion is when does exploitation in contemporary society meet the threshold of slavery as the exercise of powers attaching to the right of ownership? This section strives to uncover the relationship between the concept of trafficking in persons and the concept of slavery in law, thus highlighting the legal parameters that can be invoked in domestic criminal Courts to prosecute those who would enslave others. This will include a discussion of the threshold that can be measured to identify whether contemporary practices qualify as trafficking, slavery, servitude, or forced labor.

[1] *Prosecutor v. Kunarac, et al.*, International Criminal Court, Case No. IT-96-23/1-T, Judgment ¶¶ 775–776 (22 February 2001) (accessed from: http://www.icty.org/x/cases/kunarac/tjug/en/kun-tj010222e.pdf); Gold (2003), pp. 99, 100 (refers to trafficking in persons as 'the twenty-first century's slave trade'); Pati (2006), p. 11 (describes trafficking as 'a human rights violation that constitutes a contemporary form of slavery').

 
P. VI. S. Karenga, *A West African Model to Address Human Trafficking*,
https://doi.org/10.1007/978-3-030-88120-7_5

## 5.1 Unfolding the Concept of Ownership to Understand Conditions of Slavery

Although the practice of slavery was prohibited in natural law for centuries, the international definition of this offense was adopted in 1926 with the Slavery Convention. This instrument provides the core settled definition of "slavery" in international law and sets out the obligation for states to take 'necessary steps' to 'bring about, progressively and as soon as possible, the complete abolition of slavery in all its forms'.[2] Under Article 1(1) of the Geneva Convention, slavery is defined as: 'the status or condition of a person over whom any or all of the powers attaching to the right of ownership are exercised'.[3]

It follows that the 1926 Slavery Convention remains the authoritative definition and adduces the legal foundation for a sound analysis of what constitutes slavery. The articulation of this definition shows that slavery can be a "status" or "condition" that " demonstrates the contemporary relevance of this definition in an international legal landscape that while it universally prohibits the legal classification of people as property (slavery as a status), it must nevertheless adjudicate cases involving the commodification of persons (slavery as a condition)."[4]

Regarding the *Travaux Prépartoires* that led to the adoption of the Convention, Allain noted that attempts were made to include "conditions similar to slavery" which were designed to make clear that what was being abolished was slavery as defined in Article 1(1) of the 1926 Convention.[5] Thus, so-called 'domestic slavery and similar conditions' fall into the definition of slavery if they manifest powers attaching to the right of ownership as established by Article 1(a) of the 1926 Convention. If they do not, this form of exploitation is not covered by the Convention.[6]

In 1956, the Supplementary Convention on the Abolition of Slavery, the Slave Trade, and Institutions and Practices Similar to Slavery was adopted to abolish 'slavery, the slave trade and institutions and practices similar to slavery' as set out in its preamble.[7] Far from assimilating slavery and institutions and practices to which it is similar, the Supplementary Convention makes the following legal distinction between the two concepts:[8]

---

[2]Convention to Suppress the Slave Trade and Slavery, Sept. 25, 1926, 60 L.N.T.S 253, at Art. 2.

[3]*Id.* at Art. 1(1).

[4]Siller (2016), pp. 405, 408.

[5]Allain (2013); Allain (2008); *see also* Allain (2015).

[6]*Id.*

[7]Supplementary Convention on the Abolition of Slavery, the Slave Trade, and Institutions and Practices Similar to Slavery, Apr. 20, 1957, 226 U.N.T.S. 3.

[8]Allain, (2008), p. 264 (note 20: "This is confirmed by the fact that a proposal by Portugal to define slavery together with institutions and practices similar to slavery under the heading of 'servile status' was expressly rejected at the Diplomatic Conference negotiating the 1956 Supplementary Convention"); *Id.* at 518–519.

> (a) 'Slavery' means, as defined in the Slavery Convention of 1926, the status or condition of a person over whom any or all of the powers attaching to the right of ownership are exercised, and "slave" means a person in such a condition or status; [and] (b) 'A person of servile status' means a person in the condition or status resulting from any of the institutions or practices mentioned in article 1 of this Convention.[9]

In fact, apart from slavery, the convention enumerates and sets out the definition of four 'institutions and practices similar to slavery': debt bondage, serfdom, servile marriage, and child exploitation.

As far as forced labor is concerned, the Union of South observed the following in regard to the provision of Article 5 of the 1925 Draft Convention distinguishing slavery from forced labor: "In the first case it is slavery, because the compeller has a proprietary right in respect of the compelled. In the latter case there is some element of choice or consent on the part of the compelled."[10] The Supplementary Convention is built upon the 1926 Slavery Convention which stipulated in Article 5 the need 'to take all necessary measures to prevent compulsory or forced labour from developing into conditions analogous to slavery'; as such the 1926 "Convention dealt not so much with forced labour as with the risk of it turning into slavery."[11] The United Nations Secretary-General believed that slavery will extend to forced labor, debt bondage, or some other type of exploitation, irrespective of movement, if it is evidenced that "'any or all of the powers attaching to the right of ownership are exercised' over a person in these institutions or practices."[12]

With respect to the overall definition, the crucial question that arises is how a person is brought into the condition of slavery? Ostensibly, a determination of slavery in law should consider factors of control over human beings as key indicators of the exercise of powers of the right of ownership. Although the preparatory works that led to the definition of slavery do not provide further insightful interpretation of these "powers", the submission of the Union of South Africa made the right of ownership the test of a slavery condition, stating: "a person is a slave if any other person can...claim such property in him as would be claimed if he were an inanimate object; and thus the natural freedom of will possessed by a person to offer or render his labour or to control the fruits thereof or the consideration therefrom is taken from him."[13] Slavery involves situations of severe human rights

---

[9]U.N.T.S., *supra* note 7, at Article 7(a)(b).

[10]Allain (2008), pp. 55–56.

[11]UNGA, *Report of the International Law Commission to the General Assembly*, UNGAOR, UN Doc. A/44/10 (1989) 61.

[12]U.N. Econ. & Soc. Council [ECOSOC], Slavery, the Slave Trade, and Other Forms of Servitude: Report of the Secretary-General, UN Doc. E/2357 (27 January 1953) 28.

[13]Allain (2008), pp. 55–56, note 13. (This communication is relevant to understanding slavery as it went on to state that, '[t]he term also seems to imply a permanent status or condition of a person whose natural freedom is taken away, for from the proprietary interest of the other person in the person to whom that status attaches is implied a right of disposal of sale, gift or exchange' (emphasis in original text)).

violations where control represents an expression of property rights over the persons concerned.

This understanding of what constitutes slavery within a property law paradigm can be traced back to the Roman Empire,[14] where, because a slave was classified as a property to be owned like any other chattel, Roman Law codified issues involving slaves under property law.[15] Similarly, in 1953 the UN Secretary General elaborated the first authoritative development of what constitutes the exercise of powers attaching to the right of ownership. This refers to the power of dominion over a person (*dominica potestas*) set out in the Roman legal tradition, which was of an "absolute nature, comparable to the rights of ownership, which included the right to acquire, to use, or to dispose of a thing or of an animal or of its fruits or offspring."[16] Guided by this concept, the Secretary General described six main characteristics of slavery associated with complete control over another person:

1. the individual of servile status may be made the object of a purchase;
2. the master may use the individual of servile status, and in particular his capacity to work, in an absolute manner, without any restriction other than that which might be expressly provided by law;
3. the products of the labor of the individual of servile status become the property of the master without any compensation commensurate to the value of the labor;
4. the ownership of the individual of servile status can be transferred to another person;
5. servile status is permanent, that is to say, it cannot be terminated by the will of the individual subject to it;
6. the servile status is transmitted *ipso facto* to descendants of the individual having such status.[17]

It is important to noted that any single characteristic may be sufficient to evidence slavery and in some circumstances they might operate interdependently. For example, individuals who have become objects of transaction through purchasing and selling could be indicia of the exercise of powers attaching to the right of ownership. The use of an individual's capacity to work in an absolute manner, benefiting from their services or labor without any compensation commensurate to the value of such labor, could be considered also as indicia of powers attaching to the right of ownership being exercised over them. Finally, depending on the circumstances of the case, factors might operate interdependently in determining whether the practices are tantamount to slavery. Thus, merely detaining or keeping someone in captivity does not usually constitute slavery; compulsory labor or service must be present for this to be the case.

[14]Buckland (2001); Watson (1987), p. 66; *see also* Honoré (2012), pp. 9–16; Helmholz (2012), pp. 17–37; Cairns (2012), pp. 61–83; Drescher (2012), pp. 85–101.

[15]Watson (1987), p. 66.

[16]ECOSOC, *supra* note 12, at 27–28.

[17]*Id.* at 26–28; *see also The Queen v Tang*, 2008 HCA 39, 22 (28 August 2008).

## 5.2 Legal Parameters for Identifying Slavery Conditions

Consistent with the 1953 UN Report, the Bellagio-Harvard Guidelines on the Legal Parameters of Slavery refer also to property law to explain the substance embedded in the UN's definition of slavery and articulate its continuing relevance to contemporary slavery conditions.[18] The Guidelines thus define slavery as "[possessing or controlling] a person in such a way as to significantly deprive that person of his or her individual liberty, with the intent of exploitation through the use, management, profit, transfer or disposal of that person. Usually this exercise will be supported by and obtained through means such as violent force, deception, and/or coercion."[19] This definition provides the legal ground for the prosecution of contemporary slavery. Guideline 4 also enumerates the incidents of powers attaching to the right of ownership, which include buying, selling, or transferring a person, using a person, managing and profiting from that use, transferring a person to an heir or successor, and the disposal, mistreatment or neglect of a person.[20] However, possession remains the "foundation on which the whole superstructure of ownership rests"[21] and is therefore "the exercise of control tantamount to possession that makes possible the exercise of further powers while on the other hand, an exercise of a further power attaching to the right of ownership may serve to indicate the presence of control tantamount to possession."[22]

It is also s important to distinguish cases of slavery from other situations where, "though there has been control exercised, it does not constitute control tantamount to possession."[23] Allain highlights the trivial example of a work relationship where employers routinely make legitimate decisions about the tasks and management of their workers, expecting not unreasonably to benefit from their labor, which is subject to payment of a (fair) wage. This employment relation cannot fall within the scope of Article 1 of the 1926 Convention and it would be invectively referred to

---

[18]Hickey (2012), pp. 226–231. Honore proposed a widely -accepted list of incidents attached to ownership that are applicable to slavery situations: the right to use, the right to possess, the right to income, the right to manage, the right to the capital (including transmissibility), the right to security, the absence of term, prohibition of harmful use, liability to execution, residuary character, and rights, liberties, powers, and immunities. *See* Honore (1961), p. 113. For the full Bellagio–Harvard Guidelines, *see* Allain (2012), pp. 375–380.

[19]Regarding the 1926 definition of slavery ("the status or condition of a person over whom any or all of the powers attaching to the rights of ownership are exercised") the UN Commentary elucidates: "The definition in the Slavery Convention may cause difficulties today, as there could be no rights of ownership for one person over another. In order to solve this difficulty, an alternative definition would be 'the status or condition of a person over whom control is exercised to the extent that the person is treated like property,' or 'reducing a person to a status or condition in which any or all of the powers attaching to the right of property are exercised.'" See *Joint UN Commentary on the EU Directive – A Human Rights-Based Approach* 103 (2011).

[20]Bellagio-Harvard Guidelines on the Legal Parameters of Slavery.

[21]Honore (1961).

[22]Allain (2013), p. 122.

[23]*Id.* at 375–380.

as slavery.[24] In a similar fashion, the Australian Court considering *R v. Tang* case observed that

> [a]n employer normally has some degree of control over the movements, or work environment, of an employee. Furthermore, geographical and other circumstances may limit an employee's freedom of movement. Powers of control, in the context of an issue of slavery, are powers of the kind and degree that would attach to a right of ownership if such a right were legally possible, not powers of a kind that are no more than an incident of harsh employment, either generally or at a particular time or place.[25]

Furthermore, where factual circumstances do not disclose subjugation and absolute control tantamount to possession even though the practices are exploitative, they do not fall within the legal parameters of the definition of slavery.[26] Like clerks, labor workers in mines or domestic workers might be forced to accept less than the minimum wage under threat of dismissal; this constitutes forced labour inasmuch as "the threshold of control would have to be much higher for such an instance to constitute slavery."[27] The exercise of absolute control over another human being as a property, thus depriving them of their judicial personality, is therefore the critical element in scrutinizing labor relationships involving people in mining, agricultural labor, and prostitution to distinguish slavery from lesser servitude in order to provide protection to the victims. Similarly, a government might detain or have control over the movements of identified individuals, and at least some of the time these practices are recognized as being in pursuit of legitimate goals.[28]

With regards to the distinction between forced labor and slavery, the facts described in the 2007 *Prosecutor v Brima* case before the Special Court of Sierra are enlightening.[29] During the armed conflict in Sierra Leone, the rebels enrolled civilians in diamond mining activities and controlled them in two different ways. One witness testified that, in some cases, the rebel forces captured individuals who they then undressed, tied together, and brought to the mines "where they were forced to work at gunpoint."[30] It appears in such situations that the control exercised over the civilians was tantamount to possession, as they were completely dependent on their captors. However, in other cases civilian miners were forced under threat of violence to work by spending two days a week mining for the "Government". These individuals cannot be considered enslaved as they were free at the end of their working days to return to their homes and on other days to engage in mining

[24] Allain and Hickey (2012), pp. 915, 931.

[25] Tang, *supra* note 17, at 32.

[26] *See* Allain and Hickey (2012), pp. 936–937.

[27] *Id.* at 937.

[28] *Id.* at 931.

[29] Prosecutor v. Brima et al., Special Court for Sierra Leone, Trial Chamber, SCSL-2004-16-T (20 June 2007), ¶¶ 744–747 (which evokes the enslavement of men for the purpose of extracting forced labor in alluvial diamond fields).

[30] *Id.* at ¶ 1297.

activities for their own profit. However, they were victims of forced labour.[31] Investigating the labor dimension of trafficking in persons, Beate Andrees and Mariska Linden explained that trafficked and non-trafficked victims of forced labor often work in the same sectors, which makes it difficult to differentiate them. Notably, non-trafficked victims of forced labor exercise more agency in exiting forced labor than trafficked victims, who are maintained in the worst abusive situation.[32]

When considering an alleged case of slavery in law, the most apparent indicia of possession would be the ability to *buy or sell a person*. Because someone can only sell what he possesses in the first place, the power of a person to engage another human being in a commercial transaction or to exchange, barter, give or receive a person as gift is indicative of possession. In all cases, a person is made amenable to being the subject of a transaction only through such control, which is often established through violence or coercion.[33] For example, in the *Hadijatou Mani Koraou v. Niger* case, *HadijatouMani Koraou,* a twelve (12) year old girl of the Bouzou custom was sold for the equivalent of $400 to El Hadji Souleymane Naroua, a 46-year-old tribal chief of the Haoussa custom in Niger. She was his *Sadaka*, or "fifth wife"; that is, a woman who is taken in addition to those legally married but cannot be acknowledged as a wife under the precepts of Islam. This purchase was carried out in accordance with a practice called *wahiya*, whereby a young girl is forced into servile status, serving as both domestic servant and concubine.[34] The elements of the crime associated with the transaction in the *Prosecutor v. Kunarac* case are payment in money for the exchange, which represents the capital value of the person as a thing and the retention in custody of the person by the third party.[35] The transaction can be in kind or of a different sort in other circumstances.

However, this is not to suggest that every transaction involving human beings represents a situation of enslavement. It may indicate that slavery is present but not at a sufficient level to meet the threshold of slavery. Allain draws on the example of athletes of whom it is sometimes said that they are slaves because they are bought and sold to another club. Although their services are being bought and sold, such transactions fail to meet the threshold of slavery if evidence of control over the athlete that would amount to possession is not proven. A football player who has been forced to move cities may deem it unfair but he or she will not be compelled under threat of violence to comply; he is free to walk away. Conversely, in cases of

---

[31] Brima et al., *supra* note 29 at ¶¶ 1291–1296; *see also* ILO - Forced Labour Convention, Cf. No. 29 (01 May 1932) art. 2 ("forced or compulsory labour shall mean all work or service which is exacted from any person under the menace of any penalty and for which the said person has not offered himself voluntarily").

[32] Andrees and van der Linden (2005), pp. 55, 65.

[33] Allain and Hickey (2012), p. 933.

[34] *Koraou v. Niger*, ECOWAS Community Court of Justice, Judgment, No. ECW/CCJ/APP/0808, ¶ 8 (Oct. 27, 2008) (available at: http://www.worldcourts.com/ecowasccj/eng/decisions/2008.10.27_Koraou_v_Niger.htm).

[35] Kunarac, *supra* note 1, ¶¶ 775–776.

slavery, someone is exercising control over the victim either through actual or latent violence in such a manner that the person enslaved has no other choice than to comply.[36]

Another slavery indicia found in modern enslavement is the *transferring of a person to an heir or successor*. In traditional slavery, slaves were treated as chattel and could be conveyed to a successive generation as they were a piece of property.[37] This power to transfer a person as property is found in instances of servile marriage where a bride is purchased or acquired by offering money or services disguised as a dowry, a wife is transferred or given, and a widow inherited. It also occurs in adoption through the transfer of guardianship or child fostering.[38] Under Igbo customary law in Nigeria and many other West African countries, the prospective wife is considered to be the property of her father, and as a widow she is merely part of the heritable property of her husband to be handed over to one of the siblings of the deceased husband. Often, children are also at the disposal of their step-father.[39]

Furthermore, in chattel slavery found in Mauritania, Niger, and Mali, a slave status or condition is imposed on the children of the enslaved and "cannot be terminated by the will of the individual subject to it."[40] Therefore, in evaluating whether slavery exists in a given situation, reference should be made to the power of control over the "duration" of this condition. In investigating slavery, it is important to inquire whether the person is bound for an undetermined period of time or he is free to change their status,

Another factor involved in assessing the offense of slavery is the *use of a person* in accruing benefits that might derive from the service or labor of that person. In slavery situations, "such benefit might be the savings incurred as a result of paying little or no salary for labour or the gratification from sexual services."[41] Such cases can be found, for instance, in the forced marriages previously described in Part I where a person is used for sexual gratification,[42] or domestic servitude[43] where the servant is used to provide a service or labor for little or no pay. Similarly, during the 1991–2002 Civil War in Serra Leone, soldiers abducted young girls and women for

---

[36] Allain (2017), pp. 36, 40.

[37] Newman (2013), p. 27.

[38] Allain (2013), pp. 293–324.

[39] *Nigeria: Levirate Marriage Practices among the Yoruba, Igbo and Hausa-Fulani; Consequences for a Man or Woman Who Refuses to Participate in the Marriage; Availability of State Protection, February 2006*, UNHCR (Mar. 16, 2006), http://www.unhcr.org/refworld/docid/45f1478811.html (accessed August 18, 2021).

Report of the *Ad Hoc* Committee on Slavery (Second Session), United Nations, Economic and Social Council, 9–10 U.N. Doc. E/1998, E/AC.33/13 (May 4, 1951).

[40] ECOSOC, *supra* note 12, at 36.

[41] Allain (2012), p. 337; *see also* Allain (2017), p. 40.

[42] *Brima et al.*, *supra* note 29 (for case-law regarding prosecution of crime against humanity of forced marriage).

[43] *Siliadin v. France*, European Court of Human Rights, Application No. 73316/01, Judgment (2005).

the purpose of forced labor and forcibly took them as wives, commonly termed 'bush wives'. The rebels compel them to cook, clean, and porter under threat of death.[44] The elements inherent to determining whether a person is used by another include absolute control over the individual's movement and autonomy, unpaid labor accruing a benefit to the owner, and extreme deprivation and domination over every aspect of their life (including working conditions, housing location, sexual life, and personal decisions).[45]

Subsequent to the use of a person is the power *to manage the use of a person*. In general, to manage people does not mean to enslave them insofar as "employers make legitimate decisions on a daily basis about the management of workers."[46] When the labor relationship totally deprives the employee of choice and personal agency, then management of the use of a slave takes place. This is manifest in sex work involving African girls where the brothel owner, the so called *Madam*, delegates powers to over-seers for the day-to-day management of the prostitutes.

In such circumstances, the slave owner is typically entitled to any profit or income deriving from the labor or service of the slave. Thus, *profiting from the use of a person* constitutes exercise of power over the property one owns. For example, in the case of enslavement in agricultural fields or mining, workers are forced to harvest crops through coercion or deception, and the income and salary destined for the worker are usurped by the enslaved.[47] Furthermore, the offender might use the victim as collateral for loans, debt payments, or to reap other kinds of income and benefits through mortgaging and lending for profit. In domestic servitude, for instance, "the services performed by the enslaved child provide a sizable return on the investment in "upkeep."[48] In a similar way, Part I of this discussion raised concerns about the situations of children being sold and lent as domestic workers in Ghana and many parts of West Africa that might fall squarely under the legal definition of slavery.

Finally, owners dispose of their properties if no longer useful. This suggests that the *mistreatment or neglect of a person* falls within the parameters of slavery, inasmuch as that person is treated as a *disposable* item.[49] Bales noted that "[s] laves of the past were worth stealing and worth chasing down if they escaped. Today, slaves cost so little that it is not worth the hassle of securing permanent, 'legal' ownership. Slaves are disposable" and "[s]laveholders get all the work they can out of their slaves, and then throw them away".[50] For instance, if a bonded laborer is unable to work, "perhaps because of illness or injury, or is not needed for work, he or she can be abandoned or disposed of by the slaveholder, who bears no

---

[44] *See* Brima et al., *supra* note 29, at ¶¶ 744–747.

[45] Rassam (2005), pp. 809, 817.

[46] Allain (2017), p. 40.

[47] Allain (2017), p. 40.

[48] Bales (1999), p.21

[49] Bales (1999), p. 39.

[50] *Id.* at 35.

responsibility for the slave's upkeep."[51] Other examples of slavery situations mentioned in the previous chapter are cases in the Trokosi system, domestic servitude, begging, and mining where children are abandoned or replaced when they are deemed old or no longer effective. In the commercial prostitution industry, "[t]he brothel does have to feed the girl and keep her presentable, but if she becomes ill or injured or too old, she is disposed of. In Thailand today, the girl is often discarded when she tests positive for HIV."[52]

Such mistreatment or neglect might be planned, and would impose heavy demands that lead to physical or psychological exhaustion and may ultimately cause death if they persist.[53] As things currently stand, traffickers in persons do not want "to spend money supporting useless infants, so female slaves, especially those forced into prostitution, suffer violent, involuntary abortions. And there is no reason to protect slaves from disease or injury—medicine costs money, and it's cheaper to let them die."[54] Broadly speaking, "slavery will be manifest where the disregard for the well-being of the person is evidenced by severe physical or psychological exhaustion, which, if allowed to carry on to its logical conclusion, would entail the death of the enslaved."[55] Further to the current analysis, the following section will outline the principal features of international instruments addressing the transnational nature of trafficking in persons.

## References

Allain J (2008) The slavery conventions: the Travaux Prépartoires of the 1926 League of Nations Convention and the 1956 United Nations Convention. Martinus Nijhoff Publishers

Allain J (2012) Bellagio-Harvard guidelines on the legal parameters of slavery. In: The legal understanding of slavery: from the historical to the contemporary. Oxford University Press, p 337

Allain J (2013) Slavery in international law: of human exploitation and trafficking. Martinus Nijhoff Publishers, pp 112–113

Allain J (2015) The definition of 'slavery' in general international law and in crime of enslavement within the Rome Statute. In: The law and slavery. Brill Publication, available online at https://www.icc-cpi.int/NR/rdonlyres/069658BB-FDBD-4EDD-8414-543ECB1FA9DC/0/ICCOTP20070426Allain_en.pdf. Accessed 20 Aug 2021

Allain J (2017) Contemporary slavery and its definition in law. In: Contemporary slavery: popular rhetoric and political practice. University of British Columbia Press, pp 36, 40

Allain J, Hickey R (2012) Property and the definition of slavery. Int Comp Law Q 61:915, 931

Andrees B, van der Linden MNJ (2005) Designing trafficking research from a labour market perspective: the ILO experience. Int Migr 43:55, 65

[51] *Id.* at 36.

[52] *Id.* at 37.

[53] Allain and Hickey (2012), p. 935.

[54] Bales (1999).

[55] Allain (2017), p. 41.

Bales K (1999) Disposable people: New Slavery in the global economy. University of California Press, p 21

Buckland WW (2001) The Roman law of slavery: the condition of the slave in private law from Augustus to Justinian. The Lawbook Exchange, Ltd.

Cairns JW (2012) The definition of slavery in the eighteenth-century thinking: not the true Roman slavery. In: The legal understanding of slavery: from the historical to the contemporary. Oxford University Press, pp 61–83

Convention to Suppress the Slave Trade and Slavery, Sept. 25, 1926, 60 L.N.T.S 253, at Art. 2

Drescher S (2012) From consensus to consensus: slavery in international law. In: The legal understanding of slavery: from the historical to the contemporary. Oxford University Press, pp 85–101

Gold F (2003) Redefining the slave trade: current trends in the international trafficking of women. Univ Miami Int Comp Law Rev 11:99, 100

Helmholz RH (2012) The law of slavery and the European Ius Commune. In: The legal understanding of slavery: from the historical to the contemporary. Oxford University Press, pp 17–37

Hickey R (2012) Seeking to understand the definition of slavery. In: Allain J (ed) The legal understanding of slavery: from the historical to the contemporary. Oxford University Press, pp 226–231

Honore AM (1961) Ownership. In: Guest AG (ed) Oxford essays in jurisprudence. Oxford University Press, p 113

Honoré A (2012) The nature of slavery. In: The legal understanding of slavery: from the historical to the contemporary. Oxford University Press, pp 9–16

ILO - Forced Labour Convention, Cf. No. 29 (01 May 1932) art. 2

Joint UN Commentary on the EU Directive – A Human Rights-Based Approach 103 (2011)

*Koraou v. Niger*, ECOWAS Community Court of Justice, Judgment, No. ECW/CCJ/APP/0808, ¶ 8 (Oct. 27, 2008) (available at: http://www.worldcourts.com/ecowasccj/eng/decisions/2008.10.27_Koraou_v_Niger.htm)

Newman BN (2013) Historical perspective: slavery over the centuries. In: Burke MC (ed) Human trafficking interdisciplinary perspectives, p 27

Pati R (2006) The Miami declaration of principles on human trafficking: its genesis and purpose. Int Hum Rights Law Rev 1:11

*Prosecutor v. Brima et al.*, Special Court for Sierra Leone, Trial Chamber, SCSL-2004-16-T (20 June 2007), ¶¶ 744–747

*Prosecutor v. Kunarac, et al.*, International Criminal Court, Case No. IT-96-23/1-T, Judgment ¶¶ 775–776 (22 February 2001) (accessed from: http://www.icty.org/x/cases/kunarac/tjug/en/kun-tj010222e.pdf)

Rassam AY (2005) International law and contemporary forms of slavery: an economic and social rights-based approach. Penn State Int Law Rev 23:809, 817

Report of the *Ad Hoc* Committee on Slavery (Second Session), United Nations, Economic and Social Council, 9–10 U.N. Doc. E/1998, E/AC.33/13 (May 4, 1951)

*Siliadin v. France*, European Court of Human Rights, Application No. 73316/01, Judgment (2005)

Siller N (2016) Modern slavery' does international law distinguish between slavery, enslavement and trafficking? J Int Crim Just 14:405, 408

Supplementary Convention on the Abolition of Slavery, the Slave Trade, and Institutions and Practices Similar to Slavery, Apr. 20, 1957, 226 U.N.T.S. 3

*The Queen v Tang*, 2008 HCA 39, 22 (28 August 2008)

U.N. Econ. & Soc. Council [ECOSOC], Slavery, the Slave Trade, and Other Forms of Servitude: Report of the Secretary-General, UN Doc. E/2357 (27 January 1953) 28

UNGA, *Report of the International Law Commission to the General Assembly*, UNGAOR, UN Doc. A/44/10 (1989) 61

*Nigeria: Levirate Marriage Practices among the Yoruba, Igbo and Hausa-Fulani; Consequences for a Man or Woman Who Refuses to Participate in the Marriage; Availability of State Protection, February 2006*, UNHCR (Mar. 16, 2006), http://www.unhcr.org/refworld/docid/45f1478811.html. Accessed 20 Aug 2021

Watson A (1987) Roman slave law. John Hopkins University, p 66

# Chapter 6
# International Human Rights Laws and Trafficking in Persons

Within a human rights paradigm, trafficking in persons is first and foremost a serious violation of the victims' human rights; it is a crime against persons. The concept and scope of these human rights violations will be discussed in depth in Chap. 8 in conjunction with states' obligations according to international law. At an international level the Palermo Protocol is a piece of legislation that addresses multiple facets of trafficking.[1] The stated goal of the Convention is to undertake effective legal action to foster a "comprehensive international approach in the countries of origin, transit and destination that includes measures to prevent such trafficking, to punish the traffickers and to protect the victims of such trafficking."[2] Corresponding to these objectives, human rights law is relevant to trafficking in persons inasmuch as the victims are holders of inalienable and legally enforceable rights protecting them from abuse. The following sections explore several of the human rights violations that occur during the trafficking process and discusses the related human rights legal framework that should guide the policies adopted by states in response to such trafficking. These include the right not to be held in slavery or servitude, the right to life, the integrity and security of the person, the right to personal autonomy and freedom of movement, the right to be free from cruel or inhuman treatment, the right to equality and non-discrimination, and the right to safe and healthy working conditions.

---

[1] Braspenning (2006), p. 329, 351.

[2] Preamble of the Palermo Protocol.

 
P. VI. S. Karenga, *A West African Model to Address Human Trafficking*,
https://doi.org/10.1007/978-3-030-88120-7_6

## 6.1 The Right Not to be Held in Slavery or Servitude

Article 6 of the Slavery Convention urges contracting states to abolish slavery and similar practices in their territories and imposes an obligation to enact adequate provisions for the punishment of such infractions. Although some circumstances surrounding the trafficking in persons may not involve the "right of ownership" historically associated with slavery, they can include exploitation of the victims and deprivations of their liberty that render the situation equivalent to slavery. The parties of states shall therefore enact measures to abolish practices similar to slavery including debt-bondage and serfdom, forced marriage, and the sale/transfer of children for labor exploitation.[3]

The right not to be subjected to slavery and servitude is endorsed by the International Bill of Human Rights. The Universal Declaration of Human Rights (UDHR) also sets out in article 4 that "No one shall be held in slavery or servitude; slavery and the slave trade shall be prohibited in all their forms."[4] This prohibition is also reflected in Art 8 of the International Covenant on Civil and Political Rights (ICCPR), which protects every human being from slavery, slave trade, servitude, and forced or compulsory labor.[5] Most importantly, the right to be free from slavery or servitude is characterized as an absolute and non-derogable right under article 4(2) of the Covenant. Accordingly, states can never suspend the prohibition of slavery or servitude, even in the event of a public emergency that threatens the life of the nation. The provisions of these conventions are especially relevant in addressing the vestiges of traditional forms of slavery that still exist in West Africa, including caste–based slavery and the ritual servitude of girls (the *trokosi* system).[6]

In a similar vein, the International Covenant on Economic, Social and Cultural Rights recognizes in article 6(1) the right to work, "which includes the right of everyone to the opportunity to gain his living by work which he freely chooses or accepts."[7] Every individual has the right to be able to work, allowing him/her to live in dignity. The right to work also allows his/her family to live in dignity, and insofar as work is freely chosen or accepted, it contributes to and individual's development and recognition within the community.[8] Articles 7 and 8 further lay out the right of every human being to enjoy just and favorable conditions of work, in particular the

[3]Supplementary Convention on the Abolition of Slavery, the Slave Trade, and Institutions and Practices Similar to Slavery (1956), Article 1 and Article 6.

[4]UDHR, Article 4.

[5]Adopted by General Assembly resolution 2200 A (XXI) of 16 December 1966, United Nations Treaty Series, vol. 999, p. 171; entered into force on 23 March 1976.

[6]Slavery Convention, 1929, Art. 1: "Slavery is the status or condition of a person over whom any or all of the powers attaching to the right of ownership are exercised."

[7]ICESCR, Article 6(1), 16 December 1966: entry into force January 31976 https://www.ohchr.org/EN/ProfessionalInterest/Pages/CESCR.aspx.

[8]Committee On Economic, Social and Cultural Rights, E/C.12/GC/18, February 6 2006 para.1 https://www.refworld.org/pdfid/4415453b4.pdf.

right to safe working conditions and fair wages. The right of everyone to decide freely to accept or choose work implies that the parties of states must create the conditions to enable full enjoyment of the right along with the obligation to prohibit forced or child labor.[9]

The right to be free from slavery is afforded significant legal support in several regional instruments.[10] For example, the prohibition of slavery and forced labor set out in article 4 of the European Convention on Human Rights has been enforced by decisions made by the European Court of Human Rights. In the *Siliadin v France* case, for instance, the European Court of Human Rights held that the applicant was subjected to treatment contrary to Article 4 and kept in servitude, and thus France had breached its positive obligations under the European Convention on Human Rights.[11] A similar provision is reflected in Article 5 of the African Charter on Human and Peoples' Rights and Article 6 of the American Convention on Human Rights which prohibit the slave trade, slavery, or involuntary servitude.

## 6.2 The Right to Life, Integrity, and Security of the Person

As illustrated earlier, trafficking in persons is an inhuman act that threatens the life and the well-being of its victims. The fundamental right to life, liberty, and security for all human beings is recognized and protected in Article 3 of the Universal Declaration of Human Rights. Similarly, Article 6(1) of the International Covenant on Civil and Political Rights (ICCPR) endorses the inherent right of every person to life, mandating that "this right shall be protected by law (Article 6(1))." The Human Rights Committee has also made it clear that the protection afforded by Article 6 in so far as it concerns life is absolute. It is a supreme right from which no derogation is permitted, even in situations of armed conflict and other public emergencies.[12] The right to life is of crucial importance and its effective protection is the prerequisite for the enjoyment of all other human rights.

Along with the aforementioned international instruments, the right to life is also protected in regional treaties. For example, it is established in the African Charter on Human and Peoples' Rights that "every human being shall be entitled to respect for his life and the integrity of his person. No one may be arbitrarily deprived of this

---

[9] Committee On Economic, Social and Cultural Rights, E/C.12/GC/18, February 6 2006 para.4, 6–7 https://www.refworld.org/pdfid/4415453b4.pdf.

[10] The American Convention on Human Rights, Article 6, entered into force in 1978; African Charter on Human and Peoples' Rights, Article 5 (Adopted 27 June 1981, OAU Doc. CAB/LEG/67/3 rev. 5, 21 I.L.M. 58 (1982), entered into force October 21 1986).

[11] *Siliadin v. France*, European Court of Human Rights, Application No. 73316/01, Judgment (2005).

[12] OHCHR, General comment No. 36 (2018) on article 6 of the International Covenant on Civil and Political Rights, on the right to life, CCPR/C/GC/36, 30 October 2018, para.1 https://tbinternet.ohchr.org/Treaties/CCPR/Shared%20Documents/1_Global/CCPR_C_GC_36_8785_E.pdf.

right (Article 4)." Pursuant to other conventions related to specific violations of the right to life, the Protocol to the African Charter on Human and Peoples' Rights on the Rights of Women in Africa, Article 4(1) declares that "every woman shall be entitled to respect for her life and the integrity and security of the person. All forms of exploitation, cruel, inhuman or degrading punishment and treatment shall be prohibited." The American Convention on Human Rights Article 4(1) obligates states to protect the right to life in their domestic legislation from the moment of conception so that no one is arbitrarily deprived of their life.

## 6.3 The Right to Personal Autonomy and Freedom of Movement

Traffickers deprive victims of their autonomy and their freedom to move or travel by isolating them in their workplace. This constitutes a violation of Article 13 of the Universal Declaration of Human Rights (UDHR) and Article 12 of the International Covenant on Civil and Political Rights (ICCPR), which state that anyone lawfully within the territory of a state enjoys the right to move freely within that state and to choose their residence. Citizens of a country have the right to leave and to re-enter that state.[13] Freedom of movement has been described as an "essential condition for the free development of the person."[14] Restrictions on a person's freedom of movement provide compelling evidence supporting elements of the crime of trafficking in persons.

Moreover, trafficking in persons interferes seriously with the individual's autonomy and agency. Victims lose agency over their body, and are denied the right to make life choices including sexual and reproductive choices, and the right to choose dignified work. Article 23 of the Universal Declaration of Human Rights (UDHR) states that everyone has the right to work, to free choice of employment, and is entitled to just and favorable conditions of work and remuneration that ensure for themselves and their family an existence worthy of human dignity. In a similar vein, the International Covenant on Economic, Social and Cultural Rights (ICESCR) in Article 6 calls upon state parties to "recognize the right to work, which includes the right of everyone to the opportunity to gain his living by work which he freely chooses or accepts, and will take appropriate steps to safeguard this right."[15] The African Charter on Human and Peoples' Rights also endorses the right to free choice

[13] Article 12 of the International Covenant on Civil and Political Rights (ICCPR), 16 December 1966; Article 13 of the Universal Declaration of Human Rights (UDHR), 10 December 1948; Freedom of movement is a right protected in each of the regional human rights systems. Article 12 of the African Charter on Human and Peoples' Rights ("ACHPR"), 27 June 1981; Articles 22 (5) and 22(1) of the American Convention on Human Rights (ACHR) 22 January 1969.

[14] *Tide Mendez et al. v. Dominican Republic*, Inter-American Court of Human Rights, Judgment, Rep. No. 64/12 (29 March 2012).

[15] International Covenant on Economic, Social, and Cultural Rights, Article 6(1).

of employment, emphasizing labor rights: "every individual shall have the right to work under equitable and satisfactory conditions, and shall receive equal pay for equal work."[16] This provision is reflected in Articles 25–30 of the Convention on the Protection of the Right of All Migrant Workers and their Families, which secures minimum standards of labor conditions for migrant workers, remuneration, medical care, and social security.

The human right to health proclaimed in Article (25(1)) of the Universal Declaration of Human Rights is also recognized in Article 12 of Economic, Social and Cultural Rights, which states that everyone is entitled "to the enjoyment of the highest attainable standard of physical and mental health."[17] The right to health includes access to medical care and necessary social services, to healthy occupational and environmental conditions, protection against diseases, and rights related to sexual and reproductive health.[18] Regional human rights instruments also protect the right to health, such as the revised European Social Charter (Article 11),[19] the African Charter on Human and Peoples' Rights (Article 16),[20] and the Additional Protocol to the American Convention on Human Rights in the Area of Economic, Social, and Cultural Rights of 1988 (Article 10(1)).[21]

## 6.4 The Right to be Free from Cruel or Inhuman Treatment

Trafficking for the purpose of prostitution involves conduct that amounts to torture and inhuman or degrading treatment, which is prohibited under the Convention Against Torture and Other Cruel, Inhuman or Degrading Treatment or Punishment (CAT), Article 5 of the Universal Declaration of Human Rights (UDHR) and Article 7 of the International Covenant on Civil and Political Rights (ICCPR), and has

[16] African Charter on Human and Peoples' Rights, Article 15.

[17] International Covenant on Economic, Social, and Cultural Rights, Article 12.

[18] Frequently Asked Questions on Economic, Social, and Cultural Rights, Office of the United Nations High Commissioner for Human Rights, Fact Sheet No.33, p. 2 https://www.ohchr.org/Documents/Issues/ESCR/FAQ%20on%20ESCR-en.pdf.

[19] European Social Charter, Turin, 18.X.1961, European Treaty Series - No. 35, Article 11 "Everyone has the right to benefit from any measures enabling him to enjoy the highest possible standard of health attainable." https://rm.coe.int/168006b642.

[20] African Charter on Human and Peoples' Rights, Article 16 "Every individual shall have the right to enjoy the best attainable state of physical and mental health." http://www.humanrights.se/wp-content/uploads/2012/01/African-Charter-on-Human-and-Peoples-Rights.pdf.

[21] Additional Protocol to the American Convention on Human Rights in the Area of Economic, Social, and Cultural Rights "Protocol of San Salvador" Adopted in San Salvador on November 17, 1988 (not yet in force) Article 10(1) "Everyone shall have the right to health, understood to mean the enjoyment of the highest level of physical, mental and social well-being." https://www.oas.org/dil/1988%20Additional%20Protocol%20to%20the%20American%20Convention%20on%20Human%20Rights%20in%20the%20Area%20of%20Economic,%20Social%20and%20Cultural%20Rights%20(Protocol%20of%20San%20Salvador).pdf

attained the status of a *jus cogens* norm. The failure to protect women from sex trafficking also represents a failure to ensure the right of women to equal protection under the law. This is a well-enshrined principle of international law.

Because trafficking persons and torture are closely intertwined, the African Charter on Human and Peoples' Rights requires states to prohibit "all forms of exploitation and degradation of man, particularly slavery, slave trade, torture, cruel, inhumane or degrading punishment and treatment."[22] The Human Rights Committee explains that torture includes mental suffering as well as physical pain inflicted on someone as punishment for a crime or as an educative measure.[23] The Protocol to the African Charter on Human and People Rights provides explicitly for the right to be free from sexual violence. Article 1(j) enshrines protection against all acts of violence "perpetrated against women which cause or could cause them physical, sexual, psychological, and economic harm, including the threat to take such acts; or to undertake the imposition of arbitrary restrictions or deprivation of fundamental freedoms in private or public life in peace time and during situations of armed conflicts or wars"[24]

## 6.5 The Right to Equality and Non-discrimination

As described previously, victims of trafficking very face discrimination at work, social stigmatization, and even racist and xenophobic behaviors when they reach their country of destination.[25] The Convention on the Elimination of All forms of Discrimination Against Women (CEDAW) adopted in 1979 represents a cornerstone regarding the protection of women from any violation of their human rights on the basis of gender, including trafficking in women and prostitution. Throughout this study, stereotyped roles for women and men along with discrimination have been posited as the root cause of trafficking in persons in West Africa. The Protocol to the African Charter on the Rights of Women in Africa requires states to transform the social and cultural patterns of conduct among women and men through public education with a view to eradicating harmful cultural and traditional practices and all other human rights abuses based on gender.[26]

---

[22] African Charter, Art. 5, http://www.achpr.org/files/instruments/achpr/banjul_charter.pdf.

[23] UN Human Rights Committee (HRC), CCPR General Comment No. 20: Article 7 (Prohibition of Torture, or Other Cruel, Inhuman or Degrading Treatment or Punishment), March 10 1992, http://www.refworld.org/docid/453883fb0.html.

[24] The Protocol on the Rights of Women in Africa (2003), Article 1, entered into force in 2005.

[25] *Combating Trafficking as Modern-Day Slavery: A Matter of Non-Discrimination and Empowerment*, 43 OSCE (2012) https://www.osce.org/secretariat/98249?download=true.

[26] Protocol to the African Charter on Human and Peoples' Rights on the Rights of Women in Africa, Art 2(2), http://www.achpr.org/files/instruments/women-protocol/achpr_instr_proto_women_eng.pdf.

As mentioned previously, women in West Africa are especially vulnerable within the context of marriage. Recognizing the close link between these trends in forced labor, the Supplementary Convention on the Abolition of Slavery requires member states "to prescribe, where appropriate, suitable minimum ages of marriage, to encourage the use of facilities whereby the consent of both parties to a marriage may be freely expressed in the presence of a competent civil or religious authority, and to encourage the registration of marriages."[27] By the same token, the International Covenant on Economic, Social and Cultural Rights (ICESCR) secures the right to freely choose a spouse and, in Article 10(2), to enter into marriage with free and full consent.[28]

According to the CRC report, in March 2009 forced marriages in Burkina Faso and to a large extent in West Africa "fall outside the purview of public administration, in the forms of traditional and religious weddings which are neither recognized nor prohibited by the law."[29] The Protocol to the African Charter on the Rights of Women in Africa (2003) requires state parties to enact appropriate national legislative measures to guarantee that every marriage is "recorded in writing and registered in accordance with national laws, in order to be legally recognized;"[30] They specify the minimum age of marriage for women to be18 years,[31] and protect the right of women to "acquire their own property and to administer and manage it freely."[32]

In regard to child trafficking, the Convention on the Rights of the Child (CRC) provides a fundamental impetus that protects children from abuse and neglect within the family, reflecting the particular human rights concerns of each region to prohibit "(a) the abduction, the sale of, or traffic of children for any purpose or in any form, by any person including parents or legal guardians of the child; (b) the use of children in all forms of begging."[33] Furthermore, Article 20(1) of Convention on the Rights of the Child mandates that a child who is "temporarily or permanently deprived of his or her family environment," or in their best interests "cannot be

[27] Supplementary Convention on the Abolition of Slavery, the Slave Trade, and Institutions and Practices Similar to Slavery, Art 2, http://www.ohchr.org/EN/ProfessionalInterest/Pages/SupplementaryConventionAbolitionOfSlavery.aspx; Universal Declaration of Human Rights (art. 16(2)); Convention on Consent to Marriage, Minimum Age for Marriage and Registration of Marriages, General Assembly resolution 1763 A (XVII) of 7 November 1963, United Nations Treaty Series, vol. 521, p. 231, Art. 1(1), entered into force on 9 December 1964; UN Declaration on Human Rights Art 16(2). Read more about forced and early marriage: Analysis of the Language of Child, Early, and Forced Marriages, August 2013 at sexualrightsinitiative.com.

[28] UN Declaration on Human Rights Art 16(2).

[29] UN CEDAW and CRC recommendations on minimum age of marriage laws around the world as of November 2013, equalitynow.org, child marriage report.

[30] The Protocol to the African Charter on the Rights of Women in Africa (2003)- Art 6(d), http://www.achpr.org/files/instruments/women-protocol/achpr_instr_proto_women_eng.pdf.

[31] *Id.*

[32] *Id.*

[33] The African Charter on the Rights and Welfare of the Child, Art. 29, http://www.acerwc.org/download/the-charter-english/?wpdmdl=8410.

allowed to remain in that environment, shall be entitled to special protection and assistance provided by the State."[34]

Similarly, Art 15 of the African Charter on the Rights and Welfare of the Child, (1990) as well as the general principles of the 1989 UN Convention on the Rights of the Child (CRC) and its specific provisions, recognize the right of every child "to be protected from economic exploitation and from performing any work that is likely to be hazardous or to interfere with the child's education, or to be harmful to the child's health or physical, mental, spiritual, moral or social development."[35] To address such issues, the Convention on the Rights of the Child (CRC) requires states to provide for a minimum age for employment, appropriate regulation of the hours and conditions of employment corresponding to international human rights standards, ad be able to take appropriate sanctions to enforce these provisions.[36] The Convention on the Rights of the Child (CRC) also requires states to enforce in their domestic laws the right of every child to education (Art.28).

## 6.6 The Right to Safe and Healthy Working Conditions

Trafficking in persons for labor exploitation, particularly forced and bonded labor as a commercial sex worker, the compulsory recruitment of children for use in armed conflict, domestic servitude, the worst forms of forced labor, and other slavery-like conditions are addressed in a number of International Labor Organization (ILO) Conventions. For example, its labor standards are an effective response to trafficking for the purposes of forced labor. For instance, ILO Convention No.182 addresses the worst form of child labor punishable in domestic jurisdictions, namely:

(a) all forms of slavery or practices similar to slavery, such as the sale and trafficking of children, debt bondage and serfdom and forced or compulsory labour, including forced or compulsory recruitment of children for use in armed conflict; (b) the use, procuring or offering of a child for prostitution, for the production of pornography or for pornographic performances; (c) the use, procuring or offering of a child for illicit activities, in particular for the production and trafficking of drugs as defined in the relevant international treaties; (d) work

[34]This provision clearly echoes article 24(1) of the International Covenant on Civil and Political Rights (1976) in granting children "the right to such measures of protection as are required by his status as a minor", as well as the Convention on the Rights of the Child's article 19(1), which protects children from "all forms of physical or mental violence, injury or abuse, neglect or negligent treatment, maltreatment or exploitation, including sexual abuse, while in the care of parent(s)"; See also: U.N. Convention on the Rights of the Child, art. 9, 11, 32–34.

[35]Convention on the Rights of the Child, Article 32(1).

[36]*Id.*

> which, by its nature or the circumstances in which it is carried out, is likely to harm the health, safety or morals of children.[37]

Additionally, Domestic Workers Convention No.189 recognizes that domestic workers are entitled to the same legal and social protection as other workers. To prevent the risk of labor exploitation and trafficking in persons in the domestic work sector, member states are required to enact and enforce national labor laws, with a focus on regulating and monitoring the employment relationships between migrant domestic workers, private employment agencies, and employers. The Convention also secures specific rights to protect children from child labor.

West Africa is s one of the regions most affected by the practice of child soldiering.[38] Governments that ratify the Optional Protocol to the Convention on the Rights of the Child (CRC) regarding the involvement of children in armed conflicts (2000) make a commitment to prevent the recruitment of child combatants and protect and secure the demobilization of existing child soldiers. The Optional Protocol raises the previous minimum age for direct participation in hostilities specified in the convention on the Rights of the Child and the two Protocols Additional to the Geneva Conventions of 1949 from 15 years to 18 years.[39] Importantly, in situations where children are involved in an armed conflict, Article 6 (3) calls upon state parties to take appropriate and effective measures to "ensure that persons within their jurisdiction recruited or used in hostilities contrary to the present Protocol are demobilized or otherwise released from service as well as accord appropriate assistance for physical and psychological recovery and social reintegration."[40]

As discussed extensively in Part I, organized crime activities generate large revenues that adversely affect the legitimate economy, particularly the banking system, through untaxed profits, illicitly funded investments, and unfair business competition. The confiscation of assets or forfeiture is an import measure designed "to undermine the fiscal structure and even the survival of an organized group by seizing illicitly obtained cash and property derived from criminal activity."[41] This deprivation of property occurs under two proceedings: conviction-based

---

[37] ILO Convention on the Worst Forms of Child Labour (No.182), Art 3, http://www.ilo.org/dyn/normlex/en/f?p=NORMLEXPUB:12100:0::NO::P12100_ILO_CODE:C182.

[38] *Child Soldiers and Disarmament, Demobilization, Rehabilitation and Reintegration in West Africa, Coalition to Stop the Use of Child Soldiers*, Relief Web 3 (Dec. 2006), https://reliefweb.int/sites/reliefweb.int/files/resources/8E9E650371871EBCC125722F0049E478-csucs-gen-23nov.pdf.

[39] Article 22(2) of the African Charter on the Rights and Welfare of the Child, 1990, states: "States Parties to the present Charter shall take all necessary measures to ensure that no child shall take a direct part in hostilities and refrain in particular from recruiting any child."

[40] Optional Protocol to the Convention on the Rights of the Child on the involvement of children in armed conflict, Art 6 (3), https://www.ohchr.org/EN/professionalinterest/Pages/OPACCRC.aspx.

[41] UNODC, E4J University Module Series: Organized Crime. Module 10: Sentencing and Confiscation in Organized Crime, https://www.unodc.org/e4j/en/organized-crime/module-10/key-issues/confiscation.html.

confiscation that consists of bringing a criminal charge against the offender, or non-conviction-based confiscation that consists of a judicial action filed by the government against the suspicious asset.[42] Similarly, Articles 6, 7, 12–14 of the Convention against Transnational Organized Crime impose upon states an obligation to criminalize the laundering of the proceeds of crime and to adopt measures to combat money-laundering.[43] States must create the necessary financial intelligence to investigate money laundering practices and the investment of criminal proceeds. Prosecutions coupled with financial investigations that aim to seize criminal assets renders the business of human trafficking unprofitable and prevent the ongoing involvement of traffickers in trafficking by depriving them of their 'working capital'.[44]

In conclusion, this analysis of international law shows that criminal law and human rights standards play a complementary role and enhance one another in combating human rights violations. In fact, criminal justice strengthens the anti-trafficking strategy by facilitating the punishment of traffickers and deterring trafficking in persons whereas a human rights approach is aimed at framing "the project of alleviating the root causes of trafficking as a human rights issue" and therefore is designed to "encourage more proactive efforts to address these problems rather than the traditional assumption that such issues are solely within the province of broader development policy."[45] Indeed, an international human rights framework provides "legal and political space for the disenfranchised to begin to claim these needs as rights, and thereby bring the scope of state responsibility into sharper focus."[46]

## References

Additional Protocol to the American Convention on Human Rights in the Area of Economic, Social, and Cultural Rights "Protocol of San Salvador" Adopted in San Salvador on November 17, 1988 (not yet in force) Article 10(1), https://www.oas.org/dil/1988%20Additional%20Protocol%20to%20the%20American%20Convention%20on%20Human%20Rights%20in%20the%20Area%20of%20Economic,%20Social%20and%20Cultural%20Rights%20(Protocol%20of%20San%20Salvador).pdf

Adopted by General Assembly resolution 2200 A (XXI) of 16 December 1966, United Nations Treaty Series, vol. 999, p. 171 (entered into force on 23 March 1976)

African Charter, Art. 5, http://www.achpr.org/files/instruments/achpr/banjul_charter.pdf

African Charter on Human and Peoples' Rights, Article 5 (Adopted 27 June 1981, OAU Doc. CAB/LEG/67/3 rev. 5, 21 I.L.M. 58 (1982), entered into force October 21 1986)

African Charter on Human and Peoples' Rights, Article 15

[42] *Id.*

[43] UN Convention against Transnational Organized Crime and the Protocols Thereto, Article 6–7.

[44] U.N. Gift, *Analyzing the Business Model of Trafficking in Human Beings to Better Prevent the Crime,* OSCE 34 (2010), https://www.osce.org/cthb/69028?download=true.

[45] Chuang (2006), p. 157.

[46] *Id.*

African Charter on Human and Peoples' Rights, Article 16, http://www.humanrights.se/wp-content/uploads/2012/01/African-Charter-on-Human-and-Peoples-Rights.pdf

Analysis of the Language of Child, Early, and Forced Marriages, August 2013., sexualrightsinitiative.com

Article 12 of the African Charter on Human and Peoples' Rights ("ACHPR"), 27 June 1981

Article 12 of the International Covenant on Civil and Political Rights (ICCPR), 16 December 1966

Article 13 of the Universal Declaration of Human Rights (UDHR), 10 December 1948

Articles 22(5) and 22(1) of the American Convention on Human Rights (ACHR) 22 January 1969

Braspenning C (2006) Human trafficking in the Netherlands: the protection of and assistance to victims in light of domestic and international law and policy. Intercult Human Rights Law Rev 1:329, 351

*Child Soldiers and Disarmament, Demobilization, Rehabilitation and Reintegration in West Africa, Coalition to Stop the Use of Child Soldiers*, Relief Web 3 (Dec. 2006), https://reliefweb.int/sites/reliefweb.int/files/resources/8E9E650371871EBCC125722F0049E478-csucs-gen-23nov.pdf

Chuang J (2006) Beyond a snapshot: preventing human trafficking in the global economy. Ind J Global Leg Stud 13:157

*Combating Trafficking as Modern-Day Slavery: A Matter of Non-Discrimination and Empowerment*, 43 OSCE (2012). https://www.osce.org/secretariat/98249?download=true

Committee On Economic, Social and Cultural Rights, E/C.12/GC/18, February 6 2006 para.1 https://www.refworld.org/pdfid/4415453b4.pdf

Committee On Economic, Social and Cultural Rights, E/C.12/GC/18, February 6 2006 para.4, 6–7 https://www.refworld.org/pdfid/4415453b4.pdf

Convention on Consent to Marriage, Minimum Age for Marriage and Registration of Marriages, General Assembly resolution 1763 A (XVII) of 7 November 1963, United Nations Treaty Series, vol. 521, p. 231, Art. 1(1), entered into force on 9 December 1964

European Social Charter, Turin, 18.X.1961, European Treaty Series - No. 35, Article 11, https://rm.coe.int/168006b642

Frequently Asked Questions on Economic, Social, and Cultural Rights, Office of the United Nations High Commissioner for Human Rights, Fact Sheet No.33, p. 2 https://www.ohchr.org/Documents/Issues/ESCR/FAQ%20on%20ESCR-en.pdf

ICESCR, Article 6(1), 16 December 1966: entry into force January 31976 https://www.ohchr.org/EN/ProfessionalInterest/Pages/CESCR.aspx

ILO Convention on the Worst Forms of Child Labour (No.182), Art 3, http://www.ilo.org/dyn/normlex/en/f?p=NORMLEXPUB:12100:0::NO::P12100_ILO_CODE:C182

International Covenant on Economic, Social, and Cultural Rights, Article 12

International Covenant on Economic, Social, and Cultural Rights, Article 6(1)

OHCHR, General comment No. 36 (2018) on article 6 of the International Covenant on Civil and Political Rights, on the right to life, CCPR/C/GC/36, 30 October 2018, para.1 https://tbinternet.ohchr.org/Treaties/CCPR/Shared%20Documents/1_Global/CCPR_C_GC_36_8785_E.pdf

Optional Protocol to the Convention on the Rights of the Child on the involvement of children in armed conflict, Art 6 (3), https://www.ohchr.org/EN/professionalinterest/Pages/OPACCRC.aspx

Preamble of the Palermo Protocol

Protocol to the African Charter on Human and Peoples' Rights on the Rights of Women in Africa, Art 2(2), http://www.achpr.org/files/instruments/women-protocol/achpr_instr_proto_women_eng.pdf

*Siliadin v. France*, European Court of Human Rights, Application No. 73316/01, Judgment (2005)

Slavery Convention, 1929, Art. 1

Supplementary Convention on the Abolition of Slavery, the Slave Trade, and Institutions and Practices Similar to Slavery, Art 2, http://www.ohchr.org/EN/ProfessionalInterest/Pages/SupplementaryConventionAbolitionOfSlavery.aspx

Supplementary Convention on the Abolition of Slavery, the Slave Trade, and Institutions and Practices Similar to Slavery (1956), Article 1 and Article 6

The African Charter on the Rights and Welfare of the Child, Art. 29, http://www.acerwc.org/download/the-charter-english/?wpdmdl=8410
The American Convention on Human Rights, Article 6, entered into force in 1978
The Protocol on the Rights of Women in Africa (2003), Article 1, entered into force in 2005
The Protocol to the African Charter on the Rights of Women in Africa (2003)- Art 6(d), http://www.achpr.org/files/instruments/women-protocol/achpr_instr_proto_women_eng.pdf
*Tide Mendez et al. v. Dominican Republic*, Inter-American Court of Human Rights, Judgment, Rep. No. 64/12 (29 March 2012)
U.N. Gift, *Analyzing the Business Model of Trafficking in Human Beings to Better Prevent the Crime*, OSCE 34 (2010), https://www.osce.org/cthb/69028?download=true
UDHR, Article 4
UN Convention against Transnational Organized Crime and the Protocols Thereto, Article 6-7
UN Declaration on Human Rights Art 16(2)
UN Declaration on Human Rights Art 16(2)
UN Human Rights Committee (HRC), CCPR General Comment No. 20: Article 7 (Prohibition of Torture, or Other Cruel, Inhuman or Degrading Treatment or Punishment), March 10 1992., http://www.refworld.org/docid/453883fb0.html
Universal Declaration of Human Rights (art. 16(2))
UNODC, E4J University Module Series: Organized Crime. Module 10: Sentencing and Confiscation in Organized Crime, https://www.unodc.org/e4j/en/organized-crime/module-10/key-issues/confiscation.html

# Chapter 7
# International Criminal Law and Trafficking in Persons

The following discussion explores the potential for including trafficking in persons within the jurisdiction of international criminal courts and tribunals and examines the issues that arise when prosecuting trafficking under the charge of a crime against humanity or other inhuman acts. Trafficking in persons and its related activities is clearly a violation of both international rights standards and international criminal law.[1] The Rome Statute of the International Criminal Court makes explicit reference to the crime of trafficking in persons as a crime against humanity under the enslavement provision.[2] Enslavement "means the exercise of any or all of the powers attaching to the right of ownership over a person and includes the exercise of such power in the course of trafficking in persons, in particular women and children."[3] The International Law Commission Draft Codes for Crimes against Peace and Security of Mankind states that the concept of enslavement captures slavery and is expanded to cover the actions taken to acquire or "maintain over persons a status of slavery, servitude or forced labour"[4] and other exploitative practices found in the Supplementary Convention of Slavery. Article 7(1)(g) of the Rome Statute sets out an extensive list of sexual and gender-based crimes including rape, sexual slavery, enforced prostitution, forced pregnancy, and enforced sterilization, thus offering the possibility to prosecute acts of sexual violence as an element of trafficking in persons.

Furthermore, jurisprudence of the International Criminal Tribunal in the *Prosecutor v Kunarac* case presents a description of enslavement that is consistent with the

---

[1] Moran (2014), p. 32, 32.

[2] The Rome Statute of the International Criminal Court, Article 7(2) (c).

[3] A/CONF.183/9 (17 July 1998).

[4] *Report of the International Law Commission on the work of its forty-eighth session*, UN GAOR, 51st Sess., Supp. No.10, UN Doc. A/51/10 (1996) p. 49. http://legal.un.org/ilc/documentation/english/reports/a_51_10.pdf.

 
P. VI. S. Karenga, *A West African Model to Address Human Trafficking*,
https://doi.org/10.1007/978-3-030-88120-7_7

means elements of trafficking enshrined in the Palermo Protocol. Specifically, the Court stated that:

> "[u]nder this definition [of enslavement, which includes trafficking], indications of such enslavement include elements of control and ownership; the restriction or control of an individual's autonomy, freedom of choice or freedom of movement; and, often, the accruing of some gain to the perpetrator. The consent or free will of the victim is absent. It is often rendered impossible or irrelevant by, for example, the threat or use of force or other forms of coercion; the fear of violence, deception or false promises; the abuse of power; the victim's position of vulnerability; detention or captivity, psychological oppression or socio-economic conditions."[5]

This nexus between the material elements of the crimes of enslavement and trafficking in persons is significant as it gives the Court jurisdiction over trafficking offenses where these reach the gravity of a crime against humanity. Along with this normative foundation, it is now endorsed in court jurisprudence[6] that crimes against humanity can be charged independently of a nexus to conflict or war crimes.[7] This ensures that large scale atrocities such as trafficking in persons can be classified as crimes against humanity as they are the result of a state policy that promotes or tolerates such crimes against their own populations.[8]

The critical questions that arise are: Where do crimes against humanity-related acts and trafficking in persons meet? Who can commit crimes against humanity? Can the criminal activities of non-state actors (especially corporations) along with organized crime syndicates, which have devastating consequences and result in the deaths and suffering of civilian populations, be considered crimes against humanity? These issues will be addressed in the following section. To assess the legal potential of the International Criminal Court to exercise jurisdiction over trafficking in persons as enslavement, it is necessary to examine the various *chapeau* requirements needed to establish crimes against humanity to ensure that all relevant criteria have been considered.

[5] *Prosecutor v. Kunarac, et al.*, International Criminal Court, Case No. IT-96-23/1-T, Judgment ¶ 541-42 (22 February 2001) (accessed from: http://www.icty.org/x/cases/kunarac/tjug/en/kun-tj010222e.pdf); *See also* Elements of Crimes, Article 7(1)(c), n.11.

[6] *Id.*

[7] Section 1: Genocide, Crimes against Humanity, and War crimes, p. 202, https://www.usip.org/sites/default/files/MC1/MC1-Part2Section1.pdf; *See also* Report of the Secretary-General Pursuant to Paragraph 2 of Security Council Resolution 808 (1993), UN Doc. S/25704, ¶ 47 ( May 3, 1993); *Prosecutor v. Duško Tadić*, Case No. IT-94-1-AR72, Decision on the Defence Motion for Interlocutory Appeal on Jurisdiction, ("*Tadić* Jurisdictional Decision"), ¶ 70, (October 2, 1995).

[8] CMN, International Criminal Law Guidelines: Crimes Against Humanity, February 2017, p. 11 https://www.legal-tools.org/doc/6de633/pdf/.

## 7.1 Attack Directed against any Civilian Population

Under Article 7(1) of the Rome Statute, crimes against humanity are acts committed as part of a widespread or systematic attack directed against any civilian population in which the perpetrator had knowledge of the attack.[9] This legal requirement sets out the necessary context in which the criminal conduct of trafficking or enslavement must be inscribed. The notion of "attack" elaborated in Article 7(2)(a) includes the use of armed force as well as any non-violent attacks including discriminatory practices, psychological abuse committed multiple times, or mistreatment[10] amounting to a large scale operation carried out against any civilian population. Court Jurisprudence has defined an 'attack' as "a course of conduct involving the commission of acts of violence,"[11] and an "attack directed against the civilian population", which may be established in situations where violent acts or other criminal conduct carried out by state actors or individuals target a collective group. It is not a requirement that the attack be against the entire population of a country or a region.

In applying this interpretation, acts of trafficking in persons (exploitation of people in forced labor, prostitution, removal of organs, and servitude) can reasonably constitute an attack directed against a civilian population independently of a nexus to warfare. Although these attacks are not directed against the entire population of a country they target more than "a limited and randomly selected number of individuals within the population"[12] and are conducted in cooperation with organized crime groups.

## 7.2 Perpetrator Knowledge of the Attack

The required condition of criminal liability for the purposes of International Criminal Court (ICC) jurisdiction is that the perpetrator has committed the act prohibited (actus reus) with a guilty state of mind (mens rea).[13] Pursuant to Article 30(1) of the Rome Statute, "unlike otherwise provided, a person shall be criminally responsible and liable for punishment for a crime within the jurisdiction of the Court only if the material elements are committed with intent and knowledge."[14] It is therefore reasonable to conclude that the standard of intention laid down for enslavement

[9] Rome Statute, Article 7(1).

[10] *The Prosecutor v. Vasiljević*, Case No. IT-98-32, (Trial Chamber, November 29, 2002), para.29–30.

[11] *Prosecutor v. Jadranko Prlic*, Case No. IT-04-74-T, Judgement (TC), May 29, 2013, para.35.

[12] *Prosecutor v. Radovan Karadžić*, Case No. IT-95-5/18-T, Public Redacted Version of Judgement Issued on 24 March 2016 – Volume I of IV (TC), 24 March 2016, para. 475.

[13] Marchuk (2014), p. 8.

[14] Article 30 (1) of the Rome Statute, ICC.

under the Rome Statute is equally applicable to trafficking crime. In effect, the Palermo Protocol consolidates this existing legislation by providing that trafficking in persons occurs when the offender has committed the act with the intention (purpose) of "exploiting" the victim. Both conventions recognize that domestic legal systems may prosecute offenders on a lesser mode of criminal responsibility such as recklessness, negligence, or willful blindness.[15]

Article 30 of the Rome Statute defines the concepts of 'intent' and 'knowledge'. A person has intent when "that person means to engage in the conduct" and "means to cause that consequence or is aware that it will occur in the ordinary course of events."[16] A person has "knowledge" when he or she is aware "that a circumstance exists or a consequence will occur in the ordinary course of events."[17] The ICTY jurisprudence analyses the *mens rea* and establishes that the accused had the intent to commit the crime and knowledge "that there is an attack on the civilian population and that his acts comprise part of that attack or at least that he took the risk that his acts were part of attack which may be committed with personal reasons."[18] In the circumstances that relate to trafficking in persons, *mens rea* is a determining factor. Traffickers hold their victims in captivity and slavery with a specific intention to exploit them in forced labor, forced prostitution, organ harvesting, and other forms of abuse.[19] Similarly, the perpetrators commit acts of enslavement and crimes against humanity mentioned in Article 7 of the Rome Statute with knowledge of the nature and purpose of their criminal conduct. Thus, individuals who commit the crime of trafficking in persons exercise the right of ownership over the victim and exhibit the *mens rea* element in their offenses.[20]

An International Criminal Court (ICC) Pre-Trial Chamber ruled that it is not necessary to establish that the perpetrator knew the specific details of the attack.[21] Their knowledge of the attack in general terms may be inferred from circumstantial evidence.[22] For instance, the Court elaborated in the Katanga case that:

---

[15] UN.GIFT, *Anti-human Trafficking Manual for Criminal Justice Practitioners*, United Nations Office on Drugs and Crime (UNODC) 8 (2009), https://www.unodc.org/documents/human-trafficking/TIP_module1_Ebook.pdf.

[16] Article 30(2) of Rome Statute.

[17] Article 30(3) of Rome Statute.

[18] *Kunarac, supra* note 5, at ¶ 434; *Prosecutor v. Kunarac, et al.*, International Criminal Court, Appeals Judgement, Case Nos. IT-96-23-T and IT-96-23/1-A, ¶ 102 (12 June 2001). *See also Prosecutor v. Vasiljević*, International Criminal Case Case No. IT-98-32-T, Judgment ¶ 37 (29 November 2002).

[19] CHAPTER 5 TRAFFICKING AS CRIME AGAINST HUMANITY – ARTICLE 7 OF THE ROME STATUTE OF ICC, p. 184 https://shodhganga.inflibnet.ac.in/bitstream/10603/145318/7/ch%205.pdf.

[20] *Ibid.*

[21] *Prosecutor v. Gbagbo*, Decision on the Confirmation of Charges against Laurent Gbagbo, Pre-Trial Chamber II, ICC-02/11-01/11, 12 June 2014, para. 214.

[22] *Id.* at 35.

> knowledge of the attack and the perpetrator's awareness that his conduct was part of such attack may be inferred from circumstantial evidence, such as: the accused's position in the military hierarchy; his assuming an important role in the broader criminal campaign; his presence at the scene of the crimes; his references to the superiority of his group over the enemy group; and the general historical and political environment in which the acts occurred.[23]

Thus, in a situation of enslavement the knowledge requirement will be satisfied when it can be proven that the perpetrator committed the offense or is sufficiently connected to the crime by directly taking advantage of the situation created.[24] Similarly, an offender who has engaged in trafficking in persons would be aware that their prohibited acts are part of a criminal enterprise if they is receiving significant financial benefits and other material advantages such as labor and sexual services.

Another legal principle established in International criminal courts and tribunals which is also reflected in the Palermo Protocol is the irrelevance of consent. Relevant factors that may render consent or free will impossible and evidence a situation of enslavement include: "the threat or use of force or other forms of coercion; the fear of violence, deception or false promises; the abuse of power; the victim's position of vulnerability; detention or captivity, psychological oppression or socio-economic conditions."[25] The Palermo Protocol explicitly provides that adult consent to trafficking is irrelevant once it is established that coercion, deception, abuse of power or a position of vulnerability, or other prohibited means have been used to obtain the consent of a person.[26]

## 7.3 Attacks as Widespread or Systematic in Nature

Unlike domestic crimes, crimes against humanity include a contextual element. The criminal acts must be committed as part of a "widespread or systematic attack"[27] against the civilian population. This legal requirement sets out the necessary context in which the criminal conduct of trafficking in persons or enslavement must be inscribed.

An attack is "systematic" if the acts of violence are carried out in an organized manner with the repetition of similar types of criminal conduct on a regular basis.[28] The International Criminal Court for Rwanda supports this interpretation, defining the concept "Systematic" as "...thoroughly organised and following a regular

---

[23] *Prosecutor v. Katanga*, Decision on the Confirmation of Charges, Pre-Trial Chamber I, ICC-01/04-01/07, 26 September 2008, para. 402.

[24] *Kunarac, supra* note 5, at ¶ 592.

[25] *Id.* at ¶ 574.

[26] See Palermo Protocol, Art. 3 (b).

[27] Rome Statute, Article 7(1); See *Kunarac Appeals, supra* note 18, at ¶ 85.

[28] *Id.* at ¶ 94.

pattern on the basis of a common policy involving substantial public or private resources."[29] This can be evidenced by the existence of a preconceived plan, an ideology or policy with the possible participation of officials or authorities.

A "widespread" attack is committed on an enormous scale and involves a large number of victims.[30] Although "attack" means a course of conduct involving the multiple commission of acts carried out against civilians (Article 7(2)(a)), the notion has not been further elaborated upon in the Convention. As a benchmark, the International Criminal Tribunal for Rwanda in the *Prosecutor v. Akayesu* case suggested that the criteria of "widespread may be defined as massive, frequent, large scale action, carried out collectively with considerable seriousness and directed against a multiplicity of victims."[31] The requirement of a widespread or systematic attack is disjunctive rather than cumulative, either is sufficient to establish an offense.[32] It "excludes an isolated inhumane act committed by a perpetrator acting on his own initiative and directed against a single victim."[33] Although courts have attempted to elaborate on the meaning of the term "widespread", the critical question this raises concerns the magnitude of the atrocities that must be committed or the significant number of people that must be affected to qualify for "massive, frequent and large scale action" or "multiplicity of victims" within the criterion of a crime against humanity. Because there is no specific numerical threshold, international criminal courts and tribunals typically consider "factors such as the consequences of the attack upon the targeted population and the number of victims"[34] which is far from easy to determine when applied to practical situations.

In light of the contextual requirement, acts of trafficking in persons can sometimes reach the scale of a widespread and systematic attack targeting a specific group of people, involving more than one victim and giving rise to a crime against humanity. Regarding the organizational aspect, it has been illustrated in the preceding narrative that the Nigerian organized criminal group conducts trafficking in persons in a well-planned manner with state-like characteristics. It is a collectivity of persons sharing a common purpose and operating over a prolonged period, with an established hierarchy including a policy-making level. This criminal network has the capacity to impose the policy on its members and to sanction those who fail to

---

[29] *See Prosecutor v. Jean Paul Akayesu*, International Criminal Court, Case No. ICTR-96-4-T, Judgment, ¶580 (September 2, 1998).

[30] *Prosecutor v. Blaškić*, IT-95–14, Judgment, 3 March 2000, para. 206 (Blaškić Trial Judgment).

[31] *The Prosecutor v. Jean-Paul Akayesu*, Case No. ICTR-96-4-T, para.508 https://unictr.irmct.org/sites/unictr.org/files/case-documents/ictr-96-4/trial-judgements/en/980902.pdf.

[32] Kunarac, *supra* note 5.

[33] Yearbook of International Law Commission, Vol. II (Part Two), 94-95, U.N. Doc. A/CN.4/SER.A/1996/Add.l (Part 2) (1996) (accessed from: https://legal.un.org/ilc/publications/yearbooks/english/ilc_1996_v2_p2.pdf).

[34] Stahn (2019a), p. 58. https://www.cambridge.org/core/services/aop-cambridge-core/content/view/EFEDBED0B84359DFA281A9079047846F/9781108423205AR.pdf/A_Critical_Introduction_to_International_Criminal_Law.pdf?event-type=FTLA; See also *Kunarac Appeals*, supra note 18, at ¶ 95.

comply.[35] The conspiracy and joint enterprise activities include identification of persons; recruitment through manipulation, coercion, and document forgery; harboring, monitoring, and exploitation of the trafficked persons; and laundering of the proceeds of the crime. More broadly, traffickers work to ensure the perpetual recruitment of new victims to guarantee a profitable and flourishing business.

In addition to their impact on a large number of victims, these criminal groups have the ability to manage and control the entire operation over a large geographical area that transcends national borders. Trafficking activities can be therefore considered international offenses as they 'threaten the peace, security and well-being of the world.'[36] The United Nations War Crimes Commission has clearly laid down that crimes against humanity are prohibited acts that endanger the international community and shock the conscience of mankind, "either by their magnitude and savagery or by their large number or by the fact that a similar pattern was applied at different times and places."[37] This rationale limits the jurisdiction of international courts and tribunals to the most serious crimes. As observed by Carsten Stahn, these criteria are applied inconsistently in practice. For example, it fails to explain why terrorist attacks such as the November 2015 Paris attacks and the USA twin towers bombing in 2001 qualified as threats to peace but not as crimes against humanity.[38]

Although small-scale trafficking operations generally fall outside the scope of article 7(2)(a) of the Statute, several scholars suggest that they amount to a widespread act of violence as they can be conducted through conspiracy and joint enterprise with other organized crime syndicates and result in an increasing number of victims over the years.[39] Furthermore, attacks directed against a civilian population can be established when a single trafficked person is continuously exploited over the course of their lifetime.[40]

---

[35] *The Prosecutor v. Francis Kirimimuthaura* et al., No.: ICC-01/09-02/11, Date: 15 March 2011, Pre-Trial Chamber II, para. 12. http://www.worldcourts.com/icc/eng/decisions/2011.03.15_Prosecutor_v_Muthaura.pdf; Read also Jalloh (2013), pp. 381–441 https://digitalcommons.wcl.american.edu/cgi/viewcontent.cgi?referer=https://www.google.com/&httpsredir=1&article=1767&context=auilr.

[36] Stahn (2019b), p. 54, https://www.cambridge.org/core/services/aop-cambridge-core/content/view/EFEDBED0B84359DFA281A9079047846F/9781108423205AR.pdf/A_Critical_Introduction_to_International_Criminal_Law.pdf?event-type=FTLA.

[37] United Nations War Crimes Commission, History of the United Nations War Crimes Commission and the Development of the Laws of War (London: His Majesty's Stationery Office, 1948), 179.

[38] Stahn (2019b), p. 54.

[39] Joshua N. Aston and Dr. Vinay N. Paranjape, *Human Trafficking and its Prosecution: Challenges of the ICC*, https://www.peacepalacelibrary.nl/ebooks/files/356626199.pdf.

[40] *Id.*

## 7.4 Attacks in Furtherance to a State or Organizational Policy

Under the Rome Statute, the acts underlying a crime against humanity must be committed in "pursuant to or in furtherance of a State or organizational policy."[41] There is a lack of consensus in international criminal courts and tribunals and among scholars as to whether, under customary international law, state or organizational policy is a required element in the definition of crimes against humanity.[42] Notwithstanding this doctrinal controversy before the ICTY, Article 7(2) of the International Criminal Court introduces a 'State or organisational policy' as an independent legal requirement of crimes against humanity.[43] This is to distinguish international crimes from crimes subject exclusively to domestic laws.[44]

Regarding the concept of an organization, the major challenge in Court is to determine "the nature, type and characteristics of organisations that are deemed able to carry out a policy that implements crimes against humanity?"[45] Subsequently, the Criminal Court, when dealing with the post-electoral situation in Kenya, defined an organization as any group that has the capability to commit systematic or mass violations of human rights.[46] The Court further suggested criteria to establish whether an entity is an organization for the purposes of the Rome Statute. Specifically, these criteria could include:

> (i) whether the group is under a responsible command, or has an established hierarchy; (ii) whether the group possesses, in fact, the means to carry out a widespread or systematic attack against a civilian population; (iii) whether the group exercises control over part of the territory of a State; (iv) whether the group has criminal activities against the civilian population as a primary purpose; (v) whether the group articulates, explicitly or implicitly, an intention to attack a civilian population; (vi) whether the group is part of a larger group, which fulfils some or all of the abovementioned criteria.[47]

---

[41] Rome Statute of the International Criminal Court, art. 7(2)(a), July 17, 1998, 2187 U.N.T.S. 90.

[42] *Kunarac, supra* note 5, at ¶ 432. (footnotes omitted).

[43] CMN ICJ Toolkits, *International Criminal Law Guidelines: Crimes Against Humanity*, 35 (February 2017), https://www.legal-tools.org/doc/6de633/pdf/.

[44] Bergsmo and Tianying (2014), p. 117.

[45] Mathias Holvoet, *The State or Organisational Policy Requirement within the Definition of Crimes Against Humanity in the Rome Statute: An Appraisal of the Emerging Jurisprudence and the Implementation Practice by ICC States Parties*, 16 (2013) http://www.internationalcrimesdatabase.org/upload/documents/20131111T105507-ICD%20Brief%20%202%20-%20Holvoet.pdf.

[46] ICC, ICC-01/09–19-Corr, Decision Pursuant to Article 15 of the Rome Statute on the Authorization of an Investigation into the Situation in the Republic of Kenya, 13 March 2010, paras. 90–93 (Kenya Authorization Decision). https://www.legal-tools.org/doc/338a6f/pdf/.

[47] ICC, ICC-01/09–19-Corr, Decision Pursuant to Article 15 of the Rome Statute on the Authorization of an Investigation into the Situation in the Republic of Kenya, 13 March 2010, para. 93 (Kenya Authorization Decision). https://www.legal-tools.org/doc/338a6f/pdf/.

Based on the above-mentioned factors set out by the Court, a large number of groups or organizations could face prosecution before the International Criminal Court for crimes against humanity. Modern understandings of the policy element has been extended to cover actions not only by states or state-like organisations but also other organized entities such as terrorist organisations and political parties that direct, instigate, or encourage crimes against a civilian population.[48] For instance, given the size and the nature of the Nigerian trafficking ring, the Islamist members of *Boko Haram* alleged to have carried out trafficking, sexual slavery, and forced marriages of a large number of women and girls satisfy this policy element.[49] It can also be argued that non-state institutions and corporations that are bound to abide by international human rights law meet the legal criteria established by the Kenya Authorization Decision.[50] This broad and liberal understanding, which is supported by a number of scholars, reflects the evolution of the concept of crimes against humanity and the modern reality of international criminal justice.[51]

Trafficking in persons operates through a spectrum of criminal organizations, the policies of which are "a) to recruit, sell, transport, harbour, or transfer humans b) to profit - off of the exploitation of humans and c) to fuel demand for the human trafficking economy."[52] The organized nature of the acts involves "using the children as shields in armed conflicts, using women for sexual exploitation, exploiting women and children through forced labour and finally exploiting many cultural and ethnic groups or population."[53] In some instances, traffickers may be affiliated with the government in carrying out their sophisticated activities, thereby enhancing the economy of that country. In this regard, Article 25 of the Rome Statute provides for the individual criminal responsibility of persons or groups of persons acting with a common purpose to commit, attempt to commit, order, solicit, induce, aid, abet, facilitate, or intentionally contribute to the commission of a crime within the jurisdiction of the International Criminal Court. This covers government actors, joint enterprise syndicates, and organized criminal groups involved in the process of trafficking in persons. For example, Nigerian criminal groups that exploit women for commercial sexual purposes are well-established networks that are engaged in a

---

[48] Stahn (2019b), p. 55. https://www.cambridge.org/core/services/aop-cambridge-core/content/view/EFEDBED0B84359DFA281A9079047846F/9781108423205AR.pdf/A_Critical_Introduction_to_International_Criminal_Law.pdf?event-type=FTLA; *See also* Mathias Holvoet *supra* note 45 at. 6.

[49] ICC, Office of the Prosecutor, Report on Preliminary Examination Activities 2012, November 2012, 20-21 available at http://www.icc-cpi.int/NR/rdonlyres/C433C462-7C4E-4358-8A72-8D99FD00E8CD/285209/OTP2012ReportonPreliminaryExaminations22Nov2012.pdf.

[50] Stahn (2019b), p. 56.

[51] *Ibid.*

[52] Jane Kim, *Prosecuting Human Trafficking as a Crime Against Humanity* 9 (2011a) (unpublished J.D. thesis, Columbia Law School) (on file with Columbia Law School available at: http://blogs.law.columbia.edu/gslonline/files/2011/02/Jane-Kim_GSL_Prosecuting-Human-Trafficking-as-a-Crime-Against-Humanity-Under-the-Rome-Statute-2011.pdf).

[53] *Id.*

range of criminal activities involving madams, recruiters, transporters, receivers, brothel keepers, and document forgers as well as corrupt police officers, border guards, customs and immigration agents, and even embassy officials.

The International Law Commission has clearly expressed that the draft article on crimes against humanity "does not confine possible perpetrators of the crimes to public officials or representatives alone" and that it "does not rule out the possibility that private individuals with de facto power or organized in criminal gangs or groups might also commit the kind of systematic or mass violations of human rights covered by the article; in that case, their acts would come under the draft Code."[54] In its commentary on the policy requirement, the Commission observed: "The instigation or direction of a Government or any organization or group, which may or may not be affiliated with a Government, gives the act its great dimension and makes it a crime against humanity imputable to private persons or agents of a State."[55]

However, this precedent interpretation of organizational policy could be deemed over-inclusive as it incorporates an indefinite range of organized acts within the scope of crimes against humanity that might challenge the legitimacy of the Court. Partly in reaction to the far-reaching interpretation of crimes in precedent international Courts, the Rome Statute of International Criminal Court secured the legality principle in Article 22(2).[56] Accordingly, this states that "the definition of a crime shall be strictly construed and shall not be extended by analogy. In case of ambiguity, the definition shall be interpreted in favour of the person being investigated, prosecuted or convicted."[57] The policy element is consistently relevant and its very purpose "is to distinguish international crimes from ordinary crimes" and thus "cannot simply be inferred from the widespread or systematic nature of the attack."[58] In the same vein, Cheriff Bassiouni advocates for the preservation of conceptual boundaries and argues that crimes committed by non-state actors cannot be prosecuted in the International Criminal Court (ICC):

> Contrary to what some advocates advance, Article 7 does not bring a new development to crimes against humanity, namely, its applicability to non-state actors. If that were the case, the mafia, for example, could be charged with such crimes before the ICC, and that is clearly neither the letter nor the spirit of Article 7. The question arose after 9/11 as to whether a

[54] Yearbook of the International Law Commission, Vol. II (Part Two), 103-104, U.N. Doc. A/CN.4/SER.A/1991/Add.l (Part 2) (1991) (accessed from: https://legal.un.org/ilc/publications/yearbooks/english/ilc_1991_v2_p2.pdf).

[55] Yearbook of International Law Commission, Vol. II (Part Two), art. 18 (47), U.N. Doc. A/CN.4/SER.A/1996/Add.l (Part 2) (1996) (accessed from: https://legal.un.org/ilc/publications/yearbooks/english/ilc_1996_v2_p2.pdf) (emphasis added).

[56] Schabas (2011), p. 215.

[57] Article 22(2) Rome Statute; see also Caroline Davidson (2017) "How to Read International Criminal Law: Strict Construction and the Rome Statute of the International Criminal Court," St. John's Law Review: Vol. 91: No. 1, Article 3. Available at: http://scholarship.law.stjohns.edu/lawreview/vol91/iss1/3.

[58] Stahn (2019b), p. 56. https://www.cambridge.org/core/services/aop-cambridge-core/content/view/EFEDBED0B84359DFA281A9079047846F/9781108423205AR.pdf/A_Critical_Introduction_to_International_Criminal_Law.pdf?event-type=FTLA.

> group such as al-Qaeda, which operates on a worldwide basis and is capable of inflicting significant harm in more than one state, falls within this category. In this author's opinion, such a group does not qualify for inclusion within the meaning of crimes against humanity as defined in Article 7. . .The text [of Article 7(2)(a)] clearly refers to state policy, and the words "organizational policy". . .do not refer to the policy of an organization, but the policy of a state. It does not refer to non-state actors.[59]

Although the commentary by the International Law Commission (ILC) stated expressly that a crime against humanity is imputable to private persons,[60] organized criminal groups which operate trafficking rings in West Africa may not be subject to prosecution at the International Criminal Court (ICC) because it can be argued that their criminal act is conducted purely for financial and material gain rather than furtherance of a state policy (Rome Statute: article 7(2)(a)). It is the case that, "drug cartels or human trafficking organizations often use violence for purposes of economic gain. The primary purpose is to benefit from these activities, rather than to target the civilian population."[61]

Apart from organized criminal groups, it would also be extremely difficult to bring before the International Criminal Court (ICC) a single trafficker acting alone as "this type of isolated criminal conduct on the part of a single individual would not constitute a crime against humanity."[62] Moreover, it has been illustrated in Part I that family members, relatives, and friends are also likely to engage in trafficking; however, their activities may not be committed as part of a broader plan or policy as organized groups. The isolated acts of these offenders cannot constitute a crime against humanity. Thus, instances of trafficking in persons cannot meet the grave offense threshold of a crime against humanity as prohibited under the Rome Statute.

Although the International Criminal Court (ICC) has the legal capacity to prosecute trafficking in persons, it has not yet tried a single trafficking case in Court.[63] The first obstacle to prosecution in the International Criminal Court (ICC) is the absence of a precise definition of trafficking in persons. The trafficking clause of the Rome Statute (Article 7(1)(c)) borrows the definition of slavery laid down in the 1926 Slavery Convention. Related to this, the Women's Caucus observed that the "right of ownership" is a narrow term that impedes the potential prosecution of trafficking because traditional formulations of trafficking and slavery do not

---

[59] Cherif Bassiouni (2005), pp. 151–152.

[60] Report of the International Law Commission on the work of its forty-eighth session, UN GAOR, 51st Sess., Supp. No.10, UN Doc. A/51/10 (1996) p. 47 http://legal.un.org/ilc/documentation/english/reports/a_51_10.pdf.

[61] Stahn (2019b), p. 56.

[62] Report of the International Law Commission on the work of its forty-eighth session, UN GAOR, 51st Sess., Supp. No.10, UN Doc. A/51/10 (1996) p.47 http://legal.un.org/ilc/documentation/english/reports/a_51_10.pdf.

[63] Human Trafficking as a Crime Against Humanity: An analysis of the legal potential to prosecute human trafficking in the International Criminal Court with reference to the trafficking of Rohingya Muslims in Southeast Asia, 2014 https://www.duo.uio.no/bitstream/handle/10852/40117/LLM-PIL-THESIS-MAY-2014.pdf?sequence=1&isAllowed=y.

necessarily conflate.[64] For instance, "if persons are exploited by people other than traffickers, the continuous exercise of ownership by the traffickers is terminated, ownership may be transferred, and trafficking therefore may not be regarded as slavery."[65] The absence of an explicit definition has also been recognized as an important issue in light of the internationally established right that the accused person is entitled to know the content of the charge of enslavement.[66]

Furthermore, given the contextual elements in Article 7 and the "gravity threshold" requirements in Article 17(1)(d), it can be argued that trafficking cases in the International Criminal Court (ICC) risk being overshadowed by crimes committed in armed conflicts, disregarding its serious and global effects as an economic enterprise and human rights violation.[67] This argument is persuasive insofar as enslavement and slavery-like conditions (forced labor, sexual slavery, enforced prostitution...) are enumerated under the war crimes provision (Article 8(2)(b)). In fact, almost all cases currently referred to the International Criminal Court (ICC) involve allegations of crimes against humanity and war crimes.[68] Moreover, international criminal jurisprudence emanating from previous ad hoc tribunals such as ICTY and ICTR has interpreted enslavement and related trafficking acts as a nexus to armed conflict. The Special Court for Sierra Leone recognized "forced marriage" as a crime against humanity in the specific situation of armed conflict.[69] It therefore follows that "to prosecute human trafficking cases, the International Criminal Court (ICC) must confront the challenges of defining trafficking, the shadow of armed conflict in the International Criminal Court's (ICC) developing jurisprudence, and the risk of overlooking the gravity of human trafficking."[70] Relatedly, the following chapter will highlight states' obligations of an effective criminal justice response to trafficking in persons under international human rights law.

---

[64] Women's Caucus Advocacy In ICC Negotiations, http://iccwomen.org/wigjdraft1/Archives/oldWCGJ/icc/iccpc/062000pc/elementsannex.html.

[65] *See also* Kim (2011b), pp. 7–8 http://blogs.law.columbia.edu/gslonline/files/2011/02/Jane-Kim_GSL_Prosecuting-Human-Trafficking-as-a-Crime-Against-Humanity-Under-the-Rome-Statute-2011.pdf.

[66] Jean Allain, *The Definition of 'Slavery' in General International Law and in Crime of Enslavement within the Rome Statute*, Int'l Crim. Ct. (ICC) 12 (Apr. 26, 2007), https://www.icc-cpi.int/NR/rdonlyres/069658BB-FDBD-4EDD-8414-543ECB1FA9DC/0/ICCOTP20070426Allain_en.pdf.; *See* Article 10 UDHR, Article 14(3)(a) CCPR.

[67] Kim (2011c), p. 5 http://blogs.law.columbia.edu/gslonline/files/2011/02/Jane-Kim_GSL_Prosecuting-Human-Trafficking-as-a-Crime-Against-Humanity-Under-the-Rome-Statute-2011.pdf.

[68] *See* International Criminal Court, Situations and Cases, available at: http://www.icccpi.int/Menus/ICC/Situations+and+Cases/.

[69] *See* International Criminal Court, Situations and Cases, available at: http://www.icccpi.int/Menus/ICC/Situations+and+Cases/ (accessed August 20, 2021).

[70] Kim (2011c), p. 5.

# References

Allain J (2007) The Definition of 'Slavery' in General International Law and in Crime of Enslavement within the Rome Statute. Int Crim Ct. (ICC) 12 (Apr. 26, 2007), https://www.icc-cpi.int/NR/rdonlyres/069658BB-FDBD-4EDD-8414-543ECB1FA9DC/0/ICCOTP20070426Allain_en.pdf.; *See* Article 10 UDHR, Article 14(3)(a) CCPR

Article 22(2) Rome Statute; see also Caroline Davidson (2017) "How to Read International Criminal Law: Strict Construction and the Rome Statute of the International Criminal Court," St. John's Law Review 91(1), Article 3. Available at: http://scholarship.law.stjohns.edu/lawreview/vol91/iss1/3

Article 30 (1) of the Rome Statute, ICC

Article 30(2) of Rome Statute

Article 30(3) of Rome Statute

Aston JN, Paranjape VN. *Human Trafficking and its Prosecution: Challenges of the ICC*, https://www.peacepalacelibrary.nl/ebooks/files/356626199.pdf

Bergsmo M, Tianying S (2014) On the proposed crimes against humanity convention. Torkel Opsahl Academic E Publisher, Brussels, p 117 https://www.legal-tools.org/doc/6dea30/pdf/

CHAPTER 5 TRAFFICKING AS CRIME AGAINST HUMANITY – ARTICLE 7 OF THE ROME STATUTE OF ICC, p. 184 https://shodhganga.inflibnet.ac.in/bitstream/10603/145318/7/ch%205.pdf

Cherif Bassiouni M (2005) The Legislative History of the International Criminal Court, pp 151–152

CMN, International Criminal Law Guidelines: Crimes Against Humanity, February 2017, p. 11 https://www.legal-tools.org/doc/6de633/pdf/

CMN ICJ Toolkits, *International Criminal Law Guidelines: Crimes Against Humanity*, 35 February (2017), https://www.legal-tools.org/doc/6de633/pdf/

Elements of Crimes, Article 7(1)(c), n.11

Holvoet M (2013) The State or Organisational Policy Requirement within the Definition of Crimes Against Humanity in the Rome Statute: An Appraisal of the Emerging Jurisprudence and the Implementation Practice by ICC States Parties, 16 http://www.internationalcrimesdatabase.org/upload/documents/20131111T105507-ICD%20Brief%20%202%20-%20Holvoet.pdf

Human Trafficking as a Crime Against Humanity: An analysis of the legal potential to prosecute human trafficking in the International Criminal Court with reference to the trafficking of Rohingya Muslims in Southeast Asia, 2014. https://www.duo.uio.no/bitstream/handle/10852/40117/LLM-PIL-THESIS-MAY-2014.pdf?sequence=1&isAllowed=y

ICC, ICC-01/09–19-Corr, Decision Pursuant to Article 15 of the Rome Statute on the Authorization of an Investigation into the Situation in the Republic of Kenya, 13 March 2010a, paras. 90–93 (Kenya Authorization Decision). https://www.legal-tools.org/doc/338a6f/pdf/

ICC, ICC-01/09–19-Corr, Decision Pursuant to Article 15 of the Rome Statute on the Authorization of an Investigation into the Situation in the Republic of Kenya, 13 March 2010b, para. 93 (Kenya Authorization Decision). https://www.legal-tools.org/doc/338a6f/pdf/

ICC, Office of the Prosecutor, Report on Preliminary Examination Activities 2012, November 2012, 20-21 available at http://www.icc-cpi.int/NR/rdonlyres/C433C462-7C4E-4358-8A72-8D99FD00E8CD/285209/OTP2012ReportonPreliminaryExaminations22Nov2012.pdf

International Criminal Court, Situations and Cases, available at: http://www.icccpi.int/Menus/ICC/Situations+and+Cases/

International Criminal Court, Situations and Cases., available at: http://www.icccpi.int/Menus/ICC/Situations+and+Cases/ (accessed Agust 4, 2021)

Jalloh C (2013) What makes a crime against humanity a crime against humanity. Am Univ Int Law Rev pp 381–441. Read also https://digitalcommons.wcl.american.edu/cgi/viewcontent.cgi?referer=https://www.google.com/&httpsredir=1&article=1767&context=auilr

Kim J (2011a) Prosecuting human trafficking as a crime against humanity (unpublished J.D. thesis, Columbia Law School) 9 (on file with Columbia Law School available at: http://blogs.law.

columbia.edu/gslonline/files/2011/02/Jane-Kim_GSL_Prosecuting-Human-Trafficking-as-a-Crime-Against-Humanity-Under-the-Rome-Statute-2011.pdf)

Kim J (2011b) Prosecuting human trafficking as a crime against humanity under the Rome statute. Columbia Law School, pp 7–8. http://blogs.law.columbia.edu/gslonline/files/2011/02/Jane-Kim_GSL_Prosecuting-Human-Trafficking-as-a-Crime-Against-Humanity-Under-the-Rome-Statute-2011.pdf

Kim J (2011c) Prosecuting human trafficking as a crime against humanity under the Rome Statute. Columbia Law School, p 5 http://blogs.law.columbia.edu/gslonline/files/2011/02/Jane-Kim_GSL_Prosecuting-Human-Trafficking-as-a-Crime-Against-Humanity-Under-the-Rome-Statute-2011.pdf

Marchuk I (2014) The Fundamental Concept of Crime in International Criminal Law, 8, http://www.corteidh.or.cr/tablas/r32691.pdf

Moran CF (2014) Human trafficking and the Rome Statute of the International Criminal Court. Age Human Rights J 3:32, 32

*Prosecutor v. Blaškić*, IT-95–14, Judgment, 3 March 2000, para. 206 (Blaškić Trial Judgment)

*Prosecutor v. Gbagbo*, Decision on the Confirmation of Charges against Laurent Gbagbo, Pre -Trial Chamber II, ICC-02/11-01/11, 12 June 2014, para. 214

*Prosecutor v. Jadranko Prlic*, Case No. IT-04-74-T, Judgement (TC), May 29, 2013, para.35

*Prosecutor v. Katanga*, Decision on the Confirmation of Charges, Pre-Trial Chamber I, ICC-01/04-01/07, 26 September 2008, para. 402

*Prosecutor v. Kunarac, et al.*, International Criminal Court, Case No. IT-96-23/1-T, Judgment ¶ 541-42 (22 February 2001a) (accessed from: http://www.icty.org/x/cases/kunarac/tjug/en/kun-tj010222e.pdf)

*Prosecutor v. Kunarac, et al.*, International Criminal Court, Appeals Judgement, Case Nos. IT-96-23-T and IT-96-23/1-A, ¶ 102 (12 June 2001b)

*Prosecutor v. Radovan Karadžić*, Case No. IT-95-5/18-T, Public Redacted Version of Judgement Issued on 24 March 2016 – Volume I of IV (TC), 24 March 2016, para. 475

*Prosecutor v. Vasiljević*, International Criminal Case Case No. IT-98-32-T, Judgment ¶ 37 (29 November 2002)

*Report of the International Law Commission on the work of its forty-eighth session*, UN GAOR, 51st Sess., Supp. No.10, UN Doc. A/51/10 (1996a) p. 49. http://legal.un.org/ilc/documentation/english/reports/a_51_10.pdf

Report of the International Law Commission on the work of its forty-eighth session, UN GAOR, 51st Sess., Supp. No.10, UN Doc. A/51/10 (1996b) p. 47 http://legal.un.org/ilc/documentation/english/reports/a_51_10.pdf

Report of the Secretary-General Pursuant to Paragraph 2 of Security Council Resolution 808 (1993), UN Doc. S/25704, ¶ 47 (May 3, 1993); *Prosecutor v. Duško Tadić*, Case No. IT-94-1-AR72, Decision on the Defence Motion for Interlocutory Appeal on Jurisdiction, ("*Tadić* Jurisdictional Decision"), ¶ 70, (October 2, 1995)

Rome Statute, Article 7(1); See *Kunarac Appeals, supra* note 18, at ¶ 85

Rome Statute, Article 7(1)

Rome Statute of the International Criminal Court, art. 7(2)(a), July 17, 1998, 2187 U.N.T.S. 90

Schabas WA (2011) Introduction to the international criminal court. Cambridge University Press, Cambridge, p 215

Section 1: Genocide, Crimes against Humanity, and War crimes, p. 202, https://www.usip.org/sites/default/files/MC1/MC1-Part2Section1.pdf

See Palermo Protocol, Art. 3 (b)

*See Prosecutor v. Jean Paul Akayesu*, International Criminal Court, Case No. ICTR-96-4-T, Judgment, ¶580 (September 2, 1998)

Stahn C (2019a) A critical introduction to international criminal law. Cambridge University Press, p 58. https://www.cambridge.org/core/services/aop-cambridge-core/content/view/EFEDBED0B84359DFA281A9079047846F/9781108423205AR.pdf/A_Critical_Introduction_to_International_Criminal_Law.pdf?event-type=FTLA

Stahn C (2019b) A critical introduction to international criminal law. Cambridge University Press, p 54. https://www.cambridge.org/core/services/aop-cambridge-core/content/view/EFEDBED0B84359DFA281A9079047846F/9781108423205AR.pdf/A_Critical_Introduction_to_International_Criminal_Law.pdf?event-type=FTLA

Stahn C (2019c) A critical introduction to international criminal law. Cambridge University Press, p 55. https://www.cambridge.org/core/services/aop-cambridge-core/content/view/EFEDBED0B84359DFA281A9079047846F/9781108423205AR.pdf/A_Critical_Introduction_to_International_Criminal_Law.pdf?event-type=FTLA

Stahn C (2019d) A critical introduction to international criminal law. Cambridge University Press, p 56. https://www.cambridge.org/core/services/aop-cambridge-core/content/view/EFEDBED0B84359DFA281A9079047846F/9781108423205AR.pdf/A_Critical_Introduction_to_International_Criminal_Law.pdf?event-type=FTLA

*The Prosecutor v. Francis Kirimimuthaura* et al., No.: ICC-01/09-02/11, Date: 15 March 2011, Pre-Trial Chamber II, para. 12. http://www.worldcourts.com/icc/eng/decisions/2011.03.15_Prosecutor_v_Muthaura.pdf

The Prosecutor v. Jean-Paul Akayesu, Case No. ICTR-96-4-T, para.508 https://unictr.irmct.org/sites/unictr.org/files/case-documents/ictr-96-4/trial-judgements/en/980902.pdf

*The Prosecutor v. Vasiljević*, Case No. IT-98-32, (Trial Chamber, November 29, 2002), para.29-30

The Rome Statute of the International Criminal Court, Article 7(2) (c) A/CONF.183/9 (17 July 1998)

UN.GIFT, *Anti-human Trafficking Manual for Criminal Justice Practitioners*, United Nations Office on Drugs and Crime (UNODC) 8 (2009), https://www.unodc.org/documents/human-trafficking/TIP_module1_Ebook.pdf

United Nations War Crimes Commission (1948) History of the United Nations War Crimes Commission and the Development of the Laws of War. His Majesty's Stationery Office, London, p 179

Women's Caucus Advocacy In ICC Negotiations., http://iccwomen.org/wigjdraft1/Archives/oldWCGJ/icc/iccpc/062000pc/elementsannex.html

Yearbook of International Law Commission, Vol. II (Part Two), 94-95, U.N. Doc. A/CN.4/SER.A/1996/Add.l (Part 2) (1996a) (accessed from: https://legal.un.org/ilc/publications/yearbooks/english/ilc_1996_v2_p2.pdf)

Yearbook of International Law Commission, Vol. II (Part Two), art. 18 (47), U.N. Doc. A/CN.4/SER.A/1996/Add.l (Part 2) (1996b) (accessed from: https://legal.un.org/ilc/publications/yearbooks/english/ilc_1996_v2_p2.pdf) (emphasis added)

Yearbook of the International Law Commission, Vol. II (Part Two), 103-104, U.N. Doc. A/CN.4/SER.A/1991/Add.l (Part 2) (1991) (accessed from: https://legal.un.org/ilc/publications/yearbooks/english/ilc_1991_v2_p2.pdf).

# Chapter 8
# States' Obligations Under International Human Rights Law

Under international human rights law, the breach of human rights and its consequences lie with a contracting state rather than the perpetrator, because only states have the power and the duty to establish the laws and maintain institutions that ensure the respect and protection of such rights. An important question that will be discussed in this section is what exactly is a human rights violation? Put into perspective, why does torture (or trafficking) committed by the state, or a failure to take appropriate measures to proscribe it, constitute a violation of human rights whereas the same conduct perpetrated by a private individual is considered a crime.[1] Article 2 of the *Draft Articles* specifies the conditions required to establish the breach of an international obligation. First, there must be conduct involving some action or omission that is attributable to the state under international law. Second, the conduct must constitute a breach of an international obligation in force in that state.[2] This section discusses the nature and scope of States' Obligations under international human rights law. Additionally, insight is provided into how the Palermo Protocol operates interdependently with International Human Rights Law to balance the shared goals of preventing the crime, protecting victims, and prosecuting traffickers.

[1] Piotrowicz (2009), pp. 175, 193.

[2] *Draft Articles on Responsibility of States for Internationally Wrongful Acts*, as contained in *Report of the International Law Commission on the Work of its 53rd Session*, UN Doc A/55/10 (2000) Art. 2.



P. VI. S. Karenga, *A West African Model to Address Human Trafficking*,
https://doi.org/10.1007/978-3-030-88120-7_8

## 8.1 Conceptual and Legal Framework of States' Obligations

From a legal perspective, only states that are subjects of international law can be responsible for any violations of human rights they have committed. However, trafficking in persons and related human rights abuses are for the most part committed by non-state actors who act as private parties and whose conduct is far from attributable to the State. In the absence of any complicity or negligence by the state, it is difficult to see why trafficking in persons differs from other crimes such as murder or theft.[3] The question arises as to whether non-state criminal conduct can give rise to state responsibility, and the extent to which states can be considered accountable for trafficking-related harm?

Article 2 of the International Covenant on Civil and Political Rights (ICCPR) describes the nature and scope of the general legal obligations undertaken by states who are parties to the Convention. The provision of article 2(1) requires states "to respect and to *ensure* to all individuals within its territory and subject to its jurisdiction the rights recognized in the present Covenant."[4] Accordingly, the Human Rights Committee (HRC) considers that the term "ensure" imposes upon states' parties the duty to protect against violations by both state agents and private persons or entities.[5]

The current status of international human rights law strongly suggests that non-state actors are not bound by human rights norms, and therefore cannot be held directly accountable.[6] This position is endorsed by the Human Rights Committee of the International Covenant on Civil and Political Rights (ICCPR),[7] which states that "obligations are directed to states and do not, as such, have direct horizontal effect as a matter of international law."[8] Therefore, "private individuals or groups, i.e., non-state actors, do not have the legal capacity to violate International Human Rights Law."[9] From this perspective, "obligations imposed upon non-State actors at the international level are moral, rather than legal, in character."[10] However, this does not alter the relevancy of international human rights in combating trafficking in persons inasmuch as "[h]uman rights norms and principles may be applied

[3] *See* Szablewska (2007), p. 346.

[4] ICCPR Article 2(1).

[5] State Responsibilities to Regulate and Adjudicate Corporate Activities Corporate Activities under the United Nations' core Human Rights Treaties, OHCR, 3 (June 2007) https://www.business-humanrights.org/sites/default/files/reports-and-materials/Ruggie-ICCPR-Jun-2007.pdf.

[6] Rodley (1993), pp. 297–318; Schabas (2003), pp. 908–909.

[7] United Nations General Assembly (1966), p. 171.

[8] ICCPR Human Rights Comm., General Comment No. 31: The Nature of the General Legal Obligation Imposed on States Parties to the Covenant ¶ 8, U.N. Doc. CCPR/C/21/Rev.1/Add.13 (May 24, 2006).

[9] Olson (2009), pp. 437, 450.

[10] Obokata (2006), pp. 379, 385.

indirectly through national courts and tribunals, and the horizontal application of human rights law is possible at this level."[11] Thus, the starting point for an effective national response to trafficking in persons consists of adopting legislative measures to protect against human rights abuses and enforcing domestic laws to hold accountable those responsible for committing such crimes.[12]

In view of the foregoing assessment it is clear that "state responsibility is dependent on the link between the state and the wrongful act" and, from an individual perspective, "the conduct of a private actor must qualify as an 'act of a state'."[13] In practice, states may be reluctant to recognize a legal responsibility for trafficking and related violations of human rights, arguing for example that the primary wrong has been committed by private criminals and not by the state itself. They might also claim to have taken all appropriate measures to prevent the harm.[14] For example, in the *Chowdury and Others v. Greece* case, the government "argued that the authorities had fully complied with their positive and procedural obligations under Article 4 of the Convention with regard to the question of human trafficking."[15] They further "submitted that there had been no evidence that the authorities knew or should have been aware of facts which could give rise to well-founded suspicions that the applicants were in actual danger of being subjected to treatment contrary to that provision."[16]

Although the concept of state responsibility as it pertains to acts committed by non-state actors can raise controversy[17] due to the complex nature of trafficking in persons and its related legal framework, states nevertheless incur international responsibility for positive actions or omissions that breach their obligations under international law.[18] The CEDAW Committee underscores that "[u]nder general international law and specific human rights covenants, States may also be responsible for private acts if they fail to act with due diligence to prevent violations of rights or to investigate and punish acts of violence, and for providing compensation."[19]

---

[11] *Ibid.*

[12] Palermo Protocol, Article 5(1); ICCPR, Article 2(2); United Nations High Commissioner for Human Rights Principles and Guidelines on Human Rights and Trafficking, E/2002/68/Add.1 (2002), principle 2.

[13] Chirwa (2004).

[14] OHCHR (2014).

[15] *Chowdury and Others v. Greece*, European Court of Human Rights, Application No. 21884/15, Judgment ¶ 124 ¶ 73 (30 Mar. 2017), https://www.unipa.it/scuole/scienzegiur.ecosociali/specializzazioni/professionilegali/.content/documenti/Scaduto-Chowdury-c-Grecia.pdf.

[15] *Id.*

[17] Lutenco (2012), pp. 29–33.

[18] Responsibility of States for Internationally Wrongful Acts 2001, Article 15, United Nations (2005); *Cf.* OHCHR (2014); *State Responsibility*, A/CN.4/490 and Add. 1–7, 27(1998) (James Crawford, First report on State responsibility) http://legal.un.org/ilc/documentation/english/a_cn4_490.pdf.

[19] Committee on the Elimination of Discrimination against Women, Eleventh Session, General Recommendation No. 19: Violence Against Women, art. 9 (1989).

States are also more likely to be held accountable for the acts of individual traffickers or criminal enterprises "when their ability to influence an alternative, more positive outcome can be established."[20] In the *Velasquez Rodriguez v. Honduras* case, the Inter-American Court of Human Rights judged that "[A]n illegal act which violates human rights and which is initially not directly imputable to a State (for example, because it is the act of a private person or because the person responsible has not been identified) can lead to international responsibility of the State, not because of the act itself, but because of the lack of due diligence to prevent the violation or to respond to it as required by the Convention."[21] In such cases, the state is responsible for a human rights violation by failing to take prevention measures or respond in accordance with the required standard to address the issue, not because of the act itself.[22]

It is one thing to define the principles that govern the responsibility and content of the obligation it imposes, another to determine whether that international obligation has been breached and what the related consequences should be.[23] In light of the state's duty to act with due diligence, there are three elements a Court applies in determining whether states have violated the human rights of victims: the proximity element, the knowledge test, and the due diligence standard.[24]

The proximity element transforms the prohibited act into a human rights violation by inquiring "whether the particular harm can be linked with a particular failure by the state to take action."[25] To this end, the Court will determine whether an omission attributable to the state has contributed to the alleged harm. Such a connection can be established, for example, if the Court finds that national law and administration have failed to prohibit and punish abuses.[26] This positive obligation of states to adopt legal and policy measures in response to trafficking in persons is embedded in international human rights treaty bodies and developed in Courts' jurisprudence. For instance, in *Rantsev v. Cyprus and Russia* case, the European Court of Human Rights "considers that the spectrum of safeguards set out in national legislation must be adequate to ensure the practical and effective protection of the rights of victims or

---

[20] OHCHR (2014).

[21] *Velasquez Rodriguez v. Honduras*, Inter-American Court of Human Rights, Judgment, Rep. No. 4 (Ser. C) ¶ 172 (29 July 1988); see also the development of the concept of due diligence in *Jessica Lenahan v. United States* Inter-American Commission (2011). For example, "due diligence" is implicitly enshrined in Article 2 (1) ICESCR.

[22] OHCHR (2014).

[23] Yearbook of the International Law Commission, Vol. II, ¶ 66 (c), U.N. Doc. A/8010/Rev.l (1970) (accessed from: https://legal.un.org/ilc/publications/yearbooks/english/ilc_1970_v2.pdf).

[24] Stoyanova (2017), p. 234.

[25] *Id.* at 325.

[26] Read *L.E. v. Greece*, European Court of Human Rights, Application No. 71545/12, Judgment, ¶¶ 70–72 (21 January 2011); *Siliadin v. France*, European Court of Human Rights, Application No. 73316/01, Judgment (2005), ¶¶ 70–72; *Rantsev v. Cyprus and Russia,* European Court of Human Rights, Judgment, Application No.25965/04 , ¶ 285, (7 January 2010).

potential victims of trafficking."[27] Accordingly, this entails establishing criminal law provisions to punish traffickers, and to "put in place adequate measures regulating businesses often used as a cover for human trafficking. Furthermore, a State's immigration rules must address relevant concerns relating to encouragement, facilitation or tolerance of trafficking."[28]

The proximity element requires foreseeability of the harm.[29] For a state to be liable for human rights violations, the harmful consequences of its conduct must have been foreseeable. Thus, the state's authority must have known or ought to have known about the harm.[30] Foreseeability is the leading test in determining proximate cause between state conduct and the specific harm that has occurred. It establishes a "predictive relationship between the harm and the state conduct."[31] The foreseeability test assesses whether the state should have reasonably foreseen the potential consequences arising from its conduct and whether precaution was exercised in the steps taken toward executing obligations in good faith or due diligence.

It is also important to clarify that the predictability is not necessarily based on causality. The state's omission might simply be a factor contributing to the occurrence of the harm. Conversely, the concept of 'causality' suggests a 'but for' test, meaning that "but for the State's failure, the harm would not have happened", the predictability requires only to prove the "proximity between the harm and the state omission":[32] "[a failure to take reasonably available measures which could have had a real prospect of altering the outcome or mitigating the harm is sufficient to engage the responsibility of the State."[33] Whether a rule has been breached may depend on the knowledge of relevant state organs or agents, which requires that "the state is aware or should have been aware of the existence of a general problem."[34] In the *Hadijatou Mani Koraou v. The Republic of Niger* judgment, the Economic Community of West African States (ECOWAS) Court observed that the slavery conditions of Hadijatou Mani Koraou were brought to the attention of the state administrative authority in the Court of first instance. The fact that the national judge acknowledged the slavery status of the Applicant without denouncing it constitutes a violation of human rights as this represents tolerance, passiveness,

[27] *Id.* at ¶ 284.

[28] *Id.*

[29] Stoyanova (2017), p. 327.

[30] *Id.*; For an example of circumstances where the state was not found in violation of its positive obligation because the harm was not foreseeable, see *Rantsev, supra* note 26, at ¶ 222; and *Mastromatteov v. Italy*, European Court of Human Rights, Judgment, App. No. 37703/97, ¶¶ 178–179.

[31] Stoyanova (2017), pp. 327–328.

[32] *Id.* at 328; *See* E. and Others v. the United Kingdom, European Court of Human Rights, App. No. 33218/96, Judgment, ¶ 99 (26 November 2002).

[33] *O'Keefee v. Ireland*, [GC] App. No. 35810/09, 28 January 2014, para. 149; see also *Salakhov and Islyamova v. Ukraine*, App. 28005/08, 14 March 2013, para. 181.

[34] Stoyanova (2017), p. 329.

inaction, and abstention vis-à-vis the practice of slavery."[35] Another example can be found in the *Chowdury and Others v. Greece* case where the European Court of Human Rights (ECtHR) decided that Greece had violated human rights by not undertaking operational measures to prevent trafficking and protect victims despite the knowledge possessed by the state of press reports, an Ombudsman report, and complaints submitted to the relevant police station regarding the conditions of employment of workers in the strawberry fields.[36] Petya Nestorova made the following comments on the decision of the Court:

> Before this incident, the Greek authorities had known for years about the circumstances under which thousands of workers lived and worked in strawberry farms around Manolada, due to media reports and an Ombudsman's report which had been submitted to all relevant authorities and labour inspections, but no effective action to remedy the situation had been taken... The Court saw the situation of the workers in Manolada as a case of human trafficking for the purpose of forced labour and concluded that there had been a violation of Article 4, paragraph 2, of the European Convention on Human Rights due to the failure of the Greek authorities to fulfil their positive obligations under this article to prevent human trafficking, to protect victims, to effectively investigate the offences committed and to punish those responsible for human trafficking offences.[37]

Finally, the due diligence standard or the test of reasonableness requires interpreting positive obligations of the state "in such a way as not to impose an excessive burden on the authorities."[38] The European Convention on Human Rights (ECHR)[39] and the Inter-American Convention on Human Rights (IACHR) jurisprudences have adopted the due diligence standard as a key test in determining whether states have complied with their obligation to protect human rights. For example, in the *Gonzalez v Mexico* case, which involved systematic violence towards women in Ciudad Juarez that was linked to social class, age, and gender, the Court held Mexico to be failing in its duty to conduct due diligence to protect two girls from violence inflicted by private actors. Although Mexico knew about the sexual assault, torture, and murder of women, as a state it "did not act with the required *due diligence* to

[35] *Koraou v. Niger*, ECOWAS Community Court of Justice, Judgment, No. ECW/CCJ/APP/0808, ¶¶ 82–85 (Oct. 27, 2008) (available at: http://www.worldcourts.com/ecowasccj/eng/decisions/2008.10.27_Koraou_v_Niger.htm).

[36] Cf. *Chowdury and Others v. Greece*, *supra* note 15 at ¶¶110–115.

[37] Petya Nestorova, Executive Secretary, Secretariat of the Council of Europe Convention against Trafficking in Human Beings (GRETA and Committee of the Parties), CoE, Understanding human trafficking in the private economy-forms, industries and sectors involved, latest trends and responsibility of the private sector Conference "The Public-Private Partnership in the Fight against Human Trafficking" (Moscow, July 20–21, 2017).

[38] *O'Keefee v. Ireland* [GC] App no. 35819/09 (ECtHR, January 28, 2014) ¶144.

[39] *See Opuz v Turkey* (App no 33401/02) ECHR 9 June 2009. The Council of Europe Convention on Preventing and Combating Violence against Women and Domestic Violence (2011), article 5, has also adopted a due diligence standard in the protection of human rights: Parties shall take the necessary legislative and other measures to exercise due diligence to prevent, investigate, punish, and provide reparation for acts of violence covered by the scope of this Convention that are perpetrated by non-state actors.

prevent the death and abuse suffered by the victims adequately and did not act, as could *reasonably* be expected, in accordance with the circumstances of the case, to end their deprivation of liberty."[40] Accordingly, states have upheld their positive obligations when they can demonstrate that they have taken reasonable measures, including effective actions, to prevent violations of human rights or to punish those responsible.

The due diligence standard is embedded in many international instruments. For example, Article 4(c) of the Declaration on the Elimination of Violence against Women,[41] asserts that states have the duty to "[e]xercise due diligence to prevent, investigate and, in accordance with national legislation, punish acts of violence against women, whether those acts are perpetrated by the State or by private persons."[42] This reasonableness standard is also extended to violations of economic, social, and cultural rights by private actors. For instance, the Maastricht Guidelines assert that states are accountable for violations of economic, social, and cultural rights "that result from their failure to exercise due diligence in controlling the behaviour of such non-state actors."[43]

A substantial issue pertaining to state responsibility that may arise in the prosecution of trafficking in a cross-border or transnational context is jurisdiction *ratione loci.* Applicants may uphold in Court that the state could be held responsible for trafficking in persons where the acts and omissions of its authorities affect its nationals abroad.[44] An illustrative example can be found in the *Rantsev v. Russia* case, which involved the trafficking of a young Russian girl whose death occurred in Cyprus territory rather than the Russian state in respect of which the procedural obligation is said to arise.[45] The Russian Government argued that the circumstances leading to Ms Rantseva's death took place outside its territory and therefore "the application was inadmissible *ratione loci* in so far as it was directed against the Russian Federation. They submitted that they had no 'actual authority' over the territory of the Republic of Cyprus and that the actions of the Russian Federation were limited by the sovereignty of the Republic of Cyprus."[46] Accordingly, the Court concluded that "from the standpoint of public international law, the jurisdictional competence of a State is primarily territorial"[47] and therefore "there was no

[40] *Claudia Ivette Gonzales and Others v Mexico*, Inter-American Court of Human Rights, Series C No 205, Judgment, ¶ 284 (15 November 2009).

[41] GA Res 48/104, UN GAOR, 48th sess, 85th plen mtg, UN Doc A/48/49 (December 20, 1993).

[42] UN GAOR (1995).

[43] Adopted at Maastricht, 22–26 January 1997, [18] ('Maastricht Guidelines'). Although not legally binding, the Maastricht Guidelines have served as persuasive aids in the interpretation of economic, social, and cultural rights.

[44] *Rantsev v. Cyprus and Russia*, No. 25965/04, ECtHR, ¶204 (January 7, 2010) https://ec.europa.eu/anti-trafficking/sites/antitrafficking/files/rantsev_vs_russia_cyprus_en_4.pdf.

[45] *See* Talmon (2019), p. 99.

[46] *Rantsev v. Cyprus and Russia*, No. 25965/04, ECtHR, para. 203 (January 7, 2010) https://ec.europa.eu/anti-trafficking/sites/antitrafficking/files/rantsev_vs_russia_cyprus_en_4.pdf.

[47] *Id.*

free-standing obligation incumbent on the Russian authorities under Article 2 of the Convention to investigate Ms Rantseva's death."[48]

In conclusion, it is worth noting that the duty to protect human rights does not mean the state is responsible for all private actions that interfere with established human rights. For example, citizens have the right to security and the state has an obligation to ensure some level of security within its domestic jurisdiction through the implementation of criminal law. However "when a person is trafficked, the State has not necessarily failed to protect that right because the State cannot give an absolute guarantee of safety to all those within its jurisdiction."[49] The state would thus incur international responsibility where it failed to exercise due diligence "to prevent the violations, control and regulate private actors, investigate and, where applicable, prosecute and punish occurrences of violations, and provide effective remedies to victims."[50] Stoyanova provides an enlightening observation in this regard, stating:

> Harm, which is more proximate to state's conduct and on which the state has comprehensive knowledge, will call for more intervention by the state and, accordingly, the test of reasonableness will not be stringent from the perspective of the individual applicant (...) The harm that is more difficult to link to state conduct and knowledge thereof will imply less demanding obligations upon the state since it might not be reasonable to expect the state that it acts.[51]

The following section will delve into the wide range of policy that ECOWAS has developed in response to trafficking in persons

## 8.2 Regional Anti-trafficking Measures

In 2001 the Economic Community of West African States (ECOWAS) adopted a sub-regional approach to combat trafficking in persons with the signature of the "Declaration on the fight against trafficking in Persons" and the initial ECOWAS Plan of Action against Trafficking in Persons.[52] Since then, successive triennial plans of action have been adopted relating to the formulation and implementation of legislation, protective and preventive measures, cooperation, training and capacity building, and creating a structure for monitoring and evaluation. The initial plan of action aimed to control trafficking in persons in the sub-region, with a special focus on trafficked children.[53]

---

[48] *Id.*

[49] Piotrowicz (2009), p. 187.

[50] Chirwa (2004), pp. 17–18.

[51] Stoyanova (2017), pp. 325–326.

[52] ECOWAS (2001).

[53] U.N. Action for Cooperation Against Trafficking in Persons, *Summary of Regional and Sub-Regional Structures and Initiatives to Counter Trafficking in Persons* 4–5 (Dec. 2010),

To implement these policies, an ECOWAS Anti-trafficking Unit (TIP Unit) has been established to support and monitor member states in the development of harmonized policies, strategies, and legal instruments. Its mission is also aimed at "enhancing transnational policy cooperation, data collection on TIP, capacity-building of national staff, and facilitating police and judicial cooperation."[54] An additional task includes networking with National Focal Points (NFPs) at the domestic level to organize ECOWAS Annual Review Meetings. These are designed to monitor member states' trafficking programs while also sharing information between multi-layered stakeholders and undertaking capacity building activities.[55]

In West Africa, trafficking in persons occurs within domestic boundaries and across regional and international borders and is ultimately tied to migration. Therefore, in 2008 the ECOWAS adopted a Common Approach on Migration[56] to promote free movement of persons and safe migration, reducing the need for migrants to rely on smugglers who are prospective traffickers. Indeed, experience has shown that restrictive immigration policies force migrants to risk paying higher fees to facilitators or corrupt state actors for documentation or passage, which reduces their time and opportunities to find decent work to pay off the exploitative debt they have incurred, and also increases the possibility of being trafficked.[57]

These ECOWAS migration policies and actions are also relevant in preventing the trafficking and smuggling of migrants as they aim to address "certain root causes of trafficking such as persistent and rampant poverty, displacement of persons, forced migration and the mobility of particularly vulnerable groups such as children and women in search of economic opportunity, [security and job opportunities]."[58] For international work on trafficking in particular, a common agreed definition and bilateral agreements are useful for "collecting and sharing data and coordinating policy and assistance, as well as to criminal justice measures such as extraditing criminal suspects."[59]

---

http://un-act.org/publication/view/summary-of-regional-and-sub-regional-structures-and-initiatives-to-counter-trafficking-in-persons-december-2010/ [hereinafter *Summary of Regional and Sub-Regional Structures*].

[54] *Thematic Meeting on Trafficking in Human Beings and the Smuggling of Migrants*, Int'l Ctr. Migr. 10 (Dec. 3, 2015), https://www.rabat-process.org/images/RabatProcess/Documents/summary-debates-conclusions-thematic-meeting-porto-december-2015-trafficking-smuggling-rabat-process.pdf.

[55] *Id.*; FMM West Africa, *Counter-Trafficking Baseline Assessment* 19–21 (2017), https://fmmwestafrica.org/wp-content/uploads/2017/08/Report-of-the-ECOWAS-baseline-assessment-on-counter-trafficking.pdf.

[56] *ECOWAS Common Approach on Migration*, ECOWAS Comm. (Jan. 18, 2008), https://www.unhcr.org/49e47c8f11.pdf.

[57] Global Alliance Against Traffic in Women (GAATW) (2017), p. 5.

[58] *Training for TIP Nat'l Focal Points*, Int'l Training Ctr. of the Int'l Lab. Org., http://www.ilo.org/wcmsp5/groups/public/%2D%2D-africa/documents/publication/wcms_348047.pdf.

[59] Global Alliance Against Traffic in Women (GAATW) (2017), p. 5.

Regarding prevention, in 2000 ECOWAS, in cooperation with IOM established the Migration Dialogue for West Africa (MIDWA) as a regional consultative process to accelerate regional integration and address both the challenges and opportunities of migration, including trafficking in persons.[60] Furthermore, ECOWAS prompted a strong political commitment by developing legal and institutional frameworks to assist member states including a checklist of compliance with the Palermo Protocol, strategies for an effective National Plan of Action, and a model National Task Force and National Focal Points.[61] Accordingly, almost all ECOWAS member states signed and/or ratified the United Nations Convention against Transnational Organized Crime and its Protocols on trafficking in persons and the smuggling of migrants. They have also incorporated the provisions contained therein into their national legislations.[62] However, it is important to recognize that creating regular channels of migration in a West African context might foster conditions for the trafficking of migrant workers in the large informal sectors not covered by labor laws. Trafficking in persons and indeed irregular migration cannot be addressed in isolation from development, economic policies, and efficient labor laws designed to eliminate the risks of substandard working conditions that fuel the demand for cheap goods and services.

In terms of capacity building, ECOWAS has developed in conjunction with IOM a "Training Manual on Trafficking in Persons". This handbook contains regional case studies and good practices and "presents the definitions of trafficking in human beings and smuggling of migrants as well as general guidelines on investigation and prosecution of cases related to trafficking in human beings, with a focus on cooperation between ECOWAS member states."[63] Training courses for national Frontline Law Enforcement Officers and groups of civil society were subsequently organized and an evaluation of national legal frameworks carried out in 2006.

Regarding the protection of victims from being re-trafficked, in 2010 the Economic Community of West African States (ECOWAS) adopted a "Regional Policy on Protection and Assistance to Victims of Trafficking in Persons in West Africa" and elaborated "Guidelines on witness protection, support and assistance" as well as standard operating procedures for the protection of trafficked persons. In terms of inter-State cooperation, the Economic Community of West African States (ECOWAS) has established tools such as a "Manual on Cooperation and Networking for ECOWAS Member States" and a "Model Bilateral Agreement on cooperation and mutual legal assistance for protecting children from trans-border

---

[60] *See also The Impact of Free Movement and the Challenges of Migration*, Migr. Dialogue for W. Afr. (MIDWA) (Aug. 23, 2016), https://www.iom.int/sites/default/files/our_work/ICP/RCP/2016/MIDWA-2016-Ministerial-and-Experts-Meeting-Concept-Note.pdf.

[61] *Summary of Regional and Sub-Regional Structures*, *supra* note 53, at 4–5.

[62] U.N. Ofc. on Drugs and Crime ("UNODC"), *Regional Strategy for Combating Trafficking in Persons and Smuggling of Migrants 2015–2020*, https://www.unodc.org/documents/westandcentralafrica/UNODC_Regional_Strategy_for_Combating_TIP_SOM_West_and_Central_Africa_2015-2020.pdf; Danso (2013).

[63] UNODC (2006).

trafficking". State cooperation has also facilitated meetings between states leading to several agreements, such as those between Benin, Togo, and Gabon; Côte d'Ivoire and Mali; Nigeria and Niger; Nigeria and Benin; and Mali and Senegal. Economic Community of West African States (ECOWAS) treaties aim to promote the free movement of persons, goods, services, and capital and the right of residence and establishment between member states.[64] Similarly, the Ouagadougou Plan to Combat Trafficking in Human Beings, which was adopted in 2006, is intended to develop effective cooperation between the European Union and the African Union to prevent trafficking in persons, prosecute traffickers, and protect the human rights of the victims. The Action Plan calls on states to ratify and fully implement in their domestic legislations the provisions of the United Nations Convention Against Transnational Organized Crime (UNTOC) and the Trafficking in Persons Protocol.

Remarkably, the Trafficking Protocol under the Organized Crime Convention do not make any provision for the creation of a treaty monitoring body to review and enforce states' compliance with international legal standards. In this regard, the African Charter on Human and Peoples' Rights along with the monitoring system of the African Commission on Human and Peoples' Rights play an important role in bridging the gap between international treaty obligations and domestic laws and policies. Under Articles 55 and 56 of the African Charter on Human and Peoples' Rights, individuals can submit information or communications to the African Commission and seek remedies in cases where domestic legal proceedings fail to exercise due diligence. Furthermore, in 1998 the Protocol to the African Charter on Human and Peoples' Rights on the Establishment of an African Court on Human and Peoples' Rights (the Protocol) adopted a more judicial approach to enforcement by creating the African Court on Human and Peoples' Rights in order to complement the protective mandate of the Commission. Its decisions carry the force of law and are legally binding on whether a state party has violated the treaty. Additionally, judicial procedures such as those of the Economic Community of West African States (ECOWAS) Court of Justice and the International Court of Justice have been established to adjudicate inter-state or individual complaints alleging violations of human rights and to enforce international human rights.[65] International agreement and cooperation provide and additional layer for African law enforcement cooperation and partnership in tackling modern slavery.

[64] *Summary of Regional and Sub-Regional Structures*, *supra* note 53, at 4–5.

[65] In the *APDF & IHRDA v. Republic of Mali* case, for example, an NGO filed a complaint to the African Court alleging that certain provisions of the Malian Persons and Family Code were not in compliance with the Protocol to African Charter on Human and Peoples' Rights on the Rights of Women in Africa (the Maputo Protocol).

## 8.3 International Cooperation in Combating Trafficking in Persons

Given the cross-border nature of the crime of trafficking, a successful anti-trafficking response requires an international obligation to engage in cooperation between countries of origin, transit, and destination in fighting this crime. A West African proverb states: "Bamboo carriers concert each other before carrying their load;"[66] thus, they must agree on the direction to take, otherwise they will not be able to talk to each other again (following each other at a considerable distance) and some may want to go to the right while others want to go to the left. Similarly, concerted transnational cooperation among states is also necessary to establish a common approach and streamline legal concepts to prosecute cases of serious crime.

To enhance international cooperation in the fight against trafficking in persons, "[S]tates must recognize trafficking in persons as an extraditable offense, apply domestic anti-trafficking laws extraterritorially, and exchange information regionally."[67] Typically, in trafficking cases "alleged offenders, victims and evidence can each (or all) be located in two or more countries. The same fact can justify and give rise to criminal investigations and prosecutions in multiple jurisdictions."[68] Therefore, when offenders, victims, instruments, and assets of the crime pass through several jurisdictions, the traditional law enforcement approach, which is limited to a national jurisdiction, is non-operational. States must therefore assist each other in informal cooperation mechanisms, and develop legal tools such as extradition and mutual legal assistance to eliminate safe havens for traffickers, thereby ending the high levels of impunity they currently enjoy.[69]

In the Economic Community of West African States (ECOWAS) region, where individuals enjoy free movement and the right to residence and establishment, national authorities increasingly require the assistance of other states in ensuring successful investigation, prosecution, and punishment of transnational crime offenders.[70] When investigating and prosecuting trafficking cases, assistance

---

[66] Francois Xavier Damiba and Laurent Nare, Proverbes Mossi (Abidjan, 1999) (proverb no. 785).

[67] Mattar (2005), pp. 145, 170; *see also* OHCHR, Recommended Principles and Guidelines on Human Rights and Human Trafficking, Recommended Principles on Human Rights and Human Trafficking, principle 14.

[68] OHCHR (2010), p. 203.

[69] *Legislative Guides for the Implementation of the United Nations Convention against Transnational Organized Crime and the Protocol Thereto*, UNODC 2, at XVI (2004), https://www.unodc.org/pdf/crime/legislative_guides/Legislative%20guides_Full%20version.pdf; *Trafficking in persons: Enhancing Criminal Investigation, Prosecution and Victim/witness Protection in African and European Countries*, Africa-EU Partnership Working Group (Dec. 1, 2011), http://www.africa-eu-partnership.org/sites/default/files/documents/mme_tip_proposed_working_methodology_en_0.pdf.

[70] U.N. High Commissioner for Human Rights, Draft Compendium of Trafficking-Related Tools Developed at the Regional Level, at 39, http://www.ohchr.org/Documents/Issues/Trafficking/Dakar_draft_compendium_en.pdf.

between law enforcement agencies and judicial authorities from different countries is needed to obtain evidence in a form that is admissible in domestic Courts. Such bilateral or multilateral cooperation among states is generally governed by mutual legal assistance regulations laid out in international and domestic laws that enhance law enforcement in several ways. For instance, they allow for the summoning of witnesses, locating persons, producing documents, tracing the proceeds of crime, or issuing warrants. They supplement arrangements regarding the exchange of information obtained through the International Criminal Police Organization (Interpol), police-to-police relationships, judicial assistance, and letters rogatory. These instruments can also overcome obstacles between countries with differing legal traditions that restrict assistance to judicial authorities rather than prosecutors. In carrying out extradition, states have to ensure that, in relation to requesting mutual legal assistance, nothing will infringe upon the human rights of those whose extradition is sought.[71]

In this regard, joint efforts to address trafficking in persons among Western countries has resulted in bilateral and multi-lateral agreements on the repatriation of trafficked children, the building of a consensus on standards for a regional anti-trafficking convention, and efforts to harmonize domestic legislation.[72] Accordingly, in July 2006, the Economic Community of West African States and the Economic Community of Central States adopted an interregional plan of action (a Joint Multilateral Cooperation Agreement) on combating trafficking in persons, especially women and children in West and Central Africa. This bi-regional plan of action confirms the criminal justice response set forth in the ECOWAS Initial Plan of Action against Trafficking in Persons and extends efforts to combat trafficking into the Central African region. The related resolution and a multilateral cooperation agreement are a response to the flows of trafficking between the two regions and strengthen sub-regional initiatives to curb trafficking.[73]

However, although agreements, mutual legal assistance treaties, and extradition treaties may bear positive results in some instances, domestic and cross national jurisdiction give rise to significant legislative and procedural complexities that sometimes prevent those arrangements and treaties from acting to overcome the current challenges. For instance, perpetrators of serious crimes such as trafficking in persons usually try to escape prosecution and justice by fleeing to another country. In response to this challenge, international extradition can be applied, which is the formal process by which a fugitive who enters one country is surrendered to another for trial or punishment.[74] The law of extradition varies from country to country and

---

[71] *Legislative Guides for the Implementation of the United Nations Convention against Transnational Organized Crime and the Protocol Thereto*, UNODC 2, ¶ 217 (2004), https://www.unodc.org/pdf/crime/legislative_guides/Legislative%20guides_Full%20version.pdf.

[72] Jonathan (2003), p. 19.

[73] UNODC (2008a), pp. 171–173.

[74] U.S. Dep't of Just., U.S. Attorneys' Manual § 9–15.000 (Apr. 2018), https://www.justice.gov/usam/usam-9-15000-international-extradition-and-related-matters.

is subject to foreign policy considerations. Some countries may grant extradition only pursuant to a treaty limited to certain offenses, which entails substantive or procedural challenges; while other countries allow extradition without a treaty.

One fundamental prerequisite for the application of extradition procedures is the principle of dual criminality, wherein the law of both states must consider the alleged actions to constitute a criminal offense.[75] However, with regard to trafficking in persons, the Organized Crime Convention requires states to ensure that this crime, its constitutive acts, and ancillary offenses are extraditable under its national laws and/or extraditions treaties to avoid loopholes in jurisdiction over serious crimes and eliminate safe havens for traffickers.[76] Alternatively, "a government that denies an extradition request on the grounds that the fugitive is a national of its country should prosecute the case domestically with the same diligence as a serious domestic offence."[77]

To combat impunity in the region, the Economic Community of West African States (ECOWAS) Convention on Extradition[78] and the Convention on Mutual Assistance in Criminal Matters were established as operational tools to foster cooperation amongst state parties. Under the provisions and conditions laid down in the Convention on Extradition, states undertake to surrender to each other "all persons within the territory of the requested State who are wanted for prosecution for an offence or who are wanted by the legal authorities of the requesting State for the carrying out of a sentence."[79] This empowers national Courts of law to exercise jurisdiction in the investigation, prosecution, trial, and enforcement of penalties against offenders who seek to hide behind national borders and differences in the judicial systems of countries to escape territorial, personal, or universal jurisdiction for their crimes.[80] Similarly, the Convention on Mutual Assistance in Criminal Matters has been formulated to cope more effectively with criminal cases that have transnational implications. To this end, states are required to assist in proceedings or investigations with respect to offenses, to provide documents and

---

75 *Fact Sheet on the U.S.-UK Extradition Treaty*, U.S. Embassies and Consulates in the U.K. (Nov. 16 2011), https://uk.usembassy.gov/our-relationship/policy-history/the-u-s-uk-extradition-treaty/fact-sheet-on-the-u-s-uk-extradition-treaty/; *Read* Hafen (1992), p. 191.

76 Organized Crime Convention, Article 16. Legislative Guide to the Organized Crime Convention and its Protocols, Part I, ¶¶403, 414–417.

77 Africa-EU, *supra* note 69; United Nations Protocol to Prevent, Suppress and Punish Trafficking in Persons, Especially Women and Children, supplementing the United Nations Convention against Transnational Organized Crime, G.A. Res. 55/25, U.N. Doc. A/45/49 (Vol. I) (2001) art. 16 (10); *Id.* at 193–241; UNODC Toolkit, *supra* note 73, at 119–172; *Commentary on the Recommended Principles and Guidelines*, *supra* note 68, at 203–212.

78 ECOWAS Convention on Extradition (A/P1/8/94), adopted on 6 August 1994, entered into force December 8, 2005 http://documentation.ecowas.int/download/en/legal_documents/protocols/Convention%20on%20Extradition.pdf.

79 ECOWAS Convention on Extradition (1994).

80 Ikeora (2010), p. 107.

evidence related to criminal matters, and to facilitate search and seizure of the suspected proceeds of crime.[81]

Cooperation among states is particularly important when targeting large-scale trafficking rings; for example, joint collaboration between the Government of Ghana and neighboring countries, as well as international organizations and foreign embassies, has resulted in the prosecution of transnational cases in a successful bid to break up a trafficking ring that sent at least 50 Ghanaian women to Russia to work in the sex trade.[82] Judicial cooperation in criminal matters for similar outcomes requires "the harmonization of substantial penal legislations and the mutual judicial assistance in its major components, including extradition and police collaboration."[83]

Despite the political will expressed in the Convention on Extradition and the Convention on Mutual Assistance in Criminal Matters,[84] collaboration by West African governments with foreign countries on transnational trafficking investigations has encountered significant obstacles and challenges in the prosecuting of trafficking crimes. Subsequently, investigations and prosecutions initiated in the region have been dropped and a large number of trafficking convictions have resulted in short or suspended sentences. The *NIGERIA Attorney General vs Kingsley Edegbe* case discussed previously provides an outstanding example of this. In this case, the Government of the Netherlands asked the Attorney General of the Federation and the Minister of Justice for the extradition of Mr. Kingsley Edegbe to face trial in the Netherlands for his involvement in trafficking in persons. The judge replied that the mere signing and ratification of UNTOC by the two countries would not qualify as a treaty for the purposes of extradition. Similarly, a US Department of State report on Gambia stated that "[a] judge adjourned indefinitely the prosecution of four defendants charged with exploiting 59 women in Lebanon and Kuwait[...] because three of the suspects remained at large."[85]

To improve coordination among the various governmental agencies, the ECOWAS Plan of Action against Trafficking in Persons calls upon its member states to create a National Agency Against Trafficking in Persons and provide adequate funding and resources to ensure effective implementation of the national anti-trafficking action plan. The legal framework and policy development declared the following:

> States shall establish a National Task Force on Trafficking in Persons that will bring together relevant Ministries and Agencies in developing policy and taking action against trafficking

---

[81] *ECOWAS Convention on Mutual Assistance in Criminal Matters*, Articles 18–19; *see also* UNODC (2008b).

[82] U.S. Dep't of State, Trafficking in Persons Report 2010: Ghana (Jun. 2010), https://www.state.gov/j/tip/rls/tiprpt/2010/142760.htm.

[83] Kahombo (2010), pp. 1, 2.

[84] ECOWAS Convention on Mutual Assistance in Criminal Matters (A/P1/7/92), adopted on 29 July 1992, entered into force on 28 October 1998, 2329 UNTS 301 (ECOWAS Convention) http://documentation.ecowas.int/download/en/legal_documents/protocols/Convention%20on%20Mutual%20Assistance%20in%20Criminal%20Matters.pdf.

[85] U.S. Dep't of State, *supra* note 82.

in persons, and calling on Inter-Governmental Organizations, nongovernmental organizations, and other representatives of civil society, as necessary.[86]

The designated National Task Force is invested with the responsibility to develop recommendations for a national plan of action against trafficking in persons.[87]

Countries that have established a specific anti-trafficking agency in the Economic Community of West African States (ECOWAS) region include Nigeria (NAPTIP) and Gambia (National Agency against Trafficking in Persons). Other states do not have dedicated structures to combat trafficking, instead anti-trafficking is the responsibility of certain positions and agencies. Nevertheless, a growing number of countries have recently established anti-trafficking taskforces to coordinate their national anti-trafficking activities. For instance, Nigeria's NAPTIP directly employs immigration police, legal experts, social workers, and others and acts as a model for other national agencies in the region.[88]

Some countries have taken the initiative to set up specialized units or agencies to deal with trafficking in persons in order to promote multidisciplinary responses and to garner political support. In this sense Nigeria is a pioneer and its good practice is an example for other countries in the region to follow. Under the 2003 federal anti-trafficking law, Nigeria established the National Agency for Prohibition of Trafficking in Persons and Other Related Matters (NAPTIP) to enforce laws and foster collaboration and partnership between government bodies and civil societies within and outside Nigeria. This anti-trafficking Specialized Unit is committed at both a federal and state level to strengthen cooperation between the Attorney General of the Federation (Ministry of Justice and the Courts), Police Force, Immigration Service, Defense Intelligence Agency, Security and Civil Defense Corps, Prison Service, Welfare officials, UN agencies, and all other agencies involved in anti-trafficking activities. NAPTIP has a broad mandate to tackle trafficking in persons, covering issues such as the prosecution of perpetrators, providing protection services for victims and witnesses of trafficking, and ensuring prevention and international cooperation.

The government-interagency collaboration can be described as follows: once the Nigeria Immigration Service detects possible victims and traffickers entering or leaving the country, or front line officers encounter incidents of trafficking while on routine patrol, they are usually referred to NAPTIP for further law enforcement action. The police investigate the case and hand over the conclusions and suspects for prosecution. Because NAPTIP has trained lawyers who work in its legal department, the number of convictions has increased and more cases have now been successfully investigated and are being tried in Court.[89]

In this regard, it is important to note that, since its inception in 2003, NAPTIP has been able to demonstrate some significant achievements in the fight against

---

[86] UNODC, *supra* note 81, at x.

[87] *Id.*

[88] *Counter-Trafficking Baseline Assessment, supra* note 55, at 20–21.

[89] Hassan and Kigbu (2015), p. 249.

trafficking, especially in terms of prosecution and raising awareness. For example, in 2008 NAPTIP cooperated with law enforcement counterparts in nine European countries to break up an international ring, which led to the prosecution of more than 60 traffickers.[90] That same year, the government extradited a suspected trafficker to face trial in the United States. NAPTIP has also collaborated with other African governments including Benin, Ghana, Togo, and Cameroon on trafficking cases, most notably to repatriate victims.[91]

The Director General of NAPTIP, Julie Okah-Donli, asserts that the agency has rescued over 12,000 people, rehabilitated 6000 victims, and secured 325 convictions.[92] These remarkable outcomes are attributed to the intensified sensitization and various methods used by NAPTIP in carrying out its investigative activities, such as proactive and reactive investigations, disruptive operations, surveillance and joint operations, and other intelligence cooperation mechanisms.[93] Furthermore, in 2009 the government expressed political interest in strengthening the capacity of NAPTIP and pledged over $7 million in annual funds for its operation and activities.[94] Following this outstanding and sustained progress in combating trafficking in persons, the U.S. State Department placed Nigeria in the Tier 1 category in its 2010 Trafficking in Persons report.

The overall situation regarding trafficking in Nigeria has also improved because NAPTIP has partnered with government agencies and other non-governmental organizations (NGOs) to work in synergy to close the gaps. For instance, because NAPTIP shelters offer short-term care, the agency collaborated with NGO-run shelters when victims required longer-term care.[95] Moreover, the Catholic Church and its institutions assist government agencies in providing shelter and other social services, including family tracing and re-unification of children with their families, rehabilitation and counselling of victims of trafficking, and the provision of life and job skills.[96]

---

[90] U.S. Dep't of State, Trafficking in Persons Report 2008: Nigeria (Jun. 2008) https://www.state.gov/j/tip/rls/tiprpt/2008/105388.htm; *The Cost of Coercion: Global Report on the ILO Declaration on Fundamental Principles and Rights at Work*, ILO 42–43 (May 12, 2009), http://www.ilo.org/global/topics/forced-labour/publications/WCMS_106268/lang%2D%2Den/index.htm; *The Role of Naptip in the Control of Human Trafficking in Nigeria (2004–2009)*, Kubanni 103, http://kubanni.abu.edu.ng:8080/jspui/bitstream/123456789/1741/1/THE%20ROLE%20OF%20NAPTIP%20IN%20THE%20CONTROL%20OF%20HUMAN%20TRAFFICKING%20IN%20NIGERIA%20%282004-2009%29.pdf.

[91] U.S. Dep't of State, Trafficking in Persons Report 2008: Nigeria (Jun. 2008), https://www.state.gov/j/tip/rls/tiprpt/2008/105388.htm.

[92] *NAPTIP Rescues 12,000, Rehabilitates 6,000, Secures 325 Convictions*, Vanguard Nigeria (Sep. 13, 2017), https://www.vanguardngr.com/2017/09/naptip-rescues-12000-rehabilitates-6000-secures-325-convictions/; Kubanni, *supra* note, at 90.

[93] *Cf. Investigation and Monitoring*, Nat'l. Agency for the Prohibition of Trafficking in Persons, https://www.naptip.gov.ng/?page_id=130.

[94] U.S. Dep't of State, Trafficking in Persons Report 2010: Nigeria (Jun. 2010).

[95] U.S. Dep't of State, Trafficking in Persons Report 2014: Nigeria (Jun. 2014).

[96] Salah (2001).

To end this chapter, it is worth considering how the three branches of international law, namely international criminal law, international human rights law, and transnational criminal law, are interdependent and mutually reinforcing in combating trafficking in persons and other criminal acts.[97] For instance, Obokata pointed out that

> the common obligations imposed by all three branches of international law are prohibition of the offence and punishment of traffickers. The obligations jointly imposed by international criminal law include, but are not limited to, protection of the rights of the defendants, while the obligation to address the causes and the consequences of trafficking is imposed by international human rights law as represented by the Trafficking Protocol. Finally, an example of an obligation common to international criminal law and transnational criminal law is mutual legal assistance or international cooperation.[98]

In summary, the possibilities for African law enforcement cooperation and partnerships offer significant advantages for tackling modern slavery.

## List of Cases/Documents

Trafficking in persons: Enhancing Criminal Investigation, Prosecution and Victim/witness Protection in African and European Countries, Africa-EU Partnership Working Group (Dec. 1, 2011), http://www.africa-eu-partnership.org/sites/default/files/documents/mme_tip_proposed_working_methodology_en_0.pdf.; United Nations Protocol to Prevent, Suppress and Punish Trafficking in Persons, Especially Women and Children, supplementing the United Nations Convention against Transnational Organized Crime, G.A. Res. 55/25, U.N. Doc. A/45/49 (Vol. I) (2001) art. 16 (10).; *Id.* at 193–241; UNODC Toolkit, *supra* note 73, at 119–172; OHCHR, *Commentary on the Recommended Principles and Guidelines*, (2010) *supra* note 68, at 203–212.

*APDF & IHRDA v. Republic of Mali, AfCHPR 15, No. 046/2016 (20180).*

*Chowdury and Others v. Greece*, European Court of Human Rights, Application No. 21884/15, Judgment ¶ 124 ¶ 73 (30 Mar. 2017), https://www.unipa.it/scuole/scienzegiur.ecosociali/specializzazioni/professionilegali/.content/documenti/Scaduto-Chowdury-c-Grecia.pdf.

*Chowdury and Others v. Greece*, note 15 at ¶¶110–115

*Claudia Ivette Gonzales and Others v Mexico*, Inter-American Court of Human Rights, Series C No 205, Judgment, ¶ 284 (15 November 2009).

Committee on the Elimination of Discrimination against Women, Eleventh Session, General Recommendation No. 19: Violence Against Women, art. 9 (1989).

[97] Obokata (2006), pp. 377, 402.

[98] *Ibid.* 399–400.

*Draft Articles on Responsibility of States for Internationally Wrongful Acts*, as contained in *Report of the International Law Commission on the Work of its 53rd Session*, UN Doc A/55/10 (2000) Art.2.

*E. and Others v. the United Kingdom*, European Court of Human Rights, App. No. 33218/96, Judgment, ¶ 99 (26 November 2002).

*ECOWAS Common Approach on Migration*, ECOWAS Comm. (Jan. 18, 2008), https://www.unhcr.org/49e47c8f11.pdf.

ECOWAS Convention on Extradition (A/P1/8/94), adopted on 6 August 1994, entered into force December 8, 2005 http://documentation.ecowas.int/download/en/legal_documents/protocols/Convention%20on%20Extradition.pdf.

ECOWAS Convention on Mutual Assistance in Criminal Matters (A/P1/7/92), adopted on 29 July 1992, entered into force on 28 October 1998, 2329 UNTS 301 (ECOWAS Convention). http://documentation.ecowas.int/download/en/legal_documents/protocols/Convention%20on%20Mutual%20Assistance%20in%20Criminal%20Matters.pdf

*ECOWAS Convention on Mutual Assistance in Criminal Matters*, Articles 18–19.

*Fact Sheet on the U.S.-UK Extradition Treaty*, U.S. Embassies and Consulates in the U.K. (Nov. 16 2011), https://uk.usembassy.gov/our-relationship/policy-history/the-u-s-uk-extradition-treaty/fact-sheet-on-the-u-s-uk-extradition-treaty/;

Francois Xavier Damiba and Laurent Nare, Proverbes Mossi (Abidjan, 1999) (proverb no. 785).

GA Res 48/104, UN GAOR, 48th sess, 85th plen mtg, UN Doc A/48/49 (December 20, 1993).

ICCPR Human Rights Comm., General Comment No. 31: The Nature of the General Legal Obligation Imposed on States Parties to the Covenant ¶ 8, U.N. Doc. CCPR/C/21/Rev.1/Add.13 (May 24, 2006).

*Id.*; FMM West Africa, *Counter-Trafficking Baseline Assessment* 19–21 (2017), https://fmmwestafrica.org/wp-content/uploads/2017/08/Report-of-the-ECOWAS-baseline-assessment-on-counter-trafficking.pdf.

*Investigation and Monitoring*, Nat'l. Agency for the Prohibition of Trafficking in Persons, https://www.naptip.gov.ng/?page_id=130.

*Jessica Lenahan v. United States* Inter-American Commission (2011).

*Koraou v. Niger*, ECOWAS Community Court of Justice, Judgment, No. ECW/CCJ/APP/0808, ¶¶ 82–85 (Oct. 27, 2008) (available at: http://www.worldcourts.com/ecowasccj/eng/decisions/2008.10.27_Koraou_v_Niger.htm).

*L.E. v. Greece*, European Court of Human Rights, Application No. 71545/12, Judgment, ¶¶ 70–72 (21 January 2011).

*Legislative Guides for the Implementation of the United Nations Convention against Transnational Organized Crime and the Protocol Thereto*, UNODC 2, at XVI (2004), https://www.unodc.org/pdf/crime/legislative_guides/Legislative%20guides_Full%20version.pdf.

*Legislative Guides for the Implementation of the United Nations Convention against Transnational Organized Crime and the Protocol Thereto*, UNODC 2, ¶ 217 (2004), https://www.unodc.org/pdf/crime/legislative_guides/Legislative%20guides_Full%20version.pdf.

*Mastromatteov v. Italy*, European Court of Human Rights, Judgment, App. No. 37703/97, ¶¶ 178–179.
*NAPTIP Rescues 12,000, Rehabilitates 6,000, Secures 325 Convictions*, Vanguard Nigeria (Sep. 13, 2017), https://www.vanguardngr.com/2017/09/naptip-rescues-12000-rehabilitates-6000-secures-325-convictions/.
*O'Keefee v. Ireland* [GC] App no. 35819/09 (ECtHR, January 28, 2014) ¶144
*O'Keefee v. Ireland*, [GC] App. No. 35810/09, 28 January 2014, para. 149; see also *Salakhov and Islyamova v. Ukraine*, App. 28005/08, 14 March 2013, ¶181.
OHCHR, Recommended Principles and Guidelines on Human Rights and Human Trafficking, Recommended Principles on Human Rights and Human Trafficking, principle 14
*Opuz v Turkey* (App no 33401/02) ECHR 9 June 2009.
Organized Crime Convention, Article 16. Legislative Guide to the Organized Crime Convention and its Protocols, Part I, ¶¶403, 414–417.
Petya Nestorova, Executive Secretary, Secretariat of the Council of Europe Convention against Trafficking in Human Beings (GRETA and Committee of the Parties), CoE, Understanding human trafficking in the private economy-forms, industries and sectors involved, latest trends and responsibility of the private sector Conference "The Public-Private Partnership in the Fight against Human Trafficking" (Moscow, July 20–21, 2017).
*Rantsev v. Cyprus and Russia*, No. 25965/04, ECtHR, ¶204 (January 7, 2010) https://ec.europa.eu/anti-trafficking/sites/antitrafficking/files/rantsev_vs_russia_cyprus_en_4.pdf.
*Rantsev v. Cyprus and Russia*, No. 25965/04, ECtHR, ¶203 (January 7, 2010) https://ec.europa.eu/anti-trafficking/sites/antitrafficking/files/rantsev_vs_russia_cyprus_en_4.pdf.
Responsibility of States for Internationally Wrongful Acts 2001, Article 15, United Nations (2005).
*State Responsibilities to Regulate and Adjudicate Corporate Activities Corporate Activities under the United Nations' core Human Rights Treaties*, OHCR, 3 (June 2007) https://www.business-humanrights.org/sites/default/files/reports-and-materials/Ruggie-ICCPR-Jun-2007.pdf
*State Responsibility*, A/CN.4/490 and Add. 1–7, 27(1998) (James Crawford, First report on State responsibility) http://legal.un.org/ilc/documentation/english/a_cn4_490.pdf.
*The Cost of Coercion: Global Report on the ILO Declaration on Fundamental Principles and Rights at Work*, ILO 42–43 (May 12, 2009), http://www.ilo.org/global/topics/forced-labour/publications/WCMS_106268/lang%2D%2Den/index.htm.
*The Impact of Free Movement and the Challenges of Migration*, Migr. Dialogue for W. Afr. (MIDWA) (Aug. 23, 2016), https://www.iom.int/sites/default/files/our_work/ICP/RCP/2016/MIDWA-2016-Ministerial-and-Experts-Meeting-Concept-Note.pdf.
*The Role of Naptip in the Control of Human Trafficking in Nigeria (2004–2009)*, Kubanni 103, http://kubanni.abu.edu.ng:8080/jspui/bitstream/123456789/1741/

1/THE%20ROLE%20OF%20NAPTIP%20IN%20THE%20CONTROL%20OF%20HUMAN%20TRAFFICKING%20IN%20NIGERIA%20%282004-2009%29.pdf.

*Thematic Meeting on Trafficking in Human Beings and the Smuggling of Migrants*, Int'l Ctr. Migr. 10 (Dec. 3, 2015), https://www.rabat-process.org/images/RabatProcess/Documents/summary-debates-conclusions-thematic-meeting-porto-december-2015-trafficking-smuggling-rabat-process.pdf.

*Trafficking in persons: Enhancing Criminal Investigation, Prosecution and Victim/witness Protection in African and European Countries*, Africa-EU Partnership Working Group (Dec. 1, 2011), http://www.africa-eu-partnership.org/sites/default/files/documents/mme_tip_proposed_working_methodology_en_0.pdf.

*Training for TIP Nat'l Focal Points*, Int'l Training Ctr. of the Int'l Lab. Org., http://www.ilo.org/wcmsp5/groups/public/%2D%2D-africa/documents/publication/wcms_348047.pdf.

U.N. Action for Cooperation Against Trafficking in Persons, *Summary of Regional and Sub-Regional Structures and Initiatives to Counter Trafficking in Persons* 4–5 (Dec. 2010), http://un-act.org/publication/view/summary-of-regional-and-sub-regional-structures-and-initiatives-to-counter-trafficking-in-persons-december-2010/ [hereinafter *Summary of Regional and Sub-Regional Structures*].

U.N. High Commissioner for Human Rights, Draft Compendium of Trafficking-Related Tools Developed at the Regional Level, at 39, http://www.ohchr.org/Documents/Issues/Trafficking/Dakar_draft_compendium_en.pdf.

U.N. Ofc. on Drugs and Crime ("UNODC"), *Regional Strategy for Combating Trafficking in Persons and Smuggling of Migrants 2015–2020*, https://www.unodc.org/documents/westandcentralafrica/UNODC_Regional_Strategy_for_Combating_TIP_SOM_West_and_Central_Africa_2015-2020.pdf.

U.S. Dep't of Just., U.S. Attorneys' Manual § 9–15.000 (Apr. 2018), https://www.justice.gov/usam/usam-9-15000-international-extradition-and-related-matters.

U.S. Dep't of State, Trafficking in Persons Report 2008: Nigeria (Jun. 2008) https://www.state.gov/j/tip/rls/tiprpt/2008/105388.htm.

U.S. Dep't of State, Trafficking in Persons Report 2008: Nigeria (Jun. 2008), https://www.state.gov/j/tip/rls/tiprpt/2008/105388.htm.

U.S. Dep't of State, Trafficking in Persons Report 2010: Ghana (Jun. 2010), https://www.state.gov/j/tip/rls/tiprpt/2010/142760.htm.

U.S. Dep't of State, Trafficking in Persons Report 2010: Nigeria (Jun. 2010).

U.S. Dep't of State, Trafficking in Persons Report 2014: Nigeria (Jun. 2014).

United Nations High Commissioner for Human Rights Principles and Guidelines on Human Rights and Trafficking, E/2002/68/Add.1 (2002), principle.2

*Velasquez Rodriguez v. Honduras*, Inter-American Court of Human Rights, Judgment, Rep. No. 4 (Ser. C) ¶ 172 (29 July 1988).

Yearbook of the International Law Commission, Vol. II, ¶ 66 (c), U.N. Doc. A/8010/Rev.l (1970) (accessed from: https://legal.un.org/ilc/publications/yearbooks/english/ilc_1970_v2.pdf).

## References


Chirwa DM (2004) The doctrine of state responsibility as a potential means of holding private actors accountable for human rights. Melbourne J Int Law 5:17–18. https://law.unimelb.edu.au/__data/assets/pdf_file/0005/1680422/Chirwa.pdf

Danso SO (2013) The human being as a commodity: responding to the trafficking and trading of persons in West Africa, Kofi Annan Peacekeeping Training Centre, September 2013. http://www.kaiptc.org/kaiptc-publication/the-human-being-as-a-commodity-responding-to-the-trafficking-and-trading-of-persons-in-west-africa

ECOWAS (2001) Declaration on the fight against trafficking in persons. http://www.achpr.org/files/instruments/ecowas-declaration-against-trafficking-persons/ecowas_declaration_against_trafficking_persons.pdf

ECOWAS Convention on Extradition (1994) Article 2. The Protocol of 2005 provided for the establishment of a regional Criminal Intelligence and Investigation Bureau (CIIB) for the West African region

Global Alliance Against Traffic in Women (GAATW) (2017) Facilitating migration and fulfilling rights – to reduce smuggling of migrants and prevent trafficking in persons, 5. https://refugeesmigrants.un.org/sites/default/files/ts5_gaatw.pdf

Hafen JO (1992) International extradition: issues arising under the dual criminality requirement. BYU Law Rev 1:191

Hassan YB, Kigbu SK (2015) An assessment of the institutional framework for combating human trafficking in Nigeria. J Law Policy Glob 39:249. https://core.ac.uk/download/pdf/234650248.pdf

Ikeora MN (2010) Interstate cooperation and anti-trafficking: assessing existing approaches between Nigeria and the United Kingdom 107. https://hydra.hull.ac.uk/assets/hull:8602a/content

Cohen J (2003) Borderline slavery—child trafficking in Togo. Hum Rts Watch 15:819. http://www.hrw.org/sites/default/files/reports/togo0403.pdf

Kahombo B (2010) Judicial cooperation in criminal matters based on the ECCAS, COMESA and SADC Treaties. Afr Law Stud Libr 5:1, 2. http://www.kas.de/wf/doc/kas_20449-544-2-30.pdf?110221054310

Lutenco A (2012) The extend of state obligations in preventing and combating trafficking in human beings: challenges and perspectives for a European human rights-based approach, pp 29–33 (unpublished LL.M., Central European University) (on file in Central European University at: https://eige.europa.eu/docs/54_HU.pdf)

Mattar MY (2005) State responsibilities in combating trafficking in persons in Central Asia. Loy L A Int Comp Law Rev 27:145, 170

Obokata T (2006) A human rights framework to address trafficking of human beings. Neth Q Hum Rights 24(3)

OHCHR (2010) Commentary on the recommended principles and guidelines, 203

OHCHR (2014) Human rights and human trafficking, Fact Sheet No. 36, 11. https://www.ohchr.org/Documents/Publications/FS36_en.pdf

Olson LM (2009) Practical challenges of implementing the complementarity between international humanitarian and human rights law – demonstrated by the procedural regulation of internment in non-international armed conflict. Case West Res J Int Law 40:437, 450. https://scholarlycommons.law.case.edu/jil/vol40/iss3/5

Piotrowicz R (2009) The legal nature of trafficking in human beings. Intercult Hum Rights Law 4: 175, 193

*Rantsev v. Cyprus and Russia*, European Court of Human Rights, Judgment, Application No. 25965/04 (7 January 2010) (available at: https://ec.europa.eu/anti-trafficking/rantsev-v-cyprus-and-russia-application-no-2596504_en)

Rodley N (1993) Can armed opposition groups violate human rights? In: Mahoney KE, Mahoney P (eds) Human rights in the twenty-first century: a global challenge. Martinus Nijhoff, Dordrecht, pp 297–318

Salah R (2001) Child trafficking in West and Central Africa: an overview. UNICEF 6-7, 19 February 2001. http://www.unicef.org/media/newsnotes/africchildtraffick.pdf

Schabas W (2003) Punishment of non-state actors in non-international armed conflict. Fordham Int Law J 26:908–909

*Siliadin v. France*, European Court of Human Rights, Application No. 73316/01, Judgment (2005)

Stoyanova V (2017) Human trafficking and slavery reconsidered: conceptual limits and state's positive obligations in European law. CUP

Szablewska N (2007) Non-state actors and human rights in non-international armed conflicts. S Afr Yearb Int Law 32:346

Talmon S (2019) The procedural obligation under Article 2 ECHR to investigate and cooperate with investigations of unlawful killings in a cross-border context. Hum Rights Int Law 13:99

UN GAOR (1995) The Beijing Declaration and Platform for Action adopted by the Beijing Fourth World Conference on Women reaffirmed this principle: Report of the Fourth World Conference on Women, Annex I, UN Doc. A/CONF.177/20/Rev.1

United Nations General Assembly (1966) International Covenant on Civil and Political Rights, Treaty Series 999 (December 1966), p 171

UNODC (2006) Training manual: assistance for the implementation of the ECOWAS plan of action against trafficking in persons, at V. https://www.unodc.org/documents/human-trafficking/ecowas_training_manual_2006.pdf

UNODC (2008a) Toolkit to combat trafficking in persons, U.N. Sales No. E.08.V.14, 171–173. https://www.unodc.org/documents/human-trafficking/Toolkit-files/08-58296_tool_9-12.pdf

UNODC (2008b) Toolkit to combat trafficking in persons, U.N. Sales No. E.08.V.14. https://www.unodc.org/documents/human-trafficking/Toolkit-files/08-58296_tool_2-10.pdf

# Chapter 9
# Implementation of Human Rights Obligations in Conjunction with the Palermo Protocol

National laws play a significant role in controlling trafficking in persons as "international legal instruments depend on national level criminalization and enforcement, as well as national [. . .] policies to ensure the provision of basic services and protections of victims."[1] Accordingly, individual Economic Community of West African States (ECOWAS) countries have signed and ratified several international human rights treaties, including the Palermo Protocol; by ratifying these agreements, they have given "consent to be bound" by the treaties and to undertake legal duties to respect, protect, and fulfil human rights. The purpose of this chapter is to present analysis of the international Anti-trafficking framework enforced upon West African states to fight this crime. Upon ratification, states commit to implementing these obligations into their national domestic laws and to ensure that their policies or practices protect the rights enshrined in the treaty. Consequently, states can be held accountable under international law for any action or omission "that leads to a human rights abuse either directly or indirectly through a failure to investigate and apply the rule of law in a situation where a person or persons' rights have been compromised."[2]

This discussion examines the three core obligations, also known as the "3 P" paradigm (Prosecution, Protection and Prevention), arising from the United Nations (UN) Trafficking Protocol. These can be further broken down into the obligation to criminalize trafficking in persons, the obligation to investigate and prosecute trafficking with due diligence, the protection of and assistance given to victims of trafficking, the prevention of human trafficking by addressing its root causes, and international cooperation to implement these duties.

---

[1] Lloyd and Simmons (2015), p. 408.

[2] Budiani-Saberi and Columb (2013), p. 11.



P. VI. S. Karenga, *A West African Model to Address Human Trafficking*,
https://doi.org/10.1007/978-3-030-88120-7_9

## 9.1 Criminalization of Trafficking and Perpetrators' Criminal Liability

Article 5 of the Trafficking Protocol imposes upon states the obligation to criminalize trafficking, its component acts, and related offenses.[3] To assist states in implementing its provisions, the UNODC Model Law against Trafficking in Persons states that while establishing criminal provisions related to trafficking in persons it is essential "to ensure that national legislation adequately criminalizes participation in an organized criminal group (Convention, article 5); laundering of the proceeds of crime (article 6); corruption (article 8); and obstruction of justice (article 23). In addition, measures to establish the liability of legal persons must be adopted (article 10)."[4]

Another obligation associated with the development of legal frameworks is the provision of resources and training to enable frontline officers to enforce the law. Accordingly, Article 10(2) of the Palermo Protocol imposes upon states the duty to "provide or strengthen training for law enforcement, immigration and other relevant officials in the prevention of trafficking in persons."[5] The Guidelines on Human Rights and Trafficking further explain that states should provide law enforcement authorities such as police, border guards, and immigration officials, and adequate techniques to facilitate the effective investigation and prosecution of suspected traffickers.[6] In its concluding observations regarding Ghana's compliance with the Convention on the Protection of the Rights of All Migrant Workers and Members of Their Families, the Committee urged the State Party to:

> Increase its efforts to enforce the Human Trafficking Act, the Immigration Amendment Act and its regulations, allocate sufficient resources to implementing strategies to combat trafficking in persons and counter human smuggling and other irregular migration, and build capacity of border guards, law enforcement officials, judges, prosecutors, labour inspectors, teachers and other social service providers on the existing legal framework and

---

[3]United Nations High Commissioner for Human Rights Principles and Guidelines on Human Rights and Trafficking, E/2002/68/Add.1 (2002), principle. 12.

[4]UNODC, Model Law against Trafficking in Persons, p. 23 https://www.unodc.org/documents/human-trafficking/UNODC_Model_Law_on_Trafficking_in_Persons.pdf; *see also* Human Rights and Human Trafficking, OHCCHR, Fact Sheet No. 36, p. 34; United Nations High Commissioner For Human Rights Principles and Guidelines on Human Rights and Trafficking, E/2002/68/Add.1 (2002), Guideline 4: Ensuring an adequate legal framework.

[5]Convention Against Transnational Organized Crime, Protocol to Prevent, Suppress and Punish trafficking in Persons, Especially Women and Children, done Nov. 15, 2000, T.I.A.S.13127, Article 10(2).

[6]United Nations High Commissioner for Human Rights Principles and Guidelines on Human Rights and Trafficking, E/2002/68/Add.1 (2002), Guideline 5: Ensuring an adequate law enforcement response.

its implementation regarding both trafficking in persons, and human smuggling as well as other irregular migration.[7]

Given that, under international rights law, trafficking in persons is "defined as both a criminal offence and as a human rights violation, [...] States parties are required to address the phenomenon not only from a criminal justice framework but one that respects, protects and fulfills its obligations to uphold the human rights of persons who are most vulnerable to trafficking: its victims and its survivors."[8] A review of the relevant provisions of ECOWAS domestic legislation related to trafficking in persons reveals three typologies, both in terms of the prosecution of traffickers and the protection and reintegration of trafficked victims.[9]

The first legislative model expanded an existing broad legislative tool to include all forms of trafficking, including adults and the removal of organs. Ghana's Human Trafficking Act (Act 694) of 2005 and Nigeria's 2003 anti-trafficking law are representative of this group in terms of legislation;[10] where the law specifically criminalizes trafficking and related conduct and subjects individuals to harsher punishments.[11]

The second legislative model addresses child trafficking and comprises primarily francophone countries such as Togo and Benin. For example, in Togo the trafficking of children is considered "a serious infraction" that is defined "as the process whereby a child is recruited or kidnapped, transported, transferred, housed or accommodated," within the interior of the country or when crossing the border of the national territory "by one or more people with the purpose of exploitation."[12] Exploitation, however, appears to encompass "all activities which provide the child no economic, moral, mental or physical benefit but which by contrast, deliver to the trafficker or other individuals, either directly or indirectly, economic, moral or physical benefits."[13]

Benin's anti-trafficking law was adopted for the protection of minors and thus, criminalizes trafficking in children while excluding adults.[14] Guinean law does not

[7] International Convention on the Protection of the Rights of All Migrant Workers and Members of Their Families, CMW/C/GHA/CO/1 (September 2014) para. 45, https://www.ecoi.net/en/file/local/1114024/1930_1413884691_int-cmw-coc-gha-18155-e.pdf.

[8] Concept Note-CEDAW General Recommendation on Trafficking in Women and Girls in the Context of Global Migration, para. 8.

[9] *Borderline Slavery: Child Trafficking in Togo*, 15 Hum. Rts. Watch 8, 40 (Apr. 2003), https://www.hrw.org/reports/2003/togo0403/togo0403.pdf.

[10] Andrew and Lawrance (2012), p. 17.

[11] For more information, see Hassan and Kigbu (2015), pp. 146, 205.

[12] Official J. of the Togolese Republic, Law No. 2005-009, Chap. II, art. 3 (Aug. 3, 2005), https://www.ilo.org/dyn/natlex/docs/SERIAL/72058/72983/F1981134441/trafic%20enfants.pdf.

[13] *Id.*, art. 4.

[14] Law No. 2006-04 on the conditions of transportation of minors and the repression of child trafficking in Benin (Loi No. 2006-04 portant conditions de déplacement des mineurs et répression de la traite des enfants en République du Bénin), https://www.warnathgroup.com/wp-content/uploads/2015/03/Benin-Child-TIP-Law-French.pdf.

criminalize forms of trafficking such as debt bondage which are prohibited in the Palermo Protocol.[15] As a result, there are people living in trafficking situations in these countries who, according to the international standards, "may not be considered as trafficking victims by the national authorities as these are using legal definitions not in line with the United Nations (UN) Trafficking in Persons Protocol."[16]

Finally, the third typology is predicated on the idea that existing laws provide adequate legislative remedy and that trafficking in persons can be addressed through enhancements of existing instruments.[17] This group comprises only a few nations, the number of which is continuing to dwindle. For example, in the Ivory Coast,[18] where proper legislation is lacking, instances of trafficking are prosecuted by leveraging various provisions of laws relating to slavery, forced labor, pimping, or child stealing rather than as separate comprehensive acts. "For example, Côte d'Ivoire's Penal Code prohibits forced labor (Article 378), entering into contracts that deny freedom to a third person (Art. 376), and recruiting or offering children for prostitution (Art. 335–337), all with imprisonment and fines."[19] Because the function of criminal law is to define crimes and determine punishments, it is highly unlikely that these instruments are tailored to protect women and children or address the issue of victim assistance.

Although West African countries now recognize the crime of trafficking as an independent criminal offense and have been taking necessary measures to address it, the US Department of State has found that the sanctions for traffickers are not commensurate with the gravity of the acts committed.[20] Indeed, in Benin, the penal code and the labor law regarding trafficking into prostitution or use of forced labor provide for penalties ranging from a minimum of 2 months to a maximum of 2 years imprisonment or fines. However, none of these sentences are sufficiently stringent or commensurate with penalties incurred for other serious crimes, such as rape.[21] Similarly, Law No. 11-2014/AN criminalizes "child prostitution" and a wide range of "sale of minors" in Burkina Faso. Even though the prescribed penalties of 5–10 years imprisonment and/or a fine of 1.5–3 million FCFA (US$2399–4799) are sufficiently harsh, they are not commensurate with sentences for other serious crimes

[15] Guinea Penal Code 2016 (Article 323) https://www.warnathgroup.com/wp-content/uploads/2017/10/Guinea-Law-on-the-Criminal-Code-2016-Fra.pdf.

[16] UNODC, *Global Rep. on Trafficking in Persons 2014*, at 52 (Nov. 2014), https://www.unodc.org/documents/data-and-analysis/glotip/GLOTIP_2014_full_report.pdf.

[17] Andrew and Lawrance (2012), p. 15.

[18] U.S. Department of State TIP report in 2016 observed that draft legislation to define and criminalize the trafficking of adults and children in the Ivory Coast was pending ratification for the second year.

[19] Andrew and Lawrance (2012), p. 23.

[20] UNODC, *supra* note 16 at 51–52; Mattar (2006), p. 6.

[21] *Trafficking in Persons Report 2017*, U.S. Dep't of State (Jun. 2017), https://www.state.gov/documents/organization/271339.pdf.

when allowing for a fine in lieu of imprisonment.[22] Consequently, the failure of Economic Community of West African States (ECOWAS) to enact specific anti-trafficking legislation that imposes serious penalties on trafficking offenders constitutes a violation of the international obligations of states that are enshrined in the United Nations (UN) Protocol.

Additionally, laws and policies that institutionalize discrimination can also shape demand as a failure on the part of the state to effectively challenge discriminatory social attitudes, practices and beliefs. For instance, for decades the wives of West African customary law marriages and the daughters of such wedlock have had to contend with various oppressive, degrading, and discriminatory cultural practices, including cultural approval of "wife battery or chastisement; wife inheritance; harmful widowhood practices; payment and refund of bride-price; marginalization of women's right in the event of dissolution of customary law marriages, female disinheritance, female gender mutilation, female trafficking and Son-preference syndrome and the polygamous nature of customary law marriages, etc."[23]

These appear to be so deeply rooted in the West African cultural system that they persist despite the global upsurge in feminist jurisprudence; the most worrying aspect of this social issue is that obnoxious cultural practices such as wife battery have also been legalized in Nigerian statute books. For instance, Section 55 (1) (b) of the Nigerian Penal Code permits wife chastisement if native law or custom recognizes such "correction" as lawful and as long as it does not cause grievous bodily injuries.[24] This provision, which creates a fertile ground for violence against women, was regrettably given judicial approval in the Nigerian Court of Appeal in the *Akinbuwa v. Akinbuwa* case. Not only does the Court's decision fail to confer the corresponding right to the wife to chastise the husband, it also perpetuates gender violence and an acceptance that women have been raised to be whipped and indecently assaulted; women in Nigeria are therefore very fearful and ashamed when it comes enforcing their rights.[25]

Another factor that affects the outcome of legislation designed to address trafficking in persons concerns the political decisions made after a law is adopted. In Ghana, the domestic violence legislation was adopted in 2007; however, the

---

[22] *Id.*

[23] Ifemeje and Umejiaku (2014), p. 18; *see Africa for Women's Rights: Burkina Faso*, Wikigender (2005), http://www.wikigender.org/wiki/africa-for-womens-rights-burkina-faso/; *see generally Discrimination Against Older Women in Burkina Faso*, Convention on the Elimination of all Forms of Discrimination Against Women (CEDAW) (Jul. 2010), http://www2.ohchr.org/english/bodies/cedaw/docs/ngos/JointNGOReport_BurkinaFaso47.pdf.

[24] Penal Code (2004) Cap. (C3) §55 (Nigeria); *see Africa for Women's Rights: Senegal*, Wikigender (2015), http://www.wikigender.org/wiki/africa-for-womens-rights-senegal/; *see generally Women, Inheritance and Islam in Mali*, Agriknowledge.org (Feb. 2011), https://agriknowledge.org/downloads/kd17cs934; *see also Violence against Women in Mali: A Report to the Human Rights Committee*, World Organization Against Torture (OMCT) (2003) http://www.omct.org/files/2004/07/2409/eng_2003_07_mali.pdf.

[25] *Akinbuwa v. Akinbuwa* [1998] 7 NWLR 559, 780 (Nigeria).

implementation of the policy has been "blocked through government failure to introduce the necessary legislative instrument that will ensure the full implementation of the law."[26] The government argued that marital rape is a foreign phenomenon that would break up a large number of Ghanaian marriages if included and passed in the bill of women's rights.[27]

The considerations discussed show that ECOWAS' domestic legal frameworks only criminalize certain aspects of trafficking and therefore fail to fulfil their duty and obligations under the Palermo Protocol. According to the Protocol, the state's positive obligations entail not only a duty to adopt domestic criminal laws that prohibit and penalize trafficking and related conduct but also to ensure that the criminal law framework is enforced, thus leading to effective investigation, prosecution, and punishment with penalties proportionate to the severity of the offense.[28] Inconsistencies between national definitions and the Palermo Protocol leave a substantial number of trafficking victims unidentified and unprotected. In practice, there has also been a tendency in Courts to consider trafficking for forced labor a lesser offense and to single out trafficking for sexual purpose and slavery as the most severe.[29] In so doing, the state becomes responsible under international as well as national law for any form of human rights violations due to tolerance, passivity, omission, and abstention with regard to practice of trafficking.[30]

Finally, one of the purposes of passing legislation is to bring enduring social change in cultural practices that infringe on human rights. Unfortunately, anti-trafficking laws have thus far failed to make significant strides in curbing the issue of trafficking in persons in West Africa. Nonetheless, examples indicate that the Catholic Church plays an essential role in transforming society; because of its engagement and understanding of the culture, the Church is able to win an increasing number of y new converts and change cultural structures when addressing practices related to trafficking in persons.

---

[26] Evidence and Lessons from Latin America, Domestic Violence Laws: What Else Makes Responses to Domestic Violence Effective 6 [May 2015] http://ella.practicalaction.org/wp-content/uploads/files/Beyond%20Domestic%20Violence%20Bills_1.pdf.

[27] *Id.*

[28] Duffy (2016), pp. 375, 376.

[29] Nat'l Agency for the Prohibition of Trafficking in Persons, First Quarter Report 2017 7–8 (2017), https://www.naptip.gov.ng/wp-content/uploads/2017/05/2017-First-Quarter-Report-Modified-1.pdf; Nat'l Agency for the Prohibition of Trafficking in Persons, Data Analysis Report 2016 10–14 (2016), https://www.naptip.gov.ng/wp-content/uploads/2017/05/2016-Data-Analysis-1.pdf.

[30] *Koraou v. Niger*, ECOWAS Community Court of Justice, Judgment, No. ECW/CCJ/APP/0808, ¶85 (Oct. 27, 2008) (available at: http://www.worldcourts.com/ecowasccj/eng/decisions/2008.10.27_Koraou_v_Niger.htm.); Piotrowicz (2012), p. 182.

## 9.2 Investigating Cases of Trafficking in Persons and Prosecuting Offenders

Another legal obligation imposed upon states under international human rights laws is the responsibility to act with "due diligence" to investigate and prosecute traffickers.[31] The Inter-American Court of Human Rights made the following comments on this duty in the *Velasquez v. Honduras* case:

> The State is obligated to investigate every situation involving a violation of the rights protected by the Convention. If the State apparatus acts in such a way that the violation goes unpunished and the victim's full enjoyment of such rights is not restored as soon as possible, the State has failed to comply with its duty to ensure the free and full exercise of those rights to the persons within its jurisdiction. The same is true when the State allows private persons or groups to act freely and with impunity to the detriment of the rights recognized by the Convention.[32]

Similarly, in the *Rantsev v. Cyprus and Russia* case the European Court of Human Rights elucidated the positive obligations upon states to ensure effective investigation of alleged situations of trafficking and to implement preventive measures to protect people in such situations. In light of the facts of this case, the Court found that Cyprus had violated its obligations under Article 2 of the Convention as it had failed to conduct an effective investigation into the circumstances of Ms Rantseva's death.[33]

The obligation to investigate and prosecute is designed to punish and incapacitate those responsible for trafficking in human beings and to protect victims from harm. The main criticism that emerged following a review of criminal justice activities in Economic Community of West African States (ECOWAS) is that crimes of trafficking are significantly under-prosecuted due to the shortcomings of the law and countries' limited commitment to punishing traffickers and protecting trafficking victims.[34] During the 2014 annual review meeting on the implementation of the

---

[31] United Nations High Commissioner for Human Rights Principles and Guidelines on Human Rights and Trafficking, *Recommended Principles On Human Rights And Human Trafficking*, E/2002/68/Add.1 (2002).

[32] *Velasquez Rodriguez v. Honduras*, Inter-American Court of Human Rights, Judgment, Rep. No. 4 (Ser. C) ¶ 176 (29 July 1988); *see also Ergi v. Turkey*, European Court of Human Rights, Judgment, Application No. 23818/94 (28 July 1998); *Osman v. United Kingdom*, European Court of Human Rights, Judgment, Application No. 23452/94 (28 October 1998); *Z and Others v. United Kingdom*, European Court of Human Rights, Judgment, Application No. 29392/95 (10 May 2001).

[33] *Rantsev v. Cyprus and Russia*, No. 25965/04, ECtHR, ¶ 242 (January 7, 2010) https://ec.europa.eu/anti-trafficking/sites/antitrafficking/files/rantsev_vs_russia_cyprus_en_4.pdf.

[34] Roujanavong (2012), pp. 146–147. Wanchai Roujanavong's experience as a prosecutor sheds light on the difficulties involved in prosecuting trafficking crime and helps illuminate the problem. He described the challenges of handling trafficking cases as follows: "I found that handling a human trafficking case is much more difficult than handling a drug trafficking one for many reasons. In a drug trafficking case, the most important piece of evidence is the narcotic drug, which never changes its characteristics during arrest, investigation, prosecution, or trial. All that is needed is to send the seized drug for lab testing to prove that it is a narcotic drug. The drug does not need food,

Economic Community of West African States (ECOWAS) TIP plan of action, 546 prosecutions for the offense of trafficking in persons were reported by member states for the years 2012–2013.[35] The criminal justice response in (ECOWAS) shows that, among the countries considered in the US Department TIP report in 2016, only Nigeria reported more than 20 convictions for trafficking in persons. Of the remaining 15 countries, 10 did not report a single conviction while the other five registered fewer than 10 convictions during the year.[36] Although there may be many reasons for this low prosecution rate of, they nevertheless show that combating trafficking is not a high priority in the agendas of West African governments. Sub-Saharan Africa appears to be the region where most countries report 0–10 convictions per year with a few reporting 11 or more, whereas countries in Western and Central Europe and in the Americas tend to record high number of convictions.[37] This is illustrated in the chart (Fig. 9.1).

Experience has shown that prosecutors and law enforcement officials face several challenges[38] in interpreting trafficking laws. Indeed, legal qualification of the facts of a case in trafficking for labor exploitation can be difficult for judicial Courts. When, for example, "law enforcement agencies seek to prosecute offenses, which may not (yet) have taken place, such as an attempt at trafficking, often a particularly strong

---

clothes, shelter, physical and medical care, and other human necessities. What it needs is only a small space in a safe place, and it can stay dormant for years awaiting trial. When the trial dates arrive, the prosecutor presents the drug in front of the judge as evidence together with the report of the lab test. The drugs never deny being drugs, and the drug traffickers are severely convicted due to clear evidence.

Handling a human trafficking case is much more difficult. First of all, the officials must try their best to gain the trust of the victims to reveal their true story. Beyond revealing their experience, the officials also have to convince and encourage the victims to cooperate with them in investigation, prosecution, and trial. The officials have to provide food, shelter, clothes, physical and medical care, protect their safety, and provide for many other human needs. As humans, they cannot patiently stay for years in a shelter, inactive, awaiting trial. They or their families might be threatened or bribed by the traffickers or their networks. Some victims might disappear or change their story during the trial."

[35] *Training for TIP Nat'l Focal Points*, Int'l Training Ctr. of the Int'l Lab. Org., http://www.ilo.org/wcmsp5/groups/public/%2D%2D-africa/documents/publication/wcms_348047.pdf.

[36] The government reported 123 investigations and 59 convictions of traffickers, an increase from 103 investigations and 40 convictions in 2014. It is unclear how many of these cases actually involved trafficking charges as the government was unable to provide details. In Nigeria, NAPTIP conducted 507 trafficking investigations, completed at least 32 prosecutions, and secured 24 convictions during the reporting period. Senegal secured 1 conviction. Burkina Faso prosecuted 16 cases and convicted 9 traffickers. Ghana reported 238 potential victims of trafficking without any convictions. Benin registered 131 potential victims and convicted 4 traffickers.

[37] UNODC (2016a), pp. 51–52.

[38] Farrell et al. (2014), pp. 132, 142.

These challenges include: "uncertainty over the elements necessary to prove coercion; whether the federal law requires proof of all three elements of force, fraud, and coercion; and whether cases where children were commercially sexually exploited in the absence of a 'third party' (commonly interpreted as a pimp/trafficker) could be prosecuted by holding purchasers/exploiters accountable as third parties or as 'obtainers'."

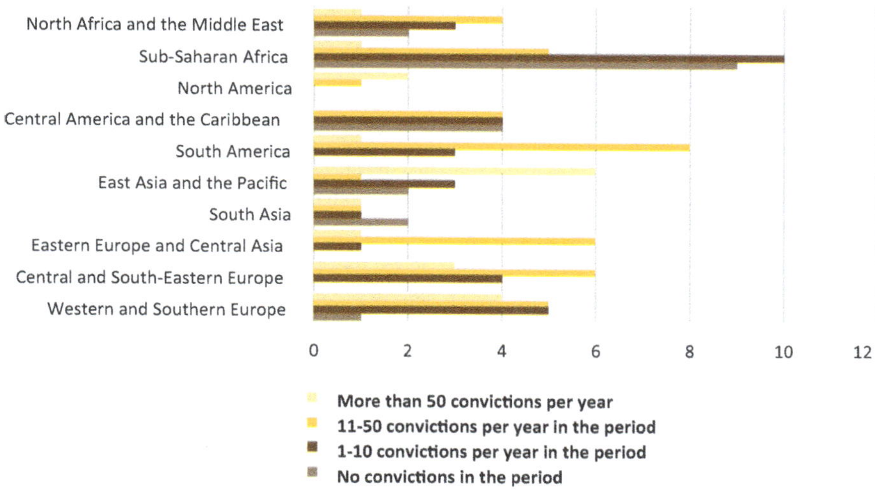


**Fig. 9.1** Number of countries reporting trafficking convictions by region and number of convictions, 2012–2014 (Source: UNODC elaboration of national data. At https://www.unodc.org/documents/data-and-analysis/glotip/2016_Global_Report_on_Trafficking_in_Persons.pdf, p. 52)

evidential base is needed to secure a conviction."[39] The difficulty that arises is that of proving that someone has 'attempted to exploit' a victim. In the case of the *Attorney-General of the Federation v. Sarah Okoya*, the accused induced six girls to travel with her to Cotonou in the Republic of Benin with the promise of flying to Spain where they would work for her as hair dressers and shop-assistants.[40] She collected various sums of money from them, supposedly to secure travel documents and flight tickets, and took them to a traditional shrine to swear allegiance and faithfulness to their "Madam" upon their arrival at their destination. In Cotonou, however, the accused stationed the girls in a hotel and informed them that they had to prostitute themselves for their sustenance; the girls rebelled against their exploiter and, with the help of the hotel manager, they fled to the Nigerian Embassy in Cotonou. The learned trial judge in this case convicted the accused of offenses charged under Section 19(1) (b) of the Trafficking in Persons Prohibition Act (Kidnapping from guardianship), and found her guilty of attempt to commit offenses charged under Section 15(a) (Procurement of any person for prostitution, pornography) and

[39] *Human Trafficking and Forced Labour Exploitation: Guidance for Legislation and Law Enforcement*, ILO 12 (Apr. 1, 2005), http://digitalcommons.ilr.cornell.edu/cgi/viewcontent.cgi?article=1021&context=forcedlabor.

[40] *Attorney General of the Federation v. Okoya*, Nigeria High Court, Suit No. B/15c/2004, Judgment 4 (2004) (available at: https://www.unodc.org/res/cld/case-law/nga/2004/attorney-general_of_the_federation_v__sarah_okoya_suit_no._b15c2004.html/Attorney-General_of_the_Federation_v._Sarah_Okoya_Suit_No._B15c2004.pdf).

Section 16 (Foreign travel which promotes prostitution) under Section 27(1) of the Act.[41]

According to the Court, in order for

> ... the offence of procuration for prostitution to be complete, the prostitution for which the girls were procured or offered must have taken place. Since the girls repulsed and aborted the prostitution intended by the accused, the accused will only be liable for attempting to procure or use them for the act. She will therefore be liable to conviction for an attempt by virtue of Section 27(1) of the Act.[42]

The outcome of the judgement in this case clearly shows that encouraging the criminalization of an attempt will never actually deter traffickers from trafficking because they will face a lesser sentence. In this case, the trafficked victims only escaped being violated by chance. This also attests to the fact that the conviction rate of offenders remains extremely low and is not commensurate with the gravity of the crime. In 2017, the government of Ghana reported seven convictions using ancillary offenses related t trafficking in persons that resulted in lesser penalties. For instance, "prosecution of a trafficker for the labor exploitation of a 15-year-old boy working on a fishing boat without pay on Lake Volta resulted in a sentence of a fine of 720 cedis ($170)."[43] Traffickers rob victims of their human dignity, violate their right to life, freedom of movement, and their right not to be subjected to degrading treatment at low risks and with exceptionally high profits. Judicial Courts in West Africa handed down punishments in criminal cases that were proportionate to the gravity of the offense committed. A propos West African juridical maxim states that, "Who steals a hen should pay with a donkey."[44]

Concerns have also been expressed that an emphasis on prosecutions in undeveloped criminal justice systems results in poor quality prosecutions that target lower level offenders; unfair and unsafe prosecutions that do not respect basic

---

[41] *Attorney-General of the Federation v. Sarah Okaja*, Suit No. B/15C/2004, 15 (December 15, 2005).

[42] Hassan and Kigbu (2015), pp. 146, 205. *Attorney General of the Federation v. M.A.*, Nigeria High Court, Suit No. B/13c/2004, Judgment (2005) (available at: https://www.unodc.org/cld/case-law-doc/traffickingpersonscrimetype/nga/2005/hon._attorney_general_of_the_federation_v._m.a.html). For a comparative analysis, see *Attorney General of the Federation v. Omoruyi*, case where the defendant was convicted of **an attempted crime** under Section 27 (1) of Trafficking in Persons (Prohibition) Law Enforcement Administration Act 2003. The judge ruled that evidence showed how the defendant obtained money to make the necessary arrangements for foreign travel for the victims. The defendant and victims knew that they were travelling to Italy for prostitution, which did not therefore constitute deceitful inducement. However, because they had not completed the act, only its preparation, the Court convicted the defendant of attempting to commit the offense of organizing foreign travel for prostitution. *Attorney General of the Federation v. Omoruyi*, High Court Edo State of Nigeria, Suit No. B/31c/2004 (2006).

[43] U.S. Dep't of State, Trafficking in Persons Report 2017 (Jun. 2017).

[44] *See generally* Francois Xavier Damiba and Laurent Nare, Proverbes Mossi (Abidjan, 1999) (proverb no 44).

**Table 9.1** Criminal law enforcement efforts related to the worst forms of child labor in Guinea-Bissau 2016 [*2016 Findings on the Worst Forms of Child Labor – Guinea-Bissau*, U.S. Dep't of Labor 4 (Sept. 30, 2017), https://www.dol.gov/sites/default/files/images/ilab/child-labor/Guinea-Bissau2016.pdf]

| Overview of criminal law enforcement | 2015 | 2016 |
|---|---|---|
| Training for investigators | | |
| Initial training for new employees | No (21) | Yes (22) |
| Training on new laws related to the worst forms of child labor | N/A (21) | N/A |
| Refresher courses provided | No (21) | Yes (22) |
| Number of investigations | 1 (23) | 0 (22) |
| Number of violations found | Unknown (21) | 0 (22) |
| Number of prosecutions initiated | 0 (21) | 0 (12) |
| Number of convictions | 0 (21) | 0 (12) |
| Reciprocal referral mechanism exists between criminal authorities and social services | Unknown | No (12) |

standards of criminal justice;[45] and the disproportionate and politically motivated targeting of certain sectors such as sex industry. More generally, the experience in poorer countries "suggests that the drive for prosecutions (largely initiated and perpetuated by the US government through the TIP Report process) is contributing to the miscarriage of justice on a significant scale as countries scramble to prove their commitment to anti-trafficking efforts in a way that will appeal to their assessors."[46] For example, in the 2016 US Department of State TIP report, the Togo "government reported 123 investigations and 59 convictions of traffickers, an increase from 103 investigations and 40 convictions in 2014. It is unclear how many of these cases actually involved trafficking charges, as the government was unable to provide details of the cases."[47]

The US Department of State labor report on Gambia and Guinea-Bissau (see Table 9.1) describes the trend in criminal justice actions across the entire region of West Africa. In 2017, the government of Gambia reported a decreased number of investigations and did not convict a trafficker for the sixth consecutive year. The Guinean embassy in Cairo identified several Guinean women exploited in domestic servitude in Egypt and arrested one of the alleged recruiters in Conakry, although he was later released. In that same year, law enforcement intercepted four groups of

[45] Barchue (2012), p. 6. Reports on Nigeria and Liberia pretrial cases have noted that criminal proceedings last for an unduly period. Detainees spend more than 3 years without being tried or having the opportunity to see a lawyer. In most instances, detainees spend more time languishing behind bars without trial than the time required as punishment for a particular crime when convicted. *See also*, Stanley (2016).

[46] Gallagher (2016), p. 1.

[47] U.S. Dep't of State, Trafficking in Persons Report 2016: TOGO (Jun. 2016).

more than 74 potential victims who were reportedly destined for forced begging or forced labor in Quranic schools. They removed the children but did not initiate any investigations into the drivers or suspected traffickers.[48]

Similarly, the government of Ghana did not report any comprehensive statistics[49] on its anti-trafficking law enforcement efforts from January 1 to December 31, 2016. The US Department of State recommended that prosecutors in the attorney general office should review trafficking case documents and lead the prosecution of such cases. In Benin, the government reportedly intercepted 19 adult female victims at the Cotonou airport who were en route to Lebanon and Kuwait, allegedly for domestic servitude purposes. One suspect in connection with these cases was arrested but was later released as the judge was unable to find any charges against him under existing trafficking prohibitions.[50]

Mali established a law against trafficking in begging in 1998; however, not one person has been convicted since its passage despite several important cases that resulted in the freeing of slaves. In Burkina Faso, an anti-begging law has been on the books since 1975 but not one slaveholder has served the prescribed 3 years jail term (although a few have been fined the equivalent of $2). In the proceedings concerning the *talibes* case in 2012, the Centre for Human Rights in a communication submitted to the African Committee of Experts on the Rights and Welfare of the Child, pointed out that "despite the presence of laws which can be used to curb the practice of child begging, the practice still lingers on in Senegal and very [few prosecuted cases] have been registered till date."[51] The applicant highlighted that this prevailing practice and its consequences in Senegal demonstrate "a lack of political will to apply the laws since the marabouts, who are religious leaders, have a very strong influence on the day to day affairs of the country. Moreover, attention was drawn to the fact that despite the various numbers of *daaras* there is a limited number of inspectors."[52]

This low or quasi-nonexistent number of prosecuted cases of trafficking in West Africa is related to the difficulties involved in obtaining the evidence needed to prove the crime and to identify and secure the arrest of suspects. Victim-witness accounts

---

[48] *Trafficking in Persons Report 2017: Guinea*, U.S. Dep't of St. (Jun. 2017), https://www.state.gov/j/tip/rls/tiprpt/countries/2017/271197.htm.

[49] *Trafficking in Persons Report 2017: Ghana*, U.S. Dep't of State (Jun. 2017), https://www.state.gov/j/tip/rls/tiprpt/countries/2017/271194.htm. Field-based research has confirmed that reliable information on prosecutions for trafficking in persons in domestic Courts remains difficult to obtain. Apart from Nigeria, statistical data remain unpublished in the region, allegedly for security purposes. In Ghana, Section 38 (1–2) of the Anti-trafficking law forbids the publication of trafficking proceedings. The purpose of this is to protect the victim's right to privacy of and prevent the media from re-victimizing them as serious exploitation by the traffickers, particularly in the commercial-sex businesses (even involuntarily), is shameful.

[50] *Trafficking in Persons Report 2017: Benin*, U.S. Dep't of St. (Jun. 2017), https://www.state.gov/j/tip/rls/tiprpt/countries/2017/271147.htm.

[51] *Sum of the Proceedings Concerning the Talibés Case*, Int'l Network for Econ. Social & Cultural Rts (2014), https://www.escr-net.org/node/366332.

[52] *Id.*

can lack credibility by appearing to conflict with the physical evidence and with common sense. For example, the absence of physical restraints and the victim's failure to escape an exploitative situation raises the question as to whether the victim was genuinely in a coercive or exploitative situation. This refers to the case of trafficking in domestic servitude in West Africa, where most victims are involved under the covert practice of child fostering or some kind of unenforceable contract. Physical evidence of violence such as unexplained bruises, cuts, or other signs of physical abuse that are typical of trafficking cases in other part of the world are lacking. Furthermore, because children of very poor villages are raised in the urban cities in a socio-cultural environment far better than that of their parents, it becomes extremely difficult to find evidence of trafficking.

The most important witness in such a case is the victim, as the prosecutor needs the testimony of those who witnessed the abuse and exploitation firsthand in order to convince the Court of what happened. In addition to securing victim cooperation and support, additional obstacles to the effective prosecution and adjudication of TIP cases are victim credibility and the need for corroborative evidence. Traumatized and suspicious victims are wary of trusting law enforcement authorities, fearing they may provide incomplete or even untruthful accounts during initial interviews.[53] However, experience has shown that many victims are more likely to give reliable stories to religious personnel in whom they confide completely and build feelings of security and trust in the legal process.

There are several factors that deter victims from giving testimony in Court;[54] one primary reason for people not filing complaints or going to authorities is that of fear. For instance, a large number of people are reluctant to report crimes out of a fear of violent retaliation by traffickers against themselves and their family members.[55] Victims subjected to a ritual oath also have a profound fear and belief that breaking the oath will result in misfortune. This raises question as to how law enforcement can gather evidence from victims subjected to ritual oaths that often result in greater psychological harm than physical harm.[56] For example, the US Department of State reported that the public prosecutor in Ghana "dropped a case against suspected traffickers arrested in November 2007 for forcing 17 women into prostitution, despite significant evidence against them, such as video recordings of them bribing immigration officials. The case was dropped when the victims, all of whom have returned to Nigeria, would not agree to testify,"[57] because they had been subjected to ritual oaths. Enlisting the assistance of the Catholic Church is therefore

[53] Gallagher (2009).

[54] Roujanavong (2012), p. 146.

[55] Convention Against Transnational Organized Crime, Protocol to Prevent, Suppress and Punish trafficking in Persons, Especially Women and Children, done Nov. 15, 2000, T.I.A.S.13127, art. 6, 24.

[56] Farrell et al. (2012), p. 52.

[57] *Trafficking in Persons Report 2009: Ghana*, U.S. Dep't of State, (Jun. 2009), https://www.state.gov/j/tip/rls/tiprpt/2009/123136.htm.

recommended to deliver trafficking victims from the fear of malevolent spiritual forces (witchcraft) that controls them. This partnership between state authorities and the Church has proved effective in the rehabilitation and reintegration of former sex trafficking victims.

Cultural barriers also impede victims' access to justice, as they are not aware they are victims of a crime punishable by law and lack the necessary capacities and resources to seek punitive action against their exploiters. Furthermore, resorting to the judicial sector to solve problems is not rooted in African mentality.[58] Importantly, victims of sexual exploitation are ashamed of what they have experienced and decide not to cooperate so that they can forget their painful memories as soon as possible.

Another major barrier to accessing justice in West Africa is the high cost of litigation and legal services in both civil and criminal matters. For instance, it has been reported that an excessive financial burden is placed on victims both before and during criminal proceedings in West Africa, thus it is not surprising that many victims do not have the means or the resources to gain access to the Courts. According to a police investigator in Ghana, the principal problems encountered in prosecuting trafficking cases relate to resource constraints, especially the logistics needed to transport victims to a Court in another town to testify.[59] To facilitate access to justice, a substantial number trafficking cases are brought to Court by Catholic Church institutions on behalf of victims who are indigent and unable to pay legal fees.[60]

Finally, the obligations of states to prosecute trafficking offenders should also include the corrupt government officials whose complicity facilitates trafficking in persons. Indeed, the United Nations Convention against Corruption, which complements the United Nations Convention against Transnational Organized Crime, requires each state party to "adopt legislative, administrative or other effective measures to promote integrity and to prevent, detect and punish the corruption of public officials."[61] As discussed in Chap. 2, corrupt public officials and law enforcement officers are reportedly bribed to include false information in genuine passports or to provide fraudulent documents to prospective labor migrants and potential trafficking victims.

Whilst the media continues to report allegations of complicity by government officials' in trafficking-related offenses, an overview of law enforcement efforts to prosecute officials is almost non-existent. For example, in 2017 the US Department of State highlighted the fact that law enforcement and the judiciary in the Economic

---

[58] *See generally* Shu-Acquaye (2013).

[59] *Protection of Victims of Trafficking in Ghana: Report from Danish Immigration Service's fact-finding mission to Accra, Ghana*, Danish Immigr. Svc. 13–14 (Jun. 2008), https://www.nyidanmark.dk/NR/rdonlyres/EB5BAEDA-0D96-46C2-B2D2-E48BA8911B2C/0/Ghanaffrapport2008.pdf.

[60] *See generally* 207/97 Afr. Leg. Aid (on behalf of Isaac and Robert Banda)/Gambia (The) (2001), http://www.achpr.org/files/sessions/29th/comunications/207.97/achpr29_207_97_eng.pdf.

[61] UNODC (2004).

Community of West African States (ECOWAS) region did not "report any investigations, prosecutions, or convictions of government officials complicit in human trafficking offenses."[62] Corruption and the unethical culture prevailing in business are primarily a moral problem that the Government alone cannot fight and resolve. In this regard, religion is effective in establishing ethical values that play an important role in moral decision-making among public servants that leads them to reject corrupt practices.[63] The Catholic Church in particular fights corruption by teaching the values of honesty, integrity, and responsibility in the work place and by calling upon public officials to purse the common good and reject the attainment of personal advantages.

## 9.3 Protection and Assistance of Trafficking Victims

Alongside its duty to prosecute, the Convention[64] and its Protocol require state parties to provide both assistance and protection for trafficking victims. Article 6 (6) of the Protocol imposes on each state the obligation to "ensure its domestic legal system contains measures that offer victims of trafficking in persons the possibility of obtaining compensation for damage suffered."[65] The Legislative Guides elaborate as follows on the nature of this corresponding obligation under the Convention:

> (a) Provisions allowing victims to sue offenders or others under statutory or common law torts for civil damages; (b) Provisions allowing criminal Courts to award criminal damages, or to impose orders for compensation or restitution against persons convicted of offences; (c) Provisions establishing dedicated funds or schemes whereby victims can claim compensation from the State for injuries or damages suffered as the result of a criminal offence.[66]

According to the OHCHR and the Special Rapporteur, the right to an effective remedy "encompasses both the substantive right to remedies and the procedural rights necessary to secure them."[67] In practice, victims often face procedural and financial difficulties when claiming remedies. In most cases, the lack of or limited access to "free legal aid is commonly cited as a barrier to victims of trafficking

---

[62] *See generally Trafficking in Persons Report 2017: Burkina Faso*, U.S. Dep't of St. (Jun. 2017), https://www.state.gov/documents/organization/271341.pdf.

[63] *See generally* Marquette (2010).

[64] UNTOC, Article 25(2): "Each State Party shall establish appropriate procedures to provide access to compensation and restitution for victims."

[65] Convention Against Transnational Organized Crime, Protocol to Prevent, Suppress and Punish trafficking in Persons, Especially Women and Children, done Nov. 15, 2000, T.I.A.S.13127, Article 6 (6).

[66] *Legislative Guide for the Implementation of the United Nations Convention Against Transnational Organized Crime and the Protocols Thereto*, 286 (UNODC 2004) para. 60.

[67] *Draft Basic Principles on the Right to an Effective Remedy*, Principle 5; A/HRC/26/18, *Summary of the Consultations held on the Draft Basic Principles on the Right to Effective Remedy for Victims of Trafficking in Persons*, para. 4 (2014).

accessing remedies and NGOs often play an important role in providing or facilitating *pro bono* legal representation."[68]

The procedural rights to a remedy may be conceived of as a range of measures "by which claims of human rights violations are heard and decided, whether by Courts, administrative agencies or other competent bodies. The second notion of remedies refers to the outcome of the proceedings, the relief afforded to the successful claimant."[69] Article 6(1) of the of the Trafficking in Persons Protocol calls on states to provide assistance during legal proceedings against the trafficker, including protection of the privacy, identity, and physical safety of the victim to the extent possible under domestic law. These procedural obligations are essential for both the identification of victims and the provision of effective remedies and adequate support services.[70] The Special Rapporteur stated clearly that "although the principle of non-criminalization [of trafficking victims] was not reflected in the Palermo Protocol, it was an important issue that had to be taken into full consideration when implementing anti-trafficking policies."[71]

As well as taking measures to further procedural rights, each state party should consider adopting legislative or other appropriate measures that provide temporary residence status to victims for the duration of their period of reflection; criminal, civil, or administrative proceedings, or even permanent residence if this is deemed to be in the best interests of the victim (Article 7).[72] Finally, Article 8 states that state parties must facilitate and accept repatriation of their nationals and permanent residents who are trafficking victims with due regard for their safety.

In light of what precedes the substantive content of the remedy required (Article 6 (6)), reparation for the harm suffered by victims encompasses a wide range of measures depending on the trafficking case. The *Draft Basic Principles on the right to an effective remedy for victims of trafficking in persons* advise that adequate reparations "may include restitution, compensation, recovery, satisfaction, and guarantees of non-repetition."[73] This document provides a more detailed description of

[68] *Providing Effective Remedies for Victims of Trafficking in Persons*, (ICAT) 14 (2016). https://www.unodc.org/documents/human-trafficking/ICAT/ICAT_Policy_Paper_3._Providing_Effective_Remedies_for_Victims_of_Trafficking_in_Persons_2016.pdf.

[69] Shelton (2000), pp. 12–13.

[70] A/HRC/26/18, *Summary of the Consultations held on the Draft Basic Principles on the Right to Effective Remedy for Victims of Trafficking in Persons*, para. 32 (2014).

[71] A/HRC/26/18, *Summary of the Consultations held on the Draft Basic Principles on the Right to Effective Remedy for Victims of Trafficking in Persons*, para. 34 (2014).

[72] A/HRC/26/18, *Summary of the Consultations held on the Draft Basic Principles on the Right to Effective Remedy for Victims of Trafficking in Persons*, para. 35 (2014).

[73] *Draft Basic Principles on the Right to an Effective Remedy for Trafficked Persons*, para. 4.https://www.ohchr.org/Documents/Issues/Trafficking/Consultation/ConsultationEffectiveRemedy/DraftBasicPrinciples.pdf; *See also Basic Principles and Guidelines on the Right to a Remedy and Reparation for Victims of Gross Violations of International and Human Rights Law and Serious Violations of International Humanitarian Law*, Adopted and proclaimed by General Assembly resolution 60/147 of 16 December 2005.

the remedial provisions that might be appropriate for trafficking victims.[74] It also emphasizes that "in the case of trafficking in persons, the responsibility of the State to provide remedies always arises and should be extended to all individuals, whether citizens or non-citizens, under its jurisdiction."[75] However, while the UN Anti-trafficking legal framework creates mandatory obligations on state parties to criminalize trafficking in persons in domestic legislation, provisions for the protection of victims are discretionary and formulated in a more exhortative language. For instance, states are only required to "consider adopting" measures in "appropriate cases and to the extent possible" to assist and protect victims of trafficking.[76] The suggestion that the Palermo Protocol might fail to provide adequate protection for human rights lies in "the fact that in 2005, the Council of Europe felt compelled to adopt its own Convention on Action against Trafficking in Human Beings, so as to include binding human rights obligations."[77]

The Legislative Guide for the Implementation of UNTOC further clarified that "the provisions of the Protocol setting out procedural requirements and basic safeguards are mandatory, while requirements to provide assistance and support for victims incorporate some element of discretion."[78] Thus, the nature of the social obligations reflected in victim protection is a 'demanding' policy dimension that entails some of the most costly measures with which to comply.[79] The legislative document explains that the costs and difficulties involved in delivering social assistance to a large group of victims in many developing countries precludes the provisions from being made obligatory, along with "the fact that they apply equally to all States parties in which victims are found, regardless of the level of socioeconomic development or availability of resources."[80]

---

[74] A/HRC/26/18, *Summary of the consultations held on the draft basic principles on the right to effective remedy for victims of trafficking in persons*, para. 19–31 (UN 2014); *Read also Providing Effective Remedies for Victims of Trafficking in Persons*, 11–12 (ICAT 2016) https://www.unodc.org/documents/human-trafficking/ICAT/ICAT_Policy_Paper_3._Providing_Effective_Remedies_for_Victims_of_Trafficking_in_Persons_2016.pdf.

[75] A/HRC/26/18, *Summary of the Consultations held on the Draft Basic Principles on the Right to Effective Remedy for Victims of Trafficking in Persons*, para. 7 (UN 2014).

[76] Convention Against Transnational Organized Crime, Protocol to Prevent, Suppress and Punish trafficking in Persons, Especially Women and Children, done Nov. 15, 2000, T.I.A.S.13127, Art. 7 (1).

[77] Allain (2015), p. 274. *Council of Europe Convention on Action against Trafficking in Human Beings and its Explanatory Report*, C.E.T.S. No. 197, at 27, 31 (2005), www.conventions.coe.int/Treaty/EN/Treaties/Word/197.doc.

[78] *Legislative Guides for the Implementation of the United Nations Convention against Transnational Organized Crime and the Protocol thereto*, Part Two. Chapter II, para. 52, (UN 2004) https://www.unodc.org/pdf/crime/legislative_guides/Legislative%20guides_Full%20version.pdf.

[79] Schönhöfer (2017), p. 153.

[80] *Legislative Guides for the Implementation of the United Nations Convention against Transnational Organized Crime and the Protocol thereto*, Part Two. Chapter II, para. 52, 62 (UN 2004) https://www.unodc.org/pdf/crime/legislative_guides/Legislative%20guides_Full%20version.pdf.

In practice, initiatives for providing effective remedies for victims of trafficking in accordance with the UN *Basic Principles and Guidelines on the Right to a Remedy and Reparation* are developing and can vary from one country to another. Most Economic Community of West African States (ECOWAS) recognize the right of irregular workers to seek protection and do not prevent undocumented workers from accessing employment tribunals to obtain compensation. These policies are relevant for the protection of trafficked persons who may be deterred from seeking legal redress because they have entered a country illegally; for example, the Human Trafficking Act in Ghana gives victims the right pursue a civil claim for restitution.[81] Furthermore, foreign victims are given the right to seek temporary residency in Ghana during the investigation and prosecution of their cases; the interior minister can also approve permanent residency if deemed to be in the victim's best interest.[82] However, the government has not reported any lawsuits for restitution or whether traffickers who were ordered to pay compensation to victims complied with the order.[83] This indicates that "even when offenders are convicted, it is unusual for victims to be compensated. Where victims are compensated, extremely low sums are awarded that are not proportionate to the magnitude of the harm suffered."[84]

Human rights provisions to assist and protect trafficking victims may be considered a burdensome responsibility by states.[85] Despite the existence of international and regional frameworks, effective remedies have remained largely inaccessible for West African states due to limited resources and a lack of dedicated infrastructure; consequently states turn a blind eye to trafficking in persons to avoid accountability.[86] For example, with regard to shelters, it has been reported that some governments have identified potential trafficking victims but have not provided any victim services, funding, or in-kind support to non-governmental organizations (NGOs) that assist victims. For instance, due to a lack of resources and miscommunication between government agencies, suspected child trafficking victims in Guinea were temporarily housed at a local prison and private houses before being transferred to a youth hall or non-governmental organization (NGO) shelters.

In general, protection centers in ECOWAS have received irregular funding, do not have an operational budget and have often relied on donations or support from

---

[81] Ghana Law, Human trafficking Act, 2005, Article 39 https://www.mint.gov.gh/wp-content/uploads/2017/06/Human_Trafficking_Act_2015-1.pdf.

[82] U.S. Dep't of State, Trafficking in Persons Report 2017: Ghana (Jun. 2017), https://www.state.gov/j/tip/rls/tiprpt/countries/2017/271194.htm.

[83] U.S. Dep't of State, 2018 Trafficking in Persons Report 2018 – Ghana, available at: https://www.refworld.org/docid/5b3e0b364.html (accessed August 17, 2021).

[84] UNODC (2016b).

[85] UNODC (2010) and Abdulrahim et al. (2009).

[86] Interview with Paulin Bambara, SG of the Ministry of Justice in Burkina Faso (Aug. 2016); U.S. Dep't of State, Trafficking in Persons Report 2014: Burkina Faso (Jun. 2014), https://www.state.gov/j/tip/rls/tiprpt/countries/2014/226690.htm. To supplement the financing of other donors, the Government of Burkina Faso has allocated the equivalent of about US$20,000 to support protection activities in 2013, including the financing of these Transit centers.

international organizations. Limited resources and a lack of trained personnel have severely reduced their efficacy and operational capacity. As part of their ethos, Catholic institutions have helped address the shortcoming of local governments by providing shelters and important social services to trafficking survivors; in these centers the religious sisters offer safety along with spiritual and psychological services to sex trafficking survivors as well as victims of forced marriage and those at risk of labor exploitation.

To enhance protection, the United Nations (UN) Protocol calls upon state parties to take the necessary measures to break the cycle of "re-victimization" among trafficked persons.[87] For instance, victims of trafficking in West Africa are at risk of being returned to an unsafe environment where they will be exposed to possible re-victimization, discrimination, and ostracism in violation of the principle of non-refoulement. The obligation of non-refoulement (non-return) is recognized as a norm of customary international law and widely accepted by states. In the context of international refugee law, this principle prevents states from returning a person to another state where they have reason to fear persecution.[88] For example, as part of a Multilateral Cooperation Agreement between the Economic Community of West African States (ECOWAS) and the Economic Community of Central African States (ECCAS) signed in 2006, the Beninese government facilitated the repatriation of five trafficked victims to their origin country (Nigeria) and partnered with the Gabonese and Congolese governments to repatriate at least 10 Beninese child trafficking victims.[89]

During this process, officials and non-governmental organization (NGO) stakeholders noted that re-trafficking was an issue in destination countries. Once child victims were reunited with their family in Benin, they were often sent back to the trafficker by their parents or their siblings them to uphold their initial agreement.[90] For others, re-victimization often occurs due to a lack of employment opportunities when they return home as well as discrimination and the various difficulties they face reintegrating into their communities. Indeed, survivors of trafficking face a significant level of stigma that has the following major components: blame, discrimination, loss of status, isolation, and shame. With respect to trafficking in persons, this stigma can arise in various ways. For example, in Nigeria the family and wider community blame survivors for their victimization, as it is believed they have chosen to enter prostitution. They may face discrimination when seeking housing or employment and also face issues achieving life milestones such as marriage as a result of their experience. Without any control over their lives, survivors often feel shame.

---

[87] *Palermo Protocol*, *supra* note 76, art. 9 (1) (b).

[88] Refugee Convention, art. 33; *see The Principle of Non-Refoulement as a Norm of Customary International Law: Response to the Questions Posed to UNHCR by the Federal Constitutional Court of the Federal Republic of Germany in Cases 2 BvR 1938/93, 2 BvR 1953/93, 2 BvR 1954/93*, UNCHR (Jan. 31 1994), http://www.refworld.org/docid/437b6db64.html.

[89] U.S. Dep't of State, Trafficking in Persons Report 2014: Benin (Jun. 2014), http://www.state.gov/j/tip/rls/tiprpt/countries/2014/226682.htm.

[90] *Id.*

Human rights advocates have argued that the exhortative language used to secure the legal rights of victims associated with their protection does not impose a strong obligation upon states, which could be detrimental to protecting victims and preventing trafficking.[91] In this regard, "the Protocol ultimately falls short of its intent to 'sufficiently protect' victims, because it fails to require nation states to prioritize the welfare of the victim above the prosecution of the trafficker."[92] Indeed,, where the United Nations (UN) Palermo Protocol has been implemented it has resulted in an imbalanced enforcement of state obligations and different levels of compliance in respect to victim protection because it "lacks formal enforcement, monitoring, and sanction mechanisms."[93] Tom Obokata argues that the weakness of the Palermo Protocol's provisions regarding the human rights obligations of nation states is supplemented by international human rights law and other international mechanisms[94] and therefore the Protocol "should be an instrument recognised as a key for promoting and implementing a human rights framework, augmenting global action against the act."[95] Analyzing victim protection efforts by states that are associated with the United Nations (UN) Anti-trafficking Protocol, Johanna Schönhöfer contends that political determinants can also drive the implementation of the international treaty and the enforcement of victim protection policies at a domestic level. This theory regarding the enforcement of anti-trafficking policies is based on an international relation system characterized by power differentials, whereby leading and powerful states influence others. Accordingly, two main reasons may drive "states to comply with international treaties lacking formal enforcement and sanction mechanisms like the UN Anti-Trafficking Protocol: they are either coerced into compliance by other states, or compliance is a strategic choice of states in order to raise their reputation and signal credible commitments.[96]

In sum, given the ongoing challenges involved in providing effective remedies to the victims, the Special Rapport has recognized that non-governmental organizations are "key partners in realizing rehabilitation through reintegration, given that they can readily gather information on the victim's family and social context and actively follow up on the victim's situation over time."[97] The efforts made by the Catholic Church strive to target the stigma surrounding trafficking and help women trafficked for sexual exploitation purposes overcome discrimination in order to fully recover from their ordeal and reintegrate into society.

---

[91] Hendrix (2010), pp. 173, 182.

[92] Shoaps (2013), pp. 931, 952.

[93] Schönhöfer (2017), pp. 153, 154.

[94] Obokata (2006), pp. 164–165.

[95] Obokata (2006), p. 165.

[96] Schönhöfer (2017), p. 157.

[97] *Summary of the Consultations Held on the Draft Basic Principles on the Right to Effective Remedy for Victims of Trafficking in Persons*, U.N. Doc. A/HRC/26/18, para. 27 (May 2, 2014), http://undocs.org/A/HRC/26/18.

## 9.4 Prevention of Trafficking in Persons

Article 9(1) under the trafficking Protocol specifies that the state has a duty to undertake comprehensive policies, programs, and other measures to prevent and combat trafficking in persons. While prosecution and the protection of victims focuses on the tangible aftermath of trafficking, prevention comprises interventions aimed at stopping harm from occurring in the first place. It constitutes the building of a safety wall. To describe this, it is useful to recall the traditional public health parable "The Upstream Story", which highlights the need to address the root causes of a health problem.[98] The parable tells of a man and woman fishing downstream.

> Suddenly a person comes down the river struggling for life. The fisherfolk pull her out. Then another comes and again must be rescued. This happens all afternoon and the fisherfolk are getting very tired from constantly pulling people from the river. Eventually they think, "We need to go upstream and find out why so many people are falling in the water". When they go upstream, they find that people are drawn to the edge to look at the river, but there is no safe way to do this. Many of them fall.
>
> The fisherfolk go to the community leaders and report the number of people who have fallen into the river. They also report that this is due to the lack of a protective barrier on the cliff. Community leaders build a wall behind which people may safely view the water. Some still fall, but there are many fewer victims to rescue.

The lesson drawn from the "moving upstream" analogy is that instead of spending all resources and energy on rescuing people, the best strategy is to prevent trafficking from even happening.[99] Thus, preventive measures are extremely important in a West African context where perpetrators include family members and even children. Interpol-Ghana has explained that many victims decline to cooperate and give evidence because it is often the victim's own family that initiated the trafficking arrangement and the trafficker is a distant relative or member of the extended family. In light of trafficking trends in West Africa, it would be an overstatement to claim that a criminalization approach may have to include the imposition of penalties on entire communities.[100]

---

[98] *Slide Presentation: Moving Upstream: The Story of Prevention* (University of Colorado, Denver), http://www.ucdenver.edu/academics/colleges/PublicHealth/research/ResearchProjects/piper/PREVENT/education/Documents/Outline1.pdf.

[99] *Id.*

[100] Opvang (2014), p. 46 [hereinafter Residency Problems]; Agrinya (2016). According to Barr, Onome Oriakhi, Caritas Nigeria's program manager for Human Trafficking and Migration, "Most times the traffickers are even relatives of the victims and it is usually difficult to use law enforcement agencies to prosecute them because victims want to protect their families. We have had an instance where a trafficked young woman refused to reveal the identity of her trafficker stating that her mother was also involved and she didn't want her mum to be punished because she meant well for her, that was why she begged her brother to take her abroad. Another one said her sister reminded her that other young girls her age were making very good money selling their bodies abroad to support their families and also told her that after a few years she would gain her freedom from her 'madam' and also start her own trafficking ring[.]"; *see* U.S. Dep't of State, Trafficking in Persons Report 2017: Guinea, *supra* note 82.

In trafficking cases involving relatives, the attitudes of anti-trafficking practitioners differ in terms of how to deal with parental responsibility. Some have expressed concern that the "punishment of parents might affect children: they are stigmatized when they have a parent in prison."[101] Furthermore, unlike developed countries where victims of trafficking have relatively strong socio-economic protection, women and children in West Africa do not have access to social, legal and medical assistance. Therefore, the prosecution of parents and relatives for the use, procuring, or offering of a child for trafficking may increase that child's vulnerability to exploitation and militate against their best interests.[102] For example, article 5 of the U.N. General Assembly's 1986 Declaration on Social and Legal Principles relating to the Protection and Welfare of Children recognizes the child's need for continued contact with his or her parents; it states that "in all matters relating to the placement of a child outside the care of the child's own parents, the best interests of the child, particularly his or her need for affection and right to security and continuing care, should be the paramount consideration."[103]

In this respect, Human Rights Watch called for "an explicit defense for parents who are genuinely deceived about the purpose of their child's recruitment, believing it to be educational or otherwise non-exploitative" and endorsed "reduced penalties for parents who reasonably but mistakenly believe that aiding and abetting child trafficking, or failing to report child traffickers to the police, is in their child's best interests."[104] Another particularly sensitive issue is the role children play as offenders and intermediaries in SECTT and trafficking in forced labor in West

[101] Andrew and Lawrance (2012), p. 25; Kraemer (2013). Ghana's Children's Act 168 prescribes the mitigation of sentences for parents to protect children from being deprived of a primary caregiver. As an alternative, the American University study recommends a "two-step prosecution process of parent traffickers." First, parent traffickers should be "arrested in every instance" but not imprisoned. Instead, following a first arrest and subsequent conviction, parents "should be required to enroll in an educational program on trafficking."172 If they "subsequently reoffend," parental custody should not be considered a defense and the minimum 5-year prison sentence mandated in the Act for trafficking offenses "should be enforced without exception." If the child is left without a "parent guardian," "the provisions of the Children's Act relating to the care of children without parents should control."

[102] Interview in the Department of Human Rights in Burkina Faso; CRC, art. 9(1) ("a child shall not be separated from his or her parents against their will, except when competent authorities subject to judicial review determine, in accordance with applicable law and procedures, that such separation is necessary for the best interests of the child"); *id.* art. 3 (1) (making the best interests of the child a "primary consideration" in "all actions concerning children"); *Borderline Slavery—Child Trafficking in Togo*, 15 Human Rts Watch 8, at VIII (2003), (available at: http://www.hrw.org/sites/default/files/reports/togo0403.pdf).

[103] G.A. Res. 41/85, *Decl. on Soc. and Legal Principles Relating to the Prot. and Welfare of Child., with Spec. Reference to Foster Placement and Adoption Nationally and Internationally*, art. 5, U.N. Doc. A/RES/41/85 (Dec, 3, 1986), http://www.un.org/documents/ga/res/41/a41r085.htm.

[104] Andrew and Lawrance (2012), p. 25; for the experience of Ghana in the prosecution of parents, *see* Heemskerk and Sertich (2011), pp. 2–7.

Africa. "[the] perpetrator in this scenario is also covered by the legislation meant to protect the victim."[105]

Because trafficking in West Africa is entrenched in cultural practices, Economic Community of West African States (ECOWAS) countries have conducted public awareness-raising campaigns to educate potential victims about the risks of migration and the consequences of trafficking in persons; these informative campaigns have targeted children, women, young people, parents, government officials, and public opinion leaders.[106] Economic Community of West African States (ECOWAS) governments have also provided extensive training to police officers, social workers, judges, teachers, labor inspectors, traditional leaders, and religious leaders on issues related to trafficking in persons. For instance, training modules have explained how to identify and provide assistance to victims, as well as provided information in investigation procedures and the prosecution of trafficking crimes.[107] It is clear that the adoption of an anti-trafficking legislative framework in West Africa has created a new awareness around the existence of trafficking and the need to educate the community. In this regard, the Catholic Church has a very important role to play in the prevention of trafficking in persons and a wide ranging platform on which to enhance awareness in society.

Education also plays a vital role in preventing women and children from becoming victims of trafficking; as mentioned in Part I, illiteracy and lack of education is an important factor rendering people susceptible to trafficking. Education this helps potential victims avoid exploitation and empowers those in captivity to escape from their slavery. Cases involving trafficking victims who have completed primary level or secondary level education show that they have managed to escape or reach out for help. For example, in the *Attorney-General of the Federation v. Sarah Okoya* case, which involved the inducement of professional hairdressers into traveling abroad for the purpose of prostitution, the victims had schooling as well as professional skills. The girls were subsequently taken into the neighboring Benin Republic, allegedly en route to Spain; when they discovered that the agent's true purpose was to engage them in prostitution, they teamed up in order to escape, despite attempts by the accused to prevent them from interacting. The girls demanded that the accused return them to Nigeria as they were not prostitutes and had no desire to become so.[108] Importantly, the girls reported the offender to the manager of the hotel and asked to be taken to the Nigerian embassy in Cotonou. The manager, accompanied by his friend, took the offender and the six girls to the embassy. The offender was

---

[105] Hawke and Raphael (2016), p. 53.

[106] *Convention Against Transnational Organized Crime, Protocol to Prevent, Suppress and Punish trafficking in Persons, Especially Women and Children*, art. 9 (2) done Nov. 15, 2000, T.I.A. S.13127.

[107] *Child Labor in Burkina Faso* 2014, U.S. Dep't of Labor 4 (2014), https://www.dol.gov/ilab/reports/child-labor/findings/2014TDA/burkinafaso.pdf.

[108] *Okoya, supra* note 40.

questioned and subsequently accused of trafficking human beings. Arrangements were immediately made to return the accused and the six girls to Nigeria.[109]

The promotion of education and schooling for children thus constitutes an effective long-term linchpin strategy to reduce their risk of becoming involved in trafficking rings and labor exploitation. At the Dakar international Forum in 2000, states committed themselves to offering "free and compulsory primary education in accordance with the United Nations Convention on the Rights of the Child (UNCRC) and other international commitments."[110] Other policy measures comprised increasing children's access to school in the early years, the prevention of school dropout through quality improvements and economic incentives, and giving second chances to working children who have missed out on an education.[111]

Despite legislative and policy commitments to the abolition of tuition fees, schooling is rarely free. There are many other costs incurred by families that involve direct and indirect financial burdens such as transport, examination papers, school uniforms, school lunch, and extra tuition.[112] While many countries have experienced impressive increments in access to education since the Dakar forum, improvements in quality have not always kept pace. For instance, the quality and availability of teacher-training and class sizes remain serious challenges affecting educational quality along with limited resources and constrained budgets. An illustrative example is provided in the *SERAP v. Federal Republic of Nigeria and Universal Basic Education Commission* case.[113]

In this case, following an investigation into the mismanagement of funds allocated for basic education in ten states of the Federation of Nigeria, SERAP (Socio-Economic Rights and Accountability Project) brought a case against the Republic of Nigeria based on the lack of adequate implementation of Nigeria's Basic Education Act and Child's Rights Act of 2004. The Applicant alleged that high level corruption and the theft of funds destined for primary education in Nigeria have negatively affected its educational system, as evidenced by the failure to train more teachers and the unavailability of books and other teaching materials. This has contributed to a denial of the right of most citizens to freely dispose of their natural wealth and resources, which forms the backbone of the enjoyment of other economic and social rights such as the right to education.

Regarding these issues, Nigeria argued that the educational objective in the Constitution of Nigeria is non-justiciable.[114] The Court dismissed the government's

---

[109] *Id.*

[110] *U.N. Econ. & Soc. Council, Education for All Monitoring Report 2015*, at 84 (2015), http://unesdoc.unesco.org/images/0023/002322/232205e.pdf [hereinafter Education for All].

[111] Salah (2001).

[112] *Education for All*, *supra* note 110 at 88.

[113] *SERAP v. Nigeria*, ECOWAS Community Ct. of Just., Suit No. ECW/CCJ/APP/12/07, Judgment (Nov. 30, 2010).

[114] *Id.*

contention that education is "a mere directive policy of the government and not a legal entitlement of the citizens," concluding that:

> once the concerned right for which the protection is sought before the Court is enshrined in an international instrument that is binding on a Member State, the domestic legislation of that State cannot prevail on the international treaty or covenant, even if it is its own Constitution. It is thus evident that the Federal Republic of Nigeria cannot invoke the nonjusticiability or enforceability of ICESCR as a means for shirking its responsibility in ensuring protection and guarantee for its citizens within the framework of commitments it has made vis-à-vis the Economic Community of West African.[115]

The enforcement of the right to education by the international Court sends a clear message that members of the Economic Community of West African States (ECOWAS) have an obligation to protect, respect, and fulfil the right to education and must be held accountable for violations or deprivations of this right.

Although governments have been steadily increasing their investments and efforts to address trafficking through education in West Africa, expectations of schools in relation to social problems have also increased. To enhance the quality of education, Catholic schools have seriously addressed the challenge posed by the spiritual and moral dimension of education with a complementary focus on the meaning and purpose of life. This type of education aims to increase young people's sensitivity to moral and justice concerns such as the respect of human dignity and trafficking in persons.[116]

States that are parties to the United Nations (UN) Convention have an obligation to adopt or strengthen legislative measures and discourage the demand that fosters all forms of exploitation related to trafficking, especially among women and children.[117] Therefore, member states should consider criminalizing the use of services offered by victims of trafficking.[118] Governments in West Africa cannot be absolved of their responsibility for generating and sustaining demand. For example, many destination countries in West Africa and Europe derive a substantial benefit from cheap foreign labor which they deliberately leave unprotected and unregulated by law. These countries in return rely heavily on the remittances of their overseas workers and are reluctant to interfere with a system that brings economic benefits because migrants who have secured a job abroad send a portion of their wages back

---

[115] *SERAP v. Nigeria and Universal Basic Education Commission*, ECOWAS Comm. Ct. Just., Suit No. ECW/CCJ/APP/08/09, Judgment, ¶ 39 (Dec. 14, 2012); Shehu (2013), p. 113.

[116] *Cf.* Graham Rossiter, *Catholic Education and Values: A Review of the Role of Catholic Schools in Promoting the Spiritual and Moral Development of Pupils* 3 (unpublished manuscript), http://citeseerx.ist.psu.edu/viewdoc/download?doi=10.1.1.577.7806&rep=rep1&type=pdf; *cf.* Jagannathan (1999), p. 8.

[117] G.A. Res. 55/25, *U.N. Convention Against Transnational Organized Crime and the Protocols Thereto*, art. 9 (5) (Sep. 29, 2003), https://www.unodc.org/unodc/en/organized-crime/intro/UNTOC.html.

[118] Kiskyte (2016). *See generally* UNODC (2008) [hereinafter UNODC Toolkit]; *cf.* OHCHR (2010), p. 203.

to their home countries to alleviate poverty for others the less fortunate.[119] The 2016 US State Department report noted that the governments of West African countries such as Benin, Togo, Cabo Verde, Ivory Coast, Liberia, and Mali had failed in their responsibilities to take systematic steps to reduce the demand for commercial sex acts or forced labor both within their countries and abroad.

In effect, trafficking in persons "is predominantly about money, profits and demand. If people don't use the products and services of the victims, and if there is no profit, [then] there is no trafficking."[120] Anti-trafficking measures implemented by Economic Community of West African States (ECOWAS) are aimed at reducing and ideally eliminating the supply that fosters trafficking in persons by prosecuting the traffickers and protecting the victims;[121] yet there has been no significant decrease in the problem, in fact it seems to be increasing. Certainly, those persons involved in trafficking are criminals deserving of punishment commensurate with their evil acts. However, what about those who purchase these commercial sexual services and the products of forced labor? Myria Vassiliadou noted that users or buyers "are upright citizens whose appetite for human trafficking services creates the incentives that make it all possible."[122] These are employers who illegally use the services of these trafficked people or force them into labor, families that rely on rural little girls for domestic help, consumers who are buying the cheap products, and clients who are raping these women and girls on an everyday basis. "So for every victim of trafficking there are many more perpetrators who sustain this trade: the clients, the customers, the users, the procurers."[123] For example, in Africa, members of the general public who are the ultimate consumers of the products of forced labor generally (out of poverty) just want to purchase their goods at the prevailing low prices without asking how their suppliers further down the line manage to achieve this outcome.[124] In this regard, the contribution of the Catholic Church's makes a profound difference in the fight against trafficking in persons in West Africa. The Church educates those members of the parish communities who are consumers and employers on how to make ethical choices to reduce the demand for trafficking. Other actions address the contemporary lifestyles and deep rooted causes that foster the demand for paid sex, body parts, and forced labor.

Consistent immigration laws could also play a part in addressing the factors that increase the risks of trafficking and help prevent migrant workers from being

---

[119] Gallagher (2013).

[120] Vassiliadou (2015), pp. 172–173.

[121] *See generally* Londo (2008).

[122] Vassiliadou (2015), p. 381; *Report on the Progress Made in the Fight Against Trafficking in Human Beings*, European Commission 13–14 (May 19, 2016), https://ec.europa.eu/home-affairs/sites/homeaffairs/files/what-we-do/policies/organized-crime-and-human-trafficking/trafficking-in-human-beings/docs/commission_report_on_the_progress_made_in_the_fight_against_trafficking_in_human_beings_2016_en.pdf.

[123] *Id.*

[124] Vassiliadou (2015), p. 471.

trafficked by focusing on the supply chains.[125] History and economic markets have shown that many goods and services prohibited by the government flourish in the black market, which is more violent and less visible. For instance, Kevin Bales contended that "...making something illegal doesn't make it cease to exist. Making it illegal only causes it to vanish from view."[126] In this regard, restrictive immigration laws and policies in destination countries particularly in Europe and the USA, enhance the growth in irregular migrants and persons trafficked from Africa. West African people willing to migrate abroad to look for a job but lack the legal means to do so, resort to findings peoples who will provide them with false documents, arrange the journey, and find them overseas employment. Once abroad, they confront legal barriers as restrictive national policies on labor migration do not allow sufficient legal immigration to fill the vacancies that exist.[127]

Today more than ever, the European Union (EU) and USA need to adopt an accurate approach to labor and immigration policies that integrates the complexity in the supply and demand of labor. In addition to a structural demand for highly-skilled migrant laborers, there is, more importantly, a high demand also for migrant workers "to cover for the care of children and elderly/disabled people, and the participation of women in paid work outside the home."[128] Therefore "increasing opportunities for legal, gainful and non-exploitative labour migration is a measure that States may take to prevent trafficking in persons."[129] Consequently a lower incidence of trafficking is reported when migration opportunities are promoted within a multilateral framework, under a bilateral agreement between the sending and receiving states, or where otherwise safe channels of migration have been created.[130] In this respect, the Catholic Church plays an important role in advocating for better laws and policies to prevent trafficking; the outcomes of these initiatives will be considered in detail in Part III.

---

[125] Report of the Special. Rapporteur on Trafficking in Persons, Especially Women and Child, ¶ 19, U.N. Doc. A/67/261 (Aug. 7, 2010), (available at: https://business-humanrights.org/sites/default/files/media/documents/special-rap-report-trafficking-7-aug-2012.pdf).

[126] Wheaton et al. (2010), pp. 114, 115–136.

[127] See *International Migration Policies Government Views and Priorities*, U.N. 29 (2013), https://www.un.org/en/development/desa/population/publications/pdf/policy/InternationalMigrationPolicies2013/Report%20PDFs/z_International%20Migration%20Policies%20Full%20Report.pdf#zoom=100.

[128] Triandafyllidou and Marchetti (2014).

[129] U.N. Secretary-General, *supra* note 117, ¶ 19.

[130] Report of the Special Rapporteur on Trafficking in Persons, Especially Women and Children, ¶ 42, U.N. Doc. A/66/283 (Aug. 9, 2011) (by Joy Ngozi Ezelio).

## 9.5 Conclusion

It is worth appraising the provisions of the Palermo Protocol that operate to impose international legal obligations upon states to criminalize trafficking in persons under domestic law and to carry out prosecutions and extradition of offenders irrespective of normal jurisdictional limits.[131] However, this approach to trafficking in West Africa has revealed several shortcomings. The first pertains to the Trafficking Protocol itself. The Covenant was primarily designed to combat transnational organized or "trafficking syndicates".[132] It has therefore prioritized criminal law enforcement provisions while victim assistance and even prevention have fallen behind. "The reasons why people are trafficked begin well before they are coerced into sex work",[133] hence there is a need to consider the conditions that create the market for trafficking in persons. In this regard, the preventive actions taken by the Catholic Church which will be described in further detail can fill this gap.

Furthermore, the enforcement of anti-trafficking legislations can be problematic. For example, the United Nations adopted the 1956 Supplementary Convention to address local practices (forced marriage, polygamy) wherein a bride is purchased. However, difficulties arose pertaining to the implementation of its provisions. While calling upon states to end the legal status of slavery manifest in forced marriage and related practices, the commission was reluctant to call on the "master to liberate his concubine, even if she did not desire her freedom" as this would "result in the concubine becoming merely a kept woman and her children would be bastardised."[134] With regard to the issue of polygamy, the Commission also observed that the enforcement of the Convention would eventually result in forcing "the less-favoured wives into a state of servitude differing little from slavery."[135] The Temporary Slavery Commission concluded that "a general amelioration of the lot of women can only be looked for in the growth of civilization and education, together with a more widespread knowledge of the right of every slave of either sex to assert his or her freedom."[136]

Adding to such considerations, members of the Economic Community of West African States (ECOWAS) have also encountered serious difficulties when carrying out prosecutions despite the criminalization of trafficking in their domestic

---

[131] Ratner and Abrams (2001), pp. 11–13.

[132] G.A. Res. 55/25, *supra* note 117, art. I ("However, the impetus for developing a new international instrument arose out of the desire of governments to create a tool to combat the enormous growth of trans-national organized crime. Therefore, the drafters created a strong law enforcement tool with comparatively weak language on human rights protections and victim assistance"); *see generally* Touzenis (2010); *see generally* Shoaps (2013), pp. 931, 952.

[133] Alcantara (2012).

[134] League of Nations, Temporary Slavery Commission, Report of the Temporary Slavery Commission adopted in the Course of its Second Session, July 13th-25th July, 1925, A.19.1925. VI, 25 July 1925, p. 8; Cf. Allain (2012), p. 186.

[135] *Id.*

[136] *Id.*

legislations. This has meant that, prosecutions rarely yield the expected results because they require witness testimony and victims are often unwilling to cooperate with law enforcement due to their beliefs about gender, family love, culture, and religion, all of which are targeted and manipulated as a means of control. West African organized crime rings perform traditional ritualized ceremonies to subjugate and silence victims using the threats of misfortune or the destruction of their loved ones by evil spirits. Given this religious aspect of the ceremony, the catholic priest is therefore in a privileged position to provide spiritual remedies and help victims escape from their traffickers and also cooperate with investigators.

As explained in part I, *Trokosi*, or ritual servitude for religious purposes and forced marriage, are rooted in the cultural practices of traditional communities. However, the cultural and religious rights of people raise serious concerns as they conflict with and violate the human rights of children and women and infringe on their freedoms. Therefore, it is unlikely that any law enforcement action alone would end the practice. The catholic experience of transforming the culture through evangelization and inculturation of the Gospel, ecclesial forums, and Catholic school education are good practices that address the cultural religious abuse of human rights.

Furthermore, trends in trafficking in persons in Africa have shown that traffickers are predominantly care providers such as family members, relatives and friends. They are often very close to the persons they subsequently exploit and whose trust they take advantage of. Surprisingly, the victims themselves (especially children) protected by the law are also trafficking their peers for labor and sexual exploitation. Additionally, in many trafficking situations involving labor exploitation, domestic servitude and forced marriages, the victims do not identify themselves as such. Countering trafficking in this context requires an inclusive approach that involves both traffickers and victims in solving the problem. The Catholic Church can play a role in this process as religion can influence individual decisions and shapes various dimensions of social life by supporting the formation of self-control, which maintains harmony in society. In effect, there is a need for sound education based on moral values to properly form people's conscience so that they can discern what is right from what is wrong; the Catholic Church's commitment in relation to catechesis, school education, and pastoral ministry in general offers a moral perspective on education and offers a potentially distinctive contribution to shaping alternative perspectives on combatting trafficking in persons.

## List of Cases/Documents

*2016 Findings on the Worst Forms of Child Labor – Guinea-Bissau*, U.S. Dep't of Labor 4 (Sept. 30, 2017), https://www.dol.gov/sites/default/files/images/ilab/child-labor/Guinea-Bissau2016.pdf.

207/97 Afr. Leg. Aid (on behalf of Isaac and Robert Banda)/Gambia (The) (2001), http://www.achpr.org/files/sessions/29th/comunications/207.97/achpr29_207_97_eng.pdf.

A/HRC/26/18, *Summary of the Consultations held on the Draft Basic Principles on the Right to Effective Remedy for Victims of Trafficking in Persons*, para. 4 (2014).

A/HRC/26/18, *Summary of the Consultations held on the Draft Basic Principles on the Right to Effective Remedy for Victims of Trafficking in Persons*, para. 32 (2014).

A/HRC/26/18, *Summary of the Consultations held on the Draft Basic Principles on the Right to Effective Remedy for Victims of Trafficking in Persons*, para. 34 (2014).

A/HRC/26/18, *Summary of the Consultations held on the Draft Basic Principles on the Right to Effective Remedy for Victims of Trafficking in Persons*, para. 35 (2014).

A/HRC/26/18, *Summary of the consultations held on the draft basic principles on the right to effective remedy for victims of trafficking in persons*, para. 19-31 (UN 2014).

A/HRC/26/18, *Summary of the Consultations held on the Draft Basic Principles on the Right to Effective Remedy for Victims of Trafficking in Persons*, para. 7 (UN 2014).

*Africa for Women's Rights: Burkina Faso*, Wikigender (2005), http://www.wikigender.org/wiki/africa-for-womens-rights-burkina-faso/; *see generally Discrimination Against Older Women in Burkina Faso*, Convention on the Elimination of all Forms of Discrimination Against Women (CEDAW) (Jul. 2010), http://www2.ohchr.org/english/bodies/cedaw/docs/ngos/JointNGOReport_BurkinaFaso47.pdf.

*Africa for Women's Rights: Senegal*, Wikigender (2015), http://www.wikigender.org/wiki/africa-for-womens-rights-senegal/.

*Akinbuwa v. Akinbuwa* [1998] 7 NWLR 559, 780 (Nigeria).

*Attorney General of the Federation v. M.A.*, Nigeria High Court, Suit No. B/13c/2004, Judgment (2005) (available at: https://www.unodc.org/cld/case-law-doc/traffickingpersonscrimetype/nga/2005/hon._attorney_general_of_the_federation_v._m.a.html).

*Attorney General of the Federation v. Okoya*, Nigeria High Court, Suit No. B/15c/2004, Judgment 4 (2004) (available at: https://www.unodc.org/res/cld/case-law/nga/2004/attorney-general_of_the_federation_v__sarah_okoya_suit_no._b15c2004.html/Attorney-General_of_the_Federation_v._Sarah_Okoya_Suit_No._B15c2004.pdf).

*Attorney General of the Federation v. Omoruyi,* High Court Edo State of Nigeria, Suit No. B/31c/2004 (2006).

*Attorney-General of the Federation v. Sarah Okaja*, Suit No. B/15C/2004, 15 (December 15, 2005).

*Basic Principles and Guidelines on the Right to a Remedy and Reparation for Victims of Gross Violations of International and Human Rights Law and Serious*

*Violations of International Humanitarian Law,* Adopted and proclaimed by General Assembly resolution 60/147 of 16 December 2005.

*Borderline Slavery: Child Trafficking in Togo*, 15 Hum. Rts. Watch 8, 40 (Apr. 2003), https://www.hrw.org/reports/2003/togo0403/togo0403.pdf.

*Borderline Slavery—Child Trafficking in Togo*, 15 Human Rts Watch 8, at VIII (2003), (available at: http://www.hrw.org/sites/default/files/reports/togo0403.pdf).

*Child Labor in Burkina Faso* 2014, U.S. Dep't of Labor 4 (2014), https://www.dol.gov/ilab/reports/child-labor/findings/2014TDA/burkinafaso.pdf.

Concept Note-CEDAW General Recommendation on Trafficking in Women and Girls in the Context of Global Migration, para. 8.

Convention Against Transnational Organized Crime, Protocol to Prevent, Suppress and Punish trafficking in Persons, Especially Women and Children, done Nov. 15, 2000, T.I.A.S.13127, Article 10(2).

*Convention Against Transnational Organized Crime, Protocol to Prevent, Suppress and Punish trafficking in Persons, Especially Women and Children*, done Nov. 15, 2000, T.I.A.S.13127, art. 6, 24.

*Convention Against Transnational Organized Crime, Protocol to Prevent, Suppress and Punish trafficking in Persons, Especially Women and Children*, done Nov. 15, 2000, T.I.A.S.13127, Article 6 (6).

Convention Against Transnational Organized Crime, Protocol to Prevent, Suppress and Punish trafficking in Persons, Especially Women and Children, done Nov. 15, 2000, T.I.A.S.13127, Art. 7 (1).

*Convention Against Transnational Organized Crime, Protocol to Prevent, Suppress and Punish trafficking in Persons, Especially Women and Children*, art. 9 (2) done Nov. 15, 2000, T.I.A.S.13127.

*Council of Europe Convention on Action against Trafficking in Human Beings and its Explanatory Report*, C.E.T.S. No. 197, at 27, 31 (2005), www.conventions.coe.int/Treaty/EN/Treaties/Word/197.doc.

*Draft Basic Principles on the Right to an Effective Remedy for Trafficked Persons*, para. 4.https://www.ohchr.org/Documents/Issues/Trafficking/Consultation/ConsultationEffectiveRemedy/DraftBasicPrinciples.pdf.

*Draft Basic Principles on the Right to an Effective Remedy*, Principle 5

*Ergi v. Turkey*, European Court of Human Rights, Judgment, Application No. 23818/94 (28 July 1998).

Evidence and Lessons from Latin America, Domestic Violence Laws: What Else Makes Responses to Domestic Violence Effective 6 [May 2015] http://ella.practicalaction.org/wp-content/uploads/files/Beyond%20Domestic%20Violence%20Bills_1.pdf.

Francois Xavier Damiba and Laurent Nare, Proverbes Mossi (Abidjan, 1999) (proverb no 44).

G.A. Res. 41/85, *Decl. on Soc. and Legal Principles Relating to the Prot. and Welfare of Child., with Spec. Reference to Foster Placement and Adoption Nationally and Internationally*, art. 5, U.N. Doc. A/RES/41/85 (Dec, 3, 1986), http://www.un.org/documents/ga/res/41/a41r085.htm.

G.A. Res. 55/25, *U.N. Convention Against Transnational Organized Crime and the Protocols Thereto*, art. 9 (5) (Sep. 29, 2003), https://www.unodc.org/unodc/en/organized-crime/intro/UNTOC.html.

Ghana Law, Human trafficking Act, 2005, Article 39 https://www.mint.gov.gh/wp-content/uploads/2017/06/Human_Trafficking_Act_2015-1.pdf

Guinea Penal Code 2016 (Article 323) https://www.warnathgroup.com/wp-content/uploads/2017/10/Guinea-Law-on-the-Criminal-Code-2016-Fra.pdf

Human Rights and Human Trafficking, OHCCHR, Fact Sheet No. 36, p. 34.

*Human Trafficking and Forced Labour Exploitation: Guidance for Legislation and Law Enforcement*, ILO 12 (Apr. 1, 2005), http://digitalcommons.ilr.cornell.edu/cgi/viewcontent.cgi?article=1021&context=forcedlabor.

International Convention on the Protection of the Rights of All Migrant Workers and Members of Their Families, CMW/C/GHA/CO/1 (September 2014) para. 45, https://www.ecoi.net/en/file/local/1114024/1930_1413884691_int-cmw-coc-gha-18155-e.pdf.

*International Migration Policies Government Views and Priorities*, U.N. 29 (2013), https://www.un.org/en/development/desa/population/publications/pdf/policy/InternationalMigrationPolicies2013/Report%20PDFs/z_International%20Migration%20Policies%20Full%20Report.pdf#zoom=100

Interview in the Department of Human Rights in Burkina Faso.

Interview with Paulin Bambara, SG of the Ministry of Justice in Burkina Faso (Aug. 2016)

*Koraou v. Niger*, ECOWAS Community Court of Justice, Judgment, No. ECW/CCJ/APP/0808, ¶85 (Oct. 27, 2008) (available at: http://www.worldcourts.com/ecowasccj/eng/decisions/2008.10.27_Koraou_v_Niger.htm.).

Law No. 2006-04 on the conditions of transportation of minors and the repression of child trafficking in Benin (Loi No. 2006-04 portant conditions de déplacement des mineurs et répression de la traite des enfants en République du Bénin), https://www.warnathgroup.com/wp-content/uploads/2015/03/Benin-Child-TIP-Law-French.pdf

League of Nations, Temporary Slavery Commission, Report of the Temporary Slavery Commission adopted in the Course of its Second Session, July 13th-25th July, 1925, A.19.1925. VI, 25 July 1925, p. 8; Cf. Jean Allain, Allain, Jean. Slavery in International Law: Of Human Exploitation and Trafficking, 186 (BRILL 2012).

*Legislative Guide for the Implementation of the United Nations Convention Against Transnational Organized Crime and the Protocols Thereto*, 286 (UNODC 2004) para. 60.

*Legislative Guides for the Implementation of the United Nations Convention against Transnational Organized Crime and the Protocol thereto*, Part Two. Chapter II, para. 52, (UN 2004) https://www.unodc.org/pdf/crime/legislative_guides/Legislative%20guides_Full%20version.pdf

*Legislative Guides for the Implementation of the United Nations Convention against Transnational Organized Crime and the Protocol thereto*, Part Two. Chapter II, para. 52, 62 (UN 2004) https://www.unodc.org/pdf/crime/legislative_guides/Legislative%20guides_Full%20version.pdf

Nat'l Agency for the Prohibition of Trafficking in Persons, Data Analysis Report 2016 10-14 (2016), https://www.naptip.gov.ng/wp-content/uploads/2017/05/2016-Data-Analysis-1.pdf.

Nat'l Agency for the Prohibition of Trafficking in Persons, First Quarter Report 2017 7-8 (2017), https://www.naptip.gov.ng/wp-content/uploads/2017/05/2017-First-Quarter-Report-Modified-1.pdf.

Official J. of the Togolese Republic, Law No. 2005-009, Chap. II, art. 3 (Aug. 3, 2005), https://www.ilo.org/dyn/natlex/docs/SERIAL/72058/72983/F1981134441/trafic%20enfants.pdf.

*Osman v. United Kingdom*, European Court of Human Rights, Judgment, Application No. 23452/94 (28 October 1998).

Penal Code (2004) Cap. (C3) §55 (Nigeria).

*Protection of Victims of Trafficking in Ghana: Report from Danish Immigration Service's fact-finding mission to Accra, Ghana*, Danish Immigr. Svc. 13-14 (Jun. 2008), https://www.nyidanmark.dk/NR/rdonlyres/EB5BAEDA-0D96-46C2-B2D2-E48BA8911B2C/0/Ghanaffrapport2008.pdf.

*Providing Effective Remedies for Victims of Trafficking in Persons*, (ICAT) 14 (2016), https://www.unodc.org/documents/human-trafficking/ICAT/ICAT_Policy_Paper_3._Providing_Effective_Remedies_for_Victims_of_Trafficking_in_Persons_2016.pdf.

*Providing Effective Remedies for Victims of Trafficking in Persons*, 11-12 (ICAT 2016) https://www.unodc.org/documents/human-trafficking/ICAT/ICAT_Policy_Paper_3._Providing_Effective_Remedies_for_Victims_of_Trafficking_in_Persons_2016.pdf.

*Rantsev v. Cyprus and Russia*, No. 25965/04, ECtHR, ¶ 242 (January 7, 2010) https://ec.europa.eu/anti-trafficking/sites/antitrafficking/files/rantsev_vs_russia_cyprus_en_4.pdf.

Refugee Convention, art. 33.

Report of the Special Rapporteur on Trafficking in Persons, Especially Women and Children, ¶ 42, U.N. Doc. A/66/283 (Aug. 9, 2011) (by Joy Ngozi Ezelio).

Report of the Special. Rapporteur on Trafficking in Persons, Especially Women and Child, ¶ 19, U.N. Doc. A/67/261 (Aug. 7, 2010), (available at: https://business-humanrights.org/sites/default/files/media/documents/special-rap-report-trafficking-7-aug-2012.pdf).

*Report on the Progress Made in the Fight Against Trafficking in Human Beings*, European Commission 13-14 (May 19, 2016), https://ec.europa.eu/home-affairs/sites/homeaffairs/files/what-we-do/policies/organized-crime-and-human-trafficking/trafficking-in-human-beings/docs/commission_report_on_the_progress_made_in_the_fight_against_trafficking_in_human_beings_2016_en.pdf.

Graham Rossiter, *Catholic Education and Values: A Review of the Role of Catholic Schools in Promoting the Spiritual and Moral Development of Pupils* 3 (unpublished manuscript), http://citeseerx.ist.psu.edu/viewdoc/download?doi=10.1.1.577.7806&rep=rep1&type=pdf.

*SERAP v. Nigeria and Universal Basic Education Commission*, ECOWAS Comm. Ct. Just., Suit No. ECW/CCJ/APP/08/09, Judgment, ¶ 39 (Dec. 14, 2012).

*SERAP v. Nigeria*, ECOWAS Community Ct. of Just., Suit No. ECW/CCJ/APP/12/07, Judgment (Nov. 30, 2010).

*Slide Presentation: Moving Upstream: The Story of Prevention* (University of Colorado, Denver), http://www.ucdenver.edu/academics/colleges/PublicHealth/research/ResearchProjects/piper/PREVENT/education/Documents/Outline1.pdf.

*Sum of the Proceedings Concerning the Talibés Case*, Int'l Network for Econ. Social & Cultural Rts (2014), https://www.escr-net.org/node/366332.

*Summary of the Consultations Held on the Draft Basic Principles on the Right to Effective Remedy for Victims of Trafficking in Persons*, U.N. Doc. A/HRC/26/18, para. 27 (May 2, 2014), http://undocs.org/A/HRC/26/18.

*The Principle of Non-Refoulement as a Norm of Customary International Law: Response to the Questions Posed to UNHCR by the Federal Constitutional Court of the Federal Republic of Germany in Cases 2 BvR 1938/93, 2 BvR 1953/93, 2 BvR 1954/93*, UNCHR (Jan. 31 1994), http://www.refworld.org/docid/437b6db64.html.

*Trafficking in Persons Report 2009: Ghana,* U.S. Dep't of State, (Jun. 2009), https://www.state.gov/j/tip/rls/tiprpt/2009/123136.htm.

*Trafficking in Persons Report 2017*, U.S. Dep't of State (Jun. 2017), https://www.state.gov/documents/organization/271339.pdf.

*Trafficking in Persons Report 2017: Benin*, U.S. Dep't of St. (Jun. 2017), https://www.state.gov/j/tip/rls/tiprpt/countries/2017/271147.htm.

*Trafficking in Persons Report 2017: Burkina Faso*, U.S. Dep't of St. (Jun. 2017), https://www.state.gov/documents/organization/271341.pdf.

*Trafficking in Persons Report 2017: Ghana*, U.S. Dep't of State (Jun. 2017), https://www.state.gov/j/tip/rls/tiprpt/countries/2017/271194.htm.

*Trafficking in Persons Report 2017: Guinea*, U.S. Dep't of St. (Jun. 2017), https://www.state.gov/j/tip/rls/tiprpt/countries/2017/271197.htm.

*Training for TIP Nat'l Focal Points*, Int'l Training Ctr. of the Int'l Lab. Org., http://www.ilo.org/wcmsp5/groups/public/%2D%2D-africa/documents/publication/wcms_348047.pdf.

*U.N. Econ. & Soc. Council, Education for All Monitoring Report 2015*, at 84 (2015), http://unesdoc.unesco.org/images/0023/002322/232205e.pdf.

U.S. Dep't of State, 2018 Trafficking in Persons Report 2018 – Ghana, available at: https://www.refworld.org/docid/5b3e0b364.html [accessed August 17, 2021]

U.S. Dep't of State, Trafficking in Persons Report 2014: Benin (Jun. 2014), http://www.state.gov/j/tip/rls/tiprpt/countries/2014/226682.htm.

U.S. Dep't of State, Trafficking in Persons Report 2014: Burkina Faso (Jun. 2014), https://www.state.gov/j/tip/rls/tiprpt/countries/2014/226690.htm.

U.S. Dep't of State, Trafficking in Persons Report 2016: TOGO (Jun. 2016)

U.S. Dep't of State, Trafficking in Persons Report 2017 (Jun. 2017).

U.S. Dep't of State, Trafficking in Persons Report 2017: Ghana (Jun. 2017), https://www.state.gov/j/tip/rls/tiprpt/countries/2017/271194.htm.

U.S. Dep't of State, Trafficking in Persons Report 2017: Guinea, *supra* note 82.

United Nations High Commissioner for Human Rights Principles and Guidelines on Human Rights and Trafficking, E/2002/68/Add.1 (2002), principle. 12.
United Nations High Commissioner for Human Rights Principles and Guidelines on Human Rights and Trafficking, E/2002/68/Add.1 (2002), Guideline 4: Ensuring an adequate legal framework.
United Nations High Commissioner for Human Rights Principles and Guidelines on Human Rights and Trafficking, E/2002/68/Add.1 (2002), Guideline 5: Ensuring an adequate law enforcement response.
United Nations High Commissioner for Human Rights Principles and Guidelines on Human Rights and Trafficking, *Recommended Principles On Human Rights And Human Trafficking*, E/2002/68/Add.1 (2002).
UNODC, *Global Rep. on Trafficking in Persons 2014*, at 52 (Nov. 2014), https://www.unodc.org/documents/data-and-analysis/glotip/GLOTIP_2014_full_report.pdf.
UNODC, Model Law against Trafficking in Persons, p. 23 https://www.unodc.org/documents/human-trafficking/UNODC_Model_Law_on_Trafficking_in_Persons.pdf;
UNTOC, Article 25(2): "Each State Party shall establish appropriate procedures to provide access to compensation and restitution for victims."
*Velasquez Rodriguez v. Honduras*, Inter-American Court of Human Rights, Judgment, Rep. No. 4 (Ser. C) ¶ 176 (29 July 1988).
*Women, Inheritance and Islam in Mali*, Agriknowledge.org (Feb. 2011), https://agriknowledge.org/downloads/kd17cs934; *see also Violence against Women in Mali: A Report to the Human Rights Committee*, World Organization Against Torture (OMCT) (2003) http://www.omct.org/files/2004/07/2409/eng_2003_07_mali.pdf.
*Z and Others v. United Kingdom*, European Court of Human Rights, Judgment, Application No. 29392/95 (10 May 2001).

## References

Abdulrahim OS, Egede SC, Taylor-Nicholson E (eds) (2009) Access to justice for trafficked persons in Nigeria: a handbook for legal actors and assistance providers
Agrinya C (2016) Hope with Caritas after escaping from trafficking. Caritas.Org, 2 May 2016. http://www.caritas.org/2016/02/hope-with-caritas-after-escaping-from-trafficking/
Alcantara A (2012) The great debate: is law enforcement alone enough to reduce human trafficking? Col Univ J Int Aff. https://jia.sipa.columbia.edu/online-articles/great-debate-law-enforcement-alone-enough-reduce-human-trafficking
Allain J (2012) Slavery in international law: of human exploitation and trafficking. Brill, p 186
Allain J (2015) The law and slavery: prohibiting human exploitation. Brill Publication, p 274. https://www.icc-cpi.int/NR/rdonlyres/069658BB-FDBD-4EDD-8414-543ECB1FA9DC/0/ICCOTP20070426Allain_en.pdf. Accessed 20 Aug 2021
Andrew R, Lawrance BN (2012) Anti-trafficking legislation in sub-Saharan Africa: analyzing the role of coercion and parental responsibility. Paper 17, Presented at Fourth Annual

Interdisciplinary Conference on Human Trafficking, Lincoln, Nebraska, 12 October 2012. http://digitalcommons.unl.edu/humtrafconf4/17

Barchue AW (2012) Pre-trial detention and the rule of law in Nigeria and Liberia, 31 December 2012. p 6. Unpublished L.L.M. thesis, Loyola University Chicago School of Law (on file with the Loyola University Chicago School of Law Rule of Law for Development John Felice Center. http://www.luc.edu/media/lucedu/prolaw/documents/BARCHUE%20PRETRIAL%20DETENTION.pdf)

Budiani-Saberi D, Columb S (2013) A human rights approach to human trafficking for organ removal. Springer Science+Business Media, Dordrecht, p 11. http://cofs.org/home/wp-content/uploads/2013/08/11019_2013_9488_OnlinePDF.pdf

Duffy H (2016) Litigating modern day slavery in regional courts. J Int Crim Just 14(375):376

Farrell A et al (2012) Identifying challenges to improve the investigation and prosecution of state investigation and prosecution of state and local human trafficking cases, p 52. Unpublished research report submitted to the U.S. Dep't of Just. https://humantraffickinghotline.org/sites/default/files/Identifying%20Challenges%20to%20Prosecution.pdf

Farrell A, McDevitt J, Owens C (2014) New laws but few cases: understanding the challenges to the investigation and prosecution of human trafficking cases. Crim Law Soc Change 61(132):142

Gallagher AT (2009) Presentation at the National Judicial College of Australia, Prosecuting and Adjudicating Trafficking in Persons Cases in Australia: obstacles and opportunities, 15 June 2009. http://traffickingroundtable.org/wp-content/uploads/2012/07/Presentation-National-Judicial-College-of-Australia.pdf

Gallagher AT (2013) Workshop presentation at the Pontifical Academies of Sciences, Pontifical Academy of Social Sciences, and World Federation of the Catholic Medical Associations: trafficking in human beings: modern slavery, 2 November 2013. http://www.endslavery.va/content/endslavery/en/publications/scripta_varia_122/gallagher.html

Gallagher AT (2016) Editorial: the problems and prospects of trafficking prosecutions: ending impunity and securing justice. Anti-Trafficking Rev 6:1. https://www.antitraffickingreview.org/index.php/atrjournal/article/view/166/169

Hassan YB, Kigbu SK (2015) Legal framework for combating human trafficking in Nigeria: the journey so far. J Law Policy Glob 38(146):205

Hawke A, Raphael A (2016) Global Study on Sexual Exploitation of Children in Travel and Tourism 2016. ECPAT Int, p 53. https://static1.squarespace.com/static/594970e91b631b3571be12e2/t/5975f0415016e132ff08e3d1/1500901444238/Global-Report-Offenders-on-the-Move-Final.pdf

Heemskerk M, Sertich M (2011) Ghana's Human Trafficking Act: successes and shortcomings in six years of implementation. Hum Rights Brief 19: 1, 27. http://digitalcommons.wcl.american.edu/cgi/viewcontent.cgi?article=1779&context=hrbrief

Hendrix MC (2010) Enforcing the U.S. Trafficking Victims Protection Act in emerging markets: the challenge of affecting change in India and China. Cornell Int Law J 43:173, 182. https://www.lawschool.cornell.edu/research/ILJ/upload/Hendrix.pdf

Ifemeje SC, Umejiaku N (2014) Discriminatory cultural practices and women's rights among the Igbos of South-East Nigeria: a critique. J Law Policy Glob 25:18

Jagannathan S (1999) World Bank, The role of nongovernmental organizations in primary education: a study of six NGOs in India, p 8. http://documents.worldbank.org/curated/en/760201468771257407/130530323_20041118114646/additional/multi0page.pdf

Kiskyte K (2016) Legal remedies for human trafficking in the United Kingdom and Lithuania 5 n. 11. Unpublished LL.M. paper, Notre Dame Law School (on file with Notre Dame Law School, https://humanrights.nd.edu/assets/205386/ht_lgl_rems_kiskytle.pdf)

Kraemer J (2013) Anti-human trafficking legislation in Tanzania and 6 countries around the world, 15 September 2013, p 25. Unpublished comment (on file with Cornell Law School)

Lloyd P, Simmons BA (2015) Framing for a new transnational legal order: the case of human trafficking. Faculty Scholarship, Paper 1698, 11, 408

Londo H (2008) Demand as a contributor facilitating the sexual exploitation of the children. Spring, Unpublished Master's thesis, Aalborg University. https://projekter.aau.dk/projekter/files/14410798/master_thesis_hanna_londo.doc

Marquette H (2010) Whither morality? 'Finding God' in the fight against corruption. Religions and Development Research Programme, Working Paper No. 41. https://www.birmingham.ac.uk/Documents/college-social-sciences/government-society/research/rad/working-papers/wp-41.pdf

Mattar MY (2006) Incorporating the five basic elements of a model antitrafficking in persons legislation in domestic laws: from the United Nations Protocol to the European Convention. Tulane J Int Comp Law 13(1):6

Obokata T (2006) Trafficking of human beings from a human rights perspective: towards a holistic approach

OHCHR (2010) Commentary on the recommended principles and guidelines, p 203

Opvang F (2014) Safe return and reintegration for victims of trafficking and victims of domestic violence facing residency problems, September 2014, p 46. http://www.opvang.nl/files/Safe_Return_Field_Research.pdf

Piotrowicz R (2012) States' obligations under human rights law towards victims of trafficking in human beings: positive developments in positive obligations. Int J Refugee Law 24:182

Ratner SR, Abrams JS (2001) Accountability for human rights atrocities in international law, 2nd edn, pp 11–13

Roujanavong W (2012) Human trafficking: a challenge to Thailand and the World Community, U.N. Asia and Far East Institute for the Prevention of Crime and the Treatment of Offenders ("UNAFEI"), 150th International Senior Seminar, August 2012. http://www.unafei.or.jp/english/pdf/RS_No87/No87_11VE_Wanchai.pdf

Salah R (2001) Child trafficking in West and Central Africa: an overview. NICEF 6, 19 February 2001. http://www.unicef.org/media/newsnotes/africchildtraffick.pdf

Schönhöfer J (2017) Political determinants of efforts to protect victims of human trafficking. Crim Law Soc Change 67

Shehu AT (2013) The enforcement of social and economic rights in Africa: the Nigerian experience. Afe Babalola Univ J Sustain Dev Law Policy 1, 2:113. https://www.ajol.info/index.php/jsdlp/article/download/122603/112151

Shelton D (2000) Remedies in international human rights law. Oxford University Press, pp 12–13

Shoaps LL (2013) Room for improvement: Palermo Protocol and the Trafficking Victims Protection Act. Lewis & Clark Law Rev 17:931, 952

Shu-Acquaye F (2013) Human trafficking: trends in Africa. Gonzaga Univ J Int Law. https://www.law.gonzaga.edu/gjil/2013/01/human-trafficking-trends-in-africa/

Stanley I (2016) Expanding access to justice for victims of pretrial injustice: reflections on the decision in Sikiru Alade v. Nigeria. Pan-Afr Yearb Law 2. https://lawyersofafrica.org/wp-content/uploads/2019/03/STANLEY-IBE-PAYL-VOL-II-2016-Article-by-Stanley-Ibe-1-1.pdf

Touzenis K (2010) Trafficking in human beings: human rights and trans-national criminal law, developments in law and practices. UNESCO, p 67. http://unesdoc.unesco.org/images/0018/001883/188397e.pdf

Triandafyllidou A, Marchetti S (2014) Europe 2020: addressing low skill labour migration at times of fragile recovery. RSCAS, p 6. https://cadmus.eui.eu/bitstream/handle/1814/31222/RSCAS_PP_2014_05.pdf?sequence=1

UNODC (2004) United Nations Convention Against Corruption, Art. 9. https://www.unodc.org/documents/brussels/UN_Convention_Against_Corruption.pdf

UNODC (2008) Toolkit to combat trafficking in persons, U.N. Sales No. E.08.V.14. https://www.unodc.org/documents/human-trafficking/Toolkit-files/08-58296_tool_9-12.pdf

UNODC (2010) Working Group on Trafficking in Persons, national approaches to compensation of victims of trafficking in persons, U.N. Doc. CTOC/COP/WG.4/2010/CRP.1, p 2, 10 October 2010. https://www.unodc.org/documents/treaties/organized_crime/COP5/CTOC_COP_WG4_2010_CRP1/CTOC_COP_WG4_2010_CRP1_E.pdf

UNODC (2016a) Global report on trafficking in persons 2016, pp 51–52. https://www.unodc.org/documents/data-and-analysis/glotip/2016_Global_Report_on_Trafficking_in_Persons.pdf [hereinafter Global Report on Trafficking in Persons 2016]
UNODC (2016b) Providing effective remedies for victims of trafficking in persons, ICAT 18. https://www.unodc.org/documents/human-trafficking/ICAT/ICAT_Policy_Paper_3._Providing_Effective_Remedies_for_Victims_of_Trafficking_in_Persons_2016.pdf
Vassiliadou M (2015) Legal and policy framework of the EU relating to criminalisation, prevention and demand reduction. The Pontifical Academy of Social Sciences Acta 20. https://dyhyjqmcimsyl.cloudfront.net/assets/files/6179/vatican-humantrafficking.pdf
Wheaton EM et al (2010) Economics of human trafficking. IOM 48 (4):114, 115–136. https://www.amherst.edu/media/view/247221/original/Economics+of+Human+Trafficking.pdf

# Part III
# Trafficking in Persons in Light of the Social Teaching of the Catholic Church

The following discussion focuses on problem-solving and decision making. The precedent development elaborated in international framework strived to galvanize legislatures and the judiciary at a domestic level to curtail, if not halt, the activities of traffickers that impinge upon human dignity. Although countries have passed legislations criminalizing trafficking in persons and have established judicial structures, laws without adequate implementation are akin to a watch dog without teeth. It does not punish or protect anyone. In addition, law enforcement efforts by their very nature are limited as they are designed to address the consequences of trafficking rather than its causes.

Given the rule of law alone cannot solve this issue, this discussion proposed an interdisciplinary approach that integrates law and Christian anthropology to develop recommendations that will achieve more positive results. In this regard, the New Haven School of international law, also called "Policy-Oriented Jurisprudence," offers an innovative conceptual framework as it applies the analytical methods of the social sciences to the prescriptive purposes of the law to create solutions to social problems.[1] The normative social goal of this jurisprudence is the maximization of shared community values and the promotion of human dignity.[2]

From a New Haven School perspective, every human being, including trafficking victims, will aspire to power, enlightenment, well-being, wealth, skills, affection, rectitude, and respect to fulfill their deepest desires and enhance their human dignity.[3] However, trafficking in persons threatens and deprives people of these values, which protected by international human rights law and national legal norms.

---

[1] Wallace Denise, *Human Rights and Business: A Policy-Oriented Perspective*. Brill | Nijhoff, 2014; Read W. Michael Reisman, Siegfried Wiessner & Andrew R. Willard, *The New Haven School: A Brief Introduction*, 32 Yale J. Int'l L. 575, 576 (2007).

[2] Land Molly, *Reflections on the New Haven School* (2013). Faculty Articles and Papers. 272; W. Michael Reisman et al., The New Haven School. A Brief Introduction, 32 Yale J. Int'l L. 575, 576 (2007).

[3] Harold D. Laswell & Myres S. McDougal, *The Identification and Appraisal of Diverse Systems of Public Order*, 53 Am. J. Int'l L. 7, 12–13 (1959).

This intellectual framework has creative potential as it is founded on the shared value of human dignity and establishes a bridge between cultures, religions, and people. To formulate further improvements, the following argument draws upon the Catholic Church's Social Teaching on human dignity[4] to elaborate recommendations that can enhance the rule of law in addressing trafficking in persons. This is because the social doctrine of the Catholic Church provides a foundational understanding of human dignity and affirms the obligation of everyone to act justly and the duty of every community to ensure all its members can live with dignity.

[4]The concept of dignity of the human person, which has become the founding value of what it is to be human was first introduced into the social and political discourse on a larger scale by Pope Leo XIII through his encyclical letter On the Origin of Civil Power (Diuturnum, 1881).

# Chapter 10
# Trafficking in Persons in the Magisterium's Documents

In 1965 Council Vatican II condemned the enslavement of human beings as a crime against one's neighbors and a "supreme dishonor to the Creator" that poisons human society.[1] The Pastoral Constitution on the Church in the Modern World (Gaudium et Spes)[2] declares that "slavery, prostitution, the selling of women and children and disgraceful working conditions where people are treated as instruments of gain rather than free and responsible persons" are insults to human dignity and "an affront to fundamental values... rooted in the very nature of the human person."[3] The Encyclical *Veritatis Splendor* (The splendor of Truth) condemns slavery as an act that is "intrinsically evil", depriving the victims of their right to liberty, dignity, security, the right not to be held in servitude, and the right to be free from cruel and inhuman treatment.

The Second Council acknowledged that women's fundamental personal rights are not universally respected and calls for the eradication of every form of social or cultural discrimination that denies women the right to choose a husband freely, embrace a state of life or acquire an education or cultural benefits equal to those

---

[1] *See* John F. Maxwell, Slavery and the Catholic Church (1975). It is worth noting that the Second Vatican Council officially corrected the Church's common teaching on slavery; *see generally* Maura O'Donohue, The Social Teaching of the Church at the Service of Humanity in Europe, Presentation to WUCWO European Conf. (Sep. 3, 2008), http://www.aptireland.org/wp-content/uploads/2012/06/odonohue_the_social_teaching_of_the_church_at_the_service_of_humanity_in_europe.pd; Barnabe D'Souza, *The Dynamics of Human Trafficking*, Pontifical Council for the Pastoral Care of Migrants and Itinerant People: People on the Move no. 117 (2012), http://www.pcmigrants.org/pom-117/souza.htm.

[2] Paul VI, Pastoral Constitution on the Church in the Modern World: Gaudium et Spes ¶ 27 (Dec. 7, 1965), http://www.vatican.va/archive/hist_councils/ii_vatican_council/documents/vat-ii_cons_19651207_gaudium-et-spes_en.html [hereinafter Gaudium et Spes]; catholic anti-slavery teaching is found principally in pontifical and conciliar documents beginning with Rerum Novarum (1891); these contain the broad doctrine of catholic social teaching and serve as an impetus for the development of local episcopal pastoral teaching.

[3] *Id.* ¶ 27, 67.

 
P. VI. S. Karenga, *A West African Model to Address Human Trafficking*,
https://doi.org/10.1007/978-3-030-88120-7_10

recognized for men.[4] In relation to, the Supreme Pontiff John Paul II wrote an apostolic letter dedicated entirely to the dignity and vocation of woman. Entitled *Mulieris Dignitatem*, it declared the following: "the Church desires to give thanks to the Most Holy Trinity for the "mystery of woman" and for every woman—for that which constitutes the eternal measure of her feminine dignity, for the "great works of God," which throughout human history have been accomplished in and through her. After all, was it not in and through her that the greatest event in human history—the incarnation of God himself—was accomplished?"[5]

In a letter to women on the eve of the Fourth World Conference on Women, to be held in Beijing in 1995, the Holy Father Pope John Paul II deplored the fact that "Women's dignity has often been unacknowledged and their prerogatives misrepresented; they have often been relegated to the margins of society and even reduced to servitude. This has prevented women from truly being themselves and it has resulted in a spiritual impoverishment of humanity."[6] The Apostolic Exhortation Ecclesia in Africa praised the dignity of African women and their specific role in the Church and society at large and "condemns, to the extent that they are still found in some African societies, all the customs and practices which deprive women of their rights and the respect due to them."[7]

Updated in 1995, the Catechism of the Catholic Church incorporates the insights of the Church magisterium, framing its anti-slavery teaching in reference to the seventh commandment which "forbids acts or enterprises that for any reason — selfish or ideological, commercial, or totalitarian — lead to the enslavement of human beings, to their being bought, sold and exchanged like merchandise, in disregard for their personal dignity. It is a sin against the dignity of persons and their fundamental rights to reduce them by violence to their productive value or to a source of profit. St. Paul directed a Christian master to treat his Christian slave no longer as a slave but more than a slave, as a beloved brother... both in the flesh and in the Lord."[8]

The Compendium of the Social Doctrine of the Church sets out fundamental elements of the Church's teaching that are related to social issues. This document contains the most extensive discussion in reference to slavery, trafficking and human rights, and reflects a serious concern with *"the painful reality* ...of ever new forms of slavery such as trafficking in human beings, child soldiers, the exploitation of

---

[4] *Id.* ¶ 29.

[5] John Paul II, Mulieris Dignitatem, on the Dignity of Women ¶ 31 (1988), http://w2.vatican.va/content/john-paul-ii/en/apost_letters/1988/documents/hf_jp-ii_apl_19880815_mulieris-dignitatem.html.

[6] John Paul II, Letter to Women ¶ 3(1995), https://w2.vatican.va/content/john-paul-ii/en/letters/1995/documents/hf_jp-ii_let_29061995_women.html.

[7] John Paul II, Post-Synodal Apostolic Exhortation Ecclesia in Africa ¶ 121 (1995), http://w2.vatican.va/content/john-paul-ii/en/apost_exhortations/documents/hf_jp-ii_exh_14091995_ecclesia-in-africa.html. [hereinafter Apostolic Exhortation].

[8] Pope John Paul, II, Catechism of the Catholic Church, Vatican ¶ 2414 (United States Catholic Conference, Inc., 2000) [available at http://www.vatican.va/archive/ENG0015/__P8B.HTM].

workers, illegal drug trafficking, prostitution."[9] The commercial exploitation of children in pornographic material, trafficking, child labor, child marriage, in armed conflicts, and in pedophilia are listed as specific injustices experienced by the majority of children in the world. These criminal acts "must be effectively fought with adequate preventative and penal measures by the determined action of the different authorities involved."[10]

In his first Apostolic Exhortation, Evangelii Gaudium (2013), Pope Francis stated that

> [t]his issue [of human trafficking] involves everyone. This infamous network of crime is now well established in our cities and many people have blood on their hands as a result of their comfortable and silent complicity... Where is the brother and sister whom you are killing each day in clandestine warehouses, in rings of prostitution, in children used for begging, in exploiting undocumented labour? Let us not look the other way (no.211).

In his 2015 World Day of Peace Message, the Supreme Pontiff formally rejected slavery and considered the phenomenon to be a pure anachronism. This message on contemporary forms of slavery issued by the Leader of the Catholic Church was presented to the heads of governments and states to call their attention to the seriousness of the issue, and the urgent need to take action.[11]

Alongside the magisterium teaching, the Church's legislative structure also contains relevant provisions tied to trafficking in persons and related practices. For instance, the Roman Catholic Canon Law (can 1083 and 930) prohibits the abduction of women either for marriage (kidnapping or elopement) or enslavement (particularly sexual slavery). A similar provision is secured in canon law 2354, requiring that any catholic (cleric and lay person) guilty of rape against a minor, of real slavery, or the selling of a human individual for any evil purpose be punished with penances, censures, and be ipso facto deprived of the right to legal actions and of any position, benefices, or dignities they may have in the Church. Usury is the most common mode of victim exploitation given, for example, the difference between the cost of the travel (US $ 200) and the income actually received from payment of the debt of US $ 4000).[12] The canon law of 1917 contains an explicit

---

[9] Pontifical Council for Just. and Peace, Compendium of the Social Doctrine of the Church ¶ 158 (2004), http://www.vatican.va/roman_curia/pontifical_councils/justpeace/documents/rc_pc_justpeace_doc_20060526_compendio-dott-soc_en.html [hereinafter Social Doctrine of the Church].

[10] *Id.* ¶ 245.

[11] Francis, No Longer Slaves, But Brothers and Sisters, World Day Of Peace ¶ 5 (Jan. 1, 2015), https://w2.vatican.va/content/francesco/en/messages/peace/documents/papa-francesco_20141208_messaggio-xlviii-giornata-mondiale-pace-2015.html; *cf.* Human Trafficking: Issues Beyond Criminalization, The Pontifical Academy of Social Sciences Acta 20, at 72 (Apr. 15, 2016), https://vista-analyse.no/site/assets/files/6179/vatican-humantrafficking.pdf.

[12] *Côte d'Ivoire/Nigeria: Combat Trafficking for Prostitution*, Human Rts Watch (Aug. 26, 2010), http://www.hrw.org/news/2010/08/26/c-te-d-ivoirenigeria-combat-trafficking-prostitution.

provision on the concept of usury and outlaws charging an excessive and unreasonable rate of interest on a loan (can 1543) (Dt 15:7-10; Lk 6:35).[13]

To fulfil its commitment to combat trafficking in persons the Catholic Church has dedicated an office to human trafficking at the United Nations. By the same token, in 1978 the Apostolic See established the Pontifical Council for the Pastoral Care of Migrant and Itinerant People which, in recent times, has monitored victims of trafficking in persons. Due to the worldwide organizational structure of the Catholic Church, "this particular Pontifical Council consists especially in encouraging the various Conferences of Bishops throughout the world to fight human trafficking and to do this with the participation of religious women and men, lay people, various Catholic associations and various movements."[14] The situation regarding conflicts and the migratory phenomenon in the region, led the episcopal conferences in West Africa to establish Commissions of Migrant and Itinerant People. Consistent with the same concern, Pope Francis issued an Apostolic Letter *Humanam Progressionem* (August 17, 2016) merging the four Dicasteries (the Pontifical Council for Justice and Peace, the Pontifical Council Cor Unum, the Pontifical Council for the Pastoral Care of Migrants and Itinerant People, and the Pontifical Council for Health Care Workers) to create the Dicastery for Promoting Integral Human Development. This institution is an expression of the Church's constitutive mission to promote "integral human development in the light of the Gospel and in the tradition of the Church's social teachings."[15] Remarkably, a section of the Dicastery deals specifically with issues concerning migrants, refugees and victims of all forms of slave trade and human trafficking.[16]

Additionally, the Church in Africa, through its continental institutions such as Symposium of Episcopal Conferences of Africa and Madagascar (SECAM), is involved in the fight against trafficking through the Caritas network in all countries and dioceses in West Africa. Furthermore, through bodies such as Commission Justice and Peace, Catholic Relief Services (CRS), and Religious NGOs, the Church offers material and pastoral support to refugees and displaced people.[17] Most

---

[13] Bonded labor is a system of usury in which the debtor has to work to pay off travel fees or any other debt without reasonable wages or no wages. The evils of bonded labor have been recognized as infringing on basic human rights and violating the dignity of work.

[14] *See generally* David Kaulemu, ed., Faith Perspectives on Migration and Human Trafficking (2012); *cf.* Stephen Fumio Hamao, Erga Migrantes Caritas Christi (The love of Christ Towards Migrants), Pontifical Council for the Pastoral Care of Migrants and Itinerant People ¶ 31 (2004), http://www.acmro.catholic.org.au/about/church-documents-on-migration/the-teaching-of-the-universal-church/other-vatican-documents/45-pontifical-council-for-the-pastoral-care-of-migrants-and-itinerant-people/file (Number of Catholic agencies including HT in their activities are: Catholic Relief Services, Caritas International, International Justice and Peace, the Leadership Conference of Women Religious, Commonwealth Catholic charities, Catholic legal immigration, the African women religious conference).

[15] Pope Francis, *Statutes of the Dicastery for Promoting Integral Human Development*, Article 1,2.

[16] *Id*, at Article 1,3.

[17] Peter Appiah Turkson, *Current SECAM-CCEE dialogue on Migration*, Pontifical Council for the Pastoral Care of Migrants and Itinerant People: People on the Move, no.109 (Apr. 2009), http://

importantly, since the creation of the Symposium of Episcopal Conferences of Africa and Madagascar (SECAM) in Kampala in 1969, a host of initiatives have been articulated in documentary form, reflecting the social teachings of the Church as a result of which universal and significant pastoral actions have been undertaken to tackle the causes of numerous social woes such as trafficking in persons.[18] From November 13th–18th, 2007 a seminar jointly organized by the Symposium of Episcopal Conferences of Africa and Madagascar (SECAM) and the Council of European Episcopal Conferences (CCEE), marking the 200th anniversary of the abolition of slavery in Africa, called for more attention to be paid to new forms of slavery taking place in Africa, such as trafficking in persons, forced labor, child soldiers, prostitution, and so on.[19]

Also worth noting are the publication on Good Governance and Democratic Transitions by the Symposium of Episcopal Conferences of Africa and Madagascar (SECAM) Justice and Peace Department, countless pastoral letters, solidarity visits, advocacy initiatives, Alternative Dispute Resolution Mechanisms (ADRM), collaborative efforts with the United Nations in the elaboration of SDGs (Sustainable Development Goals), Caritas actions with the International Cooperation for Development and Solidarity (CIDSE),[20] the European Parliament, African Union, Sub-regional Economic and Political Institutions such as the Arab League, the Economic Community of West Africa States (ECOWAS), the Southern African Development Community (SADC), and so on, all of which implement the 4 Ps (Protection, Prosecution, Prevention, Partnership).[21]

## References

Anokye G (2007) A Contribution on Children Slavery at a Round Table Discussion. In: SECAM-CCEE Seminar on the Occasion of the 200th Anniversary of the Abolition of Slavery in Africa (Nov. 13, 2007)

Caritas Africa e-Magazine, no. 27, at 6 (Sep. 2016), http://www.caritas-africa.org/Info0916.pdf

*Côte d'Ivoire/Nigeria: Combat Trafficking for Prostitution*, Human Rts Watch (Aug. 26, 2010), http://www.hrw.org/news/2010/08/26/c-te-d-ivoirenigeria-combat-trafficking-prostitution

---

www.vatican.va/roman_curia/pontifical_councils/migrants/pom2009_109-suppl/rc_pc_migrants_pom109-suppl_current-turkson.html.

[18] Caritas Africa e-Magazine, no. 27, at 6 (Sep. 2016), http://www.caritas-africa.org/Info0916.pdf.

[19] Gabriel Anokye, *A Contribution on Children Slavery at a Round Table Discussion*, SECAM-CCEE Seminar on the Occasion of the 200th Anniversary of the Abolition of Slavery in Africa (Nov. 13, 2007).

[20] Coopération Internationale pour le Développement et la Solidarité ("CIDSE"), https://www.cidse.org/who-we-are.html ("CIDSE is an international alliance of Catholic development agencies sharing a common strategy in their efforts to eradicate poverty and establish global justice").

[21] Caritas Africa e-Magazine, no. 27, at 6-9 (Sep. 2016), http://www.caritas-africa.org/Info0916.pdf.

D'Souza B (2012) The Dynamics of Human Trafficking, Pontifical Council for the Pastoral Care of Migrants and Itinerant People: People on the Move no. 117, http://www.pcmigrants.org/pom-117/souza.htm

Francis, No Longer Slaves, But Brothers and Sisters, World Day Of Peace ¶ 5 (Jan. 1, 2015), https://w2.vatican.va/content/francesco/en/messages/peace/documents/papa-francesco_20141208_messaggio-xlviii-giornata-mondiale-pace-2015.html; *cf.* Human Trafficking: Issues Beyond Criminalization, The Pontifical Academy of Social Sciences Acta 20, at 72 (Apr. 15, 2016), https://vista-analyse.no/site/assets/files/6179/vatican-humantrafficking.pdf

John Paul II, Mulieris Dignitatem, on the Dignity of Women ¶ 31 (1988), http://w2.vatican.va/content/john-paul-ii/en/apost_letters/1988/documents/hf_jp-ii_apl_19880815_mulieris-dignitatem.html

John Paul II, Letter to Women ¶ 3 (1995), https://w2.vatican.va/content/john-paul-ii/en/letters/1995/documents/hf_jp-ii_let_29061995_women.html

John Paul II, Post-Synodal Apostolic Exhortation Ecclesia in Africa ¶ 121 (1995), http://w2.vatican.va/content/john-paul-ii/en/apost_exhortations/documents/hf_jp-ii_exh_14091995_ecclesia-in-africa.html

Kaulemu D (ed) (2012) Faith Perspectives on Migration and Human Trafficking. *See generally*; *cf.* Stephen Fumio Hamao, Erga Migrantes Caritas Christi (The love of Christ Towards Migrants), Pontifical Council for the Pastoral Care of Migrants and Itinerant People ¶ 31 (2004), http://www.acmro.catholic.org.au/about/church-documents-on-migration/the-teaching-of-the-universal-church/other-vatican-documents/45-pontifical-council-for-the-pastoral-care-of-migrants-and-itinerant-people/file

Lasswell HD, McDougal MS (1959) The identification and appraisal of diverse systems of public order. Am J Int Law 53(7):12–13

Maxwell JF (1975) Slavery and the Catholic Church ("As is well known the common teaching on slavery was officially corrected by the Second Vatican Council in 1965")

Michael Reisman RW, Wiessner S, Willard AR (2007) The New Haven school: a brief introduction. Yale J Int Law 32:575, 576

Molly L (2013) Reflections on the New Haven School. Faculty Articles and Papers. 272

O'Donohue M (2008) The Social Teaching of the Church at the Service of Humanity in Europe, Presentation to WUCWO European Conf. (Sep. 3, 2008), http://www.aptireland.org/wp-content/uploads/2012/06/odonohue_the_social_teaching_of_the_church_at_the_service_of_humanity_in_europe.pd

Paul VI, Pastoral Constitution on the Church in the Modern World: Gaudium et Spes ¶ 27 (Dec. 7, 1965), http://www.vatican.va/archive/hist_councils/ii_vatican_council/documents/vat-ii_cons_19651207_gaudium-et-spes_en.html

Pontifical Council for Just. and Peace, Compendium of the Social Doctrine of the Church ¶ 158 (2004), http://www.vatican.va/roman_curia/pontifical_councils/justpeace/documents/rc_pc_justpeace_doc_20060526_compendio-dott-soc_en.html

Pope Francis, *Statutes of the Dicastery for Promoting Integral Human Development*, Article 1,2

Pope John Paul, II, Catechism of the Catholic Church, Vatican ¶ 2414 (United States Catholic Conference, Inc., 2000) [available at http://www.vatican.va/archive/ENG0015/__P8B.HTM]

Turkson PA (2009) *Current SECAM-CCEE dialogue on Migration*, Pontifical Council for the Pastoral Care of Migrants and Itinerant People: People on the Move, no.109 (Apr. 2009), http://www.vatican.va/roman_curia/pontifical_councils/migrants/pom2009_109-suppl/rc_pc_migrants_pom109-suppl_current-turkson.html

Wallace D (2014) Human rights and business: a policy-oriented perspective. Brill | Nijhoff

# Chapter 11
# Principles of Catholic Social Teaching Related to Trafficking

Pope Francis states that trafficking in persons "constitutes a grave violation of the human rights of those victimized and is an offense against their dignity, as well as a defeat for the worldwide community."[1] Combating trafficking in human beings is relevant to the principle of human life and dignity, the promotion of human rights and responsibilities, the fight against poverty, preferential options for the poor and vulnerable, the dignity of work and workers' rights, economic justice, and solidarity firmly laid down in Catholic Social Teaching.[2]

## 11.1 The Protection of Life and the Dignity of Human Persons

Human dignity is the foundation and guiding principle of the Catholic Church's teaching and action in relation to trafficking in human beings. This stipulates that, all people have dignity because they are loved and created in the image and likeness of God (Genesis 1:26–27), and are endowed with a spiritual soul.[3] In fact, among all the world's visible creatures, only human beings have a "capacity for God" (*homo est*

---

[1] Francis, *Address of Pope Francis to the New Ambassadors Accredited to the Holy See on the Occasion of the Presentation of the Letters of Credence* (Dec. 12, 2013), http://w2.vatican.va/content/francesco/en/speeches/2013/december/documents/papa-francesco_20131212_credenziali-nuovi-ambasciatori.html.

[2] *Cf.* Caritas Internationalis, The Caritas Internationalis Commitment on Combating Trafficking in Human Beings, (Oct. 2005) http://www.renate-europe.net/wp-content/uploads/2014/01/Caritas_Internationalis_commitment_on_trafficking_created_in_image_of_God2005.pdf.

[3] *Cf.* Pontifical Council for Just. and Peace, Compendium of the Social Doctrine of the Church ¶ 259 (2004), http://www.vatican.va/roman_curia/pontifical_councils/justpeace/documents/rc_pc_justpeace_doc_20060526_compendio-dott-soc_en.html; John Paul II, *Veritatis Splendor* ¶ 48 (Encyclical Letter, 6 Aug. 1993).



P. VI. S. Karenga, *A West African Model to Address Human Trafficking*,
https://doi.org/10.1007/978-3-030-88120-7_11

*Dei capax*);[4] therefore by their very existence all people are valuable and worthy of honor and esteem. This distinguishes human beings "from other creatures, notably animals, [and] underlines the uniqueness of human beings among all creatures, above all their free will, individual autonomy and capability of independent decision-making based on reason and free moral choice."[5]

The Encyclical Letter *Populorum Progressio* (On the Progress of Peoples) underscores the significance of human dignity as Pope Paul VI made the principle of "integral human development" the normative approach to pursue development goals that foster a more humane world. The encyclical explains that 'authentic development' "cannot be limited to mere economic growth. In order to be authentic, it must be complete: integral, that is, it has to promote the good of every person and of the whole person."[6] It follows from this understanding that the ultimate goal of activities towards development and progress is to enhance prosperity and human flourishing in its economic, social, political, cultural, psychological and spiritual dimensions. Thus, integral human development is a holistic vision of development which places the human person at the center of any developmental process with human dignity as a fundamental guiding value. Indeed, "human dignity forms an a priori justification for the existence of human rights, and in turn human rights becomes a means to realizing human dignity."[7] The concept of human dignity, with its universal scope across cultures provides common ground for the development of agreed priorities. Additionally, it also has the potential to engage various religious, political affiliation and secular humanistic traditions to work together to build "a world where every person, no matter what his or her race, religion or nationality, can live a fully human life, freed from servitude imposed by other people or by natural forces."[8] Thus, people are called to love others regardless of a person's race, gender, social status, disability, or history and to respect human life; such respect means ensuring that each person lives life fully, experiencing the abundance of God's love and participating in all aspects of human society. Under no circumstance, therefore, is the human person to be enslaved, manipulated, and exploited for ends that are foreign to his or her own development.[9]

---

[4] Social Doctrine of the Church, *supra* note 3, ¶ 109.

[5] Paulus Kaufman, et al., eds., Humiliation, Degradation, Dehumanization: Human Dignity Violated 1 (2011), p.1 http://www.corteidh.or.cr/tablas/r30885.pdf; Saint Irenaeus of Lyons, *Adversus Haereses*, IV, 20, 7; JOHN PAUL II, *Enc. Evangelium Vitae*, 34 "Man has been given a sublime dignity, based on the intimate bond which unites him to his Creator: in man there shines forth a reflection of God himself."

[6] Pope Paul VI (1967).

[7] Andrew M. Song, Human dignity: A fundamental guiding value for a human rights approach to fisheries?, https://www.sciencedirect.com/science/article/pii/S0308597X15002328 The International Covenant on Economic, Social and Cultural Rights states in the Preamble that "these rights derive from the inherent dignity of the human person."

[8] Populorum Progressio, *supra* note 6 at no.47.

[9] Social Doctrine of the Church, *supra* note 3, ¶ 133.

As such, the protection of human dignity has wide ranging implications for political governance, individual life, and religious assumptions. At a state and societal level, the socio-political order and its development must invariably work to the benefit of the human person, as the order of things is to be subordinate to the order of persons.[10] In this regard, the Church declares that the respect for human life and the dignity of human persons must be "a constitutive element of a civil society and its legislation."[11] It thus follows that any political, economic, social, scientific and cultural program must give primacy to each and every human being over society and state.[12] A just society can become a reality only when it is based on the respect for the transcendent dignity of the human person. The person represents the ultimate end of society.[13]

In terms of its individual and social dimensions, the call for human dignity implies a duty for every man and woman at every moment of history to ensure its defense and promotion.[14] The Catechism of the Catholic Church considers as a sin against a person's dignity and fundamental human rights, any act or cultural practices leading to the enslavement of humans. The document underscores that

> [t]he seventh commandment forbids acts or enterprises that for any reason – selfish or ideological, commercial, or totalitarian – lead to the enslavement of human beings, to their being bought, sold and exchanged like merchandise, in disregard for their personal dignity. It is a sin against the dignity of persons and their fundamental rights to reduce them by violence to their productive value or to a source of profit. St. Paul directed a Christian master to treat his Christian slave 'no longer as a slave but more than a slave, as a beloved brother, . . .both in the flesh and in the Lord.'[15]

The sexual exploitation of women and children in particular is a repugnant aspect of this trade and must be recognized as one of the offenses against life and the integrity of the human person.[16] The disturbing propensity to consider prostitution as a business or industry not only contributes to the trade in human beings, it also

---

[10]Paul VI, Pastoral Constitution on the Church in the Modern World: Gaudium et Spes ¶ 26 (Dec. 7, 1965), http://www.vatican.va/archive/hist_councils/ii_vatican_council/documents/vat-ii_cons_19651207_gaudium-et-spes_en.html; *cf.* Chigona (2012), p 22. http://www.afcast.org.zw/articles/Trafficking_final_proof.pdf.

[11]Catechism of the Catholic Church, no.2273 (2003).

[12]Pope John Paul, II, Catechism of the Catholic Church, Vatican ¶ 2235 (United States Catholic Conference, Inc., 2000) [available at http://www.vatican.va/archive/ENG0015/__P8B.HTM].

[13]Social Doctrine of the Church, *supra* note 3, ¶ 132 ("This means in no way should the human person be manipulated for ends that are foreign to his own development, or be treated as means for carrying out economic, social or political projects").

[14]John Paul II, Sollicitudo Rei Socialis ¶ 47 (Dec. 30, 1987), http://w2.vatican.va/content/john-paul-ii/en/encyclicals/documents/hf_jp-ii_enc_30121987_sollicitudo-rei-socialis.html; Pope John Paul, II., *supra* note 12, ¶¶ 1929, 2158, 2235, 2238, 2267, 2279, 2284, 2304, 2402, 2407, 2479, 2494, 2521, 2526.

[15]Catechism of the Catholic Church Church, no.2414 (2003).

[16]Gaudium et Spes, *supra* note 10.

provides evidence of a growing tendency to disconnect "freedom from the moral law and to reduce the rich mystery of human sexuality to a mere commodity."[17]

Trafficking in persons also denies the value of life, exposes victims to serious health risks, endangers the mental well-being of victims, and impedes their ability to reach their full God-given potential. For example, trafficking in prostitution is physically harmful and mentally detrimental because it increases the spread of sexually transmitted diseases, physical abuse from pimps, and can cause prostitutes to develop severe mental disorders ranging from depression to severe drug and alcohol addiction. Similarly, forced labor, forced marriage, and begging in West Africa are global phenomena seriously compromising children's freedom "which God has given [them] as one of the highest signs of his image' so that they can turn to what is good.[18] Pope Francis therefore declared "that every systematic deprivation of an individual's freedom for the purpose of personal and commercial exploitation be rejected entirely and without exception."[19]

Subsequently, in September 2013, Pope Francis approved a major updating of the criminal laws of Vatican City State, broadening the definition of crimes against children to include child prostitution, grooming of children, sexual violence, sex acts with children, and the possession and production of child pornography;[20] any Vatican employee can be tried by the Vatican court for violating those laws. In conclusion, slavery is wrong because it dehumanizes everyone—not only the victims but also the slave traders, the buyers, the corrupt officials, and even those who simply look and do not want to get involved. The sale of slaves is against the principles of justice and charity.[21]

---

[17] John Paul II, Letter to Archbishop Jean-Louis Tauran on the Occasion of the International Conference "Twenty-First Century Slavery – The Human Rights Dimension to Trafficking in Human Beings" (May 15, 2002), http://w2.vatican.va/content/john-paul-ii/en/letters/2002/documents/hf_jp-ii_let_20020515_tauran.html. [hereinafter Letter to Archbishop Jean-Louis].

[18] Pope John Paul, II, *supra* note 12, ¶ 1705.

[19] Francis, Ceremony for the Signing of the Faith Leaders' Universal Declaration against Slavery, (Casina Pio IV, December 2014), http://w2.vatican.va/content/francesco/en/speeches/2014/december/documents/papa-francesco_20141202_dichiarazione-schiavitu.html.

[20] The Pontifical Commission for the Vatican City State, Law N. VIII: Supplementary Norms On Criminal Law Matters (Jul. 11, 2013), http://www.vaticanstate.va/content/dam/vaticanstate/documenti/leggi-e-decreti/Normative-Penali-e-Amministrative/Law%20N.%20VIII%20-%20Supplementary%20Norms%20on%20Criminal%20Law.pdf.

[21] Melanie O'Connor, *Human Trafficking: The South African Sector and a Pastoral Response, with Exhortations from Africae Munus in Honour of Pope Benedict's Visit to Benin in November of 2011, in* Faith Perspectives on Migration and Human Trafficking 51 (David Kaulemu ed., 2012). [Hereinafter *Pastoral Response*].

## 11.2 The Principle of Common Good from a Cross-Cultural Perspective

Every society or culture recognizes certain values, mores, norms, and operational principles by which it seeks to promote and achieve the ideals of human dignity within the logic of that culture. Therefore, situating an analysis of African traditions and international human rights standards in a broader cross-cultural framework will not only foster cross-fertilization and mutual reinforcement, it will also contribute to a greater recognition of human rights and address trafficking in persons. In effect, people are inclined to adhere and observe the precepts of their own culture rather than those they perceive as being imposed from outside through coercion.

Contemporary North American Catholic theologians such as Lisa Cahill and David Hollenbach contend that any discussion on human rights should highlight the notion of a common good that is theologically conceived rather than emphasizing the idea of a covenant. This implies that:

> rights are not spoken of primarily as individual claims against other or society. They are woven into a concept of community which envisions the person as a part, a sacred part, of the whole. Rights exist within and are relative to a historical and social context and are intelligible only in terms of the obligations of individuals to other persons.[22]

Similarly, David Hollenbach pointed out that:

> all the doctrine and symbols of the Christian faith (creation of all persons by one God, the Universal graciousness of God toward all, the redemption of all by Christ, and the call of all persons to share in the mystery of Christ's death and resurrection) [...] are the foundation of a conception of mutual love and human solidarity that is richer than any philosophical or empirical discussion of the mutual obligations of human beings toward each other, whether liberal or Marxist.[23]

This religious perspective constitutes an important contribution to the new transnational language of human rights and human dignity. African traditions as well as the rich cultures of Asia express matters of human dignity in terms of duties to family and community, economic growth, social harmony, egalitarianism, and loyalty rather than individualism and the notion of "individual rights".[24] In addition to translating the western concept of human rights into a legal system enforced by state sanctions, the rights in *Akan* culture deriving from a general human entitlement to help their own kind, enjoy the strong backing of public opinion and the sanction of ancestors.

---

[22] Cahill (Fall 1980), p. 2, 284 https://www.jstor.org/stable/pdf/40017762.pdf.

[23] Little (1990), p. 67; Hollenbach (1979).

[24] Panikkar (1982), p. 75 http://www.sosyalarastirmalar.com/cilt5/cilt5sayi21_pdf/5_sosyoloji_felsefe/ng_thomas.pdf; Mary Yuen (2013), p. 283 https://www.stu.edu/Portals/Law/docs/human-rights/ihrlr/volumes/8/281-321-MeeYinMaryYuen-HumanRightsinChina-ExaminingHumanRightsValues.pdf.

African traditions, like any other culture in the world, contain their own contradictions.[25] However, the enforcement of brutal customs and traditions in African societies that infringe on individuals' human rights should not obscure the prevalence of human rights values across African societies. For instance, "respect for women and equality of the genders existed in many matrilineal societies in precolonial Ghana, and among the Igbo of Onitsha, in precolonial Nigeria, in West Africa."[26] The continent therefore fosters rich traditions founded on the notion of human dignity and 'humanness', as well as solidarity. As is customary in Africa, grandparents care for young children, reflecting the longstanding social expectation of intergenerational support. In *Mossi* customs specifically, as well as in other societies in West Africa, a grandmother babysits her grandchild right from the moment of their birth, helping bathe, dress, feed, and care for the baby. This establishes a bond between grandparents and grandchildren and prevents little girls becoming involved from in domestic servitude and babysitting.

Globally, advancements in public health and medical technologies along with improvements in living conditions have increased the overall population of older persons. For instance, in Africa elderly people who are 80 years and over represent 4.5%of the population according to the United Nations World Population Aging report in 2015.[27] The positive aspect of this trend is that elders can fulfil the increasing demand for child care services and fostering and thus ease the challenges faced by working mothers. Evidence from the literature has indicated that grandparents in Nigeria, South Africa, and Uganda have been largely responsible for supporting the orphans of HIV/AIDS and vulnerable children.[28]

Another illustrative example which shows that grand-parents who provide childcare and raise children outside of the foster care system are an alternative to trafficking in domestic servitude can be found in West Virginia. The national report, for example, shows that 2.4 million grandparents "are responsible for their grandchildren living with them: 29% of these grandparents are African American."[29]

---

[25] Wiredu (1990), p. 245 (claiming that the traditional beliefs of West African people (Akan and Ashanti) contain principles of human dignity and justice similar to those found in modern human rights ideology). However, it is important to clarify that these Akan beliefs in the dignity of the person were mostly restricted to the ethnic group. The Ashanti, for example, continued to supply European merchants with slaves taken as the spoils of war with neighboring states until the British declared the slave trade to be illegal in 1807.

[26] *Human Rights as a Global Conversation about Human Dignity* 3–4 (International Institute for the Advanced Study of Cultures, Institutions, and Economic Enterprise, Position Paper), http://www.interias.org.gh/sites/default/files/Position%20Paper/IIASPositionPaperHumanRights.pdf.

[27] Dep't of Econ. and Soc. Aff., World Population Ageing 2015, at 10, U.N. Doc. ST/ESA/SER.A/390 (2015), http://www.un.org/en/development/desa/population/publications/pdf/ageing/WPA2015_Report.pdf; *see generally* Aboderin (2004), p. 3, S128, http://ageboom.columbia.edu/files/2014/04/Aboderin-Gerontology.pdf.

[28] Akinyemi et al. (2016), p. 66.

[29] *West Virginia: A State Fact Sheet for Grandparents and Other Relatives Raising Children* 1, AARP Found. (May 2007), http://www.childrensdefense.org/library/data/state-data-repository/gf/grandfacts-west-virginia-2007.pdf.

Such extensive care provision is more normative among African Americans and "is rooted in West African culture and tradition and played a critical role in the United States during and after slavery and during the great migrations north after World War II."[30] Despite the changing demographic, cultural, and sociopolitical landscape of the United States, African-American grandparents play a prominent role in their grandchildren's lives.[31] An outstanding example of this is Marian Robinson, Michelle Obama's mother, who dropped everything and moved into the White House to help her daughter raise two children.

Regarding the benefits that can be derived from this, a care giving experience allows for closer bonding of grandparents with grandchildren, and a closer attachment to grandchildren impels a grandparent to undertake the caregiving role. Grandparents provide their grandchildren with family values similar to those with which the parent was raised. Those in migrant groups are therefore likely to pass on the culture, traditions and language of their country of origin to their grandchildren. Such intergenerational support comforts both the parent and child; this level of care provides flexibility, reliability, and stability in the grandchildren's lives and parents trust them. Moreover, because parents in the cities are largely low-income households, the deep involvement of grandparents in childcare significantly relieves the seemingly unaffordable costs of organized child care. As Hirshorn noted: "In so doing, grandparent caregiving stretches, reorganizes, and redefines the relationships between family members; redraws the boundaries of family and, often, of household units; and redirects the transfer of resources within the family."[32] The post-synodal apostolic exhortation Ecclesia in Africa no 42–43 highlights the fact that Africa is endowed with a wealth of cultural values and priceless human qualities which it can offer to the Churches and humanity as a whole. Africans have an acute sense of solidarity and community life; and the Pope ardently hopes and prays that "Africa will always preserve this priceless cultural heritage and never succumb to the temptation to individualism, which is so alien to its best traditions."[33]

In the *Akan* culture in Ghana, people are considered social beings who are heavily reliant on each other, especially on their kinship group. In African communal societies, there are numerous features well worth preserving and a multitude of practices that could provide ethical support to the international consensus on human rights while also preventing trafficking in persons. For instance, with regard to economic rights, traditional chiefs took charge of food storage in order to protect their communities against famine. The ethics of sharing among the family and offering hospitality to strangers is also a widespread practice in Africa that protects

---

[30] Fuller-Thomson and Minkler (2001), p. 2, 201 https://academic.oup.com/gerontologist/article/41/2/201/648323/American-Grandparents-Providing-Extensive-Child.

[31] Susan Adcox, *Grandparents Vital in African-American Families*, LiveAbout.com (Aug. 21, 2017), https://www.thespruce.com/grandparents-vital-in-african-american-families-1695850.

[32] Hirshorn (1998).

[33] John Paul II, Ecclesia in Africa ¶ 43 (Sep. 14, 1995) http://w2.vatican.va/content/john-paul-ii/en/apost_exhortations/documents/hf_jp-ii_exh_14091995_ecclesia-in-africa.html.

vulnerable individuals against starvation. These practices could buttress the internationally recognized right to food and also be adapted to enable the individual to make enforceable claims against apolitically and economically abusive African state.[34] Poverty and the denial of economic and social rights result in fewer and poorer life choices that render minorities, migrants, and women vulnerable to trafficking and related exploitation.

The *Akans* are matrilineal, which can be pictured as a system of concentric circles of matrilineal kinship relationships that encompass people in widely separated geographic regions; in these outermost dimensions a lineage becomes a clan. The circle comprises the grandmother, the mother, the mother's siblings, her own children, and the children of her sisters;[35] within this group of relatives, where the mother is the principal actor, there lies the duty of nursing an *Akan* newborn.[36] These extended relatives represent a safety net against trafficking in persons insofar as, like parents, they can provide an important measure of social and economic support for children, and may compensate for the absence of one or both parents. Furthermore, in terms of children's emotional development. there are advantages in having attachments to a number of significant adults, especially to grandparents. Studies on orphanhood and the living arrangements of children in Sub-Saharan Africa have revealed that "[a]fter parents, grandparents are the most important caregivers for single orphans, especially in the countries that have experienced large increases in the orphan rate."[37]

The right to be nursed is the first human right that is transformed dialectically into a duty to nurse one's mother in her old age. An *Akan* and *Mossi* proverb states that "if your mother nurses you to grow your teeth, you nurse her to lose hers." This is also embedded in a Yoruba adage which states "when okete (a nocturnal rodent) becomes very old, it depends on the breastmilk of her own children for survival" meaning that the younger generation, especially children, are expected to provide adequate care and look after their parents' general wellbeing during old age when

[34] *Id.* at 168.

[35] Blegne (2015), https://www.mediaterre.org/afrique-ouest/actu,20150830153532.html. In Burkina Faso and most West African countries, including Mali, there is what the oral tradition calls **joking kinship**. This relationship was allegedly established between neighboring ethnic groups and family clans during conflicts through warlike alliances, such as that between Mossis and Samos. Sometimes it has developed between people with different lifestyles. This, for example, is the case between the bobos, sedentary farmers, and the Fulani, who are nomad shepherds. Alain Joseph Sissao, a Burkinabe sociologist and a researcher at the Institute of Sciences of Societies in Ouagadougou contended that "Social stability has so far been a universally recognized and recognized reality in Burkina Faso compared to other parts of Africa where ethnic wars kill thousands of lives. It is attributed less to political action than to the strength of traditional institutions such as the alliance and kinship joking."

[36] Wiredu (1990), p. 245.

[37] Kathleen Beegle, et al., *Orphanhood and the Living Arrangements of Children in Sub-Saharan Africa* 14 (World Bank Policy Research Working Paper No. 4889, 2009), http://citeseerx.ist.psu.edu/viewdoc/download?doi=10.1.1.629.6564&rep=rep1&type=pdf.

they can no longer work to support themselves.[38] The filial duties of providing emotional support and financial help to elderly parents are significant cultural values that prevent elderly people from begging in the street.

The importance of family and community warrants far more attention among Africans;[39] many sayings from the ethnic groups in West African region can testify to this belief, which lies at the root of African communalism. For example "the cricket says that he is alone in his hole but he is not alone under the tree."[40] Or "one does not become a gravedigger for having seen the big sheep they offered the grave digger for his services",[41] meaning that an individual should not deny their family, even for a considerable profit. West African traditions also enshrine an acute sense of solidarity and the dependency of human beings on each other. "When the blind has shame, his guide has also shame"[42] meaning that what happens to a family member affects all the family. There is also the saying "Water poured upon the head, cannot avoid the face."[43] meaning that a gift granted to a family member, especially to one who is eminent, benefits all family members.

The most important ethical values flowing from the African world view of community as an ideal are 'identity' and 'solidarity'.[44] African people strongly identify themselves as integral parts of the whole community and take pride or feel shame in the group's activities, as well as committing themselves to joint projects and coordinating their behavior to realize shared ends. To show "solidarity is for people to engage in mutual aid, to act in ways that are reasonably expected to benefit each other. Solidarity is also a matter of people's attitudes such as emotions and motives being positively oriented toward others, say, by sympathizing with them and helping them for their sake."[45] In association with their fellows and collaboration with other men and women, the Catholic Church stresses that the individual should act on his own initiative for the common good.[46] Couched in more negative terms, "for people to fail to exhibit solidarity would be for them either to be uninterested in each other's flourishing or, worse, to exhibit ill-will in the form of hostility and cruelty."[47]

Identity and solidarity are separable concepts, meaning that an individual could in principle exhibit one sort of relationship without necessarily showing the other. For

[38] Akinlo et al. (2017), p. 196 http://scholarworks.wmich.edu/grandfamilies/vol4/iss1/11.

[39] *Cf. African Ethics*, Stanford Encyclopedia of Philosophy (Sep. 9, 2010), https://plato.stanford.edu/entries/african-ethics/.

[40] Damiba and Nare (1999).

[41] *Id.* Proverb no.228.

[42] *Id.* Proverb no.270.

[43] *Id.* Proverb no.279.

[44] *Id.* Proverb no.539.

[45] *Id.* Proverb no.538.

[46] John XXIII, Pacem in Terris ¶ 34 (Apr. 11, 1963), http://w2.vatican.va/content/john-xxiii/en/encyclicals/documents/hf_j-xxiii_enc_11041963_pacem.html [hereinafter Pacem in Terris].

[47] Metz (2011), p. 532, 538.

instance, members of the same family probably identify with one another, but at times may fail to protect one of their members against enslavement and related situation, and are not sympathetic toward them, thus solidarity between them is lacking. Actions such as deception, coercion, and exploitation that are characteristic of trafficking fail to honor communal relationships as:

> the actor is distancing himself from the person acted upon, instead of enjoying a sense of togetherness; the actor is subordinating the other, as opposed to coordinating behaviour with her; the actor is failing to act for the good of the other, but rather for his own or someone else's interest; or the actor lacks positive attitudes toward the other's good, and is instead unconcerned or malevolent.[48]

Communitarianism "ethics can be termed anti-egoistic as it discourages people from seeking their own good without regard for, or to the detriment of others and the community."[49] Thus, people and groups living together in a community must respect each other's rights and fulfil their duties toward one another. They must make specific contributions to the common welfare and bring their own interests into harmony with the needs of the community.[50] Harmony, friendliness, community, and sharing are great goods[51] while immorality and misbehavior such as trafficking in prostitution, forced labor exploitation, and the selling of children that threaten communal ties and subvert or undermine the sought-after good are to be avoided. "Even if it has well behaved, the hyena will not be wandering until daybreak (it would be killed because people still remember its passed misdeeds)."[52]

One of the fundamental assets West African cultures have developed consists of articulating the concept of human dignity and related duties and obligations around the values of equality, solidarity, family, brotherhood, goodness, and commonwealth. Similarly, the Catholic Church reads and interprets the modern history of human rights from the perspective of relation to others. The corresponding obligations are therefore those arising out of our individual and collective responsibilities for each other.[53] Furthermore, from the perspective of Catholic Church, the family is a rights-based institution where every person has his or her own inherent dignity in relation to society, including the family. It a basic social principle that assures everyone counts and deserves reverence. The concept of *reverence*,[54] which the Concile Vatican II uses to describe our behavior towards one another, has a much

[48] *Id.* at 527.

[49] *Id.* at 538.

[50] Pacem in Terris, *supra* note 46, ¶¶ 30, 31, 53.

[51] Sandie Cornish, *The Catholic Human Rights Tradition and the Rights of Indigenous Peoples* 15 (ACSJC Occasional Paper No. 21, 1994), http://www.socialjustice.catholic.org.au/files/CSJ-series-papers/CSJS_21_-_The_Catholic_Human_Rights_Tradition_and_the_Rights_of_Indigenous_PeoplesA4.pdf.

[52] Damiba and Nare, *supra* note 40, proverb no. 573.

[53] George Grima, *Family Rights: A Catholic Perspective* 48 (unpublished comment) (on file with the University of Malta) http://www.um.edu.mt/europeanstudies/books/CD_CSP2/pdf/ratf-ggrima.pdf.

[54] *Cf.* Gaudium et Spes, *supra* note 10, ¶ 27.

richer meaning than the conventional term *respect.* Reverence usually refers to God and "is extended to the human person to show that the attitude to the human being should reflect almost the sense of awe in the presence of someone who. . . remains a mystery"[55] and therefore cannot in any circumstance be subject to dehumanizing treatment, forced labor, forced marriage, or trafficking in prostitution.

Part I has extensively addressed West Africa where it is parents who actually give away or sell their own children into forced marriage, domestic servitude, and forced labor. Some husbands have also been known to sell their wives into prostitution. Therefore, families in West Africa fail, not only in their responsibility to enable their members to experience peace in decisive ways but also in teaching children the values of kindness, goodness, service, disinterestedness, and self-sacrifice that are the most precious fruits of love.[56] Because the family has the duty to educate its members, very close relatives who take the children away from their parents under false promises of education are failing in their responsibility to provide them with social protection to the children and facilitate their integral personal development.[57] Consequently, whoever obstructs the family right to be primarily responsible for the education of its children "undermines peace in the entire community, national and international, since he weakens what is in effect the primary agency of peace."[58]

The very "nature of the family presupposes a way of life in which the rights of all its members are respected."[59] Clearly, gender inequality and social disparities are causes that drive trafficking in persons. In fighting this current social and cultural prejudice, the encyclical Familiaris Consortio confirms "that equal dignity and responsibility of men and women fully justifies women's access to public functions."[60] The encyclical document also affirms "that the true advancement of women requires that clear recognition be given to the value of their maternal and family role, by comparison with other public roles and all other professions."[61]

Self-giving or a great spirit of sacrifice is the animating principle of a community life within the family. A particularly praiseworthy example of the highest degree of love, which is to give one's life for the person loved (cf. Jn 15:13) "is the donation of organs, performed in an ethically acceptable manner, with a view to offering a chance of health and even of life itself to the sick who sometimes have no other hope."[62] Deceased organ donation and more particularly living organ donation and

[55] Grima, *supra* note 53, at 53.

[56] *Social Doctrine of the Church*, *supra* note 3, ¶ 239.

[57] *Charter of the Rights of the Family*, Art 4(e) (Oct.22, 1983), http://www.vatican.va/roman_curia/pontifical_councils/family/documents/rc_pc_family_doc_19831022_family-rights_en.html.

[58] Benedict XVI, *supra* note 831, ¶ 5.

[59] Grima, *supra* note 53, at 49.

[60] John Paul II, *Apostolic Exhortation Familiaris Consortio* ¶ 23 (Nov. 22, 1981), http://w2.vatican.va/content/john-paul-ii/en/apost_exhortations/documents/hf_jp-ii_exh_19811122_familiaris-consortio.html [hereinafter Familiaris Consortio].

[61] *Id.*

[62] John Paul II, *Evangelium Vitae: To the Bishops Priests and Deacons Men and Women Religious Lay Faithful and all People of Good Will on the Value and Inviolability of Human Life* ¶ 86 (Mar.

transplantation is a sign of this great spirit of sacrifice, a supreme act of love, and an authentic form of human and Christian solidarity (Cf. Jn 13:34).[63]

Faced with an increasing population of patients developing organ failure and the correlative thriving of a trafficking in human organs market, Pope John Paul II urges people "to promote and encourage such a noble and meritorious act as donating" our own organ to those of our brothers and sisters who have need of it.[64] "Those who believe in our Lord Jesus Christ, who gave his life for the salvation of all, should recognize the urgent need for a ready availability of organs for renal transplants a challenge to their generosity and fraternal love."[65]

In the Catholic Church, organ transplantation is considered a way for men and women to serve the human family, giving themselves in both blood and body. Therefore, this heroic act must be appropriately recognized and promoted while combating transplant tourism, organ trafficking, and transplant commercialism.[66] One of the main problems surrounding organ trafficking, whether legal or illegal, is the exploitation of the poor; the familiar dynamic is that of organs going from the poorest and most disadvantaged people to the richest people in the United States and Europe, Middle East, and the global South to the global North. "Even in countries where organ trafficking is regulated, the poor provide the majority of organs and the rich are the beneficiaries. This goes against social justice that demands that the burdens and benefits within society be fairly distributed."[67] In West Africa, trafficking in organs that takes the form of trafficking of body parts is always to the detriment of the poor and most vulnerable in society. In November 2006, "there were reports that at least five persons in Enugu State were mutilated and killed for ritual purposes by perpetrators who worked for local politicians."[68] According to Scheper-Hughes, it is easier to trade in human body parts once they have been dehumanized "making it ethically permissible to consume (cannibalize) the body parts of the other, living or dead."[69]

---

25, 1995), https://w2.vatican.va/content/john-paul-ii/en/encyclicals/documents/hf_jp-ii_enc_25031995_evangelium-vitae.html. [herein after People of Good Will].

[63] *See generally* Scaria Kanniyakonil, *Living Organ Donation and Transplantation: A Medical, Legal and Moral Theological Appraisal* (2005).

[64] John Paul II (1985), p. 1; Pope John Paul, II, *supra* note 12, ¶ 2296.

[65] John Paul II (1990), pp. 336–337.

[66] *The Declaration of Istanbul on Organ Trafficking and Transplant Tourism*, 18 Indian J. of Nephrology 3, 135 (Jul. 2008), https://www.ncbi.nlm.nih.gov/pmc/articles/PMC2813140/.

[67] John Lee, *Trafficking in Human Beings: Modern Slavery*, Workshop at the Pontifical Academies of Sciences, Pontifical Academy of Social Sciences, and World Federation of the Catholic Medical Associations (Nov. 2, 2013), http://www.endslavery.va/content/endslavery/en/publications/scripta_varia_122/lee.html.

[68] *Nigeria Country Report on Human Rights Practices*, U.S. Dep't of St. (Mar. 6, 2007), https://www.state.gov/j/drl/rls/hrrpt/2006/78751.htm.

[69] Nancy Scheper-Hughes, *Neo-Cannibalism, Organ Theft, and Military-Biomedical Necropolitics*, EndSlavery 1 (Jan.27, 2016), http://www.endslavery.va/content/endslavery/en/publications/acta_20/scheper_hughes_panel.pdf.

Other relevant Christian values in this respect are forbearance, pardon, and reconciliation. Family communion can only be preserved if the victim has a spirit of sacrifice great enough to forgive the relatives who trafficked him/her into forced labor exploitation. For instance, Joseph forgave his brothers for selling him into slavery in Egypt and the family experienced the joy of reconciliation that brings communion and unity. In particular, "participation in the sacrament of Reconciliation and in the banquet of the one Body of Christ offers to the Christian family the grace and the responsibility of overcoming every division and of moving towards the fullness of communion willed by God."[70]

In response to child neglect, the Church's social doctrine emphasizes the role of the family in promoting children's rights as well as the family mission to provide responsible parenthood.[71] The family must devote special attention to the children and develop great respect and generous concern for their rights. This is true for every child but becomes all the more urgent when it refers to small, sick, suffering, or handicapped children;[72] individuals to whom the so-called option for the poor applies most acutely. It is also necessary for the social value of childhood to be publicly recognized in all countries and legally protected within juridical systems.[73] Thus, the Catholic Church points out the need:

> to engage in a battle, at the national and international levels, against the violations of the dignity of boys and girls caused by sexual exploitation, by those caught up in pedophilia, and by every kind of violence directed against these most defenceless of human creatures. These are criminal acts that must be effectively fought with adequate preventive and penal measures by the determined action of the different authorities involved.[74]

Supporting families should therefore be a priority when developing economic and social policies.

## 11.3 The Dignity of Work and the Rights of Workers

Human work has an ethical value and dignity; it is through work that human beings participate in God's creation and help realize his plan on earth. Work enhances human dignity and honors the gifts and talents God has given to every human being. Therefore, the trafficking of persons that turns the worker into a mere commodity (sexual objects that can be bought, sold, used, and discarded), a simple labor force with an exclusively material value, ends up distorting the essence of work and stripping it of its most noble and basic human essence.[75]

---

[70] Familiaris Consortio, *supra* note 60 ¶ 21.

[71] *Id.* ¶ 22, 28-41; *cf.* The Instruction *Donum Vitae*, 1987.

[72] Familiaris Consortio, *supra* note 60 ¶ 21, 26.

[73] Social Doctrine of the Church, *supra* note 3, ¶ 244.

[74] *Id.* ¶ 245.

[75] *Id.* ¶ 271.

In the socio-economic context of West Africa, the contribution of child "labour to family income and the national economy is indispensable, and that in any event certain forms of part time work can prove beneficial for children themselves". However the Church's social Magisterium "condemns the increase in "the exploitation of children in the workplace in conditions of veritable slavery".[76] The Church teaches that workers are entitled to a fair wage and appropriate subsidies that are necessary for the subsistence of unemployed workers and their families, the right to pensions, the right to reasonable work hours and rest to prevent work-related accidents, safe and healthy working conditions, the right to social security connected with maternity, and the right to form labor and trade unions to promote social justice.[77] Trafficking in persons infringes on all these rights.

As previously confirmed, work conditions for children in mines and plantations in West Africa are so inhuman that they are an offense to their dignity and are harmful to the workers' physical health and their moral integrity. Furthermore, those who work as prostitutes are denied their rights because they work in hazardous conditions and are perceived as objects by their clients; they are gravely mistreated and their dignity is put in peril.

Remuneration is the most important means of measuring the level of equity and also for achieving justice in work relationships. Private individuals in West Africa who engage men, women, and children in domestic work, agriculture, fishing, mining and refuse to pay a just wage, or who do not give it in due time and in proportion to the work done, commit a grave injustice (cf. Lv 19:13; Dt 24:14–15; Jas 5:4). Remuneration for labor should provide the worker with the means to sustain in a worthy manner his or her own material, social, cultural, and spiritual life. An agreed-upon salary between employee and employer is not sufficient to qualify as a "just wage", "because a just wage must not be below the level of subsistence of the worker: natural justice precedes and is above the freedom of the contract."[78]

For workers who have migrated, institutions in host countries must prevent the inequality and discrimination that facilitates the exploitation and enslavement of foreign laborers, denying them the same rights enjoyed by nationals: "Immigrants are to be received as persons and helped, together with their families, to become a part of societal life."[79]

---

[76] *Id.* ¶ 296.

[77] John XXIII, Mater et Magistra ¶ 71 (1961); Pope John Paul, II, *supra* note 12, ¶¶ 2433–2435; Social Doctrine of the Church, *supra* note 3, ¶ 301.

[78] Social Doctrine of the Church, *supra* note 3, ¶ 302.

[79] *Id.* ¶ 298.

## 11.4 Solidarity and Preferential Option for the Poor and the Vulnerable

As God walked with the refugees of the Exodus in search of a land free from slavery, the Church is committed to assisting the poor and vulnerable to enable them to participate in the life of society. It protects them by giving relief to those in most need and also provides charity, defense, and liberty to those who are deprived such as trafficking victims. In other words, the Church defends the oppressed, takes up the cause of the fatherless, and pleads the case of the widow (Isaiah 1, 17). "The Church's love for the poor is inspired by the Gospel of the Beatitudes, by the poverty of Jesus and by his attention to the poor."[80]

In modern society, "the most vulnerable among us are sold as slaves, prostitutes, organ-donors, and pawns in criminal enterprises, armed activities and conflicts."[81] Pope Francis deplores the fact that people are treated as "objects, deceived, raped, often sold many times for different purposes and, in the end, killed or, in any case, physically and mentally damaged, ending up thrown away and abandoned."[82] However, the disgrace would be more terrible if Christians who hear or read about the fate of victims feel no compulsion to share or mitigate their suffering or take actions to curb it.

Furthermore, a Preferential Option for the Poor and Vulnerable command has been developed to create conditions for them to be heard, defended against injustice, and provided with opportunities for their empowerment and the capacity to attain the fullness of their human lives. As such, we are responsible for helping those who need us most and do not have voices of their own. Scripture reminds us that "We have been bought at a great price" (cf. 1 Cor 6:20); the Lord came down to die on the Cross in order to set his people free, and "Woe [anyone] who builds his house by unrighteousness, and his upper rooms by injustice, who makes his neighbor serve him for nothing and does not give him his wages (Jeremiah 22:13).

Therefore, it is our Christian duty and also the duty of the state and the society "to do everything possible to prevent anyone in our midst from being trafficked, and to make sure that those who have fallen into the traffickers' trap are set free and are able to come home and resume their normal lives with their families, friends and community."[83] With regard to offenders, "charity and compassion demand that

---

[80] Compendium of the Catechism of the Catholic Church (2005), http://www.vatican.va/archive/compendium_ccc/documents/archive_2005_compendium-ccc_en.html.

[81] Admin-Whilssy, CBCP Pastoral Letter on Human Trafficking (Dec. 10, 2014), http://cbcp-ecy.ph/cbcp-pastoral-letter-on-human-trafficking/#sthash.F5EpdzfE.dpbs. [Hereinafter Pastoral Letter].

[82] Pope Francis, Address of Pope Francis to the New Ambassadors Accredited to the Holy See on The Occasion Of The Presentation of the Letters of Credence (Dec.12, 2013) http://www.vatican.va/content/francesco/en/speeches/2013/december/documents/papa-francesco_20131212_credenziali-nuovi-ambasciatori.html; John L. Allen, *The Francis Miracle: Inside the Transformation of the Pope and the Church*, Time (March 2, 2015).

[83] Pastoral Letter, *supra* note 81.

Christians exert every effort to free human traffickers from the motives and attractions of their illicit trade and to draw them back to genuinely good and beneficial pursuits."[84] The ultimate aim in this fight is to "drown evil in an abundance of good, and convert the wrongdoer into a source of good."[85]

In the Compendium of the Social Doctrine of the Church, the solidarity that flows from faith is fundamental to the Christian view of social relationships and political organizations. Pope Benedict XVI stated in his Encyclical on hope that: "The true measure of humanity is essentially determined in relationship to suffering and to the sufferer. This holds true both for the individual and for society."[86] "Victims of trafficking, especially sex trafficking, are stripped of their dignity in a most humiliating way and can even suffer stigmatization."[87] Traffickers "are devoid of solidarity, a sense of justice, incapable of feeling sympathy or compassion for their victim and the pain they are causing; yet they, too, are God's children and in need of conversion."[88]

## 11.5 Advocacy for Economic Justice and Debt Relief

Trafficking in persons is fundamentally a justice issue because persons who fall victim to trafficking are part of populations made vulnerable through economic injustice and other kinds of marginalization and oppressions. Among the various factors that underpin contemporary migration, international debt forms part of the background context that motivates people to migrate.[89]

But what is international debt? Like individuals and families who take out a loan to pay for a house or an education, countries with a paucity of capital borrow money from private capital markets, international financial institutions (IMF and World Bank), and governments to supplement their domestic savings in order to invest in infrastructure such as roads, public services, and health clinics; to run a government ministry; or even to purchase weapons.[90] Furthermore, like individuals, indebted countries must pay back the principal and interest on the loans they receive. However, a person who borrows money receives the credit directly and can spend it for their own benefit; "[b]ut if a country borrows money, the citizens are not

---

[84] *Id.*

[85] *Id.*

[86] Benedict XVI, *Spe Salvi*, ¶ 38 (30 Nov. 2007), http://w2.vatican.va/content/benedict-xvi/en/encyclicals/documents/hf_ben-xvi_enc_20071130_spe-salvi.html.

[87] *Pastoral Response*, *supra* note 21 at 51.

[88] *Id.*

[89] O'Connell Davidson (2013), p. 176, 179.

[90] What is the International Debt Crisis? http://www.usccb.org/issues-and-action/human-life-and-dignity/global-issues/debt-relief/what-is-the-international-debt-crisis.cfm.

necessarily notified or informed of the purpose of the loan or its terms and conditions."[91]

In practice, several governments have spent the money for legitimate purposes but financial conditions beyond their control have made loan repayment impossible whereas other have used the loans for projects that do not meet minimum standards of social, ecological, or even economic viability. At times these loans have been used to enrich a small group of people.[92] Additionally, a business or a person who falls on hard times and cannot meet his or her financial obligations over time goes bankrupt. A Court is appointed to assess the debtor's financial situation and banks then acknowledge the incapacity to fully honor the debt. At an international level there is no such procedure for countries, and no arbitrator; for the creditors, there is no court to decide whether and under what conditions a country is to pay its debt.[93]

When most African countries became independent in the 1960s, the new governments adopted a development strategy that relied heavily on foreign financing from major Western countries, the International Monetary Fund and the World Bank.[94] However, the results fell short of expectations. For all countries in the region, the standard of external debt has built up over the years to a level that is widely considered to be unsustainable. As the following table below indicates, a comparative analysis of indicators such as debt-GDP, debt-goods and services exports, and debt service-goods and services exports ratios lead to the conclusion that African foreign debt is unsustainable and unrepayable. Africa's debt as a percentage of GDP increased from 65.4& in 1993 to 67.5% in 1997. Similarly, debt service as a percentage of the earnings from the exports of goods and services averaged 27% during the same period.

In 1995 an Oxfam analysis showed that between 1990 and 1993, West African countries paid US $13.4 bn each year to their foreign creditors, equivalent to four times as much as governments in the region spent on health services. In fact, this

---

[91] *What is the International Debt Crisis*?, United States Conference Of Catholic Bishops, at http://www.usccb.org/issues-and-action/human-life-and-dignity/global-issues/debt-relief/what-is-the-international-debt-crisis.cfm. [Hereinafter *Debt Crisis*].

[92] *Id.* In the 1970s, several African leaders' preoccupation with foreign loans and investment stemmed not so much from concern for the fate of the poor as from lust for the paraphernalia of power and glory. Foreign loans provided a large and relatively inexpensive source of finance for ambitious yet unsustainable industrial programs, for expansion in the size of state bureaucracies, and for the expansion of the social service sector. Politically visible investment projects such as cathedrals, elegant airports, wide roads that lead nowhere, sports stadiums, and the accumulation of sophisticated weaponry made more political sense to statesmen than either economic growth or poverty alleviation Worse still, part of the loan money was looted and laundered to European and American banks. It has been estimated that well over US$98 billion has been stashed away by Nigerians in foreign banks, illegally acquired by its leaders as well as their family members and cronies.

*Id.*

[93] *Id.*

[94] S. Ibi Ajayi & Mohsin S. Khan, *External Debt and Capital Flight in Sub-Saharan Africa*, at http://www.imf.org/external/pubs/nft/2000/extdebt/index.htm.

amount is more than their combined spending on health and education and substantially exceeds the annual coast of US $9 bn estimated by UNICEF to meet basic human needs for health, nutrition, education, and family planning.[95] High debt levels in poor countries hinder a sovereign government's capacity to provide "social services necessary for the well-being of citizens and divert resources and energy from the pursuing of long-term development strategies."[96] Indeed, foreign debt has engendered a deep economic crisis in Africa resulting in deplorable public buildings, considerable urban unemployment, abandoned factories, potholed roads, hospitals without medicines, and schools without teaching materials, all of which form one aspect of a much wider critical problem of development that affects all populations.[97]

This resulting debt bondage has irretrievably diverted scarce resources away from productive investment and social services such as access to clean water, adequate housing, basic health care for people, and basic education.[98] This situation is crushing the lives and dignity of vulnerable children, women, and men, affecting the well-being of families, the bonds of community, and the security of the future. For West Africa, failed economic policies compounded by burdensome external debts have had a negative impact on local farmers and laborers and put pressure on the population who resort to traffickers in order to emigrate in search of a better life for themselves and their families. As underlined by the second Synod of bishop for Africa, numerous conflicts, including those involving the enrollment of children in wars in Africa, derive mainly from these unjust international structures.[99]

In his apostolic exhortation, *Tertio Millennio Adveniente*, Pope John Paul II called repeatedly for the forgiving of international debt as a sign of true solidarity, and proposed the Great Jubilee Year 2000 as an appropriate time in which to raise a voice on behalf of all the poor of the world to substantially reduce, if not cancel outright, the international debt that seriously threatens the future of many nations (TMA, no 51).[100] The problem of foreign debt is a human one and raises question

---

[95] Kanbur (2000), p. 9.

[96] Christian Barry, *Ethical Issues Relevant to Debt* 1, http://milanoschool.org/wp-content/uploads/2013/04/Barry_2006-05.pdf.

[97] Cf. NICOLA BANKS (2016), pp. 437–454 http://journals.sagepub.com/doi/pdf/10.1177/0956247816651201.

[98] Nasser Shraideh, *Foreign Debt and Poverty*, OHCHR, 1–2, https://www2.ohchr.org/english/issues/poverty/docs/sforum/spresentations/Nasser_Shraideh.pdf. In Uganda, the government spends US $3.00 per person annually on health and education and $17.00 per person annually on debt repayments. Yet one out of every five Ugandan children dies from a preventable disease before reaching the age of five. *Multilateral Debt: The Human Costs Oxfam International Position* Paper, Oxfam International (Feb. 1996), London Position Paper.

[99] Message to the People of God of the Second Special Assembly for Africa 23–33, http://www.vatican.va/roman_curia/synod/documents/rc_synod_doc_20091023_message-synod_en.html.

[100] Msgr. Dennis M. Schnurr, *A Jubilee Call For Debt Forgiveness*, United States Conference of Catholic Bishops, http://www.usccb.org/issues-and-action/human-life-and-dignity/debt-relief/jubilee-debt-forgiveness.cfm. Last year, in response to this appeal, the Holy See, our bishops' conference, and Seton Hall University co-sponsored a meeting of top policy makers, academics, church

about its legitimacy. Is the debt valid "when paying it seriously jeopardizes the survival of our peoples, when the population was not consulted before contracting the debt, and when it has not always been used for lawful purposes?"[101]

The Catholic political commitment to international solidarity has influenced and found an echo in the worldwide debt cancellation and debt relief movement that, with the support of political and social actors, including solidarity groups, development NGOs, the Africa Conference of Churches, environmental and peace groups, trade unions, and Catholic Organizations, have mushroomed in the 1990s.[102] The most outspoken and globally pervasive is the "Jubilee 2000", which was specifically meant to become a social movement that placed considerable pressure on the IFIs and the G-7 for a debt-free start to a new millennium. The principles of the biblical Jubilee and associated debt forgiveness underpinned the moral vision of this social justice campaign and played a key role in the mobilization of people of faith. This global campaign has led to a comprehensive debt reduction program. In response the World Bank, International Monetary Fund (IMF), and the African Development Bank coordinated the 1996 Heavily Indebted Poor Countries (HIPC) Initiative, supplemented by the 2005 Multilateral Debt Relief Initiative, to find a sustainable solution to Africa's debt burden. These relief programs helped 35 sub-Saharan African countries cancel US $100 billion in external debt.[103]

Taking up the words of the African Synod Fathers, Pope John Paul II urged "the Heads of State and their governments in Africa not to crush their peoples with internal and external debts." He also begged "the International Monetary Fund and the World Bank and all foreign creditors to alleviate the crushing debts of the African nations."[104] Finally, he earnestly asked "the Episcopal Conferences of the industrialized countries to present this issue consistently to their governments and to the

---

leaders, activists from creditor and debtor nations, and officials from international financial institutions to examine the ethical implications of international debt. *Id.*

[101] José Oscar Beozzo, *Santo Domingo—Latin American Bishops' Conference (1992)*, Religion Past and Present. Consulted (30 June 2018), https://doi.org/10.1163/1877-5888_rpp_SIM_025209.

[102] Relieving Third World Debt: A Call for Co-Responsibility, Justice, and Solidarity (United States Conference of Catholic Bishops, 1989).

[103] *Break the Chains of Debt*, Advocacy International, http://advocacyinternational.co.uk/featured-project/jubilee-2000; Jocelyne Sambira, *Borrowing Responsibly: Africa's Debt Challenge*, Afr. Renewal (Aug. 2015), http://www.un.org/africarenewal/magazine/august-2015/borrowing-responsibly-africa%E2%80%99s-debt-challenge.

[104] *See* Conc. oecum. Vat. II, Const.; Paul VI, Pastoral Constitution on the Church in the Modern World: Gaudium et Spes ¶ 86 (Dec. 7, 1965), http://www.vatican.va/archive/hist_councils/ii_vatican_council/documents/vat-ii_cons_19651207_gaudium-et-spes_en.html; *Populorum Progressio*, Paul VI, Encycl. (March 26, 1967), 283–284 n. 54; *Sollicitudo Rei Socialis*, Paul VI, Encycl. (Dec. 30, 1987), 534–536 n. 19. *Centesimus Annus*, Paul VI, Encycl. (May 1, 1991), 836–838; Paul VI, *Tertio millennio adveniente*, Encycl (Nov. 10, 1994), 36 no. 51; *Au Service De La Communauté Humaine : Une Approche Ethique De L'endettement International*, Pontificium Consilium de Justitia et Pace (Dec. 27 1986), at http://www.iustitiaetpax.va/content/giustiziaepace/fr/archivio/livres-et-documents/publications/%2D%2Dau-service-de-la-communaute-humaine%2D%2D-une-approche-ethique-de-.html.

organizations concerned." The situation of many African countries is so serious as to leave no room for attitudes of indifference and complacency.[105] Debt is morally "unsustainable" when keeping up with payments comes at the unacceptable cost of human development.

The Church believes trade and debt policies must be organized in light of the principles of social justice, respecting the preferential option for the poor and the requirements of the international common good. At an international level, there is a need to ensure better prices fare paid or the commodities of West African countries to increase their foreign exchange earnings; this in turn would enable West African debtor countries to build up capacity within their economies to address, on a long-term basis, the question of external debt.[106]

In addition to debt reduction, increased trade access is also needed; cotton has become a symbol of the inequities of global agricultural trade and clearly demonstrates how rich-country agriculture subsidies can have harmful impacts on farmers in developing countries. "Subsidies skew production levels and value, undermining the income of cotton farmers in developing countries."[107] West African countries are among the primary cotton producers in the world, and stand to gain significantly from reforming trade and agriculture policies; yet these efforts at economic reform and poverty alleviation measures face a depressed cotton market caused in part by the unfairness of US trade cotton practices, as the World Trade Organization (WTO) panel has shown.[108] The consequences of price volatility, increasing production costs, and unfair trading affect the livelihood of 2.5 billion small-scale farmers across the world. The most vulnerable in West Africa are women who work in their husbands' farms as a result of socio-cultural obstacles preventing them from accessing the necessary land and inputs to engage in agro-business.[109]

With limited income and a lack of information on market developments, farmers and their families are the losers in a lucrative manufacturing industry market; the financial uncertainty leads in many cases to serious social and environmental challenges resulting in insufficient investments, withholding of salaries, and incapacity to provide workers with proper working conditions, and in the worst cases s tendency to traffic children into forced labor. Hoping to increase their revenues they extend their production in land, often at the expense of sustainable, ecological. and diversified farming.

[105] John Paul II, Post-Synodal Apostolic Exhortation Ecclesia in Africa ¶ 121 (1995), http://w2.vatican.va/content/john-paul-ii/en/apost_exhortations/documents/hf_jp-ii_exh_14091995_ecclesia-in-africa.html; Patrick Claffey, *Christian Churches in Dahomey-Benin: A Study of their Socio-political Role, Brill, Leiden-Boston* 304; Colombo Sacco (1999).

[106] Omotayo Olaniyan (1996), p. 158.

[107] *Finding The Moral Fiber. Why Reform is Urgently Needed For a Fair Cotton Trade*, Oxfam International, https://www.oxfamamerica.org/static/media/files/cotton_brief101804.pdf.

[108] *Id.*

[109] OXFAM, *Unfair Trade Rules*, Oxfam Hong Kong, 2018, https://www.oxfam.org.hk/en/unfairtrade.aspx; Nkosazana Dlamini Zuma, *Agriculture in Africa,* NEPAD, (November 2013), http://www.un.org/en/africa/osaa/pdf/pubs/2013africanagricultures.pdf.

The Holy See is a member of the United Nations Conference on Trade and Development, which helps developing countries diversify their economies to benefit from the globalized economy more fairly and effectively; in the field of economic relations, and specifically pertaining to trade, the Holy See advocates for an equitable system with an ethical supplement as one of the key factors in development.[110] Relatedly, the Letter from National Conferences of Catholic Bishops to the Leaders of the G8 Nations considers "counterproductive to provide agricultural development assistance on the one hand and then to use unfair agricultural trade policies that harm the agricultural economics of poorer nations on the other."[111]

## References


Aboderin I (2004) Decline in material family support for older people in Urban Ghana, Africa: understanding processes and causes of change. J Gerontol 59B:3, S128. http://ageboom.columbia.edu/files/2014/04/Aboderin-Gerontology.pdf

Adcox S 2017) Grandparents Vital in African-American Families. LiveAbout.com (Aug. 21, 2017) https://www.thespruce.com/grandparents-vital-in-african-american-families-1695850

Admin-Whilssy, CBCP Pastoral Letter on Human Trafficking (Dec. 10, 2014), http://cbcp-ecy.ph/cbcp-pastoral-letter-on-human-trafficking/#sthash.F5EpdzfE.dpbs

African Ethics, Stanford Encyclopedia of Philosophy (Sep. 9, 2010), https://plato.stanford.edu/entries/african-ethics/

Akinlo A, Akinyemi AI, Aransiola JO, Togonu-Bickesteeth F (2017) Grandparenting in selected West African countries: implications for health and hygiene behaviours in the household. GrandFamilies: Contemp J Res Pract Policy 4:196. Available at: http://scholarworks.wmich.edu/grandfamilies/vol4/iss1/11

Akinyemi A et al (2016) Africa, ageing families. In: Shehan C (ed) 1 The Wiley Blackwell Encyclopedia of Family Studies, 66

Allen JL (2015) The Francis miracle: inside the transformation of the pope and the church, Time (March 2)

*Au Service De La Communauté Humaine: Une Approche Ethique De L'endettement International*, Pontificium Consilium de Justitia et Pace (Dec. 27 1986.), at http://www.iustitiaetpax.va/content/giustiziaepace/fr/archivio/livres-et-documents/publications/%2D%2Dau-service-de-la-communaute-humaine%2D%2D-une-approche-ethique-de-.html

Barry C, *Ethical Issues Relevant to Debt* 1, http://milanoschool.org/wp-content/uploads/2013/04/Barry_2006-05.pdf

Beegle K et al (2009) Orphanhood and the living arrangements of children in Sub-Saharan Africa 14. World Bank Policy Research Working Paper No. 4889, 2009), http://citeseerx.ist.psu.edu/viewdoc/download?doi=10.1.1.629.6564&rep=rep1&type=pdf

Benedict XVI, *Spe Salvi*, ¶ 38 (30 Nov. 2007), http://w2.vatican.va/content/benedict-xvi/en/encyclicals/documents/hf_ben-xvi_enc_20071130_spe-salvi.html


[110] *Ethical Guidelines For International Trade*, Note of the Holy See on the Preparation for the Fifth Wto Ministerial Conference (Sept. 2003), http://www.vatican.va/roman_curia/secretariat_state/2003/documents/rc_seg-st_20030910_ethics-intern-trade_en.html.

[111] Letter from National Conferences of Catholic Bishops to the Leaders of the G8 Nations (June 3, 2013) at http://www.usccb.org/issues-and-action/human-life-and-dignity/poverty/global/upload/2013-G8-Letter.pdf.

Beozzo JO (2018) Santo Domingo—Latin American Bishops' Conference (1992), Religion Past and Present. Consulted (30 June 2018), https://doi.org/10.1163/1877-5888_rpp_SIM_025209

Blegne S (2015) La parenté à plaisanterie, un bon moyen de prévention et de gestion des conflits au Burkina Faso [Joking Relationships, a Good Way to Prevent and Manage Conflict in Burkina Faso]. Mediaterre (Aug. 30, 2015), https://www.mediaterre.org/afrique-ouest/actu,20150830153532.html

*Break the Chains of Debt*, Advocacy International, http://advocacyinternational.co.uk/featured-project/jubilee-2000; Jocelyne Sambira, *Borrowing Responsibly: Africa's Debt Challenge*, Afr. Renewal (Aug. 2015), http://www.un.org/africarenewal/magazine/august-2015/borrowing-responsibly-africa%E2%80%99s-debt-challenge

Cahill L (1980) Toward a Christian theory of human rights. J Religious Ethics 8:2, 284 (Fall 1980), https://www.jstor.org/stable/pdf/40017762.pdf

Caritas Internationalis, The Caritas Internationalis Commitment on Combating Trafficking in Human Beings, (Oct. 2005). http://www.renate-europe.net/wp-content/uploads/2014/01/Caritas_Internationalis_commitment_on_trafficking_created_in_image_of_God2005.pdf

Catechism of the Catholic Church, no.2273 (2003)

*Charter of the Rights of the Family*, Art 4(e) (Oct.22, 1983), http://www.vatican.va/roman_curia/pontifical_councils/family/documents/rc_pc_family_doc_19831022_family-rights_en.html

Chigona GLM (2012) Trafficking in Human Persons: Perspectives of Catholic Thought. The African Forum for Catholic Social Teaching, p 22. http://www.afcast.org.zw/articles/Trafficking_final_proof.pdf

Claffey P, Christian Churches in Dahomey-Benin: a study of their socio-political role. Brill, Leiden-Boston, p 304

Compendium of the Catechism of the Catholic Church (2005). http://www.vatican.va/archive/compendium_ccc/documents/archive_2005_compendium-ccc_en.html

Conc. oecum. Vat. II, Const

Cornish S (1994) The Catholic Human Rights Tradition and the Rights of Indigenous Peoples 15 (ACSJC Occasional Paper No. 21). http://www.socialjustice.catholic.org.au/files/CSJ-series-papers/CSJS_21_-_The_Catholic_Human_Rights_Tradition_and_the_Rights_of_Indigenous_PeoplesA4.pdf

Damiba F-X, Nare L, Proverbes Mossi (Abidjan, 1999) (proverb no.188)

Dep't of Econ. and Soc. Aff., World Population Ageing 2015, at 10, U.N. Doc. ST/ESA/SER.A/390 (2015), http://www.un.org/en/development/desa/population/publications/pdf/ageing/WPA2015_Report.pdf

*Ethical Guidelines For International Trade*, Note of the Holy See on the Preparation for the Fifth Wto Ministerial Conference (Sept. 2003), http://www.vatican.va/roman_curia/secretariat_state/2003/documents/rc_seg-st_20030910_ethics-intern-trade_en.html

Finding The Moral Fiber. *Why Reform is Urgently Needed For a Fair Cotton Trade*, Oxfam International, https://www.oxfamamerica.org/static/media/files/cotton_brief101804.pdf

Francis P (2013a) *Address of Pope Francis to the New Ambassadors Accredited to the Holy See on the Occasion of the Presentation of the Letters of Credence* (Dec. 12, 2013), http://w2.vatican.va/content/francesco/en/speeches/2013/december/documents/papa-francesco_20131212_credenziali-nuovi-ambasciatori.html

Francis P (2013b) Address of Pope Francis to the New Ambassadors Accredited to the Holy See on the Occasion of the Presentation of the Letters of Credence (Dec.12, 2013) http://www.vatican.va/content/francesco/en/speeches/2013/december/documents/papa-francesco_20131212_credenziali-nuovi-ambasciatori.html

Francis, Ceremony for the Signing of the Faith Leaders' Universal Declaration against Slavery, (Casina Pio IV, December 2014), http://w2.vatican.va/content/francesco/en/speeches/2014/december/documents/papa-francesco_20141202_dichiarazione-schiavitu.html

Fuller-Thomson E, Minkler M (2001) American grandparents providing extensive child care to their grandchildren: prevalence and profile. The Gerontologist 41:2, 201. https://academic.oup.

com/gerontologist/article/41/2/201/648323/American-Grandparents-Providing-Extensive-Child
Grima G. Family Rights: A Catholic Perspective 48 (unpublished comment) (on file with the University of Malta) http://www.um.edu.mt/europeanstudies/books/CD_CSP2/pdf/ratf-ggrima.pdf
Hirshorn B (1998) Grandparents as caregivers. In: Szinovacz ME (ed) Handbook on Grandparenthood 200–214
Hollenbach D (1979) Claims in conflict: retrieving and renewing the catholic human rights tradition
Human Rights as a Global Conversation about Human Dignity 3-4 (International Institute for the Advanced Study of Cultures, Institutions, and Economic Enterprise, Position Paper), http://www.interias.org.gh/sites/default/files/Position%20Paper/IIASPositionPaperHumanRights.pdf
Ibi Ajayi S, Khan MS, *External Debt and Capital Flight in Sub-Saharan Africa*, at http://www.imf.org/external/pubs/nft/2000/extdebt/index.htm
John Paul II, *Apostolic Exhortation Familiaris Consortio* ¶ 23 (Nov. 22, 1981). http://w2.vatican.va/content/john-paul-ii/en/apost_exhortations/documents/hf_jp-ii_exh_19811122_familiaris-consortio.html
John Paul II (1985) Blood and Organ Donors. The Pope Speaks 30:1; Pope John Paul, II, *supra* note 12, ¶ 2296
John Paul II, Sollicitudo Rei Socialis ¶ 47 (Dec. 30, 1987), http://w2.vatican.va/content/john-paul-ii/en/encyclicals/documents/hf_jp-ii_enc_30121987_sollicitudo-rei-socialis.html; Pope John Paul, II., *supra* note 12, ¶¶ 1929, 2158, 2235, 2238, 2267, 2279, 2284, 2304, 2402, 2407, 2479, 2494, 2521, 2526
John Paul II (1990) Organ donations, address to participants at a congress on renal illness and transplants. The Pope Speaks 35:336–337
John Paul II, Ecclesia in Africa ¶ 43 (Sep. 14, 1995a). http://w2.vatican.va/content/john-paul-ii/en/apost_exhortations/documents/hf_jp-ii_exh_14091995_ecclesia-in-africa.html
John Paul II, *Evangelium Vitae: To the Bishops Priests and Deacons Men and Women Religious Lay Faithful and all People of Good Will on the Value and Inviolability of Human Life* ¶ 86 (Mar. 25, 1995b), https://w2.vatican.va/content/john-paul-ii/en/encyclicals/documents/hf_jp-ii_enc_25031995_evangelium-vitae.html
John Paul II, Post-Synodal Apostolic Exhortation Ecclesia in Africa ¶ 121 (1995c), http://w2.vatican.va/content/john-paul-ii/en/apost_exhortations/documents/hf_jp-ii_exh_14091995_ecclesia-in-africa.html
John Paul II, Letter to Archbishop Jean-Louis Tauran on the Occasion of the International Conference "Twenty-First Century Slavery – The Human Rights Dimension to Trafficking in Human Beings" (May 15, 2002), http://w2.vatican.va/content/john-paul-ii/en/letters/2002/documents/hf_jp-ii_let_20020515_tauran.html. [hereinafter Letter to Archbishop Jean-Louis]
John XXIII, Mater et Magistra ¶ 71 (1961)
John XXIII, Pacem in Terris ¶ 34 (Apr. 11, 1963), http://w2.vatican.va/content/john-xxiii/en/encyclicals/documents/hf_j-xxiii_enc_11041963_pacem.html [hereinafter Pacem in Terris].
Kanbur R (2000) Aid conditionality and debt in Africa. Routledge, p 9
Kanniyakonil S (2005) Living organ donation and transplantation: a medical, legal and moral theological appraisal
Kaufman P et al (eds) (2011) Humiliation, Degradation, Dehumanization: Human Dignity Violated 1, http://www.corteidh.or.cr/tablas/r30885.pdf
Lee J (2013) Trafficking in Human Beings: Modern Slavery, Workshop at the Pontifical Academies of Sciences, Pontifical Academy of Social Sciences, and World Federation of the Catholic Medical Associations (Nov. 2, 2013), http://www.endslavery.va/content/endslavery/en/publications/scripta_varia_122/lee.html
Letter from National Conferences of Catholic Bishops to the Leaders of the G8 Nations (June 3, 2013). at http://www.usccb.org/issues-and-action/human-life-and-dignity/poverty/global/upload/2013-G8-Letter.pdf

Little D (1990) A Christian perspective on human rights. In: An-Naim A, Deng FM (eds) Human Rights in Africa: cross-cultural perspectives. p 67

Mary Yuen M-Y (2013) Human rights in China: examining the human rights values in Chinese confucian ethics and roman catholic social teachings. St. Thomas Univ Intercultural Human Rights Law Rev 8:283. https://www.stu.edu/Portals/Law/docs/human-rights/ihrlr/volumes/8/281-321-MeeYinMaryYuen-HumanRightsinChina-ExaminingHumanRightsValues.pdf

Message to the People of God of the Second Special Assembly for Africa 23-33, http://www.vatican.va/roman_curia/synod/documents/rc_synod_doc_20091023_message-synod_en.html

Metz T (2011) Ubuntu as a moral theory and human rights in South Africa. Afr Human Rights Law J 11:532, 538

Msgr. Dennis M. Schnurr, *A Jubilee Call For Debt Forgiveness*, United States Conference of Catholic Bishops, http://www.usccb.org/issues-and-action/human-life-and-dignity/debt-relief/jubilee-debt-forgiveness.cfm

NICOLA BANKS (2016) Youth poverty, employment and livelihoods: social and economic implications of living with insecurity in Arusha, Tanzania. Int Inst Environ Dev (IIED) 28(2):437–454, http://journals.sagepub.com/doi/pdf/10.1177/0956247816651201

*Nigeria Country Report on Human Rights Practices*, U.S. Dep't of St. (Mar. 6, 2007), https://www.state.gov/j/drl/rls/hrrpt/2006/78751.htm

O'Connell Davidson J (2013) Troubling freedom: migration, debt, and modern slavery. Migr Stud 2:176, 179

O'Connor M (2012) Human trafficking: the South African sector and a pastoral response, with exhortations from africae munus in honour of Pope Benedict's visit to Benin in November of 2011. In: Kaulemu D (ed) Faith perspectives on migration and human trafficking 51

Omotayo Olaniyan R (1996) Foreign aid, self-reliance, and economic development in West Africa. Praeger, p 158

OXFAM (2018) Unfair trade rules. Oxfam Hong Kong, https://www.oxfam.org.hk/en/unfairtrade.aspx

Panikkar R (1982 Winter) Is the notion of human rights a Western concept. Diogenes 120:75. http://www.sosyalarastirmalar.com/cilt5/cilt5sayi21_pdf/5_sosyoloji_felsefe/ng_thomas.pdf

Paul VI 1965 Pastoral Constitution on the Church in the Modern World: Gaudium et Spes ¶ 26 (Dec. 7, 1965), http://www.vatican.va/archive/hist_councils/ii_vatican_council/documents/vat-ii_cons_19651207_gaudium-et-spes_en.html

Paul VI, *Populorum Progressio*, Encycl. (March 26, 1967), 283–284 n. 54

Paul VI, *Sollicitudo Rei Socialis*, Encycl. (Dec. 30, 1987), 534–536 n. 19

Paul VI, *Centesimus Annus*, Encycl. (May 1, 1991), 836–838

Paul VI, *Tertio millennio adveniente*, Encycl (Nov. 10, 1994), 36 no. 51

Pontifical Council for Just. and Peace, Compendium of the Social Doctrine of the Church ¶ 259 (2004), http://www.vatican.va/roman_curia/pontifical_councils/justpeace/documents/rc_pc_justpeace_doc_20060526_compendio-dott-soc_en.html; John Paul II, *Veritatis Splendor* ¶ 48 (Encyclical Letter, 6 Aug. 1993)

Pope John Paul, II, Catechism of the Catholic Church, Vatican ¶ 2235 (United States Catholic Conference, Inc., 2000) [available at http://www.vatican.va/archive/ENG0015/__P8B.HTM]

Pope Paul VI (1967) Encyclical Letter: Populorum Progressio. Libreria Editrice Vaticana, Vatican City, no.14

Relieving Third World Debt: A Call for Co-Responsibility, Justice, and Solidarity (United States Conference of Catholic Bishops, 1989)

Sacco UC (1999) John Paul II and world politics: twenty years of a search for a new approach. Peter's Publishers

Saint Irenaeus of Lyons, *Adversus Haereses*, IV, 20, 7; JOHN PAUL II, *Enc. Evangelium Vitae*, 34

Scheper-Hughes N (2016) Neo-Cannibalism, Organ Theft, and Military-Biomedical Necropolitics. EndSlavery 1 (Jan.27, 2016), http://www.endslavery.va/content/endslavery/en/publications/acta_20/scheper_hughes_panel.pdf

Shraideh N, *Foreign Debt and Poverty*, OHCHR, 1-2, https://www2.ohchr.org/english/issues/poverty/docs/sforum/spresentations/Nasser_Shraideh.pdf
Social Doctrine of the Church, supra note 3, ¶ 109
Song AM. Human dignity: A fundamental guiding value for a human rights approach to fisheries?, https://www.sciencedirect.com/science/article/pii/S0308597X15002328
*The Declaration of Istanbul on Organ Trafficking and Transplant Tourism*. Indian J Nephrol 18:3, 135 (July 2008), https://www.ncbi.nlm.nih.gov/pmc/articles/PMC2813140/
The Instruction Donum Vitae, 1987
The Pontifical Commission for the Vatican City State, Law N. VIII: Supplementary Norms On Criminal Law Matters (Jul. 11, 2013), http://www.vaticanstate.va/content/dam/vaticanstate/documenti/leggi-e-decreti/Normative-Penali-e-Amministrative/Law%20N.%20VIII%20-%20Supplementary%20Norms%20on%20Criminal%20Law.pdf
*West Virginia: A State Fact Sheet for Grandparents and Other Relatives Raising Children* 1, AARP Found. (May 2007), http://www.childrensdefense.org/library/data/state-data-repository/gf/grandfacts-west-virginia-2007.pdf
What is the International Debt Crisis?, United States Conference Of Catholic Bishops, at http://www.usccb.org/issues-and-action/human-life-and-dignity/global-issues/debt-relief/what-is-the-international-debt-crisis.cfm
Wiredu K (1990) An Akan perspective on human rights. In: An-Naim A, Deng FM (eds) Human Rights in Africa: cross-cultural perspectives. p 245
Zuma ND (2013) Agriculture in Africa. NEPAD. http://www.un.org/en/africa/osaa/pdf/pubs/2013africanagricultures.pdf

# Chapter 12
# The Church's Contribution to Combating Trafficking in West Africa

The precedent chapter of this study laid out the pastoral guidelines that inspire the Church's sustainable actions to address modern slavery. Drawing from the longstanding experience of the Church institutions and parishes, the following discussion will uncover the potential of a faith-based approach to challenge the factors and forces that make people vulnerable to trafficking, and support the full liberation of bonded laborers.

## 12.1 Catholic Church Institutions' Response to Trafficking

The collaboration with the Catholic Church in combating trafficking in persons has a special significance, as the Church possesses the global institutional capacity to organize international action to address this social scourge. It has acted in this regard as an effective catalyst to create anti-trafficking networks around the world to prevent and, combat trafficking and assist the victims. Relevant examples in this respect are the Catholic organizations and religious institutions in West Africa that have joined forces to form a Working Group to fight trafficking in persons. Of the many actions taken, the Nigerian Conference of Women Religious (NCWR) presented a full report of the magnitude of trafficking in persons to the Nigerian Conference of Bishops, urging them to write a Pastoral Letter on this issue.[1] A "Committee for the Support of the Dignity of Woman" (COSUDOW) was then established in 1999 with several specific goals, including advocacy and awareness programs to teach women about the dangers of prostitution. The Committee for the Support of the Dignity of Woman (COSUDOW)*)* has since become a focal point of

[1] Benedict XVI, Jesus of Nazareth, 198 (2007). A Pastoral letter on "Restoring the Dignity of Nigerian Women" was issued by the Nigerian Bishop's Conference in February 2002 and read in all Parishes on two different Sundays.

 
P. VI. S. Karenga, *A West African Model to Address Human Trafficking*,
https://doi.org/10.1007/978-3-030-88120-7_12

reference for several non-governmental organizations (NGOs) and for women in need of help.[2]

For instance, the Committee for the Support of the Dignity of Woman (COSUDOW) conducted "enlightenment/sensitization campaigns" to educate different sectors of the public on the evils of trafficking in human beings and its related consequences. Young women and school children are the target population and are reached in the village squares through market women unions, transporters associations, and other similar groups. Other enlightenment campaigns include the distribution of leaflets, media presentations, and talk shows broadcast in rural areas. Through "Advocacy Visits", the Committee for the Support of the Dignity of Woman (COSUDOW) "meets with traditional rulers and leaders of targeted groups to enlighten them on the recruitment tactics of the traffickers and to solicit their support in bringing awareness to their communities."[3] The sisters have traced victims' families, assisted and reunited victims of international trafficking with their families and communities, and provided victims with both spiritual and emotional healing.[4]

Another institutional response to trafficking can be found in Ghana. A Religious Organization known as 'Collaboration with Women in Distress' (COLWOD) was set up in 1995 by Sister Connie Gemme, Missionary Sister of our Lady of Africa to educate young girls and women in Northern Ghana on the possible dangers involved in migrating to northern and western Europe and to prevent them from falling prey to traffickers.[5] COLWOD reached out to young people in the cybercafé where offenders used an online employment search to contact potential victims with the promise of an unbelievably good job in Europe and the United States. The organization engaged churches, women in the villages, and schools in raising awareness and drawing the attention of the community to this situation. They met with the leaders of religious congregations and even took part in the Bishops' Conference in 2003 to discuss this subject. Sister Connie Gemme along with members of the organization also undertook the responsibility to travel throughout Ghana from north to south, east to west to carry out a number of workshops and seminars. A total of 150,000 brochures were distributed throughout Ghana.[6]

---

[2] *Human Trafficking*, Sisters of IHM, http://www.sistersofihm.org/what-we-do/ihm-justice-outreach-advocacy/detail.html?id=1b1839c1-886f-447d-a276-2c2fdbbaad44; Eucharia Madueke, *Human Trafficking In Nigeria: Sisters Provide Services, Seek Greater Justice For All*, Global Sister's Report, http://globalsistersreport.org/column/justice-matters/trafficking/human-trafficking-nigeria-sisters-provide-services-seek-greater.

[3] Federatie Opvang, Safe Return and Reintegration for Victims of Trafficking and Victims of Domestic Violence Facing Residency Problems 46 (Sep. 2014), http://www.opvang.nl/files/Safe_Return_Field_Research.pdf [hereinafter Residency Problems].

[4] *Id.*

[5] *Restoring dignity to street women in Tamale*, Partir Partager Prier, http://www.soeurs-blanches.cef.fr/afrique-justice-et-paix/justice-et-paix/rendre-la-dignite-aux-femmes-de-la-rue-a-tamale/.

[6] *Id.*

Similarly, on October 23, 2016, the Union of the Consecrated of the Diocese of Bobo-Dioulasso gathered at the Sisters of Our Lady of Charity of the Good Shepherd to meet with seventy-six people representing male and female religious congregations to address the issue of trafficking. The main objective of the meeting was to introduce Talithakum and set up a diocesan network with the aim of extending this network to a national level and then to francophone West African countries.[7] Other female religious institutions and individual sisters present in other West African countries are also making concerted efforts to eradicate the trafficking of women and children by promoting the education of women and girls, operating safe houses, running rehabilitation programs, and adopting a proactive role in peace-building.

This varied set of institutions are striving to develop more coordinated actions oriented toward eradicating the trafficking and smuggling of persons across national, regional, and continental boundaries. For example, the Migrants Commission of the Ghana Catholic Bishop's Conference organized a workshop in Accra from July 1 to 2, 2008 to raise awareness of the growing phenomenon in the West African sub-region. The workshop brought together 35 participants from Ghana, Togo, Benin, Nigeria, Cote d'Ivoire, Burkina Faso, Niger, Mali, Cameroon, Senegal, Sierra Leone, Liberia, as well as European partners involved in combating trafficking in persons. The objective was to share experiences and discuss strategies to mitigate or eliminate the incidence of trafficking. The workshop also provided those present with an opportunity to identify a guiding framework for the establishment of rescue, rehabilitation, and reintegration committees at regional, national, diocesan and parish levels.[8] Following this regional commitment to combating trafficking in persons, Justice and Peace Departments and Caritas in partnership with the diocesan commission for the Pastoral Care of Migrant and Itinerant People undertook and implemented awareness raising and prevention campaigns in various dioceses and parishes[9] in West Africa, with a particular focus on the protection of potential victims.

Most importantly, to perpetuate this awareness campaign the Bishops' Conference of the continent adopted February 8, the feast day of St. Josephine Bakhita, as the Day of Prayer for victims and survivors of trafficking and those who work with them.[10] In 2014, on the day earmarked for the ceremony in Nigeria, all the parishes

---

[7] *Talithakum Afrique Francophone*, Talitha kum Arise (Dec. 6, 2016), http://www.talithakum.info/news/62/talithakum-afrique-francophone.

[8] Brenda Ola, *Human Trafficking and Slavery*, N.Y.U.(May 9, 2009) http://www.nyu.edu/classes/keefer/joe/olab.pdf; *Annual Activity Report*, Caritas 13 (2008), http://www.caritas.eu/sites/default/files/ce_annualactivityreport_ed2008_en.pdf; Dadirai Chikwengo, CAFOD, *How The Sdgs And The Church Can Help The Fight Against Human Trafficking*, https://cafodpolicy.wordpress.com/2016/11/09/how-the-sdgs-and-the-church-can-help-the-fight-against-human-trafficking/.

[9] *See Notes on Human Trafficking*, http://armel.duteil.free.fr/?page=traffichumain&father=justicepaix (Caritas Guinea Conakry lack a department dedicated to trafficking and have yet to organize pastoral care for the victims).

[10] *Catholics Urged to Fight Against Human Trafficking*, NCSN (Jan. 27, 2014) http://www.cnsng.org/viewnews.php?tabnews=946.

throughout the country organized several activities and the diocesan Directors of Justice, Development and Peace mobilized the faithful for this celebration.[11] Globally, this collective response to trafficking in persons abroad and at home included announcements in churches and church bulletins; sermons with preaching points centered on trafficking during Sunday services; retreats and the formation of youth; seminars and talks on trafficking, catholic media, and catholic school awareness.[12]

Furthermore, Foyer Don Bosco has been invested to prevent children's rights abuses and improve their wellbeing in Benin (Porto-Novo). The management team, in collaboration with its partners, has organized preventive activities with the aim of raising awareness among leaders and parents as well as the children themselves on their rights and the laws that protect them. These awareness activities have increased the knowledge of the population and encouraged them to change behavior that puts children into a situation of abuse and exploitation. These groups commit themselves to protecting children in general and to report cases of abuse. Prevention activities include group support, one-to-one outreach, awareness raising, audiovisual awareness raising, sports activities, and awareness-raising meetings for master craftsmen.[13] The prevention activities of Foyer Don Bosco have reached a total of 1,015,240 persons.[14]

## 12.2 Catholic School Education to Prevent Trafficking in Persons

A common assumption in trafficking discourse is that a correlation exists between levels of education and migratory decisions that lead to unsafe and exploitive work".[15] Within this framework, a direct relationship can be drawn between access to education, school completion, and trafficking in persons. The preceding discussion showed that rampant disparities in education are a risk or vulnerability factor for trafficking and that the stereotypical victim in West Africa is portrayed as illiterate or of low level education. Therefore, education is a key priority in fighting trafficking and the investment of the Catholic Church in schooling is a highly effective measure in the prevention of trafficking in persons. For survivors starting over again as well as young people who have not been trafficked, education and job skills are important tools to prevent trafficking and or to build a new life.

---

[11] *Id.*

[12] *Id.*; *Ghana Bishops Speak. A Collection Of Communiques, Memoranda And Pastoral Letters Of The Ghana Catholic Bishops' Conference*, 17 National Catholic Secretariat (1999). [hereinafter *Collection Of Communiques*].

[13] *Rapport d'activités 2013*, Association Foyer Don Bosco 11 (Feb. 2014), http://portonovo.foyerdonbosco.org/wp-content/uploads/2014/04/Rapport_d_activites_2013.pdf.

[14] *Id.* at 9.

[15] Vijeyarasa (2015).

In addition, if trafficking is considered a result of seeking economic betterment elsewhere, a link between barriers to decent work in the domestic market and education is easily established. The socio-economic profile of women and children who fall victim to trafficking indicates that they fall into an unskilled or low-skilled category of workers and were trafficked into domestic work, tomatoes and orange harvesting, begging, prostitution, and other unskilled forms of labor. "Education creates opportunities for potential migrants to access work in the domestic market and, if they choose, to migrate for work abroad."[16] High levels of education are believed to create opportunities for professional and skilled workers to migrate legally under safe conditions. By contrast, "low levels of education are seen as an impediment for potential migrants to find work at home and/or migrate safely,"[17] giving rise to people smuggling and trafficking.

Education is also often assumed to guide individual decisions and to "increase the capacity of victims to understand, process and appreciate the risks involved when entering into a transaction."[18] Victims with low levels of education are easily deceived as they are unable to recognize the lure or overcome the risk of fraud that is potentially involved in contracts for work abroad. Indeed, migrant labor from people in this category is targeted because they "often lack the requisite support structures to defend or demand their rights, both during migration and at the new work sites. Their limited bargaining power impairs their exploitation."[19] Such an assumption gives rise to the relatively high investment of funds in anti-trafficking programs focused on education as a counter-trafficking solution.[20] Finally, "[e] ducation is also a powerful protection factor: children who are in school are less likely to come into conflict with the law and much less vulnerable to rampant forms of child exploitation, including child labor, trafficking, and recruitment into armed groups and forces."[21]

However, there is excessive amplification regarding the assumed role of school enrolment and completion as a means end trafficking in persons. Somewhat surprisingly, education and improved living conditions in West Africa is also a factor driving trafficking in persons. As highlighted in part I, the huge demand for 'house-maids' and domestic servants is a problem that has grown in concert with the apparition of a "western educated, middle/upper class . . .woman, who is addressed as 'Madam'."[22] "Almost every household that considers itself wealthy, especially among the urban middle and upper class, keeps a minimum of one 'house-maid'."[23]

---

[16] *Id.* at 11.

[17] *Id.*

[18] *Id.* at 97.

[19] Nair and Sen (2005).

[20] Vijeyarasa (2015), p. 11.

[21] *The Education Deficit*, Human Rights Watch, https://www.hrw.org/report/2016/06/09/education-deficit/failures-protect-and-fulfill-right-education-through-global.

[22] Agozino (2004).

[23] *Id.*

Thus African women with good education participate in the exploitation and abuse of their less fortunate peers in domestic servitude. This indicates that education needs a meaning, a supplement of morality, and this is where catholic school education fits in. It was catholic missions that led the founding of the first free schools run by religious orders that provided Western education to people from West Africa. The primary goal of missionaries was evangelization alongside improving the lives of the people, and schools were recognized as a preferred forum and strategy for achieving this purpose.[24] In the modern era the Church supports a large number of kindergartens, primary schools, secondary schools, and universities in West Africa.

As discussed earlier, evidence shows that in West Africa a form of education that excludes or marginalizes the moral and religious dimensions of the person can increase rather than impeded trafficking. In effect, education has amplified inequalities between women living in urban cities and those living in the remote villages that generate labor exploitation. Therefore, failing to integrate religious and moral instruction into the education of pupils can lead them into trouble. Those citizens who are called upon to take an active part in social, economic, and political life can do a disservice to the entire society. An educated citizen who lacks integrity brings insidious consequences to society: these take the form of corruption, exploitation of others, conflicts, war, intolerance, and ethno-centrism, all of which are factors driving trafficking. Therefore, the Catholic Church ensures that those who emerge from its educational institutions are people of integrity who have been provided with an authentic education.[25]

To that end, Catholic educators should bring a deeper understanding of Christian anthropology to their students along and with an understanding of what it means to be a person with inalienable dignity. Their special task is to "make human beings more human". The Sacred Congregation for Catholic Education describes this anthropological vision as follows:

> In today's pluralistic world, the Catholic educator must consciously inspire his or her activity with the Christian concept of the person, in communion with the Magisterium of the Church. It is a concept which includes a defence of human rights, but also attributes to the human person the dignity of a child of God; it attributes the fullest liberty, freed from sin itself by Christ, the most exalted destiny, which is the definitive and total possession of God Himself,

---

[24] *See, e.g.*, St. Leo, http://www.saintleo.edu/media/411879/catholic_education_in_kenya.pdf; Impact of Catholic Mission on Education in Nigeria, LinkedIn, https://www.linkedin.com/pulse/20141207174923-62892927-impact-of-catholic-mission-on-education-in-nigeria; *Christian Missions in Africa And Their Role in The Transformation Of African Societies*, Asian And African Studies 16 (2007), https://www.sav.sk/journals/uploads/102313498_Vilhanov%C3%A1.pdf; *La Contribution De L'eglise Catholique A La Formation De L'elites Africaine: Cas De La Côte D'ivoire*, http://celaf-institut.org/wp-content/uploads/2017/10/LA-CONTRIBUTION-DE-LEGLISE-A-LA-FORMATION-DE-LELITE-AFRICAINE.pdf.

[25] Provision of Quality Education in Ghana, http://kmdiocese.org/kmd/index2.php?option=com_content&do_pdf=1&id=42.

through love. It establishes the strictest possible relationship of solidarity among all persons; through mutual love and an ecclesial community.[26]

This Christian understanding of the human person has important implications for how students live and act in Catholic schools and in society. Pupils are encouraged to believe in transcendent love and to recognize the image of Christ in themselves and others, thus leading them to nurture a profound reverence for the human dignity of every person.[27] As Pope Benedict pointed out, "Only the courage to rediscover and accept the divine dimension of our being can give our souls and our society a new stability once again."[28] It is only by understanding their own dignity and loving themselves that children can cherish and protect the dignity of others from abuse and exploitation.[29]

Another essential aspect of Christian anthropology is the exhortation to love our neighbors, which implies radical inclusiveness. Christian love is expressed in catholic schools that welcome everyone without distinction. In effect, "not all students in Catholic schools are members of the Catholic Church; not all are Christians". Indeed, in countries such as Senegal, Niger, Burkina Faso, Gambia, and Mali, the vast majority of students are not Catholics. This diversity fosters a culture of dialogue, tolerance, and equality which is a panacea for conflicts and ethnic wars that fuel trafficking and slavery-like practices in the region, as highlighted in Part I. Children learn daily how to transcend their ethnic, religious, and socio-economic differences to live together in unity. In a multicultural society, an understanding of the person as fundamentally engaged in intercultural dialogue with others is relevant to building a society of fraternity and peace through solidarity. In so doing, "amidst this religious and cultural plurality, enduring and happy friendships developed between Muslims and Christians students"[30] as well as with other ethnicities.

"Moral formation and religious education also foster the development of personal and social responsibility and the other civic virtues; they represent, therefore, an important contribution to the common good of society."[31] Many benefits arising the foundation of Christian communities in West Africa were reaped from these Catholic schools. The Mission has not only contributed to the growth of moral behavior amongst the inhabitants. It has also remained a prominent and active player in the educational development of all countries in the region. Indeed, such education has

[26] Lay Catholics in Schools: Witness to Faith, The Sacred Congregation for Catholic Education ¶ 18, http://www.vatican.va/roman_curia/congregations/ccatheduc/documents/rc_con_ccatheduc_doc_19821015_lay-catholics_en.html.

[27] Marc D. Guerra, Pope Benedict XVI and the Politics of Modernity, 57–60, https://www.assumption.edu/sites/default/files/cv/140930MarcGuerra.pdf. [hereinafter the Politics of Modernity].

[28] Ratzinger (2005).

[29] The Politics of Modernity, *supra* note 962 at 58.

[30] D'Souza (2016).

[31] *Circular Letter to The Presidents of Bishops' Conferences on Religious Education in Schools*, Congregation for Catholic Education, http://www.vatican.va/roman_curia/congregations/ccatheduc/documents/rc_con_ccatheduc_doc_20090505_circ-insegn-relig_en.html.

contributed to creating the educated elite who have led the nationalist struggle for an end to colonialism and challenged slavery and apartheid in Africa. Although colonial governments saw education as a means of raising African auxiliaries for the colonial service, the mission schools used education as an instrument to facilitate the effective conversion of Africans to Christianity and to forge elites who would later be able to play an important role in shaping the direction of public affairs.[32]

As noted in Part I, the trafficking of persons for sexual exploitation and forced labor is driven by demand in destination countries. A former victim of trafficking in Florida made a compelling declaration that challenges socioeconomic stereotypes: "you don't have to be uneducated to become a victim of human trafficking." The major cause of trafficking in persons in society is greed and the desire to "make it big" coupled with unrealistic promises, and calls for a moral solution. "Science without conscience is the ruin of the soul. Politics without morality is the ruin of society."[33]

To prevent children from becoming involved in trafficking as traffickers, clients or victims, the Declaration On Christian Education (Gravissimum Educationis) aims to include in the framework of educating the young person "a positive and prudent sexual education."[34] Sexual giving belongs to married love alone and "thus becomes a power which enriches persons and makes them grow and, at the same time, it contributes to building up the civilization of love."[35] However, when sexuality is devoid of its meaning as a gift and is associated mainly with pleasure, a civilization of persons become a civilization of things "in which persons are used in the same way as things are used."[36] In this context, a woman can become an object for men to use and abuse.

[32] Jean-Marie Bouron, *Les Pères Blancs, acteurs du jeu colonial. Mission catholique et enjeux politiques en Haute-Volta au lendemain de la seconde guerre mondiale*, Université of Nantes 59-81 (2010), https://www.cairn.info/revue-histoire-monde-et-cultures-religieuses1-2010-2-page-59.htm; *Education, Western Africa (Western Colonialism)*, What-when-how, http://what-when-how.com/western-colonialism/education-western-africa-western-colonialism/.

[33] Francois Rabelais, *Gargantua and Pantagruel* (1532-64), book 2, chap. 8.

[34] *Declaration On Christian Education Gravissimum Educationis*, Congregation for Catholic Education, http://www.vatican.va/archive/hist_councils/ii_vatican_council/documents/vat-ii_decl_19651028_gravissimum-educationis_en.html.

[35] *The Truth And Meaning of Human Sexuality*, Congregation for Catholic Education http://www.vatican.va/roman_curia/pontifical_councils/family/documents/rc_pc_family_doc_08121995_human-sexuality_en.html.

[36] *Id.*

## 12.3 The Approach of the Ecclesial Forum to Harmful Cultural Practices

From the analysis set forth in Chap. 1, individuals and ethnic groups who act primarily out of a sense of cultural conviction have given rise to the thorniest issue for anti- trafficking work in West Africa. Apostolic Exhortation Africae Munus denounces the ongoing negative practices that debase and degrade women in the name of ancestral tradition and call on the Church to take responsibility in contributing to the liberation of women.[37] In response to this call, the Catholic Bishop's Conferences have upheld the dignity of human beings and prohibited relentless trafficking through their pastoral letters with respect to their specific local situations. The Archdiocese of Koupela went further in demonstrating a new strategy or method to address trafficking related practices by including forced marriage and discrimination against women in its Synod Assembly (October 27–31, 1999). The discussion on forced marriage in the Synod Assembly marked a welcome and important step in expressing not only societal opposition but also religious condemnation to such a dehumanizing act.

Synod derives from the Greek word "synodos", meaning "to walk together". The term has a rich meaning in the church body as it brings together the bishop, the priestly leadership, and lay and religious representatives throughout the diocese to discuss the most important issues affecting Church life with the purpose of promoting acceptance and encouraging the faithful in their following of Christ.[38] A diocesan synod in the Catholic Church is the most significant ecclesial forum of dialogue, discernment, and decision on important matters of faith, morality, and church discipline. It "embraces the dimensions of theological reflection, pastoral insight, visioning and governing, all within the context of a deep spiritual orientation to the wider life of the Church."[39] As such, the synod has a unique and valuable role to play in bringing about a change in the mindsets and attitudes of people and to bring renewal to the life of a diocese. The prototype of all church synods or councils is the Council of Jerusalem, which took place in 48 AD to settle deep cultural beliefs regarding circumcision and other cultural practices (Act, 15).

As part of the 100th anniversary of the evangelization of Koupela, Most Rev. Seraphin Franciss Rouamba Archbishop of Koupela convened a diocesan synod that focused on three major challenges, including forced marriage and discrimination against women. The close scrutiny given to this issue alerted the interest of the Church to the sinful state of offenders and the plight of victims living in such

---

[37] O'Connor (2012a), pp. 56, 57.

[38] *Instruction on Diocesan Syods*, Congregation for Catholic, http://www.vatican.va/roman_curia/congregations/cbishops/documents/rc_con_cbishops_doc_20041118_diocesan-synods-1997_en.html.

[39] Most Reverend Robert W. McElroy, *Embracing The Joy of Love. A Pastoral Message to the People of the Diocese of San Diego*, https://www.sdcatholic.org/Portals/0/Bishop/Documents/Embracing_the_Joy_of_Love.pdf?ver=2016-05-09-151145-653.

situations. It also drove the Church in Koupela to ponder and compare the holy image of God to the unethical behavior that some members and non-members alike had unconsciously been drawn into.[40] On this occasion, the Church deplored and condemned child marriage and forced marriage, levirate, sororate, widowhood rites, and other harmful practices, which deprive women and children of their rights and the respect due to them. This important instance of legislative power orientated the bishop toward issuing pastoral norms and formulating disciplinary and spiritual directives on this matter. It was thus decreed that parents or any individual involved directly or who were complicit in forced marriage enter a state of broken communion with the Church wherein they cannot receive any sacrament. This helps them understand the devastating effects of their sinful acts: forced marriage is not only a violation of social norms, it is also an offense against God.[41]

The synod's approach to this related trafficking practice is founded on mercy and merits further development. In the Sacred Scriptures, mercy is an extremely profound concept that promotes social harmony and individual well-being. Mercy is an act of love and kindness "that forgives a fault or an offense, leaving both parties far better off, both the one who was guilty of the offense and the one who was offended."[42] This undeserved love and unearned kindness provide the offender with an opportunity to humbly admit that they have hurt others and thus acquire the liberty to convert and begin a new path, while also softening the offended heart from the painful consequences that always come from vengeance, resentment, and anger.[43]

In order to be meaningful, mercy must involve accountability and discipline. Thus, "mercy calls a person to accept the consequences of their actions and to embrace the discipline that comes with them."[44] Although the term "discipline" in the Bible is read in conjunction with "punishment" or correction (Prov. 13:24; 22:15; 23:13–15), the hard reality of accountability is accepted by a person who desires to be virtuous, happy, and holy. The aim of the synod is to teach and guide the person involved in forced marriage toward conversion and a true reform of their life. For mercy to be a path leading to reform, "justice must discipline and admonish the person about the consequences of vice and darkness; this way, the path of goodness is understood, desired, and pursued."[45] The strategy and outcome of the synod's approach is illustrated by the following allegory.

> Picture a child being told that he cannot have dessert after dinner, but he disobeys and eats a cookie in his bed. In the morning, his mother sees the cookie crumbs. This disobedience hurts not only the child but the moral health and common good of the family.

---

[40] Awinongya (2013a), p. 15.

[41] Cf. *Assises Synodales a Koupela du 27 au 31 Octobre 1999*, (Document final du Synode Diocesain de Koupela).

[42] Kirby (2017), p. 73.

[43] *Id.* at 74.

[44] *Id.* at 76.

[45] *Id.*

> The mother has two options in terms of retribution. First, she could see the crumbs, clean them up, and never mention anything to the child. This would be a passive vengeance since it ignores the child and nurtures vice in him. This sort of reaction is born from the possible sentiments within the parent. "I don't have time for this." "I've told him not to do this before and it's just not worth the trouble; I've got to pick my battles." "I don't care. Whatever." And similar such reactions.
>
> Or she sees the crumbs, violently pulls the child into the room, screams and yells, punches the wall, and rips the covers off the bed in a fit of rage. Obviously, this is active vengeance since it causes fear and seeks to harm the person, if not physically, then psychologically.
>
> Beyond these two dramatically different options is a level-headed response that lies somewhere in the middle. The mother can choose mercy and welcome a measured form of justice at the same time. She could call the child into the room and calmly ask about the crumbs, doing her best to practice temperance, prudence, and fortitude. She'll temper her resolutions on discipline until she hears the child's explanation (and hopeful confession). Her prudence helps her assess the situation and ask the right questions to help her understand what was going on in the child's mind when he disobeyed (to hopefully help him curb future behavior away from his mindset). And her fortitude helps her keep her cool, especially if she is already tired and frustrated from the other demands of the day.
>
> If the child acknowledges that he broke a rule and shows repentance, then her discipline might be light; there will be a gentle rebuke and explanation of why disobeying is wrong. The child has to apologize and clean up the crumbs.[46]

Since the closure of the Synod, its initiatives, recommendations, and pastoral directives have been felt at every level of the lives of parishes and diocesan ministries. The celebration of the diocesan synod was truly an authentic event of grace for the Church in Koupela. It provided a moment of profound renewal and growth in their ecclesial support for the victims. Most importantly, it was provided an opportunity to awaken the conscience of potential and current offenders to the evil of their sinful behavior. As such, the Synod challenged believers to consider their relationship with God and ensure it conforms to their relationship with others.

Consequently, a significant number of families where forced marriage took place or was pending voluntarily took steps to come before their respective faithful communities and ask for forgiveness and reintegration. Notably, former offenders became participants in the general campaign against forced marriage. Religion matters because it has a positive influence on individuals, families, and entire communities and both the institution and practice are maintained over time. Moreover, a change that emanates from within is more permanent than an injunction imposed from outside.

This journey of faith and the sincere amendment of life teaches the entire faithful community how God's Spirit works in awakening and leading sinners to a radical conversion of heart. As a result, forced marriage in parishes where prevalence was high has decreased considerably. This synod therefore offers an example of good practice that has succeeded in achieving its objectives. Other ecclesial forums should therefore be convened in the region with an extended scope to include all forms of

---

[46] *Id.* at 79–80.

trafficking and related practices such as trafficking in forced labor, domestic servitude, and witchcraft, the latter of which is a force driving human sacrifice and trafficking in human body parts.[47]

The lesson that can be drawn from the previous discussion is that the synod has a compelling power of persuasion. It not only manifests ecclesial communion in a diocese, it also builds up and fosters that same unity between members. Throughout the history of the Church this ecclesial forum has been a useful instrument for implementing required moral, doctrinal, or disciplinary changes with compassion and full understanding of the pastoral needs of the faithful, who live in varying circumstances and conditions. Given the correlation between trafficking in persons and customary beliefs in Africa, the only way to implement more effective and culturally appropriate responses that will change in individuals' behavior is to reach them through the sphere of their religious convictions. Therefore, convening a diocesan synod on the social issue of trafficking and slavery-like practices constitutes a promising pathway to a renewal of church life and that of the entire society. This strategy of dialogue, education of the faithful, and discernment also enriches human rights advocacy.

This synodal approach to forced marriage especially echoes the strategy used by the non-governmental organization (NGO) International Needs Ghana in calling for the reform of *trokosi*, a traditional religious crime control practice that involves the ritual servitude of young girls. Indeed, e Christian faith based nature of this organization corroborates that assumption. To fully understand the controversy surrounding *trokosi* and how the enforcement of human rights laws that conflict with cultural and religious rights can be increasingly complex, it is important to highlight the social role played by this custom. For instance, the *trokosi* shrines perform positive functions in the community such as "healing especially from mysterious illness, help with acquiring blessings, protection, and enforcing general morality among others."[48] Ghanaian religious institutions have a long history of protecting human dignity and promoting social cohesion. They have contributed to fulfilling the moral, ethical, and spiritual needs of community members. However, some practices in the *trokosi* violate contemporary human rights standards inasmuch as the socio-political milieu which supported this system have changed. Violation of the human dignity "of the victims as a result of *trokosi* practice, takes many forms, such as enslavement, sexual exploitation and forced (child) labour, [serving time for a crime committed by another person]."[49] To eliminate harmful cultural and religious practices, the United Nations has adopted general human rights standards which it has embedded in the Universal Declaration of Human Rights and human rights conventions. As a member state of the United Nations, Ghana has pledged its cooperation in addressing the issue. Indeed, Articles 16(1) and 16(2) of the Constitution of Ghana provide that no one shall be held as a slave or be subject to servitude. Any customary practice that

---

[47] Nagle and Owasanoye (2016), p. 561.

[48] Ameh (2001), p. 186. [hereinafter *A Contextual Policy*].

[49] Asomah (2015), p. 129.

dehumanizes or jeopardizes the physical and mental wellbeing of any citizen is also recognized as a violation of article 26(2) of the 1992 National Constitution.[50]

However, despite these efforts, contemporary forms of human bondage such as forced labor, servile marriage, ritual bondage, child labor, forced prostitution, and slavery-like practices continue to thrive e in Ghana and other parts of West Africa. This indicates "that the criminal justice system is rarely an instrument of progressive social change."[51] Furthermore, evidence suggests that Ghana, like any other state, will likely justify noncompliance with human rights conventions on the basis of custom or cultural rights, and will refuse to reprimand or prosecute those whose practices violate human rights standards, especially when the customs are founded on religion.[52]

However, there are certain religious values that pose challenges to international human rights law. How can we eradicate an age-old abusive customary practice that has become so entrenched it is woven into peoples' identity and fulfils their ethical and spiritual needs?[53] In societies in which human dignity is often expressed through religion, faith is an essential element that must be taken into account in order to avoid mistakes and/or violations. Robert Kwame Ameh maintains that an approach to a belief system which is based on dialogue and education in order to conquer fear of spiritual reprisals is more effective in producing change than other means.

---

[50] UNFPA, *Liberating Slaves And Changing Minds: Starting At Grassroots*, *https://www.unfpa.org/endingviolence/html/pdf/chapter_ghana.pd*; The government of Ghana, *1992 Constitution of The Republic of Ghana*, http://www.ghana.gov.gh/index.php/constitution/395-1992-constitution-of-the-republic-of-ghana. *See also The Trokosi Practice*, *supra* note 1021 at 129–149.

[51] Ameh (2001), p. 296.

[52] Larson (1996), p. 695, 714 (examining the potential for changing the international status of women through the Beijing Conference and Platform, discussing the challenges inherent in human rights development, and analyzing how the Beijing Conference addresses those problems). *See* Bilyeu (1992), p. 457, 459.

[53] Short (2004), p. 1, https://www.newtactics.org/sites/default/files/resources/Powerful-Persuasion-EN.pdf.

[Hereinafter *Powerful Persuasion*]. Field research reports that many people visit the shrines to seek success, fortification, and protection from evil, and are reluctant to interfere with the activities of the fetish priests. *See* Veronique Mistiaen, *Virgin Wives of the Fetish Gods*, Thomas Reuters Foundation, http://news.trust.org//item/20131003122159-3cmei/. For example, Torgbi Venanua, the Tsaduma priest who owned Enyonam, a trokosi woman related: "People who do not understand the trokosi system feel it is a servitude, but it is a blessing because that girl who comes to the shrine will protect her family from harm." *Id.* In effect, fetish priests are revered figures in rural areas. *Id.* They heal people, perform rituals to protect individuals, crops and businesses, advise villagers, and deliver justice. *Id.* After ING's intervention, Torgbi Venanua finally released 200 trokosis but continued to insist they were queens rather than slaves. However, in his statement, Enyoman protested "I was no queen," "I wish I could send the government a picture of me with only a cloth around my privates and a cord around my neck." "We had no hope. We knew we'd stay at the shrine until the day we died," echoed Mercy Senahe, 34, who was sent to another shrine at the age of 9. *Id.* "Every night, the priest would come to one woman, even if she was very young. Even at that time, I knew the priest was doing something wrong, but if you tried to fight, he would beat you up. We had no one to stand up for us. When I think about it today, I still feel so pitiful and I weep." *Id.*

Legislation outlawing such practices could strengthen factors for change, although criminal law does not by itself possess the capacity to persuade proponents of a belief to adopt a change in attitudes and behavior with respect to practices that violate basic human rights.[54]

Another example which illustrates why a legal approach may not achieve the expected outcome when dealing with controversial traditional practices detrimental to women is that the large majority of African women do not have a culture of using the courts to fight for their rights. There are few instances of judicial proceedings involving allegations of human rights violations occurring as a result of controversial traditional practices in Ghana and any other West African country. The report indicates that, even in those few instances, the courts in Ghana faced a dilemma in handling the cases. Although African traditional religion is recognized by the laws of Ghana, the findings from traditional religious practices are not legally acceptable evidence in court.[55] Since the laws prohibiting harmful cultural practices have been enacted, not a single traditional priest or family member has been arrested for an abuse of human rights and an attack on the dignity and humanity of women. Consequently, the efficiency of a legal approach is limited when dealing with human rights issues arising from cultural institutions and practices with religious components.

Moreover, the legislation outlawing[56] the practice cast a dreadful fear in the population because families were afraid the curse would revisit them and in some cases resulted in driving the customary practice further underground. As a result, women and girls continued to be trapped in this system of bondage. This suggests that deep-seated beliefs and time-honored cultural practices can be changed only by persuasion and not by enforcing the law, as this cannot work without the involvement of the community. The process leading to the successful liberation of women and girls has taken more than a decade, and has involved a complex series of integrated steps. International Need Ghana (INGH), a Christian development organization, engaged respected leaders—at local and national levels—"in direct dialogue with perpetrators, victims, other community leaders, and the community at large to facilitate understanding of the practice, while providing alternatives and avenues for abandoning the practice without losing status."[57] Activists decided to

---

[54] Ameh (2004).

[55] *Id.*

[56] *Ghana Legislation Enacted Criminalize Trokosi Tradition Enslavement*, Equality Now, https://www.equalitynow.org/action-alerts/ghana-legislation-enacted-criminalize-trokosi-tradition-enslavement. Section 314 of the Criminal Code (Amendment) Act 1998 criminalizes all customary practices that involve ritual servitude, declaring: "(a) whoever sends to or receives at any place or (b) participates in or is concerned in any ritual or customary activity in respect of any person with the purpose of subjecting that person to any form of forced labour related to a customary ritual commits an offence and shall be liable on conviction to imprisonment for a term not less than three years." *Id.*

[57] Short (2004), p. 1 https://www.newtactics.org/sites/default/files/resources/Powerful-Persuasion-EN.pdf.

address the economic concerns of priests and shrine owners in the hope that such incentives would replace the economic benefits derived from having *trokosi* slaves, leaving shrines self-sufficient as well as appealing to their sense of morality.

International Need Ghana (INGH) encourages shrine owners and priests to participate in the negotiation process, providing financial assistance of US $74 to release the trokosi women and girls, and US $925 to rehabilitate the shrine and the liberation ceremony.[58] During this period, International Need Ghana (INGH) also began a program of vocational skills training for Trokosi girls to enable them to set up their own business. The program aimed to restore them emotionally and, most importantly, "to persuade the girls to leave the shrines, and to relinquish the fear of death instilled in them. Although the fetish shrines lack the high walls of traditional prisons, the girls are indoctrinated with the idea that if they leave, the wrath of the fetish will strike them dead."[59]

The most important aspect of the liberation movement that has proved successful is utilizing a powerful form of religious persuasion to solve the religious problem caused by the *trokosi* and to ensure the community recognizes that traditions are flexible and can be transformed over time and that this practice can be changed without offending the gods. The efforts of the Commission on Human Rights and Administrative Justice in conjunction with International Needs, have had some success in winning the release of 3000 women and children from 132 different shrines in Ghana. This is because they adopted a religious approach to the issue of organizing a liberation ceremony that used powerful prayers to pacify the gods of the land and to overcome the visceral fear of being cursed and the priests who once ran their lives.

Juliana Dorgbadzi, a former *trokosi* woman, testified that "fear is one of the grounds for returning to the shrine even after being granted freedom. When this fear was broken upon becoming a Christian, she felt comfortable enough to leave the shrine permanently in spite of her parents' rejection."[60] As alternatives to the practice of taking women and young girls, a suggestion was made to accept animals as objects of reparation, and people were encouraged to use the criminal justice system, specifically the police and the courts, rather than resorting to the shrines for instant justice.[61] The religious approach was therefore an effective approach that addressed the cultural and living conditions of the concerned population to help women liberate themselves from *trokosi* networks.

---

[58] Hashim (2017), p. 25 (available at: https://digitalcommons.uri.edu/cgi/viewcontent.cgi?article=1007&context=dignity).

[59] *Powerful Persuasion*, *supra* note 57.

[60] *A Contextual Policy*, *supra* note 48 at 983.

[61] *Powerful Persuasion*, *supra* note 57 at 10.

## 12.4 The Moral Role of the Church in Combating Trafficking in Persons

In Chap. 2, a clear link was drawn between trafficking in persons and both economic and social inequalities. Elabor-Idemudia, for example, asserted that economic necessity is the "underlying factor that [drives] most women and girls who engage in the sex industry whether voluntarily or by coercion."[62] Although socio-economic disparities are identified as the major cause of trafficking in persons, it is important to note that "the decline in cultural and traditional values and the collapse of the protective environment are contributing factors."[63] Indeed, if family poverty and unemployment can fully explain trafficking in persons, it is reasonable to ask why other girls in dire financial need are not involved in prostitution and trafficking activities? In his statement on trafficking, Archbishop Thomas Wenski pointed out that trafficking in persons "is not a problem which exists on far away shores and in less developed lands. It exists right here in the United States and right here in Florida."[64] This raises the question as to why trafficking occurs in developed countries where there are more job opportunities and less social and gender inequality? The answer is that so-called pimps, johns, and traffickers who abuse and exploit the less fortunate have a senseless disregard for human dignity. Those who refrain from engaging in trafficking uphold human dignity and moral norms and values.

The most invidious force driving trafficking in persons "is greed and quest for wealth on the part of the traffickers who go to any extent to deceive the victims. They are the ones who flaunt their lifestyles of unexplained wealth and use it to prey on victims' ignorance and misery."[65] Greed is a selfish and insatiable desire for material possessions, money, or power. Through catechism the Catholic Church teaches the virtue of temperance to its fellows and warns about succumbing to greed and longing excessively for riches. Jesus Christ warned, "Take care to guard against all greed, for though one may be rich, one's life does not consist of possessions"(Luke 12:15). Unlike a society that associates who someone is with what he has, Jesus' teaching reminds us that the worth and dignity of a human being is conferred by God, not by the possessions they may acquire. "And everyone should store up heavenly treasures which decay does not destroy, nor thieves can steal: love, compassion, self-denial, sacrifice, forgiveness, service..." (Matthew 6:20).

Greed is a sinful and harmful desire directed toward others and can also plunge anyone who nurses it into ruin and destruction. "The love of money is a root of all kinds of evil," (1Tim 6,9-10). Indeed, quick riches obtained whatever the means is the fashion in modern society in West Africa, and some people in their desire for wealth have strayed from human values as well their cultural values. Thus,

---

[62] Elabor-Idemudia (2003), p. 116.

[63] Ezeh (2017). [hereinafter Prostitution Among Women and Girls].

[64] *Statement of Most Reverend Thomas Wenski, Bishop of Orlando Chairman*, US Conference of Catholic Bishops on Trafficking in Human Persons, (June 9, 2004) at www.orlandodiocese.org.

[65] Prostitution Among Women and Girls, *supra* note 63 at 101.

covetousness often impels people to engage in all sorts of vices, including trafficking, either as victims or offenders to acquire wealth.[66] The principle leading to a virtuous life consists of keeping one's life free from the love of money and to be content with what one has (Heb 13:5). The religious consecrated life of numerous women and men in the Catholic Church is an outstanding witness to a dignified life led in evangelic poverty.

Norotiana Ramboarivelo Jeannoda argued that "[p]overty cannot justify human trafficking."[67] Small rural villages in North Vietnam serve as outstanding examples of communities that may experience poverty but are not involved in the trafficking business. Accordingly, one Vietnamese informant claimed "that the selling of girls only happens in the south of Vietnam and not the north because unlike the north where 'in the villages you always see the pagoda and the common house that has hundreds of years of age. . .Life there is more relaxed'."[68] Thus, a certain culture of moral relativism that gives in to the seduction of pleasure, money, and power also provides an explanation of the occurrence of trafficking in persons.

To those greedy for power, Jesus gave the following instruction: "whoever wishes to be great among you will be your servant; whoever wishes to be first among you will be the slave of all. For the Son of Man did not come to be served but to serve and to give his life as a ransom for many." (Mark 10:43–45). This passage of the scripture provides an example to Christians of how to pursue greatness with humility in their relationships with family members and also in their relationships with others. Jesus pointed out that, "the rulers of the Gentiles lord it over them, and the great ones make their authority over them felt. But it shall not be so among the believers" (Mt 20:25-26). Modern slavery is also the consequence of a culture of consumerism, and relativism "which drives one person to take advantage of another, to treat others as mere objects, imposing forced labor on them or enslaving them to pay their debts."[69] This sinful disorder "corrupts the human heart and distances us from our Creator and our neighbors, the latter are no longer regarded as beings of equal dignity, as brothers or sisters sharing a common humanity, but rather as objects."[70] Pope Paul John Paul II calls for an examination and change in "the lifestyles and models of behavior, particularly with regard to the image of women, which generate what has become a veritable industry of sexual exploitation in the developed countries."[71] The increasing demand for sex in our societies clearly elucidates the socio-cultural and economic connections between pornography,

---

66 *Id.* at 92.

67 U.S., *Trafficking in Persons,* 7, https://www.state.gov/documents/organization/258877.pdf.

68 *The Trafficked Woman, supra* note 20 at 83.

69 *Church Teachings on Slavery And Trafficking*, Justice Peace Office, http://justiceandpeace.org.au/key-ideas-and-extracts-about-slavery-trafficking/.

70 *Id.*

71 John Paul II, Letter to Archbishop Jean-Louis Tauran on the Occasion of the International Conference "Twenty-First Century Slavery – The Human Rights Dimension to Trafficking in Human Beings" (May 15, 2002), http://w2.vatican.va/content/john-paul-ii/en/letters/2002/documents/hf_jp-ii_let_20020515_tauran.html. [hereinafter Letter to Archbishop Jean-Louis].

prostitution, and sex trafficking. It all starts "with the commodification and exploitation of women and men everywhere through advertisements, internet, television, and other media."[72]

Finally, trafficking in persons is also rooted in what Pope John Paul II called a "culture of death."[73] This modern reality is characterized by the emergence of a culture that denies solidarity towards the weakest members of human society (elderly, the infirmed, immigrants, children) and promotes violence against human life (abortion). "This culture is actively fostered by powerful cultural, economic and political currents which encourage an idea of a society excessively concerned with efficiency [worldly prosperity]."[74] The most devastating form taken by this conspiracy is the legalization of abortion, which detaches the crime from any kind of social and personal responsibility. This promotion of violence against life disseminated in books and in the media has polluted and perverted people's minds in countries such as the United States. Peggy Noonan in the Wall Street Journal described what she felt is wrong with our modern culture:

> . . .I'll tell you what I think a teenager absorbs about it, unconsciously, in America. He sees a headline online, he passes a television in an airport, he hears the quick story and he thinks: "If the baby we don't let live is unimportant, then I guess I am unimportant. And you're unimportant too." They don't even know they're breathing that in. But it's there, in the atmosphere, and they're breathing it in. And it doesn't make you healthier.[75]

The threats against life are taking on vast proportions. "This conspiracy involves not only individuals in their personal, family or group relationships, but goes far beyond, to the point of damaging and distorting, at the international level, relations between peoples and States."[76] Indeed, African bishops in 2015 declared to the West their e deep concern at the resurgence of a colonialist spirit that promotes a civilization of death on the African continent by attacking "life, the family, all that is sacred, the healthy human development of our youth who are the future of Africa, the full blossoming of women and respect for our elderly – realities of which our

---

[72] UNANIMA, Stop the demand, at unanima-international.org.

[73] John Paul II, *Evangelium Vitae: To the Bishops Priests and Deacons Men and Women Religious Lay Faithful and all People of Good Will on the Value and Inviolability of Human Life* ¶ 86 (Mar. 25, 1995), https://w2.vatican.va/content/john-paul-ii/en/encyclicals/documents/hf_jp-ii_enc_25031995_evangelium-vitae.html. [herein after People of Good Will].

[74] *Id.*

[75] Peggy Noonan, *The Parkland Massacre And The Air We Breathe*, The Wall Street Journal, https://www.wsj.com/articles/the-parkland-massacre-and-the-air-we-breathe-1518739880?emailToken=bfa889e51306059a676215fcb0d22dcfBsLXVXqrBbzM%2F%2Fq%2FbqVc%2BOe4RVsno1%2Bz0LzHdaDGA%2BwpcR9j75F5ZxUPl7WYJS0o%2FEGwuHWwkrBUF2SX%2F9IOD1BRCw8oWSTLd%2B%2Fh88NlORw%3D.

[76] People of Good Will, *supra* note 73 at 12.

African cultures have such a keen sense."[77] Moral decadence leads people to see others not as subjects but only as objects to be used.

## 12.5 The Use of Traditional and Christian Family Values in Preventing Trafficking

West African socio-cultural mutation has also led to changes in family life and its dynamics. Consequently, a certain culture of relativism with little consideration of social norms and values has affected the family institution, whose structures "no longer shape and serve as models for society and its institutions."[78] A culture of transitory fashions has changed the behavior of people resulting in increased "domestic violence, family dysfunction and discrimination of women. There are changes in the forms of a relationship at a personal level, such as family conflicts and divorce"[79] temporary marriage, broken homes, a fall in the birth rate, and child neglect. These family weaknesses place children in a very precarious situation where they are at risk of being trafficked.

Culturally, traditional society in sub-Saharan Africa promotes polygamy, despite challenges the family institution might pose. For instance, research findings suggest that children and wives in polygamous families experience an unequal distribution of household duties which can lead to jealousy, competition, and the disruption of family resources.[80] This is buttressed by the presumption that the traditional family in West Africa "makeup paves a way for human trafficking because of the polygamous nature [of marriage] and large family size."[81] Adults and especially children are coerced into unions where they involuntarily engage in acts similar to those undertaken by victims of trafficking for sexual and forced labor.

The Catholic Church in West Africa, especially in modern times, has unceasingly taught the doctrine on family and marriage. Christian marriage is defined in the 1983 Code of Canon Law as a 'covenant', "by which a man and a woman establish between themselves a partnership of the whole of life, [which] by its nature [is] ordered toward the good of the spouses and the procreation and education of offspring."[82] Partnership of the whole life and well-being of the spouses marks the fundamental difference between Christian matrimony and other forms of life

[77] *Common Declaration of the Bishops of Africa and Madagascar*, SECAM, para. 4-5 http://www.cultura.va/content/dam/cultura/docs/pdf/Adoukonou/declaration.pdf. at https://agendaeurope.wordpress.com/2015/09/24/african-bishops-tell-the-west-stop-spreading-the-culture-of-death/.

[78] Awinongya (2013b), p. 30.

[79] Prostitution Among Women and Girls, *supra* note 63 at 72.

[80] *A Contextual Policy*, *supra* note at 48.

[81] Prostitution Among Women and Girls, *supra* note 63 at 72.

[82] *See The Celebration Of The Christian Mystery*, Catechism of the Catholic Church, http://www.vatican.va/archive/ccc_css/archive/catechism/p2s2c3a7.htm.

companionship. Feely exchanged consent between a man and a woman is an indispensable condition of marriage. The Code of Canon Law of 1983 emphasizes the importance of consent as follows: "A marriage is brought into being by the lawfully manifested consent of persons who are legally capable. This consent cannot be supplied by any human power."[83] At this juncture it is important to note the transforming dialogue initiated in this encounter between Christian values and African traditional cultures. Christian marriage is "rooted in the contracts of its partners",[84] which sets it apart from other forms of gendered violence, bondage, and servile status.

Conversely, the community dimension of marriage is the salient feature of the traditional society in Africa. African cultures emphasize that marriage is as much an alliance between families as it is between two individuals (the bride and groom). In effect, this union of two people drawn together by love must fit into larger social kinship ties. This "new emphasis on personal values in marriage (mutual love, personal choice, a desire for self-fulfillment, etc.)"[85] brought by Christian tradition does not exclude the social values embedded in traditional marriage but provides avenues for the inculturation of the Gospel message into African family life. In practice, experience shows that a successful marriage always draws its strength from social support in times of difficulty. In African society, when a serious argument arises between the spouses threatening the marriage with collapse, relatives and perhaps the elders of the clan will involve themselves in order to save the marriage. The stability of the African family stems in a large measure from this type of community support for couples and the shared responsibility for children's upbringing.[86] Thus, a community watch initiative for the protection and prevention of the trafficking of children can dwell on these traditional values of family and human solidarity, previously mentioned in the cross-cultural analysis.

In line with this discussion, it is also worth noting that couples who stay together their whole life create a conducive atmosphere of love that keeps their family members safe from abuse and neglect and therefore prevents children from moving. Indeed, the family institution is considered the main source of material and emotional support for children's wellbeing. In this regard, "the African traditional and Christian beliefs reinforce the values attached to loving bonds between parents and children, filial duty, responsibility and respect, parental obligations and responsibilities of mutual support within a closely-knit family network."[87]

---

[83] *Id.*

[84] Paul VI, Pastoral Constitution on the Church in the Modern World: Gaudium et Spes ¶ ¶ 48,1 (Dec. 7, 1965), http://www.vatican.va/archive/hist_councils/ii_vatican_council/documents/vat-ii_cons_19651207_gaudium-et-spes_en.html.

[85] *Marriage And The Family In Africa*, Cormac burke, http://www.cormacburke.or.ke/node/288.

[86] *Id.*

[87] A Study on Street Children in Zimbabwe, 99 at https://www.unicef.org/evaldatabase/files/ZIM_01-805.pdf.

Given that Christian marriage is a sacrament, the Code of Canon Law requires "personal preparation for entering into marriage, so that the spouses are disposed to the holiness and the obligations of their new state."[88] Thus, in all the parishes in West Africa, marriage preparation is given prominence. Marriage preparation is a continual work of catechesis beginning with the preparation for marriage which aims to help the engaged "understand the meaning of the responsible and mature love of the community of life and love which their family will be, a real domestic church which will contribute toward enriching the whole Church."[89] It continues in the celebration of the sacrament of matrimony, and later throughout the entire lifespan of the spouses, so that they can preserve their fidelity even in difficult times. Significant Apostolic movements, Groups, and Associations such as the Cana-Jericho Brotherhood, Tiugung Bulli, the Teams of Our Lady (la Fraternité Cana-Jéricho, Tiugung Bulli, les Equipes Notre Dame etc), which have developed pastoral care for the family, provide moral education and guidance for couples and their families.

Experience shows that various reasons can lead to the irreversible breakdown of a marriage, including the death of a spouse. After separation, spouses experience the pain of loneliness, isolation, and at times the feeling of abandonment, especially when they consider themselves to be the innocent parties. As described in the first section, men and women with a history of failed relationships are more likely to travel abroad (Gambia, Ghana) for sex tourism, craving a holiday 'romance', attention, and genuine emotional attachment. As many as 600,000 women from Western countries have allegedly engaged in sex tourism with impoverished young men in return for money or goods; the statistics for men are likely to be substantially higher.[90]

To prevent these people from heading down hill, the Church and the ecclesial community are making themselves increasingly available to these wounded human beings. The parish community offers the potential for healing and relieving in a significant way the loneliness of the widowed within their midst. Associations of widows in parishes are providing social and especially meaningful spiritual aid to widows. Days of recollection, annual retreats tailored to uplift and inspire the widowed to a new fullness of life in Christ, are a readily available means of changing the outlook of the widowed in African society regarding the possibilities of a greater union with Christ.

It is commendable that several separated couples and widows, after the death of their spouse, have consecrated to God their remaining years in an unmarried state.

---

[88] Canon Law of the Catholic Church, CIC can. 1063, 2, CCEO can. 783, §1; *see also Preparation for The Sacrament of Marriage*, Pontifical Council for the Family, http://www.vatican.va/roman_curia/pontifical_councils/family/documents/rc_pc_family_doc_13051996_preparation-for-marriage_en.html.

[89] *Id.*

[90] Julie Bindel, *Thought It Was Just Men Who Flew Abroad For Squalid Sexual Kicks? Meet The Middle-Aged, Middle-Class Women Who Are Britain's Female Sex Tourists*, Daily Mail, http://Www.Dailymail.Co.Uk/Femail/Article-2401788/Sex-Tourism-Meet-Middle-Aged-Middle-Class-Women-Britains-Female-Sex-Tourists.Html.

They have thus chosen to lead a life of perfect chastity for the love of God and to abstain from sexual pleasure for the rest of their lives in order to devote themselves more freely to the meditation of divine things and better experience the elevations of the spiritual life.[91] However, there is an urgent need for the establishment of a specific ministry for separated couples to show concern for their spiritual life, solidarity, understanding, and provide them with practical help in preserving their fidelity to the catholic moral doctrine, even in their current difficult situation. It must also help them cultivate the need to forgive, which is inherent in Christian love, and to be ready, perhaps, to return to their former married life.

As a consequence of our society in mutation, concerns now arise in relation to the widespread practice of cohabitation, which does not lead to marriage and sometimes even excludes it. Similar situations include: the single-parent family, polygamy, marriages with the consequent problem of a dowry, migration and the reformulation of the very concept of the family, and the influence of the media on popular culture in its understanding of marriage and family life.[92] Cohabitation or "free" unions (or live-in partnerships) without any public recognized institutional bond, either civil or religious, can have grave religious and moral consequences (loss of a religious sense of marriage as the covenant of God with his people, deprivation of the grace of the sacrament, grave scandal) as well as social consequences (destruction of the concept of the family, weakening of the sense of fidelity, possible psychological damage to children, the strengthening of selfishness).[93] The Church reaches out to couples in these difficult situations to provide compassionate and respectful contact, enlightening them patiently and charitably, and showing them the witness of the Christian family life to smooth the path for them so that they can regularize their situation. Many parishes in Burkina Faso provide an opportunity on Palm Sunday for couples living in cohabitation to regularize their matrimony and hundreds of couples every year gather for these community celebrations.

The Christian family is a "domestic church" with an evangelizing and missionary task.[94] Indeed, Christian families in Africa are living witnesses to the way in which unity of marriage and responsible parenthood bring about changes in society, transforming the culture from within and rendering it new. The outstanding example of catholic married couples challenges the issue of polygamy and related practices. Nowadays, young girls who complete secondary school education are turning away

---

[91] *Encyclical of Pope Pius XII On Consecrated Virginity to our Venerable Brothers, The Patriarchs, Primates, Archbishops, Bishops, And Other Local Ordinaries In Peace And Communion With The Apostolic see*, Sacra Virginitas, http://w2.vatican.va/content/pius-xii/en/encyclicals/documents/hf_p-xii_enc_25031954_sacra-virginitas.html.

[92] *Synod of Bishops, Pastoral Challenges to the Family in the Context of Evangelization*, Preparatory Document, http://www.vatican.va/roman_curia/synod/documents/rc_synod_doc_20131105_iii-assemblea-sinodo-vescovi_en.html.

[93] *Pastoral Care of the Family*, Faith Seeking Understanding, http://fsubelmonte.weebly.com/40-pastoral-care-of-the-family.html.

[94] Catechism of The Catholic Church, *You Shall Love Your Neighbor as Yourself*, http://www.vatican.va/archive/ccc_css/archive/catechism/p3s2c2a4.htm.

from polygamous marriages and entering monogamous marriage. This trend is now spreading widely in the midst of an increasingly educated class in Africa.

As discussed in Chap. 1, elderly people are vulnerable to use and abuse. Honor and respect towards seniors lie at the heart of the Catholic social tradition. The fourth commandment expresses the relationship of children toward their parents as positive duties to be fulfilled and required as follows: "Honor your father and your mother, that your days may be long in the land which the Lord your God gives you" (Ex. 20:12; Dt 5:16). The scope of this commandment encompasses "honor, affection, and gratitude toward elders and ancestors."[95] Observing the fourth commandment brings spiritual fruits, peace, and prosperity. Conversely, a failure to respect causes great harm to communities and to individuals.[96] "As much as they can," adult children are required to provide their parents with "material and moral support in old age and in times of illness, loneliness, or distress."[97] "My son, be steadfast in honoring your father; do not grieve him as long as he lives. Even if his mind fails, be considerate of him; do not revile him because you are in your prime. . .Those who neglect their father are like blasphemers; those who provoke their mother are accursed by their Creator." (Sirach 3:12-13, 16). This echoes a proverb from Niger that states, "The donkey gives birth so that her back can rest" implying that grown up children should help elderly people. Children in Africa represent insurance and security for their parents in old age.

Although this duty of children towards their parents is the most universal, conditions of work in modern societies require mobility as distances separate family members from each other and families also assume new burdens that often prevent them from looking after their elderly parents who become outcasts or are merely tolerated as a useless burden. Faced with this situation, "[t]he pastoral activity of the Church must help everyone to discover and to make good use of the role of the elderly within the civil and ecclesial community, in particular within the family."[98] The Catholic Church exhorts us to draw heavily upon the culture, beliefs, values, and lifestyle of the African people and those from elsewhere to make policies that recognize the elderly are a particular and significant asset for the development of the family insofar as they often have the charisma to bridge generation gaps.[99] Jomo Kenyatta, in his book Facing Mount Kenya, highlights the principle of African seniority and related societal inclusivity:

> As a man grows old, his prestige increases according to the number of age grades he has passed. It is his seniority that makes an elder almost indispensable in the general life of the community. His presence or advice is sought in all functions. In religious ceremonies, the

[95] *Id.*

[96] *Id.*

[97] *Id.*

[98] Familiaris Consortio, *supra* note 60 ¶ 27.

[99] *Id.*

elders hold supreme authorities. The custom of the people demands that the elder should be given his due respect and honour.[100]

Along with health programs, pastoral visits, and material support for elderly people, the Catholic Church has gone further than other churches in demonstrating a social concern and providing a vision for elderly care in Ghana. The Conference of Bishops in Ghana now operates an institution of Socio-Economic Development (SED) to express the Church's commitment to the integral development of human beings. SED functions at three levels: the National level, the Diocesan level, and the Parish level. At each level, SED promotes development activities to restore the dignity of elderly people and provide them with meaningful engagement in the community so that they become gradually self-reliant.

By asserting their dignity through development, they are able to protect their integrity in the midst of modernizing changes that have eroded their status and role in society. Because parishes are located in rural areas as well as in urban centers, the Church works to bridge the gap between the urban and rural with the provision of social services aimed at reducing migration, unemployment, and the breakdown of the extended family organization.[101]

Consequently, in 1993 the Catholic Church in Ghana established St Vincent de Paul Day Centre for the aged with the following goals and objectives:

1. To create a meeting place for older people that promotes friendship and thereby brings some happiness into their lives.
2. To provide a daily nutritious meal for older people attending the center.
3. To offer the aged a range of medical, social, and material assistance to improve their health and wellbeing.
4. To serve as a community awareness forum to support respectful care of the elderly and mobilize resources to solve problems.

This senior day care center is a gathering place for elderly people who have been neglected by their relatives or have lost their jobs, and attend the center while their loved ones are working. In addition to social services and a range of recreational activities, the priest of Sacred Heart Catholic Church and Catholic Sisters of the Saint Vincent de Paul society cater for the spiritual needs of members. Notably, the center enrolls the elderly irrespective of their religious affiliations. Singing and praying do not reflect a strong catholic tradition, facilitating fellowship within the members of the community. This initiative to provide a daily nutritious meal coupled with free medical care ensures that elderly people enjoy total wellbeing and remain dignified members of society.[102]

[100]Nana Araba, *Rapid Urbanizations and Living Arrangements of Older Persons in Africa*, Center Soc. Pol'y Stud. 297, https://pdfs.semanticscholar.org/fbef/a761418b8fb2cbee7dfb7390dec68966f569.pdf.

[101]Ayete-Nyampong, *A Study of Pastoral Care of the Elderly in Africa: An Interdisciplinary Approach With Focus On Ghana*, 279, Author House S (2014). [hereinafter *Care Of The Elderly*].

[102]*Id.* at 93.

An interview carried out with the elderly at the Centre on February 6, 1996 provided insightful information regarding the average number of people attending the center, the size of their nuclear families, the level support, if any, received from the extended family, and any source of anticipated help. The results showed an average of nineteen elderly people in attendance, the mean age of whom was 74 years. They were parents to an average of 4 children (89.5%). Only 10.5% of the elderly did not receive any support from the extended family. In terms of which organization or group they expect to help them, 29% stated the Government, 42% the Church, 13% General, 8% Voluntary Organizations, and 8% had no idea.[103] The creation of senior centers aims to prevent abuse of seniors and adults with disabilities and to reduce trafficking in the elderly for the purposes of organized begging in the street.

Another example of a community based center for elderly people is the *Delwende* Center[104] established by the Catholic Church in Ouagadougou in 1966 and directed by the Missionary Sisters of Our Lady of Africa. This center takes care of 410 women accused of being sorceresses along with other women in dire need.[105] Since the Center first opened, numerous awareness-raising efforts to mobilize public opinion for intensified action against social exclusion have been made by the religious sisters in collaboration with the Archdiocese of Ouagadougou, the National Commission of Justice and Peace of Burkina Faso, Social Welfare and National Solidarity, and many other non-profit organizations. There are clear signs that the center has had a positive impact on the citizens of Burkina Faso. For instance, Sister Hortência Sizalande, head of the *Delwende* Center reports that:

> in February 2013, a 27-year-old man came to *Delwende* in search of his mother after a forced separation of 22 years! He was five when his mother was driven from her village. He now came to take her back to live with him and his new family, his wife and daughter. Tradition does not yet allow his mother to return to the village. Thus, they will live in Ouagadougou where he has home and work. It is certain that whatever happens, the child cannot forget his mother nor the mother forget his child. This woman is so happy despite everything she has experienced.
>
> Another day of happiness was on April 29, 2013, when a few years after the death of her husband, a widow came to seek her mother-in-law in Ouagadougou. The old woman had spent 22 years in *Delwende*, but she was so delighted to go with her daughter-in-law![106]

The outstanding achievements of the Center can be seen in the inexorable change of attitudes and cultural beliefs that lead to women being accused of witchcraft and also the extent of outreach to the youth. For an ordinately long time, people, especially children, were afraid of these women, whereas today street vendors sell

[103] *Id.* at 93.

[104] Can be translated as "in the hands of God." *Delwende Center in Ouagadougou*, Missionary Sisters of Our Lady of Africa, http://www.msolafrica.org/index.php/en/our-mission/africa/burkina-faso/448-delwende-center-in-ouagadougou. [hereinafter *Delwende Center*].

[105] *Burkina Faso: Centre De Solidarité Pour Sorcières Présumées*, Afrik, http://www.afrik.com/article8157.html. [hereinafter *Burkina Faso*].

[106] *Delwende Center*, *supra* note 104.

bread, peanuts and various commodities to the grandmothers in the center and many people come to buy their cotton and vegetables. Their faces show no expression of fear or any desire to sell as quickly as possible and leave the premises. More importantly, in all the parish churches in Ouagadougou, pastors are calling upon the faithful community to sponsor those living in the center and give them community support. Since then, some young people and families have adopted a "yaaba" (granny) whom they visit regularly and exchange presents with.[107] The center now has a large influx of visitors including youth groups, benevolent individuals and organizations, that come to socialize and offer support to the inhabitants of the centers.

Another notable change is that the aged women, with the support of the Ministry of Social Welfare, are engaging in an economic activity that prevents them from begging while at the same time improving their living conditions so that they can regain their dignity as women. They spin raw cotton in the center that will then be sold, which previously had been almost unimaginable. People are no longer afraid to buy from them, which proves that the outreach is effective.[108] This is the result of the tremendous work of the Missionary Sisters of Our Lady of Africa together with the efforts of the various television programs that have highlighted the work of the *Delwende* Center. It also reflects the success of the public awareness campaign that has educated the public to abandon the tradition of accusing some of being a 'soul-eater'.[109]

The above survey in Ghana and that of a large number of elderly people in Delwende Center shows the extent to which support within the extended family has decreased, resulting in people placing their hope in the new community church for support, namely the Community-Based Home Care for the Aged. This challenges the Christian Church in West Africa to point the way forward in developing relevant care programs to tackle the problems of ageing and promote the potentialities of ageing.[110] Support for elderly people should not be left to themselves or their relatives alone but should instead be seen as a community and a global national concern.

Just as the Catholic Church has given a new orientation to its mission after the second Vatican Council to implement development programs, other Christian Churches, the Muslim religion, and traditional religions in West Africa "ought to redefine their mission so that whilst they concentrate on saving souls for heaven, they would also maintain the wellbeing and quality of life of humans on earth before their souls arrive in heaven".[111] At the 66$^{th}$ Synod of the Church at Takoradi in Ghana in August 1995, a former Moderator of the Presbyterian Church of Ghana made an insightful analysis in his speech that is highly compelling:

---

[107] *Id.*

[108] *Burkina Faso, supra* note 105.

[109] *Id.*

[110] *Care of the Elderly, supra* note 101 at 93.

[111] *Id.* at 96.

> In evangelism, we show keen interest in able-bodied people and neglect the old, the infirm and the housebound. In Europe the elderly are housed in special homes. People are employed to look after them. Some are fed, cleaned and dressed by nurses or people trained to do so. What do we do? Our elderly people live with families in their own homes. Because of the rapid social change, many sons and daughters have moved to the cities. The elderly are beginning to face loneliness and isolation. What the church does for these people is to [visit them in] a while to administer Holy Communion, [but often] the minister is in a hurry. He has to serve many people that day that he has to rush. There is very little time for chat. We must realise that apart from physical infirmity, the elderly have the additional difficulty of seeing their loved ones dying one after the other. For them bereavement is a constant process, and increasing loneliness is a real threat to their lives. [Furthermore] they feel shaken by change which is unleashed almost every day. . .The time is ripe for the church to train people to look after elderly people. It is our duty to start a ministry for the aged and infirm for Hebrews 13:7 tells us: "Remember your leaders, those who first spoke God's message to you"; and the Lord Jesus also says in Matthew 25 ". . .naked you clothed me; when I was ill you came to my help. . .[112]

## 12.6 The Promotion of Social and Economic Justice

For many decades the Catholic Church in West Africa has played a critical role in the development of the region, providing essential social services to the most vulnerable and empowering communities to thwart the root cause of trafficking in persons. Caritas and Foundation John Paul II for the Sahel are involved in programs that encourage agricultural development as well as animal husbandry, improve access to potable water and sanitation systems, protect the environment, and provide support for income-generating activity projects. The rationale for this is to make local economic activities of the population worthwhile and the returns lucrative enough to counter the attractiveness of trafficking. The provision of alternative employment as a means of livelihood for the youths that are most vulnerable to the lure of traffickers should further stem the flow of trafficking overseas.[113]

As discussed previously, women and girls in West Africa have low status in society and face difficulties accessing education and a means of livelihood, particularly as they are less likely to have land and capital and are paid lower wages. This limits their ability to effect change, challenge discrimination, or safeguard themselves against traffickers who lure them into life-saving employment opportunities. In this context, the economic empowerment of women represents a key factor in anti-trafficking strategies. Sources have shown that some girls from West Africa travel purposely to the capital cities of Europe to make money as prostitutes. Others go there lured by the promise and hope of a job, or even the prospect of marriage. Some men are known to either allow or compel their own wives to engage in this

[112] *Care of the Elderly, supra* note 101 at 93 (citing Beeko 1995).

[113] *Preventing Human Trafficking And Modern Slavery*, Santa Marta Group, http://santamartagroup.com/wp-content/uploads/2016/11/SMG-Progress-Brochure-031116.pdf.

business in order to make ends meet.[114] Parents may feel forced to one child in order to have enough money to feed the rest of the family. Poverty is therefore one of the driving factors that make individuals vulnerable to trafficking. Lack of resources, particularly job opportunities, is a harsh reality to escape from. Women and children especially often become desperate enough to undertake any kind of work, putting their health at risk as well as their human dignity.

Financial services can empower families to resist the root causes of trafficking in persons and thus play a crucial role. For instance, they enable the poor to participate in the creation of wealth, access food and decent housing, and ensure an education for their children. To enable the poor to access a system of Community funding and Proximity more easily, the Caritas Abomey initiated the Savings and Internal Lending Communities (SILC) Project with an affordable requirement for membership and subscription to credits.[115] Since 2007, an average of 4400 people each year, primarily women, despite their meager revenues, have been able to save from 12,000,000 (US $22,630) to 48,000,000F CFA (US $90,522). They give loans to one another to develop income-generating activity. In 2011, for example, the total amount of cumulative savings was 81,236,250F CFA (US $153,537). Capacity building that empowers the poor is therefore a way to alleviate the effect of pervading precariousness.[116]

Governments in West Africa have adopted laws mandating free compulsory schooling. However, this law is not enforced and poor children are often unable to attend school because their families cannot pay all the costs connected with schooling such as uniforms, books, examination fees, and other fees that form part of a "free" education. The Catholic Church, with the support of partners in Europe and the USA, is providing school sponsorship to rural school children in West Africa. With proper education, these boys and girls, who one day may become parents, will continue to nurture the correct values and set examples to the next generation of women and men to enable them to realize their full potential. In this way, the trafficking of children can slowly be curbed.

To improve access to education, OCADES Caritas Burkina (Organisation Catholique pour le Développement et la Solidarité) has built 13 school buildings, granted 1327 scholarships, rehabilitated 37 classrooms, and distributed 323 sets of equipment and 4653 school kits.[117] Consequently, the fostered girls who used to engage in domestic work, especially in the cities, are now enrolled in schools. The number of girls involved in domestic labor is therefore clearly diminishing and this is happening in numerous cities in Burkina Faso where some villages have a low or zero level of unschooled children.

---

[114] *Collection Of Communiques*, *supra* note 12 at 12–11.

[115] *Food crisis in West Africa*, Caritas Africa Info (July 2012) 9 at http://www.caritas-africa.org/info0712.pdf. [hereinafter *Food crisis*].

[116] *Food crisis*, *supra* note 115 at 12.

[117] *Rapport Annuel Consolidé 2012 de l'OCADES Caritas Burkina*, Ocades, http://ocadesburkina.org/rapport-annuel-consolide-2012-de-locades-caritas-burkina/.

Another outstanding example of good practice has been identified in Benin., where, to prevent school drop-out, trafficking, and exploitation of children, the Don Bosco Foyer has since December 2011 initiated with the support of Enrique Castillo, Carmen Sanchez and friends a program to support vulnerable families.[118] In 2013, more than 433 families were supported with amounts awarded for the development of income-generating activities ranging from 30,000F CFA (US $57) to 100,000F CFA (US, $200). The total amount allocated was 24,345,000F CFA (US $46, 012). Women have submitted applications for support through centers for the social promotion of the five municipalities of intervention (Porto-Novo, Missérété, Adjarra, Dangbo, and Sakété) and through selected NGOs and associations. This form of solidarity has also been supported by awareness programs for beneficiaries that are related to underdevelopment problems: illiteracy, schooling of children, family and reproductive health, and so on. Remarkably, not a single child of these beneficiaries is on the street at risk of trafficking.

## 12.7 Reducing Demand to Prevent Trafficking in Persons

The moral teachings of the Church on marriage and sexuality condemn people who provide and demand commercial sexual services. This is a factor that has contributed to the increase in trafficking in persons. Consumer demand is generated directly by people who actively or passively buy goods or services of trafficked labor; for example, the household father who buys chocolate blended with beans picked by a trafficked adolescent on a cocoa farm or the tourist who buys a cheap T-shirt made by a trafficked youth in a sweatshop.[119] This kind of demand indirectly influences trafficking even though the household father and the tourists do not specifically ask traffickers to exploit children.

Such demand facilitates trafficking directly "because it is generated by the people who stand to make a profit from the transaction."[120] Such persons include pimps and brothel owners, the various intermediaries involved in the trafficking process, and corrupt factory owners or farmers who exploit trafficked labor to save costs in order to keep their prices low and profits flowing.[121] Our purchasing habits contribute as well as our "lifestyles and models of behavior" also add to the demand for

[118] *Rapport d'activités 2013*, Association Foyer Don Bosco 14 (Feb. 2014), http://portonovo.foyerdonbosco.org/wp-content/uploads/2014/04/Rapport_d_activites_2013.pdf.

[119] UNODC, Working Group on Trafficking in Persons, *Good Practices And Tools In Demand For Exploitative Services*, at 8, (Jan. 27-29, 2010), https://www.unodc.org/documents/treaties/organized_crime/2010_CTOC_COP_WG4/WG4_2010_3_E.pdf.

[120] *Combating Trafficking in Children for Labour Exploitation in West and Central Africa: Synthesis Report*, ILO 30–31 (Dec. 1, 2001), http://www.ilo.org/ipec/Informationresources/WCMS_IPEC_PUB_776/lang%2D%2Den/index.htm.

[121] *Id.*

exploitative labor.[122] At one of its sessions, The Pontifical Academy of the Social Sciences (PASS) concluded that one of the most critical components involved on preventing trafficking from occurring is that of reducing the high demand that drives the high volume of supply.

In this context, the Catholic Church assumes a pastoral responsibility to promote general morality and call the faithful community and the entirety of society to holiness. The conference of bishops in Ghana in its Advent pastoral letter to the nation and especially to the youth, emphasizes the immense moral and spiritual damage caused by trafficking in commercial sex. "Prostitution is not only immoral and sinful, it is also a misuse of the body and its senses as given by God. It is a degradation of the human person created in the image and likeness of God himself, and called to communion with God in Jesus Christ through the indwelling of the Holy Spirit."[123] Mary Dorothy Ezeh acknowledged that our modern society "is concerned with the problem of prostitution in general but more with human trafficking because of the devastating and unhealthy threat it poses to sexual morality, to family life, to health, to the welfare of women and girls and young men."[124]

In this regard, a variety of ministries in all parishes give proper moral training to the youth in order that they may live lives of holiness, uprightness, and integrity. Globally, the demand for sexual exploitation in the form of child sex tourism is rooted in an economically-based degradation of human sexuality, the human person, and human work. The Church thus calls tirelessly for the re-sanctification of the human person, a re-sanctification of sexuality, and the re-sanctification of human work.[125]

Additionally, slavery dehumanizes not only the victims but also the slave traders, the buyers, the corrupt officials, and even those who are observer sand do not want to get involved.[126] The Vatican Council has stressed that trafficking poisons human society, but it does more harm to those who practice it than those who suffer the injury.[127] From a Christian standpoint, the "client" is in a certain sense enslaved and therefore needs more than social condemnation; they too must be helped to face their deeper problems and find other ways of dealing with their personal needs. They are also a child of God who needs to be educated that buying sex from a prostitute does not solve the problems that arise from loneliness, frustration, or a lack of true relationships.

---

[122] John Paul II, Letter to Archbishop Jean-Louis Tauran on the Occasion of the International Conference "Twenty-First Century Slavery – The Human Rights Dimension to Trafficking in Human Beings" (May 15, 2002), http://w2.vatican.va/content/john-paul-ii/en/letters/2002/documents/hf_jp-ii_let_20020515_tauran.html.

[123] Ghana Catholic Bishops' conference, *Advent Pastoral Letter, Message to our Nation and Especially our Youth on Drug-trafficking and Prostitution*, 14 (Ghana Bishops speak 1995).

[124] Prostitution Among Women and Girls, *supra* note 63 at 78.

[125] *How to Bring About Normative Change in The Demand For Trafficked Persons*, End Slavery, http://www.endslavery.va/content/endslavery/en/publications/acta_20/porpora.html.

[126] O'Connor (2012b), p. 51.

[127] Gaudium et Spes, *supra* note 104, ¶ 27.

To address employers' demand for exploitable laborers, in 1931 the International Christian Union of Business Executives (UNIAPAC) was established on the occasion of the 40th anniversary of the Encyclical "Rerum Novarum" in Rome with a mission "to promote a vision of business built on the dignity and respect of the human person and the promotion of the common good."[128] Today, UNIAPAC has become an ecumenical organization that brings together Christian Business Leaders Associations in 40 countries in Europe, Latin America, Africa, and Asia, and represents more than 30,000 highly active global business executives working in various leading sectors of the world economy.[129] This model, based on Christian social thought, invokes a true change in business attitudes and has tremendous potential to bring about more responsible and sustainable economic, social, and human progress as well as curbing labor exploitation.

In Africa, UNIAPAC works "to put in evidence certain challenges of the Africa society currently such as the good administration of the economy, the good government, the social responsibility of the companies for the human person's promotion and of the commonwealth as well as the challenge of the cultural and religious pluralism."[130] Kevin Bales observed that slavery has invaded our lives each day as even before we get to work, we are "eating, wearing, walking and talking slavery." "Every one of us, every day, touches, wears and eats products tainted with slavery. Slavery-made goods and commodities are everywhere in our lives."[131] What is especially troubling is to inspect the long chains that supply our shirts and sneakers, our tee shirts and blouses, and realize that our low prices come at the high price of the slave labor of men, women, and children. Research has also revealed the connection between trafficking in persons and the celebration of Halloween. According to the International Council of Shopping Centers, Americans are expected to spend about $11.3 billion on costumes, candy, decorations, and other Halloween goodies, and most of this chocolate is made by Kraft, Hershey's, and Mars.[132] We therefore need to make the problem of trafficking prominent and personal in our lives and be willing

---

[128] Naughton, *Respect in Action*, St. Thomas University, https://www.stthomas.edu/media/catholicstudies/center/ryan/publications/publicationpdfs/subsidiarity/RespectInActionFINALWithAcknowlCX.pdf. [hereinafter *Respect in Action*].

[129] Pontifical Council for the Laity, *International Associations of the Faithful*, http://www.vatican.va/roman_curia/pontifical_councils/laity/documents/rc_pc_laity_doc_20051114_associazioni_en.html#INTERNATIONAL%20CHRISTIAN%20UNION%20OF%20BUSINESS%20EXECUTIVES.

[130] UNIAPAC-Africa, Strategic Plan 2014-2016. *Leading with Responsibility*, http://uniapacafrica.org/wp-content/uploads/2015/04/Plano-estrat%C3%A9gico-PT-UNIAPAC-Africa-2014-2016-.pdf.

[131] Bales and Soodalter (2009), p. 6.

[132] Janet H. Cho, *Halloween-Loving Americans Will Spend About $125 On Candy, Consumes and Decorations This Year*, Cleveland, http://www.cleveland.com/business/index.ssf/2014/09/halloween-loving_americans_will_spend_about_125_on_candy_costumes_and_decorations_this_year.html.

to work with others to eradicate slave labor from our homes and dinner tables by becoming "ethical consumers."[133]

Consume pressure can spark collaboration among enterprises to address child labor and the ethical choices made by consumers can also have a significant impact on reducing the profits and related incentives that fuel the trafficking business. Through the efforts of UNIAPAC, the Catholic Church thus brings a significant contribution to social change in the formation of 'ethical consumers.' UNIAPAC believes:

> that consumers, who in many cases have buying power well above the mere subsistence level, exert significant influence over the economic reality through their personal decisions whether to spend, invest or to save. Purchasing power must be used within the context of the moral demands of justice and solidarity, and in one with well-defined social responsibilities.[134]

Thanks to increased awareness, a growing number of consumers care about moral issues and the general idea of combining ethics with purchasing is becoming a mainstream concept that takes "into account not only the price and quality but also the presence of correct working conditions in the company as well as the level of protection on the natural environment in which it operates, to steer the behaviour of producers."[135]

Those who are skeptical about ethical consumerism argue that companies which actively pursue social responsibility invest more in workers' safety but are not rewarded by the consumer. This is because global consumers tend to regularly look for good deals and ignore the social impact of the products they purchase. However, individuals have been found to display ethical and political practices in their lifestyles in connection with ethical consumerism. For example, recycling, ethical investments and charity giving are all actions indicative of ethical consumerism.[136] In fact, "most people will at least sometimes behave ethically even when they have to sacrifice something, usually cash, for their morals."[137] Charity Navigator reports that in 2013 the USA alone gave $335.15 billion to charity. This clearly reveals the willingness of people to part with their money for an ethical and just cause. Additionally, a new image of the consumer is now emerging with people buying hybrid cars, organic foods, environmentally-friendly detergents, and Warby Parker glasses. There is anecdotal evidence to suggest that ethical consumer values

---

[133] *David B.* Couturier, Consumerism And The Many Faces Of Human Trafficking. A Franciscan Theology of Stuff, https://cmsm.org/wp-content/uploads/2015/10/FranciscanTheology_Couturier.pdf.

[134] The Profit of Values: *A Christian Vision Of Corporate Social Responsibility A For Of Management For Long-Lasting Enterprises*, Uniapac, 16 (2008), http://www.uniapac.org/filesPDF/The%20Profit%20of%20Values.pdf.

[135] *Ibid.*

[136] Tracey Bedford, *Ethical Consumerism: Everyday Negotiations in The Construction of an Ethical Self, 200-01* http://discovery.ucl.ac.uk/1318018/1/314135.pdf.

[137] Irwin (2015), https://hbr.org/2015/01/ethical-consumerism-isnt-dead-it-just-needs-better-marketing.

exist, but these have to be drawn out with better marketing so that they become both a lifestyle and a new behavior.[138]

Drawing from their experience, UNIAPAC and its national associations:

> believe that an economy and business inspired and motivated to serve man as an end in itself, are from a social perspective as well as an economical one more efficient in generating added value than an economy and business that is only guided by the financial interests of a few and that considers man as a tool to serve their individualistic interests.[139]

Therefore, Catholic Church-inspired organizations are committed to raising awareness in the business environment so that ethical management practices which promote quality ways of living make sustainable use of natural resources, create conditions for the integral personal development of employees, and also serve the common good. In doing so, they will optimize stakeholders' interests and "create lasting success for companies because respected employees—those who have been entrusted with the agile deployment of their creativity—are best able to adapt to the ever evolving and complex demands of the business world."[140]

Consumer choices are also a key determinant in the context of trafficking in persons. In the Encyclical Caritas in Veritate, the Catholic Church reminds us that as consumers we have a specific social responsibility: "It is good for people to realize that purchasing is always a moral—and not simply—economic act."[141] The fair trade movement created by CRS and promoted in the Catholic Church parishes in Ghana is a small but significant response to this call.[142]

---

[138] *Id.*; *Global Consumers are Willing to put their Money where their Heart is when it comes to goods and services from Companies committed to social Responsibility*, Nielsen, http://www.nielsen.com/us/en/press-room/2014/global-consumers-are-willing-to-put-their-money-where-their-heart-is.html; Delphine Allaire, *Green Churches Label Targets Ecological Conversion*, La Croix International, https://international.la-croix.com/news/green-churches-label-targets-ecological-conversion/5651; In response to the challenge of climate change and environmental destruction, on September 2017 the French Catholic Bishops Conference, the Protestants' Federation, the Assembly of Orthodox Bishops, and the Council of Christian Churches will launch the "Green Church" label, targeting an "ecological conversion" of parishes covering five themes: liturgical celebrations and catechesis, buildings, parish land and property, community and global engagement, and individual lifestyles. The proposal to celebrate a Time for Creation during these five weeks was made by the Third European Ecumenical Assembly in Sibiu in 2007. *Id.*

[139] *A Christian Vision of Corporate Social Responsibility*, *supra* note 134 at 16.

[140] *Respect in Action*, *supra* note 128; Statement Of Catholic Church-Inspired Organizations Related to Decent Work and the Post-2015 Development Agenda, http://www.caritas.org/includes/pdf/advocacy/CatholicInspiredStatDecentWork13.pdf; Vocation of the Business Leader at http://www.uniapac.org/home/Library.

[141] Pope Benedict XVI, Encyclical Letter Caritas In Veritate 66 (Jun. 29, 2009), http://w2.vatican.va/content/benedict-xvi/en/encyclicals/documents/hf_ben-xvi_enc_20090629_caritas-in-veritate.html.

[142] *Baseline Study on Newly Fairtrade Certified Cocoa Producer Organizations in Côte d'Ivoire and Ghana Terms of Reference - May 2013*, Fair Trade Africa, http://www.fairtradeafrica.net/wp-content/uploads/2010/06/FTA_FLO_TOR_Callfortender_Baseline_Ghana_CDI_.pdf; *Oversight of Public and Private Initiatives to Eliminate the Worst Forms of Child Labor in the Cocoa Sector of Cote d'Ivoire and Ghana*, September 2010 at http://www.pjcvt.org/dbpjc/wp-content/uploads/

Broadly speaking, fair trade is a social and economic movement that seeks, through private enforcement, "to help producers in developing countries get a fair price for their products so as to reduce poverty, provide for the ethical treatment of workers and farmers and promote environmentally sustainable practices."[143] The use of fair trade organizations to certify that goods have been produced free of child labor and with fair wages paid to workers is a private solution to addressing the root causes of child labor and influence the trading and purchasing behavior of consumers.[144] "[U]nlike prosecutions that focus on a small number of the resulting problems of child labor and trafficking, fair trade focuses on improving incomes, working conditions, health and education of a large number of workers."[145]

## 12.8 Building a Network of Interfaith Leaders to End Trafficking

Other determinants of trafficking in Africa described in part I include ethnic fragmentation as a result of different traditions and languages, conflict, internally displaced persons, and religious conflicts. Africa is a mosaic of people (3000 distinct ethnic groups) with great linguistic and cultural diversity (over 2000 languages are spoken in the continent). The Catholic Church carries out advocacy and works on dialogue, social cohesion, reconciliation and peacebuilding initiatives among parties involved in violent conflicts and civil and tribal war (Ecclesia in Africa no.45).[146]

Through Justice and Peace Commissions, the Church is engaged in the civic formation of citizens and with assisting in the electoral process in several countries (for example, Mali, Ivory Coast, Togo, Nigeria, Burkina Faso). As such, the contributes to educating people by awakening their consciences and their sense of civic responsibility. This particular educational role is appreciated by a great many countries which recognize the Church as a peacemaker, an agent of reconciliation, and a herald of justice (AM no 23).

---

2012/02/Final-Fourth-Annual-Report.pdf; Read The principles of Fair Trade at http://www.fairtraderesource.org/uploads/2009/06/CRS-Chocolate-Lesson-Plans.pdf.

[143] Merriam-Webster Dictionary, *Fair Trade*.

[144] Shima Baradaran and Stephanie Barclay, Fair Trade And Child Labor, 39–41 at http://hrlr.law.columbia.edu/wp-content/uploads/sites/10/2016/03/Baradaran_Barclay-1.pdf. [hereinafter Fair Trade]; de Pelsmacker (2005), p. 50, 51.

[145] *Id.* at 1.

[146] Of all the mechanisms of crisis resolution initiated on the African continent, the Catholic Church has been regularly solicited as an actor of choice to play a catalytic role, calling for dialogue and reconciliation. For example, in Togo, the presidency of the national conference organized from 1st to 15th of February 1990 for the advent of democratic renewal was untrusted to Archbishop Isidore de Souza; bishop Nicodeme Barrigah-Benissan, presided over the commission of truth, justice, and reconciliation. *Id.*

The Church cohabits with the followers of traditional African religions as well as with Christians and Muslims. In countries such as Senegal, good relations exist between Christians and Muslims. In others, the local Christians are merely second-class citizens. Thanks to the outreach of the Catholic Church towards other religions, positive experiences in terms of relations with Muslims in some regions of Africa brings hoper that these forms of collaboration will increase in number and become even more effective. In numerous countries, Christians and Muslims have created associations for dialogue and the promotion of peace and justice. In some places, Christians and Muslims even take part in common days of fasting and prayer.[147] These initiatives contribute to preserving peace and preventing trafficking in persons in West Africa.

Political instability in West Africa is consider an important factor that impels a large number of civilian populations to flee their countries in pursuit of prosperity elsewhere. This large migration flow presents "an opportunity for criminal organizations, such as smugglers and human traffickers to take advantage of the mass movement of people."[148] To prevent forced displacement and the subsequent vulnerability of persons to trafficking "[t]he Catholic Church uses its moral authority to act as a mediator in case of crises [by] publishing roadmaps for improving governance [and] criticizing the ruling elite, but trying to avoid violence."[149] In this regard, the Bishops' Conference of Burkina Faso published a courageous, forward-looking Declaration to the Nation in late March 2012 dealing, amongst other things, with the conditions needed for peaceful and democratic political development. Their declaration criticized the way ruling elites have attempted to modify the political system in order to stay in power.[150]

Significantly, the Catholic Church is also well positioned to fill a local leadership vacuum in West Africa and federate community members. An illustration of this can be seen in its involvement in the resolution of "isolated conflicts, including inter-ethnic disputes over power and control, intra-ethnic disputes over chieftaincy

---

[147] *II Special Assembly For Africa The Church In Africa In Service To Reconciliation*, Justice And Peace, 27 at http://www.vatican.va/roman_curia/synod/documents/rc_synod_doc_20060627_ii-assembly-africa_en.html.

[148] *Amy Weatherburn*, The Effects Of Political And Social And Economic Factors On Human Trafficking, 15, at https://www.researchgate.net/publication/284725360_The_effects_of_political_and_socio-economic_factors_on_human_trafficking.

[149] Most Reverend Seraphin F. Rouamba was president of the Concertation Comity in Burkina Faso and of other political structures during the transition in 1991 that allowed to the country to change from an exception regime to a democratic regime. Most Reverend Anselm Titiama Sanon presided over the "Rapport du college des sages" in 1999 after the social and political crisis following the assassination of Nobert Zongo, a journalist who uncovered a scandal involving the brother of the President.

[150] *Lettre Pastorale Des Evêques Aux Fils Et Filles De L'eglise Famille De Dieu Qui Est Au Burkina Faso Et Aux Hommes Et Femmes De Bonne Volonte*, http://www.catholique.bf/index.php/documents-des-eveques-du-burkina-niger/765-lettre-pastorale-des-eveques-du-burkina-sur-la-mise-en-place-du-senat.

succession, land-disputes and election related tensions"[151] in Northern Ghana. To address these recurring conflicts, the Catholic archbishop of Tamale, Most Rev. Phillip Naameh, decided to focus his initial apostolate as Bishop of Damongo on creating the Northern Ghana Peace Project in 1995, which later evolving into the Center for Conflict Transformation and Peace Studies (CECOTAPS), to complement the efforts of the NSC.[152]

Furthermore, human rights abuses and child soldiering in West Africa have been attributed to instability and war. During the civil war in Liberia, the Catholic Church made a significant contribution to establishing peace. When the United States publicly withdraw their support to help end the Liberian civil war, due to lack of a vital interest in Liberia, the Religious Leaders of Liberia (both Christian and Islamic clerics) made a determined effort to intervene in the conflict as mediators of peace and thus end the First Liberian Civil War.[153]

## 12.9 Supporting the Prosecution of Offenders

As previously discussed, organized crime syndicates traffic girls for commercial sexual exploitation abroad using *ju-ju* or *voodoo* practices to bind them to their traffickers, thereby preventing them from cooperating with the police. They forbid their victims from revealing their identity and the nature of the transaction. They also bind them emotionally into compliance with the agreed terms and conditions. NAPTIP confirmed that many victims who are intimidated by ju-ju are in a state of psychological trauma, and the oath that they victims have sworn is a serious matter to them. In some cases, NAPTIP has "raided ju-ju shrines and reclaimed the items that were used to establish the oath and NAPTIP has counselled victims in order to help them overcome their fear."[154]

Without effective support for victims in such situations, it is extremely difficult to increase the number of prosecutions as victims must be made to feel safe from physical as well as psychological harm and be confident enough to come forward

[151] William A Awinador-Kanyirige, *Ghana's National Peace Council*, Global Centre for the Responsibility to Protect (2014), http://s156658.gridserver.com/media/files/awinador-ghana-national-peace-council.pdf.

[152] *Id.*

[153] George Klay Kieh, Religious Leaders, Peacemaking, and the First Liberian Civil War, http://www.religionconflictpeace.org/volume-2-issue-2-spring-2009/religious-leaders-peacemaking-and-first-liberian-civil-war.

[154] Protection of victims of trafficking in Nigeria. Report from Danish Immigration Service's fact-finding mission to Lagos, Benin City and Abuja, Nigeria 9 to 26 September 2007, 2-24 at https://www.nyidanmark.dk/nr/rdonlyres/bad16bf3-a7c8-4d62-8334-dc5717591314/0/nigeriatrafficking2007finalpdf.pdf; *See* Upper Tribunal (Immigration and Asylum Chamber), The Immigration Acts, Heard at Field House, On 18th, 19th and 20th July 2016, HD (Trafficked women) Nigeria CG [2016] UKUT 00454 (IAC).

and recount their story. The police station, for instance, is not an appropriate environment in which to break a religious oath, which is supposed to result in a curse of madness. Law enforcement action is not able to cover this spiritual dimension of fear of the spirits and the sense of guilt invoked by denouncing family members involved in the trafficking process. These acts exceed their functions and simultaneously reveal the lacuna in criminal justice.[155] "A spiritual battle must be fought with spiritual weapons."[156]

Measures to enhance support for victims must take into consideration the culture and the context from which the victims come. In effect, many girls have travelled with a lucky charm. However, telling them that the magic, known in Nigeria as *ju-ju*, has no power is counterproductive. The spell makes them c become uncommunicative. Whether they believe it or not, the risk of something terrible happening to their family is real. The only salvation they can find lies in the service of Catholic priests ministering exorcisms. The Italian authorities therefore enlisted Catholic priests to conduct exorcisms to break "voodoo spells" placed on terrified Nigerian migrant girls by traffickers who forced them to work as prostitutes.[157]

Victims of trafficking show spontaneous confidence in civil society organizations, including faith-based and church structures, accompanying them during the legal procedures. For example, in Burkina Faso the Church is strengthening the judiciary system, making access to a fair trial possible for the most vulnerable in society including victims of trafficked and forced labor as well as forced marriage and domestic violence. OCADES-Caritas in Burkina Faso plays a vital role in assisting victims of trafficking and slavery to engage with the criminal justice system to file claims, pursue prosecutions, and obtain legal compensation following the completion of criminal cases involving their traffickers. Hundreds of paralegal members of Justice and Peace commissions have been trained in all the dioceses in Burkina Faso to assist the most vulnerable members of society.[158] This support is critical, not only in improving legal outcomes but also in improve the victims' experience of the criminal justice system.

Of special relevance in this respect is the information I obtained from field research undertaken in Burkina Faso. The Sisters of Good Shepherd in Bobo

---

[155] Giordano (2015), p. 211, 216 (available at: http://www.journals.uchicago.edu/doi/pdfplus/10.1086/683272).

[156] *Centuries Old Advice On How To Fight and Removed Evil* Spirts, Mystics, http://www.mysticsofthechurch.com/2010/08/how-to-get-rid-of-evil-spirits-demons.html.

[157] Hannah Roberts, *"I Had A Nest Of Insects Inside My Body, I Wanted To Die": Revealed, How Italian Priests Are Conducting Exorcisms To Break "Voodoo Spells" Put On Terrified Nigerian Migrant Girls By Traffickers Who Force Them To Work As Prostitutes*, Daily Mail, http://www.dailymail.co.uk/news/article-3140330/I-nest-insects-inside-body-wanted-die-Revealed-Italian-priests-conducting-EXORCISMS-break-voodoo-spells-terrified-Nigerian-migrant-girls-traffickers-force-work-prostitutes.html; Nigeria Sex Trafficking, EASO Country of Origin Information Report, http://www.refworld.org/pdfid/5631cf0a4.pdf.

[158] *Burkina Faso: Comment Faciliter L'acces A La Justice Des Populations Rurales?*, ABC Burkina, www.abcburkina.net.

Dioulasso (Burkina Faso) recounted that they were also involved in the prosecution of traffickers and were successful in ensuring two perpetrators were prosecuted. This

> partnership between law enforcement and religious women is an example of how the work in caring for victims can support prosecutions. By working with these populations, sisters gain the trust of victims and are often the recipients of their disclosures. While the victims do not speak with the police when present for a raid, they will speak to the sisters.[159]

Catholic Church organizations such as the International Catholic Child Bureau (BICE) also appear to have good working relationships with local governments in West Africa, particularly when it comes to facilitating the protection of victims and the prosecution of suspected perpetrators of trafficking. In the case *Public Ministry and 14 minors represented by their parents v Mito Yoyo, Sabi-Ifon Ayouba, Babatounde Emmanue*, which involved the trafficking of children in agricultural labor, the offenders made a financial agreement with parents to hand over their children for a sum of 200,000F CFA (US $336.95) or a motorcycle. In return, the children were taken on a long and perilous journey to rural Nigeria and assigned to work one year in cassava fields where they were ruthlessly exploited. On the night of January 24, 2011, the bus carrying the 27 children was intercepted in Atakpame by the National Gendarmerie Research Brigade. The children were then entrusted to the BICE Togo for reintegration and follow-up.

Pursuant to Article 2 of the Criminal Procedure Code, BICE constituted itself as a civil party and filed a criminal procedure against three defendants, charging them with trafficking of minors. The Court of Appeal of Lomé found the defendants and imposed a prison sentence on all three. The defendants were also ordered to pay the International Catholic Child Bureau the sum of 247,000F CFA (US $416.14) as compensation for the care provided to the fourteen children. The defendants were also ordered to pay the costs of the process.[160]

During the field work in Burkina Faso, the secretary of the Ministry of Human Rights highlighted positive cooperation between government agencies and religious-based organizations in the protection of victims and the detection, investigation, and prosecution of perpetrators. The Ministry of Human Rights continually receives referrals from OCADES/Caritas and religious-affiliated institutions regarding trafficking in persons.

---

[159]Mary Leary, Religion and Human Trafficking, Caritas in Veritate Foundation, 8, http://www.fciv.org/downloads/Mary%20Leary.%20Religion%20and%20Human%20Trafficking.pdf.

[160]Extrait Du Jugement Add, https://www.unodc.org/res/cld/case-law/tgo/2011/add_n__8811_html/Jugement_du_tribunal_dAtakpame.pdf; Contribution du Bureau Internation Catholique de L'Enfrace a L'Examen Perlodique Universel (EPU) de la Republique du Togo, http://bice.org/app/uploads/2014/10/Rapport_BICE_EPU_TOGO_S12_14_oct_2011_fr.pdf.

## 12.10 Counseling and Spiritual Support

In light of its preferential option for the poor, the Church is an institution actively involved in the social life of the community. It carries out social services in all regions of Africa, particularly in the areas of education, health, and human services for poor families.[161] While attending to needs of people in West Africa, churches are often at the front line when dealing with trafficking in persons. Cultural patterns lead people to consider their priests and religious nuns as the primary source of help for their socio-economic problems and more especially for their family and personal concerns. Trafficking in persons is a personal drama and an individual trauma that often drives people to ask for pastoral counselling from their religious leaders.[162] Therefore, it is necessary to understand the importance of spiritual counselling to those affected by trafficking and the role played by the priest in prevention and healing the wounds.

For the purpose of this study, attention was given to parishes in Burkina Faso with a high incidence of migration abroad and therefore more exposure to trafficking. In these parishes, interviews were conducted with priests regarding their experiences of counseling people affected by trafficking in persons. Many priests reported receiving phone calls from parishioners abroad asking for counselling on labor abuse. Usually these migrants look for guidance in a situation where they are defenseless before an abusive employer who is taking advantage of their immigration status and withholding their wages.

Priests also reported situations where young people came to them seeking prayers and moral support before leaving the country to work abroad. Some people may come asking for a thanksgiving mass having obtained the visa. A priest recounted his advice as follows "...I always tell them to be hard workers and to earn their life honestly and to be surrounded by good friends. Avoid being involved in drugs alcohol and women...And if God blesses your adventure, remember your loved ones you left behind...they rely on your financial support." Another priest reported that a father working abroad resorted to pastoral counseling regarding his decision to take his wife and his children with him to Canada. He needed support in making such a difficult decision and was concerned about the best interests of his family. It must also be noted that many pastors and religious sisters in rural areas have been confronted with the victims of child marriage.

Finally, several priests admitted that they were involved in the immigration process for financial support as well as counseling. One pastor was asked for money by his parishioner who won the U.S. Green Card Lottery but could not afford the flight ticket. Furthermore, individuals in the faith community may also come across victims of trafficking in the course of unrelated programs. For example, during counseling or confession the priests may encounter cases of domestic

---

[161] Ferris (2005), p. 318 at https://www.icrc.org/eng/assets/files/other/irrc_858_ferris.pdf.

[162] *The Partnership Between The State and The Church Against Trafficking in Persons*, MPRA, https://mpra.ub.uni-muenchen.de/20306/1/MRoman_final.pdf.

violence that raise suspicions of trafficking. The findings of this interview indicated that religious leaders are embedded in the social life of their local communities and are actively involved in counseling and offering primary assistance to victims and people affected by trafficking in persons.

Experience also shows that the only place where victims controlled by their traffickers are allowed to go to without close scrutiny is the local church or place of worship. Foreign national victims are often very wary of the authorities and find it difficult to trust them for fear of what might happen to them and therefore turn instead to the Church for relief services and protection. Father Antoine Chenu of the Catholic Mission of Arlit in Niger recounts that some migrants come to parish prayer because they are Christians or they come to ask for help because they are already in need. Some ask for confession, a rosary, and a blessing![163]

As a rule, victims tend to come out from under the shade during police raids. However, victim reporting and police raids do not identify all trafficking victims as is the case for the vast majority of trafficking victims in West Africa. It therefore appears that non-judicial methods of victim identification must be employed to complement existing methods. Accordingly, the Sisters of Good Shepherd, whose mission is to fight trafficking and prostitution, continue to conduct outreach activities to meet the girls at their "place of work" in the brothel, in bars, or on the lonely roads and streets of the city of Bobo-Dioulasso. They pray and share the Gospel with them and listen to their life stories. This initiative encourages them to leave the road or the brothel and join the rehabilitation program in the center. The religious women run a house where they welcome those girls who wish to renounce prostitution, join the rehabilitation, and have access to medical care, counseling, financial support, adequate housing, opportunities for further training, and legal services.

Additionally, these religious women have a special advantage in that they are unaffiliated with government authorities. As such, they are considered ideally suited to providing adequate support to victims by building trust and a sense of security between the abused and the local police. When it comes to identification and rescue of the victims, the Committee for the Support of the Dignity of Woman established by the Nigeria Conference of Religious Woman provides an outstanding example of cooperation with the police in the country of destination in facilitating the rescue of a victim by gathering information about them through hotlines and relatives. Finally, the religious women also involve the families of trafficked victims, where possible, in monitoring the safety of their children following their return.[164]

The experience of trafficking victims can be so painful that forgiving is difficult. Thus, one of the greatest spiritual needs of a victim is leading her/him to forgive her/his traffickers and reconcile with them. Carine Agossou, a psychologist working

---

[163] Père Antoine Chenu, Mission catholique d'Arlit, in Carrefour de migrations Carrefour de solidarités, 41, http://ccfd-terresolidaire.org/IMG/pdf/brochure_gao_def_tbd.pdf.

[164] Federatie Opvang, Safe Return and Reintegration for Victims of Trafficking and Victims of Domestic Violence Facing Residency Problems 47 (Sep. 2014), http://www.opvang.nl/files/Safe_Return_Field_Research.pdf [hereinafter Residency Problems].

at the Don Bosco Center in Porto-Novo, the capital city of Benin, which cares for more than 200 victims of child trafficking, explained: "The children don't understand. . .They say, 'why have they done this to me?' And when it's the people who should be protecting them—the people who should be keeping them safe and sound—that's very hard to accept."[165]

Spiritual care and healing are indispensable in helping the children to forgive those who exploited and hurt them so much and to bring about reconciliation.[166] The fifth petition of the Our Father prayer begs God to "forgive us our trespasses as we forgive those who trespass against us." Helping victims connect to their faith tradition is a great source of healing. In this respect, priests, religious, and other members of Christ's faithful play an indispensable role in the journey to bring about the full spiritual healing of victims. "A victim of trafficking is created in the image and likeness of God" and therefore "pastoral care for victims of trafficking is tailored towards restoring the victim to [their] dignity and to restore all [of their] inalienable rights. In the care for such victims, they must be treated with utmost respect and compassion."[167]

Traffickers are also affected by their evil doing. This belief that oppression and abuse harm both the victim and the offender is expressed in an Igbo proverb that states: "The rain beats the slaves as well as the slave driver." There are times when things may actually go wrong in the trafficking process, resulting in a loss of money. The risk of being caught, tried and convicted drains the offenders psychologically and emotionally and they bear shame and a loss of integrity once caught. Indeed, family members who played any role in the process of procurement, transportation, harboring, and exploitation experience a state of guilt that may result in their feeling haunted, although they may at times have been blinded by the positive effect of increased income (money) and improved financial status. The family involved in trafficking suffers stigmatization once the business enters the public domain with repatriation of the victims.[168]

Thus, from a Christian standpoint, the trafficker is also a victim, a brother and sister to be converted. Sisters therefore extend their outreach to both the exploiters and the exploited.[169] The trafficker is capable of rising again from the ashes and Pope Francis appeals to everyone not to forget the dignity which is ours:

> Human beings, while capable of the worst, are also capable of rising above themselves, choosing again what is good, and making a new start, despite their mental and social

---

[165] *BENIN: Salesian Missionaries Provide Hope and Healing to Victims of Child Trafficking*, Mission Newswire, http://missionnewswire.org/benin-salesian-missionaries-provide-hope-and-healing-to-victims-of-child-trafficking/.

[166] A Holistic Support for Victims of Human Trafficking, 10 at file:///C:/Users/irie/Downloads/sr-nwaonuma-traffick-100414.pdf. [hereinafter Holistic Support].

[167] *Id.*

[168] Ogugua V.C. Ikpeze and Sylvia C. Ifemeje, Dynamics of Trafficking in Nigerian Women and Globalization, 47, http://citeseerx.ist.psu.edu/viewdoc/download?doi=10.1.1.899.5242&rep=rep1&type=pdf.

[169] Holistic Support, *supra* note 166 at 9.

> conditioning. We are able to take an honest look at ourselves, to acknowledge our deep dissatisfaction, and to embark on new paths to authentic freedom. No system can completely suppress our openness to what is good, true and beautiful, or our God-given ability to respond to his grace at work deep in our hearts.[170]

The chaplaincy programs provided by the Catholic Church to prison inmates encourage them to seek spiritual formation and participate in worship. The US Conference of Bishops believes that genuine religious participation and formation is a road to spiritual healing, renewal, and rehabilitation for those who have committed crimes.[171] Additionally, volunteers from parishes reach out to prisoners and their families, offering help and hope to those caught up in crimes and the criminal justice system. Jesus Christ himself, who was also in prison, called on his followers to visit the imprisoned and take care of the sick, including victims of crime.

## 12.11 Protection of Trafficking Victims and Reintegration Strategies

The Catholic Church makes a valuable contribution in the work in the work it performs against trafficking in West Africa by establishing and operating shelters and centers that provide accommodation, safe havens, counseling, legal assistance, and professional skills training to victims of trafficking.[172] The survivors also receive information about their human rights as well as their rights as victims of trafficking or domestic violence. For example, the Committee for the Support of the Dignity of Woman (COSUDOW) works conjointly with the Anti Human Trafficking Unit of the Nigeria Police Force to provide a safe place for victims and also protect them from being re-trafficked. Along with its partner organizations in Europe, the Committee for the Support of the Dignity of Woman (COSUDOW) also coordinates the return of trafficking victims to Nigeria using family tracing and implements a process of reconciliation to prepare the immediate family and the community to receive returnees and support them in the process of reintegration.[173]

Survivors of trafficking face a significant stigma that includes the following major components: blame, discrimination, loss of status, isolation, and shame. With respect

[170] *See* Laudato Si Alliance Protect Earth-Dignify Humanity, https://www.laudatosi.org/laudato-si/spirituality/.

[171] Responsibility, Rehabilitation, and Restoration: A Catholic Perspective On Crime and Criminal Justice at http://www.usccb.org/issues-and-action/human-life-and-dignity/criminal-justice-restorative-justice/crime-and-criminal-justice.cfm.

[172] *A Christian Reponses to Human Trafficking,* Faith Perspectives, https://www.stltoday.com/lifestyles/faith-and-values/civil-religion/a-christian-response-to-human-trafficking/article_3a15d8ea-54cf-11e0-8c3c-0017a4a78c22.html.

[173] USAID, The Rehabilitation Of Victims Of Trafficking In Group Residential Facilities In Foreign Countries, 20, http://pdf.usaid.gov/pdf_docs/Pnadk471.pdf. [hereinafter The Rehabilitation Of Victims].

to trafficking in persons, this stigma can occur in various ways. For example, in Nigeria the family and the wider community blame survivors for their victimization when, for example, they have chosen to enter prostitution. As a result of their experiences, they may face discrimination when seeking housing or employment as well as other issues when they try to achieve important life milestones such as marriage. Without any control over their lives, survivors often feel shame as a result of their victimization.

In seeking to reintegrate victims into society, the Catholic Church and its institutions help women trafficked for sexual exploitation purposes to overcome the stigma and discrimination arising from their abuse so that they can fully recover from their ordeals. Ndioro Ndiaye, Deputy Director General for the International Organization for Migration, observed that:

> [b]y breaking down the stigma and by empowering trafficked women to step forward and speak of their experiences, global efforts to counter human trafficking, particularly of women and girls for sexual exploitation, will be much more successful. But this can only be done by tackling ignorance and prejudice among the public at large as to why women fall prey to traffickers.[174]

The Bishops of Africa commit themselves "to ensuring a person-centered, holistic, human rights-based and non-judgmental approach with regards to survivors of trafficking"[175] in the service they provide. In the field, organizations such as the Committee for the Support of the Dignity of Woman (COSUDOW), Association Foyer Don Bosco, and religious women in West Africa work within affected communities to help families and community members understand what has happened to these children and to encourage them to forgive and accept the victims.

Additionally, access to vocational training and job opportunities play an important role in offsetting the stigma attached to sex trafficking as they facilitate the sustainable social integration of victims by increasing their future employment prospects, confidence, and life skills. This is a way forward to attaining financial autonomy and developing a sense of control over reintegration and a sense of worth and capacity. Given that many women and children have often been denied access to school and educational opportunities, Benin center provides literacy programs for everyone and assists ambitious students wishing to pursue academic studies at the University. Others are enrolled in vocational training to help them diversify and augment their sources of income from petty-trading. Girls aspire to training in sewing, hairdressing, knitting, tie-and-dye, embroidering, and catering while boys

---

[174] More Needs to Be Done to Address Stigma and Discrimination Towards Women Trafficked for Sexual Exploitation at https://www.iom.int/statements/more-needs-be-done-address-stigma-and-discrimination-towards-women-trafficked-sexual.

[175] *Final Message From The Conference On Human Trafficking Within And From Africa Held In Abuja, Nigeria From 5th-7th Of September 2016*, Caritas Internationalis, http://www.caritas.org/includes/pdf/coatnet/NigeriaConf16/DeclarationConferenceNigeria16.pdf.

prefer to be trained in barbering, mechanical work, and carpentry or become truck drivers.[176]

In addition to these activities, Association Don Bosco also conducts agro-pastoral farming. To that end, the center provides training in food crops and market gardening, cuniculture (breeding and raising domestic rabbits), fish farming, pig breeding, laying hens, and palm oil production.[177] The center also strives to educate inmates in basic practical agricultural skills, including the cultivation of fruits and vegetables and coping strategies to address the risks associated with climate variability, which include control of farmland degradation, management of soil fertility, crop diversification, animal production, and sale of livestock.[178]

The fieldwork for this dissertation, which was conducted in 2016 in Ghana, Togo, and Burkina Faso at UNICEF and several other charity organizations found that many of the opportunities for education and vocational training offered to trafficked women and children in West Africa were not ambitious enough and do not necessarily guarantee success. Such initiatives send victims back to what society terms "women's work", which is underpaid and poorly protected by labor laws. Such trades reflect patterns of gender inequality that contributed to women being trafficked in the first place. An anti-trafficking advisor observed that "it may not be appropriate to train a young woman to be a hairdresser if she is then sent back to a village where people can only afford to get their hair cut twice a year — this occupation will not sustain her."[179] Computer training and bookkeeping may also be inappropriate in a market where the victims will be competing with more highly educated peers.[180]

Nevertheless, despite the difficulties inherent in reintegration, the Committee for the Support of the Dignity of Woman (COSUDOW) reports several stories of successful reintegration. Examples of these include happy marriages for some of these women after their stay at the center; happy reintegration where survivors live on their own in dignity and feel fulfilled; reunification of trafficking victims with their families; and freedom from forced labor.[181] Some women have been economically empowered and are now happily married with children. Even some of the men deported from European countries who were part of the Bakhita Villa family have

---

[176] The Challenge of Resettling those who Have Been Trafficked, with Special Reference to Nigeria at http://www.endslavery.va/content/endslavery/en/publications/acta_20/bonetti.html; Nigeria struggles against human trafficking at http://www.dailymail.co.uk/wires/ap/article-3287824/Nigeria-struggles-against-human-trafficking.html.

[177] Rapport d'activités, Association Foyer Don Bosco 23 (Feb. 2014), http://www.plateformehaiti.be/images/pdf/GTEF_-_RAPPORT_ACTIVITES_octobre_2013_-_f%C3%A9vrier_2014.pdf.

[178] *See* Climate Change in the Sahel A Challenge for Sustainable Development at http://www.agrhymet.ne/PDF/pdfeng/specialChCang.pdf.

[179] The Rehabilitation Of Victims, *supra* note 173.

[180] *Id.*

[181] Q & A with Sr. Patricia Ebegbulem, Rescuing and Rehabilitating Victims of Trafficking in Nigeria https://secam.org/q-a-with-sr-patricia-ebegbulem-rescuing-and-rehabilitating-victims-of-trafficking-in-nigeria/.

also been empowered with the assistance of generous donors.[182] Helping victims to become more self-sufficient and contribute to the national economy can assist mental rehabilitation, which can offset any alienation and the need for people to leave their communities to find work abroad and run the risk of being re-trafficked.[183]

## References

A Christian Reponses to Human Trafficking, Faith Perspectives, https://www.stltoday.com/lifestyles/faith-and-values/civil-religion/a-christian-response-to-human-trafficking/article_3a15d8ea-54cf-11e0-8c3c-0017a4a78c22.html

A Holistic Support for Victims of Human Trafficking, 10 at file:///C:/Users/irie/Downloads/sr-nwaonuma-traffick-100414.pdf

A Study on Street Children in Zimbabwe, 99 at https://www.unicef.org/evaldatabase/files/ZIM_01-805.pdf

Agozino B (2004) Pan African issues in crime and justice. Routledge

Allaire D. Green Churches Label Targets Ecological Conversion, La Croix International, https://international.la-croix.com/news/green-churches-label-targets-ecological-conversion/5651

Ameh RK (2001) Child Bondage in Ghana: a contextual policy analysis of Trokosi. Simon Fraser University, p 186

Ameh RK (2004) Human rights, gender and traditional practices: the Trokosi system in West Africa. In: Kalunta-Crumpton A, Agoni B (eds) Pan-African Issues in Crime and Justice. Routledge

*Annual Activity Report*, Caritas 13 (2008), http://www.caritas.eu/sites/default/files/ce_annualactivityreport_ed2008_en.pdf

Araba N. Rapid urbanizations and living arrangements of older persons in Africa. Center Soc Policy Stud p 297. https://pdfs.semanticscholar.org/fbef/a761418b8fb2cbee7dfb7390dec68966f569.pdf

Asomah JY (2015) Cultural rights versus human rights: a critical analysis of the trokosi practice in Ghana and the role of civil society. Afr Human Rights Law J 15:129

Assises Synodales a Koupela du 27 au 31 Octobre 1999, (Document final du Synode Diocesain de Koupela)

Awinador-Kanyirige WA (2014) Ghana's National Peace Council. Global Centre for the Responsibility to Protect. http://s156658.gridserver.com/media/files/awinador-ghana-national-peace-council.pdf

Awinongya MA (2013a) The understanding of family in ghana as a challenge for a contextual ecclesiology. University of Munich, p 15

Awinongya MA (2013b) The understanding of family in Ghana as a challenge for a contextual ecclesiology. University of Munich, p 30

Ayete-Nyampong (2014) A study of pastoral care of the elderly in Africa: an interdisciplinary approach with focus on Ghana. Author House S, 279

Bales K, Soodalter R (2009) The slave next door. Human trafficking and Slavery in America Today. University of California Press Berkeley, p 6

[182]Human Trafficking: Interview with Sr. Patricia Ebegbulem at http://www.catholicstand.com/human-trafficking-interview-with-sr-patricia-ebegbulem/.

[183]The Limitations of Necessary Criminalisation: Developing a Comprehensive and Holistic Response to Modern Slavery, 6 at http://www.endslavery.va/content/endslavery/en/publications/acta_20/hyland.pdf.

Baradaran S, Barclay S. Fair Trade and Child Labor, 39–41 at http://hrlr.law.columbia.edu/wp-content/uploads/sites/10/2016/03/Baradaran_Barclay-1.pdf

*Baseline Study on Newly Fairtrade Certified Cocoa Producer Organizations in Côte d'Ivoire and Ghana Terms of Reference - May 2013*, Fair Trade Africa, http://www.fairtradeafrica.net/wp-content/uploads/2010/06/FTA_FLO_TOR_Callfortender_Baseline_Ghana_CDI_.pdf

Bedford T. *Ethical Consumerism: Everyday Negotiations in The Construction Of An Ethical Self, 200-01* http://discovery.ucl.ac.uk/1318018/1/314135.pdf

Beeko AA (1995) Presbyterian Church of Ghana: 66th Synod Moderatorial Address at Takoradi, 2-3 Acrra

Benedict XVI, Jesus of Nazareth, 198 (2007)

BENIN: Salesian Missionaries Provide Hope and Healing to Victims of Child Trafficking, Mission Newswire, http://missionnewswire.org/benin-salesian-missionaries-provide-hope-and-healing-to-victims-of-child-trafficking/

Bilyeu AS (1992) Trokosi - the practice of sexual slavery in Ghana: religious and cultural freedom vs. human rights. Ind Int Law Comp Law Rev 9:457, 459

Bindel J. Thought It Was Just Men Who Flew Abroad For Squalid Sexual Kicks? Meet The Middle-Aged, Middle-Class Women Who Are Britain's Female Sex Tourists. Daily Mail, http://Www.Dailymail.Co.Uk/Femail/Article-2401788/Sex-Tourism-Meet-Middle-Aged-Middle-Class-Women-Britains-Female-Sex-Tourists.Html

Bouron J-M (2010) Les Pères Blancs, acteurs du jeu colonial. Mission catholique et enjeux politiques en Haute-Volta au lendemain de la seconde guerre mondiale. Université of Nantes, pp 59–81, https://www.cairn.info/revue-histoire-monde-et-cultures-religieuses1-2010-2-page-59.htm

Brenda Ola, Human Trafficking and Slavery, N.Y.U. (May 9, 2009). http://www.nyu.edu/classes/keefer/joe/olab.pdf

Burkina Faso: Centre De Solidarité Pour Sorcières Présumées, Afrik, http://www.afrik.com/article8157.html

Burkina Faso: Comment Faciliter L'acces A La Justice Des Populations Rurales?, ABC Burkina, www.abcburkina.net

Can be translated as "in the hands of God." *Delwende Center in Ouagadougou*, Missionary Sisters of Our Lady of Africa, http://www.msolafrica.org/index.php/en/our-mission/africa/burkina-faso/448-delwende-center-in-ouagadougou

Canon Law of the Catholic Church, CIC can. 1063, 2, CCEO can. 783, §1

Catechism of The Catholic Church, *You Shall Love Your Neighbor as Yourself*, http://www.vatican.va/archive/ccc_css/archive/catechism/p3s2c2a4.htm

*Catholics Urged to Fight Against Human Trafficking*, NCSN (Jan. 27, 2014). http://www.cnsng.org/viewnews.php?tabnews=946.

Centuries Old Advice On How To Fight And Removed Evil Spirts, Mystics, http://www.mysticsofthechurch.com/2010/08/how-to-get-rid-of-evil-spirits-demons.html

Chenu PA. Mission catholique d'Arlit, in Carrefour de migrations Carrefour de solidarités, 41, http://ccfd-terresolidaire.org/IMG/pdf/brochure_gao_def_tbd.pdf

*Christian Missions in Africa and Their Role in The Transformation Of African Societies*, Asian And African Studies 16 (2007), https://www.sav.sk/journals/uploads/102313498_Vilhanov%C3%A1.pdf.

*Church Teachings on Slavery and Trafficking*, Justice Peace Office, http://justiceandpeace.org.au/key-ideas-and-extracts-about-slavery-trafficking/

*Circular Letter to The Presidents of Bishops' Conferences on Religious Education in Schools*, Congregation for Catholic Education, http://www.vatican.va/roman_curia/congregations/ccatheduc/documents/rc_con_ccatheduc_doc_20090505_circ-insegn-relig_en.html

Climate Change in the Sahel A Challenge for Sustainable Development at http://www.agrhymet.ne/PDF/pdfeng/specialChCang.pdf

*Combating Trafficking in Children for Labour Exploitation in West and Central Africa: Synthesis Report*, ILO 30-31 (Dec. 1, 2001), http://www.ilo.org/ipec/Informationresources/WCMS_IPEC_PUB_776/lang%2D%2Den/index.htm

Common Declaration of the Bishops of Africa and Madagascar, SECAM, para. 4–5 http://www.cultura.va/content/dam/cultura/docs/pdf/Adoukonou/declaration.pdf. at https://agendaeurope.wordpress.com/2015/09/24/african-bishops-tell-the-west-stop-spreading-the-culture-of-death/

Contribution du Bureau Internation Catholique de L'Enfrace a L'Examen Perlodique Universel (EPU) de la Republique du Togo., http://bice.org/app/uploads/2014/10/Rapport_BICE_EPU_TOGO_S12_14_oct_2011_fr.pdf

Dadirai Chikwengo, CAFOD, *How The Sdgs And The Church Can Help The Fight Against Human Trafficking*, https://cafodpolicy.wordpress.com/2016/11/09/how-the-sdgs-and-the-church-can-help-the-fight-against-human-trafficking/

David B. Couturier, consumerism and the many faces of human trafficking. A Franciscan Theology of Stuff, https://cmsm.org/wp-content/uploads/2015/10/FranciscanTheology_Couturier.pdf

de Pelsmacker P (2005) Consumer values and fair-trade beliefs, attitudes and buying behaviour. Int Rev Pub Non Profit Market 2:50, 51

*Declaration On Christian Education Gravissimum Educationis*, Congregation for Catholic Education, http://www.vatican.va/archive/hist_councils/ii_vatican_council/documents/vat-ii_decl_19651028_gravissimum-educationis_en.html

D'Souza MO (2016) Catholic philosophy of education: the church and two philosophers. McGill-Queen's University Press

e.g., St. Leo., http://www.saintleo.edu/media/411879/catholic_education_in_kenya.pdf

*Education, Western Africa (Western Colonialism)*, What-when-how, http://what-when-how.com/western-colonialism/education-western-africa-western-colonialism/

Elabor-Idemudia P (2003) Race and gender analyses of trafficking: a case study of Nigeria. Canadian Woman Stud 22:116

*Encyclical of Pope Pius XII on Consecrated Virginity to Our Venerable Brothers, The Patriarchs, Primates, Archbishops, Bishops, And Other Local Ordinaries in Peace and Communion with the Apostolic See*, Sacra Virginitas, http://w2.vatican.va/content/pius-xii/en/encyclicals/documents/hf_p-xii_enc_25031954_sacra-virginitas.html

Eucharia Madueke, Human Trafficking In Nigeria: Sisters Provide Services, Seek Greater Justice For All, Global Sister's Report, http://globalsistersreport.org/column/justice-matters/trafficking/human-trafficking-nigeria-sisters-provide-services-seek-greater

Extrait Du Jugement Add, https://www.unodc.org/res/cld/case-law/tgo/2011/add_n__8811_html/Jugement_du_tribunal_dAtakpame.pdf

Ezeh MD (2017) Human trafficking and prostitution among women and girls of Edo State, Nigeria Possibility of Rehabilitation Through Education and Prevention. Xlibris UK

Federatie Opvang, Safe Return and Reintegration for Victims of Trafficking and Victims of Domestic Violence Facing Residency Problems 46 (Sept. 2014), http://www.opvang.nl/files/Safe_Return_Field_Research.pdf

Ferris E (2005) Faith-based and secular humanitarian organizations. 87 Number 858, 318 at https://www.icrc.org/eng/assets/files/other/irrc_858_ferris.pdf

Final Message from the Conference on Human Trafficking Within and From Africa Held in Abuja, Nigeria From 5th-7th of September 2016, Caritas Internationalis, http://www.caritas.org/includes/pdf/coatnet/NigeriaConf16/DeclarationConferenceNigeria16.pdf

*Food crisis in West Africa*, Caritas Africa Info (July 2012) 9 at http://www.caritas-africa.org/info0712.pdf

*Ghana Bishops Speak. A Collection of Communiques, Memoranda and Pastoral Letters of the Ghana Catholic Bishops' Conference*, 17 National Catholic Secretariat (1999)

Ghana Catholic Bishops' Conference (1995) Advent Pastoral Letter, Message to our Nation and Especially our Youth on Drug-trafficking and Prostitution. Ghana Bishops Speak, p 14

*Ghana Legislation Enacted Criminalize Trokosi Tradition Enslavement*, Equality Now, https://www.equalitynow.org/action-alerts/ghana-legislation-enacted-criminalize-trokosi-tradition-enslavement

Giordano C (2015) Lying the truth practices of confession and recognition. Univ Chicago Curr Anthropol 56:211, 216 (available at: http://www.journals.uchicago.edu/doi/pdfplus/10.1086/683272).

Global Consumers are Willing to put their Money where their Heart is when it comes to goods and services from Companies committed to social Responsibility, Nielsen, http://www.nielsen.com/us/en/press-room/2014/global-consumers-are-willing-to-put-their-money-where-their-heart-is.html

Guerra MD. Pope Benedict XVI and the Politics of Modernity, 57-60, https://www.assumption.edu/sites/default/files/cv/140930MarcGuerra.pdf

Hashim MN (2017) Tradition and culture in Africa: practices that facilitate trafficking of women and children. Dignity J Sex Exploit Viol 2:25 (Available at: https://digitalcommons.uri.edu/cgi/viewcontent.cgi?article=1007&context=dignity)

*How to Bring About Normative Change in The Demand for Trafficked Persons*, End Slavery, http://www.endslavery.va/content/endslavery/en/publications/acta_20/porpora.html

Human Trafficking, Sisters of IHM, http://www.sistersofihm.org/what-we-do/ihm-justice-outreach-advocacy/detail.html?id=1b1839c1-886f-447d-a276-2c2fdbbaad44

Human Trafficking: Interview with Sr. Patricia Ebegbulem at http://www.catholicstand.com/human-trafficking-interview-with-sr-patricia-ebegbulem/

II Special Assembly For Africa The Church In Africa In Service To Reconciliation, Justice And Peace, 27 at http://www.vatican.va/roman_curia/synod/documents/rc_synod_doc_20060627_ii-assembly-africa_en.html

Ikpeze OVC, Ifemeje SC. Dynamics of Trafficking in Nigerian Women and Globalization, 47, http://citeseerx.ist.psu.edu/viewdoc/download?doi=10.1.1.899.5242&rep=rep1&type=pdf

Impact of Catholic Mission on Education in Nigeria, LinkedIn, https://www.linkedin.com/pulse/20141207174923-62892927-impact-of-catholic-mission-on-education-in-nigeria

Instruction on Diocesan Syods, Congregation for Catholic, http://www.vatican.va/roman_curia/congregations/cbishops/documents/rc_con_cbishops_doc_20041118_diocesan-synods-1997_en.html

Irwin J (2015) Ethical consumerism isn't dead, it just needs better marketing, Harv Bus Rev (Jan. 12, 2015), https://hbr.org/2015/01/ethical-consumerism-isnt-dead-it-just-needs-better-marketing

Janet HC, Halloween-loving Americans will spend about $125 on candy, consumes and decorations this year. Cleveland, http://www.cleveland.com/business/index.ssf/2014/09/halloween-loving_americans_will_spend_about_125_on_candy_costumes_and_decorations_this_year.html

John Paul II, Evangelium Vitae: To the Bishops Priests and Deacons Men and Women Religious Lay Faithful and all People of Good Will on the Value and Inviolability of Human Life ¶ 86 (Mar. 25, 1995), https://w2.vatican.va/content/john-paul-ii/en/encyclicals/documents/hf_jp-ii_enc_25031995_evangelium-vitae.html

John Paul II, Letter to Archbishop Jean-Louis Tauran on the Occasion of the International Conference "Twenty-First Century Slavery – The Human Rights Dimension to Trafficking in Human Beings" (May 15, 2002a). http://w2.vatican.va/content/john-paul-ii/en/letters/2002/documents/hf_jp-ii_let_20020515_tauran.html

John Paul II, Letter to Archbishop Jean-Louis Tauran on the Occasion of the International Conference "Twenty-First Century Slavery – The Human Rights Dimension to Trafficking in Human Beings" (May 15, 2002b), http://w2.vatican.va/content/john-paul-ii/en/letters/2002/documents/hf_jp-ii_let_20020515_tauran.html

Kieh GK. Religious Leaders, Peacemaking, and the First Liberian Civil War, http://www.religionconflictpeace.org/volume-2-issue-2-spring-2009/religious-leaders-peacemaking-and-first-liberian-civil-war

Kirby J (2017) Kingdom of happiness. Saint Benedict Press, p 73

La Contribution De L'eglise Catholique a la Formation De L'elites Africaine: Cas De La Côte D'ivoire., http://celaf-institut.org/wp-content/uploads/2017/10/LA-CONTRIBUTION-DE-LEGLISE-A-LA-FORMATION-DE-LELITE-AFRICAINE.pdf

Larson EL (1996) United Nations Fourth World Conference on Women: action for equality, development, and peace (Beijing, China: September 1995). Emory Int Law Rev 10:695, 714

Laudato Si Alliance Protect Earth-Dignify Humanity, https://www.laudatosi.org/laudato-si/spirituality/

Lay Catholics in Schools: Witness to Faith, The Sacred Congregation for Catholic Education ¶ 18, http://www.vatican.va/roman_curia/congregations/ccatheduc/documents/rc_con_ccatheduc_doc_19821015_lay-catholics_en.html

Leary M. Religion and Human Trafficking, Caritas in Veritate Foundation, 8, http://www.fciv.org/downloads/Mary%20Leary.%20Religion%20and%20Human%20Trafficking.pdf

Lettre Pastorale Des Evêques Aux Fils Et Filles De L'eglise Famille De Dieu Qui Est Au Burkina Faso Et Aux Hommes Et Femmes De Bonne Volonte., http://www.catholique.bf/index.php/documents-des-eveques-du-burkina-niger/765-lettre-pastorale-des-eveques-du-burkina-sur-la-mise-en-place-du-senat

Marriage and the Family in Africa, Cormac burke, http://www.cormacburke.or.ke/node/288

Merriam-Webster Dictionary, Fair Trade

Mistiaen V. Virgin wives of the fetish gods. Thomas Reuters Foundation, http://news.trust.org//item/20131003122159-3cmei/

More Needs to Be Done to Address Stigma and Discrimination Towards Women Trafficked for Sexual Exploitation. at https://www.iom.int/statements/more-needs-be-done-address-stigma-and-discrimination-towards-women-trafficked-sexual

Most Reverend Robert W. McElroy, Embracing the Joy of Love. A Pastoral Message to the People of the Diocese of San Diego, https://www.sdcatholic.org/Portals/0/Bishop/Documents/Embracing_the_Joy_of_Love.pdf?ver=2016-05-09-151145-653

Nagle LE, Owasanoye B (2016) Fearing the dark: the use of witchcraft to control human trafficking victims and sustain vulnerability. Sw Law Rev 45:561. Available at: http://www.swlaw.edu/sites/default/files/2017-04/5%20Fearing%20the%20Dar.pdf

Nair PM, Sen S (2005) Trafficking in women and children in india, Orient Longman, 147, New Delhi

Naughton, Respect in Action. St. Thomas University, https://www.stthomas.edu/media/catholicstudies/center/ryan/publications/publicationpdfs/subsidiarity/RespectInActionFINALWithAcknowlCX.pdf

Nigeria Sex Trafficking, EASO Country of Origin Information Report, http://www.refworld.org/pdfid/5631cf0a4.pdf

Nigeria struggles against human trafficking at http://www.dailymail.co.uk/wires/ap/article-3287824/Nigeria-struggles-against-human-trafficking.html

Noonan P. The Parkland Massacre and the Air we Breathe. The Wall Street Journal, https://www.wsj.com/articles/the-parkland-massacre-and-the-air-we-breathe-1518739880?emailToken=bfa889e51306059a676215fcb0d22dcfBsLXVXqrBbzM%2F%2Fq%2FbqVc%2BOe4RVsno1%2Bz0LzHdaDGA%2BwpcR9j75F5ZxUPl7WYJS0o%2FEGwuHWwkrBUF2SX%2F9IOD1BRCw8oWSTLd%2B%2Fh88NlORw%3D

Notes on Human Trafficking. http://armel.duteil.free.fr/?page=traffichumain&father=justicepaix

O'Connor M (2012a) Human trafficking: the South African sector and a pastoral response, with exhortations from Africae Munus in Honour of Pope Benedict's Visit to Benin in November of 2011. In: Kaulemu D (ed) Faith perspectives on migration and human trafficking. p 56, 57

O'Connor M (2012b) Human trafficking: The South African sector and a pastoral response, with exhortations from Africae Munus in Honour of Pope Benedict's visit to Benin in November of 2011. In: Kaulemu D (ed) Faith Perspectives on Migration and Human Trafficking 51

Opvang F. Safe Return and Reintegration for Victims of Trafficking and Victims of Domestic Violence Facing Residency Problems 47 (Sep. 2014), http://www.opvang.nl/files/Safe_Return_Field_Research.pdf

*Oversight of Public and Private Initiatives to Eliminate the Worst Forms of Child Labor in the Cocoa Sector of Cote d'Ivoire and Ghana,* September 2010 at http://www.pjcvt.org/dbpjc/wp-content/uploads/2012/02/Final-Fourth-Annual-Report.pdf

*Pastoral Care of the Family*, Faith Seeking Understanding, http://fsubelmonte.weebly.com/40-pastoral-care-of-the-family.html

Paul VI, Pastoral Constitution on the Church in the Modern World: Gaudium et Spes ¶¶ 48,1 (Dec. 7, 1965), http://www.vatican.va/archive/hist_councils/ii_vatican_council/documents/vat-ii_cons_19651207_gaudium-et-spes_en.html

Pontifical Council for the Laity, *International Associations of the Faithful,* http://www.vatican.va/roman_curia/pontifical_councils/laity/documents/rc_pc_laity_doc_20051114_associazioni_en.html#INTERNATIONAL%20CHRISTIAN%20UNION%20OF%20BUSINESS%20EXECUTIVES

Pope Benedict XVI, Encyclical Letter Caritas In Veritate 66 (Jun. 29, 2009), http://w2.vatican.va/content/benedict-xvi/en/encyclicals/documents/hf_ben-xvi_enc_20090629_caritas-in-veritate.html

*Preparation for The Sacrament of Marriage*, Pontifical Council for the Family, http://www.vatican.va/roman_curia/pontifical_councils/family/documents/rc_pc_family_doc_13051996_preparation-for-marriage_en.html

Preventing Human Trafficking And Modern Slavery, Santa Marta Group, http://santamartagroup.com/wp-content/uploads/2016/11/SMG-Progress-Brochure-031116.pdf

Prostitution Among Women and Girls, *supra* note 63 at 78

Protection of victims of trafficking in Nigeria. Report from Danish Immigration Service's fact-finding mission to Lagos, Benin City and Abuja, Nigeria 9 to 26 September 2007, 2-24 at https://www.nyidanmark.dk/nr/rdonlyres/bad16bf3-a7c8-4d62-8334-dc5717591314/0/nigeriatrafficking2007finalpdf.pdf

Provision of Quality Education in Ghana. http://kmdiocese.org/kmd/index2.php?option=com_content&do_pdf=1&id=42

Q & A with Sr. Patricia Ebegbulem, Rescuing and Rehabilitating Victims of Trafficking in Nigeria. https://secam.org/q-a-with-sr-patricia-ebegbulem-rescuing-and-rehabilitating-victims-of-trafficking-in-nigeria/

Rabelais F, Gargantua and Pantagruel (1532-64), book 2, chap. 8

Rapport Annuel Consolidé 2012 de l'OCADES Caritas Burkina, Ocades, http://ocadesburkina.org/rapport-annuel-consolide-2012-de-locades-caritas-burkina/

Rapport d'activités, Association Foyer Don Bosco 23 (Feb. 2014), http://www.plateformehaiti.be/images/pdf/GTEF_-_RAPPORT_ACTIVITES_octobre_2013_-_f%C3%A9vrier_2014.pdf

*Rapport d'activités 2013*, Association Foyer Don Bosco 11 (Feb. 2014a), http://portonovo.foyerdonbosco.org/wp-content/uploads/2014/04/Rapport_d_activites_2013.pdf

*Rapport d'activités 2013*, Association Foyer Don Bosco 14 (Feb. 2014b), http://portonovo.foyerdonbosco.org/wp-content/uploads/2014/04/Rapport_d_activites_2013.pdf.

Ratzinger J (2005) The Yes of Jesus Christ. The Crossroad Publishing Company

Read the principles of Fair Trade. at http://www.fairtraderesource.org/uploads/2009/06/CRS-Chocolate-Lesson-Plans.pdf

Respect in Action, supra note 128; Statement Of Catholic Church-Inspired Organizations Related To Decent Work And The Post-2015 Development Agenda, http://www.caritas.org/includes/pdf/advocacy/CatholicInspiredStatDecentWork13.pdf

Responsibility, Rehabilitation, and Restoration: A Catholic Perspective on Crime and Criminal Justice. at http://www.usccb.org/issues-and-action/human-life-and-dignity/criminal-justice-restorative-justice/crime-and-criminal-justice.cfm

*Restoring dignity to street women in Tamale*, Partir Partager Prier, http://www.soeurs-blanches.cef.fr/afrique-justice-et-paix/justice-et-paix/rendre-la-dignite-aux-femmes-de-la-rue-a-tamale/

Roberts H. "I Had A Nest Of Insects Inside My Body, I Wanted To Die": Revealed, How Italian Priests Are Conducting Exorcisms To Break "Voodoo Spells" Put On Terrified Nigerian Migrant Girls By Traffickers Who Force Them To Work As Prostitutes, Daily Mail, http://www.dailymail.co.uk/news/article-3140330/I-nest-insects-inside-body-wanted-die-Revealed-Italian-priests-conducting-EXORCISMS-break-voodoo-spells-terrified-Nigerian-migrant-girls-traffickers-force-work-prostitutes.html

Short E (2004) Powerful persuasion combating traditional practices that violate human rights. Center for Victims of Torture 1, https://www.newtactics.org/sites/default/files/resources/Powerful-Persuasion-EN.pdf

*Statement of Most Reverend Thomas Wenski, Bishop of Orlando Chairman*, US Conference of Catholic Bishops on Trafficking in Human Persons, (June 9, 2004). at www.orlandodiocese.org

*Synod of Bishops, Pastoral Challenges to the Family in the Context of Evangelization*, Preparatory Document, http://www.vatican.va/roman_curia/synod/documents/rc_synod_doc_20131105_iii-assemblea-sinodo-vescovi_en.html

*Talithakum Afrique Francophone*, Talitha kum Arise (Dec. 6, 2016), http://www.talithakum.info/news/62/talithakum-afrique-francophone.

The Celebration of the Christian Mystery, Catechism of the Catholic Church, http://www.vatican.va/archive/ccc_css/archive/catechism/p2s2c3a7.htm

The Challenge of Resettling those who Have Been Trafficked, with Special Reference to Nigeria at http://www.endslavery.va/content/endslavery/en/publications/acta_20/bonetti.html

The Education Deficit, Human Rights Watch, https://www.hrw.org/report/2016/06/09/education-deficit/failures-protect-and-fulfill-right-education-through-global

The Limitations of Necessary Criminalisation: Developing a Comprehensive and Holistic Response to Modern Slavery, 6 at http://www.endslavery.va/content/endslavery/en/publications/acta_20/hyland.pdf

The Partnership Between The State and The Church Against Trafficking in Persons, MPRA, https://mpra.ub.uni-muenchen.de/20306/1/MRoman_final.pdf

The Profit of Values: *A Christian Vision of Corporate Social Responsibility a for of Management for Long-Lasting Enterprises*, Uniapac, 16 (2008), http://www.uniapac.org/filesPDF/The%20Profit%20of%20Values.pdf

*The Truth and Meaning of Human Sexuality*, Congregation for Catholic Education http://www.vatican.va/roman_curia/pontifical_councils/family/documents/rc_pc_family_doc_08121995_human-sexuality_en.html

U.S., *Trafficking in Persons,* 7, https://www.state.gov/documents/organization/258877.pdf

UNANIMA, Stop the demand, at unanima-international.org

UNFPA, Liberating Slaves and Changing Minds: Starting at Grassroots, https://www.unfpa.org/endingviolence/html/pdf/chapter_ghana.pd; The government of Ghana, 1992 Constitution of The Republic of Ghana, http://www.ghana.gov.gh/index.php/constitution/395-1992-constitution-of-the-republic-of-ghana

UNIAPAC-Africa, Strategic Plan 2014-2016. *Leading with Responsibility*, http://uniapacafrica.org/wp-content/uploads/2015/04/Plano-estrat%C3%A9gico-PT-UNIAPAC-Africa-2014-2016-.pdf

UNODC, Working Group on Trafficking in Persons, Good Practices and Tools in Demand for Exploitative Services, at 8, (Jan. 27-29, 2010), https://www.unodc.org/documents/treaties/organized_crime/2010_CTOC_COP_WG4/WG4_2010_3_E.pdf

Upper Tribunal (Immigration and Asylum Chamber), The Immigration Acts, Heard at Field House, On 18th, 19th and 20th July 2016, HD (Trafficked women) Nigeria CG [2016] UKUT 00454 (IAC)

USAID, The Rehabilitation of Victims of Trafficking In Group Residential Facilities In Foreign Countries, 20, http://pdf.usaid.gov/pdf_docs/Pnadk471.pdf

Vijeyarasa R (2015) Sex, slavery and the trafficked woman: myths and misconceptions. Routledge, p 11

Vocation of the Business Leader at http://www.uniapac.org/home/Library

Weatherburn A. The Effects of Political and Social and Economic Factors On Human Trafficking, 15, at https://www.researchgate.net/publication/284725360_The_effects_of_political_and_socio-economic_factors_on_human_trafficking

# Chapter 13
# Recommendations and Solutions

Extensive research has brought to the forefront substantial and compelling evidence to show that trafficking in persons is one of the most substantive issues now facing the West African region. An analysis of trafficking in the Economic Community of West African States (ECOWAS) focused on predominant forms of trafficking occurring in this region such as trafficking in mines, domestic servitude, forced marriage, begging, forced commercial exploitation, and religious ritual practices. Victims of these crimes are trafficked within their countries from rural to urban areas, between neighboring countries, and across different continents.

To address the problem of trafficking in the region, Economic Community of West African States (ECOWAS) countries have adopted legislative, administrative, and institutional measures in line with their ratification of the UN Trafficking in Persons Protocol. Despite these anti-trafficking policies, outlawed practices continue to prevail because legislation enacted in the Economic Community of West African States (ECOWAS) countries only criminalizes certain aspects of trafficking defined by the UN Trafficking in Persons Protocol and its implementation often falls short. This has resulted in an extremely low number of convictions and a remarkable increase in the number of victims detected.

Although human rights law is a necessary means by which to achieve a society where all persons are treated with respect and dignity, the law alone is not a sufficient instrument for realizing human rights and improving people's lives. Not all rights are legally enforceable. This discussion therefore offers several insights inspired by the Catholic tradition, which when added to a legal analysis of international human rights, will help achieve a more holistic approach toward tackling the scourge of trafficking in persons.



P. VI. S. Karenga, *A West African Model to Address Human Trafficking*,
https://doi.org/10.1007/978-3-030-88120-7_13

## 13.1 Awareness Raising and Sensitization Through All Parishes

According to a well-known African proverb, "When the hyena acquires a bag, the kids avoid the market."[1] Thus, to be "forewarned is forearmed." Indeed, someone who knows about a problem or a situation before it happens is prepared to face it. The Roman Catholic Church has always advocated to protect the lives and dignity of vulnerable migrants and has championed public awareness campaigns in its parishes through Sunday services, youth gatherings, Catholic media, and in Catholic schools. This public awareness program strives to educate Catholics and the general public on the reality of human rights and migration issues and strives to forewarn potential victims. The goal of evangelization is to change structural beliefs and behaviors by working diligently to awaken the consciences of potential perpetrators and vulnerable people, uprooting the culture of enslavement as well as sorcery and witchcraft that fuel the demand for trafficking and the commercialization of organs and body parts.

To facilitate a church-based anti-trafficking campaign, it would be necessary to establish a Human Trafficking Ministry in all Dioceses of the West African region. The Church plays a critical role in supporting survivors of trafficking in persons. It helps them find love, faith, acceptance, new life, and a family on their journey towards healing. A Human Trafficking Ministry will facilitate this community action and will go a long way toward showing how trafficking in all its forms has become a priority in the pastoral action plan of the dioceses in West Africa. An important suggestion to make in this regard is that the feast of St. Josephine Bakhita on February 8th should be a day on which the entire region of West Africa reflect on the Church's efforts to contain trafficking in persons. The episcopate should consider this a moment of teaching by issuing an insightful pastoral letter that aims to reach their flock as well as the general audience.

## 13.2 Improvement of Livelihood and Dignity of the Most Vulnerable

Another preventive action worthy of note is the commitment the Catholic Church has made to fighting abject poverty in Africa since the missionary era. Through the solidarity and financial resources deriving from overseas churches, the Catholic Church has tackled the root cause of migration by promoting various development and welfare programs throughout the region. These actions comprise both physical and spiritual poverty alleviation, sustainable livelihoods, community development, economic empowerment of women, child sponsorship programs, education, health

[1] Proverbes Mossi (Abidjan 1999), at no. 315.

provision, and vocational training. Their purpose is to improve life conditions and contribute significantly to reducing the level of socio-economic vulnerability that so often makes victims available for traffickers.

This action is in line with the preferential option for the poor that is rooted in the scriptures and the life of Jesus Christ. The Catholic Church believes that the long-term solution to trafficking in persons lies in a form of prevention that provides income earning opportunities for vulnerable people and upholds human dignity. This model can be found in the book of Kings (2 Kg 4), where a desperate widow reached out to ask prophet Elisha for help because she was burdened with heavy debt and the creditors had threatened to take her two sons as slaves. Elisha then performed a miracle to produce enough oil to pay off the widow's debt and protect both her and her children from exploitation and enslavement. In performing this miracle, the prophet involved them in an earning income activity and God provided for the widow's immediate needs to pay off her debts and keep her children from slavery. After the debt was paid, the remaining income was used to make provisions for the future.

## 13.3 Responsible Consumer Practices

The primary reason why trafficking in persons is flourishing in society is because of consumers' voracious demand for cheap goods, cheap workers, and cheap sex. The Catholic Church calls on everyone to recognize their own slavery footprint and the effect that their behavior and consumption have on the trafficking business. In a globalized world economy with an immense number of slaves working in manufacturing, agriculture, mining, and domestic services the odds are that the commodities each of us eat, drink, wear, drive or even text are tainted by modern day slavery. Purchasing is a moral act and making individual ethical purchasing decisions has a large cumulative impact on efforts to eradicate trafficking in persons. In fact, buying from companies that make slave-free and fair-trade products not only affirms their ethical practices, it also influences other companies to take similar actions.

Through evangelization and its moral teachings, the Church addresses the demand for commercial sexual services by educating people on the need for equal and respectful relationships between genders; family values of fidelity, love, and unity; and awareness campaigns specifically targeted at clients. Sexual relationships should be used for what they were properly intended, namely for the procreation of children and the expression of love and communion between husband and wife. Thus, Christian families in the West Africa can mitigate trafficking in persons and related issues by modelling a positive lifestyle that influences others.

To discourage the demand for inexpensive labor that leads to trafficking, the Catholic Church is promoting a model of good management, fair wages, and ethical investment through the creation of ethical employer associations such as UNIAPAC. These adhere to codes of conduct that protect the rights of their workers and promote fair labor practices. This is a promising initiative that needs to be extended to all countries and should also encompass the informal labor sector as it is this that leads to abuse and violations of the rights of migrant workers and fosters trafficking. In a similar vein, Catholic Relief Services created the Ethical Trade movement to instill in people and in culture ethical purchasing behavior founded on the core values of the Catholic faith. The goal is to address trafficking in persons, migration, and climate change. This powerful force for change helps educate consumers about responsible purchasing and mobilizes citizens to campaign for better policies that improve the well-being of the world's most vulnerable workers. To support this Catholic Church initiative, the Coalition of Catholic Organizations Against Human Trafficking (CCOAHT) has gone a long way toward demanding slave-free seafood labels that provide consumers with the information need to make moral purchasing decisions.

## 13.4 Catholic School Education to Combat Human Trafficking

Another spearhead against trafficking in persons is academic education, which can serve as a long term measure to bring about change. In West Africa, government and private schools have co-existed with mission schools. In general, however, Catholic-sponsored schools and seminaries distinguish themselves by providing a holistic education and maintaining top performance in national examinations. The Church extends its education mission to public schools through religious education, catechism, youth ministry, masses, spiritual guidance, and confession.

Catholic schools and universities that are particularly infused with the values of human life and dignity are ripe environments in which to incubate anti-trafficking activities. These education centers consolidate the development of the common good as they conduct academic studies that enhance human rights and therefore improve the community's quality of life; they also inspire campus and community actions that foster intercultural dialogue to prevent trafficking in persons. As initial learning and information portals, Catholic Church educational institutions support trafficking prevention efforts through education and awareness-raising among their student population and in their surrounding communities. The United States Conference of Catholic Bishops has developed an anti-trafficking kit for parishes and schools to educate people about trafficking from a Catholic perspective, equipping students and the wider community with related knowledge and skills r to prevent the deleterious consequences of forced labor and commercial sexual exploitation.

Other academic programs such as St. Thomas University School of Law's LL.M./J.S.D. Program in Intercultural Human Rights are directly involved in the phases of protection and prosecution. They are incubators for research pertaining specifically to trafficking in persons and offer specialized training and assistance to law enforcement officials, lawyers, healthcare providers, teachers, students, researchers, religious institutions, and the wider community on issues pertaining to trafficking in persons. Several schools and programs explicitly seek to educate and engage the students in taking action. For example, many schools and campuses have student clubs dedicated to awareness, prayer, and services for victims.[2]

## 13.5 The Catholic Church in Partnership with Trafficking Stakeholders

Trafficking in persons is a community concern. There is an African proverb that says: "When the hyena catches the child of the unloved woman, go and help her because it could come to take the child of the favorite."[3] A hyena is a dangerous predator in West Africa that preys on young sheep and calves. It is particularly lethal to children. To chase it out of the village, inhabitants must band together with burning torches and shout at the animal. Frightened by the noise and fire, the hyena will run away. In the same way, it is necessary for communities to band together to keep traffickers away before they can ruin more lives.

In this sense, the Catholic Church has made partnership a centerpiece of its anti-trafficking efforts. Itis taking the leading role in West Africa by calling on local churches, traditional and Muslim religions, law enforcement agencies, clergy, and religious congregations to leave aside their differences and together carry out trafficking and conflict prevention campaigns within their communities. Such peacebuilding initiatives undertaken by Catholic Church leaders are more likely to promote sustainable peace in the region by addressing the socio-cultural and political dynamics that give rise to violent conflicts.

To expand this partnership around the world, in 2014 the Holy See launched the Santa Martha Group to implement collaborative initiatives with all stakeholders (governments, law enforcement agencies, civil society, and organizations of religious inspiration) to eradicate trafficking in persons. This is highly appropriate as modern day slavery is a transnational crime that requires a coordinated international response. The primary objective of the Santa Martha Group is to develop a worldwide network with church institutions, law enforcement authorities, religious sisters, and civil society to secure the prosecution of offenders, provide pastoral care to victims, and prevent trafficking in persons. The Coalition of Organizations and Ministries Promoting the Abolition of Slavery at Sea (COMPASS) in the USA and International Union of Superiors General (UISG) are also good examples of partnerships that exist to eradicate trafficking in persons.

---

[2]A Review of Anti- Human Trafficking Activities at U.S. Catholic Colleges and Universities by Foundations and Donors Interested in Catholic Activities, December 2017, http://files.constantcontact.com/e2cade8c301/7d3229cd-6cd8-4558-9206-30d3edf3f584.pdf.

[3]Proverbes Mossi, *supra* note 1 at no 571.

## 13.6 Putting Faith into Action through Advocacy

The Catholic Church identifies itself as the "voice of the voiceless". Undoubtedly, direct assistance to immigrants and people who have been victims of trafficking is essential. However, for the root causes of the scourge to be stopped, advocacy is also necessary. In the majority of countries, episcopal conferences at a national and regional level constitute the most influential presence of religious advocacy by the Catholic Church. Alongside regional episcopal conferences, the Church encompasses a vast array of institutions or non-governmental organizations (NGOs) that lobby local governments to develop anti-trafficking policies and promote decent works. These catholic institutions may also have observer status in some of these organizations in order for them to carry out advocacy on behalf of the Catholic Church for migrants and victims of trafficking in different settings.

The assembly of bishops fulfills its prophetic role by releasing pastoral letters and statements to teach and guide people in religious matters as well as in social justice, human rights concerns, and political affairs. For example, faced with rising levels of uncontrolled and illegal immigration supported by organized trafficking groups, the Association of Episcopal Conferences of Anglophone West Africa (AECAWA) issued a communiqué in August 2009 to express their concerns about the consequences of labor migration. The goal of catholic advocacy is to inform governments, churches, religious bodies, and people of the region about the challenges and benefits associated with migration. To reduce incentives for irregular migration, the Regional Episcopal Conference of bishops recommends that national governments address the root causes of trafficking in persons, including unemployment, and implement regional integration agreements to protect the rights of migrants.

This initiative by the Catholic Church in West Africa links to a growing network of Catholic NGOs and national church institutions across the world that champion the reform of public policies that make migration beneficial for people on the move as well as for communities in the countries of origin, transit and destination. Advocacy by the United States Conference of Bishops for migrants and comprehensive immigration reform has been the most inclusive approach that creates social awareness. It involves families and individuals who then carry out this advocacy in their daily lives and take actions to change the general culture and public opinion.

## 13.7 Healing and Restoration in Christ

Aftercare is a vital component of rehabilitation and recovery for trafficked victims. In particular, religious congregations have developed faith-based services for victims that include safe housing, medical assistance, psychological and spiritual support, legal assistance and financial help, family and relative tracing, as well as counseling and job training to support eventual independent living. Alongside these protective and reintegration services, the Catholic Church makes a distinctive contribution by addressing the emotional and spiritual needs of victims. Like Jesus Christ, victims of trafficking "have been betrayed by those who claimed to love them, sold [them] for money [and] stripped and de-humanized [them]."[4] They struggle with shame and low self-esteem as well as feelings of guilt and resentment. Spiritual healing is therefore the best hope victims have of overcoming the lifelong suffering, brokenness, and trauma caused by trafficking. In these centers, victims discover the God of love and mercy through the compassionate care of the Christians who accompany them. This personal journey of healing and recovery is enhanced with spiritual resources, whether this is prayer support, retreats, or the sacrament of reconciliation that is designed to lift the spirits of the survivors and instill in them a positive image of themselves.

The loving support of the community also constitutes a healing remedy for victims. The local church is a welcoming community, a family where survivors can find unconditional love, acceptance, faith, support, and a new life. Indeed, a great number of trafficking victims come from abusive and broken families and the church has therefore assumed the role of a new family where they feel protected and they belong. In this fellowship community, survivors encounter brothers and sisters who sympathize with their plight, as expressed in the letter to the Corinthians "If one part of the body suffers, all the other parts of the body suffer with it."[5]

## References

A Review of Anti-Human Trafficking Activities at U.S. Catholic Colleges and Universities by Foundations and Donors Interested in Catholic Activities, December 2017. http://files.constantcontact.com/e2cade8c301/7d3229cd-6cd8-4558-9206-30d3edf3f584.pdf

Damiba F-X, Nare L, Proverbes Mossi (Abidjan, 1999)

Grasska D. Healing from human trafficking. Social Ministry San Diego, http://socialministrysandiego.com/healing-from-human-trafficking/

[4]Denis Grasska, *Healing from Human Trafficking*, SOCIAL MINISTRY SAN DIEGO, http://socialministrysandiego.com/healing-from-human-trafficking/.

[5]I Cor 12:26–27.

The manufacturer's authorised representative in the EU is Springer Nature Customer Service Centre GmbH, Europaplatz 3, 69115 Heidelberg, Germany. If you have any concerns regarding our products, please contact ProductSafety@springernature.com

Printed and bound by CPI Group (UK) Ltd, Croydon, CR0 4YY
30/09/2026
02225332-0010